GEORGE WASHINGTON'S GENERALS AND OPPONENTS

Their Exploits and Leadership

BOOKS BY GEORGE ATHAN BILLIAS

AMERICAN CONSTITUTIONALISM ABROAD: Selected Essays
in Comparative Constitutional History
Editor and Contributor

AMERICAN HISTORY: Retrospect and Prospect
Editor and Contributor

THE AMERICAN REVOLUTION: How Revolutionary Was It?
Fourth Edition 1989
Editor

ELBRIDGE GERRY: Founding Father and Republican Statesman

THE FEDERALISTS: Realists or Ideologues?
Editor

GENERAL JOHN GLOVER AND HIS MARBLEHEAD
MARINERS

INTERPRETATIONS OF AMERICAN HISTORY: Patterns and
Perspectives, 2 volumes, Sixth Edition 1992
Editor and Contributor

LAW AND AUTHORITY IN COLONIAL AMERICA:
Selected Essays
Editor

MASSACHUSETTS LAND BANKERS OF 1740

PERSPECTIVE ON EARLY COLONIAL HISTORY
Editor and Contributor

GEORGE WASHINGTON'S GENERALS AND OPPONENTS

Their Exploits and Leadership

Edited by

GEORGE ATHAN BILLIAS

DA CAPO PRESS • NEW YORK

Library of Congress Cataloging in Publication Data

George Washington's generals and opponents: their exploits and leadership / edited by
George Athan Billias.—1st Da Capo Press ed.
    p.   cm.
First work originally published: George Washington's generals. New York: Morrow,
1964; 2nd work originally published: George Washington's opponents. New York: Mor-
row, 1969.
Includes indexes.
ISBN 0-306-80560-X
1. United States—History—Revolution, 1775-1783—Biography. 2. Generals—United
States—Biography. 3. United States. Army—Biography. 4. Generals—Great Britain—Biogra-
phy. 5. Admirals—Great Britain—Biography. 6. Great Britain. Army—Biography. 7. Great
Britain. Royal Navy—Biography. I. Billias, George Athan, 1919–   . II. George Washington's generals. 1994. III. George Washington's opponents. 1994.
E206.G46 1994
973.3'3'0922—dc20   93-33603
[B]   CIP

Grateful acknowledgement is made to:

Alfred A. Knopf, Inc. for permission to reprint the maps entitled "The Theater of War
    in New York and New Jersey," "The Northern Theater of War," and "The Campaign
    of 1781" from *Portrait of a General* by William B. Willcox, © copyright 1962, 1964
    by William B. Willcox.
Harper & Row, Publishers, Incorporated, for permission to reprint the map entitled
    "Campaigns in New York State" from *The American Revolution 1775-1783* by John
    Richard Alden (Harper & Row, 1954).
The Macmillan Company for permission to reprint the map entitled "Seat of War in the
    Southern States 1775-1781" from *The War of the Revolution* by Christopher Ward.
Longmans, Green & Co. Limited for permission to reprint the map entitled "The Carib-
    bean and Central America" from *War for America 1775-1783* by Piers Mackesy.

First Da Capo Press edition 1994

This Da Capo Press paperback edition of *George Washington's Generals and Opponents*
brings together in one volume *George Washington's Generals*, originally published in
New York in 1964, and *George Washington's Opponents*, originally published in New
York in 1969. They are reprinted by arrangement with the author.

Published by Da Capo Press, Inc.
A Subsidiary of Plenum Publishing Corporation
233 Spring Street, New York, N.Y. 10013

To my son, Stephen W. Billias,
and his bride, Bela Breslau,
who love and appreciate
the meaning of American liberty.

Contents

Volume I
George Washington's Generals

Volume II
George Washington's Opponents

Volume I
GEORGE
WASHINGTON'S
GENERALS

Preface

THIS BOOK presents a literary portrait gallery of George Washington's generals. Surprising as it may seem, the last book of essays devoted solely to Revolutionary War military leaders was written more than a century ago. Three developments in recent years have shed new light on America's military leadership in the War for Independence—the appearance of Douglas Southall Freeman's monumental study of Washington, the publication of a number of full-scale biographies of other generals, and the discovery of more manuscript materials. The purpose of the present volume is to re-examine the careers of the most important Continental army commanders in the light of these new findings, hoping thereby to lead the reader to a better understanding of how America won the war.

Within these pages the reader will encounter many of the outstanding military figures of the Revolution: Washington, "god of the army"; Charles Lee, the brilliant but unorthodox ex-British officer who dreamed of altering the art of warfare to suit the peculiar genius of the American people; Philip Schuyler, the New York aristocrat who was as capable as he was cool toward the Yankees in his army; Horatio Gates, the cautious but competent professional soldier; the gifted Nathanael Greene, who was, after Washington, perhaps the best general in the Continental army; John Sullivan, the contentious Irishman who spent as much time battling congressmen as he did the British; brash, ambitious Benedict Arnold, who prior to his defection proved to be one of the army's bravest and boldest battlefield commanders; Benjamin Lincoln, the steady New Englander; the fledgling Frenchman, Lafayette, who was so eager to impress Washington; portly Henry Knox, who earned Washington's rare affection by his faithful service and tireless energy; dashing Anthony Wayne, who was not "mad" but a military romanticist; and the burly frontiersman, Daniel Morgan, whose flair for guerrilla warfare bedeviled the British.

This set of essays does not pretend to account for all the major commanders of the Continental army. The generals treated here were selected on the basis of two criteria: the significance of their contribution to the war effort; and the fact that they served alongside Washington in some capacity or campaign—hence the title of this volume. Had space permitted, essays might have been included on at least three other figures who also meet these criteria—Rochambeau, Putnam, and von Steuben.

Every one of the essays is by a specialist in his subject. Each contributor was asked to prepare an essay covering primarily one man's military career in the Continental army and placing proper emphasis upon the relative importance of his contribution to America's victory. The authors were not always in agreement, but in the best interests of scholarship I have allowed their judgments to stand unaltered.

As editor, I must express my appreciation to many persons who improved this volume in a number of ways. To my contributors, I am grateful for the good grace with which they accepted my suggestions and criticisms. Of the historians who helped me, I relied most upon the literary talents of two close friends—Professor Herbert J. Bass, of the University of Maine, and Dean Milton M. Klein, of Long Island University. They gave most generously of their time in reading these essays and I profited immensely from their wise advice. I am indebted also to Lois Dwight Cole—my co-worker and editor at William Morrow and Company—for her sympathetic and imaginative assistance in preparing this book for press. Messrs. Nathan Cohen and Stanley Shapiro, of Worcester, Massachusetts, patiently drew the maps for this volume. The following fellow historians shared their ideas with me, read parts of the manuscript, or offered expert advice in certain areas: Professor John R. Alden, of Duke University; Professors Gerald N. Grob and George H. Merriam, of Clark University; Dr. Clifford K. Shipton, of the American Antiquarian Society; and Dr. John D. R. Platt, of Independence National Historical Park. Staff members of the American Antiquarian Society, Clark University Library, and Worcester Public Library eased the burdens of my research. My wife, Joyce B. Billias, as in the past, shared my labors; without her loving help, cheerful encouragement, and patience this book could not have been completed.

G.A.B.

Introduction

AMERICA'S victory in the Revolutionary War came as a surprise to many people. Even some of the combatants were amazed at the war's outcome. Washington himself predicted in 1783 that posterity might one day label the patriot triumph as "fiction" rather than fact. "For it will not be believed," he went on to say, "that such a force as Great Britain has employed for eight years in this Country could be baffled in their plan for Subjugating it by numbers infinitely less, composed of Men oftentimes half starved; always in Rags, without pay, and experiencing, at times, every species of distress which human nature is capable of undergoing."

Behind Britain's defeat lay many factors—French aid, flaws in British strategy, the distance of three thousand miles between England and America, the rugged terrain of the New World, and the necessity of having to reconquer a vast territory in order to win. But America's victory could not have been achieved without the efforts of George Washington and his generals. Despite defeats, an undisciplined army, and supply shortages, these officers stubbornly fought on until they brought to a successful conclusion the longest war this country has ever waged.

America's success appears all the more surprising when one considers that the Continental army leaders were essentially military amateurs at the outbreak of the war. How amateur American generals managed to defeat trained British professionals puzzles some military historians to this day. It is true, of course, that many Americans had had previous combat experience in the French and Indian War. But field operations in the French War provided valuable training only for enlisted men and officers in the lower echelons; they did little to prepare provincial officers for the problems of high command.

Consider, for a moment, Washington's own case. Having served five years as regimental commander along the Virginia frontier, he had, by 1775, a more active war record than most colonists. Yet in spite of his military background, he was poorly prepared to assume the post of commander-in-chief and confessed his "want of experience to move upon a large Scale." Commanding a regiment of several hundred men along a 300-mile frontier was hardly adequate training for the huge task of handling an entire American army numbering in the thousands on a continent encompassing 200,000 square miles. His combat experience was scanty at best and confined for the most part to small-scale operations against French and Indians in woodland warfare. His firsthand knowledge of certain branches of the army was extremely limited—he had never commanded a cavalry unit, employed massed artillery, or administered medical or supply installations of any great size. Because British regulars relegated him to a comparatively junior rank, he was never called upon to help formulate strategy.

Younger generals such as Henry Knox, Anthony Wayne, and Nathanael Greene, who were not of age to serve during the French War, had even less experience. These men came into the army straight from civilian life and were forced to acquire most of their military expertise from books. Propelled into the higher ranks of the Continental army with lightning rapidity, they continued to rely heavily upon book learning to solve many of their military problems. History offers few more comic examples of amateurs in combat than the scene that took place in front of the Chew House at Germantown in the fall of 1777. When the attack was momentarily held up, Washington began debating with his generals as to what the next move should be. Significantly, it was Henry Knox who settled the argument. Having owned a book store in Boston before the war, Knox was well-read in matters of tactics and strategy; he won his point simply by quoting from the writings of one of Europe's leading military men.

Of the generals appointed to the Continental army in 1775, only three could properly be regarded as professional soldiers—Charles Lee, Horatio Gates, and Richard Montgomery. All had been officers in the British army, had seen service in the French War, and had remained with the regulars in the postwar period. Yet even among these professionals, experience in the upper echelons of command was quite limited. Charles Lee reached the rank of lieutenant colonel in the British regulars long after his active service in America and Portugal—though he did gain more knowledge and experience while serving with foreign armies in Central Europe and the Balkans. Gates, who became a major, spent most of his time in military administration and never commanded a considerable body of troops. Montgomery rose only to the rank of captain. Nor was the advice of the professionals available to Washington for very long. Of the three, only Gates was still with the Continental army at the close of the conflict; Montgomery was killed in the first year of fighting and Lee held no important post after 1778.

Throughout the war, Washington was joined by other professionals and soldiers of fortune from the armies of Europe. Such officers frequently proved to be more trouble than they were worth. The commander-in-chief was forced to find places for them in order to placate Congress; at the same time he had to be careful not to disappoint jealous American generals who were equally deserving of higher rank. The commission given to the Frenchman, Phillipe du Coudray, for example, brought forth letters threatening resignation from three Americans—Nathanael Greene, John Sullivan, and Henry Knox. Thomas Conway and Johann de Kalb, who had both been in the French service, caused difficulties of a different sort; they hinted or proposed that Washington be replaced as head of the army.

Although certain foreign generals had much to offer in the way of expert military knowledge, their contributions to final victory on the whole were rather limited. The Comte de Rochambeau influenced strategy by pressing upon Washington, in 1781, the idea of attacking Cornwallis in Virginia rather than Clinton in New York. Louis du Portail, the efficient Frenchman, became the army's most competent engineer, and von Steuben, the Prussian drillmaster, its finest disciplinarian. Lafayette arrived in America innocent of battle and stayed on to win his spurs in combat as well as the affection of his commander-in-chief. But with the possible exception of Rochambeau, none of these officers made a contribution so decisive as to affect the outcome of the war. It is safe to say that, despite the presence of foreign professionals, the generalship of the American army maintained its amateur standing during the early war years.

Yet this very amateurism at the outset contributed, in part, to America's success, and enabled the colonists to make a contribution to the art of warfare. By refusing to fight according to the formal rules employed by professional soldiers in the eighteenth century, Americans developed new techniques of fighting. In an era when Europeans were still depending upon Prussian tactics that emphasized massed linear formations, the Americans frequently resorted to the thin skirmish line. The British put a premium on volley firing, which made up in firepower what it lacked in accuracy; the Americans encouraged individually aimed fire and showed a greater appreciation of military technology by substituting rifles for muskets in some of their units. The colonials were quick to recognize the value of fast, light infantry and demonstrated more military flexibility in employing swiftly moving forces for hit-and-run tactics. Their readiness to carry on winter campaigns and to march and fight at night also violated to some degree the code by which Europeans normally conducted warfare.

The American approach to warfare, however, was no conscious effort to introduce new military methods. For the most part, the amateurs tried to ape the professionals. Washington sought to model the Continental army along the lines of the British army by stressing drill and discipline, emphasizing distinctions in rank between officers and enlisted men, and insisting upon longer terms of enlistment. His aim was to create an army of regulars capable of meeting British troops on their own terms. An amateur himself, Washington had little faith in militia forces unless they were properly trained. Paradoxically, it was professionals like Lee and Gates who saw some military potential in short-term irregulars.

If George Washington and his generals were not military men primarily, where did they hail from and what was their background? A glance at the first group of fourteen generals commissioned by Congress in June, 1775, is revealing. Only three of this number—Washington, Lee, and Gates—had lived in the South. Of the remaining eleven generals, nine were Yankees and two Yorkers. This sectional imbalance was to continue throughout the war; most of the eminent military leaders were born or resided in the North. All fourteen men emerged from the upper or middle classes—some, like Washington, were great aristocratic landowners; others, like William Heath, owned less land but were prosperous; one was a lawyer, another a doctor, and a third a well-to-do artisan. Only three, so far as is known, held a college degree. Although a high number—about three-fourths—had seen active military service before the Revolution, relatively few had held a rank above major or commanded a unit larger than a battalion.

Their civilian activities were often of as much importance in preparing these men for a military career as was their active service in the field. The executive ability which Washington developed as a plantation owner—by supervising men, planning complex agricultural and commercial activities, and directing the efforts of a slave labor force—served him well as commander-in-chief. Philip Schuyler's previous experience as a part-time merchant along the Hudson eased his task of collecting supplies for the Continental army. And the habit of command demanded of men who led New England town meetings was precisely the same quality of leadership needed to take troops into battle. This ability of American generals to put their peacetime pursuits to good wartime use helps to account in part for the success of the patriots against British professionals.

Politics as well as peacetime experience played an important part in qualifying many men for an appointment in the army. Washington, as is well known, was picked primarily for political rather than military reasons. Similar motives governed the selection of many of his colleagues. Congress could rarely commission a general solely on the basis of merit. Conditions in the Continental Congress being what they were, state, not national, considerations were paramount. In certain instances—as in the case of Benedict Arnold in February, 1777—deserving individuals were passed over for promotion because of such political pressures.

Although political influence was a factor in selecting generals, remarkably few misfits reached that rank. The few who did, like old Israel Putnam, were rapidly replaced in responsible positions by younger and more able men. Others, such as the cantankerous John Sullivan, prepared the way for their own downfall by antagonizing congressmen. Most generals, however, showed an unusual capacity for learning. By conducting combat operations, they slowly mastered the art of warfare and by 1783 had become as professional as their adversaries in most respects.

Despite their growing professionalism, almost none of the military leaders of the Revolution emerged as first-rate generals. Amateurism, politics, and prudence resulting from feelings of inferiority when faced by British regulars inhibited the development of any outstanding commanders. Few had an opportunity to command forces of sufficient size to enable them to demonstrate a grasp of precise tactics or grand strategy. Of those who served for more than half the war, only Washington, Greene, and Arnold could be considered above average in ability.

Washington towered above his colleagues and deserved the title "Atlas of America" bestowed upon him by a French officer. To the position of commander-in-chief he brought great traits of character—an unflinching sense of responsibility, tenacity of purpose, and steady courage. His qualities of leadership alone must be reckoned among the more important influences in winning the war. But he also had serious shortcomings. His portrait as revealed in the pages that follow is often an unflattering one; he sometimes tried to shift the blame for his errors onto the shoulders of others, suspected that a "junto" was out to unseat him, and proved overly sensitive to criticism. As an army commander, he was inclined to rely too much upon his staff for advice and to employ faulty tactics on occasion. He never once defeated the enemy's main army in a major engagement on the open field. Despite these deficiencies, Washington was probably the man best qualified for the post of commander-in-chief in terms of military ability and temperament. While he was by no means as indispensable as historians sometimes have represented him to be, it is unlikely that the Continental army would have fared better under any one of its other top-ranking commanders.

One of Washington's greatest attributes was his genius in the art of managing men. Although he could not inspire genuine affection among the rank and file because of a certain hauteur and coldness in his personality, Washington had a profound effect upon the members of his official family. His ability to contend with jealous colleagues, to assess the relative strengths and weaknesses of his subordinates, and to cope with misfits and malcontents enabled him to weld a few fellow officers into some semblance of an American high command. It is not too much to suggest that Washington's gifts as a general were more political than military and that his unique contribution to the Continental army resulted not from his grasp of strategy and tactics but rather from his skill in handling America's military leaders. By shaping some of these men in his own image, he produced commanders who could rightly be called George Washington's generals.

GEORGE ATHAN BILLIAS

Clark University

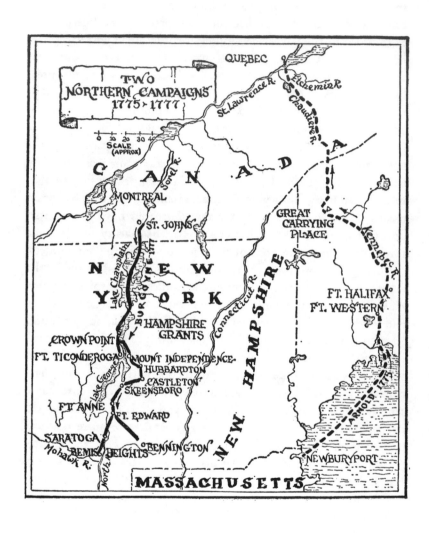

TWO
NORTHERN CAMPAIGNS
1775 ▸ 1777

SCALE
(APPROX)
0 10 20 30 40

QUEBEC

St. Lawrence R.

Etchemin R.

Chaudière R.

C A N A D A

MONTREAL

Sorel R.

ST. JOHNS

GREAT
CARRYING
PLACE

Kennebec R.

N E W

Lake Champlain

BURGOYNE 1777

Connecticut R.

FT. HALIFAX
FT. WESTERN

Y O R K

HAMPSHIRE
GRANTS

N E W   H A M P S H I R E

CROWN POINT

FT. TICONDEROGA

MOUNT INDEPENDENCE
HUBBARDTON

Lake George

CASTLETON
SKEENSBORO

FT. ANNE

FT. EDWARD

ARNOLD 1775

SARATOGA

BENNINGTON

Mohawk R.

BEMIS HEIGHTS

North R.

NEWBURYPORT

MASSACHUSETTS

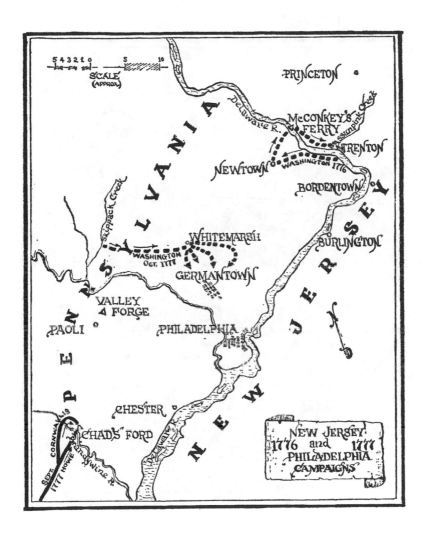

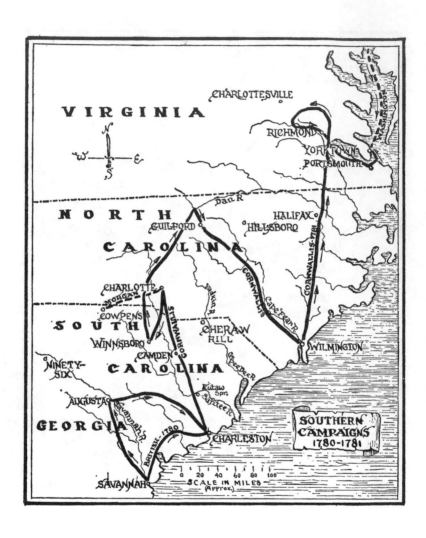

SOUTHERN
CAMPAIGNS
1780-1781

GEORGE WASHINGTON'S GENERALS

George Washington:

GEORGE WASHINGTON'S GENERALSHIP

MARCUS CUNLIFFE

University of Manchester, England

At first sight there is not much to be said about George Washington's generalship. At least, there is little new to be said. With hardly an exception, his contemporaries and biographers alike have agreed that he was an exemplary leader. Not even his few detractors have denied that he possessed certain essential attributes. To begin with, he was personally brave. In the fighting on Manhattan in September 1776, at Princeton in the following January, and at Germantown in September 1777, he displayed conspicuous courage. Tall, handsome, dignified, an expert horseman, he *looked* the part of a commander. He had great physical stamina; unlike some of his generals he was able to survive years of arduous campaigning without a serious illness. While less well educated than a number of his associates, he managed to express himself, in conversation and correspondence, with clarity and vigor. He was a methodical and energetic administrator. However despondent he might appear in private correspondence, he never wavered in his public insistence that the American cause was righteous and would triumph. Nor did he ever waver in his loyalty; the British admiral, Rodney, hopelessly misread his character in assuring Lord George Germain (as late as December 1780) that "Washington is certainly to be bought—honours will do it." [1] Then, early in the struggle he realized that crisis could be defined as peril plus opportunity. The limitations of his command—miscellaneous and inexperienced troops, inadequate equipment and supplies, lack of naval vessels—must determine military policy. "[W]e should on all occasions," he told the President of Congress in September 1776, "avoid a general Action, or put anything to the Risque, unless compelled by a necessity, into which we ought never to be drawn." [2] But these words were written at a time of grave danger, when his troops were raw, hard-pressed and considerably outnumbered. He never ceased to seek out the possibility of what he liked to call a "brilliant stroke": a sudden assault, that is, like the one across the Delaware in December 1776. And when he felt more confidence in the quality of his men, he did not shun large-scale encounters. Finally, though he had a high sense of his own reputation, he resisted the temptation to abuse his authority. No scandal, financial or moral, attached to his name. If he kept a punctilious record of the expenses owed him by the United States, he took no pay for his services. If British propaganda alleged that he had a mistress, the *canard* gained no credence. More important, he made it plain beyond doubt that he cherished no overweening dream of military dictatorship. In emergency Congress twice entrusted him with exceptional powers. Some of his officers were prepared to hint in 1783 that he might become king of the new nation. In such situations he responded with the utmost rectitude. No wonder that the contrast was so often drawn between his own career and that of Napoleon Bonaparte.

On all this there is virtually no argument. But to probe deeper, to offer any reassessment of Washington's relative military talent, or of his standing vis-à-vis his brother generals or the Continental Congress, is difficult. Some of the evidence we need—for example, on the true nature of the so-called Conway Cabal—is lacking and probably never will be available. And the story has become too fixed in its main outlines. Between us and what might be a fresher truth lie all the famous tableaux, apocryphal or authentic. Through portraiture we see Washington as elegant, severe, unruffled. We recall a whole sequence of static scenes:

Washington being placed in nomination for the chief command by John Adams at Philadelphia in June 1775; Washington reviewing his army on Cambridge Common a couple of weeks later; Washington sharing the miseries of the Valley Forge winter of 1777–78 with his men, yet (in our minds' eye) less affected by the cold than they; Washington rebuking Charles Lee at Monmouth Court House in June 1778, his soldiers broiled and parched, yet himself neither thirsty nor perspiring though angry enough with Lee; Washington superb in triumph at Yorktown, when Cornwallis surrenders to him in October 1781; Washington equally superb in his fatherly wisdom, when he puts on his spectacles to reply to the Newburgh Address of his discontented officers in March 1783; Washington bidding farewell to his officers, who now weep, at Fraunces Tavern in December of the same year. With such scenes are associated smaller vignettes: of nice young Lafayette, gruff old Steuben, jealous Gates and Conway, robust John Stark, comical Artemas Ward, villainous Arnold, loyal Greene, fat Knox; of Major André the British spy, so polite as to be almost masochistic; and of the Continental Congress, peevish, erratic, self-important. The total effect is like that of an old-fashioned engraving in which a central subject or person (Washington) is surrounded by a decorative border of tiny subordinate figures. The achievements of others are dwarfed, and made to seem dependent upon Washington's direction.

An awareness of this disparity accounts for much of the carping or malicious comment about him that circulated among such prominent soldiers and civilians as Joseph Reed, Charles Lee, Benjamin Rush, James Lovell, and John Adams. Admired, deferred to, secure in seniority, Washington (as they saw it) could easily afford the luxury of *noblesse oblige*, just as the wealthy, well-born Lafayette could easily rise to a nobility of conduct that endeared him to Washington but made him an exasperating example for a hard-up comrade like "Baron" de Kalb.

The nature of the war itself creates further difficulties of interpretation. Though we call it the Revolutionary War, or the

War of Independence, it was also a civil war—less so than the War Between the States, but enough to blur conventional military evaluations. It was an improvised, ambiguous struggle. We do well to remember, for instance, that John Stark, the hero of Bennington, had a brother William who fought on the opposite side and was killed in the Battle of Long Island in August 1776.[3] The British were not sure how to regard the conflict. The simplest answer was to call it a rebellion. Indeed, the British might have noted that such disturbances were apparently subject to a thirty-year cycle: 1775 was preceded by the Jacobite risings of 1745 and 1715, and by Monmouth's rebellion of 1685. The difference was that the American rebels were more remote, and the extent of their threat to British power less starkly obvious. So George III's advisers and generals fell into confusions over strategy and policy comparable to those that were later to perplex Abraham Lincoln. Both sides complained bitterly, and with reason, that they did not know where they stood, or where they ought to stand in a war that was much easier to lose than to win.

In the circumstances, British generalship was so hesitant and mediocre at major moments that Washington's own prowess is not easy to determine. When he tried to write this portion of his biography of the American commander-in-chief, Washington Irving confessed his bewilderment. The military campaigns, he said, reminded him of two drunk men trying to hit one another yet failing to connect. An English observer (in *The Gentleman's Magazine* of August 1778), while seeking of course to denigrate Washington, admitted to a similar inability to make sense of events:

> Nature has certainly given him some military talents, yet it is more than probable that he will never be a great soldier. . . . He is but of slow parts, and these are totally unassisted by any kind of education. Now, though such a character may acquit itself with some sort of eclat, in the poor, pitiful, unsoldierlike war in which he has hitherto been employed, it is romantic to suppose he must not fail, if ever it should be his lot to be opposed by real military skill.

The anonymous commentator continues:

> He never saw any actual service, but in the unfortunate action of Braddock. He never read a book in the art of war of higher value than Bland's Exercises; and it has already been noted, that he is by no means of bright or shining parts. If, then, military knowledge be not unlike all other; or, if it be not totally useless as to all the purposes of actual war, it is impossible that ever Mr. Washington should be a great soldier. In fact, by the mere dint and bravery of our army alone, he has been beaten whenever he has engaged; and that this is left to befall him again, is a problem which, I believe, most military men are utterly at a loss to solve.

The author is ungenerously inaccurate. Washington had had several years of soldiering in the French and Indian War. He had "heard the bullets whistle" more than once, before and after Braddock's disaster at the Monongahela. And it would strain the imagination to see the actions at Trenton and Princeton as proofs of British military superiority. Still, the commentator's puzzlement is understandable. For whatever reasons, and with the doubtful exception of Monmouth Court House, Washington *did* get the worst of all the major engagements he had a hand in during the first half of the war. The English writer goes on:

> It should not be denied . . . that all things considered, [Washington] really has performed wonders. That he is alive to command an army, or that an army is left him to command, might be sufficient to insure him the reputation of a great General, if British Generals any longer were what British Generals used to be. In short, I am of the opinion . . . that any other General in the world than General Howe would have beaten General Washington; and any other General in the world than General Washington would have beaten General Howe.[4]

Without taking the last observation too seriously, perhaps we can agree that Washington came very near to catastrophe in the latter part of 1776. With a little more persistence and audacity from Howe, the army led by Washington might have been destroyed. If so, and if he himself had fallen into British hands, the struggle might have continued and Washington would have been dismissed by posterity as a well-intentioned but outmatched amateur.

The situation—to return to the perspective of the period—was certainly novel. As this *Gentleman's Magazine* assessment indicates, the war defied measurement according to European standards. It was a civil war, or a rebellion, or a popular patriotic rising, or a mixture of all three. Washington was a novice, with a reputedly limited intelligence; and yet he had "performed wonders."

In the final analysis the two most decisive factors were perhaps not personal but geographical: the huge extent of America and the width of the Atlantic. We have said that Washington's own eminence has made the activities of his officers seem minuscule. Geography, as Washington Irving came to feel, had a similar diminishing effect upon the commanders of both sides. A third factor, the French alliance, could be held almost equally decisive. Its inception might be counted as a diplomatic rather than a military success, while the all-important victory at Yorktown may be seen primarily as a Franco-British affair—a blow struck in a century-long contest.

If we attach some weight to such elements, what are we left with by way of an estimate of George Washington's generalship? It seems that there must be some scaling-down of the wilder claims: claims, it must be said, that he did not advance on his own behalf and that have not been asserted by reputable historians in the past half-century. We must discard the legend, disproved but still lingering on in folklore, that Frederick the Great ever sent Washington a sword with the engraved inscription, "From the oldest soldier in Europe to the greatest soldier in the world." [5] Instead, let us consider dispassionately his stature as a fighting general, or field commander; and secondly, as an organizing general, or commander-in-chief.

Washington's talents as a field commander were in truth not tested often enough, or upon a big enough scale, to rank him automatically with the prodigies of military history. Like the other American generals at the beginning of the war, he was after all deficient in experience. At the outset this recognition weighed upon them to a perhaps undue extent. None of them had had much formal training on the European pattern. They were at best veterans of colonial warfare, unaccustomed to the handling of large bodies of troops or to the employment of special arms such as cavalry. Washington never had the responsibility for campaigns on the Napoleonic scale, not to mention those of the American Civil War. This is not to maintain that he would have failed to rise to the occasion, but simply to note that the giant occasion did not present itself. We can only guess what his "ceiling" of achievement might have been in the tactical disposition of one big army confronting another.[6]

On the debit side, military historians tend to agree that Washington made mistakes. Possibly he was too ready to shift the blame for a reverse onto a subordinate. This has been said of his treatment of Nathanael Greene after the loss of Fort Washington, and of his more peremptory reaction to Charles Lee at Monmouth Court House. The evidence against him is by no means conclusive; and indeed few senior soldiers in history could be held entirely innocent of such a charge. Washington's record is, for example, no worse and probably better than that of Stonewall Jackson in this respect. As for actual mistakes, he is most commonly accused of the following:

Long Island (August 1776): Splitting his army between New York and Brooklyn; failure to appreciate the value of cavalry for reconnaissance purposes, and so being taken by surprise through a flank attack; failure to give close supervision to General Israel Putnam's dispositions, which led to raw troops fighting without benefit of entrenchments.[7]

Fort Washington (November 1776): The loss of 3,000 men when the Fort was captured through his own indecision.[8]

Brandywine (September 1777): Failure to use his Light Horse to gather information of enemy moves, or in other ways to anticipate Howe's flank attack; general lack of firm direction.[9]

Germantown (October 1777): Reliance upon too intricate a plan of battle.[10]

Campaigns of 1777: A strategic error in deciding to march south against Howe's invasion of Pennsylvania, instead of joining Gates and Schuyler so as to crush Burgoyne in the north and then swing south, with reinforcements from the Northern army, against Howe.[11]

These charges are not without substance. In extenuation, it should be said that most soldiers, even celebrated ones, make mistakes. Stonewall Jackson, brilliant in the Shenandoah Valley in 1862, was abominably sluggish in the Peninsula fighting a few weeks later. Washington's errors, significantly, were concentrated in the first half of the war, when he was a learner in command of learners, face to face with professionals. Probably Howe could have destroyed him at the end of 1776. But Howe hesitated; Washington's response was the splendidly impudent *coup* at Trenton. It was a raid rather than a battle; part of the plan miscarried; but the effect upon American morale was tremendous. It was as needed a victory, at the time, as was the more ripely comprehensive and more thoroughly professional victory at Yorktown five years later. The difference in the scope and context of the two engagements defined the distance that Washington and his army had traveled in skill, in offensive capacity, and in assurance. Valley Forge and the French alliance represent the turning point. After the winter of 1777–78, the troops close to Washington began to correspond to the notion he had always stressed: namely, that America must have a disciplined national force, as trained and tried as the best European ranks that could be brought against them.

Here we come to a point that is worth stressing. Ever since the Revolution, Americans have been debating the respective merits of professional and of amateur soldiery. It has been a heated debate, for it embodies quite fundamental divisions of opinion as to the true nature of American nationalism and democracy. The contenders have both managed to find ammunition in their interpretation of the Revolutionary War. The professionals cite Washington's highly critical references to the militia, and to all short-term enlistments; the conflict was won, they believe, by the Continental regiments. The amateurs dwell upon the battles in which the militia fought stoutly, and upon the superior qualities of initiative, patriotism, and ingenuity which derive from an amateur tradition. George Washington, the Virginia planter, could be seen as the highest product of this essentially civilian approach to warfare.[12]

That he retained some "civilian" characteristics is undeniable. His deference to Congress, and to civilian authority generally, may be seen in this light. It is arguable that the tactics to which he sometimes resorted show a refreshing freedom from military orthodoxy, and that the British generals were hopelessly hidebound. No doubt the achievements of Washington's lieutenants —Greene, Knox and Morgan especially—are striking illustrations of amateur proficiency. But the professional-amateur debate is misleading in various ways. On the British side, many of the officers prided themselves on a dilettante approach to warfare. Nor do we give proper credit to the Americans if we caricature the British conduct of operations as a series of brutally stupid frontal attacks on the Bunker Hill pattern. On occasion the British showed considerable enterprise. One example of this would be Grey's night assault on Anthony Wayne at Paoli in September 1777, when the British killed, wounded, or captured nearly 400 Americans for the loss of only 8 of their own men. On the American side, amateurishness may have been evident—perhaps all too evident—in the war's initial stages. But after two or three years of campaigning, Washington, his officers, and his Continental rank-and-file had become professionals in all important respects.[13]

This was what Washington himself ardently desired. He did not visualize himself as a guerrilla leader, a will-of-the-wisp harassing the stolid British like some brigand chief. From the start he strove to build an army able to meet the British in open battle and beat them at their own game.[14] He knew that this was only a dream in the early stages, and acted accordingly. But it was no idle dream; it was an ambition that he labored to fulfill. As his correspondence shows, he hammered away at the task of creating an army officered (as far as possible) by gentlemen, observing strict discipline, properly armed, accoutered, paid, rewarded, punished. His was no doubt a sensible conservatism: even the most revolutionary armies discover the advantages of well-established procedures and hierarchical distinctions. "Let us have a respectable Army," was his plea from 1776 onward, "and such as will be competent to every exigency." In other words, an army much like that of Howe or Rochambeau.[15]

But George Washington was not merely a field commander, though he maintained his headquarters in the field with whatever troops seemed to be best placed for his manifold purposes. He was commander-in-chief. The limits of his authority could not be exactly defined, in a situation without precedent. Even if a precise definition could have been formulated, much else would have remained hazy. He had a large but vague jurisdiction. His commission came from the Continental Congress, a body speaking for a then nonexistent nation. Congress entrusted him with considerable powers. But Congress itself was only a comity, or perhaps more accurately a committee, of thirteen semi-sovereign states. Washington was clearly senior in rank to all the other generals. But what control was he to exercise, theoretically or actually, over armies that might be several hundred miles away from his own headquarters? To what extent could he give orders to the French military and naval leaders when their expeditions began to arrive in 1778? Who was to formulate strategy? With whom was he to communicate, and on what terms—governors of states, other commanders, the President of Congress, the Board of War? If he lost favor, was he removable?

Like the rest of his countrymen, Washington had to proceed by trial and error. That he did err now and then seems both undeniable and forgivable. His appointment was meant to sym-

bolize the spirit of union. In 1775 such spirit was more an as-
piration than a reality. Through indiscreet early letters he let it
be known that he, the Virginian, was not much impressed by
New England's military prowess. Some harm was done. He had
one or two awkward passages with the French, again through
indiscreet and possibly disingenuous correspondence which fell
into the wrong hands. For a prudent man he sometimes expressed
himself with dangerous candor in letters to his family and to
friends in and out of Congress. Yet he learned by his mistakes.
He shed all trace of Virginia localism, until he, more than any
other person or any institution or symbol, became synonymous
with America's cause. And compared with most of his prominent
fellow countrymen—soldiers and civilians—he was a model of
discretion. His letters are sometimes angry and self-righteous;
they are never whining, silly or malicious.

It was both a strength and a weakness of his position that he
seemed, in more than one sense, irreplaceable. In retrospect the
critical mutterings of 1776–77, in Congress and among certain
army officers, strike us as petty and perhaps even treasonable.
We find it absurd that Washington's military policy should be
subject to the scrutiny of the five men whom Congress constituted as the Board of War and Ordnance in June 1776. What
assistance could be rendered by such a member of the Board as
the utterly unmilitary John Adams? It was replaced in 1777 by
a new Board not composed of congressmen. But was this not
even worse, when intrigue might place disgruntled army officers
upon it? Or what of the six special committees sent by the Continental Congress to inquire into the army's affairs? Knowing
what befell Gates at Camden—or thinking we know—we wonder how anyone could have entertained the notion of substituting
him for Washington in the supreme command.

But this is hindsight, and a hindsight which may be cruelly
unfair. On the whole Congress and Washington worked together
well—fantastically well if we compare their relations with those
between Congress and Lincoln's wretched generals in the Civil
War. The boards and special committees of Washington's day

had next to nothing in common with the inquisitorial Committee on the Conduct of the War. They were anxious to help, and rendered all the aid within their power. It is doubtful whether there was any serious and concerted scheme to supplant Washington. There was something of a crisis of confidence in 1777–78. His more demonstratively enthusiastic supporters may have persuaded him that an organized plot existed. In the subsequent jockeying for position certain officers—Conway, Gates, Mifflin—may have been identified as a coalition hostile to Washington. Whether they were is dubious. Washington and posterity have treated them with marked disdain.

Whatever the inner history of a situation that may have had *no* inner history, Washington emerged as the undisputed commander, at the head of a group of competent and devoted officers. If there was a plot, it hardly deserves the name. If there was a counterstroke by Washington, it was far from being a Putsch.[16] In the long run, the effects of the entire episode were probably beneficial. The army could rely on Washington to put its case before the country; Congress could feel reasonably sure that with Washington in command there was no risk of subversion by a military junto. It would have been amazing if there had been no friction, no dissension, no backbiting. Once his position was secure, Washington was able to display a remarkable magnanimity. True, he complained unceasingly of the difficulties in his path. The war dragged on and on. The French had their own views of fruitful strategy. There were ominous mutinies in the Continental line. Yet there was a good deal more acrimony in the British camps and council chambers, and far more in that later American conflict of 1861–65.

Washington's ultimate success may owe as much to British limpness as to his own firmness. It has been plausibly maintained that the British situation was impossible from the start, and that no amount of brilliance in leadership could have offset the formidable disadvantages of having to fight an unpopular war, with resources strained by other global commitments, in a terrain in which merely to feed or move an army—let alone fight major battles—was an administrative problem of daunting dimensions.[17] The surrender of Cornwallis could not have been encompassed without the French fleet and army. Washington's own growing military capacity would have counted for little if his generals, junior officers, and enlisted men had not grown commensurately in competence and assurance. The heroic efforts of Greene, Knox, Lafayette, and others ought not to be underrated in the apportionment of credit. Greene was accurate as well as warmhearted in writing to Knox after Yorktown:

> Colonel Lee who has lately returned from the Northern Army says you are the genius of it, and that everything is said of you that you can wish. . . . Your success in Virginia is brilliant, glorious, great and important. The commander-in-chief's head is all covered with laurels, and yours so shaded with them that one can hardly get sight of it.[18]

As Washington himself was quick to acknowledge, there was room for more than one set of laurels.

Nevertheless, his devoted subordinates and his admiring French allies gladly yielded to him a major share of the glory. We may discount some of their compliments as flattery or as formal rhetoric. Yet they knew him, closely and testingly, from day to day and month to month. If he had been indecisive, or unduly arrogant, nervous, or reckless, he could not have won and held their respect. The British army no doubt labored under handicaps; yet those of Washington's army were sometimes very similar. Long after the war, John Adams is said to have growled that Washington was "a block of wood!" [19] If he really made the remark, which is likely enough, it can be understood as an oblique commendation, a grudging testimony to the vital elements of straightforwardness, consistency, and reliability in Washington's character. He won, that is, by taking to the field and staying there: by tenacity rather than by Napoleonic *brio*. Though he could be dashing in action, his overriding service to America lay in his steadfastness. He was a fixed point in a shifting universe.

Washington's role in the War of Independence was extraor-

dinary. There are no close historical parallels. Yet two comparisons can be made, each of which helps to remind us that the
commander-in-chief was only in part a military leader. The two
comparisons are with Charles de Gaulle and Dwight D. Eisenhower. Like de Gaulle, though with less conscious purpose on
his part, George Washington symbolized his country and its will
to resist. The new nation insisted upon endowing "His Excellency" George Washington with charismatic glamour.[20] He
was able to sustain the role with remarkable modesty, all things
considered, as well as with remarkable dignity. Like the French
leader, he was a figure of exceptional strength of purpose. And
like General Eisenhower, he was a coalition general for a large
part of the war. A great proportion of his work went on in
conference and in correspondence. Some of his activities were
political, or diplomatic, rather than military, as when he had to
deal with British offers to negotiate, or with French military
and naval chiefs. As with General Eisenhower, major strategic
plans usually lay outside his scope; but their implementation
often depended upon his advice. Despite his charismatic authority, he was more a mediator than a dictator. He communicated
with governors of states, with Congress, with the Board of War,
with the whole gamut of overlapping jurisdictions. In this respect, indeed, we might say that he was a dictator: a dictator of
letters, not of decisions. If his charismatic symbols were those
of the flag, the sword, the beautifully caparisoned horse, his
day-to-day responsibilities were more appropriately symbolized
by the chairman's gavel, the memorandum, the agenda, and the
secretary's quill. It was his task, and his talent, to preside, to
inform, to adjudicate, to advise, to soothe, to persuade, to anticipate, to collaborate. He had to weld the states together, as far
as he could; to co-operate with the French, harmonizing America's aims and theirs; to reconcile the competing claims of different theaters of war; to face the consequences, in terms of
mounting pride and estrangement, of having managed to create
a professional army; to remember that though a master of men,
he was the servant of his country and of Congress.[21] A co-or-

dinator, he had to learn how to stay near the scene of military action and yet not allow local problems to narrow his vision. A more mercurial figure might well have lost patience. A more genial one might have found his popularity was too cheaply purchased, and so too rapidly dispersed. For most of the war he had to stand on the defensive, reacting to British pressures. But when the chance came, in 1781, he showed that years of parleying had not eroded his spirit. At a vital moment he seized the initiative, like an ideal coalition leader, in ensuring that he and the French for once acted in entire harmony. In earlier episodes he may perhaps now and then have picked the wrong alternative in what he called his "choice of difficulties." Should he, for instance, have marched north instead of south in 1777? Should he, failing that, have retained the 3,000 men he sent to reinforce Schuyler and Gates? He made up his mind and acted, without vain regrets. He sent help to another army at the expense of his own immediate command. Can we imagine such a response from, say, General George B. McClellan?

What irony has accrued to those grudging judgments from *The Gentleman's Magazine!*

> Now, though such a character may acquit itself with some sort of eclat, in the poor, pitiful, unsoldierlike war in which he has hitherto been employed, it is romantic to suppose he must not fail, if ever it should be his lot to be opposed by real military skill. . . .

If and perhaps. History can only answer that it was Washington who stayed the course; it was Howe and Clinton and Cornwallis who headed back home to their firesides and their extenuating speeches and memoirs.

FOOTNOTES

1. Quoted in Henry S. Commager and Richard B. Morris, eds., *The Spirit of 'Seventy-Six: The Story of the American Revolution as told by Participants*, 2 vols. (Indianapolis, 1958), II, 703.
2. Letter of September 8, 1776, in John C. Fitzpatrick, ed., *The Writ-*

ings of George Washington, 39 vols. (Washington, D.C., 1931–44), VI, 28.

3. Maldwyn A. Jones, *American Immigration* (Chicago, 1960), pp. 53–54.

4. "Particulars of the Life and Character of General Washington, Extracted from a Letter in Lloyd's Evening Post of Aug. 17, Signed An Old Soldier," *The Gentleman's Magazine*, Vol. XLVIII (August 1778). This is conveniently reprinted in Martin Kallich and Andrew MacLeish, eds., *The American Revolution Through British Eyes* (Evanston, 1962), pp. 111–13.

5. The results of various scrutinies of the legend are summarized in Francis V. Greene, *The Revolutionary War and the Military Policy of the United States* (New York, 1911).

6. "His courage is calm and brilliant, but to appreciate in a satisfactory manner the real extent of his . . . ability as a great . . . captain, I think one should have seen him at the head of a greater army, with greater means than he has had, and opposed to an enemy less his superior. At least one cannot fail to give him the title of an excellent patriot, of a wise and virtuous man, and one is . . . tempted to ascribe to him all good qualities, even those that circumstances have not yet permitted him to develop." This is the rather feline opinion of Colonel de Broglie, a young French nobleman who joined his regiment in 1782. W. S. Baker, *Character Portraits of Washington* (Philadelphia, 1887), pp. 18–21. Perhaps its coolness, unusual for this late stage of the war, has something to do with family history. Four years earlier, another de Broglie was being hinted at as a candidate for what would in effect have been the chief command in America. See Douglas S. Freeman, *George Washington*, 6 vols. (New York, 1948–54), IV, 99.

7. F. V. Greene, *op. cit.*, p. 41; Christopher Ward, *The War of the Revolution*, 2 vols. (New York, 1952), I, 229; George F. Scheer and Hugh F. Rankin, *Rebels and Redcoats* (Cleveland, 1957), p. 174.

8. This criticism has been most sharply formulated by Bernhard Knollenberg, in *Washington and the Revolution: A Reappraisal* (New York, 1940), pp. 129–39.

9. For some representative comments, see Willard M. Wallace, *Appeal to Arms: A Military History of the American Revolution* (New York, 1951), p. 139; John R. Alden, *The American Revolution, 1775–1783* (New York, 1954), p. 123; Freeman, *op. cit.*, IV, 488; and Scheer and Rankin, *op. cit.*, pp. 240, 293–94.

10. Ward, *op. cit.*, I, 364–71; Alden, *op. cit.*, p. 125; Scheer and Rankin, *op. cit.*, p. 244.

11. One of the first books in Washington historiography to express serious reservations as to the commander-in-chief's military prowess (including his failure to understand the value of cavalry) was Charles Francis Adams, Jr., *Studies Military and Diplomatic, 1775–1865* (New York, 1911). For the campaigns of 1777 see pp. 132–49.

12. One stout upholder of this view is John A. Logan, *The Volunteer Soldier of America* (Chicago, 1887), p. 484: "No amount of preliminary technical education could have made a greater general of the hero of Trenton, Princeton, and Yorktown. His genius was natural, and bloomed into the perfection attained under the developing influence of actual warfare."

13. There are intelligent comments on these matters in Walter Millis, *Arms and Men* (New York, 1956), pp. 32–33; Daniel Boorstin, *The Americans: The Colonial Experience* (New York, 1958), pp. 364–71; Theodore Ropp, *War in the Modern World* (Durham, 1959), pp. 71–80; and Alfred Vagts, *A History of Militarism*, revised ed. (New York, 1959), pp. 92–101.

14. An excellent recent study is Russell F. Weigley, *Towards an American Army: Military Thought from Washington to Marshall* (New York, 1962). See especially pp. 1–7.

15. By the closing stages of the war he had gone far enough in this direction to astonish discriminating Frenchmen, although previously Mifflin and other generals had enjoyed a reputation for being somewhat more effective disciplinarians. "I had expected to see," wrote the Comte de Ségur, "unkempt soldiers and officers without training. . . . I saw a well-disciplined army presenting in every detail the very image of order, reason, training and experience." Chastellux was equally impressed: "When one sees . . . the General's guards encamped within the precincts of his house; nine waggons, destined to carry his baggage, ranged in his court; . . . grooms taking care of very fine horses belonging to the General Officers and their Aides de Camp; when one observes the perfect order . . . within these precincts, . . . one is tempted to apply to the Americans what Pyrrhus said of the Romans: *Truly these people have nothing barbarous in their discipline!*" Gilbert Chinard, ed., *George Washington as the French Knew Him* (Princeton, 1940), pp. 37, 57. If these officers had visited Washington's headquarters in 1776 or 1777, instead of 1781 or 1782, they would of course have found a more rough-and-ready atmosphere.

16. The undercurrents of hostility and rivalry are closely analyzed in Knollenberg, *op. cit.*, pp. 30–77, and in Kenneth R. Rossman, *Thomas Mifflin and the Politics of the American Revolution*

(Chapel Hill, 1952), pp. 91–139, as well as in Freeman, *op. cit.*, IV, 581–611. An older account, which assumes that opposition to Washington was organized, is Louis C. Hatch, *The Administration of the American Revolutionary Army* (New York, 1904), pp. 23–34.

17. See Eric Robson, *The American Revolution in its Political and Military Aspects* (London, 1955), pp. 93–152.

18. Greene to Knox, December 10, 1781, quoted in North Callahan, *Henry Knox: General Washington's General* (New York, 1958), p. 190.

19. An anecdote relating to *circa* 1816, recorded by John G. Palfrey; see *William & Mary Quarterly*, 3rd series, XV (January 1958), 93–94.

20. Seymour Martin Lipset, *The First New Nation: The United States in Historical and Comparative Perspective* (New York, 1963), pp. 16–23.

21. Edmund C. Burnett, *The Continental Congress* (New York, 1941), has some fascinating detail on Congress and the army. See for example pp. 442–67 for the period in 1780 when a committee of Congress visited Washington's headquarters.

BIBLIOGRAPHY

Burnett, Edmund C., *The Continental Congress*. New York, 1941. Explores the complicated relationships of the commander-in-chief with his civilian colleagues and mentors.

Cunliffe, Marcus, *George Washington: Man and Monument*. Boston, 1958. Treats Washington's symbolic as well as military role.

Fitzpatrick, John C., ed., *The Writings of George Washington*, 39 vols. Washington, 1931–44. Perhaps the best way of putting oneself in Washington's place is to read selected letters from these volumes. The portions dealing with the war years number some 10,000 pages.

Freeman, Douglas S., *George Washington: A Biography*, 6 vols. New York, 1948–54. The essential work on Washington. Volumes IV and V relate to the Revolutionary War and they are thorough, dispassionate, and admirably indexed. Washington's military qualities are interestingly assessed at the end of Volume V.

Frothingham, Thomas G., *Washington, Commander in Chief*. Boston, 1930. An older work that is laudatory in tone but still of some value.

Knollenberg, Bernhard, *Washington and the Revolution: A Reappraisal*. New York, 1940. The most searching critical comment to be found on Washington.

Miller, John C., *Triumph of Freedom, 1775–1783*. Boston, 1948. A solid contribution as a general account of the war.

Sparks, Jared, ed., *Correspondence of the American Revolution, Being Letters of Eminent Men to Washington, 1775–1789*, 4 vols. Boston, 1853. Supplements the work of Fitzpatrick.

Charles Lee:

THE SOLDIER AS RADICAL

JOHN W. SHY

Princeton University

THE reputation of Charles Lee has long suffered by comparison with that of George Washington. He is traditionally remembered as a troublemaker—one who confounded Washington by disobeying orders, intriguing for the position of commander-in-chief, and calling for a court-martial with the hope of casting his superior into oblivion. Lee may have even betrayed the Revolution itself because of his malice toward Washington. His conduct after dismissal from the army has been debated so long as a political, not a military, question that Lee's modern biographer has subtitled his book, *Traitor or Patriot?* [1] But in all these evaluations, the result has been to judge rather than to understand an extraordinary human being.

To understand Lee in depth, a psychiatrist instead of a historian is probably required. Certainly he would have benefited from psychiatry had such a medical practice existed in his day. Born as the youngest child of a prominent family near Chester, England, he grew up in a home environment created by the early death of five out of seven children. The only other survivor was his elder sister Sidney. Disliked by his mother, he lavished much of his affection on Sidney, who like himself never married. He grew to be a tall, skinny, ugly young man, remarkable for his slovenly personal habits and coarse speech. His sex life seems to have been of the transient kind, and in those instances where he became interested in some woman he seems to have been rebuffed. There were hints, but no more than that, of homosexuality.[2] Besides his sister, the only serious rivals for his affection were his dogs. It may be that Lee's love for dumb animals was the only kind of uncomplicated relationship of which this most complex personality was capable.

If Charles Lee conversed as he wrote, then the mid-twentieth-century label for him would be "compulsive talker." It appears that Lee would say almost anything. He was equally unrestrained in his letters. Rarely did he include a request that his views be kept confidential. More often than not, he suggested his letters be printed. His published attacks on Washington after the court-martial caused even Lee's remaining friends to turn away in disgust. When Lee turned sour, and his frenetic energy that had helped sustain the American cause in 1776 was turned against the commander-in-chief two years later, then another modern label is suggested: the "true believer," the fanatic whose very strength lies in his lack of balance, judgment, and self-restraint.[3]

Washington, with all the understatement of a Virginia gentleman, called Lee "fickle" long before he knew the worst about him. Washington's biographer, Douglas Southall Freeman, another Virginia gentleman who understood perfectly the vocabulary of his subject, hated Lee with a passion that he had some difficulty in controlling.[4] At best, Freeman ceased to take Lee seriously, treating him as a two-dimensional, unbalanced man. Many historians, led on perhaps by Lee's own admission of "the distemper of my mind," have been willing to do likewise.[5]

Members of the Continental Congress took Lee with utter seriousness, however, when the time came to organize an American army in June, 1775. For a man of forty-three, and a citizen of an empire at peace for more than a decade, he had an impressive military record. At the age of fourteen he had received a commission in his father's regiment. While still in his early twenties, he served as lieutenant in one of two British regiments sent to America from Ireland in early 1755 under the command of Major General Edward Braddock. Scanty evidence suggests that Lee first met Washington that spring on the disastrous expedition against Fort Duquesne, when Lee's regiment was shot to pieces and Braddock killed in an ambush by French-led Indians.[6]

Lee's regiment, the 44th Foot, moved northward into New York as Britain's war with France expanded in North America. Vigorous recruiting, by Lee and others, brought the 44th back to strength, so that it soon was composed primarily of native Americans. The regiment was in the Albany area during 1756, where Lee had time to study Iroquois culture, acquiring an Indian consort and a Mohawk name—"Boiling Water"—in the process. In 1757, he went on the abortive expedition against Louisbourg, but service the next summer was more rugged. By then a captain and company commander, Lee had two ribs smashed by a musket ball before the French earthworks around Ticonderoga. He was several months recovering from his wounds, but spent some of his convalescence criticizing his superior for the conduct of a campaign that ranks with Braddock's march for misfortune and bloodshed.

The next two campaigns in which Lee participated brought about the fall of Canada. He was at the siege of Niagara, went on a hazardous mission from Niagara to Fort Pitt, and then accompanied the main attack in 1760 down the St. Lawrence which ended with the taking of Montreal. With the capture of Montreal, fighting came to an end on the American mainland.

Lee got leave to go to England, rather than vegetate with his messmates in the American wilderness, and soon was promoted to major in a newly-raised regiment. When Spain jumped into the war in early 1762, the British response was an expedition to the Iberian Peninsula. Lee served there under Brigadier General John Burgoyne, and each won his brightest victory when Burgoyne ordered and Lee led a daring and successful raid upon a Spanish encampment.

Peace came to Britain in 1763, but by 1765 Lee was off to other wars. He went to Poland where civil strife threatened, carrying letters of introduction to Stanislas Poniatowski—King of Poland, former lover of Catherine the Great, and reputedly one of the most enlightened and liberal minds of his age. Though Lee became royal aide-de-camp, he saw no action and, after a visit to Constantinople, returned to England. In 1769, when Stanislas lost control of his kingdom as the result of a revolt, and Russian armies began moving into Poland to give him "support," Lee returned to Warsaw. Commissioned a Polish major general without command, he joined the huge Russian army in Moldavia, and watched it grapple with an even larger Turkish army. Then, sick and disgusted, he went slowly home to England by way of Hungarian spas and Italian beaches. He had seen in his travels through Poland what civil war could be: rebel bands so active that "it is impossible to stir ten yards without an escort of Russians," and vicious fighting methods "about as gentle as ours was in America with the Shawenese and Dellawars." [7]

During the years after 1755, while Washington was patrolling a comparatively quiet Virginia frontier and worrying about the price of tobacco, Lee had been exposed to a variety of military experiences. More important, his experience had profoundly affected him, because he was that rarity in any age—the soldier who is also an intellectual. He had attended good schools, knew classical and modern languages and literature, and was especially fond of Shakespeare. But above all, he had studied military theory and tactics. John Adams, who came to know Lee "very thoroughly," modestly admitted that Lee was the only American officer who had read more than he had on the history and art of war.

If the active service which guided his military study was deficient in any respect, it was in its comparative lack of experience with the "conventional" warfare epitomized by Frederick the Great. Lee had seen the highly disciplined Prussian battalions move slowly through their intricate linear tactical formations, but no document records that he was especially impressed. On the contrary, he expressed contempt for "Hyde Park tactics" and recollected that British regulars became effective in the French and Indian War only after they had forgotten everything they had learned on the parade grounds at home. His less studious and stay-at-home contemporaries were apt to regard Prussian military methods as the proper models for warfare, but Lee knew better. Between his books, travels, and combat experience in irregular warfare, he had become something of a military radical, prone to doubt the accepted practices of his day.[8]

His radicalism was not solely the product of experience and study, nor was it confined to military affairs. By temperament he was disposed to attack or question the assumptions and conventions that most men lived by. Quiet loyalty did not stand high in his scale of values and three British commanders in America had felt the sting of Captain Lee's tongue and pen. The King of England himself was not immune. When George III granted Lee an audience in order to receive a letter from Stanislas of Poland, and began to apologize for his inability to offer Lee military preferment, the latter stopped him short by coolly observing: "Sir, I will never give your Majesty an opportunity of breaking your promise to me again." [9]

Some have used this broken promise to explain Lee's readiness to serve on the American side in the Revolution. But the truth lies deeper. Lee's personal and family connections were with the Whig politicians who opposed the policies of young King George in the 1760's. He was not satisfied, however, with the narrow ground of opposition taken by the Whig aristocrats. Instead, Lee repeatedly attacked the very principle of monarchy itself. He called Switzerland "those bless'd regions of manly Democracy" (when *democracy* was still a dirty word), and darkly alluded to making himself a good soldier "for purposes honest, but which I shall not mention." [10] It was not only a disgruntled half-pay officer who tendered his services to Congress in 1775, but a man whose whole life seemed preparation to fight against arbitrary, corrupt monarchical authority in the name of American freedom.

Members of Congress were impressed by Lee, for political as well as military reasons. Shrewd, learned men like John Adams would have detected a mere military adventurer. But Lee talked to them earnestly and knowledgeably about Rousseau and the rights of man; he shared their fondness for the now-forgotten Whiggish historian, Mrs. Catherine Macaulay; and he wrote a biting pamphlet explaining why American militiamen could fight more effectively than British regulars. Once Virginia had been placated with the appointment of Washington as commander-in-chief and Massachusetts was satisfied by the naming of Artemas Ward, some delegates from these two provinces proposed Lee as third-ranking general. When Congress hesitated, Washington himself requested Lee's appointment and the issue was settled in June, 1775.[11]

From that time until the early fall of 1776, there can be no question that Lee lived up to the highest expectations of his supporters. To the Boston siege in the summer of 1775 he brought the organizational, tactical, and engineering skills that were so badly needed. There are glimpses in the records of Lee working tirelessly to improve the new American army—riding, observing, writing, correcting, and commending. James Warren, who was disturbed by Lee's lack of conventional manners, described Lee's activity for Sam Adams: "[Lee] came in just before dinner, drank some punch, said he wanted no dinner, took no notice of the company, mounted his horse, and went off again to the lines." [12]

Washington, dividing his army into three divisions, gave Lee the northernmost command, facing the Charlestown peninsula and British position on Bunker Hill. Lee's brigadiers were Nathanael Greene, of Rhode Island, and John Sullivan, of New Hampshire. In late July, he was exhorting Sullivan to use all his manpower to complete the fortifications, adding: "For God's sake finish and strengthen the abattis." By late August, when a British attack over the Charlestown neck against Lee's position seemed imminent, the Americans were able to move first. With 1,200 men as a work party and twice as many to cover them, Sullivan moved forward and in a single night entrenched Ploughed Hill, within point-blank range of Bunker Hill. The

British countered with a violent artillery and naval bombardment, but the work had been done too well; Lee's division stood fast.[13]

Confidence in Lee's abilities soon spread throughout the army. Greene wrote of Lee's "genius and learning," and William Thompson, colonel of riflemen, reported that he was "everyday more pleased with General Lee." [14] As winter came on and the likelihood of British naval raids on American ports grew, Washington ordered Lee to Rhode Island to lay out defensive positions, and later to New York on a similar mission. It is clear that Lee was a trouble shooter, a key man to be sent to points where danger threatened.

When it became apparent in February, 1776, that the American expedition against Canada had failed, and that the British soon would withdraw from Boston to attack somewhere to the southward, American leaders were in a quandary as to what to do with Lee. "We want you at N. York— We want you at Cambridge— We want you in Virginia—" wrote John Adams. "But Canada seems of more Importance than any of those places," he continued, "and therefore you are sent there." [15] But the estimate of the situation changed almost before Lee received this letter, and Congress ordered him south instead. At Baltimore, Williamsburg, and Norfolk, Lee did all he could to strengthen defenses. Then in May came definite word that a British fleet was moving off the Carolinas, probably toward Charleston. Lee set out immediately for that city.

From Boston to Norfolk, Lee had contributed his military expertise at the crucial, formative stage of American resistance. The defenses that he had planned and begun at Newport and New York would later crumble before determined British attacks, but he had made those places far stronger than they had been before. Of greater importance, however, was his political activity between December, 1775, and May, 1776. During those trying months, people on the American seaboard outside Boston were wavering. There had been little fighting and many people, caught up in the shadowy state between war and peace and loyalty and treason, made small compromises with British officials. There seemed to be a tendency to listen more closely to loyalist neighbors now that an abstract argument had become immediate and concrete, and to postpone any violent or decisive action as long as possible. Lee moved through this murky world of indecision like a flame. In Newport and New York, he made suspected Tories swear an elaborate oath.[16] In New York and Virginia, he disarmed them or moved them from militarily sensitive areas. When fence-sitters living under the guns of British ships used their vulnerability as an excuse for inaction, Lee told them to move out where they could not be threatened. He demanded that the Revolutionary authorities in New York, Maryland, and Virginia stop communicating with their royal governors, and make a clean break.

Lee antagonized and upset civil officials wherever he went, but he also shocked them out of their lethargy. He had been an outspoken advocate of an immediate declaration of American independence since October, 1775. Lee supported the idea of independence partly for diplomatic reasons, but primarily as a means of crystallizing the popular will to fight before it was eroded by confusion and delay. He saw clearly that a successful Revolution needed much more than an army in the field; it required action at the grass-roots level—determination and efficiency among its supporters, and firm control over its enemies. The extralegal political bodies that had sprung up since 1774 were to provide the basis of this action, but their members in general had been unwilling to usurp the essential function of government by using coercion in a systematic way. Everywhere he went, Lee pushed the new holders of power toward this last and decisive step—the step that meant treason and no turning back.[17]

He made an effort to be tactful in his direct dealings with Revolutionary officials, but he let himself go in his reports to Congress and to Washington. Wherever he saw vacillation, or interest in conciliation with the British government, it sickened him and he said so. When he could not obtain civilian co-operation in New York, he moved against Tories and suspects on his own initiative and justified his conduct on the basis of military necessity. Congress, frightened by any encroachment of the military on civil authority, reprimanded him gently.[18]

What Washington thought about Lee and his behavior at this time is more interesting. When he sent Lee to New York, he had accurately predicted that Congress would not support Lee, but would be "duped" by the lukewarm New York government. Two months later, as if in response to Lee's rhetorical question, "Are we at war or are we not?", he wrote: "It is a great stake we are playing for, and sure we are of winning if the Cards are well managed. Inactivity in some, disaffection in others, and timidity, in many may hurt the Cause; nothing else can. . . ." And of Lee himself: "General Lee . . . is the first Officer in Military knowledge and experience we have in the whole Army. He is zealously attach'd to the Cause, honest and well meaning, but rather fickle and violent I fear in his temper. However as he possesses an uncommon share of good Sense and Spirit I congratulate my Countrymen upon his appointment. . . ." [19] Whatever his doubts, Washington was equally uncompromising in the face of fear and uncertainty.

When Lee arrived at Charleston in early June, 1776, he found less trouble with Tories and more preparation for defense than he had elsewhere. But Charleston was not ready to resist the British force that had appeared on the horizon almost as Lee rode into town. Islands, rivers, marsh, shoal and deep water created a problem for the defender nearly as complex as the one Lee had met in fortifying New York.[20] There was a half-finished fort on Sullivan's Island, east of the city and commanding the entrance to the harbor. Both Lee and the British commanders saw its weaknesses: it could not protect the city from a determined attack, could be flanked by sea from the west and by land from the east, and might well be a trap for its garrison. Lee wanted to abandon the fort, but too much labor and prestige were invested in it. The hour was late and he finally agreed to complete the fort and to make it as defensible as possible, though he was still dubious about its strength. By erecting batteries, building bridges, digging trenches, and clearing fields of fire, he managed to keep pace with the slow-moving councils of the invaders.[21]

Lee angered more than one Charleston worthy with his "hasty and rough" manners, his demands for speed and obedience, and his insistence that white men do work usually reserved for Negro slaves. He made life miserable for Colonel William Moultrie, the easy-going commander of the fort, and alienated William Henry Drayton, future chief justice of South Carolina. When the British finally launched their attack on June 28, it came in the form of a naval assault on the fort itself. The enemy plan was both unimaginative and badly executed. In part, this was because Lee had managed to eliminate most other tactical choices. Moultrie's men drove off the attackers with heavy losses and suffered few casualties themselves.

In the report he submitted after the battle, Lee gave full credit to the Carolinians for the victory. He admitted he "had once thoughts of ordering the Commanding officer to spike his guns," but that the "cool courage" of the garrison, which "astonished and enraptured" him, had made it unnecessary. Moultrie, he concluded, "deserves the highest honors." [22] Lee, in fact, had been on the verge of replacing Moultrie when the attack began, and after its repulse continued to harass the colonel with directions and questions—"Is your Gate finish'd? How is the Bridge? I beg you will inform me. . . ." [23] After Lee's disgrace and death, Moultrie and Drayton's son each wrote memoirs of the Revolution, and one might expect to find in them two hostile witnesses. But John Drayton thought that "however disagreeable General Lee's manners were, . . . there is much reason for being thankful, that he was sent on to command. . . ." [24] Moultrie concurred: ". . . his coming among us was equal to a reinforcement of 1000 men . . . he taught us to think lightly of the enemy, and gave a spur to all our actions." [25]

Lee was at the peak of his career when Congress ordered him, on August 8, to return to New York. The war was going badly.

Before Lee arrived, Washington suffered a sharp reverse in the Battle of Long Island in late August and was forced to evacuate his position. Many in the American army began comparing Washington's dark defeat with Lee's shining victory in Charleston. Washington's army was then driven from New York City and lower Manhattan. The army retreated to Harlem Heights, where it was exposed on both flanks to envelopment by British amphibious attack, and Congress was directing the commander-in-chief to hold the forts located near the ends of the present George Washington Bridge. More than one American officer looked to Lee's arrival as the only salvation of the army.

When he finally reached New York and saw the situation, Lee responded to it just as he had responded to every new turn in his life—sharply. He wrote to Horatio Gates that he disliked the position of the army and that Congress was a herd of stumbling cattle. Washington, said Lee, was wrong to let the legislators interfere with military strategy.[26]

As at Charleston, Lee seemed to appear just in the nick of time. In a well-executed amphibious operation, Howe landed most of his force on the north shore of Long Island Sound on October 12, threatening Washington's left flank and rear. Lee took command in that sector on the fourteenth. Tench Tilghman, one of Washington's aides, described the effect: "You ask if General Lee is in Health and our people feel bold? I answer both in the affirmative. His appearance among us has not contributed a little to the latter." [27] The troops in Lee's command fought a skillful delaying action, Howe co-operated by not pressing too hard, and Washington was able to extricate his army from Manhattan and march safely to White Plains.

As soon as Lee joined Washington at White Plains, the two generals reconnoitered the lines together. Lee saw serious flaws in the position and recommended a movement northward to the next ridgeline. Washington agreed, but immediately received a report that British troops were preparing for an attack. There was no time to deploy, and Washington could only alert his command and tell his generals, rather lamely, "do the best you can." [28] Their best was not good enough to hold a faulty position, and the American army was again driven back.

There was a lull in the fighting in early November until Howe suddenly turned southward to swoop down upon the American garrison at Fort Washington, which had been left as a pocket in the British rear on upper Manhattan. When Washington was sure that Howe had left White Plains, he crossed the Hudson with all the troops who came from states south of that river, leaving Lee with about 7,500 New Yorkers and New Englanders on the east side. From that day—November 12—there was never again a meeting of the minds between the two men, and Lee's career began its downward run.

It may well be that their minds had never met at all. When they had first inspected the troops around Boston in June, 1775, both had agreed that the officers as a group were woefully incompetent. But their reports showed a significant difference in evaluating the rank and file. Washington seemed to doubt whether Yankees could ever be good soldiers; ". . . an exceeding dirty and nasty people," he wrote to Lund Washington, and to Richard Henry Lee he described "an unaccountable kind of stupidity in the lower class of these people." [29] Nothing comparable is to be found in Lee's correspondence.

Lee explained in one letter that British officers were fatally underestimating Yankee soldiers as a result of the French and Indian War. In that conflict, "the regulars attributed to a difference of materials in their men what, in fact, ought to have been attributed solely to ignorance of method." [30] This letter to Edmund Burke was admittedly propaganda, but his reports to Benjamin Rush can be trusted. In one of them, he stated his belief in a close connection, not separation, between military and civil affairs: "Duke Ferdinand," who reportedly had criticized the failure to assault the British garrison inside Boston, "is beyond dispute a very great soldier," wrote Lee. "But if he is at the same time a Philosopher he wou'd not dictate the same measure to different Troops—if the Army before Boston had been Russians, Boston must have been ours . . . but They are not Russians

. . . the men (as I observ'd before) are excellent materials. . . . Our new Army will I hope and believe be good." [31] The military virtues of a free people were different in kind from those of a peasant army, he observed, and military organization and tactics had to take account of the differences. Among the American troops, Lee had doubts only about the southern soldier because Virginians and Carolinians seemed not quite ready for republicanism; but even on this point he had soon changed his mind.[32]

Nearly every step taken by Lee as general in the American army had shown a consciousness of the political aspects of the war. He was obsessed with the idea of maintaining the morale of his men and creating the proper attitude among the civilian population. He even capitalized upon his own eccentric behavior in order to gain these ends. Whether recommending that a pro-American Jesuit be sent to the army in Canada, or suggesting that unarmed Virginians be trained in the use of spears, Lee constantly emphasized the psychological aspects of warfare.[33] Washington, on the other hand, was far more in tune with the mid-eighteenth-century concept of warfare—an era in which war and society were carefully separated and the soldier fought primarily because he was more afraid to disobey than to die. Washington and Lee looked at the same troops, but where the Virginia planter saw only surliness and disobedience, the British radical saw alertness and zeal.

If the war had not gone badly, perhaps the divergence of their views never would have been of any consequence. During the first year of the Revolution, when the two men played complementary rather than clashing roles, their assignments were nicely suited to their respective attitudes. But Lee's success and rising reputation, coupled with Washington's record of failure from August to November, were bound to bring a change. Relations between the two had remained friendly, and Lee's barbs had been aimed only at Congressional interference with Washington. It is likely, however, that the incident on the lines at White Plains in late October had shaken Lee's confidence in his commander.

By the end of November, it is certain that this confidence was destroyed.

On November 16, Lee expressed an opinion which he directed to Joseph Reed, Washington's adjutant general: "I cannot conceive what circumstances give to Fort Washington so great a degree of value and importance as to counterbalance the probability or almost certainty of losing 1400 of our best Troops." [34] Washington had decided not to evacuate Fort Washington when Nathanael Greene convinced him that the fort was defensible, and that the troops could be withdrawn across the river whenever necessary. Greene was soon proved wrong on both points. On the day that Lee wrote his letter to Reed, Howe assaulted the fort, capturing not 1,400 but 3,000 men, and inflicted one of the worst American defeats of the Revolution. Several years later, Washington confessed there had been "warfare in my mind and hesitation which ended in the loss of the Garrison." [35] Lee, when he heard the news, by all accounts went wild. Someone told Benjamin Rush that he cried out in anger and grief, ". . . had it been called Fort Lee, it would have been evacuated long ago." [36] His first letter to Rush after the loss was certainly indiscreet, though a close reading reveals the principal target of his wrath was Congress, not Washington.

Before Lee could recover from this shock, he learned that the garrison of Fort Lee, on the New Jersey side, had almost been surprised by a similar attack. Washington at this time was known to be fleeing across the Hackensack River. On the heels of this news Lee received an incredible letter from Joseph Reed, dated November 21: "I do not mean to flatter," wrote Washington's most trusted staff officer, "nor praise you at the Expence of any other, but I confess I do think that it is entirely owing to you that this Army & the Liberties of America so far as they are depending on it are not totally cut off. You have Decision, a Quality often wanting in Minds otherwise valuable. . . ." [37] There was more in the same vein, including the hint that Reed was speaking for the whole army. It is hardly surprising that Lee, upon reading these words, lost his equilibrium, never to regain it.

From the time he received Reed's letter until his capture by the British on December 13, Lee was no longer the subordinate ready to give unquestioning obedience to his commander.

The events of Washington's retreat across New Jersey are usually treated as the prelude to the Trenton–Princeton campaign—the most brilliant stroke of his military career. In this context, Lee's failure to join him becomes just one more gloomy aspect of a situation so dismal that it provoked Thomas Paine to begin a pamphlet with the words, "These are the times that try men's souls." It is as difficult to quarrel with success as it is with some traditional ideas about George Washington. But the traditional view does less than justice to the actual course of events.

After the fall of the Hudson forts, Washington repeatedly urged Lee to move west of the river and join him, although the wording of these orders was more or less equivocal. The truth is that Lee did not want to move, and he used every possible excuse to delay. Some of the excuses seemed good ones: enlistments throughout the American army expired at the end of the year, but Lee's troops, unlike Washington's, would be marching farther from home rather than closer to it. Lee was afraid, with reason, that his army would simply fall apart. It was winter, many of the men were sick and some were literally naked, and there seemed little chance to find adequate shelter on the other side of the Hudson. Washington's retreat was along the main road between New York and Philadelphia, but Lee would have to follow a longer and rougher route and perhaps expose his army to capture. Was Washington's order militarily sound? He justified it by expressing fear that Howe's objective was Philadelphia; Lee disagreed, and thought that Howe wanted no more than to clear East Jersey for use as winter quarters. We know now that Lee was right in his estimate, Washington wrong.[38] The excuses make an impressive list, but the fact remains that Lee disobeyed.

Lee had never before allowed obstacles to stand in his way when he thought some course of action was necessary. In fact, he took pleasure in overcoming such obstacles. In this case, the explanation is that he considered the orders given by Washington not only unnecessary but unwise. When Washington scuttled back across New Jersey, resistance in the state collapsed. British observers were delighted by the submissiveness of the inhabitants, loyalists came out of hiding everywhere, and there were even reports of Tory militia units rounding up known "rebels." Washington himself knew why this had happened; he had written to Lee that the people of New Jersey "will expect the Continental Army to give what support they can, or failing in this, will cease to depend upon or support a force, from which no protection is giv'n to them." [39] But the need to maintain popular support by protecting people and property, and the need to keep a Continental army intact and united, had become conflicting demands on American strategy. It was obvious to Washington that, however painful the choice, the army was more important than the people if the war were to be won. To Lee, it was not at all obvious. He had a different conception of what to do with a revolutionary war on the brink of failure, and being no longer willing to trust Washington's judgment, he intended to be guided by that conception. Lee meant, as he so incautiously phrased it, to commit a "brave, virtuous kind of treason," and "to reconquer . . . the Jerseys." [40]

His plan for doing so, from all indications, was based on the use of militia forces. The militia was the last line of local defense. When militiamen did not fight to defend their locality or at least to make existence there dangerous for small bodies of the enemy, then the rest of the people were sure to submit, hoping for gentler treatment at the hands of the British and Germans in return for good behavior. But militiamen would not automatically spring to arms in time of danger. They were afraid. They lacked the confidence that comes with training and experience, and their companies and regiments were much too small to fight without help. Militiamen had to be encouraged, they had to be organized, and they had to be supported by Continental troops until there were enough active militia units to support one another. Lee would co-operate with Washington, but he would do so by creating zones of resistance that could deny General Howe the fruits of his recent victories. As the end of the year approached and one-year soldiers prepared to go home, Washington damned the militia and called on Congress for a professional army of long-service volunteers.[41] Lee was doing the opposite. Forget long-service enlistment, he wrote Benjamin Rush, and get soldiers on any terms you can. Draft every seventh man from the militia, Lee begged James Bowdoin of Massachusetts, and he praised a "people" who had "virtue enough to . . . oblige every citizen to serve in his turn as a soldier." [42]

Lee knew on November 21 that he was supposed to join Washington. From his camp north of White Plains, he could have had his whole command across the Hudson at Peekskill no later than November 26. He actually completed the crossing nine days later, on December 5. He was at Morristown, about fifty miles away from the crossing, on December 8—not an unreasonable rate of march for men "so destitute of shoes that the blood left on the rugged frozen ground, in many places, marked the route they had taken." [43] The delay east of the Hudson had been used to re-enlist soldiers, to clear upper Westchester of Tories and irregulars like Robert Rogers and his "Queen's Rangers," and to give Massachusetts and Connecticut time to replace the departing Continentals with militia. As Lee moved through New Jersey, he arrested Tories and called out the militia. He established a base for the militia in the Morristown area. Some successful raids were conducted and the New York militia under George Clinton started moving to join him. Northern New Jersey began to present a considerably different picture from the one Washington had seen as he retreated south to the Delaware leaving the state to the mercy of the British.

Three times—on December 3, 5, and 7—Washington sent messengers to find Lee. There can be no doubt that the commander-in-chief was exasperated by the tardiness of his subordinate. But there was once good evidence, of which only traces remain, that Washington was not sure himself of just what he should do next. Unfortunately, the letters have disappeared that could prove this indecision beyond a doubt. On December 8, Lee wrote a reply to accompany the messenger sent by Washington on December 5. In his letter, Lee said he had learned that Washington was "considerably reinforced," and he referred to "your Excellency's idea of surprising [New] Brunswick." If such a letter was sent to Lee with the messenger on December 5, it no longer exists. The implication that Washington had proposed or agreed to some plan of raids on the British flanks and rear is borne out by a second letter from Lee, on December 8. The third messenger, sent by Washington the day before, had just arrived, and Lee expressed surprise that his information about reinforcements had been wrong. Lee then wrote: "Your last letters proposing a plan of surprises and forced marches convinced me that there was no danger of your being obliged to pass the Delaware; in consequence of which proposals I have put myself in a position the most convenient to cooperate with you by attacking their rear."

Lee had referred to "letters" from Washington. These may have been the letters of December 2 and 3, which Washington said he wrote but which no longer exist, or the letter of December 5, if there ever was one. Likewise the letter sent by the messenger on December 7 is not to be found. But the internal evidence is unmistakable; some or all of these missing letters must have presented to Lee an image of a commander still unsure and wavering between alternatives.[44]

None of this, of course, can excuse Lee. After he received the peremptory order on December 8 to make haste, he remained near Morristown. In his last letter to Washington before his capture, he revealed himself in the final sentences: "The Militia in this part of the Province seem sanguine. If they could be assured of an army remaining amongst 'em, I believe they would raise a considerable number." [45] Apparently he had tried to swing Washington around to his view, and failing, he was ready to disobey. On December 12, he unwisely accepted an invitation to stay at an inn at Baskingridge, several miles from his camp. That night, he complained about Washington to his old comrade, Horatio Gates: ". . . *entre nous,* a certain great man is most damnably deficient— He has thrown me into a situation where I have my choice of difficulties—if I stay in this Province I risk myself and Army and if I do not stay the Province is lost for ever." [46]

The next morning Lee was taken prisoner by a patrol of British cavalry. Ironically, he was captured by members of a unit he had once commanded in Portugal. For a time, there was danger that he would be hanged as a British officer waging war on his King. Instead, he was finally exchanged in April, 1778. Had he been put to death, he probably would have gone down in history as one of America's heroes.

But it was not to be. In the mid-nineteenth century, a document was found, unquestionably in Lee's handwriting, dated March 29, 1777, in the family papers of one of the British commissioners then in New York. It called into question Lee's whole career in the Revolution because it was a plan to end the war. The document began by expressing concern for continued bloodshed on both sides. It then proposed that British sea power be used to support an army controlling a line from the upper Chesapeake Bay to Narragansett Bay, or Alexandria–Annapolis–Philadelphia–New York–Newport. Such a deployment was supposed to rally the Tories, to "unhinge and dissolve the whole system of defence," and to end the war two months after its execution.

The discoverer of the plan believed it proved Lee's treason. His chief biographer, however, is of the opinion that it was intended to trick Howe into his fruitless expedition to Philadelphia in 1777.[47] Curiously enough no reference to the plan has ever been found in any other contemporary document. But Lee's recommendations to Congress after his release were based on a similar analysis of the strategic situation, so there is little room to doubt its authenticity. The plan itself seemed sound, though rather ambitious for the forces available to Howe. It was characteristic of Lee to argue that encouragement and protection of loyalists were the true keys to pacifying America. From the American point of view, the plan was fairly humane, for it proposed no raids or harsh policies. One can only guess why Lee wrote it: to save his neck, to mislead Howe, to strike at Washington, perhaps simply to become a participant again instead of a bystander—it would have been perfectly in character for Lee to do such a thing.

Upon his release, Lee had another plan ready, this one for Washington and Congress. In it, he proposed a reformation of army organization and tactics, and analyzed the strategic choices for the campaign of 1778. His discussion of tactics and organization showed that his ideas had not changed. He stressed the value of simplicity and the need for American warfare to fit the American genius. "If the Americans are servilely kept to the European Plan," he wrote, "they will make an Awkward Figure, be laugh'd at as a bad Army by their Enemy, and defeated in every Rencontre which depends on Manoeuvres." The exact meaning of these ideas became clearer when he discussed strategy. He believed that it was madness to think of fighting British regulars on their own terms; to do so would be to forsake the natural advantages of the American position. The idea "that a Decisive Action in fair Ground may be risqued is talking Nonsense." Instead, "a plan of Defense, harassing and impeding can alone Succeed." If necessary, the Americans could base their operations on the rough country west of the Susquehanna, where British regulars would not dare penetrate. In short, Lee had driven his earlier thinking toward its logical conclusion, and was proposing a war waged along guerrilla lines.[48]

Nothing could have been further from Washington's mind. Throughout the winter and spring at Valley Forge, he and Steuben had planned and trained the army according to the "European Plan," as Lee had put it. Steuben has often been quoted on the difference between Europeans and Americans as soldiers, but if he learned to explain to Americans why they were being trained, it was only to shape them better to the conventional European form of tactics. It is likely, in fact, that Lee's plan was aimed directly at Steuben's program, for Lee had hardly arrived in the American camp when he succeeded in having Steuben's powers as inspector general curtailed.[49]

Lee, however, could arouse little interest in his own plan. Both in Congress and among the senior officers of the army, he had gained a following among those men who disliked Washington or doubted his ability. But their preference for Lee was a matter of personalities rather than military theories. If any of them fully understood Lee's military arguments, they probably were puzzled or dubious. Although they preferred Lee, they lacked his radical perceptions, and they must have been attracted more by the promise of an army composed at last of *real* soldiers, able to fight redcoats and Germans in the open field. During his year in New York, the war seemed to have moved beyond Charles Lee.

Washington received Lee warmly, but may not have been altogether happy to have him back. By this time Washington had learned of the disloyal letters exchanged by Lee and Joseph Reed. Because of illness and a desire to visit Congress, Lee did not join the army until May 20. Sir Henry Clinton, who had succeeded Howe, sat in Philadelphia with the bulk of the British forces. The crucial questions for Washington were: when and where would Clinton move, and what should the American army do once the British began to march? Lee had been back on duty less than a month when, on June 18, Clinton evacuated Philadelphia, crossed the Delaware, and began marching across New Jersey toward New York City. Within a few hours, the American vanguard under Lee's command had begun to move from Valley Forge on a parallel course.

The events of the next ten days were complicated and remain controversial.[50] Washington twice called a council of war, on June 17 and 24, both of which revealed that he and his generals were torn between two desires: one was to fight; the other, not to get hurt. Most wanted some "partial attack," but all agreed that a "general action" was to be avoided. The key issue was whether a "partial attack" would necessarily entail a "general action." [51]

Lee advised caution, and for the record, most of the council went along with him. But Wayne, Lafayette, Greene, Knox, and certainly the young aide, Alexander Hamilton, wanted to strike a blow before Clinton reached New York. Hamilton described the council of war at Hopewell, New Jersey, on the twenty-fourth, as doing "honor to the most honorab[le] body of mid-wives and to them only." [52] No one was completely happy with the compromise that was reached. When Washington decided to detach 1,500 men from his 10,000 to harass the British flank and rear, the detachment seemed either too large or too small.

Lee, at first, declined the command of the force. But then Washington decided to send another 1,000 and to put Lafayette in charge of all detached forces—over 4,000 Continentals and 1,000 New Jersey militia. At this point, Lee asserted his right as senior major general and asked for the command because it now included almost half the army. Washington agreed, and on June 27 Lee caught up with his troops around Englishtown.

Six miles east, at Freehold, lay the flank of the British column, stretching four miles along the road to Sandy Hook. The weather continued suffocatingly hot. Lee had argued against any action east of Princeton, down in the lowland where British cavalry superiority could prove decisive. Even Hamilton, so ardent for battle, suddenly feared that the main body, at Cranbury ten miles west of Englishtown, was not close enough to support the vanguard effectively. But now it was too late. On the twenty-seventh, Washington ordered Lee to attack the British rearguard over terrain that neither general had reconnoitered.

The approach to Freehold from Englishtown was along a road that ran on the high ground between two branches of swampy, westward-flowing Wemrock Brook.[53] In order to reach the British flank, Lee had to pass three ravines, created by the brook and its tributaries, that crossed the American axis of advance. The plan was to wait until the British column was on the march. But conflicting reports about British movements caused some confusion as Lee's command got under way from Englishtown early on the morning of the twenty-eighth. Soon after, the leading American units made contact with the British beyond the farthest, or eastern, ravine. Lee ordered Wayne to the front with reinforcements and told him to keep the enemy engaged. The action was on the left, with Freehold and the roads through it on the American right flank. The British were marching away toward the northeast. Lee meant to send most of his remaining troops behind and to the left of Wayne, thus cutting off and enveloping Clinton's rearguard, which Wayne had pinned down. But Clinton, to whom the attack was no surprise, anticipated the American maneuver. He held Wayne with minimum forces, halted the rearmost of the two British divisions and sent it back down the road through Freehold against the American right.

The action took on a pinwheel pattern, with Clinton, able to use the road, outracing Lee, who had to cross rough, wooded, and boggy ground. The American general, Charles Scott, who led the first element following Wayne, ran into Wayne in the woods instead of going behind and to Wayne's left. Neither Scott nor Wayne seemed to understand Lee's concept of the operation, and in the rapidly changing situation the system of mounted aides carrying messages merely added to the confusion. Lee was forced to order troops to Scott's right, toward Freehold, and placed Lafayette in charge of them. As Lafayette advanced and then fell back before the returning British division, Scott watched from across the 1,000-yard gap that separated him from Lafayette. Afraid that he was going to be cut off when he saw the American troops moving rapidly back toward Freehold, Scott began moving his own men to the rear without orders and without informing Lee. Wayne soon followed.

Once the American half of the pinwheel had ceased to turn, a large part of Lee's command was in danger of being cut off. It might be trapped against one of the ravines and wiped out. With most of his force now marching instead of fighting, Lee had to move all of his units across the middle ravine and take up a defensible position. He gave the necessary orders, but in the noise and confusion he was unable to contact his scattered subordinates. At this point Washington arrived on the scene, and he and the hot and exhausted Lee exchanged some sharp words. The day ended better than the Americans deserved. They finally retreated to a strong position on the westernmost ravine and fought off repeated British attacks. Washington could claim a victory, but it was a soldier's victory; none of the senior commanders—Scott, Wayne, Lafayette, Lee, or Washington—had performed with distinction. Clinton smiled at the American claim. From his point of view, the British had conducted a model rearguard action.[54]

Without doubt, Washington's sharp words precipitated Lee's ruin. Lee had reached the end of his patience: his advice on strategy had been rejected; his opinion in council was ignored; and while he was in the process of saving the army from a defeat he had foreseen, he was insulted. This was too much! Lee wrote to Washington, demanding an explanation of the treatment accorded him. He had not been dealt with fairly, he claimed. No doubt, he said, Washington's behavior had been "instigated by some of those dirty earwigs who will forever insinuate themselves near persons in high office." Washington replied that Lee would be given an opportunity to clear or hang himself. Lee fired back a letter referring to the "tinsel dignity" of Washington's office. In a third letter, Lee demanded a court-martial. His wish was soon granted.[55]

Lee was tried on three charges: disobedience of orders by not attacking; "making an unnecessary, disorderly, and shameful retreat"; and disrespect toward the commander in-chief. No one who carefully reads the record of trial, examines the ground, and considers the British side of the battle would find Lee guilty of the first two charges. But no one who reads his letters to Washington will believe him innocent of the third. Under the circumstances an acquittal on the first two charges would have been a vote of no-confidence in Washington. Lee was convicted on all counts, with the wording of the second charge considerably softened. He was given the absurd sentence of suspension from command for one year.

The rest of the story is not pretty. Lee and his friends lobbied in Congress to disapprove the findings of the court-martial. A number of delegates must have squirmed, as did Gouverneur Morris when he wrote to Washington: "General Lee's Affair hangs by the Eye Lids. . . . Granting him guilty of all the

Charges it is too light a Punishment. And if he is not guilty . . . there would be an Injustice in [delegates] not declaring their Opinion." John Laurens expressed his fear to Alexander Hamilton that "the *old faction*," meaning Richard Henry Lee and Sam Adams, might recruit a majority in Charles Lee's favor. But Benjamin Rush was soon complaining that delegates had begun to "talk of *state necessity* and of making justice yield in some cases to policy." The sentence was confirmed, though the vote was surprisingly close.[56]

Lee retired to his Virginia farm and vented his spleen for the rest of his life. He was subsequently dismissed from the army for a disrespectful letter to Congress and had to fight a duel with John Laurens for his public attacks on Washington. To Lee and his few remaining intimates, Alexander Hamilton was "the son of a bitch" who had been out to ruin him and who had perjured himself at the trial.[57]

Lee's few remaining years were rather pathetic ones. He lived in quarters that were more like a barn than a house. There was no glass in the windows, and the rooms were marked out by chalk lines on the floor. In a pitiful letter to his sister, he recalled being asked years ago when he would stop wandering, and reminded her of his reply—". . . whenever I could find a Country where power was in righteous hands." He felt further from his goal than ever, and concluded, "I may be a pilgrim to all eternity." [58] And so he was. Not long before his death in 1782, he was busily drawing up Utopian plans for a military colony in the West.

The contribution of Charles Lee to the Revolution was substantial, though perhaps difficult to measure. His services should not be minimized in the light of what finally happened to his career. As the partisan Rush recalled, "He was useful in the beginning of the war by inspiring our citizens with military ideas and lessening in our soldiers their superstitious fear of the valor and discipline of the British army." [59] At a glance, this would seem to contradict the judgment of Alexander Graydon: ". . . if he committed a fault it was because he was too respectful of the enemy; and that he was too scientific, too much of a reasoner . . ." [60] But Graydon's statement contains the link between these two views of Lee: ". . . too much of a reasoner." Intellectual that he was, Lee tried to see the Revolution as a consistent whole, with every aspect in rational harmony with every other. It was a fight by free men for their natural rights. Neither the fighters nor the cause were suited to the military techniques of despotism —the linear tactics, the rigid discipline, the long enlistments, the strict separation of the army from civic life that marked Frederick's Prussia. Lee envisioned a popular war of mass resistance, a war based on military service as an obligation of citizenship. He sought a war that would use the new light-infantry tactics already in vogue among the military avant-garde of Europe, the same tactics the free men at Lexington and Concord had instinctively employed.[61] Such men could not be successfully hammered into goose-stepping automatons and made to fire by platoons, but properly trained and employed, they could not be defeated. Here lay the solution to any apparent contradiction in his opinion of American soldiers as against British regulars.

Nathanael Greene's campaign in the South, and, on a far larger scale, the early campaigns of the French Revolutionary War, were to confirm Lee's prophetic insight.[62] But to Washington—a practical man not given to theorizing—this was all madness. He never seriously considered resorting to a war of guerrilla bands drawn from the militia. He would have recoiled with horror from such an idea.[63] Such strategy would change the war for independence into a genuine civil war with all its grisly attendants—ambush, reprisal, counterreprisal. It would tear the fabric of American life to pieces. It might even undermine the political process, and throw power to a junta—a committee of public safety with a Lee, not a Washington, as its military member.

Historians have often noted that the American Revolution was a "conservative" revolution, with surprising stability of institutions and continuity of leadership. But few have noticed that it was also militarily conservative, and that its conventional strategy served as a buffer for American society and politics. If

Washington's strategy had failed, as it almost did in 1776, then the Revolution would have collapsed or turned sharply leftward. Charles Lee was one who, by his alienation from the world to which other men were adjusted, could dimly see the full range of possibilities. He might then have had a chance to translate his vision into reality. Probably the true blessing of his unhappy career is that he never got the chance.

FOOTNOTES

1. John R. Alden, *General Charles Lee, Traitor or Patriot?* (Baton Rouge, 1951).
2. There are three hints, all of which are susceptible to other interpretations. One is in a letter to his sister, December 23, 1763, *Lee Papers, New York Historical Society Collections*, 1871–74, I, 48; hereinafter referred to as *Lee Papers*. Another is in a letter about Lee when he was staying at Lucca, during his return from the second journey to Poland; it is quoted in a note by Alden, *op. cit.*, p. 317, n. 15. The third is the attempt by his first biographer, Edward Langworthy, to prove that Lee liked women, rumors to the contrary notwithstanding; in *Lee Papers*, IV, 163–64.
3. The description is borrowed from Eric Hoffer, *The True Believer* (New York, 1951).
4. Douglas Southall Freeman, *George Washington* (New York, 1948–57), especially Vols. IV and V.
5. Lee to Sidney Lee, March 28, 1772, *Lee Papers*, I, 110.
6. See Lee to Washington, May 9, 1776, *ibid.*, II, 12, for an indication that Lee was on Braddock's march with Washington.
7. Lee to George Colman (the elder), May 8, 1769, *Lee Papers*, I, 81–82.
8. He mentioned a proposed visit to Silesia to see a Prussian military review in a letter from Warsaw to the Earl of Charlemont, June 1, 1765, *ibid.*, 41. His view of the French and Indian War is best expressed in his influential pamphlet, *Strictures on . . . A "Friendly Address to All Reasonable Americans . . ."* (Philadelphia, 1774), in *Lee Papers*, I, 162.
9. The three commanders were Loudoun, Abercromby, and Amherst. For the encounter with the King, see Horace Walpole, *Last Journals* (London, 1910), I, 404–05.
10. Lee to Sidney Lee, March 28, 1772, *Lee Papers*, I, 111.
11. In particular, see the letters of John Adams in Edmund C. Burnett,

ed., *Letters of Members of the Continental Congress* (Washington, D.C., 1921–36), I, 136–37; hereinafter, Burnett, *Letters*.

12. James Warren to Sam Adams, July 9, 1775, in William V. Wells, *The Life and Public Services of Samuel Adams* (Boston, 1866), II, 316.

13. Lee to Sullivan, July 24, 1775, *Lee Papers*, I, 199. Historians usually credit Washington or Sullivan with the movement forward to Ploughed Hill, but contemporary accounts describe it as Lee's action. See the *Virginia Gazette*, October 21, 1775, and *The Magazine of American History*, VIII (1882), 125.

14. George W. Greene, *The Life of Nathanael Greene* (New York, 1867), I, 131; Thompson to his brother, September 10, 1775, in William T. Read, *The Life and Correspondence of George Read* (Philadelphia, 1870), 112.

15. John Adams to Lee, February 19, 1776, *Lee Papers*, I, 312.

16. For a sympathetic eye-witness account of Lee's effect in Newport, see Franklin B. Dexter, ed., *The Literary Diary of Ezra Stiles* (New York, 1901), I, 646–47.

17. Letters expressing his attitude during these months are in *Lee Papers*, I, 233 ff. Curtis Nettels, *George Washington and American Independence* (Boston, 1951), describes the problems of this period and puts Lee's activity in proper perspective.

18. For the politics of this resolution, see Burnett, *Letters*, I, 329, 339, 354, 389, 405, and 408.

19. To John Augustine Washington, March 31, 1776, in John C. Fitzpatrick, ed., *The Writings of George Washington* (Washington, D.C., 1931–44), IV, 450–51. All quotations from Washington's letters are from the Fitzpatrick edition unless otherwise noted. This work is referred to hereinafter as Washington, *Writings*. Lee's question was asked in a letter to Robert Morris, January 23, 1776, *Lee Papers*, I, 255.

20. Lee to Washington, February 19, 1776, *ibid.*, 309.

21. See Eric Robson, "The Expedition to the Southern Colonies, 1775–1776," *English Historical Review*, LXVI (1951), 535–60, for the British side.

22. Lee to Washington, July 1, 1776, *Lee Papers*, II, 100–03.

23. Lee to Moultrie, July 7, 1776, *ibid.*, 126.

24. John Drayton, *Memoirs of the American Revolution* (Charleston, 1821), II, 313 and 280 ff.

25. William Moultrie, *Memoirs of the American Revolution* (New York, 1802), I, 141.

26. Lee to Gates, October 14, 1776, *Lee Papers*, II, 261–62.

27. Tilghman to Duer, October 17, 1776, quoted in Henry P. Johnston,

The Campaign of 1776 Around New York and Brooklyn (New York, 1878), p. 271. See also note on p. 270.

28. The incident is recounted by Major General William Heath, who was not sympathetic to Lee in general, in Rufus R. Wilson, ed., *Heath's Memoirs of the American War* (New York, 1904), pp. 87–88; hereinafter Heath, *Memoirs*.

29. Washington to Lund Washington, August 20, and to Richard Henry Lee, August 29, 1775, Washington, *Writings*, III, 433 and 450.

30. Lee to Burke, December 16, 1774, *Lee Papers*, I, 147.

31. Lee to Rush, November 13, 1775, *ibid.*, 216.

32. Lee to Rush, October 10, 1775, *ibid.*, 212.

33. *Ibid.*, 332, and 417–18.

34. *Ibid.*, II, 283.

35. Washington to Reed, August 22, 1779, Washington, *Writings*, XVI, 152.

36. Rush to John Adams, September 21, 1805, in Lyman H. Butterfield, ed., *Letters of Benjamin Rush* (Princeton, 1951), II, 906; hereinafter, *Letters of Rush*.

37. Reed to Lee, November 21, 1776, *Lee Papers*, II, 293–94.

38. Howe to Germain, November 30, 1776, in Peter Force, ed., *American Archives*, 4th series (Washington, D.C., 1837–53), V, 926.

39. Washington to Lee, November 21, 1776, *Lee Papers*, II, 296.

40. His words about "treason" were used in another connection to James Bowdoin, November 22, 1776, *ibid.*, 303, but they do indicate his state of mind. He wrote of reconquering New Jersey to Heath, December 9, 1776, *ibid.*, 340.

41. See Freeman, *op. cit.*, IV, 232–90.

42. Lee to Rush, November 20, 1776, and to Bowdoin, November 30, 1776, *Lee Papers*, II, 289 and 324.

43. Heath, *Memoirs*, 107.

44. The sequence of letters, and the indications that some letters are missing, are found in *Lee Papers*, II, 326–44, and Washington, *Writings*, VI, 318–42. For further evidence that Washington was neither quite as desperate in early December nor as certain about what Lee should do as tradition suggests, see the letters in Greene, *op. cit.*, I, 280–85.

45. Lee to Washington, December 11, 1776, *Lee Papers*, II, 345.

46. Lee to Gates, December 12/13, 1776, *ibid.*, 348.

47. The document is printed in *Lee Papers*, II, 361–66. It is discussed by George H. Moore, *The Treason of Charles Lee* (New York, 1860); in *Lee Papers*, IV, 335–427; and by Alden, *op. cit.*, pp. 174–79.

48. "A Plan for the Formation of the American Army . . . [April, 1778]," *Lee Papers*, II, 383–89.

49. Alexander Hamilton to Elias Boudinot, July 26, 1778, in Harold C. Syrett and Jacob E. Cooke, eds., *The Papers of Alexander Hamilton* (New York, 1961–   ), I, 528–29; hereinafter, *Hamilton Papers*.

50. There is no satisfactory account of the Monmouth campaign. What follows is based on the record of Lee's court-martial, except where noted (*Lee Papers*, III, 1–208) and on several visits to the ground itself.

51. Nathanael Greene best expressed the optimistic view of the American strategic dilemma to George Washington, June 24, 1778, quoted in Theodore Thayer, *Nathanael Greene, Strategist of the American Revolution* (New York, 1960), p. 244. Greene wrote: "People expect something from us. . . . I think we can make a partial attack without suffering them to bring us to a general action."

52. Hamilton to Boudinot, July 5, 1778, *Hamilton Papers*, I, 510.

53. Every published sketch map of the battle of Monmouth that I know of is misleading and inaccurate. The best one, surprisingly, is in Jared Sparks, ed., *The Writings of George Washington* (Boston, 1834–37), V, 430. William S. Stryker, *The Battle of Monmouth*, William S. Myers, ed. (Princeton, 1927), makes no attempt to plot the battle graphically. The most important contemporary map is reproduced in Louis Gottschalk, *Lafayette Joins the American Army* (Chicago, 1937), p. 222.

54. William B. Willcox, ed., *The American Rebellion; Sir Henry Clinton's Narrative of His Campaigns, 1775–1782* (New Haven, 1954), pp. 91–98. Clinton, who did not like Lee, thought Lee had been unjustly treated.

55. The letters are in *Lee Papers*, II, 435–38.

56. Morris to Washington, October 26, 1778, Burnett, *Letters*, III, 465; Laurens to Hamilton, December 5, 1778, *Hamilton Papers*, I, 593; Rush to William Gordon, December 10, 1778, *Letters of Rush*, I, 220; Alden, *op. cit.*, pp. 253–54.

57. The epithet was used by Major John Eustace, Lee's aide; Eustace to Lee, November 28, 1779, *Lee Papers*, III, 394.

58. Lee to Sidney Lee, December 11, 1781, *ibid.*, 464–65.

59. Benjamin Rush, *Autobiography*, George W. Corner, ed. (Princeton, 1948), pp. 155–56.

60. Alexander Graydon, *Memoirs of a Life* (Edinburgh, 1822), pp. 337–39.

61. Lee had expressed keen interest in light infantry to Sidney Lee,

March 1, 1761, *Lee Papers*, I, 29. For the rapidly growing European interest in light infantry tactics and partisan warfare at this time, see Max Jähns, *Geschichte der Kriegswissenschaften* (Munich and Leipzig, 1889–91), III, 2710–20.

62. For a brilliant account of the military revolution that accompanied the political revolutions of the late eighteenth century, see Robert R. Palmer, "Frederick the Great, Guibert, Bülow: From Dynastic to National War," in Edward M. Earle, ed., *Makers of Modern Strategy* (Princeton, 1941), pp. 49–74.

63. Marcus Cunliffe, *George Washington: Man and Monument* (Boston, 1958), in the third chapter of his book was the first to develop the idea of Washington as a military conservative.

BIBLIOGRAPHY

Alden, John R., *Charles Lee, Traitor or Patriot?* Baton Rouge, 1951. The thorough, sympathetic study that Lee deserves.

Bunbury, Sir Henry, "Memoirs of Charles Lee," in *The Life and Correspondence of Sir Thomas Hanmer*. London, 1838. A brief account, inferior to Langworthy's, but containing some information not available elsewhere because Sir Henry was a maternal second cousin to Lee.

Fiske, John, "Charles Lee, The Soldier of Fortune," in *Essays Historical and Literary*, 2 vols. New York, 1902, I, 55–98. Fiske, a great popularizer of American history, built his unfavorable interpretation of Lee on Moore's essay; probably Lee's reputation will never recover.

Langworthy, Edward, *Memoirs of the Life of the Late Charles Lee, Esq.* London, 1792. The first biography of Lee, by an admiring Georgian who, as a delegate to Congress, voted to disapprove the findings of the court-martial.

Lee Papers, 4 vols. *New York Historical Society Collections*, 1871–74. New York, 1872–75. Unusually important because of the subsequent loss of many of the originals. The works by Langworthy, Bunbury, Sparks, and Moore, listed here, are conveniently reprinted in Volume IV.

Moore, George H., *The Treason of Charles Lee*. New York, 1860. Not a biography, but a tract using the recently discovered Plan of March, 1777, in an uncritical way to prove Lee a traitor.

Patterson, Samuel W., *Knight Errant of Liberty: The Triumph and Tragedy of General Charles Lee*. New York, 1958. The latest biography, but comparable to Alden's only in its sympathy for its subject.

Sparks, Jared, *Life of Charles Lee*. Boston, 1846. Although Sparks has a bad reputation as an uncritical admirer of George Washington, his life of Lee shows careful research and balanced judgment on Washington's worst enemy.

Philip Schuyler:

THE GENERAL AS ARISTOCRAT

—•••—

JOHN H. G. PELL

Long Island University

PHILIP SCHUYLER enjoyed George Washington's friendship, high regard, and complete loyalty as did few other generals in the Continental army. Some commanders, like Gates and Lee, started out as trusted colleagues, but soon fell from Washington's favor. Others, like Putnam and Sullivan, were given important positions by the commander-in-chief, but were found lacking in ability. Schuyler, however, remained in the esteem of his fellow aristocrat, Washington, throughout the entire war.

Washington and Schuyler first met on May 15, 1775, when Schuyler arrived to attend the Second Continental Congress in Philadelphia. The two men took an instant liking to one another because they had so much in common: both were in their early forties; both had been large landowners; and both had acquired managerial experience in running huge estates—Schuyler in New York and Washington in Virginia. The similarities did not end there. Both men had been amateur soldiers of long standing prior to 1775. They had served in the French and Indian War, enduring the rigors of frontier campaigning, learning the ways of the colonial militia, and fighting alongside British regulars. Both men were also political leaders in their communities, having served in their respective provincial assemblies. It was little wonder, then, that they became fast friends and remained close for the rest of their lives.

Philip Schuyler was born in Albany on November 11, 1733, the eldest son of Johannes and Cornelia Van Cortlandt Schuyler. The Schuylers, one of the great landed families in upper New York, were generally regarded as the first family in Albany in terms of wealth, social standing, and political prestige. To say that Schuyler was born with a silver spoon in his mouth was, if anything, an understatement.

As befitted a member of the Dutch aristocracy, he received a fine education. At the age of fifteen, he was sent to New Rochelle to study under a talented minister of the French Protestant Church. He soon mastered the French language and became so proficient in mathematics that in later years he corresponded with David Rittenhouse, the famed astronomer, about the mathematics of astronomy. Besides his formal education, Schuyler learned to converse in the tongue of the Mohawk Indians after taking numerous trading trips into the wilderness of western New York.

By the time Schuyler was twenty, he was tall—as tall as George Washington—thin, with aquiline features, brown eyes, and reddish brown hair. He was powerfully built and had the commanding presence required of a good soldier. Despite his fine physique, he was rarely in excellent health. He kept suffering attacks of rheumatic gout—a disease that dogged him throughout his entire life.

When the French and Indian War broke out, Schuyler was commissioned a captain, in 1755, and raised a company of militia to join General William Johnson's expedition against Crown Point. The campaign got underway in late August, and Schuyler had his first taste of combat in a skirmish against the French at Lake George on September 8, 1755. Because of his knowledge of French, the young captain was assigned the duty of escorting prisoners back to Albany. While he was at home, Schuyler took advantage of a brief furlough to marry Catherine Van Rensselaer, the talented daughter of Colonel Johannes Van Rensselaer of Greenbush. Within a few weeks after his wedding, however, the new bridegroom was back at Fort Edward trying to build up a depot of military stores.

In the spring of 1756, Schuyler served under Colonel John Bradstreet on an expedition to carry provisions to Oswego. This meant traveling almost due west from Albany mostly by canoe up the Mohawk River, through Lake Oneida, down the Oswego River into Lake Ontario. During this campaign Schuyler learned a great deal about transporting men and supplies by canoe and bateau through wilderness waterways. Although he resigned his commission the following year, he continued to supply provisions to the army and earned a substantial income.

Schuyler returned to the military service in 1758, this time as deputy commissary. He was with General James Abercromby when the ill-fated attempt was made to take Ticonderoga in early July. This disaster was counterbalanced by the capture of Fort Frontenac in late August, during which Schuyler served under Colonel Bradstreet. Both campaigns provided Schuyler with an opportunity to learn more about military organization and the problems of logistics.

He served the following year when another army gathered at Albany, under the leadership of General Sir Jeffrey Amherst. Schuyler's logistical talents by now were widely known, and during this expedition he was employed for the most part at Albany in collecting and forwarding supplies to the army. Occasionally he made trips to the forts on the frontier. On one of these visits, Schuyler met Paul Revere, who presented him with a beautifully inscribed rum horn.[1]

Altogether Schuyler participated in four major campaigns during the French and Indian War. He had ample opportunity to study at first hand the problems of feeding, housing, and transporting supplies to troops stationed on the New York frontier. This experience was to prove valuable, for the future general was to face similar situations in the same region during the Revolutionary War.

The year 1763 marked not only the close of the French and

Indian War but the final settlement of the estate of Philip Schuyler's father. Schuyler inherited thousands of acres in the Mohawk Valley and along the Hudson River. From his Uncle Philip's estate he received even more land in the Saratoga patent and the old Schuyler homestead near West Troy. The Saratoga patent was to become Schuyler's favorite area of all his estates. He conducted lumbering operations there, developed water power for his sawmills and gristmills, maintained a small fleet of vessels on the Hudson for trading purposes, and leased a group of small farms to tenants.

Successful in business, Schuyler soon began to take a serious interest in politics. In 1768, he was elected to the Assembly and quickly became identified with those who were hostile to Parliament's interference with colonial commerce and industry. He sat in the Assembly for the next seven years. Although he never openly sympathized with the radicals among New York's Sons of Liberty, Schuyler constantly fought against the pro-British faction in the colony—the DeLancey–Colden coalition.

In January, 1775, Schuyler introduced a motion in the Assembly calling for repeal of the recent acts of Parliament for raising a revenue in America, extending the admiralty courts, and depriving American subjects of trial by jury. The resolution was adopted and sent as a petition to the King. It was forwarded to Edmund Burke, who was then serving as colonial agent for New York in England.

When the New York delegates were named to the Second Continental Congress, Schuyler was among those appointed. By the time Congress convened in Philadelphia in May, 1775, fighting had already broken out at Lexington and Concord. In forming an army to fight the British, Congress asked the New York Provincial Congress that an officer be nominated to command the American troops in that province. The answer was not long in coming:

Courage, prudence, readiness in expedients, nice perception, sound judgment, and great attention, these are a few of the natural qualities which appear to us to be proper. To these ought to be added an extensive acquaintance with the sciences, particularly the various branches of mathematical knowledge, long practise in the military arts, and above all a knowledge of mankind. On a general in America, fortune also should bestow her gifts that he may rather communicate lustre to his dignities than receive it and that his country, his property, his kindred and connections, may have sure pledges that he will faithfully perform the duties of his high office and readily lay down his power when the general weal requires it. Since we cannot do all that we wish, we will go as far towards it as we can. And therefore you will not be surprised to hear that we are unanimous in the choice of Colonel Philip Schuyler.[2]

Acting upon this recommendation, Congress appointed Schuyler as one of the four major generals under Washington on June 19, 1775.

Washington and Schuyler left Philadelphia together and rode toward New York City. After remaining in New York for a few days, Washington continued on his way to Cambridge. Before leaving, however, he handed Schuyler his orders:

You are to take upon you the command of all the troops destined for the New York department and see that the orders of the Continental Congress are carried into execution, with as much precision as possible. . . . Your own good common sense must govern you in all matters not particularly pointed out as I do not wish to circumscribe you within narrow limits.[3]

Thus, Schuyler became commander of what came to be called the Northern Department and commandant of the Northern army.

Schuyler spent the next few weeks in New York City organizing supply lines and recruiting troops to strengthen the garrisons at Ticonderoga and Crown Point. These two northern outposts constituted New York's first line of defense. The British forces in Canada under the command of Sir Guy Carleton were stationed at three places—St. Johns, the principal British stronghold between Lake Champlain and the St. Lawrence River, Montreal, and Quebec. Realizing that if Carleton invaded New York he would sail down Lake Champlain, Schuyler began building an American fleet. The same craft that were built to defend against a British invasion might also be employed to transport troops to the north if the Americans decided to mount an offensive against Canada.

Schuyler left New York City early in July and traveled north in order to be present as the building of the fleet got underway. Upon reaching Lake George, he was shocked at the lack of discipline and vigilance shown by the troops guarding the area:

> About ten o'clock last night I arrived at the landing place, at the north end of *Lake George,* a post occupied by a captain and one hundred men . . . the whole guard, like the first, in the soundest sleep. With a penknife only I could have cut off both guards. . . .[4]

Despite this discouraging reception, Schuyler quickly went about putting the American defenses in order. By the end of July, he was able to report to Washington: "I have now one boat on the stocks, which I hope will carry near three hundred men; another is putting up today." [5] Orders were issued to the commanding officers at Crown Point and Fort George warning them to exercise greater vigilance in guarding their posts.[6]

In the weeks that followed, Schuyler showed many of the same qualities of organization and planning in building up the defenses on Lake Champlain that had enabled him to become such a success in civilian life as a businessman. Soldiers were sent into the forests to fell choice timbers for building boats and making oars. A field hospital was organized to care for the sick and wounded. Schuyler also located a powder mill on the Hudson and proceeded to make arrangements to have powder shipped up the river to Albany and thence to Ticonderoga. His correspondence for this period was filled with requests for carpenters, tools, pitch, oakum, nails, rope, and numerous other items required for building sailing vessels.

At the same time, Schuyler kept up a constant stream of correspondence with Washington, the New York Provincial Congress, and the Continental Congress in Philadelphia. Alarmed by reports received from the north, the Continental Congress practically granted Schuyler dictatorial powers in mid-July:

> The dispatches from General Schuyler being taken into consideration, *Resolved*, that Gen[era]l Schuyler be empowered to dispose and employ all the troops in the New York department, in such manner as he may think best for the protection and defense of these colonies, the tribes of Indians in friendship and amity with us, and most effectually to promote the general Interest, still pursuing, if in his power, the former orders from this Congress, and subject to the future orders of the commander in chief.[7]

Schuyler then turned his attention to the problem of winning the friendship of the powerful Iroquois Indian tribes in New York. This was not an easy thing to do. The Iroquois had traditionally sided with the British in their wars with the French, and it would be difficult to woo and hold their affections. But Schuyler had been dealing with the Indians since boyhood days and understood the redmen as few whites did. He invited the Indian chiefs to meet him at Albany, and a number of them arrived early in August accompanied by 700 braves. Many of the Indians attended the parley wearing ruffled shirts, Indian moccasins and stockings, and blankets trimmed with silver and wampum.

After a few days of opening festivities, the conference got underway. Before long, Schuyler was able to report to Washington that he had been successful. "[A]pprehensive that we should request them to take arms in our cause, they explicitly declared that it was a family quarrel," he wrote, and that "they would not interfere." [8] Under the circumstances, this settlement was the best that could be expected. The treaty cleared the way for the major military operation in northern New York which the Americans had planned.

Congress for some time had been proposing an invasion of Canada with the hope of inducing a fourteenth colony to revolt. Schuyler, along with his energetic second in command, Brigadier General Richard Montgomery, were ordered to seize any points in Canada vital to the security of the colonies. Launching an expedition from Crown Point, Montgomery went north in the direction of St. Johns in August, with Schuyler following on his heels. At about the same time, a second small army led by Benedict Arnold set out from Massachusetts to march through the Maine woods to meet the force from New York at Quebec. If the two armies succeeded in linking up at Quebec, Arnold was instructed that "in case of a union with General Schuyler you are by no means to consider yourself as upon a separate and independent command but are to put yourself under him and follow his directions." [9]

Schuyler and Montgomery advanced toward St. Johns during the early days of September. After reaching their objective, the Americans retired a few miles south and laid siege to the British garrison.[10] At this point Schuyler fell sick and was forced to return to Ticonderoga, leaving the Northern army under the command of Montgomery.[11]

What appeared at first to be a misfortune for the Americans in losing their ranking officer soon proved to be a blessing. Schuyler's skillful handling of supply problems from Ticonderoga prevented a complete collapse of the Northern army from starvation. As Montgomery wrote to his superior officer from "Camp South Side St. Johns" a few weeks later: "Your diligence and foresight have saved us from the difficulties that threatened us; we are no longer afraid of starving. . . ." [12]

Although his condition improved, Schuyler decided to remain at Ticonderoga. It was well that he did, for the flow of supplies to Montgomery's force might have ceased from sheer neglect. As he noted in one letter:

> Near a thousand barrels of provisions lay exposed to the weather at Lake George and such was the laziness of the scoundrels that in twenty two days preceding my arrival here they had not brought over more than they have since done in six. The same negligence had prevailed in building batteaux at this place. I have been under the necessity of employing the blacksmiths in making nails. In short, I am as crusty as an old woman at all this rascality.[13]

Schuyler could not stand the inefficiency of the undisciplined soldiers under his command and wrote to Washington: "If Job had been a General in my situation, his memory had not been so famous for patience." [14]

Montgomery, a brilliant and resourceful officer, went on to capture St. Johns and Montreal in quick succession, but lost his life in a futile attempt to take Quebec on December 30, 1775. With the failure to capture Quebec, the Canadian offensive came to a halt and the Americans could only maintain a weak cordon around the city throughout the rest of the winter. Although Schuyler had not been present during most of the campaign, the failure of the Canadian offensive discredited the New York general with many of the New Englanders. Behind this antagonism lay the sectional jealousies between Yankees and Yorkers that had been evident all along in the Northern army. Most New Englanders disliked Schuyler because he had supported New York's land claims in a boundary dispute between Massachusetts, New Hampshire, and New York over the region that was later to be the state of Vermont. Moreover, Schuyler's haughty ways and aristocratic airs did not set well with Yankee troops, who entertained more democratic ideas.

Despite his waning popularity, Schuyler continued to serve the army stranded in Canada to the best of his ability. He divided his time between Ticonderoga and Albany doing what he could to help the beleaguered troops. By keeping the lines of supply open, he was able to send them food, supplies and reinforcements. When Congress appointed commissioners to evaluate the political situation in Canada, Schuyler entertained them and provided vital information. [15] By this time it was clear that Canada was irretrievably lost and that the remnants of the army before Quebec would have to retreat back to New York.

Congress sent out a succession of new commanders to head the forces in Canada. The first was Brigadier General John Thomas, who decided to raise the siege against Quebec in May, 1776. When Thomas died of smallpox, Brigadier General John Sullivan, a New Hampshire lawyer, was named commander. Then, in June,

1776, Congress appointed Horatio Gates as head of the retreating army. This last appointment touched off a bitter dispute between Gates and Schuyler as to just who was in command of the Northern Department. Congress had left the matter vague by stating that Gates was to command those forces stationed in Canada, but making no mention of what was to happen once the troops reached American soil. The two generals quarreled constantly, since each had some basis for his claim.

During the last days of June, Schuyler and Gates began meeting in Albany to plot the future strategy of the army. Realizing that the command of Lake Champlain was the key to the strategic situation, Schuyler wrote to General Sullivan, who was still in command of the retreating American army at the time: "By keeping a naval superiority on the lake we shall be able to prevent the enemy from penetrating into the inhabited part of these colonies . . ." [16]

Sullivan by this time had retreated farther southward down Lake Champlain and had encamped his army at Crown Point, a few miles north of Ticonderoga. Schuyler, accompanied by Gates and Benedict Arnold, met him there early in July and reviewed the remnants of the exhausted army. After a council of war was held on July 6, the army was ordered to retreat even farther, to Ticonderoga and Mount Independence on the opposite shore of Lake Champlain.

In Philadelphia, Congress became increasingly aware of the delicate situation that had arisen regarding the command of the Northern Department. The army in Canada no longer existed as a separate entity, and on July 8, Congress resolved:

> . . . that General Gates be informed, that it was the intention of Congress to give him the command of the troops whilst in Canada, but had no design to vest him with a superior command to General Schuyler.[17]

Thus the issue between the two jealous generals was settled for the time being.

Through the summer and fall of 1776, the generals worked in

harmony. This was fortunate for the Americans because a British army led by Sir Guy Carleton had started to move south from Canada to invade New York at that time. Dividing their duties, the American commanders made preparations to stop Carleton. Schuyler, maintaining his headquarters at Albany for the most part, sought to recruit some militia to throw against the invaders. Gates took command of the field forces inside the fortress at Ticonderoga. Benedict Arnold was put in charge of building the fleet at Skenesborough.

Carleton in the meantime halted his advance to build a British fleet at the northern end of Lake Champlain. On October 11, 1776, the American fleet commanded by Benedict Arnold engaged the British fleet off Valcour Island. Although Arnold's fleet was destroyed, it served its purpose—the British had delayed so long in building their own naval force that Carleton was forced to return to Canada because winter was coming. Schuyler's role in turning back this first major British invasion from the north was an important one: he had suggested the strategy of maintaining naval superiority on Lake Champlain and had begun building the fleet that made it necessary for the British to stop and construct one of their own.

Despite the fact that his efforts had been successful, Schuyler continued to be harassed by New Englanders. In the course of the summer campaign he had ordered Crown Point evacuated on the grounds that the post was too weak to be held. Some of the officers at Crown Point, all of whom were Yankees, signed a remonstrance declaring that the abandonment of the post would leave Lake Champlain open to the enemy and expose the New England colonies to an invasion. Washington also expressed his disapproval of the removal of the troops from the fort. Indignant that his judgment had been questioned, Schuyler demanded a court of inquiry into his conduct of the campaign. When his request was not met, he submitted a letter of resignation in mid-September. Congress, however, refused to accept his resignation and sent him assurances of respect and appreciation.

In the spring of 1777, Schuyler was attacked again by New

Englanders—this time by the Yankee delegation in Congress. As a result of two flimsy charges brought against him, Schuyler was reprimanded by the Congress. In March, 1777, he was actually deprived of his command of the Northern army and Gates was put in charge. Two months later, the legislators reversed themselves and reinstated Schuyler.

Throughout these ordeals, Schuyler continued to do the best he could for the Northern army with the slim resources available to him. In the spring of 1777, he even went so far as to furnish some of his own funds to buy food for the troops. Since Gates and Arnold had departed, Schuyler sent his most able field officer, Major General Arthur St. Clair, to Ticonderoga to take command of the fort and garrison there. After looking the situation over, St. Clair wrote back: "If the enemy intend to attack us, I assure you, sir, we are very ill-prepared to receive them. The whole amount of Continental troops, fit for duty is one thousand five hundred and seventy-six . . . we cannot reckon upon more than twenty-two hundred men . . ." [18]

Schuyler also sent scouts into Canada to try to find out what the enemy were doing. On their return, on June 10, 1777, he wrote to General Washington: "Last evening two Canadians who had been sent into Canada returned . . . I cannot believe that there are so many troops in Canada as they report nor do I believe that General Burgoyne was there on the 10th of May." [19] Unfortunately the report was all too true. General Burgoyne with a force of British and German soldiers was scheduled to leave Three Rivers in May to launch the second major British invasion from the north.

Schuyler proceeded to Ticonderoga because it was here that the Northern army was expected to make its stand. The fortress, described as the "American Gibraltar," was assumed to be an unassailable citadel. But Schuyler's report on its condition was gloomy:

> I was in hopes to have found the post in a better state of defense than it is . . . I was very disagreeably disappointed to find the

troops at Ticonderoga so miserably clad and armed . . . many are literally barefooted and most of them ragged . . . the huts built last campaign . . . consumed in the course of the winter . . . as fire wood . . . the enemy cannot be ignorant how very difficult if not impossible it will be for them to penetrate to Albany unless in losing Ticonderoga we should lose not only all our cannon but most of the army designed for this department.[20]

After determining the situation at Ticonderoga, Schuyler returned to Fort George to gather provisions and to make certain that his supply lines were in good working order. A brief time later, he was at Saratoga, writing to Pierre Van Cortlandt, president of the New York Provincial Congress: "Having brought affairs at Tyconderoga in some better train than I found them I left the necessary directions for carrying on the work . . . St. Clair . . . does not imagine they mean a serious attack on Tyconderoga." [21]

St. Clair was mistaken. General Burgoyne arrived before Ticonderoga on July 3 with a splendidly equipped army of more than 7,000 men. St. Clair had only 3,000. On July 5, he held a council of war and decided to evacuate Ticonderoga.[22] Burgoyne had hauled heavy artillery to the summit of Sugar Loaf Hill, about a mile from the fortress, and was in a position to bombard it.

Schuyler was amazed to learn that St. Clair had withdrawn from Ticonderoga. He knew that the fortress had been insufficiently manned, but the thought that it would be abandoned without a fight simply had not occurred to him. When he wrote to Washington, he communicated the bare facts of the evacuation and nothing more.[23] Unaccompanied by any explanation, the news of the fall of Ticonderoga spread throughout the country and Schuyler soon found himself subjected to severe criticism. In New England and elsewhere, he was accused of treachery for presumably delivering the fortress over to the enemy.

Although discouraged by this turn of events, Schuyler continued his efforts to halt Burgoyne's advance. He established his headquarters at Fort Edward, a strategic location on the upper

Hudson. From this post he could command both the main routes leading south from Ticonderoga: one by Lake Champlain, Skenesborough, and Wood Creek; the other by Lake George and the Hudson. When Burgoyne decided upon the former route, Schuyler made ready to stop him at Fort Anne some fifteen miles north of Fort Edward.

Writing to Colonel Long, commander of Fort Anne, Schuyler urged him, on July 7, to make a stand: "I have sent a detachment to your assistance with some ammunition and doubt not but it will be well expended. . . . I expect General Nixon with a Brigade tomorrow or next day. I hope when General St. Clair and General Nixon and the other troops from below arrive that we shall be able to do a little more than merely keep them at Bay." [24] But two days later, Schuyler had to report to Washington: "The enemy followed the troops that came to Skenesboro as far as Fort Ann where they were yesterday repulsed notwithstanding which Col. Long contrary to my express orders evacuated that post. . . . I am here at the head of a handful of men not above fifteen hundred without provisions. . . ." [25]

Burgoyne had advanced from Canada to Skenesborough at the southern end of Lake Champlain—a distance of nearly one hundred and fifty miles—in a few weeks. It was to take him a full month to advance the few miles from Skenesborough to a position south of Fort Edward. It was this month—from July 7 to August 7—that ultimately cost him the campaign. If Schuyler was not Washington's equal as a great military leader or Arnold's equal as a dashing field officer, he was the perfect commander for a delaying operation. He did everything in his power to slow down Burgoyne's progress. Trees were chopped down across the wagon tracks the British were to use. Bridges were removed or destroyed. Huge boulders were rolled into Wood Creek, diverting its waters across Burgoyne's route. Cattle were driven off and crops put to the torch to deny the enemy any food. Although Burgoyne's main column was not attacked, his advance parties were harassed unmercifully.

While slowing down Burgoyne's army, Schuyler made every

chusetts Historical Society, *Proceedings*, XLIII (April–June, 1910), p. 580.

10. Bellamy Partridge has alleged—though without producing any evidence to substantiate the charge—that Howe's failure on several occasions to press home his advantage against the enemy was directly attributed to his friendly feelings toward the Americans and to his hopes for a reconciliation. See Partridge, *Sir Billy Howe* (London and New York, 1933), pp. 98–99, 101–03, 148–51, 168, 241–42.

11. The famous historian of the British army, Sir John W. Fortescue, who was always ready to blame politicians rather than generals, exculpated Howe on these grounds. See John W. Fortescue, *A History of the British Army*, 13 vols. (London, 1899–1930), III, pp. 174–75, 204, 208, 397–98.

12. Howe's most persuasive modern advocate has been Troyer S. Anderson. In *The Command of the Howe Brothers during the American Revolution* (New York and London, 1936), Anderson noted that Howe had to act as military commander and as peacemaker simultaneously; that he was beset by immense logistical problems because all supplies had to be sent from England; that he had to conduct operations over vast distances; and that he found fewer loyalists prepared to make personal sacrifices for George III than ministers in England believed. According to Anderson, Howe's caution and avoidance of risks were due to the precariousness of his position. Because British losses could not speedily be replaced, Howe felt bound to conduct operations with prudence in order to minimize the chances of a serious defeat.

13. This argument was, in effect, that of Fox, Burke, and Chatham, who believed from the first that the colonies could not be recovered by force. The same thesis appears in the works of Whig historians, notably in George O. Trevelyan's *History of the American Revolution*, 2 vols. (London, 1899–1903).

14. Lewis B. Namier, *The Structure of Politics at the Accession of George III* (London, 1929), pp. 32–33.

15. Quoted in *ibid.*, p. 31.

16. Anderson, *op. cit.*, p. 48.

17. *Ibid.*, p. 49.

18. *Ibid.*, p. 50.

19. Skene to North, January 23, 1775, Historical Manuscripts Commission, *Dartmouth MSS.*, II, p. 262.

20. Germain to Suffolk, June 16 or 17, 1775, Historical Manuscripts Commission, *Stopford-Sackville MSS.*, II, p. 2.

ists and Indians, advanced eastward from Lake Ontario intending to join up with the British general at Albany. Led by Lieutenant Colonel Barry St. Leger, this force marched down the Mohawk Valley until it reached Fort Schuyler. There the American garrison put up a stout defense and St. Leger was forced to place the fort under siege. Learning of the garrison's plight, Schuyler sent off a relief expedition under Benedict Arnold. When the siege was raised, St. Leger abandoned his efforts to reach Albany and turned back to Lake Ontario. These three parts of Schuyler's strategy—delaying the advance of Burgoyne's main army, protecting the Northern army's eastward flank in the vicinity of Bennington, reinforcing and rescuing the garrison of Fort Schuyler to the westward—all were successful, but they occurred just prior to Gates's assumption of command. As Nathanael Greene wrote: "This Gentleman is a mere child of fortune. The Foundation of all Northern Successes was laid long before his arrival there!" [33]

The people of Albany remained loyal to their leading citizen, even though his military career had suffered an eclipse. Upon Schuyler's return to the community, they addressed a memorial to him expressing their gratitude in the following words:

> . . . our warmest thanks, are justly your due, for having so eminently distinguished yourself in the preservation of the remains of our small and dispersed Army; by collecting them together, and effecting their safe retreat from Fort Edward, to their present Encampment near Half Moon, without loss of men, Artillery, Baggage, or Stores, and . . . in defiance of the most strenuous efforts of a vastly superior Army, greatly elated by their easy acquisition of the Fortress of Ticonderoga.[34]

Schuyler was relieved of command of the Northern army on August 19, 1777; almost two months later to the day, Burgoyne surrendered to Gates. There can be little doubt that much of the credit for the defeat of Burgoyne's expedition belongs to Schuyler. He had delayed and harassed Burgoyne's army with a force that was one-third of the size of the enemy's, lured the foe far from the main base of supplies in Canada, and denied the British any opportunity of replenishing their dwindling food supplies. Moreover, it was largely due to Schuyler's efforts that New York had been able to garrison the fort in the Mohawk Valley to oppose the sweep of the British right wing under St. Leger. But it was Gates, not Schuyler, who was destined to reap the fruits of all these labors.

After his retirement to Albany, Schuyler was kept informed of the course of events by his friends in the Northern army. When the British surrendered, he made a trip to Saratoga and was introduced to Burgoyne and other enemy generals. Despite the fact that Burgoyne's troops had destroyed his fine country house during the course of military operations, Schuyler greeted the British general graciously and offered him the hospitality of his home in Albany. He was equally kind to the families of the vanquished enemy. Madame Riedesel, wife of the German general, left this interesting account of her first meeting with Schuyler:

> I confess that I feared to come into the enemy's camp, as the thing was so entirely new to me. When I approached the tents, a noble-looking man came toward me, took the children out of the wagon, embraced and kissed them, and then with tears in his eyes helped me also to alight. "You tremble," said he to me, "fear nothing." "No," replied I, "for you are so kind, and have been so tender toward my children, that it has inspired me with courage." He then led me to the tent of General Gates, with whom I found Generals Burgoyne and Phillips, who were upon an extremely friendly footing with him. . . . The man, who had received me so kindly, came up and said to me, "It may be embarrassing to you to dine with all these gentlemen; come now with your children into my tent, where I will give you, it is true, a frugal meal, but one that will be accompanied by the best of wishes." "You are certainly," answered I, "a husband and father, since you show me so much kindness." I then learned that he was the American General Schuyler.[35]

Madame Riedesel and Burgoyne accepted Schuyler's invitation to spend some time with him at his home in Albany. There they were received in a friendly manner and shown every mark of respect. Even General Burgoyne was deeply moved by this magnanimity, and remarked to General Schuyler, "Is it to me, who have done you so much injury that you show so much kindness!" "That is the fate of war," replied the New Yorker, "let us say no more about it."

Schuyler's concern with military affairs continued long after he lost command of the Northern army. He was plagued by the persistent rumors that he had been disloyal in losing the fortress at Ticonderoga.[36] To clear himself of these charges, Schuyler insisted upon a court of inquiry into his conduct of the campaign. Although the Continental Congress was reluctant to hold such a court-martial, Schuyler remained adamant, claiming that he would not feel free until he had a hearing.[37]

The charge that Schuyler had responded to enemy efforts to win him over has gained credence among historians after the discovery of certain data revealed by Major John Ackland, a British army officer. Ackland, who was attached to Burgoyne's staff, accompanied the British general to Schuyler's residence in Albany. When Burgoyne departed for Boston, Ackland remained with the Schuylers along with his beautiful wife, Lady Harriet, who was pregnant.[38] Eventually an exchange was arranged for Ackland so that he could take Lady Harriet to New York and from there back to England. Early in January, 1778, with the arrangements completed, Schuyler sent the couple to New York in one of his sleighs.

Sir Henry Clinton, commander of the British garrison in New York, closely questioned Ackland about Schuyler's views. Ackland revealed that in his conversations with Schuyler the American general did not appear to favor the break with Great Britain. If the British would abandon their policy of taxation without representation and would not insist upon unconditional surrender by the Americans, Schuyler was said to be ready for some kind of settlement between the two sides.

Sir Henry remembered these conversations and nearly eight years later—in 1785—wrote a memorandum on the subject:

Among others of the Saratoga Convention army who came in to
see me was Major Ackland who informed me that he had had many
conversations with L.S. that he was certain he was a staunch friend
to Government; and that he was authorized by him to open a correspondence between us; that he wished me to settle a cipher and
said he had his authority to declare if the Commissioners would
promise on their part that taxation would be given up and unconditional submission not insisted upon, he would join Government
with all his force.[39]

In 1793, Sir Henry wrote a second memorandum:

General Schuyler was the Person. His motives were interested. In
the first place till Ticonderoga was taken Burgoyne could not advance. It was the wish of Schuyler that he might because the Vermonters his bitter Enemys and who claim the greatest part of his
Estates, would in that case be obliged to disclose themselves, if they
joined the Kings troops, Schuyler would have been hearty with the
Americans; if on the contrary they should oppose the Kings troops
Schuyler would certainly take the opposite side for reasons in both
cases very obvious. The Vermonters had acquired so much credit
with the Americans by their spirited exertions against Burgoyne's
army that Schuyler was decided in the part he was to take and
thence his proposal to me through Major Ackland . . .[40]

Despite this damaging evidence, the charge of treason against
Schuyler does not appear to rest upon a very solid foundation.
There are no other scraps of evidence available on this subject,
and it is not even clear that the "L.S." referred to in the first
memorandum was Schuyler. Since all of the Schuyler estates lay
to the west of the Hudson, these lands were not claimed by Vermont as was implied. Finally, there is the dubious credibility of
Sir Henry Clinton as a witness. To provide an alibi for the failure of his campaign in America, Clinton actually forged a false
order from his superiors and included it in his memoirs after the
war—which raises a question of validity regarding everything
that Clinton ever wrote.

Schuyler's court-martial was held on October 1, 1778, at the
headquarters of Major General Benjamin Lincoln in Pawling,

New York. He was charged with neglect of duty for not being present at Ticonderoga during the crucial weeks prior to the taking of the fortress.[41] Schuyler produced an imposing array of witnesses and letters to show the steps he had taken to strengthen the Ticonderoga defenses.[42] As a result, he was acquitted with honor. The following spring, Schuyler formally resigned his commission as general.

Schuyler, however, continued to serve his country in many ways. He remained a member of the Board of Commissioners on Indian Affairs and advised Washington on the expedition that was sent against the tribes in the Mohawk Valley in 1779. When he went to Congress in 1779 and 1780 as a member of the New York delegation, he used his influence to emphasize the Indian menace along the northern frontier. His intimate knowledge of Indian affairs proved most valuable because many of the members of Congress had not dealt with such matters at first hand.

Although he was no longer in the army, Schuyler rendered great service to General Washington on military matters. During the spring and summer of 1780, he served as chairman of the committee at Washington's headquarters, helping to reorganize the army's staff departments and to devise ways of gaining more effective co-operation with the French forces stationed in America.[43] When Washington suggested that Schuyler accept another position in 1781, the New Yorker replied:

> Your Excellency draws too favorable a conclusion when you suppose me competent to the business of the War Department . . . I cannot suppose that Congress will offer it . . . since I have . . . in writing declared my intention never to hold any office under them unless accompanied with a restoration of my military rank . . .[44]

During July, 1781, General Washington maintained his headquarters at Peekskill, where he could keep an eye on nearby New York City. Contemplating an offensive action against the British garrison there, he turned to his old friend Philip Schuyler to build bateaux to transport troops down the Hudson River.[45]

Although a full-scale attack on the city never materialized, Schuyler built 100 boats at Albany for the army.[46]

Washington's trust in Schuyler was demonstrated once again when he sought the New Yorker's assistance in dealing with the movement that was afoot to make Vermont a British province. When the Continental Congress hesitated to admit the independent Republic of Vermont to the Confederation, General Haldimand of the British army contacted the authorities in Vermont and proposed that they rejoin the empire. Washington decided to keep a close eye on the situation, and he turned to Schuyler for advice. To open correspondence with Thomas Chittenden, the president of Vermont, Washington sent a letter addressed to him through Schuyler. The commander-in-chief asked Schuyler to look the letter over before forwarding it. All these moves were conducted in the greatest secrecy because Washington noted: "I do not wish to have my writing to him publicly known." [47] Eventually the British negotiations with the Vermonters broke down and Haldimand's efforts failed.

After the war had come to a close, Schuyler continued to hold important public offices on the state and national levels. Like many of the great landlords in New York, he supported the movement in favor of the Federal Constitution. Co-operating with his son-in-law, Alexander Hamilton, he worked hard to secure ratification of the Constitution in his state. He went on to represent New York in the first Senate of the United States and became an ardent champion of Hamilton's financial program. After a short term, he was defeated for re-election by Aaron Burr in 1791. Six years later he defeated Burr for the same seat, but was forced to resign because of ill-health in January, 1798.

Schuyler's few remaining years were sad ones. His loyal friend George Washington died. His brilliant son-in-law, Alexander Hamilton, was killed by Aaron Burr in a duel. And his devoted wife Catherine died of apoplexy in 1803. The loss of his wife hastened his own death on November 18, 1804. On the day of his funeral, the *Albany Gazette* reported: "The streets were lined with people, doors and windows were filled and even the house tops were not without spectators to behold the melancholy procession and to pay their last offices of respect to the deceased." [48]

Those who knew Schuyler well appreciated fully his great services to the Continental army. What was his contribution to the cause of American independence? From the beginning of the Revolution to its end, the British Ministry correctly realized that the way to suppress the rebellion was to take possession of the north–south water highway extending from Montreal to New York and thus split the rebellious colonies in two. After 1775, both Montreal and New York were in the possession of the British and the target was, therefore, Albany, lying halfway between. By building a fleet, or rather a series of fleets, on Lake Champlain, Schuyler prevented a British advance in both 1775 and 1776. By obstructing Burgoyne's advance in July and August 1777, he gained valuable time to allow the patriots to assemble the militia forces required to win a victory. When Gates arrived to take command, Burgoyne's troops had been defeated at Bennington and Fort Schuyler, and the balance of power had already turned in favor of the Americans.

A general by force of circumstances rather than by choice, a revolutionary who had more to lose than to gain from change, Schuyler helped to determine the outcome of the war. Burgoyne's surrender at Saratoga has been called the turning point of the war and Schuyler's contribution to that major success entitles him to a place of prominence among the military leaders of the Revolution.

FOOTNOTES

1. The rum horn is included in the Fort Ticonderoga Museum Collection.
2. *Journals of the Provincial Congress, Provincial Convention, Committee of Safety and Council of Safety of the State of New York, 1775–1776–1777*, 2 vols. (Albany, 1842), I, 33.

3. Washington to Schuyler, June 27, 1775, Schuyler Letter Books, LV, No. 1, New York Public Library; hereinafter, N.Y.P.L.

4. Schuyler to Washington, July 18, 1775, Peter Force, ed., *American Archives* (Washington, D.C., 1837–46), 4th series, II, 1686; hereinafter, *American Archives.*

5. Schuyler to Washington, July 31, 1775, Schuyler Letter Books, I, N.Y.P.L.

6. Orders, July 25, 1775, Schuyler MSS, Henry E. Huntington Library, San Marino, California.

7. Worthington Chauncey Ford, ed., *Journals of the Continental Congress,* 35 vols. (Washington, D.C., 1905–22), II, 194.

8. Schuyler to Washington, August 27, 1775, *American Archives,* 4th series, III, 442

9. Washington to Arnold, September 14, 1775, *ibid.,* 766.

10. Schuyler to Washington, September 20, 1775, *ibid.,* 751–52.

11. Schuyler to Montgomery, September 16, 1775, Schuyler Letter Books, I, N.Y.P.L.

12. Montgomery to Schuyler, September 2, 1775, Schuyler MSS, I, N.Y.P.L.

13. Schuyler to Montgomery, September 29, 1775, Schuyler Letter Books, I, N.Y.P.L.

14. Schuyler to Washington, September 26, 1775, *American Archives,* 4th series, III, 808.

15. *Journals of the Continental Congress,* IV, 219.

16. Schuyler to Sullivan, June 28, 1776, Schuyler MSS, Massachusetts Historical Society.

17. *Journals of the Continental Congress,* V, 526.

18. William Henry Smith, *Life and Public Services of Arthur St. Clair,* 2 vols. (Cincinnati, 1882), I, 399–400.

19. Schuyler to Washington, June 10, 1777, Schuyler Letter Books, XX, N.Y.P.L.

20. Schuyler to Congress, June 25, 1777, Schuyler Letter Books, XXI, N.Y.P.L.

21. Schuyler to Van Cortlandt, June 27, 1775, Houghton Library MSS, Harvard University.

22. "St. Clair Court-Martial Proceedings," *Collections of the New York Historical Society for the Year 1880* (New York, 1881), pp. 33–34.

23. John C. Fitzpatrick, ed., *Writings of George Washington,* 39 vols. (Washington, 1931–44), VIII, 377; hereinafter, Washington, *Writings.*

24. Schuyler to Long, July 7, 1777, Schuyler Letter Books, XXV, N.Y.P.L.
25. Schuyler to Washington, July 9, 1777, *ibid.*
26. Schuyler to Washington, July 10, 1777, *ibid.*
27. Schuyler to Tenbroeck, July 10, 1777, *ibid.*
28. Schuyler to Fellows, July 11, 1777, *ibid.*
29. Schuyler to Nixon, July 11, 1777, *ibid.*
30. *Journals of the Continental Congress,* VIII, 596.
31. *Ibid.,* VIII, 603–04.
32. Washington, *Writings,* IX, 11–12.
33. Theodore Thayer, *Nathanael Greene, Strategist of the American Revolution* (New York, 1960), 214.
34. Memorial, Inhabitants of Albany to Schuyler, August, 1777, Schuyler Letters, N.Y.P.L.
35. Baroness Frederika Riedesel, *Letters and Journals relating to the War of the American Revolution and the Capture of the German Troops at Saratoga,* translated from the original German by William L. Stone (Albany, 1867), pp. 134–36.
36. *Journals of the Continental Congress,* IX, 901.
37. Schuyler to President of Congress, November 29, 1777, Schuyler Letter Books, XXII, N.Y.P.L.
38. F. J. Hudleston, *Gentleman Johnny Burgoyne* (Indianapolis, 1927), p. 201.
39. Sir Henry Clinton Memo, 1785, Clinton Papers, William E. Clements Library, Ann Arbor, Michigan.
40. *Ibid.,* 1793.
41. "The Trial of Major General Schuyler, October, 1778," *Collections of the New York Historical Society for the Year 1879* (New York, 1880), p. 26.
42. *Ibid.,* p. 25.
43. Washington to Duane, May 14, 1780, Washington, *Writings,* XVIII, 356–57.
44. Schuyler to Washington, February 25, 1781, Sparks Transcripts, Houghton Library, Harvard University.
45. John Fitzpatrick, ed., *The Diaries of George Washington, 1748–99,* 4 vols. (Boston, 1925), II, 247.
46. *Ibid.,* II, 248.
47. Washington to Schuyler, January 8, 1782, Schuyler MSS, Huntington Library, San Marino, California.
48. *Albany Gazette,* November 22, 1804.

BIBLIOGRAPHY

Lossing, Benson J., *Life and Times of Philip Schuyler*, 2 vols. New York, 1872–73. The oldest but still the best biography of Schuyler.

Mayer, Brantz, ed., *Journal of Charles Carroll of Carrollton, during his Visit to Canada in 1776, as one of the Commissioners from Congress.* Baltimore, 1845. Contains important information for a study of the Canadian expedition of 1776.

New York Historical Society, "The Trial of Major General St. Clair, August, 1778," in *Collections*, 1880. New York, 1881. A valuable document about the surrender of Fort Ticonderoga in July, 1777.

New York Historical Society, "The Trial of Major General Schuyler, October, 1778," in *Collections*, 1879. New York, 1880. The equal of the St. Clair court-martial, as a source on the loss of Fort Ticonderoga in July, 1777.

Nickerson, Hoffman, *The Turning Point of the Revolution: or Burgoyne in America.* Boston & New York, 1928. This is one of the most useful and reliable works on the American Revolution and especially on the Burgoyne campaign of 1777.

Schuyler, George W., *Colonial New York: Philip Schuyler and His Family*, 2 vols. New York, 1885. It is more a work on the history of New York than on Philip Schuyler; has only a small section on him.

Sellers, Charles Coleman, *Benedict Arnold: The Proud Warrior.* New York, 1930. A well done popular biography. It contains good descriptions of the Quebec expedition, Saratoga, and Schuyler at St. Johns. The author is sympathetic toward Schuyler.

Tuckerman, Bayard, *Life of General Philip Schuyler.* New York, 1903. Contains information on Schuyler's military career that cannot be found elsewhere.

Horatio Gates:

PROFESSIONAL SOLDIER

———————

GEORGE A. BILLIAS

Clark University

THE place of Horatio Gates in American history presents a paradox. By virtue of his victory in the most decisive battle of the war for independence, Gates deserves to be ranked among the founding fathers of the republic. His triumph at Saratoga, which is regarded rightly as one of the crucial battles in American and world history, marked the turning point of the Revolution. A professional soldier among generals who were mostly amateurs, Gates contributed much in molding the Continental army into an effective fighting force. But instead of being remembered with gratitude for his good deeds, Gates has gone down in history as "a weakling, a bungler, and a marplot." He remains a sinister figure in the minds of many Americans. In the words of Allan Nevins, Gates has been made "the whipping boy . . . of the Revolution." [1]

Two American generals, whose reputations lie poles apart, have prevented Gates from taking his proper place among the eminent men of his generation. One was the Revolution's greatest war hero, George Washington; the other, its most infamous traitor, Benedict Arnold. The so-called Conway Cabal—an alleged plot to oust Washington in favor of Gates as head of the Continental army—caused Gates to go down in history as a general who was disloyal to his commander-in-chief. Benedict

79

Arnold's daring attacks and dashing role at Saratoga led many historians to give Arnold, not Gates, the credit for that important victory. As a result, Gates remains the Revolution's most controversial military figure.

Gates hardly looked the part of a soldier. At the pinnacle of his career at Saratoga, he seemed much older than his fifty years. He was stooped in stature, ruddy-cheeked, had thinning gray hair, and wore spectacles perched precariously on the end of his long nose. Even his conversation was that of an old man, for he had a habit of using homely proverbs to illustrate his points. Little wonder that his men called him "granny Gates."

Appearances can be deceiving, however. This gray-haired, grandfatherly figure was a tough and experienced professional soldier. Military matters were his main concern throughout much of his adult life. He started soldiering at an early age and practiced his profession in two armies for almost a quarter of a century. Prior to accepting a commission in the Continental army, he could boast of fifteen years' service as an officer in the British regulars. When Congress appointed him a general in 1775, no other high-ranking officer, with the possible exception of Charles Lee, had seen more years of active military duty or knew as much about the business of warfare.

Horatio Gates was born the only child of Robert and Dorothea Gates, on July 26, 1727, probably at Maldon, England. Too much has been made of the fact that he sprang from humble origins. It is true that his mother was a housekeeper for the Duke of Leeds, but her occupation helped rather than hurt her son's career. Junior officers in the British army purchased their commissions and as a result such positions usually were acquired by those whose families possessed money and influence. Under ordinary circumstances, one of Gates's low birth would have had little chance of entering the officer class. Because of his mother's association with the Leeds household, however, Horace Walpole offered to become his godfather and namesake.[2] This connection with a prominent family probably helped Gates to gain his first army position. His father, a minor government official, assisted

Horatio's military career by providing the money to purchase the commission.[3]

Gates left England for an overseas assignment at an early age. He had barely turned twenty-two when he came to America as a volunteer with Edward Cornwallis, governor of Nova Scotia.[4] Stationed in this isolated northern outpost in 1749–50, the young officer set about learning the ways of garrison life. Cornwallis soon appointed him captain lieutenant in Warburton's regiment and in 1754 made it possible for him to purchase his captain's commission.[5] By a strange quirk of fate, Cornwallis helped to promote the very man who was destined to lead an American army against the governor's own nephew, Lord Charles Cornwallis, in the Revolutionary War.

During his stay in Nova Scotia, Gates took two steps that increased his chances for advancement. In 1754 he married Elizabeth Phillips, the eldest daughter of an army officer. Although her father did not hold high rank, the Phillips family had proper upper-class connections in England. Elizabeth, moreover, had been left a little money of her own.[6] But in the long run, his wife's ambitions may have hindered Horatio's career in the American army. General Charles Lee once called her "that Medusa . . . [who] governs with a rod of Scorpions." [7] Perhaps even more damaging to her husband's future was the quarrel Elizabeth Gates had with Martha Washington.

Gates cultivated also the friendship of General Robert Monckton, lieutenant governor of Annapolis Royal. This gallant and generous soldier used every opportunity to promote the career of his protégé. Gates for his part was genuinely fond of the bachelor general, and named his first and only son, Robert, in Monckton's honor.

When the French and Indian War broke out, Gates was sent south to join General Braddock's army in Virginia as captain of an independent company. He had little chance to gain combat experience. On his first day under fire, Gates was badly wounded when a musket ball tore through his body. Braddock's men had been ambushed by a force of French and Indians who fought frontier style from behind logs, thickets, and trees. As the red-coats huddled together, the enemy pouring a hail of arrows and lead into their ranks, a lowly private—one Francis Penfold—saved Gates from almost certain death by carrying him to safety from the battlefield. This incident may account for the warmth with which Gates always treated the common soldiers under his command. When he learned that Private Penfold needed help in later years, Gates offered him the hospitality of his home:

> Come and rest your firelock in my chimney corner, and partake with me; while I have my savior Penfold shall not want.[8]

The French and Indian War served as a kind of dress rehearsal in preparing Gates for his role in the Revolution. Fighting against the French afforded him an opportunity to test his talents for military leadership under combat conditions. He also encountered the tactics employed in frontier fighting, traversed some of the same terrain he was to battle upon in later years, saw the colonial militia in action, and gained valuable experience in dealing with the Indians. But his combat experience was limited because he commanded only small units on the lower echelons for the most part.

Gates mastered the details of military administration as well as leading troops into battle. He began serving as brigade major, or military secretary, to one British general—Stanwix—in 1759. When his old friend Monckton became Stanwix's successor in 1760, Gates served him in a similar capacity. The following year General Monckton was appointed governor of New York and brought along his young brigade major to do the desk work.

Toward the close of 1761, Gates sailed with Monckton on an expedition against the French-held island of Martinique in the West Indies. The conquest was carried off with great success. Although Gates took little part in the fighting, he served with such distinction that Monckton commended him to the attention of King George III as a "deserving officer." Selected for the honor of carrying the news of victory back to England, he was rewarded by being commissioned a major in 1762 at the age of thirty-four.[9]

When the war ended, he returned to England only to find that further advancement in the army was practically impossible. His low birth and limited resources, coupled with the fact that the British army was reverting to a peacetime footing, killed his chances for promotion. He became embittered and turned to "guzzling and gaming" for a time. By the mid-1760's, his military career seemed at an end. He was retired from active service in the Royal American Regiment and placed on half-pay. At about the same time, he underwent a religious conversion and began leading a quiet life in the English countryside.

During his years of retirement, Gates maintained an active interest in American political affairs. He had been linked with the Livingston-Whig faction while serving in New York and met many of the budding politicians who later led America down the road to revolution.[10] As the breach between the colonies and mother country widened, he showed his sympathies lay with the patriots.

Gates had acquired a reputation in England as a "red hot republican" by the year 1770.[11] His republicanism probably was motivated in large part by his frustrated ambitions in both social and military circles. As a servant's son living on a meager pension he found it difficult to rise in English society. He was often entertained by the nobility but such contacts only heightened his sense of frustration. He apparently felt that he had no future and that his friends either could not or would not help him.[12]

It was in this mood of dissatisfaction with English class barriers that Gates began to think of moving to the New World. In the spring of 1772, he wrote to George Washington, with whom he had served under Braddock almost twenty years before, to inquire about the possibility of buying an estate in the colonies. He sailed for America that same summer and in 1773 purchased a Virginia plantation which he called appropriately enough "Traveller's Rest." Gates seemed to take the name of his estate to heart; for the next two years he participated little in

public life beyond accepting an honorary commission as lieutenant colonel in the Virginia militia.

The outbreak of the Revolutionary War presented Gates with
a second chance for an active army career. He was too shrewd
an opportunist to pass up the possibilities that the military situation offered to someone with his background and experience.
Though it meant fighting against his former King and country,
he accepted a commission as brigadier general to become the first
adjutant general of the American army. His appointment as
general must have been a source of great satisfaction to Gates,
for it was a rank he could never have hoped to attain in the
British army.

He had a real flair for administration and quickly became
Washington's right-hand man in organizing the new American
army at Cambridge in July, 1775. By writing the first army regulations and maintaining military records, he brought some
semblance of order to the chaotic situation facing the new commander-in-chief. His professional experience enabled him to set
up procedures for recruiting new soldiers and for training older
ones. Efficient, hard-working, and loyal, he was able to relieve his
chief from many time-consuming clerical chores. Washington
was quick to recognize his merits as an administrator, and long
after Gates had left the post of adjutant general, the commander-
in-chief kept trying to persuade him to return.[13]

As a member of Washington's staff, Gates also had an opportunity to voice his views on strategy. The British army was
cooped up inside Boston during the last half of 1775 and hemmed
in on land by a semicircle of American troops. While other generals were suggesting an offensive to drive the besieged British
into the sea, Gates was in favor of remaining on the defensive.
Knowing how touchy the British government was to mounting
military expenses, he proposed to strike a blow at Parliament's
most sensitive spot—the pocketbook. "Boston Dirt will be a
Dollar a Bushell to the English Treasury," he argued. "The
Army, the Fleet, seventy Transports, and an Infinity of Cutters
&c in constant pay." [14] Like most military men in 1775, he

anticipated a short war and counted upon the costs of a stalemate to force Britain to abandon her policy of coercion.

When it became increasingly clear that a prolonged war was in prospect, Gates advocated a strategy based on caution. "Our Business," he wrote early in 1776, "is to Defend the main Chance; to Attack only by Detail; and when a precious advantage Offers." [15] In effect, this was the policy he was to follow during the early years of the war.

Caution was Gates's most outstanding characteristic in tactics as well as strategy. Throughout the siege of Boston, he opposed any rash moves. He voted against Washington's bold scheme for attacking the city across the ice. When a plan was proposed for seizing Dorchester Heights, Gates voted to postpone it.[16] But the majority of Washington's staff disagreed with him and approved the plan that finally resulted in driving the British out of Boston in March, 1776.

Cautious as he was on military matters, Gates found himself among the radicals on the political question of American independence. Few men, except the "brace of Adamses"—John and Sam—were more rabid for independence than this Englishman. Gates chided John Adams for failing to persuade Congress to break with Great Britain early in 1776. For those who wanted to steer a middle-of-the-road course, Gates quoted this couplet:

> The Midd[l]e way, the best, we sometimes call,
> But 'tis in Polliticks no way at all.[17]

Gates's politics had no adverse effects upon his military career, for he was promoted to major general in May, 1776. One month later, his first assignment to command American forces in the field came when he was ordered to take charge of the Northern army retreating from Canada into New York. By the time Gates reached his new command, the army at Crown Point was facing a major crisis.

Disease, desertion, and dissension had shattered the Northern army. Smallpox raged in the ranks and soldiers were dying in great numbers. The militia, discouraged by successive defeats, were melting away. There was a problem of divided command: General Philip Schuyler, a New York Dutch patroon-turned-patriot, claimed, with some justification, that Congress had made *him* head of the Northern army. To make matters worse, an Anglo-German army clad in scarlet and blue led by the capable Sir Guy Carleton was poised to sweep south down Lake Champlain upon the Americans.

Gates already had demonstrated his great gifts as a military organizer while helping Washington form the American army at Cambridge; he showed these same qualities in meeting the threat of this first major British invasion from the north. While Carleton busied himself building a fleet during the summer of 1776, Gates prepared to meet the enemy on both land and water. He began whipping his battered army back into shape and plunged into a shipbuilding race with the British.

Gates's primary success was in restoring the morale of the Northern army and instilling his troops with a fighting spirit. Within weeks after his arrival, one officer wrote: "Generalship is now dealt out . . . by our worthy and well-esteemed General Gates, who is putting the most disordered Army that ever bore the name into a state of regularity and defense." The new-found confidence of the troops was reflected in his next remark: "If our friends in *Canada* . . . will wait a few days, we will give them a very proper reception." [18] Gates himself reported two months later: "The army here are in good spirits and think only of victory." [19]

One way Gates helped to achieve this military miracle was by showing a deep concern for the physical welfare and well-being of his men. Realizing that smallpox posed a greater threat to his troops than the enemy, he bent all of his efforts to combat the disease. Sick soldiers were isolated immediately, the "pernicious practice" of inoculation was halted for fear it might spread the disease, and desperately needed medical supplies were procured.[20] By early September, he could report to the President of Congress: "Thank Heaven, the smallpox is totally eradicated from among us." [21] When the damp climate led to fever and the ague in the

army, Gates won the affection of his men by ordering huge bon-
fires built and by issuing extra rations of rum.

The army's morale improved also as bickering between the
generals diminished. Gates showed admirable restraint in his
initial dealings with the difficult Dutchman, Philip Schuyler.
After Congress had confirmed Schuyler as head of the Northern
Department, Gates took his defeat gracefully and served faithfully under him for the remainder of the campaign. Although
Schuyler was named over-all commander, Gates was put in
charge of all the forces in the field at the foot of Lake Champlain.

In preparing his defenses on land, Gates decided with Schuyler
that the Northern army should make its main stand at Fort
Ticonderoga, the so-called "American Gibraltar." However,
when Gates ordered the army to withdraw from the crumbling
fortifications at Crown Point, Washington and General Israel
Putnam wrote that they disapproved of his decision. Instead of
resenting the criticism directed against him, Gates gently chided
the proud Putnam, who had helped to build the fort, with this
bit of good humor:

> Every fond mother dotes on her booby, be his imperfections
> ever so glaring, and his good qualities ever so few.
> *Crown-Point* was not indeed your immediate offspring,
> but you had a capital hand in rearing the baby . . .
> why should you not be fond of Crown Point? [22]

For all his good-natured bantering, he stoutly refused to order
the army back to Crown Point.

Gates also played an important part in preparing the fleet that
fought on the waters of Lake Champlain. He personally hand-
picked fiery Benedict Arnold to serve as fleet commander.[23] The
task of shipbuilding was placed primarily in Arnold's hands, but
he could not have accomplished as much as he did without the
assistance of his superior. Gates efficiently rounded up skilled
ship carpenters to work on the makeshift fleet, sought out sea-

faring supplies, and recruited seasoned sailors to man some of the craft.

Gates not only helped to create the Champlain fleet—he directed its operations. The fleet operated as his naval arm and the general dictated naval strategy through his orders to Arnold. The cautious Gates conceived the role of his fleet to be a defensive one. In his eyes, it was to serve as a counterweight to the British naval force in opposing the invasion. Gates wrote to Arnold in August warning him to stay near the American end of the lake and to take "no wanton Risk" nor to make any "unnecessary Display of Power." [24]

His instructions went unheeded. Arnold, spoiling for a fight, took matters into his own hands by bringing on an engagement with the British fleet off Valcour Island on October 11–13. Despite a gallant running battle, the British smashed the Champlain fleet, swept the American ships off the lake, and Carleton's army moved down to occupy Crown Point.

Carleton may have won the naval battle, but it cost him the campaign. Valuable time had been lost while he halted his army to build a larger fleet than that of Gates. Even after defeating Arnold, Carleton still had to contend with the second line of American defense—the army inside Fort Ticonderoga. The British general probed the outer works of the rocky fortress but found them too strong to be stormed. His troops were not equipped for a winter campaign and it was too late in the season to begin a siege. There was little else for him to do but re-embark his army in early November and return to Canada.

Gates deserves much credit for turning back Carleton—though historians usually have given all the glory to Arnold. Because of Gates's rare abilities as a military organizer, the Americans were able to mount strong defenses on both land and water. He made a disciplined army out of what had once been a disorganized mob, took up a position at Ticonderoga where the fortifications were more formidable, and blocked the British advance until the approach of winter forced Carleton to retreat. Gates should share the honors with Arnold as builder of the

Champlain fleet and events were to show that his defensive naval strategy was sound. By halting this first British invasion, Gates not only saved the Northern army and Fort Ticonderoga—he also gave the patriots precious time to prepare for the second major British invasion from the north.

Gates remained at Ticonderoga until December, 1776, when he was ordered to march south with troops to reinforce Washington. Had he wished to be disloyal to his commander-in-chief, he had his opportunity at this time. The New York Committee of Safety urged him to disobey Washington's orders and to join his men with those of General Charles Lee. Their plan was to create a separate army independent of Washington's command to fight in the Hudson Highlands. Gates did not hesitate; he continued marching toward Washington and sent one of his aides to turn down the New York proposal.[25]

After a winter commanding troops in Philadelphia, Gates was ordered back to Ticonderoga in March, 1777, to take charge of the forces there. By this time his bitter controversy with Schuyler over the command of the Northern army had broken out into the open again. Both men had their champions in Congress. John and Sam Adams were Gates's strongest backers. Gates tried to lobby in his own behalf, but did his cause more harm than good by losing his temper with members of Congress. The Gates–Schuyler feud reflected little credit on either man, and it brought out the worst side of Gates's nature by showing him to be petty and vindictive where matters of rank and authority were concerned. After shuffling the two commanders back and forth, Congress finally removed Schuyler in favor of Gates in August, 1777.

The immediate cause for Schuyler's removal was the loss of Ticonderoga. While jealous American generals were contesting for command of the Northern army, "Gentleman Johnny" Burgoyne had started his southward drive down the Lake Champlain–Hudson River corridor with the aim of sealing off New England from the rest of the states. The British general scored a stunning surprise victory on July 6, 1777. He occupied a high peak known as Mount Defiance which overlooked Ticonderoga, and pointing his cannon downward, forced the Americans to withdraw from the fortress without a fight.

Gates, who had a keen eye for terrain, had long warned of this threat to Ticonderoga. In 1776, he tried without success to persuade his superior, Schuyler, to occupy the strategic summit. When Gates himself was in command of Ticonderoga the following year, he ordered his engineer, Thaddeus Kosciuszko, to reconnoiter the ground to determine if guns could be dragged to the top of Mount Defiance. Kosciuszko reported that such a move was a distinct possibility. Before Gates could do anything about the problem, however, he had been replaced by Schuyler. Even after he had gone south, Gates kept writing back to point out this flaw in the Ticonderoga defenses. But his warnings were ignored until it was too late.[26]

The Northern army was thoroughly demoralized by the time Gates returned to assume supreme command in mid-August. Spirit and discipline among the troops had deteriorated to the point where one officer described the army as "rabble." "Would to God Gates would arrive," he sighed. The army's mood changed from despair to confidence with startling suddenness once Gates came on the scene. "From this miserable state of despondency and terror," wrote the same officer, "Gates' arrival raised us, as if by magic. We began to hope and then to act." [27]

Gates had an electrifying effect upon the Northern army for a number of reasons. For one thing, he held a high opinion of the New England troops that formed the backbone of his army. Yankee soldiers responded by showing a great affection for this little gray-haired general who came to be known as "the darling of the New Englanders." [28] Gates also earned the respect of his men by sharing with them the rigors of camp life. As Sam Adams noted of Gates, "He . . . has the Art of *gaining the Love of his Soldiers* principally because he is *always present* with them in Fatigue and Danger." [29]

Schuyler, on the other hand, was as much loathed as Gates was loved. In part, this reaction was the result of the sectional strife that existed between Yankees and Yorkers. But the Dutchman also earned the enmity of his men because he spent much of his time at his upstate mansion, was haughty and rude to the common soldier, and was suspected by some Yankees of having secret dealings with the enemy.[30]

Besides gaining the confidence of his men, Gates restored the army's effectiveness by insisting upon strict military discipline. He had already achieved a reputation as an outstanding disciplinarian. While serving as adjutant general, he had introduced stiff military regulations and was hailed in later years as "the father of . . . discipline of the American army in 1775." [31] When he was commander of the Northern army, both friend and foe testified to Gates's ability in this regard. Benjamin Rush—who admittedly was anti-Washington—claimed that Gates was a better disciplinarian than the commander-in-chief. "I have heard several officers who have served under General Gates compare his army to a well regulated family," he wrote. "These same gentlemen have compared General Washington's imitation of an army to an unformed mob." [32] Less biased and more meaningful was the praise from a fellow professional, General Burgoyne, who inspected Gates's army after his capture at Saratoga and reported back to his superiors in England: "The standing corps which I have seen are disciplined. I do not hazard the term; but apply it to the great fundamental points of military institution, sobriety, subordination, regularity and courage." [33]

Just about the time that Gates took command of the army, the military situation began to swing slowly in favor of the Americans. Burgoyne's invasion plans had suffered two serious setbacks. To the west the British right wing, under veteran Barry St. Leger, driving down the Mohawk Valley was checked at Oriskany and eventually began falling back toward Canada. In the east two lumbering German contingents conducting a raid for supplies near Bennington were routed by scrappy John Stark and Seth Warner. Despite these reverses and the slow progress Burgoyne was making because of Schuyler's delaying tactics, the handsome British general confidently continued his thrust southward toward Albany.

In early September, Gates dealt Burgoyne's plans a sharp blow by a shrewd stroke of propaganda. Swarms of Indians accompanied the British and despite orders to the contrary carried out raids in which women and children were killed. Although the warriors had slain other victims, Gates deliberately chose the case of Jane McCrea to publicize these Indian atrocities. The circumstances surrounding her death could not have been more dramatic, for the comely young woman was killed while waiting to meet her lover. Gates did not allow the fact that she was a Tory sympathizer and her fiancé a Tory officer to stand in the way of making her a patriot martyr.

Weeks after her death, Gates sent a stinging letter of rebuke to Burgoyne filled with sweeping indictments of Indian atrocities with torch and tomahawk. He denounced the British general for hiring "the Savages of America to scalp Europeans and Descendants of Europeans," and accused him of paying "a Price for . . . each Scalp so barbarously taken." Dwelling at some length on the sad fate of Jane McCrea, Gates pictured her in glowing terms as a "young lady lovely to the sight," of "virtuous character" and "amicable disposition." He added a final touch of pathos by describing her as dressed in her bridal finery at the time of her death.[34] That Gates was resorting to propaganda was clear from his gleeful remark to a friend that he had given Burgoyne "a Tickler upon Scalping." [35] His letter proved to be most effective. By playing on the fears of the local inhabitants, Gates persuaded more militiamen to join his army.

More important than the McCrea incident in turning out the militia was Gates's effectiveness as a leader of such troops. Unlike most American generals, he had great confidence in short-term soldiers and showed a keen understanding of their temper. It was his announced policy never to call up the militia until almost the very moment they were needed.[36] Once they had finished their tour of duty, he was quick to thank them and to send them packing off to home.[37] For these reasons—plus the fact that

it was fall and most farmers had already harvested their crops—
he received unprecedented support from the militia during the
Saratoga campaign. "The farmers left their ploughs," reported
an enemy officer, "the smith his anvil, cobbler and tailor followed . . . [and] the militia came marching in from all the
provinces of New England." [38] By the close of the campaign,
the militia probably outnumbered the regulars in the Northern
army.

Gates showed the same sensitivity to terrain during the Saratoga campaign as he had at Ticonderoga. When he assumed command, the American camp was located on level ground at the
mouth of the Mohawk River. Had he remained on such terrain
it would have favored the British, because it allowed them to
employ their artillery and close-rank formations more effectively. In early September, however, Gates marched his army
north and eventually took up a position on Bemis Heights—a
strategic bottleneck located in one of the narrow passes which
lay across Burgoyne's path to Albany.[39] Here the terrain in
front of the American lines was rugged, rolling country, covered
with dense woods except for a few scattered farm clearings and
wagon trails. Gates improved on the natural defenses by having
Thaddeus Kosciuszko fortify the position with a series of batteries and breastworks. With the right wing of his army resting
on the Hudson River and his left on the high ground to the
west, Gates dug in and waited for the British to approach.

On the morning of September 19, Burgoyne, resplendent in
his bright scarlet and white uniform, stepped out to lead his
troops against Gates's prepared position. The battle that followed
has come to be known as the First Battle of Saratoga. Although
in sight of the American defenses for two days, the British general was forced to grope his way forward blindly. Indians and
British scouts who attempted to reconnoiter the ground were
driven back inside their lines by long-range fire from American
sharpshooters. Gates, on the other hand, knew from the reports
of the sentinels he had posted high in the treetops that Burgoyne's army was advancing in three widely separated columns.

Gates ordered two units to take up a position well in front of the American lines to meet the attackers gathering on his left flank. One outfit was the famous corps of light infantry dressed in faded brown hunting shirts and leggings, led by the burly rough-and-ready frontiersman, Colonel Daniel Morgan. Armed with their long rifles, these marksmen were not only deadly in their aim but equally adept at the hit-and-run tactics used in fighting Indian style. Gates was so impressed with the idea of a select corps that he soon created one of his own. Choosing 300 crack musketmen from his army to serve as light infantry, Gates equipped them with bayonets and ordered their commander, Major Henry Dearborn, to act in conjunction with Morgan's men. These two advance elements collided with Burgoyne's column of troops as they came crashing through the woods to enter the clearing at Isaac Freeman's farm.

Most of the fighting that day centered about the clearing at Freeman's farm and the surrounding woods. Morgan's men were in their element fighting in the forest, but Burgoyne was hampered in his efforts to employ the traditional British tactics that relied heavily on cannon and close-rank military formations. Both Burgoyne and Gates fed more troops into the battle as the fighting raged on into the afternoon. Gates, as was his custom, remained well to the rear, directing the battle from his headquarters. When night began to fall, he ordered the Americans to pull back inside their lines, leaving the British in possession of the battlefield.

Burgoyne claimed a technical victory because he held the disputed ground, but in reality the battle was a success for Gates. British losses were nearly twice those of the Americans—about 600 casualties as compared to 320. Much more important was the fact that Burgoyne's advance had definitely come to a halt. The following day the British went over to the defensive and began building a system of field fortifications hardly a mile from the American lines. Gates still stood between the British and Albany—the community where they hoped to find winter shelter and a food supply. As autumn turned the leaves from green to golden brown, time began running out for Burgoyne as it had for Carleton the year before.

There was no lull between battles. Gates kept putting pressure on the British. Each night raiding parties slipped out to attack enemy pickets and Burgoyne's men were forced to sleep with their weapons nearby. During daylight, American snipers posted in the treetops picked off officers and men who were so bold as to show themselves.

Burgoyne's predicament grew more and more desperate with each passing day. The morale of his men was deteriorating, his food supply of salt pork and flour was petering out, and desertions were reducing the size of his army. The Americans meanwhile were swelling their numbers as more militiamen kept coming into camp. A relief expedition under Sir Henry Clinton was pushing its way slowly up the Hudson toward the rear of Gates's army, but Burgoyne held little hope for immediate help. There was nothing left but to attack. When the British general personally led a reconnaissance-in-force against the left wing of the American army on October 7, 1777, it resulted in the Second Battle of Saratoga.

Gates had sized up his opponent well. Burgoyne was an "old gamester," he wrote just before the battle. "Perhaps his despair may dictate to him to risque all upon one throw." [40] Gates was ready, therefore, when Burgoyne emerged from his lines with 1,500 troops to probe the American position. Turning quietly to his military aide, he said, "Order on Morgan to begin the game." A three-pronged attack was developed to drive the British back inside their own lines.

While the American attack was proceeding according to plan, Benedict Arnold suddenly appeared upon the battlefield. Gates and Arnold had been friends earlier, but in the course of the Saratoga campaign ill-feeling sprang up between them. Arnold sulked because he felt he had not received the credit due him for his role in the First Battle of Saratoga. After a violent quarrel between the two men, Gates relieved his unruly subordinate of his command. Although he was acting without orders, the bold and dashing brigadier rode out to do battle. Rallying soldiers about him, he led a gallant charge against the Breymann redoubt—a key position in Burgoyne's fortifications. Lunging forward, Arnold carried the redoubt, and exposed the enemy's lines. When the battle came to a close, Burgoyne's position was no longer defensible.

The British army began retreating to the north and after a brief delay, Gates took up pursuit. He neatly cut off any possibility of escape, and by October 13, Burgoyne's army was virtually encircled. For several days the shooting war gave way to a war of words as the two generals negotiated. Burgoyne finally laid down his arms in accordance with a convention signed near the village of Saratoga on October 17. Gates, fearful of the threat to his rear posed by Clinton's relief expedition, did not insist upon an unconditional surrender. Even Washington was forced to confess that Gates's situation was so critical that he was in no position to demand a "more perfect Surrender." [41]

Many have given Arnold the glory for the Saratoga triumph as a result of his spectacular feat in turning the tide of the battle. The truth of the matter is, Gates had already set the stage for an American victory by his quiet organization and cautious strategy. Realizing that time and the terrain were in his favor, his strategy was to settle deep behind his fortifications, letting Burgoyne wear himself down in fruitless probes against the American position. He was determined to deny the British the opportunity of a pitched battle. Although both actions were fought in front of the American lines, Gates carefully kept a large part of the Northern army back inside his fortifications at all times. Arnold and Morgan should not be denied a share of the honors for their valiant fighting in the field and Schuyler should be given his due for the delaying tactics that slowed Burgoyne's advance to a crawl, but the primary credit for capturing the enemy's army belongs to Gates. He had fought the right kind of campaign at the right time and place. Gates's caution and Burgoyne's recklessness made inevitable an American military success.

The victory had world-shaking consequences. The British suffered their greatest defeat of the war up to that time when 5,700 men, about one-fifth of the regular forces stationed in America, laid down their arms. The Hudson River, lifeline of the patriots, remained in American hands and the British campaign to cut off New England collapsed. Most important of all, France was so heartened by the success at Saratoga that she openly entered the war and began providing the foreign aid which eventually made possible America's independence. As John Adams so aptly noted in a letter from Paris, "General Gates was the ablest negotiator you ever had in Europe." [42]

For a self-made man, Gates was exceedingly modest in this most triumphant hour of his life. On the day of the Saratoga surrender, he wrote to his wife:

> The voice of fame, ere this reached you, will tell you how greatly fortunate we have been in this department. Burgoyne and his great army have laid down their arms . . . to me and my Yankees. Thanks to the Giver of all victory for this triumphant success. . . . Tell my dear Bob not to be too elated at this great good fortune of his father. He and I have seen days adverse, as well as prosperous. Let us through life endeavor to bear both with an equal mind.[43]

In giving his son such philosophical advice, Gates seemed almost to have a premonition of what lay in the future. His good fortune was soon overshadowed by misfortune.

Shortly after the Saratoga victory, a serious rift developed between Gates and Washington. Relations between the two generals soured when Gates wrote directly to the Continental Congress to break the news of his success rather than writing to Washington. Matters became more strained when the commander-in-chief complained that Gates was tardy in returning reinforcements loaned to him for the campaign against Burgoyne. The fact that most Americans were contrasting Gates's brilliant victory at Saratoga with Washington's gloomy defeat at Germantown did not help the situation any. At this point, General Thomas Conway, a veteran of the French army serving in the American forces, wrote Gates a letter criticizing Washington as a "weak General." News of the letter reached the commander-in-chief, who jumped to the conclusion that Gates was a member of a "Junto" engaged in "machinations" for "getting me out of the way." [44]

The Conway Cabal—or supposed plot to supplant Washington with Gates as supreme commander—seems to have little basis in fact. While it is true that Washington had critics both in Congress and the army, historians have been unable to uncover much evidence to indicate that there was such a conspiracy. No one ever dared to propose on the floor of Congress that Washington be removed. Gates certainly never committed himself on the matter. The key to the Conway Cabal, as one historian has suggested, may well lie in Washington's extreme sensitivity to criticism rather than in Gates's "machinations." [45]

The war's strain was beginning to tell on the health of the aging Gates. Among other things, he had been suffering from diarrhea.[46] Soon he was expressing the hope that the Saratoga campaign would be his last. Writing to his wife in September, 1777, he remarked, ". . . a General of an American army must be everything, and that is being more than one man can long sustain. This campaign must end my military labors." [47] But Congress would not let him go. In November he was appointed to the Board of War and spent the winter of 1777 reorganizing the American army.

As president of the Board of War, Gates was technically superior to Washington. It is clear that Congress had intended only to honor him for his Saratoga victory and not to humble or humiliate the commander-in-chief in any way. Gates, however, used his position to lord it over Washington and was both petty and rude. Without so much as consulting the commander-in-chief, he drew plans for an invasion of Canada. When the plans fell through, he vented his anger by squabbling with Washington over some negligible expenses that had been incurred in anticipation of the invasion. It was, according to Gates's biographer, the "pettiest thing he ever did." [48] Relations between the two generals as a result remained cool and distant.

Fortunately Gates and Washington were assigned to different commands during most of 1778 and 1779. The more miles between the two men the better both seemed to like it. In the spring of 1778, Gates expressed the desire to take to the field once more and was assigned to a post in the Hudson Highlands. Here he refuted the rumor that it was cowardice that kept him off the Saratoga battlefield by fighting a pistol duel with Colonel James Wilkinson. Gates thrice offered himself as a target without once trying to hit his opponent.

In the fall of 1778, he was sent to command the troops in Massachusetts—a sector where there was no fighting going on. When Washington offered him command of the expedition to be launched against the Indians in the Mohawk Valley in 1779, he turned it down on the grounds that he was neither young nor energetic enough for the task. He accepted instead the command at Providence, Rhode Island, where he spent more time fighting patriot profiteers than he did the enemy. After this tour of duty, Gates was given his choice of a command along the Hudson or a position in the main army. He asked, however, that he be given a furlough to see his family. His request was granted at the end of 1779 and he spent several months at Traveller's Rest.

Gates was called out from semi-retirement when Congress offered him command of the Southern army in June, 1780. The military situation in the South at the time was critical. The British had just won their greatest victory of the war by capturing Charleston and an American army numbering 5,500 men. Despite the sardonic remark supposedly made to him by Charles Lee—"Take care lest your Northern laurels turn to Southern willows"—Gates accepted the assignment. He joined his little army in Hillsboro, North Carolina, and immediately began laying plans for stopping the British invasion in the upper South.

He had few illusions about his chances of success. In the kindly letter written to Benjamin Lincoln whom he was replacing, Gates revealed his misgivings:

> The series of Misfortunes you have experienced, since you were doom'd to the Command of the Southern Department, has affected

me exceedingly. I feel for you most sensibly.—I feel for myself who am to succeed to what? To the command of an Army without Strength—a Military Chest without Money. A department apparently deficient in public Spirit, and a Climate that encreases Despondency instead of animating the Soldiers Arm.[49]

Despite the apparent hopelessness of the situation, he set out upon a task which he had done so often and so well in the past— to organize an army into an effective fighting force.

Gates soon discovered that the South was a far different theater of operations than the North. Food and forage were hard to come by: there were no supply depots; the distances involved were vast; and the commissary services proved to be notoriously inefficient. Believing supply to be "the Mainspring of Military Motion," he urged that depots be established immediately. Without them, Gates warned, "our Army is like a dead whale upon the Sea Shore—a monstrous Carcass without Life or Motion." [50] But nothing was done. His troops were forced to live off the country while on the move and their marching rations soon were reduced to an unhealthy diet of green corn and unripe peaches.

There was also a great difference between the Southern militia forces and those of the North. Because of his striking success at Saratoga, Gates was inclined to place too much confidence in short-term troops. The Yankee and Yorker farmers, however, who turned out to fight Burgoyne's invasion were defending their own homes and families. In the South the theater of operations covered a much wider area and the militia were often forced to fight far from their firesides. When they did so, they frequently fought with less urgency. Although short-term troops in the South proved effective in guerrilla warfare and in certain battles such as the Cowpens, the militia under Gates turned out to be untrained, undisciplined, and thoroughly unreliable.

Within forty-eight hours after his arrival in late July, Gates broke camp and ordered his army to advance toward the British garrison at Camden, South Carolina. He has been severely criticized for his decision in taking the most direct route to his objective—one which passed through a desolate region filled with loyalists—rather than a more roundabout approach through more prosperous country controlled by patriots. He had two reasons for choosing the more difficult route: by moving quickly, he hoped to deny the British time to rush reinforcements to the Camden garrison; he was anxious also to reach General Richard Caswell, an unruly militia officer who was ignoring orders to join the main army. Despite dysentery, famine, the summer's heat, and threats of mutiny, Gates whipped his ragged, hungry soldiers forward to a junction with Caswell. Unbeknownst to Gates, however, Lord Cornwallis had arrived at Camden with reinforcements.

Driving deep into the enemy's territory, Gates appeared to be abandoning his cautious strategy at Saratoga for bolder measures. Ironically, he now found himself in the same situation in the South as Burgoyne at Saratoga. With supplies dangerously low, he felt compelled to strike a blow against the enemy before his army fell apart from sheer starvation. In early August, Gates wrote Governor Thomas Jefferson:

> I . . . hope your Excellency is doing all in Your power to supply your half Starved Fellow Citizens. Flour, Rum and Droves of Bullocks, should without Delay be forwarded to this Army or the Southern Department will soon want one to defend it.[51]

On a dark summer night outside the village of Camden, the two armies encountered one another unexpectedly. Gates found himself facing a fighting general in the bold and vigorous Cornwallis. The British commander had only 2,200 troops against Gates's 3,000. But two-thirds of Cornwallis' men were hardened veterans, including the famed and feared British legion of Banastre Tarleton. Only one-third of the Americans were soldiers from the Continental army, the rest were militia.

Gates could have avoided a battle by a withdrawal, but he decided to stand and fight. His position was a good one. His flanks were covered on both sides by swamps and there was cover for his men in the open pine forest to his front. Moreover, he had the concurrence of a council of war. Just before the battle, he called a meeting of his generals and asked: "Gentlemen, what is best to be done?" General Stevens, commanding the militia, answered, ". . . is it not too late *now* to do anything but fight?" [52] There was a brief moment of silence. Gates then ordered his generals to their stations.

The battle opened at daybreak on the morning of August 16. The British began advancing on the American right wing. When Gates's adjutant came riding up to report that the time was ripe for the Virginia militia on the left wing to attack, the general replied: "Sir, that's right—let it be done." [53] It was his last battle order of the day.

As the Virginians stepped out in ragged formation, Cornwallis sent his regulars forward on a charge. With a wild cheer, the British fired one volley and then rushed forward with their glittering bayonets. Frightened by this awesome sight, the Virginians dropped their guns and fled in sheer terror. They were soon joined by the North Carolina militia. As the entire American left wing collapsed, Gates rode into the midst of the panic-stricken men, trying in vain to rally them. "They ran like a Torrent," he reported, "and lost all before them." [54] Wheeling his horse into the milling throng, Gates tried a second time to stop their flight. It was all to no avail. While engaged in these efforts, Gates was spotted by British cavalrymen who sped after him in pursuit.[55] Spurring his horse, Gates galloped to safety, leaving the battlefield far in the rear. Cornwallis then turned most of his troops upon the Continentals and soon overwhelmed them.

Camden was one of the most crushing defeats of the entire war. Cornwallis, at the cost of only 320 British casualties, inflicted heavy losses of nearly 650 on the Continental veterans alone—to say nothing of the militia. The Southern army lay shattered, for most of the scattered militia never returned. When Gates gathered together the broken remnants of his force there were only 700 Continentals left. The road to North Carolina and Virginia lay open to Cornwallis.

Gates must bear much of the blame for the Camden debacle.

He made a grave tactical error by positioning his untrained militia face-to-face with the best British regiments. By putting too much faith in raw militia, Gates helped to bring about his own defeat. "His passion for Militia, I fancy will be cured," wrote Alexander Hamilton, "and he will cease to think them the bulwark of American liberty." [56]

Camden ruined Gates's military reputation. In addition to the humiliation of a disastrous defeat, he was accused of cowardice for leaving the battlefield. The fact that Gates galloped almost 200 miles from the battlefield in three days was used to taunt him. He explained that his purpose had been to reach the main base at Hillsboro where he could regroup his forces, but his critics interpreted his flight differently.[57] "[W]as there ever an instance of a General running away as Gates has done from his whole army?" asked Alexander Hamilton. Then, adding up the number of miles the fifty-three-year-old general had ridden, Hamilton added sarcastically, "It does admirable credit to the activity of a man at his time of life." [58] Because of Camden, Congress removed Gates from his command in October, 1780, and ordered a court of inquiry into his conduct of the battle.

Gates retired once more to Traveller's Rest. Besides his military misfortunes, he was grieving over the recent death of his son, Robert. He repeatedly insisted that a court be called to review the Camden battle. But Congress would not comply with his demands. In fact, in the summer of 1782, Congress repealed its resolve for an inquiry and reinstated Gates into the army. With his self-respect restored, he rode north to Washington's headquarters on the Hudson. Once there, he became the second ranking officer in the Continental army. Although his relations with Washington remained friendly on the surface, there is some evidence that he was involved in the Newburgh Address—a protest to the commander-in-chief by disgruntled army officers.[59]

Gates left the army for the last time in 1783 to hurry home to the bedside of his dying wife. After her death, he remained in retirement at his Virginia plantation. In 1786 Gates married Mary Vallance, an heiress with a fortune close to a half million dollars. His wife's fortune enabled him to live comfortably in his declining years. Though his own lot was easy, Gates did not forget his old comrades and spent large sums of money aiding less fortunate army veterans.

In 1790 he put Traveller's Rest up for sale and moved to New York City, where he purchased an estate called Rose Hill Farm. Upon selling his Virginia plantation, he called his slaves together and announced to them that they were free men. He became a Jeffersonian Republican, as might be expected of one with his liberal views, serving a single term in the New York legislature in 1800–01. He died at Rose Hill Farm on April 10, 1806, at the age of seventy-eight.

No honest appraisal of Gates's generalship can fail to concede that he had certain serious shortcomings. His conduct of the Camden battle reveals his limitations as a tactician. In his relations with Congress, he was too high-handed and demanding for his own good. His greatest defect, however, was his inability to work smoothly with his colleagues. Quarrels among American generals were quite common, but Gates seems to have been more contentious than most. Had he ever been made commander-in-chief, it is probable that his feuds with Washington, Schuyler, and Arnold would have wrecked the American army.

For all his shortcomings, Gates's virtues outweighed his vices. Few military men contributed more to the cause for independence. He was a key figure in halting two major British invasions and was largely responsible for winning the most decisive battle of the war. Although by no means a great general, he displayed considerable talent as an organizer and administrator. But the greatest secret of Gates's success lay in his qualities of leadership. He had few peers in the Continental army as a disciplinarian. By treating the common soldier with a kindness uncommon in that day, he inspired their confidence and was almost always able to rouse them to a fighting pitch. As a professional soldier he could view his career with pride; he had helped to create an army, defeat the enemy, and to secure the independence of his adopted country.

FOOTNOTES

1. Samuel W. Patterson, *Horatio Gates: Defender of American Liberties* (New York, 1941), p. vii.
2. Horace Walpole, *Journal of the Reign of King George the Third from year 1771 to 1783* (London, 1859), II, 200.
3. Robert Gates was Surveyor of Customs at Greenwich. George Sackville to Robert Gates, September 23, 1748, Gates Papers, New York Historical Society. Hereinafter the New York Historical Society will be cited as N.Y.H.S.
4. Edward Cornwallis to Robert Gates, March 18, 1749/50, Gates Papers, N.Y.H.S.
5. Commission as Captain, September 13, 1754, Gates Papers, N.Y.H.S.
6. Will of Thomas Parker, September 10, 1742, Gates Papers, N.Y.H.S.
7. Charles Lee to Robert Morris, June 16, 1781, *New York Historical Society Collections*, VI, 458.
8. Hezekiah Niles, *Principles and Acts of the Revolution in America* (New York, 1876), p. 496.
9. Charles Townshend to Gates, April 26, 1762, Gates Papers, N.Y.H.S.
10. Milton M. Klein, "The American Whig: William Livingston of New York" (Columbia University, Unpublished Dissertation, 1954), pp. 506–07.
11. Thomas Hayes to Gates, May 16, 1770, Gates Papers, N.Y.H.S.
12. Elizabeth Gates to Lady Galway, August 1, 1772, Gates Papers, N.Y.H.S.
13. John C. Fitzpatrick, ed., *Writings of George Washington* (Washington, D.C., 1931–44), VII, 267.
14. Patterson, *op. cit.*, p. 53.
15. Massachusetts Historical Society, *Proceedings*, LXVII, 141.
16. Clifford K. Shipton, *Biographical Sketches of Those Who Attended Harvard College in the Classes 1746–1750*, etc. (Boston, 1962), XII, 372.
17. Massachusetts Historical Society, *Proceedings*, LXVII, 138.
18. Matthias Ogden to Aaron Burr, July 26, 1776, *American Archives*, 5th series (Washington, 1848), I, 603.
19. Gates to Schuyler, October 24, 1776, *ibid.*, II, 1257.
20. Gates to Jonathan Trumbull, August 11, 1776, Gates Papers, Houghton Library, Harvard University; General Orders, July 17, 1776, *American Archives*, 5th series, I, 654; Dr. John Morgan to Gates, September 1, 1776, *ibid.*, II, 106.
21. Gates to President of Congress, September 2, 1776, *ibid.*, I, 1268.

22. Gates to Putnam, August 11, 1776, *ibid.*, I, 900.

23. Gates to President of Congress, July 29, 1776, *ibid.*, I, 649.

24. General Gates' Orders and Instructions for the Honourable Benedict Arnold, Esq. etc. . . . August 7, 1776, Gates Papers, N.Y.H.S. Gates agreed to Arnold's move to the vicinity of Valcour Island, but his letter approving the shift to this position was sent on October 12, after the battle on Lake Champlain had been fought. See also *American Archives*, 5th series, II, 440–81, 591, 1015, for important instructions from Gates to Arnold.

25. Resolves of the Committee to Cooperate with General George Clinton, December 8, 1776, *ibid.*, III, 1126; Robert Livingston to Gates, December 8, 1776, *ibid.*, 1127; and William Duer to Gates, December 9, 1776, *ibid.*, 1128.

26. Gates to Arthur St. Clair [n. d.], cited in John Armstrong Memorial, December 4, 1831, Sparks MSS 49. 1 (7), Houghton Library, Harvard. John Trumbull also claimed to be the first to recognize that Ticonderoga was vulnerable from Mount Defiance.

27. Udney Hay to George Clinton, August 13, 1777, cited in John Armstrong Memorial, Sparks MSS, Houghton Library, Harvard; and H. A. Washington, ed., *Writings of Thomas Jefferson* (Washington, 1854), VIII, 496.

28. Ray W. Pettengill, ed., *Letters from America 1776–1779* (Boston, 1924), p. 98.

29. Edmund Burnett, *Letters of the Members of the Continental Congress* (Washington, 1923), II, 413.

30. James Thacher, *A Military Journal During the American Revolution* (Boston, 1827), p. 86.

31. Lyman H. Butterfield, ed., *Letters of Benjamin Rush* (Princeton, 1951), II, 767. Hereinafter *Benjamin Rush Letters*.

32. *Ibid.*, I, 159–60.

33. John Burgoyne, *State of the Expedition from Canada*, 2nd ed. (London, 1780), Appendix, pp. xcvi–xcviii.

34. Gates to Burgoyne, September 2, 1777, Gates Papers, N.Y.H.S.

35. Gates to Governor Trumbull, September 4, 1777, Gates Papers, N.Y.H.S.

36. *Ibid.*

37. See, for example, Gates to Colonel Hide, November 9, 1776, *American Archives*, 5th series, III, 623.

38. Pettengill, *op. cit.*, p. 98.

39. It is not clear whether Gates or Kosciuszko selected the site at Bemis Heights, but as supreme commander Gates had the ultimate authority on this matter.

40. Horatio Rogers, ed., *Hadden's Journal and Orderly Books* (Albany, 1884), p. lxxxiv.
41. Bernhard Knollenberg, *Washington and the Revolution* (New York, 1940), p. 29.
42. Francis Wharton, ed., *Revolutionary Diplomatic Correspondence of the United States* (Washington, D.C., 1889), II, 664.
43. Frank Moore, ed., *Diary of the American Revolution* (New York, 1860), I, 511.
44. Massachusetts Historical Society, *Proceedings*, LVIII, 317.
45. Knollenberg, *op. cit.*, pp. 65–77.
46. Benjamin Rush to Thomas Jefferson, *Benjamin Rush Letters*, II, 858.
47. Gates to Elizabeth Gates, September 22, 1777, Gates Papers, N.Y.H.S.
48. Patterson, *op. cit.*, p. 265.
49. *Magazine of American History*, V, 283.
50. *Ibid.*, pp. 281, 284.
51. Julian P. Boyd, ed., *Papers of Thomas Jefferson* (Princeton, 1951), III, 525.
52. Otho W. Williams, "A Narrative of the Campaign of 1780," in William Johnson, *Sketches of the Life and Correspondence of Nathanael Greene* (Charleston, 1882), I, 493.
53. *Ibid.*
54. Gates to Washington, August 20, 1780, Gates Papers, N.Y.H.S.
55. *Magazine of American History*, V, 277–78.
56. Hamilton to Duane, September 6, 1780, in Harold C. Syrett and Jacob E. Cooke, eds., *Papers of Alexander Hamilton* (New York, 1961), II, 420. Hereinafter *Hamilton Papers*.
57. Gates to Washington, August 20, 1780, Gates Papers, N.Y.H.S.
58. Hamilton to Duane, September 6, 1780, in *Hamilton Papers*, II, 421.
59. Douglas S. Freeman, *George Washington: A Biography* (New York, 1952), V, 437.

BIBLIOGRAPHY

Billias, George A., *General John Glover and His Marblehead Mariners.* New York, 1960. Shows the striking change in attitude that took place in the Northern army when Gates assumed command.

Emmett, Thomas A., ed., "The Southern Campaign 1780: Letters of Major General Gates from 21 June to 31 August." *Magazine of American History*, V (New York, 1880), 281–320. The letters of Gates covering the Camden campaign.

Knollenberg, Bernhard, *Washington and the Revolution*. New York, 1940. Contains the best brief appraisal of Gates's contribution to the American military cause. Gives a much less biased view of the relations between Gates and Washington.

Nickerson, Hoffman, *The Turning Point of the Revolution*. Boston, 1928. The standard work on the Saratoga campaign and quite fair on some points toward Gates.

Patterson, Samuel W., *Horatio Gates, Defender of American Liberties*. New York, 1941. The only full-scale biography of Gates, but far too uncritical and laudatory in approach to be of much value.

———, *Horatio Gates Reconsidered*. New York, 1941. A short address by Gates's biographer before the Saratoga Historical Society that contains some views not expressed in the longer work.

Shipton, Clifford K., "Horatio Gates," in *Biographical Sketches of Those Who Attended Harvard College in the Classes 1746–1750 with Bibliographical and Other Notes*, Vol. XII of *Sibley's Harvard Graduates*, 370–80. An informative sketch of Gates's life that catches the essence of the man.

Swiggert, Howard, *Forgotten Leaders of the Revolution*. New York, 1955. Contains a character sketch of Gates in one of the chapters.

Thacher, James, *A Military Journal during the American Revolutionary War*. Boston, 1827, pp. 437–44. Has one of the early biographical sketches of Gates by one of his contemporaries.

GEORGE WASHINGTON

ANTHONY WAYNE

HENRY KNOX

Independence National Historical Park Collection

NATHANAEL GREENE

DANIEL MORGAN

LE MARQUIS DE LAFAYETTE

HORATIO GATES

BENEDICT ARNOLD

JOHN SULLIVAN

BENJAMIN LINCOLN

PHILIP SCHUYLER

CHARLES I

Nathanael Greene:

REVOLUTIONARY WAR STRATEGIST

——•——

THEODORE THAYER

Rutgers University

GENERAL WASHINGTON was greatly impressed with Nathanael Greene the very first time the two men met. When the handsome and engaging Rhode Islander reported for duty with the army at Cambridge in the summer of 1775, Washington quickly sized him up as an "object of his confidence." [1] A keen judge of character, Washington became convinced within a year that if he were killed or captured Greene was the best qualified of all his generals to succeed him as commander-in-chief.

Time proved that Washington had taken the correct measure of his man. After fighting alongside Washington in the North for five years, Greene finally was given a command of his own in the South. Within the short space of a single year, he reorganized the Southern army, fought several bloody battles, and compelled Lord Cornwallis to relinquish most of the territory the British had conquered in South Carolina and Georgia. Greene somewhat humorously summed up the secret of his success in these words: "There are few generals," he wrote, "that have run oftener, or more lustily than I have done. But I have taken care not to run too far, and commonly have run as fast forward as backward, to convince the Enemy that we were like a Crab, that could run either way." [2] Greene's strategy and Cornwallis' impetuosity eventually sent his Lordship drumming down the road to Virginia and defeat at Yorktown.

Nathanael Greene literally appeared out of nowhere to become in the words of one soldier "the greatest military genius" of the war for independence. Many Revolutionary War generals had had previous military experience, but he had none. Greene was, moreover, a Quaker opposed to war for religious reasons. But when England's colonial policies became unbearable, he discarded his pacifism, joined a military association, and threw himself wholeheartedly into the struggle for liberty and independence.

As a boy, Greene had little formal education. It was not because his family lacked the means, for his father along with some of his uncles owned a forge that produced iron anchors and chains for sailing ships. Rather, it was because his father was "a man of industry" who brought up his children "to business." "Early, very early," wrote Greene, "when I should have been in the pursuit of Knowledge, I was digging into the Bowels of the Earth after Wealth." [3] But a precocious youth, he soon discovered the world of books and learning. In time he accumulated a fine library of more than two hundred books on history, religion, law, philosophy, and most important of all, military science. One of the first volumes he acquired was a copy of Euclid, which he kept by his side at the forge, sweating over every theorem until he had mastered the whole book.

This self-taught, awkward anchorsmith from Coventry, Rhode Island, reported to Washington at the age of thirty-three as brigadier general at the head of his colony's three Continental regiments. Why was this unsophisticated youth chosen when others appeared to be better educated or more experienced for the command? The answer lay in Greene's rare qualities of leadership and his sound grasp of military affairs. From the time of the Boston Tea Party, he spent his spare moments reading military manuals, studying the lives of great generals, and drilling the local Kentish Guards. He put his newly-acquired knowledge to use as a member of the legislative committee charged with the responsibility of preparing Rhode Island's defenses in 1775. Consequently, when the General Assembly cast about for an officer to lead its "Army of Observation," Greene was a logical choice. He went from the rank of private in the Kentish Guards to that of brigadier general in the Continental army in less than two months.

When Greene first reported to Washington, the commander-in-chief saw before him a rather stocky, good-looking man, five feet ten inches tall with sparkling blue-gray eyes. Like Washington, Greene cut a fine athletic figure, despite a slight limp caused by an accident during his youth. The commander-in-chief immediately was impressed by the young man's astute comments concerning certain problems then confronting the army. He was amused, too, by the way the Rhode Islander seasoned his remarks with homespun witticisms. Greene's sunny disposition and winning ways soon offset the lack of polish he had shown upon entering the military service. Henry Knox, Washington's artillery commander, noted that Greene "came to us, the rawest, the most untutored being" he ever saw, but in less than a year, he was the equal in military knowledge "to any General Officer in the army, and very superior to most of them." [4]

One year prior to his entry into the army, Greene had married pretty Catherine Littlefield, of Block Island. Kitty, as she was called, was the life of any party she attended. Washington, who had an eye for feminine charm, was naturally attracted to her and at one social affair he is said to have danced with her all of three hours without stopping. During the war, Kitty became a frequent visitor to Nathanael's headquarters and her presence helped to brighten the drabness of army life. When Cornwallis surrendered, she made a long and arduous trip to South Carolina to be with her husband until the war ended.

After serving through the long and sometimes boring Boston siege, Greene accompanied the Continental army to New York in the spring of 1776. Washington by this time regarded the Rhode Islander as one of his best divisional commanders and put him in charge of the Brooklyn defenses where the first British blow was expected to fall. But when General Howe did arrive in the early summer of 1776, Greene, who had just received his promotion to rank of major general, was sick abed with a fever. He was removed to New York City to recover and was not on hand when his comrades-in-arms were whipped soundly in the Battle of Long Island. Henry Knox was of the opinion that if Greene had been there "matters would have worn a very different appearance. . . ." Greene, on the other hand, modestly observed, "I have not the vanity to think the event would have been otherwise had I been there, yet I think I could have given the commanding general a good deal of necessary information. Great events, sometimes depend upon very little causes. . . ." [5]

Recovering from his illness, Greene was placed in charge of the forces guarding the shores of New Jersey. Within his jurisdiction was Fort Washington, a strategic bastion high on the rocky heights at the northern end of Manhattan Island. Fort Washington was destined to be Greene's most costly mistake of the entire war. After the British had landed and occupied the lower end of Manhattan, enemy ships sailed safely past the guns of Fort Washington to the wide waters of the Hudson farther north. When Washington removed the major part of his army from New York's Westchester County into New Jersey in mid-November, the peril to the fortress increased. Greene, however, strongly advised Washington to hold on to the post.

Then Greene compounded his error by reinforcing the garrison so that more troops poured into the impending trap. If Howe attacked, Greene was convinced, the Americans, fighting behind breastworks, could give the British a bloodbath similar to the one at Bunker Hill. In any event, he argued, the fort could be evacuated at any time by small boats from the Jersey shore. Until such a move seemed necessary, the Rhode Islander was for holding Fort Washington, since it might prevent the British from launching a drive into New Jersey or posing a threat to General Charles Lee's division in Westchester County. Most of the other generals, including Israel Putnam and Hugh Mercer, agreed with the young strategist. Indeed, Greene's views were regarded so highly that Washington was persuaded to hold the seemingly impregnable fortress for a little while longer. "His Excellency, General Washington, has been with me several days," reported Greene. "The evacuation of Fort Washington was under consideration but finally nothing concluded on." [6]

General Howe suddenly appeared before the fort on November 15 and demanded that the garrison surrender. In answer to the British ultimatum Greene ordered Colonel Robert Magaw, commander of the fort, to stand fast. That evening while crossing the Hudson, Washington met Greene and Putnam as they were returning from a last-minute inspection. Both generals, Washington discovered, were convinced that the fortress could withstand the threatened attack. Although apprehensive of the outcome, the commander-in-chief let Greene's orders stand and returned to spend the night in New Jersey. Early the next morning Washington, Greene, and several other officers recrossed the Hudson to Fort Washington and arrived just as Howe opened up his attack with about 10,000 soldiers. Although the Americans numbered less than 3,000, Greene was still confident that all would go well.

Magaw's men fought valiantly, but the overwhelming odds soon began to tell. As the fort's outer defenses started to crumble, Washington boarded a boat and was rowed to safety. Greene begged to remain behind to direct the battle, but Washington would not hear of it for fear of losing his pugnacious young general.

The stunning news that Magaw had surrendered reached Greene as he returned to his headquarters. With the fall of Fort Washington, some 3,000 soldiers and quantities of badly needed military supplies were lost. Greatly chagrined, Greene sat down and poured out his anguish in a letter to his good friend Henry Knox: "I feel mad, vexed, sick, and sorry; Never did I need the consoling voice of a friend more than now." [7]

Greene's military reputation took a plunge as a result of the Fort Washington fiasco. Men began inquiring if he were really the "Heaven born genius" he had been called. Washington entertained some doubts as to whether or not he had overrated

Greene. Although Washington never openly charged Greene with the loss of Fort Washington, his failure to come to the Rhode Islander's support caused the blame to fall squarely on the shoulders of his subordinate. As commander-in-chief and superior officer at the scene of action, Washington was, in fact, the one primarily responsible for the costly mistake.

Greene's prestige suffered, but the setback was only temporary. Washington apparently charged off the loss to the fortunes of war and before long was again relying on the quick-thinking Greene for advice and counsel. But the fall of Fort Washington had the effect of making both generals more cautious. Washington and Greene henceforth placed more emphasis upon tactics calculated to wear down the enemy to a point where the patriots could assume the offensive.

After playing a prominent role in conducting the masterly retreat of the ragged American army as it fled across New Jersey, Greene participated in the Battle of Trenton. He commanded one wing of Washington's task force which launched a surprise attack on the Hessian garrison during the early hours of the morning after Christmas day. The triumph of American arms which followed lifted the sagging hopes of the patriots. During the battle, Greene wrote his wife that he went "thirty hours in all the Storm without the least refreshment." [8]

Heady with victory, Greene with some other officers tried to persuade Washington to "push on" to attack the neighboring German garrison at Burlington. But Washington could not be swayed and refused to risk his precious gains for higher stakes. In retrospect, it appears that the commander-in-chief made a mistake by not acting on Greene's advice, for the Germans at Burlington were so stunned and demoralized by the Trenton defeat they might have made an easy mark. Washington, himself, is said to have regretted later that he had not seized "the golden opportunity." [9]

Fortune smiled again upon American arms with the victory at Princeton early in January, 1777. Riding his spirited dark horse, Greene once more was in the thick of the battle. Besides the victory, Greene was particularly pleased that the commander-in-chief was depending upon him for advice. Writing to Kitty, Greene noted he was enjoying "the full confidence of his Excellency General Washington." Indeed, he added, "the more difficult and distressing our affairs grew," the more Washington had relied upon him.[10]

After the army had gone into winter quarters at Morristown, Washington sent Greene off to Congress in March, 1777, to acquaint the politicians with the pressing needs of the Continental army. Among other things, the commander-in-chief was hoping that Congress would create three new positions for the rank of lieutenant general and that Greene would be nominated as one of the high-ranking officers. But Congress failed to act on Washington's recommendation. Despite the fact that he had not been promoted, Greene was not unhappy about leaving Philadelphia, for he was convinced that Congress was little more than a useless debating society. "The Congress have so many of those talking gentlemen among them," he observed, "that they tire themselves and everybody else with their long labored speeching that is calculated more to display their own talents than to promote the public interest."[11]

Upon his return to the army at Morristown, Greene was given a series of important assignments. With Henry Knox, the portly artillery commander, he was sent in May to view the defenses along the strategic Hudson Highlands. He had no sooner completed his inspection than Washington sent him to Middlebrook, New Jersey, to select a safe position from which the army might launch its summer campaign. Greene chose a spot high up on the first range of the Watchung Mountains. Here the Continental army took up a position and defied all attempts by General Howe to bring on an engagement. Finding that Washington could not be dislodged or lured from his eagle's nest, Howe finally pulled his troops out of New Jersey.

Howe next sought to capture the American capital, Philadelphia. After landing at the head of the Chesapeake Bay, the British general outmaneuvered Washington on a warm day in early

September at the Brandywine River. While his forces made a feint at the American center at Chad's Ford, Howe sent the major part of his army on a wide end sweep to outflank the American left wing under General John Sullivan. Although he had been anticipating a flank attack, Sullivan was caught by surprise and his line soon collapsed under the superior weight of the enemy. When word reached Washington at Chad's Ford of the impending disaster, he ordered Greene to hasten to the rescue. Greene's division, made up of many Virginians, raced four miles through broken country in less than fifty minutes. Reaching a strategic spot called Sandy Hollow, Greene set up a defensive line and opened his ranks to allow Sullivan's battered division to scramble through to safety. Then he closed his lines and confronted the enemy, holding the British at bay until darkness fell. Under this protection, the whole American army was able to pull back without further harassment and to lick its wounds from the more than 1,000 casualties suffered.

Despite the fact that he had saved part of the American army, Washington failed to mention Greene's division in his report of the Brandywine battle to Congress. Unhappy at the omission, the Rhode Islander mentioned the matter to the commander-in-chief. Washington is said to have answered: "You Sir, are considered my favorite officer: Weedon's brigade, like myself, are Virginians: should I applaud them for their achievement under your command, I shall be charged with partiality, jealousy will be excited, and the service injured." [12] Washington's policy was to bend over backward so that he would not be charged with favoritism to his own state and Greene was forced to suffer in consequence.

Early in October, after Howe had succeeded in taking Philadelphia, Washington attempted a surprise attack upon the main body of the enemy encamped at Germantown. Greene led the left wing of the army into the attack. Unfortunately his men lost their way in the darkness and fog and arrived forty-five minutes late at their appointed place. Washington's initial advantage began to ebb as a heavy fog rolled in during the early

morning and allowed the enemy time to recover and get reinforcements. With the tide of battle running against him, Washington prudently ordered a retreat. Once more a battle with a
promising beginning had come to a disappointing end. Washington was asked after the battle if the failure was caused by
Greene's tardy arrival. "Not at all," replied the commander-in-
chief, "the fault lay with ourselves." [13] The fog had been so intense that even General Howe's dog lost his way in the mist and
Washington returned him to his owner under a flag of truce.

Both Washington and Greene came under severe criticism as
the defeats in Pennsylvania were compared with Gates's glowing
victory at Saratoga. The grumbling grew more ominous with
each passing day. James Lovell, the Massachusetts congressman,
warned that "the list of our disgusted patriots is long and formidable and their Resentments keen against the reigning Cabal."
By the "reigning Cabal," he meant the officers upon whom
Washington leaned for advice—Greene, Knox, Lafayette, and
Joseph Reed. Greene was generally considered to be the one
closest to the commander-in-chief and consequently he was
blamed for influencing Washington in the wrong direction. Despite the fact that Greene was under fire in Congress at the
time, Washington took the opportunity to state once again that
he desired the Rhode Islander to succeed him as commander-in-
chief in the event he were killed or captured.[14]

No matter how highly Washington regarded Greene, the latter never would have been made commander-in-chief if Lovell
and like-minded congressmen had had their way. Greene, according to Lovell, was the "languid Counsellor" whose strategy
had brought about the loss of Philadelphia. Because of the
mounting attacks upon himself and Washington, Greene finally
felt compelled to take up his pen to answer his detractors. Comparisons between the Philadelphia and Saratoga campaigns were
unfair, he noted. Howe's army had been far more powerful than
Burgoyne's and Washington had performed a great feat in maintaining a force in the field capable of opposing the British near
Philadelphia. As for Gates, he was "a child of good fortune"

according to Greene, and one whose success "was laid long before his arrival there." [15]

Criticism of both Washington and Greene soon died down as the result of the so-called "Conway Cabal." This supposed plot to replace Washington with Gates as commander-in-chief of the Continental army revealed the extent of Washington's popularity, and his detractors quickly changed their tune and halted their attacks upon him. One congressman wrote to Greene "that the Junto [in Congress] are alarmed at their unpopularity on account of their malevolent machinations, & now deny all their Practices." [16]

While the army was in winter quarters at Valley Forge, Washington decided to seek a replacement for Thomas Mifflin, the quartermaster general. Affairs in that department had fallen into such a sorry state that only a person with unusual administrative abilities could set matters right again. In desperation, he turned to Greene, who had been gathering provisions for the army. Although the Rhode Islander did not relish the thought of leaving behind a battlefield command, he accepted the post out of deference to Washington's wishes. After one year on the job, Greene had some second thoughts about his decision. "There is a great difference between being raised to an office, and descending to one," he wrote. "Had I been an inferior officer I might have thought myself honored by the appointment. But as I was high in rank in the army, I have ever considered it derogatory to serve in this office." [17]

Despite his dissatisfaction with the position, Greene quickly proved his worth. Through his efforts, the Continental army was ready when it came time to begin campaigning again in the summer of 1778. Greene's preparations, declared Washington, "enabled us, with great facility, to make a sudden move with the whole Army and baggage from Valley Forge in pursuit of the Enemy." [18] Considering the obstacles that beset him, Greene's achievements were little less than miraculous. Laboring long hours, he managed to keep the army going from season to season despite shortages of funds, supplies, and means of transportation.

If he gained little glory as quartermaster general, Greene did pocket some rather handsome profits. He was allowed, according to practice of the day, a commission of 3 per cent on all funds expended by his department. These profits he divided equally with his two assistants. Critics were soon charging that Greene and his associates were making a fortune at the expense of their country. Greene admitted the financial compensation was attractive, but declared the recompense was small considering that he had been deprived of his command in the field. All in all, he earned a total of $170,000 measured in terms of specie.

Large as this amount was, Greene cannot be accused of padding the army's accounts or buying overpriced goods. It is true that he issued some army contracts to his relatives in Rhode Island, but he saw nothing wrong with nepotism so long as the army received its supplies in good condition and at the going market price. At the close of the war, Greene was under suspicion of having speculated with army funds, but the charges were never proved.[19]

While serving as quartermaster general, Greene tried also to assert that he had a right to command troops in battle. Such was the understanding, he maintained, when he took the administrative post. Much to his displeasure, however, Washington failed to support his claim when the question became an issue in 1779. Greene, in reality, had little to complain about on the question of command. He was always consulted by Washington on strategy and tactics and participated in all the councils of war. During the Battle of Monmouth, he fell heir to Lee's command when Washington summarily ordered Lee from the field. Because of Greene's intimate knowledge of his state, he served under Sullivan during the Rhode Island campaign of 1778. Washington also gave him a command at Springfield, New Jersey, in June, 1780.

Greene's opportunity to resign as quartermaster general and to return to a full-time command in the field came in the summer of 1780. Having run out of funds, Congress decided supplies and money could only be procured by requisitions drawn from the states. Greene was convinced such a system would not work and tendered his resignation. Some members of Congress reacted bitterly to his stubbornness and wanted to discharge him from the service altogether. Washington came to Greene's defense and warned Congress that dire consequences would follow if he were dismissed. The commander-in-chief worked out a compromise and persuaded the disgruntled Greene to continue as quartermaster until a suitable replacement was found.

While Greene was having his set-to with Congress, the country was shocked to learn of the crushing defeat of General Gates by Lord Cornwallis at Camden, South Carolina, in August, 1780. With the British in almost undisputed possession of South Carolina and Georgia, the way seemed clear for Cornwallis to sweep north into North Carolina and Virginia. The patriot cause south of the Potomac looked hopeless.

Fortunately, Congress left the choice of the new commander to replace Gates as head of the Southern army to Washington. It was a foregone conclusion that he would pick Greene and once the appointment was announced, there was universal acclamation within the army. The sentiment of most military men was succinctly summed up by one officer up North who wrote: "If anything is to be expected from the abilities and exertions of a single person, I think no one will be more likely to answer every reasonable expectation than this amiable officer. There can be no better proof of his worth than the universal regret all ranks among us feel at the idea of parting with him." [20]

Greene decided to go south at once. He left his headquarters at West Point in October, 1780, in such a hurry that he missed seeing his wife who was coming over from Rhode Island to be with him. "My dear Angel," he wrote hastily to Kitty. "What I have been dreading has come to pass. His Excellency General Washington by order of Congress has appointed me to the command of the Southern army." Greene made one last desperate effort to contact his wife at Fishkill, New York. "But alas," he wrote, "I was obliged to return with bitter disappointment. My longing eyes looked for you in all directions, and I felt my heart leap with joy at the sound of every carriage." [21]

Upon reaching Philadelphia, Greene did everything in his power to procure supplies for his new command. Because he was convinced that cavalry units would prove of great value in the southern theater of operations where hit-and-run tactics were employed, he made a special effort to raise more horsemen. By a happy coincidence, "Light-Horse Harry" Lee and his famed legion of 150 dragoons was available and the unit was assigned to him. The legion would strengthen the company of horse under Lieutenant Colonel William Washington already serving in the South. Besides these two veteran outfits, Greene was counting upon using mounted militia—provided he could get such irregulars to co-ordinate their moves with those of the main army.

Throughout the rest of his trip, Greene stopped at all the leading towns in Maryland and Virginia to urge local authorities to raise both troops and arms. The prospects, however, looked bleak. The farther south he traveled, the more apparent it became that except for food his supplies would have to come mainly from the North. Greene wrote letter after letter to the Congress spelling out his needs in great detail. But his attention was not always directed toward military problems. Sometimes trotting down the dusty roads, the conversation turned to other subjects and an aide-de-camp recalled years later how on one occasion Greene had led a brilliant discussion of great Latin poets.

One of Greene's primary concerns was to gather a staff of experienced officers to assist him. He lost his most valuable subordinate when he was forced to leave Baron von Steuben behind in Virginia to supervise recruiting and the procurement of supplies. He gained another, however, when Colonel Edward Carrington, a first-rate officer, agreed to serve as his quartermaster general. At Hillsboro, North Carolina, he encountered the Polish engineer, Thaddeus Kosciuszko, and promptly put him to work improving transportation facilities and building supply magazines. Another excellent addition to his staff was Colonel William R. Davie, a famed cavalryman and expert swordsman who became Greene's commissary general. Davie was reluctant to accept the post, claiming he knew nothing about keeping money or accounts, but Greene told him he could take the job with a clear conscience because there were no funds in the military chest to manage.

Upon his arrival at Charlotte, North Carolina, Greene found what remained of the shattered Southern army. All that was left after the Camden battle were 2,000 ragged and famished creatures who resembled scarecrows more than soldiers. Discouraging as the outlook appeared, Greene decided not to retreat or to abandon North Carolina. Instead, he hoped to keep Cornwallis at arm's length while he rebuilt his army with the help of local leaders. Greene sized up the situation so quickly that within twenty-four hours, according to one officer, he understood the problems confronting him better than Gates ever had.[22]

The military picture in the South brightened a bit for the Americans about the time Greene arrived on the scene. In October, 1780, a small band of mountaineer militia had met and defeated a British force made up mainly of loyalists atop King's Mountain in South Carolina. Unknown to all, King's Mountain was to be the turning point of the war in the South. Cornwallis still had an army that was far superior in numbers to any force Greene could put in the field, but the British soldiers were scattered throughout South Carolina and Georgia in numerous small forts and garrisons. After the British defeat at King's Mountain, these occupied states grew restless, and Cornwallis did not dare to enlarge his main force at the expense of the garrisons. Consequently he was forced to fall back to Winnsboro, South Carolina, where he waited for reinforcements from Virginia. Once they arrived, he hoped to crush Greene as he had Gates at Camden.

Greene was fully aware of the dangers facing him. If Cornwallis were left unmolested at Winnsboro, he would be able to strengthen his force by enlisting local loyalists and could overwhelm the Southern army once reinforcements arrived. Something had to be done to distract Cornwallis and prevent a British buildup. Greene decided to take a bold move. He would split his little army in the face of an enemy who was superior in size and fighting ability—a dangerous tactic that, if not successful, could result in complete disaster. To assist him in his plan Greene called upon Brigadier General Daniel Morgan, a tough old frontier fighter who had served brilliantly in the Canadian and Saratoga campaigns earlier in the war. Greene ordered Morgan to take 700 light troops plus some cavalry and to circle to the north of the British at Winnsboro. From his position above the British, Morgan could harass the enemy and discourage any loyalists who might think of enlisting under Cornwallis. Greene in the mean¬ time would be free to move to a more favorable location and to rebuild his army unmolested.

Once Morgan had departed, Greene marched the rest of the Southern army to Cheraw Hill, South Carolina, 75 miles east of the British at Winnsboro and over 100 miles away from Morgan. Despite the fact that his army was divided, Greene was satisfied with his moves. He summed up his strategy in these words:

> I am here in my camp of repose, improving the discipline and spirits of my men, and the opportunity for looking about me. I am well satisfied with the movement, for it has answered thus far all the purposes for which I intended it. It makes the most of my inferior force, for it compels my adversary to divide his, and holds him in doubt as to his own line of conduct. He cannot leave Morgan behind him to come at me, or his posts of Ninety-Six and Augusta would be exposed. And he cannot chase Morgan far, or prosecute his views upon Virginia, while I am here with the whole country open before me. I am as near Charleston as he is, and as near Hillsborough as I was at Charlotte; so that I am in no danger of being cut off from my reinforcements.[23]

While Greene was working hard to whip his army into shape, his lieutenants in the field kept the enemy off balance by scoring a series of minor victories in South Carolina. Operating in the region of Ninety-Six to the west of Winnsboro, William Washington's horsemen swept down upon a sizable force of loyalist militia and wiped them out. Other victories over loyalist bands in the area further disenchanted any recruits who might have thought of joining the British. General Francis Marion, the famed "Swamp Fox," following Greene's orders, pounced upon British supply trains in the lowlands. Henry Lee's dragoons meanwhile were carrying on guerrilla warfare in the region between Winnsboro and Orangeburg.

Greene gained even more precious time when the British reinforcements under General Alexander Leslie were tardy in reaching South Carolina. Tossed by winds and gales at sea, the transports with 2,500 men aboard did not reach Charleston until mid-December. After disembarking, Leslie's march into the interior was delayed for lack of wagons. It was the middle of January, 1781, before the British reinforcements arrived near the scene of action.

With Leslie's men drawing near, Cornwallis decided it was time to march against Morgan's force. Once it was destroyed, he could turn upon Greene for a showdown. To smash Morgan's men, Cornwallis picked Colonel Banastre Tarleton, the cavalry leader known as the "Green Dragoon." Tarleton's force was made up of crack troops—350 dragoons and 800 trained infantry. Morgan had about the same number of soldiers, but many of his men were untrained militia. In one of the most remarkable engagements of the Revolution, Morgan scored a stunning victory over Tarleton at the Battle of Cowpens on January 17.

As soon as Cornwallis learned the news of Tarleton's defeat, he fairly panted for revenge. He tried to intercept Morgan, hoping to recapture the British prisoners taken at Cowpens. But the wily old frontiersman raced for the Catawba River at the best speed he could make and crossed the stream two days ahead of the pursuing British. By the time Cornwallis reached the Catawba, the winter rains had swollen the stream to a point where it was unfordable.

Temporarily safe from pursuit, Morgan rested his men and reported his position to Greene. In a daring ride through a country infested with Tories, Greene galloped 125 miles with a small escort to join Morgan and to direct his march. In Morgan's camp, the two generals sat down to discuss strategy. Morgan wanted to take to the mountains where his troops would be safe from pursuit. Greene turned down the idea. Instead, he ordered Morgan to march for Salisbury, North Carolina, where the rest of the Southern army was headed. Morgan, disagreeing with this dangerous strategy, declared he would not be answerable for what might happen if he had to retreat through North Carolina. "Neither will you," Greene is said to have replied, "for I shall take the measure upon myself." [24]

If the North Carolina militia turned out in sufficient force, Greene planned to fight it out with Cornwallis. But if they did not respond, he would retreat all the way to Virginia, if necessary. Greene's plan was bold and daring but not foolhardy in its conception. He was well aware of the risks involved and warned, "Our prospects are gloomy notwithstanding these flashes of success." [25]

Realizing that Cornwallis would cross the Catawba as soon as the river subsided, Greene sent riders through the countryside to rouse the patriot militia. He was hoping that a sufficient number of men would turn out to delay Cornwallis' crossing temporarily. The delay would allow Morgan time to reach Salisbury and to cross over the next river, the Yadkin. But the militia failed to respond. In fact, rather than gaining strength, Greene lost some of his best troops. Just twelve hours before Cornwallis began crossing the Catawba, the Virginia militia whose enlistments had expired cut out of the army and headed for home.

Greene waited in vain at the rendezvous where the militia were supposed to gather. When it became clear that none were coming, he set out for Salisbury in a driving rain. By the time the British reached the river crossing, the only troops there to oppose them were a handful of North Carolina militiamen who had been with Morgan since the beginning of the campaign. Even these troops fled in confusion after exchanging a few shots with the enemy and the British pressed on their pursuit.

Determined to catch his prey, Cornwallis burned his baggage and mounted two men on each horse in order that he might move more rapidly. Morgan, however, had too much of a head start. The Americans reached Salisbury safely and crossed the Yadkin easily, for Greene had had the foresight to collect numerous small craft at one spot on the river. Cornwallis, on the other hand, had no means of getting his army across the stream.

Angered by his failure to trap his quarry, Cornwallis ordered a furious bombardment on the American camp across the Yadkin, but because of the river's high banks the cannonade did little more than amuse the patriots. During the bombardment, one British gunner concentrated his fire on the roof of a certain building unaware that it was Greene's headquarters. Shingles and boards went flying as the gunner found his mark. Greene, who was inside, went right on writing his reports. "His pen," reported one officer, "never rested but when a new visitor arrived, and then the answer was given with calmness and precision, and the pen immediately resumed." [26] From Salisbury, Greene carried away 1,700 muskets he had found stored for use by the militia. The sight of the muskets and the failure of the militia to respond stirred Greene to cry out in anguish in one letter: "O that we had in the field as Henry the Fifth said, some few of the merry thousands that are idle at home!" [27]

Leading Morgan's men, Greene finally reached Guilford Court House, North Carolina, where he linked up with the main army that had arrived from Cheraw Hill. Despite repeated calls for more militia, few men came into camp to offer their services. Feeling that his army was still too small to risk a battle, Greene decided to continue his retreat to the Dan River and to cross over into Virginia. Cornwallis by this time was drawing near with the hope of pinning Greene's army up against one of the rivers.

Greene at this point came up with another of his stratagems. He detached a sizable force under Colonel Otho H. Williams and ordered him to march toward the upper fords of the Dan, making it appear that he intended to cross the river at that point. Greene's intent was to draw Cornwallis away from the main army which would take the road leading in the opposite direction toward Irwin's Ferry lower down on the Dan. There Kosciuszko was waiting with boats to take the army over.

Back at the Yadkin, Cornwallis had been forced to march miles upstream before he found a suitable place to ford. When he learned the Americans were heading for the upper fords of the Dan, he felt he had Greene at his mercy. Pointing his march toward the upper fords, Cornwallis hurried out to head off his foe. To his astonishment, the force under Williams which he was following suddenly wheeled about and started back toward Irwin's Ferry. Greene, by that time, had gained a whole day's march and was well on his way to the crossing.

The race to the Dan, some seventy miles away, was on. Greene's little army trudged along clay roads that turned into slippery mud as the rains began to fall. His men suffered terribly. Hundreds of soldiers were without shoes and left bloodstains behind to mark the army's route. Without tents the ill-clad troops were forced to huddle by campfires or inside makeshift bough shelters to keep from freezing at night. Greene suffered along with the men. One evening he and John Rutledge, the South Carolina governor, found shelter against the cold rain in an abandoned hovel. During the night, they awoke and accused one another of kicking. When the kicking continued, they examined their bed of straw and discovered that a hog had joined them in the night to get out of the cold.

While the main army was heading for the Dan, Colonel Williams followed them keeping just a step ahead of Cornwallis. To prevent the enemy from circling around his camp, Williams kept half his men patrolling at night while the rest snatched a few hours of sleep. He often began marching as early as three in the morning. When his men were far enough ahead of Cornwallis, Williams permitted them to stop and cook rations to last through the next twenty-four hours.

Although they were often in sight of Williams' task force, the British were never able to overtake the Americans and to force them into a battle. Tarleton's dragoons sometimes attempted to rush the light troops while crossing streams, but such brushes usually ended up with British losses because the horsemen under "Light-Horse Harry" Lee and William Washington were more than a match for Tarleton's troopers. Most of the time the British were content to trudge along in the footsteps of their retreating foe. "The demeanor of the hostile troops," wrote Lee, "became so pacific in appearance, that a spectator would have been led to consider them members of the same army." [28]

At long last, Colonel Williams and his exhausted men received the welcome news that Greene had crossed the Dan. The report spread rapidly through the line and with one voice the men gave a shout of joy. General Charles O'Hara, leading Cornwallis' advanced corps, heard the cry and guessed its meaning. By the time O'Hara reached the Dan, he glimpsed the last of Washington's cavalry swimming across the river to the opposite shore. Greene's army had reached sanctuary at last.

Greene summed up his historic retreat in a letter to Thomas Jefferson. He was "almost fatigued to death," he wrote, "having had a retreat to conduct for upwards of two hundred miles, maneuvering constantly in the face of the enemy, to give time for the militia to turn out and get off our stores." [29] The British were as high in their praise of Greene's exploit as were his own countrymen. Tarleton wrote that "Every measure of the Americans during their march from the Catawba to Virginia, was judiciously designed and vigorously executed." [30]

Cornwallis longed to pursue Greene further, but he dared not. His men were tired and sick and his supplies were dangerously low. There was little else to do but to turn back. Cornwallis retreated to Hillsboro, North Carolina, hoping to replenish his supplies and to enlist more loyalists. Only a handful of loyalists joined his force, however, and he found few supplies.

The initiative now passed to Greene. Determined to give Cornwallis as little time as possible to build up his army, Greene recrossed the Dan into North Carolina late in February, 1781. Lee's legion and Washington's cavalry were sent on ahead to harass the enemy and to frighten the loyalists from joining the British. Pressed by Greene, Cornwallis fell back slowly. At

Guilford Court House in mid-March, Greene decided it was time to fight. It was a sound strategic move. As Tarleton so aptly noted, "A defeat of the British would have been attended with the total destruction of Earl Cornwallis's infantry, whilst a victory at this juncture could produce no very decisive consequences against the Americans!" [31]

Greene's ranks were swelled by this time with new units from the Continental army and fresh bodies of militia. His force was nearly twice the size of the British; Greene had 4,200 men and Cornwallis about 2,000. But the armies were more evenly matched because more of Cornwallis' troops were veterans. Both generals joined in battle confident of victory.

Greene rose early on the morning of March 15 and mounting his horse, gave last-minute instructions to his officers. While riding about he often paused to rub his upper lip as was his habit when thinking out a problem. His battle formation according to Tarleton was "unexceptionable," and his choice of ground excellent. He stationed his troops in three lines at the crest of a long rise with some open ground on their front. Despite these well-laid plans, however, the opening encounter was nearly disastrous. Greene's front line, made up of North Carolina militiamen, ran from the field after delivering but one volley. His second line, composed mainly of Virginia militia, stood their ground for a time. But they too were slowly pushed back through some woods and finally retired in confusion. Now it was up to Greene's third line of Continentals from Maryland, Delaware, and Virginia. Fortunately, his third line held firm.

The fighting grew desperate and bloody and the battle hung in the balance. Cornwallis' force on occasion was threatened with complete destruction. To prevent an American breakthrough at one point, Cornwallis ordered his gunners to fire grapeshot into the thick of the fighting even though it meant killing some of his own men. For an instant Greene himself was in grave danger of being killed or captured when he rode through the din and smoke to get a better view of the battle. He had almost reached the British line before one of his aides shouted at him to turn back. After a bitter two-hour struggle, Greene ordered a retreat. His ammunition was running low and the enemy had broken through the Maryland regiment to threaten his whole line.

Cornwallis won a technical victory at Guilford Court House, but it was a costly one. Tarleton marked the battle as a great disaster for British arms. Fully one-quarter of Cornwallis' fine army had been knocked out of action. Too weak to continue the campaign, Cornwallis retreated to Wilmington on the coast, where he could be supplied by sea. His withdrawal left Greene the master of North Carolina.

More significant, perhaps, than the retaking of North Carolina, was the effect the campaign had on Cornwallis' thinking. Convinced that British control could not be sustained in the Carolinas as long as Virginia remained an American supply base, Cornwallis made a fateful decision. He would march into Virginia and join the British forces already there. Greene, he was quite sure, would follow him and the combined sections of the British army would make short work of destroying the Southern army. After Greene was crushed, organized resistance in the South would cease and the states below the Potomac would become conquered provinces once more.

But Cornwallis miscalculated. As soon as he was well on his way to Wilmington, Greene broke off his pursuit and turned south to swoop down upon the British forts and garrisons in South Carolina and Georgia. With the help of local partisans like Francis Marion, Thomas Sumter, and Andrew Pickens, he hoped to take all the enemy posts except Savannah and Charleston. After driving the enemy from the interior, Greene planned to leave behind some local forces to contain the British at the two southern cities while he marched his army northward to confront Cornwallis once again.

When Greene's strategy to move into South Carolina became known in the North, it evoked high praise. Lafayette thought Greene's decision was "a great piece of generalship." Richard Henry Lee declared that "like Scipio" Greene had "left Cornwallis in N. Carolina and pushed into S. Carolina intending no doubt to compel the British general to relinquish his prospects this way, or find his southern conquests wrested from him, if he does not return to defend them." In Virginia, Jefferson saw the wisdom of Greene's move and wrote: "North as well as South Carolina being once in the Hands of the Enemy may become the Instruments of our Subjugation and effect what the Enemy themselves cannot. The British may harass and distress us greatly but the Carolinas alone can subdue us." [32]

Marching into South Carolina in the spring of 1781, Greene suffered a repulse at the hands of Lord Rawdon at Hobkirk's Hill, near Camden. This battle only served to arouse his fighting spirit and he wrote doggedly, "We fight, get beat, rise, and fight again." [33] He ran into trouble once more at Ninety-Six when reinforcements led by Rawdon arrived on the scene to lift the siege Greene had imposed on the strong British garrison there. But while he was keeping Rawdon occupied, Greene's subordinates captured all of the small forts in South Carolina except those in the vicinity of Charleston. With the coming of summer and the stifling heat, Greene withdrew his tired troops to the High Hills of the Santee to rest. Rawdon evacuated Ninety-Six and all but the lower part of South Carolina was now back in American hands.

Greene kept himself informed on developments in the North while conducting his Southern campaign. Upon learning that a powerful French fleet was expected in American waters that summer, he sensed the opportunity this would have afforded him had he been able to dash back into Virginia. With the cooperation of the French fleet, he might cut off the British army in Virginia from outside help and Cornwallis' fate would be sealed. This was to be the future course of events at Yorktown, but it was Washington and Rochambeau, not Greene, who were destined to trap Cornwallis.

While the Yorktown campaign was beginning to take shape, Greene marched down from the High Hills of the Santee. The British forces in South Carolina and Georgia were still formidable. If Cornwallis managed to break free from Lafayette in Virginia before Washington and Rochambeau arrived and retreated south, there was a possibility that Greene might be crushed between two British armies. To prevent this, Greene sought to destroy the enemy in South Carolina by a full-scale attack on the British army at Eutaw Springs on September 8, 1781. Before the battle, he was joined by Marion, Pickens, and other local militia leaders itching for a fight. During the bloody struggle that followed, both sides suffered heavily. The British claimed a technical victory because they were in possession of the field when the fighting was over. But, as in all Greene's battles in the South, the results were decisively in favor of the Americans. British losses were so heavy that the enemy were forced to relinquish all territory in the state outside of Charleston.

Praise for Greene again ran high after the Eutaw Springs battle. Henry Knox wrote, "The exalted talents of General Greene have been amply displayed in North and South Carolina—without an army, without Means, without anything he has performed wonders." From Holland, John Adams wrote that Eutaw Springs was "quite as glorious for the American arms as the capture of Cornwallis." [34]

Although Cornwallis surrendered at Yorktown in October, 1781, fighting continued in the deep South. The British were bottled up inside Charleston but they were so well entrenched that Greene could do no more than clamp a tight siege on the city by land. If Admiral de Grasse had sailed for Charleston with the French fleet after the Yorktown victory, Greene was convinced the city would have fallen. But the French admiral had orders to return immediately to the West Indies. It was not until December, 1782, that the British finally evacuated Charleston. Fearing the British might resume hostilities, Greene kept a small force together despite the gradual disintegration of his army. After the peace treaty was formally ratified, he disbanded what remained of his army and prepared to leave for home. With his faithful soldiers gone, Greene said he felt "like Sampson after Delilah cut his locks." [35]

When Greene rode northward, he was greeted everywhere as a conquering hero. All along his route, he was honored by banquets, meetings, and celebrations. At Alexandria, while Greene lay ill with a fever, a public gathering was held in his behalf. The principal speaker voiced the sentiment of all when he declared that Greene had "the honor of proving to the World that circumstances of the greatest distress . . . can be nobly surmounted by brave men . . . under the command of wise, virtuous, and persevering Leaders." [36]

Upon reaching Philadelphia, Greene found himself as famous in the North as the South. As much as possible, however, he avoided public demonstrations, preferring as he did the company of old friends like Clement Biddle, Charles Pettit, and Robert Morris. At Trenton, a spot that brought back many memories, Greene met General Washington. Together they rode to Princeton, where Congress was sitting. From Congress, Greene received permission to return home as a civilian. As a symbol of its appreciation of his services in the Carolinas, Congress presented him with two brass cannon captured in the South. When he arrived at Newport, Rhode Island, the town turned out to greet him. "In this mighty Revolution," declared the principal speaker, "Which regard the Rights of Humanity for its Base, we feel a Pride . . . that a Citizen of this State had brightened the Paths of Glory. . . ." [37]

In the postwar period, Greene returned south to live at Mulberry Grove, the beautiful plantation near Savannah given to him by the state of Georgia for his military services. He struggled for a few years to get his plantation in operation and to find relief from a ruinous debt contracted while he was still in the army. Worn out by the strains of war and worried by debts, he succumbed to an infection and died at the age of forty-four in June, 1786.

Thomas Jefferson acknowledged long afterward that Greene was second to none among the Revolutionary War generals. Francis Kinloch, a congressman who fought in the war, declared the Rhode Islander was "the greatest military genius produced by the War for Independence." [38] With the passing of years, such appraisals of Greene by his contemporaries seem justified. In the North he gave Washington sound advice, his mistake at Fort Washington notwithstanding, and he performed brilliantly at Brandywine and other battles. In the South, Greene's strategy and daring played a major role in the final undoing of British power in that region. Carrying on a warfare of attrition, Greene harassed Cornwallis to the point that he decided to abandon North Carolina for Virginia. After marching away from Cornwallis, Greene carried out a whirlwind campaign that enabled him to free much of the deep South from complete subjugation. Always a great leader and a deadly strategist, he deserves to be remembered as the logical successor to the commander-in-chief had anything ever happened to Washington in the course of the war.

FOOTNOTES

1. George Washington Greene, *Life of Nathanael Greene, Major General in the Army of the Revolution* (New York, 1867–71), II, 417. Hereinafter G. W. Greene.
2. Greene to Henry Knox, July 18, 1781, Greene Papers, Connecticut Historical Society.
3. Greene to Samuel Ward, Jr., September 26, 1771, Greene Papers, Rhode Island Historical Society.
4. Alexander Garden, *Anecdotes of the American Revolution* (Brooklyn, 1865), I, 65.
5. Knox to John Adams, September 25, 1776, *Proceedings of the American Antiquarian Society*, V, 56, 217; G. W. Greene, *op. cit.*, I, 207.
6. Theodore Thayer, *Nathanael Greene: Strategist of the American Revolution* (New York, 1960), p. 118.
7. Henry P. Johnston, *The Campaign of 1776 around New York and Brooklyn* (Brooklyn, 1878), p. 284.
8. Greene to his wife, January 10, 1777, Greene Collection, V, 88, William Clements Library.
9. William Gordon, *History of the Rise, Progress and Establishment of the Independence of the United States of America* (London, 1788), II, 296.
10. G. W. Greene, *op. cit.*, I, 310–11.

11. Greene's letter, May 20, 1777, Greene Papers, Rhode Island Historical Society.
12. G. W. Greene, *op. cit.*, I, 457.
13. *Ibid.*, II, 483–85, 500–02.
14. John Clark to Greene, January 10, 1778, Greene Collection, II, William Clements Library; G. W. Greene, *op. cit.*, II, 1–40.
15. Douglas Southall Freeman, *George Washington: A Biography* (New York, 1952), IV, 592–611; G. W. Greene, *op. cit.*, II, 2.
16. George Lux to Greene, May 26, 1778, Greene Collection, II, William Clements Library.
17. G. W. Greene, *op. cit.*, II, 466, 505–06.
18. *Ibid.*, II, 86, 512; John C. Fitzpatrick, ed., *The Writings of George Washington* (Washington, D.C., 1934), XII, 277.
19. Thayer, *op. cit.*, pp. 229–38, 413–20.
20. Samuel Shaw, *The Journals of Major Samuel Shaw* (Boston, 1847), pp. 82–83; G. W. Greene, *op. cit.*, II, 374–75, 377–78.
21. G. W. Greene, *op. cit.*, II, 381–94; Greene to wife, October 14, 1780, Greene Collection, X, William Clements Library; Thayer, *op. cit.*, p. 280.
22. Henry Lee, *Memoirs of the War in the Southern Department of the United States* (Philadelphia, 1812), I, 244–45; Elkanah Watson, *Men and Times of the Revolution* (New York, 1856), p. 259.
23. G. W. Greene, *op. cit.*, III, 131–32.
24. Gordon, *op. cit.*, IV, 59.
25. Greene to John Mathews, January 23, 1781, Greene Papers, Bancroft Collection, New York Public Library.
26. G. W. Greene, *op. cit.*, III, 161.
27. Greene to Steuben, February 3, 1781, Greene Papers, XVIII, William Clements Library.
28. Lee, *op. cit.*, I, 289–90.
29. G. W. Greene, *op. cit.*, III, 174.
30. Banastre Tarleton, *History of the Campaign of 1780 and 1781 in the Southern Provinces of North America* (London, 1787), p. 229; Greene to Jefferson, December 15, 1781, Greene Papers, Bancroft Collection, New York Public Library.
31. *Ibid.*, p. 277.
32. *Letters of Richard Henry Lee* (New York, 1912–14), II, 218–19; Julian Boyd, *The Papers of Thomas Jefferson* (Princeton, 1952), V, 541; Greene to Joseph Reed, March 18, 1781, Reed Papers, IX, New York Historical Society.
33. Greene to Luzerne, June 22, 1781, Greene Collection, XXXI, William Clements Library; Greene to Lafayette, May 23, 1781, Greene Papers, Library of Congress.

34. Knox to John Adams, October 21, 1781, *Proceedings of the American Antiquarian Society*, XVI, 225; Charles Francis Adams, *The Works of John Adams* (Boston, 1852), VII, 487.
35. Greene to Charles Pettit, July 29, 1783, Reed Papers, X, New York Historical Society.
36. Greene Papers, VII, 330, Library of Congress.
37. Greene to Malgine, Channing, and Goodwin, November 29, 1783, Greene Collection, LXXXIX, William Clements Library.
38. Paul Leicester Ford, *The Works of Thomas Jefferson* (New York, 1905), XII, 246; Francis Kinloch, *Letters from Geneva and France* (Boston, 1819), II, 142.

BIBLIOGRAPHY

Alden, John R., *The South in the Revolution 1763–1789*. Baton Rouge, 1957. Contains a brief but accurate account of Greene's campaigns in the South.

Caldwell, Charles, *Memoirs of the Life and Campaigns of the Hon. Nathanael Greene*. Philadelphia, 1819. An older work that is very inaccurate.

Freeman, Douglas S., *George Washington: A Biography*, 6 vols. New York, 1954. Volumes III and IV contain excellent accounts of Greene's contributions to the campaigns in the North.

Greene, Francis V., *General Greene*. New York, 1893. An old and incomplete account of Greene's life, but one that is especially good on military analysis.

Greene, George W., *Life of Nathanael Greene*, 3 vols. New York, 1867–71. The most comprehensive biography of Greene and written by his grandson. A mine of information on Greene's life, but lacks critical analysis of both the men and events of the Revolution.

Johnson, William, *Sketches of the Life and Correspondence of Nathanael Greene*. Charleston, 1822. A useful biography for a detailed account of Greene's southern campaigns.

Pratt, Fletcher, "Nathanael Greene: The Quaker Turenne," in *Eleven Generals: Studies in American Command*. New York, 1949. A brief and illuminating sketch.

Thayer, Theodore, *Nathanael Greene: Strategist of the Revolution*. New York, 1960. The most recent biography of Greene.

John Sullivan:

LUCKLESS IRISHMAN

CHARLES P. WHITTEMORE

South Kent School

OF ALL Washington's generals, John Sullivan deserves the reputation of a fighter, whether in the field or in the halls of Congress; for when this fiery Irishman was not busy warring with the British, he found time to take on Congress or his colleagues. But throughout his entire career, battling either friend or foe, Sullivan was dogged by bad luck. His failure to succeed against the British might be explained by his not having battle experience—though he was no worse off in this respect than many of his fellow officers. Because he had been a small town country lawyer, one might expect John Sullivan to have acquired the knack of getting along well with people, but he was a contentious soul and had no trouble finding ways to irritate those about him. Like so many men who complain of ill-luck, Sullivan helped to bring on many of his own misfortunes. The same driving ambition that caused him to make errors on the field of battle, also caused him to alienate politicians in Congress. He strained for success with every fiber of his being, sought the plaudits of the crowd, and strove without letup to advance his own welfare. In the end it was Sullivan's ambition that brought him down and ended his military career before the Revolutionary War was concluded.

John Sullivan came from a humble background. His parents

arrived from Ireland as redemptionists, or indentured servants, in the 1730's and settled in Somersworth, New Hampshire, where John was born on February 17, 1740. His father, a schoolteacher, gave his son a far better education than most boys could expect in those years. For a time the family lived in Berwick, Maine, a frontier community across the border from New Hampshire. When he was eighteen, Sullivan read law with Samuel Livermore, and shortly afterward launched out on a practice of his own. After his marriage to Lydia Worster in 1760, he moved from Berwick to Durham, New Hampshire, which was to be his residence for the rest of his life.

Even at this early stage in his career, his contentious streak became evident. Overly zealous in suing for debts owed him, he once antagonized some of his neighbors to the point where they formed an armed mob to storm the house at which he was staying. He became a passionate hater of Great Britain, and soon advocated independence. His driving ambition made him a talented politician in spite of his tendency to irk people, and New Hampshire chose to send him to the First Continental Congress. Upon his return in November, 1774, he urged his fellow townsmen to co-operate in economic coercion against the mother country, organized a raid upon the British fortress in the Portsmouth harbor, and found himself on the road to Philadelphia to attend the Second Congress in May, 1775. He was now ready for any eventuality, and brought much fire and zeal to the task facing him.

In June, 1775, Sullivan left Congress to go to Boston to assume his duties as a brigadier general. His appointment to so high a rank came as no surprise. As a former major in the militia and spokesman of the patriot forces in New Hampshire, Sullivan was a logical choice.[1] His striking appearance lent dignity to his new command, for although he was of middling stature, he stood erect. His black, piercing eyes and his ruddy complexion helped give him the look of a daring leader. And time would show that he had the qualities needed for combat—courage, energy, and enthusiasm.

General Sullivan's military career may be considered as having three phases. At first he was completely cocky, absolutely convinced of his own ability, and daring almost to the point of being foolhardy. During the siege of Boston, for example, he wrote that the Americans would "take possession of the town, or perish in the attempt." [2] When Washington sent him to take command of the pathetic little army in Canada, Sullivan still was confident, and only after he knew for sure that he faced quick disaster did he reluctantly order a retreat. His clumsy performance and capture at Long Island were somewhat redeemed by his part in the successes at Trenton and Princeton, after he had been exchanged as a prisoner of war. Thus ended the first phase: he was still cocksure despite his setbacks.

The second phase of Sullivan's career came in the last half of 1777, when he suffered successive defeats at Staten Island, Brandywine, and Germantown. With severe criticism buzzing about his head, Sullivan seemed unnerved. Confidence began giving way to caution as he entered the third phase. Thanks to the caution that came with experience, Sullivan performed competently from this point on. He proved a sound commander during the Rhode Island campaign in the summer of 1778, although his handling of the French allies left much to be desired. His final contribution was his march into the Indian country in the Finger Lakes district of New York in 1779. Sullivan had come into his own by this time. He was now the careful tactician stalking an elusive prey. His scorched-earth policy dealt the Indians a blow from which they never fully recovered.

Sullivan's role in the early stages of the war was a relatively minor one. After joining the new American army in Cambridge in July, 1775, he commanded a brigade in the force that kept the British penned up inside Boston. Whenever Washington's staff met to discuss strategy, Sullivan joined those who advised against any attempts to attack the enemy during the summer or fall. He preferred to wait, he said, until winter. True to his word, Sullivan led an abortive assault to seize outbuildings and barracks on Bunker Hill, late in December. The attempt failed and with it went Sullivan's first chance to gain military glory.

The British remained in Boston until the following spring, and the two armies did little else but glower at one another. The military stalemate came to an end when Washington captured Dorchester Heights in March, 1776, and the British decided they must evacuate the city. As the enemy prepared to embark, the energetic Sullivan galloped down to where he could have a good look at Bunker Hill. There he saw sentries with shouldered firelocks standing guard, but they stood suspiciously motionless. Putting his spyglass to his eye, Sullivan saw that the "sentries" were effigies left by the departing redcoats. Convinced that the siege was over, he moved forward with a small party and "bravely took a fortress Defended by Lifeless Sentries." [3]

The joy of outlasting the British was dampened by Sullivan's controversy with the New Hampshire legislature regarding his right to appoint militia officers. When the militia was threatening to leave at the end of 1775, Sullivan set out to re-enlist as many of the men as would listen to his pleas. He even took the liberty of making some of the men officers, a prerogative which the legislators at home claimed for themselves. Displeased by Sullivan's actions, they criticized him for highhandedness. Always a touchy man, Sullivan did not take the reproach lightly. Soon he would be off to New York, he wrote, then "those persons will . . . have no more fear of the Destruction of their Liberties from a person who has spent more money undergone more Fatigue and oftener Risqued his Life than any other person in your Province. . . ." [4]

His ego bruised, Sullivan set off for New York City in March with the rest of Washington's army. He did not linger there for long, for he was soon on his way upstate to take reinforcements to the Northern army invading Canada. No sooner had he arrived than he learned he must assume command in place of John Thomas who was dying of smallpox. The Canadian campaign was crumbling, and Sullivan should have had enough sense to order an immediate retreat. But he wanted to fight, and this seemed to him to be the time to show Washington and Congress that here was an Irishman eager to strike blows at the British. Glory was just around the corner and to retreat seemed ridiculous in his eyes. He stubbornly insisted upon a raid at Trois Rivières. Even after his men were defeated there, he still would not consider pulling back. "I now think only of a glorious Death or a victory obtained against Superiour numbers," he wrote.[5] But an army riddled with smallpox cannot fight, and even Sullivan was finally forced to face the inevitable. As Sullivan told the story, however, it was not the certainty of defeat that caused him to withdraw. Instead he blamed his dispirited army, the desire of some officers to resign, and the possibility that his men might not stand up to the British as his reasons for turning back to New York. The retreat, surprisingly enough, was orderly and efficient, although the agony of pain and illness which his unhappy men had to endure was a nightmare. On July 1, 1776, the shabby remnants of a once confident army reached Crown Point, thereby bringing to an end America's attempt to win the "fourteenth colony."

Shortly after his return, Sullivan learned that Congress was sending on Horatio Gates to supersede him as commander in the Northern Department. He smarted at the setback. Sullivan was not the type of man to stand idly by and let Gates move in without opposition. Unbeknownst to Sullivan, however, Washington had assessed his candidacy at the time Congress was considering the matter, in these frank words:

> [Sullivan] . . . is aiming at the Command in Canada. . . . Whether he merits it or not, is a matter to be considered; and that it may be considered with propriety I think it my duty to observe . . . that he is active, spirited, and Zealously attach'd to the Cause; that he does not want Abilities, many Members of Congress, as well as myself, can testify. But he has his wants, and he has his foibles. The latter are manifested in a little tincture of vanity, and in an over desire of being popular, which now and then leads him into some embarrassments. His wants are common to us all; the want of ex-

perience to move upon a large Scale; for the limited, and contracted knowledge which any of us have in Military Matters stands in very little Stead; and is greatly over balanced by sound judgment, and some knowledge of Men and Books; especially when accompanied by an enterprizing genius, which I must do Genl. Sullivan the justice to say, I think he possesses. . . .[6]

Washington's appraisal confirmed the congressmen in their opinion that a more experienced man was needed in the Northern Department. But Sullivan had no intention of settling for second place and in a fit of pique he requested leave to go to Philadelphia so that he might submit his resignation. This episode was but the first of many temperamental blasts from the constantly irate Irishman.

In Philadelphia, some of his friends soothed him and sought to dissuade him from handing in his resignation. Sullivan eventually acceded to their request. It is just as well he did. Congress had been prepared to give him a "rap on the knuckles," to use Thomas Jefferson's words.[7] Sullivan, however, never saw it that way, and remained quite unaware that he had antagonized anyone. In fact, he felt he had been quite shabbily treated.

It was in such a truculent frame of mind that Sullivan faced his next military assignment on Long Island. He still was full of confidence, convinced that he was one of Washington's better officers. He had just been promoted to major general, and was most eager to show his talents. The Battle of Long Island, fought August 27, 1776, would be the proving ground. To protect New York City, Washington had scattered his army in three separate locations: Manhattan Island, Long Island, and along the New Jersey shore. The force on the western tip of Long Island guarding the entry into New York's inner harbor was commanded by Nathanael Greene. When Greene became ill in August, his command was given to Sullivan. Joseph Reed, Washington's adjutant, thought little of the choice, claiming that Sullivan "was wholly unacquainted with the ground or country." [8] Israel Putnam was likewise disgruntled because he wanted the assignment for himself.

The patriot forces on Long Island took up a position behind the breastworks on Brooklyn Heights controlling the East River and New York City. In front of the redoubts and entrenchments, about a mile and a half away, ran a ridge of hills. In these hills some American units stood guard at the passes, for this would have to be the British route of entry to the American position at Brooklyn—unless the British chose to swing far to the right to enter the pass that opened on Jamaica Road behind the ridge. But who in Washington's army expected the enemy to make such a detour?

On August 22, 1776, the British ferried troops from Staten Island to Long Island. A battle was obviously in the offing, but Washington was not sure what to do next. At this point he apparently had second thoughts about placing Sullivan in charge on Long Island. He sent Putnam over to take command instead. But the tough old Connecticut farmer, although brave and vigorous, was no tactician and was incapable of handling the large command of about 9,000 troops.

Historians, unfortunately, have never been able to determine the definite scope of Putnam's command. Consequently it is hard to pin down just who was responsible for the American defeat that followed.[9] Most likely Sullivan had command of the forces outside the Brooklyn breastworks, although he denied this later, claiming that another American general—Lord Stirling—had this honor. Yet Sullivan certainly acted as though he had authority to protect the approaches to Brooklyn Heights. On August 23, he ordered regiments to all the passes except the one which opened upon the Jamaica Road. There he sent only a patrol of five men. This was a fantastic piece of misjudgment on his part. The total inadequacy of the weak forces at the passes and puny guard at the Jamaica Pass should have been obvious to any competent military commander. Yet Washington toured the lines on the eve of the battle and seemed satisfied with the disposition of the troops. The commander-in-chief was far from keen on this occasion; his better days still lay ahead.

Sullivan, who was commanding the center of the American

lines, had little inkling of the masterful attack which the British were about to unfold. While General James Grant and the Hessians under Von Heister assaulted the passes on the morning of the twenty-seventh, General Howe along with Lord Percy was circling the American left for a flanking attack. The British had moved out on the previous evening and soon learned of the small patrol at the Jamaica Pass. They hoped to reach Sullivan's rear before the Americans even knew of their whereabouts.

Howe's plan succeeded brilliantly. When dawn came, Sullivan found himself hotly committed along his front in the middle of the American lines. But he was able to hold his own. Suddenly firing broke out behind him as Howe completed his encirclement. Fighting furiously, Sullivan tried to break through to the lines at Brooklyn Heights, but with no success. His men were overrun and the general himself was forced to surrender to three Hessian soldiers in a cornfield. After his dreams of military glory, Sullivan's surrender seemed ludicrous.

The Battle of Long Island ended with a serious defeat of the American forces. The patriots found themselves driven into a tight little defense perimeter on Brooklyn Heights, barely two miles wide and one mile deep. At this time the British undoubtedly could have overwhelmed them and pushed them into the sea. Fortunately, however, Howe chose not to press his advantage and Washington escaped by an amphibious midnight evacuation back to the island of Manhattan. This safe withdrawal was the only bright spot in the American efforts.

Was Sullivan responsible for the turning of the American left and the defeat that followed? The question is not easy to answer, as it hinges upon the issue of who was in command of the lines in front of the Brooklyn defenses. Sullivan certainly must share some of the blame for the poor watch kept at the Jamaica Pass. Washington also must assume some blame for failing to spell out more clearly the duties of his subordinates and for the poor deployment of troops in front of the Brooklyn breastworks. But what really had happened was that a professional, William Howe, had won by outsmarting the American amateurs. Sullivan summed up the battle best by saying: "General Howe was too old for us." [10]

Sullivan, now a captive aboard the ship of Lord Richard Howe, William Howe's brother, found the admiral likewise "too old" for him. The captured American received the polite treatment so typical of eighteenth-century warfare. He soon fell under the influence of Lord Howe, who was most anxious to serve as conciliator between England and her rebellious colonies and kept telling Sullivan why the Americans should come to terms. At first Sullivan paid little attention to Howe's persuasive efforts, but gradually he gave way and consented to carry a message to Congress seeking reconciliation.

It is not easy to explain Sullivan's willingness to serve as Howe's errand boy. Certainly no one in Washington's army was more anxious to whip the British than the New Hampshire Irishman. But apparently Lord Howe had convinced Sullivan that the British were ready to make major concessions in giving up taxation and the control of internal policy. Sullivan, at least, thought Howe had gone that far, but the British admiral later denied it. Allowed to leave on his parole, Sullivan went off to Philadelphia to talk with the delegates in Congress.

The members of Congress, still displeased over Sullivan's petulance earlier in the summer, were not so gullible as the captured general. John Adams, for example, was not the least bit impressed by Sullivan's stories of British change of heart. Leaning over toward Benjamin Rush, Adams whispered that he wished "the first ball that had been fired on the day of the defeat of our Army had gone through his [Sullivan's] head." In Adams' mind Sullivan was no less than a "decoy duck whom Lord Howe has sent among us to seduce us into a renunciation of our independence." [11] In his summary of the episode, John Adams, who was thoroughly annoyed, had nothing to say that would credit Sullivan. He wrote:

The conduct of General Sullivan, in consenting to come to Philadelphia, upon so confused an errand from Lord Howe, though his situation, as a prisoner, was a temptation, and may be considered as some apology for it, appeared to me to betray such want of penetration and fortitude, and there was so little precision in the information he communicated, that I felt much resentment, and more contempt, upon the occasion, than was perhaps just. The time was extremely critical. The attention of Congress, the army, the States, and the people, ought to have been wholly directed to the defense of the country. To have it diverted and relaxed, by such a poor artifice and confused tale, appeared very reprehensible.[12]

Nothing came of the British peace overtures. The delegates were wary of taking the bait, and after an inconclusive conference between the two sides, the matter came to a close. Sullivan, however, gained his exchange and by the end of September had rejoined Washington's army in New York.

Despite the many reverses he had suffered, Sullivan was not downhearted. Fortunately for his morale and for the patriot cause, the Battles of Trenton and Princeton around the turn of the year allowed the patriot army to demonstrate to the British that it had some fight left. In the Trenton battle, Sullivan crossed the Delaware with Washington's main task force, took half of the men and cannon, and marched along the road close to the river to strike at the southern end of town. The result was a quick victory and a bag of prisoners. At Princeton, Sullivan's column was not positioned to be in the main fight, but his men took part in the pursuit that followed. These two surprising victories gave Washington the time he needed and he settled in Morristown for the winter. Sullivan had proved to be a tireless and brave fighter, whether in the heartbreaking defeats suffered earlier or in the victories at Trenton and Princeton. The first phase of his military career had come to a close.

Sullivan entered 1777 with high hopes that better days lay ahead now that the Americans had had some success. But he was doomed to be disappointed. During the winter he fell ill from a digestive disorder, most likely a peptic ulcer.[13] That a man of such a mercurial and excitable nature had an ulcer is understandable. Nor did he help matters by drinking heavily. Doctors warned him to stop, but to no avail. "Spirits I must never again use but with the Greatest Caution (if at all)," was the way Sullivan casually stated the matter. But throughout the rest of his life, John Sullivan remained a heavy drinker.[14]

The general's ulcer was not soothed by the report that Arthur St. Clair had been given the command at Ticonderoga, a post that Sullivan had wanted for himself. The news caused another of Sullivan's outbursts. He sent a whining letter to Washington in March complaining that he had been passed over for a separate command and offered to resign since the commander-in-chief had shown such little confidence in him. Washington's stinging reply was abrupt and to the point:

> Do not, my dear General Sullivan, torment yourself any longer with imaginary Slights, and involve others in the perplexities you feel on that Score. No other officer of rank, in the whole army, has so often conceived himself neglected, Slighted, and ill treated, as you have done, and none I am sure has had less cause than yourself to entertain such Ideas. Mere accidents, things which have occurred in the common course of Service, have been considered by you as designed affronts.[15]

These caustic words silenced Sullivan, but not for long. In June when he learned that a French officer, Philippe du Coudray, had been granted a major general's commission to command the artillery and engineers and to be responsible only to Washington and Congress, Sullivan burst forth again. This time he had some support. Nathanael Greene and Henry Knox were also furious that Du Coudray was outranking them. There was a mild storm when the three generals threatened to resign. But Congress refused to give way and expected an apology from the American generals. No apology was forthcoming. Fortunately for the patriot cause, Du Coudray foolishly rode his horse across the deck of a ferry and drowned in the Schuylkill. The Frenchman's drowning brought an end, for the time being, to the promotion problem.

Irked by his failures and anxious to win a victory of his own,

Sullivan planned an independent raid on Staten Island from the New Jersey shore in the summer of 1777. On the morning of August 22, Sullivan moved his men across to Staten Island and at first met with some success. But as the hours went by, he ran into trouble. His officers could not maintain strict discipline and the men began to straggle and plunder. As though the unruly men were not enough trouble, chaos and confusion arose from a misunderstanding about the rendezvous whence the men were to recross to New Jersey. Although Sullivan had taken some prisoners, he also had lost some men so that his neat *"coup"* was somewhat of a failure. Congress was beginning to have some doubts about Sullivan's ability and a crisis approached, both for the American army and the Irishman's future.

When Howe invaded Pennsylvania in late August to capture Philadelphia, Sullivan faced the most bitter controversy of his career. Washington marched his men to face Howe southwest of Philadelphia and took up his position along the Brandywine in September to halt the Britisher's advance. The most likely place for the enemy to cross was at Chad's Ford and there Washington placed several brigades. To Sullivan he gave the key assignment of guarding the right flank at Brinton's Ford, just above Chad's Ford. The American lines were not unlike those at Long Island, except this time Washington was determined not to allow the British to march around him as they had a year before.

Sullivan did not assume his post at Brinton's Ford until the eve of the Battle of Brandywine on September 11. Before taking command, he visited Washington's headquarters on the night of September 10, for a briefing, and at that time he was told to have men reconnoiter as far north as Buffington's Ford, the fork at which two branches of the Brandywine joined. Washington assured him he need not worry about the fords beyond Buffington's because there were no likely crossing places for at least twelve miles to the north and there were light-horse units scouting in that direction to warn of any surprise flanking move. Lulled into a false sense of security, Sullivan reported to his command and made no move to check Washington's information that there were no places to cross immediately north of Buffing-ton's Ford. He had little time to study the terrain, for the battle was soon joined.

Early that morning, Howe moved some of his forces to Chad's Ford, giving the impression that he was about to attack the American center. At the same time, he sent Lord Cornwallis on a wide sweeping march north to cross the Brandywine well above Buffington's Ford and to fall upon the American right wing under the hapless Sullivan. Once again Howe was using the tactics of Long Island, and the inept Americans were to be an easy prey.

Yet Sullivan could not get Long Island out of his mind, and as a result he was wary of a flank attack. He expected such a move, at least he claimed so later, but unfortunately he failed to take proper initiative to check on possible crossing places. On two separate occasions during the morning, he sent word to Washington that some flanking move was coming. Washington, who had received other reports of a flanking march, thought it would take the enemy some time to make such a move and to be in position to attack. If Howe chose to divide his army, a tactic frowned upon by many, Washington thought the time had come to take advantage of the daring British move. It seemed as though he had a perfect opportunity to strike at the British stationary force at Chad's Ford. After attacking the force in front of him, Washington thought he would have plenty of time to regroup his forces to meet the reported movement on his flank. Making his decision, the commander-in-chief ordered Sullivan to cross the Brandywine to assist him in attacking the enemy's stationary unit.[16]

Just as Sullivan was getting ready to move, Major Joseph Spear of the Pennsylvania militia rode up to report that there was no sign of the enemy in the branches of the Brandywine. Sullivan was in a quandary; the facts seemed to run counter to his own opinion of a flanking attack. He quickly relayed Spear's report, with his own conclusion that his earlier information about a flanking march was "wrong," to Washington.[17] The confused Washington hesitated momentarily, for he dared not order an assault if there were any possibility that the enemy facing him was at full strength across Chad's Ford.

The lull continued until about two o'clock in the afternoon, when another messenger rode up to General Sullivan, bringing an intelligence report from Colonel Theodorick Bland, who was scouting for Washington. Bland's message was short and alarming. The enemy were at Sullivan's rear barely two miles away! What Sullivan had been expecting all along, until fooled by Spear's account, had actually come to pass. Although not quite sure of the location of the enemy, Sullivan began to deploy his troops. He hardly had time to do so. Within an hour and a half about 7,000 British troops were pressing upon him, and by four o'clock the attack had become general. Some of Sullivan's men were still not in place. The enemy's rapid approach threw his division into a panic and soon the whole line was giving way. Fortunately, Nathanael Greene arrived on the scene and with Sullivan's help managed to turn the rout into an orderly, if hard-pressed, retreat. It had been a bad day for the Americans, who suffered 1,000 casualties and were forced to move in the direction of Philadelphia. The capital could not be saved much longer.

The next few weeks following the defeat at Brandywine were bitter ones for John Sullivan. Members of Congress demanded his removal for what appeared to be poor performance at both Staten Island and Brandywine. Sullivan's most outspoken critic was Thomas Burke, of North Carolina, whose charges carried extra weight because he had been on hand and witnessed parts of the battle. Burke levied two major complaints against Sullivan—faulty intelligence and incompetent deployment of troops: he censured Sullivan for passing on Spear's inaccurate information to Washington and claimed the New Hampshire general had handled his troops badly in the battle. Both charges were unfair. Washington said that Sullivan was correct in relaying Spear's message, although possibly Sullivan should have attempted to evaluate the information for the commander-in-chief. There is a good chance, though, that the faulty information saved Washington from an embarrassing beating had he chosen to cross Chad's Ford to attack the British stationary force, for the British were far stronger than he had estimated. Burke's second complaint that Sullivan brought his men into action by a circuitous rather than a direct route had some basis of fact. But it may be said in Sullivan's defense that he did not know where the adjoining patriot forces were located at the time or the exact position of the attacking enemy. His reaction to events as they unfolded was logical and reasonable, but he lacked brilliance.

Congress, however, was more interested in finding a scapegoat on whom to blame the battle than in explanations. To the members, Sullivan looked like the logical man to be sacrificed. He had been consistently unlucky, had failed as yet to win a major victory, and had never endeared himself to the delegates in his earlier relations. Congress voted to recall the unhappy general until an inquiry could be made into his conduct, not of the Brandywine battle, but of the ill-fated Staten Island raid. Washington, fearful of losing one of his top officers, persuaded the politicians to delay Sullivan's recall until the military crisis in Pennsylvania had passed.

Washington's gesture on Sullivan's behalf brought the Irishman small consolation. Faced with an inquiry on Staten Island and with criticism for incompetence at Brandywine, Sullivan was thoroughly angered. He hoped Washington would speak favorably of his actions at Brandywine, and asked the commander-in-chief to come to his defense, but Washington demurred on the grounds that he had not been in Sullivan's sector. All he could say to comfort the irate subordinate was, "Some have condemn'd your disposition [at Brandywine] tho' time perhaps wd. not allow a better but none have accused you of want of bravery, and exertion, that I have heard of." [18] Sullivan's own reaction to the attack on his reputation was a pathetic whine: "I am the butt against which all the darts are levelled." [19]

In the midst of all this bickering came another battle, this time at Germantown, the site of Howe's main encampment.

Washington's army moved out on the night of October 3, 1777, and in four widely separated columns headed toward the enemy. Once again Sullivan had a major assignment, command of the right wing, but this time Washington accompanied him, probably to shield the unfortunate New Hampshire man from any further criticism. As the morning of October 4 opened, the Americans had some initial success, but then a variety of factors —fog, confusion, and lack of co-ordination—deprived them of the victory they desired so ardently. Instead of achieving the triumph which had been close at hand, the patriots had to tumble backward from the field of battle, and Sullivan's men retreated with the rest. Although the retreat in no way was Sullivan's fault, some insinuated that his division had been the first to quit the battle. This time, however, Washington was quick in coming to his subordinate's assistance and he silenced the critics.

While the repercussions over Germantown were still in the air, the inquiry on Staten Island was held. Sullivan was quickly cleared of any blame, and the members of the court unanimously agreed that the expedition had been well-planned and with better luck would have been a stunning success. With this favorable decision given some publicity, Sullivan found that criticism of his conduct at Brandywine began to abate. Now exonerated of any negligence, Sullivan joined Washington's men as they prepared for the harsh winter at Valley Forge during the remainder of 1777 and the early part of 1778. The second phase of Sullivan's military career had concluded. Although he continued to be somewhat cocky, his defeats had had a sobering effect. He was no longer what Benjamin Rush called him—"in the field a madman." [20] The third phase lay ahead, and it would be his best and most productive one, thanks to the caution Sullivan had learned from bitter experience. He was to gain the independent command that he had so eagerly sought. With this new responsibility would come a more able performance.

Although he changed his tactics on the battlefield, Sullivan remained as peevish as ever. At Valley Forge, he constantly pestered Washington for leave to go home to recoup his financial losses. When told he could not be spared, he complained that he still was hoping for an independent command. It was an unhappy John Sullivan who wrote to Washington:

> I Reallize my Command as high in The Army at the Same time Consider it as arising from mere Fortuitous Circumstances & not from any notice that has been taken of my Constant & faithful Services—In fact I have never yet had a post assigned me where there was Even a probability of Acquiring Honor Those posts are Either Reserved for older or for younger officers (more in favor Than myself) I have often Sensibly felt The Degrading prefference given to others & have Suffered it So far to operate upon me: That I am now unhappy in the Service—I am willing as heretofore to Live upon my own fortune in the Service a Campaign or Two Longer provided I can have an opportunity of putting my affairs in Such a Situation as will afford me the necessary Subsistance but if I might have my Choice it would be that Some more Suitable person Should fill my place in the Army & I be permitted to Retire.[21]

Washington finally had all he could take of Sullivan's complaints and gave way to the Irishman's pleas for a better post. From his commander-in-chief Sullivan got a choice assignment— command over the forces in Rhode Island in the spring of 1778. It was his first independent command since the debacle in Canada two years earlier. Soon Sullivan became the envy of the rest of the military, for he was destined to be the first American general to conduct joint operations with the new foreign allies, the French. "You are the most happy man in the World. What a child of fortune," wrote Nathanael Greene.[22]

Sullivan busily prepared for battle, writing frantic letters to the New England governors requesting troops and supplies. In gathering munitions for his expedition, he became so greedy that he roused the anger of General William Heath, commander of the Eastern Department at Boston. But Sullivan was determined to let nothing stand in his way. With the French in the fight, he had every intention of launching a devastating attack upon the

British in Newport. Visions of glory danced in front of him. The Comte d'Estaing's fleet, which had given up operations in New York waters, arrived off Newport on July 29 for action, but it was not until August 8 that Sullivan's forces were sufficient in number to begin the assault. Considering the short time at his disposal for building an army, Sullivan had done a commendable job. Now fortune seemed to be in his camp, for Washington had sent on veteran regiments under Greene, and the New England states had forwarded militia. To this land force were to be added D'Estaing's sixteen ships with 4,000 troops aboard. With all this military might converging on the Newport garrison that was cut off from help, Sullivan seemed assured of success.

Sullivan and D'Estaing had agreed upon a plan calling for the French to force the entrance to Narragansett Bay and to land north of Newport—a spot from which they could co-operate with the American forces. On August 8, 1778, the French moved into the channel between Conanicut and the island of Rhode Island, today called Aquidneck. Sullivan was supposed to cross from the mainland at Tiverton on August 10, the day the French were told to land. But when Sullivan discovered that the British had left their fortifications at the northern part of the island to pull back to Newport, he impatiently moved across a day earlier than planned, much to the annoyance of the French leader. D'Estaing, however, managed to keep up with the Irishman and landed some troops on the opposite side of the island on the same day. It looked as though the British were about to be caught in a vise.

Suddenly the customary Sullivan ill-luck occurred and brought a quick change to the scene. A British fleet appeared off the coast and D'Estaing, after hastily re-embarking his troops, put out to engage the enemy. Despite Sullivan's pleas that he wipe out the British garrison immediately, D'Estaing was adamant that the enemy fleet be disposed of first. On August 11, no sooner had the French dipped over the horizon in pursuit of the British than a storm lashed forth from the northeast, whipping not only the ships at sea but also Sullivan's tattered forces standing on Rhode Island. Once the storm had abated, word came that the French would sail for Boston to repair the damage to their ships rather than assist in the attack upon Newport.

Frustrated by the near victory that had eluded him, Sullivan lashed out at the new allies. He wrote a stinging letter to D'Estaing spelling out the ruinous consequences that would ensue if the French persisted in going on to Boston. Then after D'Estaing's ships did sail, Sullivan and his officers prepared a remonstrance accusing the French of not living up to their agreement to attack Newport. These foolish words may have soothed the frantic Sullivan, but they failed to bring back the French and did little to start the alliance off on a satisfactory course. Lafayette was irate because of the slanders against his fellow countrymen; Sullivan, however, was oblivious to the fact that he had been indiscreet.

Convinced at last that the French fleet was not going to return immediately, Sullivan gave his full attention to the campaign on land. His army had marched to Newport and placed the town under siege. He then had three alternatives: continue the siege, attack, or retreat. After talking the matter over with his officers, he decided to retreat from Newport and to continue the siege from a greater distance. There he would wait for D'Estaing's return.

Without the French, Sullivan seemed to have small hope of taking Newport; his retreat made sense. But he did not take into account one crucial factor: he failed to foresee what the enemy might do. The British had no intention of remaining bottled up. As Sullivan fell back to take up a new position at Butt's Hill, British redcoats and Germans clad in blue and yellow came out of their lines and advanced down two roads toward him. For the first time in his military career, Sullivan was to have over-all direction of a battle. At Long Island, Trenton, Princeton, Brandywine, and Germantown some senior officer had been present. Now he was on his own. In the fight that followed on August 29, Sullivan managed to repulse the enemy. But although

Sullivan bombastically claimed a complete victory, the losses on both sides were equal.

The stalemate could not last. When Sullivan learned that British reinforcements were sailing toward Newport, he wisely ordered an amphibious retreat. The withdrawal was beautifully executed and was completed under the cover of darkness without the loss of a single man, or any guns or supplies. He had not moved a moment too soon, for British reinforcements appeared on the scene the very next day. The new troops and the naval forces that accompanied them would have trapped Sullivan's men.

In the days that followed, Sullivan was at his worst. He sniped at the French, whom he felt had let him down. He also accused his suppliers of providing him with inadequate service and vented his wrath upon the commissary department under Jeremiah Wadsworth. Sullivan never hesitated to fight his own comrades when no British were about.

When spring of 1779 approached, however, Sullivan found that he had a new assignment to challenge his energies. Washington asked him to undertake a punitive expedition against the Indians in the Finger Lakes district of New York. Too often the savages had devastated the frontier settlements of Pennsylvania and New York, and the Wyoming and Cherry Valley massacres were fresh in the minds of many Americans. Retaliation became a necessity and the commander-in-chief decided to send some of his troops against the marauding Indians.

Washington's plan called for a two-pronged invasion of the land of the Six Nations. Sullivan, with three brigades and a regiment of artillery with small cannon, was to enter the redman's country from the south by way of the Susquehanna River and to march north. General James Clinton was to march along the Mohawk River and to turn south to meet Sullivan. Once joined, the two men would jointly carry out their assignment against the enemy. Washington's instructions to Sullivan were brief but to the point: destroy the Indian settlements and capture as many prisoners as possible. If any Indians sued for peace they were to

be told to attack Fort Niagara, the British stronghold to the
north, as proof of their loyalty to the American cause.

In May, Sullivan arrived in Easton, Pennsylvania, the starting
point for his expedition. This time he had every intention of
succeeding and caution dictated his every move. Unfortunately
he placed his needs too high. He wanted to have 3,000 men with
him, in addition to the guards and boatmen, although it was
estimated that the enemy numbered no more than 1,400 men.
His demands for men and matériel were insatiable, causing Alexander Hamilton to write: "General Sullivan appears to be very
anxious to have his supplies of every kind forwarded to him,
that he may begin his career—He is in his usual pother; but
dispatch is certainly very desirable." [23] In mid-June, Sullivan
was ready at last and marched toward Wyoming (Wilkes-Barre,
Pennsylvania), whence he planned to march into the territory
of the Senecas.

Some had hoped that the expedition would not tarry at Wyoming, but the careful Sullivan still felt his supplies were not
adequate. He refused to move on until he got what he wanted.
His long delay is hard to excuse. He should have started toward
the Seneca land long before he did, but instead he carped at his
suppliers and at the Board of War for insufficient support. Someone had to crack down on Sullivan, and Washington curtly told
him that his demands for more men were unreasonable.

It was the end of July before Sullivan finally moved out for
Tioga (Athens, Pennsylvania). With him were 2,000 men, 1,200
packhorses and 700 beef cattle. His numbers were to swell to
4,000 men when Clinton joined him. Certainly this was no light
expeditionary force trying to move swiftly through Indian country; it was a fully equipped army starting upon an invasion of
alien land.

At Tioga, Sullivan built a fort and waited for Clinton to arrive. Once Clinton had joined him on August 22, Sullivan set out
for one of the largest Indian settlements in the region at Newtown—a site near present-day Elmira, New York. It was here
that the Indians, with loyalist support, decided to make their

stand on August 29. The fight at Newtown showed that Sullivan was no longer the "madman" Benjamin Rush had dubbed him. Although he had overwhelming numerical superiority, he showed extreme caution and fought the unorganized redmen as though he were battling a formidable foe on a grand scale. The Indians offered resistance at first, but then thought better of it and fled. After entering Newtown, Sullivan razed huts, destroyed crops, and burned fields to deny the Indians food and shelter in the future.

The rest of the story is much the same: the story of a moving army, burning and destroying as it marched against no resistance. His army had one slight mishap when a small scouting party was ambushed and the two survivors were tortured by the Indians. Sullivan gained revenge by putting to the torch the Indian stronghold at Genesee (near Cuylerville, New York). Although he was now only fifty miles from the Niagara River, Sullivan did not push on toward Fort Niagara. Instead, he turned his army toward Tioga and began a long march back. On October 8, he reached Wyoming, where he took leave of his troops to report to Washington that his mission was finished.

Sullivan's campaign had accomplished much. His soldiers had destroyed more than forty Indian villages with their orchards and food plots, and he had seized more than 160,000 bushels of beans and corn. He had met and defeated the enemy once in pitched battle. If Sullivan had failed to take any Indians captive, or had caused few to sue for peace, he had significantly reduced their military strength for the time being. That winter the Indians were to suffer for lack of supplies, and not until 1780 were they able to resume their sporadic raids.

Ironically, Sullivan's most successful venture led to his retirement. He had complained and criticized once too often. His barbed remarks aimed at the Board of War during the Indian campaign had created powerful enemies. Members of the Board told Congress that the general's criticisms were unjustified. When Sullivan offered his resignation in November, 1779, citing poor health as his principal reason, he expected Congress to respond by giving him temporary leave. Instead, Congress accepted his resignation and Sullivan's military career came to a close.

He returned to Durham hoping to settle down to a quiet domestic life. But after his four-year stint in the army, he found it hard to sit still for long. In September, 1780, he entered the Continental Congress to serve as representative from New Hampshire for one year. All of his energy went into the war effort and the approaching problem of peace negotiations. His career as a legislator, however, was marred by the same mistakes he had exhibited as a military man. He showed bad judgment, for example, in accepting a loan from the French minister in Philadelphia, the Chevalier de la Luzerne. There is no evidence that the loan was ever repaid, or that it was intended to be. The French certainly looked upon the loan as an investment in gaining a voice in Congress. Although Sullivan never subordinated America's interests in legislation, he did show a marked partiality toward French policy. During this same time the British made an effort to woo Sullivan over to their side, using his captive brother, Daniel, as bait. Sullivan's behavior may have been somewhat strange with regard to these British moves, but in no way did he compromise the American position.[24] Nothing ever came of the British overtures.

In August, 1781, Sullivan headed back for New Hampshire bringing to an end his years on the national scene. He became an important figure in New Hampshire politics, acting as attorney general and holding three terms as president of the state in the late 1780's. Always a nationalist in his outlook, he helped put down New Hampshire's counterpart to Shays' Rebellion and gave his full support to the ratification of the Federal Constitution. Washington appointed him a Federal district judge in 1789, but he was unable to sit upon the bench beyond the spring session of 1792.

The few remaining years of his life were tragic ones. He rapidly deteriorated into senility either as a result of a nervous disease that grew progressively worse, or from excessive drinking, or both. He died at the age of fifty-five on January 23, 1795, and was buried in the little family cemetery on the knoll behind his home.

Sullivan's reputation as one of Washington's generals has paled with the passing of years partly because he never had a brilliant victory. Yet Washington always held a good opinion of this battling Irishman, and found him to be a loyal, albeit a difficult, officer. Sullivan never shirked his duty or sought an easy assignment. When given a mission he fought hard and gave his best. But too often his best was not good enough. Luck, which must accompany any successful military man, did not choose to march with John Sullivan.

FOOTNOTES

1. There were some, however, who argued that John Stark or Nathaniel Folsom would have been a better choice. See George W. Nesmith, "Services of General Sullivan," *Granite Monthly*, I, No. 11 (April, 1878), 325–30; Howard P. Moore, *A Life of General John Stark of New Hampshire* (Boston, 1949), p. 209.

2. Sullivan to John Adams, December 21, 1775, in Otis G. Hammond, ed., *The Letters and Papers of Major-General John Sullivan* (1930–39), I, 152.

3. Sullivan to John Adams, March 19, 1776, *Massachusetts Historical Society Proceedings*, XIV (1876), 284.

4. Sullivan to New Hampshire Committee of Safety, March 14, 1776, Hammond, *op. cit.*, I, 187.

5. Sullivan to Philip Schuyler, June 12, 1776, *ibid.*, 234.

6. Washington to President of Congress, June 17, 1776, in John C. Fitzpatrick, ed., *The Writings of George Washington* (1931–44), V, 152; hereinafter Washington's *Writings*.

7. Thomas Jefferson to R. H. Lee, July 29, 1776, in Edmund C. Burnett, ed., *Letters of Members of the Continental Congress* (1921–36), II, 28.

8. Joseph Reed to William Livingston, August 30, 1776, in Thomas W. Field, "Battle of Long Island," *Long Island Historical Society Memoirs* (Brooklyn, 1869), II, 397.

9. Since no records have been found limiting Putnam's command, Douglas Freeman assumes it "was real, and not merely titular." Douglas S. Freeman, *George Washington*, 6 vols. (New York, 1948–54), IV, 155n. Henry Knox wrote somewhat ambiguously that Putnam commanded on Long Island with a number of other

generals. Knox to Lucy Knox, August 26, 1776, Knox Papers, III, 28, Massachusetts Historical Society.

10. Edward H. Tatum, Jr., ed., *The American Journal of Ambrose Serle* (San Marino, California, 1940), p. 84.

11. Burnett, *op. cit.*, II, 70n.

12. C. F. Adams, ed., *The Works of John Adams* (Boston, 1856), III, 80–81.

13. Sullivan to Washington, February 9, 1777, Hammond, *op. cit.*, I, 315.

14. Sullivan to Washington, August 7, 1777, *ibid.*, 424; see also William Plumer, "John Sullivan," *New Hampshire State Papers*, XXI, 825.

15. Washington to Sullivan, March 15, 1777, in Washington, *Writings*, VII, 290–91.

16. Sullivan to John Hancock, October 6, 1777, in Hammond, *op. cit.*, I, 475–76; Freeman, *op. cit.*, IV, 476.

17. Freeman, *op. cit.*, IV, 476.

18. Washington to Sullivan, September 20, 1777, in Washington, *Writings*, IX, 242.

19. Sullivan to John Adams, September 28, 1777, in Hammond, *op. cit.*, I, 471.

20. Benjamin Rush, "Historical Notes of Dr. Benjamin Rush, 1777," *Pennsylvania Magazine of History and Biography*, XXVII, No. 2 (1903), 147.

21. Sullivan to Washington, February [?], 1778, in Hammond, *op. cit.*, II, 21.

22. Greene to Sullivan, July 23, 1778, *ibid.*, II, 103–04.

23. Hamilton to Nathanael Greene, May 22, 1779, Nathanael Greene Papers, V, No. 59, American Philosophical Library.

24. See Bibliography.

BIBLIOGRAPHY

Amory, Thomas C., *Daniel Sullivan's Visits . . . to General John Sullivan in Philadelphia.* Cambridge, Mass., 1884. Contains interesting information on the British attempt to win Sullivan over when he was in Congress in 1781.

———, *General Sullivan Not a Pensioner of Luzerne.* Boston, 1875. Argues that Sullivan was not in the pay of the French while in Congress.

———, *The Military Services and Public Life of Major-General John Sullivan.* Boston, 1868. This is the first biography and is of value for information on the family and for anecdotal material.

Cook, Frederick, ed., *Journals of the Military Expedition of Major General John Sullivan*. Auburn, N.Y., 1887. Contains many diarists' accounts of the march against the Six Nations. Should be supplemented by the Flick material listed below.

Flick, Alexander C., ed., "New Sources on the Sullivan–Clinton Campaign." New York Historical Association, *Quarterly Journal*, X, July and October, 1929.

———, *The Sullivan–Clinton Campaign in 1779*. Albany, 1929. Both of the Flick entries contain many valuable diaries and letters on the march against the Six Nations.

Hammond, Otis G., ed., "Letters and Papers of Major-General John Sullivan," 3 vols. *New Hampshire Historical Society Collections*, XIII to XV, 1930–39. This collection contains most of the Sullivan letters in existence, and is essential reading for understanding of the man.

New Hampshire Provincial and State Papers, 40 vols. Concord and Manchester, N.H., 1867–1943. This is an invaluable collection of source material for the history of New Hampshire in the early years.

Scott, Kenneth, "Major General Sullivan and Colonel Stephen Holland." *New England Quarterly*, XVIII, September, 1945. An interesting treatment of the British overtures to Sullivan in 1781, which suggests that Sullivan may have considered these overtures— a supposition which this author does not accept.

Whittemore, Charles P., *A General of the Revolution: John Sullivan of New Hampshire*. New York, 1961. A recent treatment of the general and contains a full bibliography.

Benedict Arnold:

TRAITOROUS PATRIOT

WILLARD M. WALLACE

Wesleyan University

FEW generals in the Continental army demonstrated greater qualities of leadership than Benedict Arnold, but not one proved, in the end, so disloyal. Arnold was an extremist in his actions, and his behavior has usually evoked a vehement response. Until his act of treason, men were always divided in their opinions of him; after it, his countrymen were unanimous in condemning him. Because of the disgrace into which he fell, his contributions to the patriot cause have often been forgotten or ignored. That the most perfidious traitor in American history should have rendered heroic service to the country he subsequently betrayed, has seemed incredible to many. Treason itself was a most shocking act to the Revolutionary generation. To none was this more so than to General Washington, who had given his trusted lieutenant command of West Point. Washington never recovered his former good opinion of Arnold, but the passing of time and the work of numerous scholars have now enabled people to appreciate the value of Arnold when he was loyal and to comprehend a little more clearly his defection, without condoning it.

Arnold was born on January 14, 1741, in Norwich, Connecticut. Descended from an early governor of Rhode Island bearing the same name, Arnold spent a lively boyhood, but one not unmixed with sadness and disaster. His father, likewise called Bene-

163

dict, had married a wealthy widow, Hannah Waterman King, whose family was among the local colonial aristocracy. All went well for a time with the Arnold fortunes. Then the elder Benedict Arnold overextended his mercantile ventures, lost heavily, and consoled himself at the local taverns, from which his young son often had to lead him home. While Arnold was attending school in Canterbury, yellow fever struck at his family. His mother, now deprived of all but two of her six children, and with her husband a heavy charge on her, bade Arnold constantly to keep in mind his duty to himself and his Maker.

With the family's fortunes declining, his mother was forced to withdraw him from school. Once home, the spirited boy frequently broke loose from parental control. His feats of strength, agility, and daring earned him a position of leadership among his peers. One Thanksgiving, Arnold and a number of other boys undertook to roll barrels from a nearby shipyard to the village green for a bonfire as a boyish prank. When the local constable interrupted the fun, Arnold offered to fight him on the spot. Instead of arresting him, the officer dragged the angry boy home to his mother.

Unable to handle the rebellious youth, his mother turned for assistance to her cousins, Daniel and Joshua Lathrop, graduates of Yale College. They ran one of the largest and most prosperous drug stores in eastern Connecticut and agreed to take the boy on as an apprentice. He remained with them for years, leaving on at least two occasions, however, to enter the army for brief terms of service during the French and Indian War. Arnold's mother died in 1759 and his father, two years later. Once his apprenticeship was completed, he sailed for Europe, bought large stocks of supplies, and set up an apothecary's shop in New Haven. He kept in close contact with the only surviving member of his immediate family, his sister Hannah, who became his able assistant.

But Arnold was not satisfied to remain a simple apothecary. Buying shares in a number of ships, he soon developed a lively trade with Canada, the West Indies, and Central America, and sailed as one of his own shipmasters. Like many merchants of the period, he resorted to smuggling in defiance of British customs laws and became a leader of the more radical political element in New Haven.

At the same time Arnold had a keen eye for respectability. He built a fine house, kept a small stable of horses, and dressed in the style befitting a gentleman. In appearance he was short but powerfully built, with black hair, dark skin, and light blue eyes. Before long he caught the eye of Margaret Mansfield, daughter of the sheriff in New Haven, and they were married in 1767. His wife soon bore him three sons—Benedict, Richard, and Henry.

Just prior to the Revolution, the Governor's Second Company of Guards was formed, a militia organization consisting of sixty-five New Haven "gentlemen of influence and high respectability." A vigorous man with a fiery and commanding presence, Arnold was a logical and successful candidate for the commission as captain. He made it clear from the outset that his company would not stand idly by should hostilities commence between the colonies and the Crown.

When news of the fighting at Lexington and Concord reached New Haven, Arnold started his company marching toward Cambridge within twenty-four hours. The selectmen at first refused his request for powder, but when he told David Wooster, who sought to intercede, that he would break open the powder magazine by force, the town fathers handed him the keys. "None but Almighty God shall prevent my marching!" Arnold had exclaimed when defied. As it happened, none did, nor Providence either.[1]

Arnold was eager for action while the American army lay inactive in the siege lines around Boston. He proposed to the Massachusetts Committee of Safety, in April, 1775, that he be empowered to capture Fort Ticonderoga, a strategic post rich in artillery and other military supplies. After several days of pondering, the Committee finally assented; the need of the army for siege guns and fieldpieces was too compelling. Arnold promptly left Cambridge for Ticonderoga, raising recruits as he went, largely from Massachusetts.

Unfortunately for his high hopes of accomplishing the feat alone, Arnold had revealed information about the war matériel at Ticonderoga to Colonel Samuel Parsons, another Connecticut officer. Parsons, upon his return to the Hartford area, discussed plans with several important politicians for a swift raid north, and soon Connecticut had its own expedition underway. Agents were sent into Vermont to mobilize more men, and Ethan Allen, leader of the Green Mountain Boys, was approached with the idea of commanding Connecticut's force.

Passing through western Massachusetts, the Connecticut group was joined by forty men with two officers who were to haunt Arnold for years to come. One was Major John Brown, an agile-minded, fast-talking lawyer who had recently been in Montreal and who also entertained the notion of capturing Ticonderoga. He was married to the sister of Arnold's cousin, Oliver Arnold, attorney general of Rhode Island, a man whom Arnold disliked intensely. The other nemesis was Colonel James Easton, a tavern-keeper who was neither gentle nor genteel.

At the Catamount Tavern in Bennington, where the Green Mountain Boys held forth with shouts and rum, both the Connecticut force and the small Massachusetts force under Arnold were surprised to find Ethan Allen raring to go against Ticonderoga. He, too, had an eye on the fortress, knowing that it was garrisoned by only a small detail of the 27th Foot under Captain William Delaplace. Apparently all Allen had been waiting for was some kind of authorization beyond his own impulse. He accepted the Connecticut commission, sent word out to the Boys, and presently led the Connecticut force and his own hard-drinking, quarrelsome fighters in the direction of the fort at the foot of Lake Champlain.

Arnold discovered to his chagrin that his authorization from the Massachusetts Committee of Safety meant nothing to Allen and that unless he could persuade Allen to relinquish command, the glory of the capture would be denied him. But arguing with

the Vermonter was like arguing with the north wind. The best
Arnold could do was to win an agreement from Allen that he
might accompany, but not command, the force. On May 10, the
Americans surprised the small British garrison, which yielded,
according to Allen, upon his demand "in the name of the great
Jehovah and the Continental Congress." Arnold was completely
ignored by the raucous Green Mountain Boys, who celebrated
their bloodless seizure of the fort by breaking open the garrison's
rum kegs and getting roaring drunk; or, as Allen euphemistically
wrote, his Boys "tossed about the flowing bowl."

Frustrated, Arnold presently encountered further humiliation.
In camp the Boys jeered him and even shot at him. When a report was prepared for the Massachusetts authorities, informing
them of the Ticonderoga conquest, Arnold engaged in a violent
quarrel with Colonel Easton who was to deliver the message.
Small wonder that Arnold found two captured British officers
better company than his own countrymen.

At length, however, more of Arnold's recruits arrived aboard
a schooner seized by Allen's men from a Tory proprietor. Because Arnold was an experienced seaman, Allen sent him to raid
St. Johns at the northern end of the lake and to seize a sloop
moored there. Arnold brought her back to Ticonderoga and
armed her. With the Green Mountain Boys disbanding, he was
gradually gaining control over the situation both at Ticonderoga
and Crown Point, which had also been taken. Allen was still
around to dispute the command, however, and the only point on
which the two men saw eye-to-eye was the necessity of invading
Canada.

While Arnold and Allen were in the midst of planning a Canadian invasion, Colonel Easton returned from his mission to
Massachusetts. Almost at once Arnold had another quarrel with
him because he felt Easton had done his best to diminish Arnold's
reputation while delivering the report. When Easton refused to
accept Arnold's challenge to a duel, the fiery Connecticut captain used the toe of his boot on the man. Presently Arnold was
gratified to see both Allen and Easton leave. Thereafter he pro-

ceeded with his plans for a Canadian invasion, specifying that there should be no Green Mountain Boys involved.

His period of gratification was limited. Colonel Benjamin Hinman arrived from Connecticut with a thousand men. Though Arnold refused to turn over his command, a Massachusetts committee arrived on the scene and ordered Arnold to place himself at Hinman's service. Arnold resigned and, in a fit of pique, discharged his men. His temper scarcely improved when many of his men were recruited by Easton, who had popped up again, with John Brown as his second in command. Arnold went off in a huff to Albany, where at the suggestion of General Philip Schuyler he dashed off a letter to the Continental Congress regarding the situation at Ticonderoga. He also began an accounting of his expenses for the Massachusetts Congress.

His experience in the Champlain area had been a bitter one. Granted that he was a hot-tempered person, impatient and restless, and that his behavior toward Easton was inexcusable, Arnold still had grounds for being angry at the shabby treatment he had received. Most of the men with whom he dealt had neither the legal authority nor the military insight he possessed. Some had cut his reputation to shreds behind his back in their presentations to the Massachusetts authorities and the Continental Congress. Barnabas Deane, who was on the scene, declared that Arnold had been "greatly abused and misrepresented by designing persons." Arnold, moreover, had been the unhappy victim of the rivalries between Massachusetts and Connecticut, both of whom were contending for the military honors of taking Ticonderoga. When Massachusetts acknowledged Connecticut's claims of supremacy on Lake Champlain, it is not difficult to understand Arnold's conclusion that the Bay Colony had renounced both him and its own authority. Since it was a humiliation he could not endure, he left. That it might have been even more honorable to remain than to depart seems not to have occurred to him.[2]

Arnold's stay in Albany was cut short by news of his wife's sickness. Hastening home, he found her already in her grave and his three boys in his sister's care. Hannah, in fact, had become a second mother to them. She had taken charge of Arnold's business affairs as well as his family, and when, on returning from Albany, he fell ill with a serious attack of the gout, Hannah nursed him through that, too.

Though not wholly recovered, Arnold rode up to Cambridge to settle his accounts with the Massachusetts Congress. Once again, he received questionable treatment. The authorities expressed dissatisfaction with a number of items, including Arnold's difficulty in accounting for sums he claimed to have expended from his own funds. They were willing to give him only about half of what he said he had spent. This amount was so far short of what Arnold expected that he turned his accounts over to Silas Deane, who reported them to the Continental Congress. After a careful scrutiny, the Congress refunded the balance to Arnold.

During the summer of 1775, Congress began planning a Canadian invasion. The main effort would be made by an army under General Schuyler, of New York, who was to seize St. Johns, Chambly, and Montreal, then move down the St. Lawrence to Quebec. When illness prevented Schuyler's participation, General Richard Montgomery assumed command and captured the three towns by early November.

But this drive was only one arm of a pincers movement; the other was a march through the rugged Maine wilderness to Quebec. Arnold, among other men, had drawn up a plan for such an expedition, and Washington proposed his name to Congress for the command. He was commissioned a colonel in the Continental army and began busily making preparations. His plan was to follow the network of waterways consisting of three rivers, the Kennebec, Dead, and Chaudière. Washington wrote Schuyler that Arnold would compel the British commander, General Carleton, to withdraw to Quebec, thus facilitating Schuyler's advance. If, on the other hand, Carleton remained at Montreal, Quebec would fall an easy mark for Arnold. To the delight of Arnold, who always did his best work in an independent capacity, Schuyler agreed to give him a free hand.

The wilderness march has been celebrated in historical narrative and fiction.[3] The march was a remarkable feat under incredibly difficult conditions largely occasioned by nature but complicated by the faulty construction of the wrong kind of craft for river navigation. In the annals of American military history, it still stands as a classic.

Arnold rose magnificently to the great trust Washington placed in him. Notwithstanding their dissimilarities in physical size, social background, experience, and disciplined character, both were energetic men capable of superb leadership. But even Washington's faith in Arnold could not compensate for the lateness of the season. Arnold went into a flurry of conferences, ordering bateaux built on the Kennebec, mustering guides and supplies, organizing a force of about a thousand men, and assembling ships to transport them from Newburyport to the Kennebec. The expedition, consisting of three rifle companies from Pennsylvania and Virginia and ten companies with muskets from New England, finally sailed. Arnold reached Gardiner on September 22, where he ordered a number of the green-lumbered bateaux rebuilt, and then went on to Fort Western. Once there, he divided his little army into four divisions, the leading division under the harsh but able frontiersman from Virginia, Captain Daniel Morgan, who was to make a road across the Great Carrying Place between the Kennebec and the Dead, and the rearguard under Lieutenant Colonel Roger Enos, of Vermont. By the twenty-ninth, all divisions had shoved off from Fort Western.

With cold weather coming early in Maine, Arnold pushed his men along. It was not easy, for the river was often shallow and rocky, and the bateaux, weighing 400 pounds apiece, had to be carried around numerous falls. Arnold retained his cheerfulness despite the shocking discovery that the bateaux were falling apart and many of the provisions were already ruined. At the Great Carrying Place, with the men's shoulders raw and blistered, downpours turned the portage into a sea of yellow mud. Some men drank the water and came down almost at once with nausea and diarrhea. Still resolute, Arnold lent a helping hand here and an encouraging word there. At the same time he wrote Washington, expressing the hope that the commander-in-chief would not be too critical of the slow progress made thus far. He wrote also to Schuyler, informing the New Yorker that they might be meeting soon at Quebec.[4] The Schuyler letter was given to an Indian named Eneas, who was presumed trustworthy; but the Indian delivered the letter to the British instead.

Although Arnold had sounded a note of optimism, subsequent developments proved his hopes for a swift trip were unfounded. The Dead River overflowed its banks in a torrential rain lasting three days. Bateaux foundered, units marching by land lost their way in the morass, and rations began running out. Arnold called his officers together to inform them he intended to push ahead to the Canadian settlements and bring back supplies. It is possible that had he remained, he might have prevented the desertion of Colonel Enos, who carried back most of what was left of the food with his rear division. As it was, if Arnold had not rushed across the Height of Land and down the roaring, rock-strewn Chaudière to send back bullocks and flour, the rest of the army would have starved to death. With game driven away by the weather and the passage of so large a body of troops, the exhausted, half-frozen, famished men were down to meals of boiled moccasins and a gruel of shaving soap. Many, in fact, were dying in the snow when food supplies arrived from Arnold in the nick of time. He personally saved the life of one young man, who, despite Arnold's infamy, testified later to the regard with which the soldiers held their leader. Another soldier spoke of the troops being "inspired . . . with resolution" by their commander's "firmness and zeal." [5]

Washington's gratitude was profound when he learned that Arnold had finally reached the St. Lawrence with more than 600 men. "It is not in the power of any man to command success; but you have done more—you have deserved it," he wrote Arnold. "My thanks are due, and sincerely offered to you," he con-

tinued, "for your enterprizing and persevering spirit." He wrote
Schuyler that Arnold's "merit" was "great." [6]

Warm as this praise was, Arnold would have been deserving
of more commendations had he been able to take Quebec. When
Eneas handed his letter to the British, however, reinforcements
came racing from Montreal in an effort to protect Quebec.
Though Arnold assembled canoes to cross the St. Lawrence, a
wild storm arose to prevent his crossing for three days. By the
time the river waters had calmed, reinforcements reached Quebec to strengthen the shaky garrison. Eluding two men-of-war
and their patrol boats, Arnold finally slipped his men into
Wolfe's Cove, paraded them before the walls, but could not persuade the British to come out and fight as Wolfe had done with
Montcalm sixteen years before.

Presently Arnold retired to Pointe aux Trembles, where he
waited for Montgomery. After having taken Montreal, Montgomery was deeply embarrassed by the departure of a large part
of his army for home because enlistments had expired. He
brought only 300 men to add to the Kennebec column, which he
admired for "a style of discipline . . . much superior to what I
have been used to see in this campaign." [7]

Though the combined columns moved back to Quebec, what
to do next became a troublesome problem. Carleton had reached
the city by ship, and his garrison was twice as large as the
American force. Smallpox had broken out among the Americans,
and the enlistments of many of Arnold's soldiers were to expire
on the last day of the year. The two leaders decided, therefore,
to attack the city on the first stormy night. To their relief snow
started to fall late in the afternoon of December 30, and in the
dark and stormy night that followed, the Americans launched
their attack. Montgomery was to lead a force against the lower
town from Wolfe's Cove and Arnold against the lower town
from St. Roque.

From the very start things went wrong. A deserter alerted
the British to the impending attack. Montgomery fell almost at
once, and his second in command refused to press the attack and

turned back. Arnold drove furiously against the British but went down with a bullet in the leg. Though burly Daniel Morgan took over and fought with great gallantry, he and hundreds of the troops, lacking the knowledge of the Quebec streets that Arnold possessed, were trapped and forced to surrender.

Now in sole command, Arnold refused to give up the siege. From his hospital bed he issued orders to keep the city under harassment. He dashed off letters to Washington and the Continental Congress, and appealed for assistance to his fellow Connecticut officer, General David Wooster, commanding the troops at Montreal. "I have no thought of leaving this proud town," he wrote his sister Hannah, "until I first enter it in triumph." [8]

It was not to be. True, he received recognition that delighted him. Wooster praised him, Washington sent congratulations and appointed him commander of a new regiment being raised, and Congress unanimously promoted him to brigadier general. But meager reinforcements, smallpox, and the lukewarm reception from the Canadians prevented him from doing anything decisive at Quebec.

When Wooster arrived on the first of April to take over the command, Arnold faced the humiliating prospect of again resuming a lieutenant's role. His horse solved the problem for him by slipping on the ice and mauling Arnold's game leg so painfully that he asked permission to withdraw to Montreal. Later he explained to Schuyler that had Wooster chosen to consult him about plans, he might have remained. [9]

At Montreal, Arnold was kept busy. He received a delegation from Congress whose aim was to bring the Canadians into an official alliance. This effort at diplomacy failed. Then Arnold plunged again into military affairs. When Wooster was succeeded by General John Thomas, who was subsequently forced to withdraw from Quebec, Arnold checked an attack on Montreal from the west by British and Indians. He carried out the evacuation of Montreal as the defeated and smallpox-stricken army began its retreat toward Lake Champlain. Ordered by the Congressional delegation to seize from the Montreal merchants whatever was needed to sustain the army, Arnold plundered thoroughly, though on a legal basis. He remained in the city until Carleton's fleet was sighted. Then, accompanied by young Captain James Wilkinson, he joined the new commander of the Northern army, General John Sullivan, at St. Johns. When the army subsequently withdrew in mid-June to Ile-aux-Noix, Arnold was the last to leave the Canadian shore. He accompanied the remnants of the shattered invading army as they retreated southward to Crown Point.

During the summer of 1776, as the British were preparing their thrust down the Lake Champlain corridor, Arnold was fighting legal, not military, battles. He was deeply involved in a court case rising over the plundering of the Montreal merchants for provisions and supplies. Many of these goods were ruined and stolen during the retreat from Chambly, where they had been sent, and Arnold was the officer held responsible. Colonel Moses Hazen, a Canadian who had wavered between the British and the Americans and finally chose the latter, had refused to take charge of the goods. At least this was the story given by one witness, Major Scott, who claimed that Arnold then had been forced to accept the responsibility. Charges and counter-charges flew back and forth; Arnold accused Hazen of laxness in allowing the goods to be stolen and Hazen charged Arnold with stealing from the Montreal merchants. Hazen ultimately insisted upon a court-martial to clear his name.

When the trial got underway, Arnold found himself in more difficulty than the defendant. The court refused to admit Scott, Arnold's principal witness, on the grounds that he was prejudiced. Arnold's hot temper boiled over. He protested the refusal as unprecedented and unjust, and dressed down the court members in scathing language. The court retaliated by demanding an apology, and Arnold refused, offering, instead, to give "any gentleman of the court the satisfaction his nice honor may require." [10] Court members responded by demanding Arnold's arrest.

The quarrel went through channels to the newly appointed

commander of the Northern army, General Horatio Gates, who sent the trial record on to the Continental Congress. In May, 1777, the Board of War, ruling on a charge that Arnold had plundered the Montreal merchants for his own gain, exonerated him. As to the demand for Arnold's arrest, Gates responded by dismissing the court. He explained to Congress, "The United States must not be deprived of that excellent officer's service at this important moment." [11]

The "important moment" to which Gates alluded, pertained to desperate American efforts to counter the British threat gathering in the north. With no roads the length of Lake Champlain, Carleton was putting together a fleet at the northern end to be manned by the Royal Navy. Arnold at an earlier date had stressed to Washington the need for building an American fleet on the lake. Washington approved, and appeals went throughout New England for woodsmen, carpenters, armorers, and crewmen. Gates placed Arnold in charge of the construction of the rowgalleys and gondolas at Skenesborough, and a flotilla put together with green lumber and armed with swivel guns and small cannon rapidly took shape.

Once the fleet was built and ready for action, Gates summoned Arnold to Ticonderoga to take command of it. The Connecticut general was ordered to sail down the lake, but he was given instructions to retire if the British appeared with a greater force. Arnold made an initial cruise in August and kept the British under surveillance during September. Discovery that the British not only matched his fleet but possessed heavier vessels with superior firepower was disturbing, though not dismaying, intelligence. As he appraised the situation, it appeared that a defensive effort would be his best course and that the most defensible position was not near Ticonderoga but between high, thickly wooded Valcour Island and the western shore. In several letters to Gates he explained the situation and his choice of the Valcour Island position, offering to return if Gates did not approve. Gates replied that he was gratified to learn that Arnold and the fleet "ride in Valcour Bay, in defiance of our foes in Canada." [12] By a stroke of irony Gates's letter was dated October 12, when Arnold's fleet had already suffered heavy casualties and was desperately trying to get back to Ticonderoga.

Carleton's fleet sailed south and engaged Arnold on October 11. Though Arnold's position was strong, the major British vessels, superior in every way except fighting heart, were too powerful for the Americans. Arnold fought a furious seven-hour battle, losing the schooner *Royal Savage* and the gondola *Philadelphia* and many casualties. In operating their guns, the Americans were exposed not only to the enemy fleet but also to the galling musketry of hundreds of Indians whom the British had landed on Valcour Island and the mainland.

That night, after the British drew off to refit and fog settled down over the lake, Arnold held a council of war and listened grimly to his captains' reports. Capture appeared inevitable. But Arnold was resourceful. He proposed to move southward that night between the British ships and the shore, each vessel showing a hooded lantern in the stern. Silently, like gray ghosts, the crippled American ships slipped through the dark waters. From out in the lake came the sound of hammers and saws as carpenters repaired the damage to the British fleet, while ashore the glow of campfires was visible and the Americans could hear the howling of the Indians as they anticipated the morrow's fight and the scalps they would lift.

Fortunately Arnold's maneuver proved successful, and, with morning, his squadron was clear of the enemy and on its way to Ticonderoga, which a number of ships reached safely. The breeze was light, however, and a few of the shattered vessels wallowed along in a half-sinking condition. Carleton caught up with them on the thirteenth off Split Rock. Lingering behind in his own row-galley, the *Congress,* to cover the retreat, Arnold fought a bloody rearguard action and ran his ship ashore rather than surrender. After setting fire to the *Congress,* he and the blood-stained survivors of his crew slipped through an Indian ambush and soon arrived at Crown Point.

Critics leaped on Arnold at once. He had lost the fleet, or at least eleven of the sixteen ships, and his action failed to prevent Carleton from seizing Crown Point and moving on toward Ticonderoga. But the great naval historian, Alfred Thayer Mahan, has pointed out that Arnold recognized that the purpose of a fleet is to contest control of the waters and to impose delay even if victory is impossible. Admiral Mahan, therefore, has defended Arnold's choice of the Valcour position. True, the British naval victory had been complete, but the sheer construction of the American fleet had long delayed Carleton's advance. Moreover, Arnold's fight had given some indication of the fierceness of the resistance Carleton might meet on land, resistance that might frustrate him until the snows arrived to put an end to campaigning. Carleton approached Ticonderoga, but declined to lay siege owing to the lateness of the season. He retired to Canada, confident that nothing could prevent the capture of Ticonderoga in the spring. It was a happy decision for the Americans because it may well have saved the young republic whose main army under Washington was suffering humiliating reverses in the New York campaign.[13]

The winter that followed was a stormy one professionally and emotionally for Arnold. John Brown, his old nemesis, dragged up a series of charges against him, claiming that Arnold had been guilty of "great misconduct" on the march through Maine, had attempted treason at Ticonderoga, and had lost the Lake Champlain fleet because of incompetence. Gates refused to countenance the charges, but he was obliged by regulations to send them on to Congress. Arnold's other enemy, Colonel Hazen, hauled him before a military court on a charge of slander and won a decision. Undoubtedly, however, the event that troubled Arnold most of all was the fact that he was on a mission in Rhode Island when the Battle of Trenton took place. Arnold hated missing the spirited attack. His personal life suffered as well. He sought the hand of Elizabeth Deblois of Boston, daughter of a Tory, and, to his chagrin, the girl rejected him.

His rebuffs were far from ended. Congress dealt his pride the greatest blow by promoting five brigadier generals, every one

junior to him, to the rank of major general in February, 1777.
Arnold, who was the oldest brigadier by date of commission in
the Continental army, was passed over. Congressmen explained
that in their voting they gave "due regard . . . to the line of succession, the merit of the persons proposed, and the quota of
troops raised, and to be raised, by each state." [14] Once again
political considerations had robbed him of military rewards due
him.

Washington was disturbed when he learned what had happened; he had not even been consulted. He wrote Arnold, bidding him do nothing hasty and acknowledging that the refusal
of Congress to promote him revealed "a strange mode of reasoning." [15] The commander-in-chief was in a delicate position in
view of his high regard for civil authority and his need of good
officers. A number of the latter were likewise so indignant at
having been passed over by Congress that they threatened to
resign. Arnold's case was so flagrant, however, that Washington
sought, on the one hand, to appease his scrappy little general
and, on the other, to find out from friends in Congress whether
the action was the result of accident or design.[16] He was no more
successful in getting a satisfactory answer to his inquiry than he
was in calming Arnold. The Connecticut officer considered the
action of Congress "an implied impeachment" on his character,
and was convinced that he had enemies in Philadelphia who had
worked against him. Hence he requested and received permission
to go to the capital to plead his case.[17]

How successful he might have been without additional considerations to support his cause is a matter of speculation. Many
congressmen undoubtedly shared the feelings of John Adams
who wrote his Abigail that he was "wearied to death with the
wrangles between military officers . . . scrambling for rank and
pay like apes for nuts." [18] But on the way to Philadelphia, Arnold
had the good fortune to perform a distinctive service. While he
was visiting his family in New Haven, the British landed near
Norwalk and raided Danbury, leaving it in flames. When Arnold
heard the news, he helped raise the countryside and harassed the

enemy's withdrawal. He lost one horse, had another wounded, and was nearly captured and killed. This valiant fight persuaded Congress to appoint him a major general on May 2. For some unexplained reason, however, his seniority was not restored.

Arnold was still indignant about the tardiness of Congress in settling his accounts for the Canadian campaign. The records were in wretched condition owing to the lack of finance officers, to the exigencies of the military situations, and to the loss of many of Arnold's papers on the lake. Brown, of course, had long been busy alleging that the discrepancies were explicable; "Money is this man's god," he said in a handbill published in Pittsfield on April 12, "and to get enough of it he would sacrifice his country." [19] Although Brown's crystal ball was working well for the future, it was evidently less revealing for the past. The Board of War cleared Arnold's character and conduct, and even John Adams confessed that the Connecticut man had been "basely slandered and libeled." [20]

However cordial Congress might appear, that body persisted in its refusal to restore his seniority. Arnold chafed mightily. Washington supported him loyally, pointing out to Congress that "he has always distinguished himself, as a judicious, brave officer, of great activity, enterprize and perseverance." [21] These kind words had no effect on Congress, and Arnold angrily resigned his commission in July, 1777.

But the very day he wrote his letter of resignation, Washington recommended Arnold as the logical officer to help General Schuyler in stopping the alarming advance of Burgoyne's invading army that had just captured Ticonderoga. This was too attractive an opportunity to miss. Arnold sought a suspension of his resignation, then hurried northward to assist Schuyler. After he was gone, Congress voted down a motion to restore his seniority. Some members of Congress questioned the propriety of a military man like Arnold having challenged the authority of the ruling civilian body.[22] For his part, Arnold never forgot or forgave the slights dealt him by the Continental Congress.

Upon his arrival at the Northern army headquarters, Arnold

had the misfortune once again to step into the middle of another rivalry between states. The army was composed mostly of New Englanders and New Yorkers, who mixed about as well as oil and water. There had been antagonism between the two in peacetime over conflicting land claims, and during the war the antipathy manifested itself in military circles by the Schuyler–Gates feud. Most New Englanders despised Schuyler and wanted Horatio Gates to be named commander. New Yorkers, on the other hand, backed Schuyler and wanted no part of Gates. Arnold had occasion to be grateful to both generals, but perhaps his recent experiences with Congress made him particularly sympathetic toward Schuyler, who was having similar difficulties.

From his initial task of slowing Burgoyne's progress through the woods toward the Hudson and Albany, Arnold presently left on a mission to the Mohawk Valley. As Burgoyne pushed southward, another force, composed of Tory regiments and Indians under Colonel Barry St. Leger, drove eastward from Fort Oswego on Lake Ontario and laid siege to Fort Schuyler. If the fort fell, the way would be open to Albany, where a junction with Burgoyne was to be effected. The post held out valiantly under Colonel Peter Gansevoort. An attempt by old General Nicholas Herkimer to relieve the fort ended when his Tryon County militia were ambushed in a thickly wooded ravine at Oriskany. Conditions soon becoming desperate at Fort Schuyler, Gansevoort slipped an officer through the enemy lines at night with an urgent plea to General Schuyler for help. When Schuyler called for a volunteer from among his officers to lead a rescuing expedition, none, least of all any of the New Englanders, offered to go— with one exception, Benedict Arnold.

The hazardous situation was one that Arnold met with a skillful blend of force and guile. He had fewer than a thousand men in his relief column, and there was no prospect of aid from the Tryon County militia, who had been thoroughly intimidated by their experience at Oriskany. On approaching the fort, Arnold halted. Among his prisoners was a man named Hon-Yost Schuyler, a distant relative of General Philip Schuyler, who was due to hang for his part in planning a Tory uprising. But Hon-Yost, besides being a Tory, was also a half-wit and well known to the Indians, who regarded him as being under the protection of the Great Spirit. When Hon-Yost's mother and brother pleaded with Arnold for Hon-Yost's life, Arnold said that he would spare him provided he went into the Indian camp and told the Indians that Arnold was coming with an enormous army. The Schuyler family agreeing, Arnold kept the brother as hostage and sent out Hon-Yost. First, however, he had the half-wit's coat shot full of bullet holes. To confirm Hon-Yost's information, and also to keep an eye on him, a friendly Oneida runner was dispatched behind him.

True to his word, Hon-Yost burst among the British Indians with his terrifying tale of near-capture by Arnold's overwhelming numbers. When the Indians asked just how many troops were coming with the dreaded American general, Hon-Yost pointed to the leaves on the trees. Staggered by the news, the Indians had scant chance to recover before the Oneida appeared with similar information, and then still another runner behind him. With whoops of dismay the Indians dashed for the woods, pausing only to drink up the British liquor and scalp a few Tory soldiers who straggled in the rush for safety. When Arnold, marching hard, came up to Fort Schuyler, he found the besiegers gone and the garrison as incredulous as it was joyful.[23]

Once back with the main army, Arnold discovered that Burgoyne's German troops had lost at Bennington and that Gates, who had replaced Schuyler, was a less congenial commander than the New Yorker. In fact, trouble between Gates and Arnold was not long in developing. During the first battle between Burgoyne's army and that of Gates at Freeman's Farm on September 19, the two American generals had a difference of opinion over the kind of battle that should be fought. Gates, who had fortified his lines, was content for the most part to wait behind a protected position for the British to approach. The impetuous Arnold favored an attack upon the enemy in front of the American lines. In the initial stages of the battle that followed, Gates allowed Arnold to lead some troops on the left wing against the British and to engage the enemy considerably ahead of the American breastworks. But as the battle progressed, Gates grew cautious, refused reinforcements, and restrained Arnold by ordering him to remain in the rear at main headquarters. Arnold was furious because he was confident that if he had received reinforcements, he could have delivered a decisive victory.[24]

Arnold's indignation, already simmering, really boiled over as a result of two other incidents. He learned that a number of troops had been removed from his command without his knowledge and he was apprised of the fact that Gates had not given credit to his division in the battle report on Freeman's Farm that was sent to Congress. Arnold at once bulled his way into Gates's headquarters, and a bitter argument ensued. When the Connecticut general, unable to contain his anger and disgust, requested permission to leave the area, Gates deprived him of his command for insubordination.[25]

Arnold, on sober second thought, was reluctant to leave with the showdown with Burgoyne imminent. Instead, he hung around camp, sulking in his tent and complaining to his aides, who were former aides to Schuyler. When Burgoyne made his last effort against Gates at Bemis Heights, on October 7, Arnold was thus without a command. Though the Americans had such superiority of numbers and fought so valiantly that there was little likelihood of a British victory, the outcome was still in doubt as the late afternoon wore to a close. Gates, whose headquarters was two miles from the scene, had little actual control over what was happening in the field.

The situation was too much for Arnold. Striding restlessly back and forth in front of his tent, the frustrated officer listened to the roar of the battle and fired impatient questions at his aides, who were trying to keep him informed of the progress of the fighting. News of the indecisive nature of the contest suddenly infuriated him. Forgetting his pique as well as the fact that he had no official command, he ordered his horse saddled and galloped to the sound of the guns.

His appearance at first startled, then exhilarated the troops. Regiment after regiment broke into cheers as the bay mare with its blue-coated rider dashed to the front. Seeing a Connecticut brigade moving up, Arnold waved his sword in response to their cheers and shouted, "God bless you! Now, come on boys, if the day is long enough, we'll have them all in hell before night!" He led them in two furious assaults, and the second momentarily broke the enemy's center. When the British rallied, Arnold slid to the right, picked up two more brigades, and stormed the enemy's line again. Reinforced, the redcoats held fast.

Arnold now swung his horse to the left and spurred between the two armies under a hail of British lead. Finding the Connecticut brigade again, he swept a force of Canadians and Indians out of a number of cabins in front of a powerful German redoubt guarding Burgoyne's right flank. If this redoubt could be taken, the flank would be uncovered and Burgoyne would have to withdraw from the field. Fortunately a force was at hand, Daniel Morgan's crack riflemen and two regiments in support. Dashing up to them, Arnold pointed his sword at the redoubt. The men greeted him with a shout and followed him in a fierce charge against the position. Though the Germans fought hard, the American pressure was so severe that the defense finally crumbled. Arnold, a torrent of troops behind him, burst into the entrenchments.

But at the very moment of victory, the mare went down before a storm of bullets, and a German soldier fired point-blank at Arnold. The little general fell, severely wounded in the same leg that had been hit at Quebec. "I wish it had been my heart," he said bitterly to the stretcher party that quickly reached him. Perhaps more than any single officer he had been responsible for the decisive American success that day. Ten days later, without further action, Burgoyne capitulated; and the triumph brought France to the side of the young republic.[26]

From this point on, Arnold's career with his countrymen ran downhill, and at a steadily accelerating pace. Though Congress restored his seniority in grade shortly after Burgoyne's capitulation, the action came too late to save his pride. Furthermore, he was crippled for life, one leg shorter than the other, a sharp blow indeed for a man who was a remarkable athlete and gloried in physical prowess. With Arnold's wound only partially healed, Washington appointed him commandant of the city of Philadelphia, which the British had evacuated in June, 1778.

All of Arnold's vanity and pride came to the fore in his new command. It was not simply the duties of the assignment that were responsible, it was also because of his marriage to Peggy Shippen. Margaret Shippen was the youngest of the three vivacious, fun-loving daughters of Edward Shippen, a prominent jurist whose cousin, William Shippen, was surgeon general of the Continental army. Like many of the Philadelphia girls, Peggy had greatly enjoyed the dances and parties that had enlivened the British occupation. When Sir Henry Clinton took the British army back to New York, Philadelphia became something of a social desert for these girls. Peggy especially missed Captain John André, a handsome young staff officer, who had paid her a good deal of attention. Arnold met the restless Peggy at a party during the summer and lost his heart to her. She, in turn, was impressed by the virile charm of the wounded hero, yet neither she nor Judge Shippen was enthusiastic when Arnold sought her hand in marriage. Arnold was so persistent in his wooing, however, that Peggy finally succumbed; and the judge assented, somewhat hesitantly, to the marriage. The wedding took place in early April of 1779, with Arnold's leg still so weak that he had to be supported by a soldier during the ceremony. At the time he was thirty-eight years old; Peggy, eighteen.

Though marriage into one of Philadelphia's leading families brought Arnold great social status, in his pursuit of Peggy and his attempts to keep her in the style to which she was accustomed, he was forced to live far beyond his means. Hard-pressed, he developed a number of money-making schemes, most of them of a dubious character. These included speculating in real estate, trying to get hold of property belonging to Tories who had fled from the city, issuing a pass to a ship in which he subsequently

invested contrary to a regulation of the Pennsylvania authorities, and using government wagons to save his own property
from capture. Arnold's enemies were not slow in pointing to the
impropriety of his actions. Of enemies, moreover, he had no lack,
particularly within the Council of Pennsylvania, which as a
civilian political body deeply resented any military authority.
The radical patriots within both the Council and the Continental
Congress criticized him likewise for his lavish entertaining and
his association with Tories. Finally the Council preferred charges,
and Arnold, on Washington's advice, demanded a court-martial.
Though Arnold defended himself vigorously, the court-martial
refused to clear him of two charges, issuing the pass and using
government wagons, and it sentenced him to receive a reprimand
from Washington. The commander-in-chief, in April, 1780, accordingly pronounced Arnold's conduct with respect to the pass
"peculiarly reprehensible" and with respect to the wagons, "Imprudent and improper." [27]

Stung though he was by the reprimand, Arnold already had
been sufficiently hurt and angered by the spring of 1779 that
in May he had opened negotiations with the British. Why he
should have committed treason must remain a matter of speculation. That the financial reward was an inducement is beyond
doubt; Brown had been at least partially correct in his prediction
that money meant much to Arnold. But there were other motivations. He was deeply humiliated, affronted, and angered by
the treatment he had received at the hands of the Massachusetts
Congress, the Continental Congress, and the Council of Pennsylvania. There is no doubt, moreover, that he considered himself
unappreciated and deserted by his own countrymen, in whose
service he had been crippled. A man of greater moral stature
might have been able to take this treatment in stride, but not
Arnold. For that matter, few generals had escaped criticism—
even Washington was subjected to caustic comments from officers and politicians concerning his military capacity. But though
there were hot words, grumbling, some resignations, and a few
dismissals, outright treason of a gross nature was the exception

among higher officers.[28] It is possible, too, that Arnold mistrusted the French alliance; certainly after the treason he said this was so. Even if one grants this possibility earlier, it is difficult to be certain how potent an influence it was in his decision. A conviction of betrayal by his countrymen, injured pride, and avarice were probably the principal motivations for his treason.

One is on surer ground in conjecturing about his wife's involvement and influence. For years Peggy's innocence was freely conceded by Arnold's worst enemies. Recent research, however, has revealed that she both knew of his negotiations and aided him with them.[29] She may have merely confirmed his will, but the admiration she acquired for the British during the occupation and the friendships she developed were not likely to lead her to discourage her husband's disgust with his own compatriots.

The story of Arnold's betrayal of the American cause is a fascinating one.[30] Through a number of intermediaries, a long correspondence ensued with John André, who remembered Peggy from the British occupation of Philadelphia. Now serving as adjutant general of the British army and Sir Henry Clinton's intelligence chief, André understood the value of a defection as important as Arnold's. Yet if Arnold was cautious, so was Clinton. As a pledge of Arnold's sincerity, Clinton wished the Connecticut general to bring about the surrender of a sizable force. Arnold saw his chance to do so by securing command of West Point, which he proposed to surrender for £10,000. Washington temporarily disconcerted him by offering him the left wing of the army—an opportunity for fame and action that would have delighted him in earlier years. Hastening to plead his physical incapacity, he was given the West Point command instead.

To complete the details of the surrender of West Point, André left New York on September 20, 1780, for his clandestine meeting with Arnold. General Clinton, in the meantime, was laying plans for a swift move up the Hudson. When the sloop *Vulture* from which André landed was forced by an American battery on Tellers Point to drop down the river, the decision was made for André to return to the British lines by land. He was carrying in his pocket a pass from Arnold and in his sock documents for Clinton written by Arnold. Captured on the way back by irregulars, André was turned over to American authorities when the documents were discovered. Luckily for himself, Arnold was apprised of the capture in time to dash to the *Vulture* in his barge. André subsequently went to his death as a convicted spy and Arnold passed out of American service.

The traitor received ample rewards from the British for his defection. He was given a commission as a British Provincial brigadier general, with solid footing as a cavalry colonel in the regular establishment, whose half-pay he drew after retirement for as long as he lived. Full pay as a colonel amounted to £450 a year, while as a Provincial brigadier he drew an additional £200. Though Arnold had failed to bring about the surrender of West Point and its garrison, Clinton granted him the full £6,000 that André had been commissioned to offer, plus £315 as expense money. The former Connecticut businessman at once invested £5,000 of the capital sum with the Court bankers for £7,000 in consolidated annuities at 4 per cent. The British likewise rewarded his family. In 1782, the King authorized an annual pension of £500 for Peggy. Each of Arnold's children by Peggy— and there were five who survived—received a pension of £100, while Arnold's three young sons by Margaret Mansfield were given commissions in the British army with half-pay as long as they should live. The Crown subsequently awarded the traitor and his family a total of 13,400 acres from among its lands in Canada reserved for American Tories.[31]

Generous as the British were to Arnold, they never completely trusted him as an officer in their service. Though he conducted a raid into Virginia and led the tragic expedition to New London, the British declined to give him an important command. After Cornwallis' surrender at Yorktown, Arnold took his family to London, where he encountered both respect and contempt but found no employment. Presently he moved to Canada—to St. John, New Brunswick—and entered the shipping business. The transplanted Tories in St. John hated him. On one occasion they blamed him for a fire that destroyed his warehouse, accusing him of wanting to collect the insurance, even though he was out of the country at the time.

Eventually Arnold moved his family back to London and tried to secure a command when the war with revolutionary France broke out. Denied a chance at another military career, he traded with the West Indies, where he was well thought of, and invested in privateering ventures which turned out badly. Rejected once again in his request for military service, he died in 1801, forlorn and almost forgotten in Britain.[32] His wife outlived him by only three years, but had the satisfaction of seeing her children started in respectable careers in which they were to attain a mild fame. Arnolds have performed well since then, and a number have risen to high rank in Britain's subsequent wars, including the Second World War. If none has achieved such military importance as their ancestor, the tireless and deadly "Dark Eagle" as the Indians called him, none has put self-interest or injured pride before honor.

FOOTNOTES

1. For Arnold's early life, see Willard M. Wallace, *Traitorous Hero: The Life and Fortunes of Benedict Arnold* (New York, 1954), pp. 5–37; James Thomas Flexner, *The Traitor and the Spy* (New York, 1953), pp. 3–19; Malcolm Decker, *Benedict Arnold, Son of the Havens* (New York, 1932), pp. 1–33; Isaac N. Arnold, *The Life of Benedict Arnold*, 3rd ed. (Chicago, 1897), pp. 15–36.
2. For Arnold's part in the seizure of Ticonderoga and his subsequent experiences in the Champlain area with Allen and others, see Wallace, *op. cit.*, pp. 37–54; Flexner, *op. cit.*, pp. 41–58; Justin H. Smith, *Our Struggle for the Fourteenth Colony*, 2 vols. (New York, 1907), I, 107–92; John Pell, *Ethan Allen* (London, 1929), pp. 74–108; *Collections of the Connecticut Historical Society* (Hartford, 1860), I, 165–88.
3. The best accounts are: Kenneth Roberts, *March to Quebec, Journals of the Members of Arnold's Expedition* (New York, 1947); Justin H. Smith, *Arnold's March from Cambridge to Quebec* (New

York, 1903); John Codman, *Arnold's Expedition to Quebec*, 2nd ed. (New York, 1901).

4. Arnold's letters to Washington and Schuyler, both dated October 13, 1775, may be found in Roberts, *op. cit.*, pp. 70–73.

5. *Ibid.*, pp. 301, 347–48, 552.

6. For Washington's letters to Arnold and Schuyler, both dated December 5, 1775, see John C. Fitzpatrick, ed., *The Writings of George Washington*, 39 vols. (Washington, D.C., 1931–44), IV, 147, 148. Hereinafter cited as Washington, *Writings*.

7. Montgomery to Schuyler, December 5, 1775, in Peter Force, ed., *American Archives*, 9 vols., 4th series (Washington, D.C., 1837–53), IV, 189. Hereinafter cited as *American Archives*.

8. Arnold to Hannah, January 6, 1776, in Roberts, *op. cit.*, p. 109. For the Quebec assault, see Arnold's letters of December 31, 1775, and January 2, 1776, in *ibid.*, pp. 102–06. See also, for letters of January 6 and 14, *American Archives*, 4th series, IV, 589, 674, and Carleton's report in *ibid.*, p. 656. For other accounts see Smith, *op. cit.*, II, 113–47; Allen French, *The First Year of the American Revolution* (Boston, 1934), pp. 614–20; and North Callahan, *Daniel Morgan, Ranger of the Revolution* (New York, 1961), pp. 100–08.

9. Arnold to Schuyler, April 20, 1776, in *American Archives*, 4th series, V, 1098–100.

10. *Ibid.*, 5th series, I, 1273.

11. Gates to John Hancock, September 2, 1776, in *ibid.*, 5th series, I, 1268.

12. The Arnold–Gates correspondence may be found in *ibid.*, 5th series, II, 440, 481, 591, 1015.

13. For Admiral Mahan's opinions, see *The Major Operations of the Navies in the War of American Independence* (Boston, 1913), pp. 13–26. For other accounts, see Christopher Ward, *The War of the Revolution*, John Richard Alden, ed., 2 vols. (New York, 1952), I, 393–97; Gardner W. Allen, *A Naval History of the American Revolution*, 2 vols. (Boston, 1913), I, 161–79; Wallace, *op. cit.*, pp. 110–20.

14. Gaillard Hunt, ed., *Journals of the Continental Congress*, 34 vols. (Washington, D.C., 1904–37), VIII, 132–33; hereinafter, *Journals of Cont. Cong.*

15. Washington to Arnold, March 3 and April 3, 1777, in Washington, *Writings*, VII, 234, 352–53.

16. Washington to Richard Henry Lee, March 6, 1777, in *ibid.*, VII, 251–52.

17. Arnold to Washington, March 14 and 26, 1777, in Jared Sparks, ed., *The Writings of George Washington,* 12 vols. (Boston, 1835), IV, 345–46.

18. Charles Francis Adams, ed., *Familiar Letters of John Adams and His Wife Abigail Adams during the Revolution* (New York, 1876), p. 276.

19. Carl Van Doren, *Secret History of the American Revolution* (New York, 1941), p. 159.

20. *Journals of Cont. Cong.,* VII, 372–73, VIII, 372–73, 382; Adams, *op. cit.,* p. 276.

21. Washington, *Writings,* VIII, 47–48.

22. The motion to restore Arnold's seniority was defeated sixteen to six, and Congressional comment was bitter, pro and con. Henry Laurens, of South Carolina, who thought "the reasoning upon this occasion was disgusting," said that Arnold was rejected "not because he was deficient in merit or that his demand was not well founded but because he asked for it and that granting at such an instance would be derogatory to the honour of Congress." See E. C. Burnett, ed., *Letters of Members of the Continental Congress,* 8 vols. (Washington, D.C., 1921–36), II, 585, 442, 445.

23. For the relief of Fort Schuyler, see Wallace, *op. cit.,* pp. 141–44; Flexner, *op. cit.,* pp. 163–67; Ward, *op. cit.,* II, 489–91.

24. Arnold's part in the action on September 19 is discussed in Hoffman Nickerson, *The Turning Point of the Revolution* (Boston, 1928), pp. 308–16, 473–77; Flexner, *op. cit.,* pp. 170–73; Ward, *op. cit.,* II, 504–12, 941–42; Wallace, *op. cit.,* pp. 146–48, 326–32.

25. Differing views of the Arnold–Gates quarrel may be found in Samuel W. Patterson, *Horatio Gates* (New York, 1941), pp. 159–63, and Wallace, *op. cit.,* pp. 149–53. For an especially sharp criticism of Arnold's role in the whole campaign ending at Saratoga, see Lynn Montross, *Rag, Tag and Bobtail: The Story of the Continental Army, 1775–1783* (New York, 1952), pp. 217–27.

26. Accounts of the action on October 7 may be found in Nickerson, *op. cit.,* pp. 356–68; Ward, *op. cit.,* II, 526–31; Flexner, *op. cit.,* pp. 180–84; Patterson, *op. cit.,* pp. 166–68; Wallace, *op. cit.,* pp. 1–2, 154–59.

27. For Arnold's courtship of and marriage to Margaret ("Peggy") Shippen, his commercial transactions, and his troubles with civilian authorities, see Wallace, *op. cit.,* pp. 162–92; Flexner, *op. cit.,* pp. 217–53; John C. Miller, *Triumph of Freedom, 1775–1783* (Boston, 1948), pp. 530–35; Van Doren, *op. cit.,* pp. 168–93; Arnold, *op. cit.,* pp. 222–64.

28. The most comprehensive study of treason during the Revolution is the excellent monograph by John Bakeless, *Turncoats, Traitors and Heroes* (Philadelphia, 1959).

29. Wallace, *op. cit.*, pp. 193–259.

30. See the accounts by Van Doren, *op. cit.*, pp. 193–371; Flexner, *op. cit.*, pp. 253–393; Wallace, *op. cit.*, pp. 193–259. See also Sir Henry Clinton, *The American Rebellion*, William B. Willcox, ed. (New Haven, 1954), pp. 214–18, 462–66.

31. Arnold's rewards are discussed in detail in Wallace, *op. cit.*, pp. 261–63, 365–66.

32. For Arnold's career after the treason conspiracy, see Willcox, *op. cit.*, 235–37, 243–44, 250–55, 276–78, 482–83, 505–06, 565–67; Arnold, *op. cit.*, pp. 329–98; Van Doren, *op. cit.*, pp. 371–88; Flexner, *op. cit.*, pp. 356–65; Wallace, *op. cit.*, pp. 260–309; J. G. Taylor, *Some New Light on the Later Life and Last Resting Place of Benedict Arnold and His Wife Margaret Shippen* (London, 1931).

BIBLIOGRAPHY

Callahan, North, *Daniel Morgan, Ranger of the Revolution.* New York, 1961. A biography of the officer closely associated with Arnold in the Quebec and Saratoga campaigns.

Clinton, Henry, *The American Rebellion*, William B. Willcox, ed. New Haven, 1954. A biased treatment, but of great value, by the British commander-in-chief, with discussions of Arnold's treason and his service in the British army following his defection.

Flexner, James T., *The Traitor and the Spy.* New York, 1953. A remarkably interesting, unique, tri-cornered study (despite the dual title) of Arnold, André, and Peggy Shippen, containing a good deal of original information.

Nickerson, Hoffman, *The Turning Point of the Revolution.* Boston, 1928. The most competent account of the Saratoga campaign, with a careful evaluation of Arnold's role.

Roberts, Kenneth, ed., *March to Quebec, Journals of the Members of Arnold's Expedition.* New York, 1947. A compilation of journals, some written on a daily basis under the most trying conditions, that makes fascinating reading.

Smith, Justin H., *Our Struggle for the Fourteenth Colony*, 2 vols. New York, 1907. A detailed and objective history of the attempt to acquire Canada, with attention to Arnold's early efforts on Lake Champlain, his march through Maine, and his subsequent experiences in Canada.

Van Doren, Carl, *Secret History of the American Revolution*. Garden City, 1941. Contains a superb close analysis of Arnold's treason, with the inclusion of the Arnold–André correspondence.

Wallace, Willard M., *Appeal to Arms: A Military History of the American Revolution*. New York, 1951. A useful one-volume history of the war.

————, *Traitorous Hero: The Life and Fortunes of Benedict Arnold*. New York, 1954. The most complete Arnold biography of recent years.

Benjamin Lincoln:

OLD RELIABLE

—•—

CLIFFORD K. SHIPTON

American Antiquarian Society

BENJAMIN LINCOLN as a soldier had all the traditional virtues of a New Englander—reliability, sobriety, and common sense. He took both victory and defeat in his limping stride, for he participated in the great victories at Saratoga and Yorktown, and, between them, had the dubious distinction of surrendering the Southern army at Charleston. After the Revolution he served with wisdom and success against Shays' rebels. Fat, lame, and undramatic, he has been neglected by historians who are naturally attracted by more dashing men.

He was born the son of Colonel Benjamin and Elizabeth Lincoln, of Hingham, Massachusetts, on January 24, 1733. The Colonel was a farmer and maltster by trade, but held an important political office on the colony's Council. After receiving "a good common education," young Benjamin took to farming for a living and prospered enough to marry Mary Cushing, of Pembroke, in 1756. The next year he was elected town clerk, an office his father and grandfather had held before him. He followed his father's footsteps in military as well as political circles. Appointed an adjutant in Colonel Lincoln's militia regiment, the Third Suffolk, he eventually worked his way up in the ranks to succeed his father as commander.[1]

With the advent of the Revolutionary War crisis, he took a

much stronger Whig position than most Hingham inhabitants, and this gave him much more influence than his native ability might have won for him. He served on the town's Committee of Safety and was sent as the Hingham representative to several provincial congresses. In October, 1774, he was elected commissary by the Massachusetts Provincial Congress.

In his new position, Lincoln pressed for the reorganization of the militia and helped to replace Tory officers with reliable Whigs appointed by the governor and Council. When fighting broke out, he mustered the Second Suffolk regiment on April 19 and marched to Cambridge. But on the news that the British regulars had retired into Boston, he left the regiment and rode up alone to take his place in the Provincial Congress.

At Watertown, Lincoln was promptly chosen muster master of the army of Massachusetts. By July he had been appointed president of the Provincial Congress, the chief executive post in the rebel government. When that Congress transformed itself into the General Court, Lincoln was elected to the Council. During the winter of 1775–76, he went home to make saltpeter and to strengthen popular sentiment. In May he headed a town committee which instructed the representatives to support independence if Congress declared it.

In 1776, Lincoln had his first taste of combat. The Council appointed him major general, and co-operating with Artemas Ward, who commanded the Continental forces in Massachusetts, he broke the blockade of the port of Boston, on June 13, 1776, by driving off H.M.S. *Renown*. After the Battle of Long Island, the General Court ordered him to take a draft of militia by way of Rhode Island to reinforce the army in New York. On Washington's orders he conferred with Governor Trumbull about attacking Long Island, but the situation of the commander-in-chief became critical before the assault could be mounted. Lincoln joined the Continental forces and commanded the right wing at the Battle of White Plains on October 28, 1776. Then, while the armies moved to winter quarters, he hastened back to Providence to get more militia.

In January 1777, Lincoln arrived at Peekskill and led the right wing in Heath's attempt to recapture Fort Independence. When this movement failed, he crossed the Hudson, and on February 11, led the first of his regiments into Washington's camp. General Charles Lee, who didn't like deacons in uniform, accused him of trying to prevent the sending of Massachusetts militia to join Washington,[2] but the commander-in-chief, although he didn't like other deacons, had no such doubts about this one. Writing to Congress about Lincoln, he said:

> I should not do him justice were I not to add that he is a Gentleman well worthy of Notice in the Military Line. He Commanded the Militia from Massachusetts last Summer . . . much to my satisfaction, having prov'd himself on all occasions an active, spirited, sensible Man. I do not know whether it is his wish to remain in the Military Line, or whether, if he should, any thing under the Rank he now holds in the State he comes from, would satisfy him; how far an appointment of this kind might offend the Continental Brigadiers I cannot undertake to say.[3]

Congress decided to ignore the feelings of the other generals, and on February 19, 1777, appointed Lincoln a major general in the Continental line.

The new general was stationed at Bound Brook, New Jersey, the post nearest the British army. At daybreak on April 13, 1777, a force under Cornwallis made a sudden attack. The American outposts ran without giving the alarm, and the British were within 200 yards of Lincoln's headquarters before he was warned. He mounted and galloped to rally his force; one of his aides who was a little slower in mounting was captured. Lincoln gathered his men, got them off before two converging columns of the enemy could close, and took up a position in a valley in which he could present a narrow front. Cornwallis ate his luncheon in the Bound Brook headquarters, and then retired to Brunswick taking Lincoln's baggage with him. The American general returned and ate his dinner as usual at headquarters.

Other generals experienced far worse defeats in the north,

where the evacuation of Ticonderoga so angered the New England leaders that they wrote to congressmen saying that the quota of militia called for by the Northern army could not be raised unless Lincoln was appointed to command it. Washington had already made up his mind to the same end, and had written Schuyler telling him he was sending Lincoln to command the militia:

> This Gentleman has always Supported the Character of a judicious, brave, active Officer, and as he is exceedingly popular and much respected in the State of Massachusetts . . . he will have a degree of influence over the Militia, which cannot fail being very advantageous. I have destined him more particularly to the command of them, and I promise myself it will have a powerful tendency to make them turn out with more cheerfulness, and to inspire them with perseverance to remain in the field.[4]

Washington might have added, as others did, that Lincoln had "gained the love and respect of all men" with whom he had served, and that his division was sorry to see him leave.[5] No one ever suggested that he was a brilliant soldier or a good judge of men; his popularity rested on his obvious integrity, and that was what the Northern army needed now that suspicions were being voiced that Schuyler was dealing with the enemy.

In July, 1777, Lincoln took up his station at Manchester, Vermont, rallied the fleeing inhabitants, served as contact between the army and the New England governments, and organized the militia as it came in. On the news of the Battle of Bennington he marched to join Stark, arrived after the fighting was over, and sent out three columns of militia which cut Burgoyne's lines of communication with Canada. He did this without informing his superior, Gates, lest news of the movement be intercepted.

In September, Lincoln joined Gates at Stillwater, where as second in command he led the right wing. During the Second Battle of Saratoga on October 7, he commanded the defensive works. That night he led out the force sent to relieve the troops who were holding the ground gained during the day. The next morning he led a reconnoiter which, considering the conflicting reports later circulated, had better be described in his own words:

> I entered an open cart path, which led through the wood, rode in it some distance, and did not discover any troops till I turned an angle in the road. Then a body of men opened to my view. At first, I could not distinguish them by their dress from our own troops, two of them having scarlet clothes, others being in blue, (the Hessian uniform), and some being clad like our militia. A few of our men, two or three in a company, had British uniforms taken in a prize; the other Continental troops were in blue, while our militia resembled in dress the people of the country who had joined the army. In this state of uncertainty I continued my route until I was within a few yards of them so near as perfectly to discover my error. As soon as the enemy perceived this, and that I was checking and turning my horse, I saw the two in British uniform present and fire.[6]

A ball shattered his right ankle. He exclaimed, "The rascals have struck me," [7] and rode back. The enemy could easily have captured him, but fearing that he was a decoy, did not follow.

Lincoln was carried to Albany, where part of the broken bone had to be cut out. Three months later he was taken home on a couch in a sleigh. For several years the wound kept breaking open and pieces of bone working out; when it healed the leg was two inches shorter than the other. Washington presented him and Arnold with "shoulder and sword knots" in recognition of their wounds and service. In September, 1778, Congress sent him to command in the Southern Department, where what was needed was not a brilliant soldier but a man who could gather and control the militia; any pitched battle was sure to be a disaster.

Lincoln arrived at Charleston on December 4, 1778, and set himself to the task of organizing an army. When he heard that the great British force which had sailed from New York had landed in Georgia, he started down to halt their northern advance, but the commanders in the upper country on whom he called for assistance could not help because their forces were being pinned down by loyalist companies. Still more frustrating, he reported to Washington, was the unco-operative spirit of the state government:

> I found . . . that the army, to use Major General Howe's own words, "has been in a state of abject dependence on the civil authority." Indeed the continental officer, commanding in this department, had not had it in his power, from the want of supplies which he could controul, to march the troops, without the consent of the President of South Carolina, however urgent the necessity. —I hope things will be better settled, and that I never shall be driven to the hard necessity of altercating with the civil power.[8]

Only three days later that hard necessity presented itself. He had requested President Lowndes to instruct the keeper of the state arsenal to issue arms and supplies to the North Carolina Continentals who had just arrived, and had been told:

> His Excellency cannot think of delivering these stores while this State is in so precarious a situation with respect to the enemy . . . it would be betraying a trust reposed in him to do it; —they were purchased for the defence of this State—it would never do to leave themselves defenceless— No: he would deliver them, should he receive an order of Congress for it.[9]

Besides this lack of co-operation, he complained, he was hindered by the vice and corruption which had sprung up during the war to such a degree that if the Americans were saved it would not be because of their merit.

Lincoln had hoped to invade East Florida, but the small forces he could raise could do no more than occupy upper Georgia. Even here he met with disaster, for at Brier Creek on March 3, 1779, the incompetence of General Ashe cost the Americans an estimated third of the Southern army. Instead of placing the blame on "that good man," where it really belonged, he sheltered Ashe from the wrath of his countrymen.[10] The Georgians, less charitable, hated him for a century.

Once more building up his army, Lincoln again moved into Georgia in April, 1779. General Prevost evaded him and made a feint toward Charleston which he turned into a serious invasion when he found a great part of the population neutral or friendly. Lincoln got there before him and formed a junction with the forces under Governor Rutledge and General Moultrie. Their combined force was greater than that of the British and loyalists, but the spirit was weak. A council, in which Governor Rutledge and a majority of the members of the upper house of the South Carolina legislature participated, authorized negotiations with Prevost on the basis of an agreement that the state stand neutral for the rest of the war. Before anything could be accomplished in this direction, Lincoln brought up his forces and compelled Prevost to retire to an island in the harbor, where he attacked him and could have captured his army had promised reinforcements come up.

Prevost escaped to Savannah, but Lincoln reported to Congress that his own troops were melting away and unless there were immediate reinforcements from the North there would soon be no army. Knowing that little would be done in this direction, he asked and received, in June, 1779, permission to retire and relinquish the command to Moultrie. However, that general and the Council of South Carolina unanimously asked him to remain; reluctantly he consented.

It is hard to see why General Lincoln was so popular in the South. He was not a romantic figure, for his weight was usually around 224 pounds, and it sagged. He was so methodical that he accomplished much with little inconvenience or hurry, and thus gave the impression of sloth. His manners were of a kind more common in New England than the South, for he was pious, and he always frowned on profanity and impropriety; he was temperate, frugal, and an early riser. He had no use for military affectations of honor, and refused to be provoked into duels. Once when a quarrelsome officer tried to goad him at headquarters table, he said coldly:

> I apprehend, Sir, you are disposed to take too much liberty. If you repeat any thing of this kind, I shall be obliged to tell this company facts, which I know respecting you, that will make their hair stand on end.[11]

This was enough to silence that officer. Of his military personality, there is much testimony like this:

> His composure and self-possession, his exemption from any apparent weakness or folly, uniform discretion and integrity made him revered, whilst the goodness of his disposition, and his frank and cordial manners, engaged affectionate regard. He knew how to exercise command without exciting aversion. Paying deference to the rights and feelings of others, whether present or absent, his own were not likely to suffer injury or insult. . . . By an expressive look, which was understood, by an anecdote, by pleasant irony, or more directly, he was sure to notice and to repress any symptoms of impertinence or rudeness which might show in his presence.[12]

Much of the civil war which the South was then suffering was waged, on both sides, more for plunder than for patriotism. But Lincoln did his best to suppress this "licenciousness" even at the risk of alienating the militia support which he so desperately needed. Denouncing both the cruelty and political stupidity of plundering, he insisted that individuals who collected Tory goods "forfeit them to the public." Equally troublesome at times was the social consciousness of the Southern officers. In the Northern army a militia captain might be a cobbler who would cheerfully repair the shoes of his men, but one of Lincoln's South Carolina captains was haled into a court of inquiry for "ungentlemanly Behaviour in associating with a private Soldier." [13] Because physical labor was the badge of the black man, the general found it very difficult to get his soldiers to work on the defenses which were everywhere necessary, and by way of setting an example, he would spend whole days with the work details, sometimes handling pick and shovel himself. Considering the climate and his weight, this was heroism. He could also be brutally hard when necessary; he ordered the instant hanging of a colonel apprehended in the act of riding out to the enemy with plans of the Charleston fortifications in his pocket.

When D'Estaing landed before Savannah in September, 1779, Lincoln marched at once to join in the siege. The count hoped to conquer Georgia for France, and in dealing with Prevost he

said, "I apprise your Excellency that I have not been able to refuse the army of the United States uniting itself with that of the
King," and he demanded the surrender of Savannah "in the name
of the King of France." [14] Lincoln firmly protested this attitude
and insisted on being the spokesman for the allies. Prevost had
asked D'Estaing for permission to send the women and children
out of the city, but Lincoln tartly informed him that this was
only a transparent play for time, and that the blood of the civilians would be on the head of the British command. For this he
was denounced in the British press like "Beast Butler" of another
generation.

When it became apparent that Savannah could not be reduced
by siege, the allies planned an assault, which was promptly betrayed to the British. In the dark of the morning of October 9,
1779, Lincoln and D'Estaing led the main column, which in the
face of a withering fire fought its way through the abatis and
planted two standards on the parapet, but a second column led
by Count Dillon lost its way in the dark. After D'Estaing had
been twice wounded and Pulaski killed, the allies withdrew.
Because of the season the French fleet had to leave the coast, and
Lincoln sadly retired toward Charleston. A lesser man would
have blamed the count for the disaster, but Lincoln's report to
Congress was eminently fair:

> Our disappointment is great, and what adds much to our sense of
> it, is the loss of a number of brave officers and men. . . . Count
> D'Estaing has undoubtedly the interest of America much at heart,
> this he has evidenced by coming to our assistance, and his constant
> attention during the siege; his undertaking to reduce the enemy by
> assault, when he despaired of effecting it otherwise; and by bravely
> putting himself at the head of his troops, and leading them to the
> attack. In our service he has bled; I feel much for him, for while
> he is suffering the distress of painful wounds, he has to combat
> chagrin.[15]

Back in Charleston, Lincoln resumed the effort to get the state
to support the Continental effort. In vain he tried to get the

Assembly to permit the enlistment of Negroes, the draft of militia to fill the Continental battalions (general practice in the North), and the placing of the militia when in the field under the Continental articles of war. For fear of smallpox, masters refused to send their slaves to work on the fortifications, so the general himself spent every day from dawn to dark on the works. The Assembly made Governor Rutledge dictator and then dissolved, but Lincoln could get no more co-operation from the governor than from the legislature.

In February, 1780, Sir Henry Clinton had landed a great army and begun a slow advance toward Charleston. Lincoln had small hope of withstanding a siege, but he knew that if he withdrew the Continental forces to the up country, the state would make a separate peace. He had with him a large surplus of experienced Continental officers whom he might have sent away, but he still had some faint hope that the Carolinians would rally and send militia who might be placed under their command. He waited too long, and the officers were trapped with him when Clinton arrived before the town in April.

Lincoln rejected the first summons to surrender, but within two weeks failing food supplies compelled him to offer to evacuate the town if given a ten-day truce in which to withdraw his army; naturally the British rejected his proposal.[16] When word of this got out, a delegation of citizens appeared before the Council and informed the general that if he attempted to withdraw the troops and leave them to the British, they would cut up his boats and open the gates. After this there was nothing to do but make the best terms possible. On May 9, Clinton again demanded that the town surrender, but Lincoln replied that the proposed terms were inadmissible. The next day the civilians asked him to accept the British terms. The militia, meantime, seeing the flags passing back and forth, decided that it was all over, abandoned the defensive works, and straggled into town. Lincoln had himself been in the front lines night and day, and had not taken his uniform off for two weeks. When he dragged himself back into town he met the lieutenant governor and the

Council who joined in the demand that he surrender. Now he could only accept the inevitable. An amused British officer reported the events of the next day:

> The Lincolnade was acted on the 12th of May. General Leslie, with the Royal English Fusileers and Hessian Grenadiers, and some Artillery, took possession of the Town, and planted the British Colours by the Gate, on the Rampart, and Lincoln limp'd out at the Head of the most ragged Rabble I ever beheld. . . . They were indulged with beating a Drum, and to bring out their Colours cased. . . . The Militia, poor Creatures, could not be prevailed upon to come out. They began to creep out of their Holes the next Day.[17]

It was reported that the militia promptly took the oath of allegiance to the King and happily marched off with Cornwallis. When the news of the "Lincolnade" reached the back parts of South Carolina, one regiment of militia seized their officers, marched into Charleston, and surrendered them to the British.[18] Hundreds who had refused to serve under Lincoln flocked to enlist in the loyalist regiments, and some of the most trusted members of the Council who had worked with him now became willing collaborators with Sir Henry Clinton. The amused British reported that nothing could equal the hatred which the Carolinians now showed for the northern rebels, whom they blamed for misleading them.

It is an amazing fact that none of this hatred rubbed off on Lincoln as it did on Ashe. Francis Bowen, who was the last historian to read the voluminous Lincoln correspondence, declared that it did not show one word of reproach or complaint leveled against him by the Carolinians, indeed not even an insinuation that he had shown injustice, partiality, neglect, or incompetency.[19] Equally amazing is the fact that Lincoln never excused his defeat by pointing out the contrast between their lack of co-operation with him and their quick turn to loyalism. In later years when these Carolinians sent their sons to Harvard, it was Lincoln whom they asked to look after them.

Paroled and back in Philadelphia on June 23, 1780, Lincoln

asked for a court of inquiry to investigate his conduct at Charleston, but no one ever showed any interest in such a procedure. At the Harvard commencement a month later, when Benjamin Lincoln, Jr., took his M.A. in course, the general was voted an honorary degree. There were no qualifications to his welcome in Massachusetts; even so ardent a Whig as William Gordon urged that there was no better person than Lincoln to be the first governor under the new constitution.[20]

He had no political ambitions, however, and in September he was at Elizabethtown with the British Major General Phillips, negotiating a general exchange of prisoners which would release them both from their parole. When this was achieved, Washington wrote kindly to Lincoln:

> I am of the opinion, that your influence and exertions in procuring the State's quota of Troops for the War, providing funds for the subsistance of them, and Magazines, will be of infinitely more importance in your own State this winter, than it can be to become a mere spectator, or fellow-sufferer of hunger and cold . . . which I expect the small remains of our Army will have to encounter in a very short time, and more than probably to contend with during the winter. But at the same time I give this as an opinion; I leave you at full liberty to pursue the bent of your inclination and judgment.[21]

Lincoln spent the winter in Massachusetts, and in June, 1781, joined Washington's army on the North River. His first assignment was to cut off Delancey's loyalist regiments then at Morrisania, but they took alarm and escaped. In July, he tried in vain to draw the British out of their fortifications around New York. When in August word arrived of the opportunity to corner Cornwallis at Yorktown, Lincoln led the southward dash of the army. Six weeks later he opened the trenches before the town, and during the siege he commanded the allied right. On November 19, it was he who conducted the British garrison of Yorktown through the allied army drawn up in two lines to the field of surrender. The terms of capitulation were substantially those imposed upon him at Charleston the year before. Throughout the negotiations he was very careful not to "mortify" the conquered. Then he led the army back to the Hudson.

The system of committee management of the departments of the Federal Government had failed, and while Lincoln was busy at Yorktown he was appointed the first Secretary of War. The appointment was an excellent one, for more than anyone else he enjoyed the confidence of the army officers, who were bitter at what they considered to be the neglect of Congress. While most politicians were ardent supporters of the interests of their economic groups or geographical areas, Lincoln had more perspective. He felt keenly the situation of the poor debtors who had claims against the United States, but he also saw that their interests would not be served in the long run by policies which destroyed the public credit.[22] He spent two uncomfortable years in Philadelphia waiting for the peace which would permit him to resign. As he sat in his office, he pondered the preceding years and came to the conclusion that although the war had hurt his generation more than the British economic policy which had brought it on would have done, his children would reap the benefits. He did not share Washington's antipathy for the loyalists, but urged Massachusetts to encourage the return of all but the most recalcitrant. When he met returnees like Ward Chipman, he greeted them kindly and over a bottle of wine gave them the news of their Boston friends.[23] In October, 1783, Lincoln resigned from the War Office and returned to civilian life in Hingham.

With the outbreak of Shays' Rebellion in 1786, he was forced to don his uniform once more. Governor Bowdoin appointed him commander of the Massachusetts militia, one obvious reason being his popularity in the western part of the state as the result of his services in the Saratoga campaign. On January 20, 1787, he marched from Boston to relieve General Shepherd who was holding the arsenal at Springfield. As he rode through the snow with his plodding column, Lincoln watched curiously the expressions on the faces he passed, and at the first stopping place he reported back to Bowdoin:

There is now in this part of the Country a fine field for the sporting
fancy of the Physiognomist, to range in: I never had any knowledge
of the art, but since I left your Excellency, if I read truly, I have
seen in many countenances the open smile of approbation and the
most perfect good wishes that Heaven would prosper us, while in
others a sullen anxiety marked every line of the faces, and they
seemed to mutter a wish, that destruction might over take us. These
however are few, and I think we shall in general receive the kindest
welcome.[24]

And how did the people of that day see General Lincoln?

He was about five feet nine inches in stature, and of so uncom-
monly broad person, as to seem to be of less stature than he was.
His gray hair was combed back from his forhead, unpowdered, and
gathered in a long queue. His face was round and full, his eyes blue,
and his complexion light. He was usually dressed in a blue coat, and
light under clothes, and wore a cocked hat. . . . His speech was with
apparent difficulty, as though he were too full. The expression of
his countenance was exceedingly kind and amiable. His manner was
very gracious. . . .[25]

The most significant quality of the Hingham Cincinnatus at
this time was his entire lack of the usual military pomp, prolixity,
and tediousness. When he spoke it was with brevity, and often
with gentle wit. He liked people, particularly young people, and
he concerned himself with their personal problems. He delighted
in children, and they loved him in turn. Perhaps his most famous
characteristic was his somnolency:

This was not occasioned by age, but was constitutional. In the
midst of conversation, at table, and when driving himself in a
chaise, he would fall into a sound sleep. While he commanded the
troops against the Massachusetts insurgents, he dictated dispatches,
and slept between the sentences. His sleep did not appear to disturb
his perception of circumstances that were passing around him. He
considered this an infirmity, and his friends never ventured to speak
to him of it.[26]

As Lincoln plodded westward through the bitter January
weather, he pondered the disadvantages under which he acted.

Chief of these was the fact that he moved under civil authority, so that when he came up with the insurgents he could, unless they fired upon him, do no more than read the Riot Act, upon which they could quietly disband to come together in some other place. He had a vision of marching around, Riot Act in hand, until his troops collapsed from exhaustion and the insurgents quietly took over the western counties. Fortunately Shays did not see this opportunity. On January 25, 1787, he sent Lincoln proposals that both armies should disband and all proceedings against the insurgents be suspended until the people could have a proper hearing before the General Court.[27] The general replied that he had no authority to compromise, and urged the rebels to submit. On January 27, he reached Springfield and without stopping to rest his exhausted troops, crossed the Connecticut and scattered the insurgents on the western side while another column of his army proceeded up the river on the ice.

Having thus cut the rebellion in two, Lincoln sat down at Hadley on January 30, 1787, and wrote to Shays:

> Whether you are convinced or not of your error, in flying to arms; I am fully persuaded that before this hour, you must have the fullest conviction upon your own minds, that you are not able to execute your original purposes. Your resources are few, your force is inconsiderable and hourly decreasing, from the disaffection of your men; you are in a post where you have neither cover nor supplies, and in a situation in which you can neither give aid to your friends, nor discomfort to the supporters of good order and government. Under these circumstances you cannot hesitate a moment to disband your deluded followers. If you should not, I must approach and apprehend the most influential characters among you. Should you attempt to fire upon the troops of government, the consequences must be fatal to many of your men the least guilty.[28]

When this message failed to produce a mass surrender, the general tried to divide the insurgents by offering to intercede with the government for any privates who might lay down their arms. To the representatives of the towns who came to him asking mercy for the insurgents, he replied that he felt keenly for the distress of those unhappy and misled men who were in arms against their country, and that in his effort to reclaim them without bloodshed he had hitherto restrained his troops from firing; the decision to shed blood would be made by Shays.[29]

This did not mean that Lincoln would not try to capture or scatter the insurgents without bloodshed, and on the night of February 3–4, 1787, he struck at their headquarters at Petersham. His own account is the best:

> At 8 o'clock, our troops were in motion; the first part of the night was light, and the weather clement, but between 2 and 3 o'clock in the morning, the wind shifting to the westward, it became cold and squally, with considerable snow: The wind arose very high, and with the light snow that fell the day before, and was falling, the paths were soon filled up, the men became fatigued, and they were in a part of the country, where they could not be covered in the distance of eight miles, and the cold was so increased that they could not halt in the road to refresh themselves. . . . We arrived here about nine o'clock, exceedingly fatigued by a march of 30 miles, part of it on a deep snow and in a most violent storm. When this abated the cold increased, and a great part of our men are frozen in some part or other. . . . We approached this town nearly in the centre where Shays had covered his men; and had we not been prevented by the steepness of the hill, and the depth of the snow, from throwing our men rapidly into it, we should have arrested very probably one half his force, for they were so nearly surprised as it was, that they had not time to call in their out parties, or even their guards.[30]

Having broken up the eastern army of insurgents, Lincoln moved quickly to the west. Setting up his headquarters in Pittsfield, he sent mobile parties in every direction, apprehending or disarming those who had "made an improper use of their arms." By February 20, he could report that the former rebels were hourly coming in to submit, and he pointed out to Bowdoin that a mild policy would check the flight of others from the state. The governor of Vermont agreed to disarm the refugees who might make trouble, and on Lincoln's request Governor George

Clinton led a body of New York militia nearly to the line in order to co-operate. There were still many armed insurgents hovering on the borders, many of them wishing to return and submit but still capable of throwing the whole region into civil war. Only Lincoln's "delicately Cautious" policy, as Bowdoin described it, prevented this and trouble with the other states. Writing of the impending trial of the captured insurgents before the Supreme Judicial Court, the general said:

> I hope they will [be merciful] and do it with a grace, and that she may evidence a disposition to forgive and to embrace Cordially those who are forgiven To regain the affections of the deluded and to bring them to order and to esteem government.[31]

In March, Lincoln was appointed by the General Court to head a commission that went through the insurgent regions, where it set at liberty most of the prisoners and collected the few ringleaders who were to be tried. There were still dangerous rebels in Vermont and New York, and Bowdoin asked Congress to commission Lincoln as an officer of the United States so that he might hunt them down, but fortunately this did not become necessary. On June 10, the general was allowed to resign his special commission, but he continued to serve as major general of the Suffolk militia.

In postwar politics, Lincoln's influence was not great because his attachment to Washington made the Hancock party suspicious of him. When the Constitution of the United States began to operate, the President appointed him the first collector of the Port of Boston. He also served the Washington administration as commissioner plenipotentiary to negotiate a peace with the Indians of the South, and, in 1793, to treat with the Western Indians at Sandusky. President Adams considered appointing him commander-in-chief, so naturally the Jeffersonians did not make use of his services. In 1809, he resigned the office of collector while under political fire, and on May 9, 1810, he died in the house in which he was born.

FOOTNOTES

1. Family manuscripts in the Massachusetts Historical Society contain some of Benjamin Lincoln's military commissions.
2. New York Historical Society, *Collections*, 1872, p. 273.
3. John C. Fitzpatrick, ed., *The Writings of George Washington*, VI, 408.
4. *Ibid.*, VIII, 459.
5. Timothy Pickering, October 22, 1777, in Pickering MSS, V, 59, Massachusetts Historical Society; hereinafter, Mass. Hist. Soc.
6. Francis Bowen, "Life of Benjamin Lincoln," in Jared Sparks, *The Library of American Biography*, 2nd series, XIII, 262.
7. Mass. Hist. Soc., *Collections*, 3rd series, VI, 284. Ebenezer Matoon's contradictory account apparently confuses the events of the seventh and the eighth.
8. Benjamin Lincoln, Letter Book, December 19, 1778, Mass. Hist. Soc.
9. *Ibid.*, December 22, 1778.
10. *Ibid.*, March 3, 1779.
11. Mass. Hist. Soc., *Collections*, 2nd series, III, 251.
12. *Ibid.*
13. *South Carolina Historical and Genealogical Magazine*, XVI, 179.
14. Bernhard A. Uhlendorf, *The Siege of Charleston* (Ann Arbor, 1938), p. 173.
15. Mass. Hist. Soc., *Collections*, 1st series, II, 180.
16. The documents exchanged during the siege are printed in *The Siege of Charleston* (Albany, 1867), p. 91 ff.
17. *Ibid.*, pp. 129–30.
18. *New York Royal Gazette*, June 8, 1780, 2/3; June 17, 2/4; July 1, 3/2.
19. Francis Bowen, *op. cit.*, pp. 352–53.
20. Mass. Hist. Soc., *Proceedings*, LXIII, 440.
21. A. J. Bowen, *Fifty-Five Letters of George Washington* (New York, 1907), p. 28.
22. Benjamin Lincoln to Artemas Ward, September 13, 1782, in Artemas Ward MSS, Mass. Hist. Soc.
23. Essex Institute, *Historical Collections*, LXXXVII, pp. 216–17.
24. Shays MSS, January 21, 1787, Mass. Hist. Soc.
25. William Sullivan, *The Public Men of the Revolution* (Philadelphia, 1847), p. 128.
26. *Ibid.*, p. 129.

27. The originals of this and a number of other key documents are in the Shays MSS, Mass. Hist. Soc.
28. Hartford *American Mercury,* February 5, 1787, 3/2–3.
29. Knox MSS, February 1, 1787, Mass. Hist. Soc.
30. Hartford *American Mercury,* February 12, 1787, 3/3–3.
31. Knox MSS, March 1, 1787, Mass. Hist. Soc.

BIBLIOGRAPHY

Adams, James T., *New England in the Republic 1776–1850.* Boston, 1926. Has a brief account of Lincoln's part in quelling Shays' Rebellion.

Alden, John R., *The South in the Revolution, 1763–1789.* Baton Rouge, 1957. Contains a short but accurate survey of Lincoln's southern campaigns.

Bowden, A. J., *Fifty-Five Letters of Washington to Benjamin Lincoln 1777–1779.* New York, 1907. A calendar of some interesting letters exchanged between the two generals.

Bowen, Francis, "Life of Benjamin Lincoln," in Jared Sparks, ed., *The Library of American Biography.* Boston, 1864, 2nd series, XIII, 205–434. Provides one of the longer and more complete accounts of Lincoln's life.

Lawrence, Alexander A., *Storm Over Savannah.* Athens, Georgia, 1951. Describes Lincoln's role in the Savannah campaign with Comte d'Estaing in 1779.

Nickerson, Hoffman, *Turning Point of the Revolution.* Boston, 1928. Highlights Lincoln's contribution to the victories in the Saratoga campaign.

Thacher, James, *Military Journal During the American Revolutionary War.* Boston, 1827, pp. 400–10. One of the earliest biographical sketches of Lincoln.

Uhlendorf, Bernhard A., ed., *Siege of Charleston.* Ann Arbor, 1938. Lincoln as seen through enemy eyes during the Charleston campaign.

Marquis de Lafayette:

EAGER WARRIOR

HOWARD H. PECKHAM

William Clements Library

OF THE twenty-nine major generals who served during the American Revolution, few were more devoted to the commander-in-chief than the Marquis de Lafayette. Certainly no one drew more expressions of affection from the forbidding dignity of George Washington than the ebullient young Frenchman. What began on Washington's part as the resigned acceptance of still another condescending French adventurer ripened into paternal attachment, nurtured by filial esteem and love. The relationship surprised Washington's compatriots and astonished Lafayette's friends. To be sure, Lafayette was the youngest of the generals, and Washington twenty-five years his senior. The difference in age no doubt helped to frame the father–son attitudes that developed, but it does not explain the warmth of regard on both sides. Nor is it enough to say that Washington represented the type of man Lafayette longed to be but never could because of his temperament—though it might be sufficient to say on the other side that the young marquis was the kind of son the Virginian would have loved to have had. It was the coincidence of Washington as a man and a symbol of an ideological struggle that made him the idol of this young aristocrat who was dissatisfied with himself.

Lafayette belonged to the rural aristocracy of his native land.

His father, the Marquis de Lafayette, was an army colonel and minor seignior with an estate at Chavaniac in Auvergne, in southern France. Gilbert de Motier was born in the family château on September 6, 1757. His father was killed at the Battle of Minden two years later by a cannon ball allegedly from the British battery of Captain William Phillips, a name to remember. When Gilbert was eleven he was sent to Paris to be put in school. Two years later both his mother and his maternal grandfather died. Suddenly the young marquis came into great wealth which was ably managed and increased for him. Countryfied though he might be, he was richer by far than most of his noble acquaintances.

Early in 1772, when he was fourteen and a half, his great-grandfather arranged for his marriage to Marie Adrienne de Noailles, aged twelve and a half. She was the daughter of the Duc d'Ayen, who was eager to tap the Lafayette fortune, and granddaughter of the noted Duc de Noailles. Adrienne was not told of the arrangement for more than a year. By that time she had become acquainted with Lafayette and was quite fond of him. The marriage ceremony, eagerly entered by both parties, took place on April 11, 1774, and the young couple set up residence in Paris.

Presumably Lafayette had reached his full growth by this time. He stood about five feet nine inches tall, was rather lanky and pale in coloring. His sandy hair verged on red, his eyes were hazel. More noticeable were a receding forehead and a pointed nose. No one called him handsome, yet he seemed to have an animated countenance and pleasant manner. Lafayette possessed few of the qualities required for the gay social life at Versailles: he was shy in company, awkward in sports and dancing, a poor drinker, and generally uncomfortable in the glittering royal court.

His youthful virtues are harder to fathom. Reserved though he appeared, he had a warm and affectionate nature capable of high enthusiasm and great devotion. He loved the military life. By it he hoped to achieve recognition and distinction, possibly to compensate for his feelings of inferiority at court. But after a long war with England, France was at peace. Lafayette had been made an officer in the Noailles regiment of dragoons and after his marriage was promoted to captain. Although he could look forward to gradual promotion, his career did not promise excitement.

There must have been more to the youth than this limited ambition. He probably did a great deal of reading on his own—especially in the military field. Otherwise, it is impossible to explain the ease with which he exercised a major general's command in the Continental army two years later. Similarly, there is no documentary evidence that Lafayette grew introspective about his wealth and position, or speculated on the rights of peasants and city populace, or was touched by the writings of such liberals as Rousseau or Voltaire. It is difficult, however, to believe that thoughts of social and political reform were utterly foreign to him. If so, then his enthusiasm for the American cause in 1777 was an incredibly sudden adoption of strange doctrine. Six or seven years later, Lafayette declared that he had always had republican leanings, but the statement has been suspect because it was written after the American Revolution ended victoriously. The truth is that what went on in Lafayette's mind—and it was an observant, active mind—between 1775 and 1777 is simply not known.

In the summer of 1775, he attended a dinner at which the revolt in America was discussed with admiration because of France's long enmity toward England. Lafayette thereafter seems to have followed Washington's campaigns. But at the end of the year a new minister of war determined to reform the French army, and one of his measures was to ease out those officers who had had no real military experience. Captain Lafayette found himself a reserve officer, with small prospect of promotion unless France went to war. Small wonder, then, that his interest in a distant war increased.

In July of 1776, Silas Deane arrived in Paris, the first representative of the American colonies sent abroad. On his own initiative, he began engaging European army officers to serve in America by promising them high rank and good pay in the Continental army. Deane was glad to sign up Colonel Johann Kalb, dubbed Baron de Kalb, who had served in the French army, and promised him a major generalship in America. By December 1, 1776, seventeen French officers were enlisted in addition to several who had crossed the Atlantic earlier. The example of these officers fired Lafayette's imagination. De Kalb took him to Deane. Rather surprisingly, the nineteen-year-old Lafayette asked for the rank of major general in America, largely to win his father-in-law's permission to go. He accompanied that request with another surprise: he would not take any pay, only expenses. The eager Deane agreed on December 7, 1776.

The party of French officers preparing to embark for America was stopped at Le Havre by the French government and returned to Paris. It was now hinted to Lafayette that if he would buy a ship for the voyage, the group could slip away secretly. The notion appealed to him; a merchant ship was found and the sale consummated early in March, 1777. Fifteen French officers and Edmund Brice, who was a friend of Deane's secretary, were to rendezvous at Bordeaux. After some delay the *Victoire* sailed on April 20 directly for Charleston, South Carolina. In Paris, Lafayette's defiant exploit made him a hero to all the liberals, just as he was considered an errant hothead in the salons of the conservatives.

In a letter to his young wife, Lafayette tried to excuse his leaving her so abruptly by declaring his devotion to liberty and calling America the hope of all humanity. If this was just an idea and not a philosophy, as his biographer Gottschalk insists, it is still difficult to believe that it was a rationalization that occurred to him on the high seas when he had time to think.[1] The coming change in his public character from what it appeared to his friends at home was even more startling.

Escaping all British cruisers, the *Victoire* anchored near midnight in Georgetown Bay on June 13, 1777. Lafayette, De Kalb, and Brice went ashore on North Island and found themselves on

the summer estate of Major Benjamin Huger of the South Carolina militia. That surprised southern gentleman readily played
host, and from this moment on Lafayette delighted in everything he saw in America.

What Lafayette and his companions did not know was that
the Continental Congress and General Washington were fed up
with French adventurers demanding high rank, some of them
bearing "contracts" from the enthusiastic Silas Deane. When
Lafayette and his friends reached Philadelphia, he was the only
one who impressed Congress. He was asked whether he would
accept a commission as major general dating from that day (so
he would not supersede any existing major generals), without
pay, and without claim to commanding a division. This was
hard bargaining, but Lafayette agreed.

Congress thereupon voted Lafayette the rank of major general
on July 31 and sent him a sash. That night he was invited to
dinner at the City Tavern to meet Washington, who had just
entered Philadelphia with some troops in search of the elusive
Howe. The commander-in-chief was prepared only to dislike
another Frenchman foisted on him, especially one so young and
inexperienced. But he was impressed by the earnest and respectful youth; by the modesty of his motives, his eagerness to learn,
his exquisite manners and his efforts to speak English. Lafayette
found his anticipation more than realized, for he believed he
could recognize true nobility in the face and demeanor of Washington. The Virginian made a point of speaking privately to
Lafayette, inviting the volunteer to mess at his headquarters and
to accompany him next day on an inspection of Philadelphia's
defenses. The young man was elated.

Lafayette's deference and charm soon made him the most popular man at headquarters. He risked this favorable impression,
however, by writing directly to Congress and hinting to Washington about getting a division to command. This was in complete disregard of the earlier stipulation to which he had agreed.
One of his motives for doing so was to make a place for some of
his French companions, who remained in Philadelphia begging

for commissions. His appeal was unexpectedly strengthened by letters to Congress from Deane and Franklin saying that a warm reception of Lafayette would help the American cause in France, and a private letter to Washington from Franklin asking him to take a personal interest in the youth so as to preserve him from unnecessary risk. Along with these letters came Count Casimir Pulaski, hero of the unsuccessful Polish war for independence, who expressed a willingness to serve under Lafayette. In consequence of these endorsements, Washington explained to Lafayette that though Congress could not yet grant him a command, he himself would be glad to be regarded as the young man's "father and friend." The marquis was more than satisfied —he was deeply touched and honored. From this moment on he had a living ideal before him, such as he had never known before. The familiar relationship not only molded Lafayette's character but even affected the self-possessed Washington by drawing a rare ray of warm affection from him.

When the British transports headed up the Chesapeake, Washington moved his headquarters down to Wilmington on August 25. Lafayette took part in councils of war, marched and countermarched with various troop units. He observed his twentieth birthday on September 6. Three days later a war council directed the army to Chad's Ford on Brandywine Creek, 26 miles southwest of Philadelphia. Here was the spot where the British and Hessian forces probably would try to cross. On the morning of September 11, the enemy appeared marching in two columns. The one commanded by Major General Wilhelm Knyphausen stopped at Chad's Ford and made as if to cross. Cannon and musket fire were exchanged.

Washington, with Lafayette at his side, grew more concerned about the second column, under Lord Cornwallis, that marched away from Chad's Ford. The commander-in-chief alerted Sullivan, who commanded his right wing, but Sullivan could not see the column. Cornwallis continued far beyond Sullivan before crossing the creek, then turned back, coming in sight of Sullivan's flank about four o'clock. Meanwhile, Lafayette, sensing that Knyphausen did not intend to force a crossing, had obtained Washington's permission to move over to the right wing. He joined Stirling's division just before Cornwallis struck.

Although he had never been under fire before, Lafayette exhibited great bravery and command ability. Dismounting, he rallied the men in Conway's brigade to hold against the British. In the close fighting he was hit by a bullet that passed through his leg below the calf. Blood ran out of the top of his boot, and his aide Gimat insisted he remount and ride into the woods. Greene's brigade turned and came up just before Washington did. They held Cornwallis at bay until the American left wing could pull back. Knyphausen then crossed the ford, and the outgeneraled American forces fled toward Chester, 12 miles away. Dr. John Cochran, Washington's personal physician, slapped a hasty bandage on Lafayette's leg as they joined the retreat.

It was dusk when Lafayette reached the stone bridge across Chester Creek. He stopped and gathered up scattered fugitives, forming the men into lines and reassuring them. When Washington came up there was a semblance of order, and the flight was stopped. Lafayette was carried into a house and set on a table so that Dr. Cochran could finish attending to his wound. The marquis was voluble and in high spirits; he had demonstrated that he was no oranamental soldier. But Washington sent him to Philadelphia by boat.

While Lafayette was recuperating, Washington was pushed away from Philadelphia after warning Congress he could not protect the capital. Residents and delegates alike began to flee and Congress resolved to meet in York. A boat moved Lafayette up to Bristol on September 16. Congressman Henry Laurens did not leave Philadelphia until the nineteenth. He picked up Lafayette in his coach and deposited him two days later in Bethlehem, where the Moravian brethren were caring for American wounded.

Lafayette remained at Bethlehem about three weeks, captivating the Moravians by his admiration for their faith and institutions. On his return to headquarters about the middle of October, he still limped and could not wear a boot, but he was ready to take up military duties again. He was also something of a hero. De Kalb wrote home to the French War Department that "No one deserves more than he the esteem which he enjoys here. He is a prodigy for his age, full of courage, spirit, judgment, good manners, feelings of generosity and of zeal for the cause of liberty on this continent." [2] It was an accurate summary.

On November 20, General Nathanael Greene led a brigade into New Jersey to strengthen Fort Mercer against Cornwallis. Lafayette asked to join him. Four days later Lafayette took a detachment of 300, mostly militia, north of Gloucester to observe Cornwallis' camp. They ran into a Hessian outpost of 350 men with two cannon. Lafayette charged them and drove them back, then disengaged at dusk. The enemy lost 60 men in killed, wounded, and captured; Lafayette had one officer killed and five men wounded. He had conducted an independent command with skill and coolness, and his casual reference to the engagement in a letter to Henry Laurens, now president of Congress, earned him fresh regard: "I was there nothing almost but a witness, but I was a very pleased one in seeing the behaviour of our men." [3]

There was no holding the marquis from command of a division now. Washington did not want him to return to France in disgust and so with Congress' approval, Lafayette was given the Virginia brigades of Woodford, Muhlenberg, and Scott, formerly commanded by Major General Adam Stephen. The new command was announced on December 4.

Lafayette avoided the factions jealous of Washington because he recognized that Washington was the Revolution and that should he be reduced in power or replaced, the whole cause would collapse. Considering his age and experience, how Lafayette could handle himself so adroitly would be a mystery if he had not revealed his method in a letter to his father-in-law on December 16: "I read, I study, I examine, I listen, I think, and out of all that I try to form an idea into which I put as much common sense as I can. I shall not speak much for fear of saying foolish things; I will risk still less for fear of doing them, for I am not disposed to abuse the confidence which they have deigned to show me. Such is the conduct which until now I have followed and will follow." [4] To judge the young man by his enthusiasms or Gallic expression of his feelings is to miss the sober reflections of a maturing mind. Washington was a shrewd judge of character and never would have warmed to Lafayette if he had been only a superficial ingratiating romantic.

Lafayette scrupulously looked after his men, spending his own money when Congress failed to provide them necessities. Nor was he backward in suggesting to Washington certain changes and innovations from French military practice. The Board of War now proposed to Congress an expedition into Canada that won approval. Lafayette was given the command, to impress the French-Canadians.

Going to Albany to assume command, he consulted three fellow generals all of whom declared that the obstacles to success were insurmountable. The troops were less than half the number promised; no food, clothing, sleighs, or ammunition were ready, and soldiers in the Northern Department were long in arrears on their pay. Angry and deflated, Lafayette wrote to the Board of War for a new assignment. He happily rejoined Washington at Valley Forge on April 8, 1778, and saw what another adventurer, the pseudo-Baron von Steuben from Prussia, was doing toward training the troops.

Lafayette was soon overjoyed to learn that France had allied herself openly with the young republic. Announcement of the Franco-American treaty was made at Valley Forge on May 5. More than ever, the young marquis regarded himself as the spokesman for his country in America.

Lafayette next saw action during a probing march toward Philadelphia on May 18, when he went to discover what the enemy was doing. With a reconnaissance force of 2,200, Lafayette set out and, contrary to Washington's suggestion, established a camp on Barren Hill, halfway to the city. It was a good, defensible position, however, from which to reconnoiter. He posted some militia at Whitemarsh to protect two fords, but for reasons unknown they did not remain there. From a deserter Howe learned of this neglect and set out the next night to get behind Lafayette, using three columns of troops. Warned barely in time, Lafayette extricated himself from the trap, deceived one of Howe's columns, and forced the enemy to retire into Philadelphia chagrined. Moving in a circle, Lafayette returned to Barren Hill and then proceeded back to Valley Forge. If he erred in camping on the same spot two nights in a row and in trusting too much to militia, Washington was yet willing to say: "Upon the whole, the Marquis came handsomely off." [5]

It was now apparent to everyone that the British were going to evacuate Philadelphia. To the question of what the American army should do, the council of generals recommended following the enemy on its road of retreat without bringing on a set battle. Howe had resigned, and his second, Sir Henry Clinton, had become commander-in-chief. He "is a military pedant, somewhat blunderer, and nothing more," Lafayette characterized him, and it was not a bad estimate.[6]

By noon on June 18, Washington learned that the British had pulled out of Philadelphia, crossed the Delaware, and were marching northeast across New Jersey. Immediately he started six brigades in pursuit under Generals Lee and Wayne. At dawn the next day the main army marched out of Valley Forge led by Lafayette's division. When Lee came within striking distance of Clinton's column, he urged avoidance of a clash. Lafayette opposed him in council, and it was finally decided to send a small detachment to annoy the enemy's rear. The eager Frenchman begged to lead it. Washington agreed, asking only for Lee's consent. Lee readily granted it, since he did not want the blame that would come from failure of this effort. Washington then raised the "detachment" to 5,200 men and ordered Lafayette to pursue Clinton. When Lee learned of the increased size of the corps Lafayette was given, he was jealous and demanded that as second in command he should lead it. Washington hesitated, and Lee appealed to Lafayette to save his somewhat suspect "honor." The Frenchman was touched and said that if he did not meet the enemy within twenty-four hours he would turn over the corps to Lee.

Unfortunately for the American cause, Lafayette could not catch up to Clinton within the prescribed time limit. Despite intense heat he pushed his brigades to Hightstown and then onto the road to Monmouth Court House, getting ahead of his provisions. Washington ordered him to Englishtown and sent Lee to support him. The older man took command upon joining. So it was that on June 28, a cautious general was in charge when the American advance came up with the British near Monmouth. Lee developed no plan of action and had few orders to give. Getting into a favorable position to cut off Clinton's rearguard, he muffed the attack and ordered a partial withdrawal. His unit commanders were confused by his orders, and Lee permitted a general retreat, though he knew that Washington was coming up with the main army.

Washington appeared before noon and saw his advance force in retreat. Finding Lee, he rebuked him publicly, took personal command, and reversed the movement. He sent Lafayette back to the main army to form and command the second line of attack. At the front Washington pushed the advancing British back toward Monmouth. The dreadful heat took its grim toll, and the battle broke off with darkness. Clinton had no intention of renewing it, and at midnight he stole away, having suffered a great number of casualties.

Washington's horse had dropped dead from the heat, and when Lafayette came up to him, the two slept under a tree together. Lee was court-martialed and suspended from the army. The Continentals turned up to White Plains, New York, and encamped. Both sides were now back where they were in October, 1776. If only the incompetent Lee had been kept from command of the advance, there is little doubt that under Lafayette a vigorous thrust would have crippled Clinton and perhaps insured a decisive victory by Washington.

The French alliance soon produced its first joint military operation. Comte d'Estaing, who was both an admiral and a general, reached Maryland with sixteen ships and some French marines aboard. To everyone's disappointment, his largest warships were too big to enter New York harbor, and the French were directed to Rhode Island. Newport was garrisoned by 6,000 British, and Sullivan was encamped nearby with 3,000 Continentals and militia. Washington sent Lafayette and Greene with 2,000 reinforcements, and called for the New England states to supply more militia. D'Estaing indicated he would be happy to place his French marines under Lafayette's command.

The allied attack on Newport never materialized. D'Estaing was uneasy about being bottled up in Narragansett Bay by a British fleet. He had started to put some of his troops ashore, however, when Admiral Howe appeared on the horizon with thirty sail, on August 9, 1778, offering to do battle. D'Estaing immediately weighed anchor to meet the British, but a severe storm of gale force prevented a decisive sea fight. The storm scattered and damaged both fleets, and D'Estaing brought his crippled squadron back to Rhode Island only to inform Sullivan that he had to proceed to Boston for repairs.

Sullivan now had more troops than the British, and he tried to persuade D'Estaing to stay for a joint attack. But the admiral sailed away, much to Sullivan's disgust and Lafayette's embarrassment. Sullivan launched an unsuccessful attack on August 29. Lafayette was not present, having been dispatched on the twenty-seventh to Boston to learn what D'Estaing's intentions were. He felt himself very much in the middle, forced to defend D'Estaing and uphold the French alliance in the face of critical public outcry.

He remained on duty in Rhode Island until late September, when he asked for permission to go home for a visit. Washington readily assented, and Lafayette sailed from Boston on January 11, 1779, carrying messages from Congress to Franklin and from Ambassador Gérard to Foreign Minister Vergennes as well as testimonials of his own services to the American cause. The Atlantic was crossed in the short time of twenty-three days, the passengers surviving a brief mutiny.

Lafayette's reappearance in Paris was as dramatic as his exit from France. His cousin, the Prince de Poix, was giving a party on February 11, and suddenly about midnight Lafayette burst in, to be cheered and embraced by all the guests—an authentic hero and celebrity home from the wars. Officially he was still under the displeasure of the King for having run off without royal permission, but a week of house arrest placated His Majesty. Lafayette then was free to be lionized. Indeed, the King promoted him from a reserve captain to lieutenant commander of the King's Dragoons, which, in European fashion, cost him 80,000 livres for the commission.

Lafayette and Franklin met at last, and each was taken by the other. John Adams was now also in Paris. As requested by Congress, Lafayette spoke to them about the previously planned invasion of Canada with French help. Franklin approved, but Adams preferred that France help America with her navy. Premier Maurepas and Vergennes heard the persuasive youth, but were not moved. Lafayette himself soon became diverted by the prospect of a more exciting venture, and in a few months learned that the Continental Congress had changed its mind about Canada.

The new venture planned by the ministry involved Spain, which declared war on England in June, 1779. French troops had been quietly gathered in Normandy and Brittany for an invasion of England. Lafayette was named aide to the commander. This bold undertaking was to begin as soon as the combined French and Spanish fleets had cleared the English Channel. Lafayette worked feverishly at Le Havre gathering supplies for a force of 30,000.

Admiral d'Orvilliers finally sailed into the Channel in August with a combined fleet of 66 French and Spanish ships. He blockaded Plymouth for three days while the French army made ready to embark for Falmouth. Then a severe storm blew the navy out of the Channel, and a British squadron sailed in. D'Orvilliers returned for a decisive engagement, but the smaller British force skillfully avoided battle. The French admiral gave up the chase early in September. His fighting strength reduced by sickness and dangerously low on his supply of stores, D'Orvilliers disgustedly returned to France.

It was November before the invasion army was disbanded and Lafayette could leave Le Havre. He was now showing a genuine interest in human rights—Irish discontent and the condition of his own serfs—but his fondest dream was still to lead an expeditionary force to America. Premier Maurepas was reluctant to send off a French army, but Vergennes favored it because he believed that America was the best place to strike England. A letter received from Washington in January, 1780, said he would welcome such military aid. The ministry acceded to the new appeal, but hesitated over the commander. Their decision was to ask Lafayette to resume his rank in the American army and to name the Comte de Rochambeau to command the expeditionary force. Rochambeau was fifty-five years old, a veteran of the Seven Years' War, and had been a major general for nineteen years.

Jaunty as ever, Lafayette was not offended, as he recognized that his youth and lack of experience were against him. He was instrumental in having Rochambeau's instructions include the stipulation that the French army should act only under the orders of Washington so as to prevent its falling under the authority of Congress. Moreover, he won the promise of clothing and munitions for American troops. He was to set off at once to carry the good news to Washington.

Arriving in Boston at the end of April, 1780, Lafayette was welcomed by cannon, bells, bands, and officials. Although he drank up this tribute, he was not happy by what he saw and heard. The country was just emerging from a particularly harsh winter, taxes and prices were exorbitant, paper currency had depreciated greatly, the Congress was held in low regard, the army was hungry and small. Charleston, South Carolina, was under siege by the British.

The main army was at Morristown, New Jersey, and Lafayette set off on the long ride. Washington did not try to hide his delight that the marquis was coming back. No doubt he had missed his youthful confidence and high spirits, his warm and loyal devotion, and his faith in the common cause. Lafayette reached the Morristown camp on May 10, to be welcomed by all.

His message to Washington prompted the commander-in-chief to plan an attack on New York as soon as Rochambeau should arrive. In the meantime the Continental army would have to be enlarged, and Washington could think of no one better qualified than Lafayette to go to Philadelphia and gain authorization from Congress. Then came news that General Lincoln had surrendered Charleston on May 12, and that Clinton was returning to New York. Washington still persevered in his plan to attack New York, but Rochambeau's army of 5,000 men did not arrive at Newport, Rhode Island, until mid-July. The delay had enabled an English squadron to reach New York, and an attack on the city seemed out of the question.

Rochambeau requested a personal meeting, but as Washington was conferring with a visiting committee from Congress, he sent Lafayette instead. The marquis soon discovered there was a problem of divided command. The French admiral, Du Ternay, insisted on superiority at sea before he would blockade New York, and Rochambeau would not act without naval control in local waters. This meant asking Paris for more ships and troops. It was clear that nothing could be attempted that summer. Lafayette again was disappointed by his countrymen, because he believed New York could be taken by an attack on land by the combined armies. The stalemate continued.

Lafayette was given command of a new corps of 1,850 light infantry, a kind of elite mobile division. Divided into two brigades, it included a cavalry unit under Major "Light-Horse Harry" Lee. Lafayette worked to develop an *esprit de corps* and spent his own money on uniforms and equipment. The war news almost countered his efforts. In August, Gates was routed by Cornwallis in Camden, South Carolina, in a battle that cost the life of Lafayette's old friend, Baron de Kalb. Lafayette was sufficiently discouraged to wish that Washington would make

himself dictator for the sake of the public welfare. His democratic faith at this point was not unshakable.

In the middle of September he and several officers accompanied Washington to Hartford for a meeting with Rochambeau
and Du Ternay. On the way they learned that the English naval
force at New York had been reinforced. The commanders agreed
that unless the French could gain naval superiority around the
city, the allies should attempt an expedition somewhere in the
South.

On their way back to camp, Washington's party again stopped
off at West Point, where Arnold commanded, on the fateful
twenty-fifth of September. Arnold had held a treasonable meeting with Clinton's adjutant general, Major John André, and
arranged to surrender West Point and its garrison to the British
for handsome pay and honors. Word was now received by Arnold
that André had been captured within the American lines on the
Hudson, and that suspicious papers in his boot were being forwarded directly to Washington. Fleeing from his quarters just
before Washington rode up, Arnold took to a boat and was
rowed down the Hudson to a British ship. Washington was
shocked and numbed by Arnold's defection. Lafayette, along
with thirteen other officers, tried André and sentenced him to
hang as a spy.

After this excitement, matters reverted to normal idleness,
broken only by Admiral de Ternay's sudden death in December.
Lafayette was mortified by Rochambeau's cautiousness. He
feared for the alliance and the honor of France if some action was
not taken in 1781. Action was just as necessary for America;
Lafayette could see that his friends were plainly running out of
funds. He put these arguments together in an urgent code letter
to Vergennes, another to the Prince de Poix, and another to
Franklin. He asked for men, ships, and cash. His pleas were
echoed by Washington and Rochambeau.

In the interim of waiting, Lafayette's constitutional impatience
and his eagerness to provoke battle asserted themselves in proposals for several small attacks. Washington, always more real-

istic, admired Lafayette's boldness but cautioned him that "we must consult our means rather than our wishes; and not endeavour to better our affairs by attempting things, which for want of success may make them worse." [7] This attitude was foreign to the youth, but instructive.

Lafayette also sharpened his comprehension of political liberty by talking with the Duc de Chastellux and writing to a new friend, Dr. James McHenry. Though still a defender of French institutions, he was learning from his American experience to question and to doubt.

In February, 1781, Washington decided to help Virginia, which had been invaded by a British force under the turncoat Arnold. Lafayette marched south at the head of 1,200 Continentals to reinforce Steuben and try to bottle up the British inside Portsmouth so that a French fleet on its way could close the door of an escape by sea. He proved to be a master at wheedling supplies where none seemed to exist. In mid-March, the incoming French fleet was attacked by a British squadron and forced to turn north. Arnold was able to receive reinforcements and supplies, and the contemplated allied clamp was broken. The marquis' hopes of gaining glory by bagging Arnold were dashed.

Lafayette went back to Annapolis, where his men were waiting. General Nathanael Greene in the meantime was in North Carolina pleading for reinforcements, and Washington ordered Lafayette to go to his assistance. At first Lafayette was loath to stay in the South, fearing he would be too far away when French reinforcements arrived and the long delayed attack on New York took place. Then he learned that the commander of the reinforcements brought to Arnold was Major General William Phillips—the man whose battery had killed his father in 1759. Lafayette took after him in a hurry. To reach Richmond with greater speed, he impressed wagons and had half of his men ride and half walk, with the two changing positions at regular intervals. He arrived at Richmond in the last days of April, barely before the British. Steuben, whose militia had dwindled to a thousand men, kept falling back slowly up the James River until he joined Lafayette. The British came within sight of the city, burned some hogsheads of tobacco, swore at Lafayette, then turned back down the river.

The military maneuvering continued, though most of it was inconclusive. As tensions tightened on him, Lafayette was not without humorous self-knowledge. "I have so many Arrangements to make, so many difficulties to Combat, so many enemies to deal with," he wrote to Alexander Hamilton, "that I am just that much of a general as will make me an Historian of misfortunes, and nail my name upon the Ruins of what good folks are pleased to Call the Army of Virginia . . . To speak truth I was afraid of myself as much as of the Enemy. Independence has rendered me the more cautious, as I know my warmth." [8]

By mid-May, the situation in Virginia had altered considerably. Lord Cornwallis, moving up from North Carolina, took over command of those British forces that had lost their leader when General Phillips died of fever. Convinced that British control in the deep South could not be restored while Virginia remained a major supply and training base, Cornwallis was determined to make the state a major theater of operations. There was a rapid British buildup of forces, and Cornwallis soon had 7,200 men to mop up Virginia. Lafayette, who by this time held practically an independent command in the state, could muster no more than 2,500—half of whom were militia. Yet the young man whom Cornwallis sneeringly dubbed "the boy" proceeded to teach the veteran lord something of a lesson in the war of maneuver. "I am therefore determined to scarmish, but not to engage too far," he wrote to Washington, adding with a wink, "I am not strong enough even to get beaten." [9]

Lafayette had to abandon Richmond as Cornwallis approached, moving northward in a line parallel to the British but holding himself between them and certain American supply depots. He was maneuvering also in the direction of his coming reinforcements. Near Fredericksburg, Wayne joined him with 900 veterans in early June. Then Colonel Campbell, who had fought at King's Mountain, arrived with 600 mounted riflemen. Lafayette called also for General Daniel Morgan, who was home on sick leave.

After failing to catch the Frenchman, Cornwallis raided deep into Virginia. He sent Tarleton riding off to Charlottesville in a wild attempt to capture Governor Thomas Jefferson. The results were almost successful, but Tarleton bagged only a few lowly legislators rather than a governor. A force of British rangers under Major John Simcoe set off in pursuit of Steuben, but the Prussian eluded the stab and marched his 450 men toward Lafayette. As the young marquis was reinforced and more militia began turning out to halt the British invasion, Cornwallis decided to move back toward Williamsburg where he expected to find new orders. Lafayette, his force now swelled above 5,000, discarded the role of rabbit and turned upon the hounds.

When Cornwallis first veered toward a supply depot at Albemarle Old Court House, Lafayette by forced marches beat him to it. Cornwallis pulled away toward Richmond, and then to avoid battle, began marching eastward toward Williamsburg. Lafayette followed on his heels. Five miles from the old colonial capital, there was a small clash on June 26, but it was the British who broke it off. As Professor Gottschalk has pointed out, most Americans believe that Cornwallis ran because Lafayette chased him, whereas in reality Lafayette chased him because he ran.[10] The marquis gave out the former impression to raise the morale of Virginia. Throughout this phase of the campaign he had handled himself admirably, and no one could have done better. Washington was not flattering when he wrote to a friend: "He possesses uncommon Military talents, is of a quick and sound judgment, persevering, and enterprizing without rashness, and besides these, he is of a very conciliating temper and perfectly sober, which are qualities that rarely coincide in the same person."[11]

At Williamsburg, Cornwallis found frantic letters from Sir Henry Clinton. The British commander-in-chief had never given His Lordship permission to leave the Carolinas, and as he was planning to strike at Philadelphia again, he did not want to get committed in Virginia. Therefore he ordered Cornwallis to take up a defensive post on the coast and send part of his army up to New York for the Philadelphia project.

Clinton had no sooner posted these orders than he found his plans overturned. News came from France to Rochambeau that a large French fleet would reach America in July or August. Washington met with the French general at Wethersfield, Connecticut, and they perfected plans to attack New York City. Washington wrote this news to Lafayette, and Clinton read the intercepted letter. Panicked, Clinton wrote again to Cornwallis that he needed all the men from Virginia who could be spared. The irritated Cornwallis decided to move to Portsmouth and headed for the James River.

Lafayette was right after him. At the crossing on July 6, Wayne rushed up on what he thought was the rearguard, but the main body of British lay hidden just beyond them. When they burst out on Wayne's 900 men, he realized that to call retreat would bring on a rout. So he bluffed the enemy and ordered an attack! Lafayette came up and helped the men when they recoiled from overpowering numbers. The Pennsylvanians pulled back half a mile in good order, and Cornwallis resumed his crossing of the river. Lafayette had two horses shot out from under him and suffered casualties of 139 killed, wounded, and captured. The British losses were less.

As the Virginia militia began to go home, Lafayette established a camp at Malvern Hill, halfway between Williamsburg and Richmond, and kept Wayne reconnoitering on the south side of the James. Having calmed down, Clinton changed his mind and told Cornwallis to keep his troops and occupy a port that would provide a good naval station for warships, preferably on the Chesapeake. Not knowing of these fresh orders, Lafayette was puzzled when on the last day of July, Cornwallis shifted his men by water to Yorktown and the hamlet of Gloucester, across the York River.

Lafayette moved his troops eastward to the head of the York River and set about badgering and imploring General Nelson, who had succeeded Jefferson as governor, for men and supplies. He could not understand why Cornwallis was fortifying himself, but soon after the middle of August he received exciting news from Washington. The French fleet under Admiral de Grasse was coming up from the West Indies to the Chesapeake; Lafayette must not let Cornwallis escape and might expect aid from the North. Lafayette acknowledged "the most beautifull prospect that I may ever behold." [12]

To prevent Cornwallis' escape southward, he shifted men south and east around to Portsmouth and alerted the North Carolina militia. His intelligence service now included one of Cornwallis' servants. Arrival of General du Portail, Washington's best engineer, about August 26, gave Lafayette the latest news. Not only was De Grasse coming, but so was the Rhode Island squadron, and so were the combined armies of Rochambeau and Washington! Lafayette drew his noose tighter. On August 30, De Grasse hove in sight—34 ships, 3,100 marines, and crews of several thousand. Cornwallis' hope of rescue by sea was gone.

A tardy British fleet appeared on the horizon on September 6, and De Grasse sailed out of the lower bay to meet it. An all-day battle damaged the English seriously and they broke off, though they hovered around several days before turning back to New York. De Grasse returned to the bay. Lafayette fell sick with the fever, but he got up on September 14, to rush out and embrace Washington and Rochambeau, who had arrived ahead of their troops. Late that night after a joyful reunion supper, De Grasse sent word that the Rhode Island squadron had joined him with siege guns.

With American and French forces pouring in, the siege of Yorktown began. The presence of Major General Lincoln, who outranked Lafayette, placed the marquis under him in command of two brigades, including his old light infantry. It fell to Lafayette's division to storm one of the British redoubts outside the Yorktown wall. The assault was capably handled by Lieutenant Colonel Alexander Hamilton in a matter of minutes on the night of October 14. The French seized the other redoubt, and both were incorporated into the tightening ring Washington drew around the beleaguered post. The next night Cornwallis tried a sortie that failed. On the seventeenth he opened negotiations to surrender, and on the nineteenth he signed the capitulation. Lafayette insisted that the British be allowed no honors because they had denied Lincoln the same privilege at Charleston the year before. No one viewed the surrender ceremonies with more pleasure and satisfaction than the marquis. It was the glorious culmination of a long wait.

After the fall of Yorktown, Lafayette applied for a furlough for France. He was to seek reinforcements for Rochambeau and another fleet. Stopping at Philadelphia, he was thanked by Congress for his services and asked to consult with Benjamin Franklin in Paris about getting a loan from France. Lafayette proceeded to Boston, where he boarded the *Alliance* commanded by Captain John Barry. They sailed on December 23, and Lafayette was back in Paris on January 20, 1782. The King promptly promoted him to *maréchal de camp* (major general) in the French army. He was honored and congratulated by everyone, and crowds gathered wherever he made an appearance.

Franklin, now troubled by the gout, made good use of the young man in obtaining a loan. The ministry agreed also to reinforce Rochambeau. Then England's war ministry fell, and the British began to show signs of desiring peace. During the negotiations, Lafayette did yeoman service as liaison between the French foreign minister and the American peace commission composed of Franklin, John Adams, and John Jay. By stalling, the American commissioners forced England to recognize American sovereignty before negotiating a treaty.

France and Spain in the meantime had decided to send D'Estaing to the West Indies and offered Lafayette command of the troops aboard the French fleet. He set off for Cadiz in November. Late in December, word reached the fleet that a preliminary treaty of peace had been signed between England and the United States. France signed a separate treaty on January 20, 1783, and the expedition to Cadiz was called off. Lafayette, who had consciously tried to model his deportment as a diplomat after Washington, sent his congratulations to his idol. "I cannot but envy the happiness of my grand children when they will be about celebrating and worshipping your name. To have one of their ancestors among your soldiers, to know he had the good fortune to be the friend of your heart, will be the eternal honour in which they shall glory. . . ." [13]

Both Lafayette's energy and his humanitarianism asserted themselves in a peacetime proposal he made to Washington: he and the Virginian should purchase together a small plantation and experiment in employing freed Negroes as tenants. It would be a demonstration of how slavery might be abolished. Matured by his experience and observations in America, Lafayette was on his way to becoming a true and thoroughgoing liberal. America, indeed, shone as the example to French radicals of what might be done by a transfer of political power from the King and nobles to the people. There was a great difference, however, in the two peoples, and Lafayette's political efforts in France were destined for disaster.

The young marquis returned to America in August, 1784. Beginning with an ovation in New York, he was wildly received by everyone. Washington entertained him at Mt. Vernon, fulfilling a wartime promise. Three states made him and all his male heirs citizens. When he returned to Paris, he threw himself into various reform movements and ably assisted Jefferson in promoting increased trade with the United States.

With the outbreak of the French Revolution, Lafayette was recognized in the initial stages as a national leader. In 1790, he was probably the most popular person in France. But he was a moderate, and as the revolution fell into excess he was denounced by the terrorists and imprisoned from 1792 to 1797. Although President Washington sought his release, it was Napoleon who finally had him freed. Settling down in La Grange, forty miles from Paris, he retired from public life for a short time. The years had taken his fortune, but the United States Congress now voted him almost $25,000 for his unpaid services and later gave him 11,500 acres of land in Louisiana. His wife died in 1807. After Napoleon's defeat at Waterloo, Lafayette sat in the Chamber of Deputies from 1818 to 1824, always voting on the liberal side.

In 1824, President Monroe invited the aging warrior to visit America as the nation's guest. His triumphal tour has never been matched. Most of his distinguished colleagues were dead and some were forgotten, but Lafayette's name was still a household byword. He moved through the southern states to the Mississippi, then up that river and the Ohio, across New York and into New England. The great circle tour lasted a year. He was greeted everywhere with banquets, balls, parades, fireworks, special music, speeches, and testimonials of respect and affection. Congress restored his fortune by voting him the sum of $200,000. Fifty-five towns and counties were named in his honor. He was touched, inspired, proud, and grateful. His charm enchanted everyone.

Lafayette had less success with his republican ideas in France than abroad. In the 1830 revolution he was offered the presidency of the French Republic but decided his country was not yet ready for that form of government. Instead he accepted Louis Philippe as "King of the French" hoping for a monarchy with republican institutions. His idea was doomed to fail. He died on May 20, 1834, still dreaming of a pure republic for France. He was buried in Paris, his grave covered with soil from Bunker Hill, a gesture by which the United States laid claim to him.

What remains to be said of this exuberant Frenchman who was an American major general? Perhaps he was bumptious in regarding himself as the spokesman and representative of France in America, but his presumption was so infused with good will that few could take offense. He did, in fact, succeed in promoting better relations between the two countries. Throughout the war he showed a remarkable facility for being amiable to all factions in Congress and in the Versailles court. For his diplomatic services alone, Lafayette is deserving of high praise.

He was equally untiring in concocting schemes for military

offensives. Personally brave to the point of recklessness, he gave watchful care to his men and actually held them in high regard, contrary to most foreign officers. In battle he displayed good judgment, matching his field generalship with a talent for wheedling supplies from barren cupboards. Like Washington, he respected the democratic process while pushing against its slowness. Devoted to the American cause, he not only risked his life but opened his ample purse. His motive was partly glory for the sake of reputation, yet it was not all self-promotion. There was also idealism and commitment to principles. Although he learned the weaknesses of republics and the pitfalls of liberty, his faith in self-government remained. He outlasted and outshone the self-righteous Jacobins of his own country.

In speaking of himself he was modest, even deprecating, but it was more humorous than truthful. When he asked for something for himself, he revealed immense self-assurance. It is difficult in assessing one so young to say whether his American experience changed his character or hastened its liberal growth. If at the beginning of 1777 he was only a wealthy aristocrat, shy and without social conscience, as innocent of political philosophy as he was of military operations, by the end of the year he was revealed as aggressive in manners, courageous in perils and proposals, enthusiastic about the libertarian ends of the Revolution, and devoted to Washington as a person and as a symbol. The contrast appears too great for a harvest from barren ground. Clearly he developed rapidly under Washington's tutelage and returned to France a ready leader of men and ideas in the movement to liberalize the French monarchy.

FOOTNOTES

1. Louis R. Gottschalk, *Lafayette Comes to America*, pp. 137, 141.
2. Gottschalk's translation in *Lafayette Joins the American Army*, p. 53, of a letter from De Kalb to St. Paul, November 17, 1777, in *American Historical Review*, XV (1910), 563.
3. *South Carolina Historical Magazine*, VII (1906), 55.

4. Quoted in *Lafayette Joins the American Army*, p. 92, from Lafayette's *Mémoires*, I, 133–34.
5. Washington to G. Morris, May 29, 1778, in John C. Fitzpatrick, ed., *The Writings of George Washington*, XI, 485; hereinafter cited as Washington, *Writings*.
6. Lafayette to Laurens, June 12, 1778, *South Carolina Historical Magazine*, IX (1908), 4.
7. Washington to Lafayette, October 30, 1780, in Washington, *Writings*, XX, 267.
8. Lafayette to Hamilton, May 23, 1781, in Harold C. Syrett and Jacob E. Cooke, eds., *The Papers of Alexander Hamilton*, II, 643–44.
9. May 24, 1781, in Gottschalk, ed., *The Letters of Lafayette to Washington*, p. 198.
10. Gottschalk, *Lafayette and the Close of the American Revolution*, pp. 270–71.
11. Washington to Joseph Jones, July 10, 1781, in Washington, *Writings*, XXII, 353.
12. August 21, 1781, in *The Letters of Lafayette to Washington*, p. 220.
13. February 15, 1783, in *ibid.*, p. 259.

BIBLIOGRAPHY

Chinard, Gilbert, *The Letters of Lafayette and Jefferson*. Baltimore, 1929. These letters reveal much about Lafayette's services to the United States after his return to France.

Gottschalk, Louis R., *Lafayette Comes to America*. Chicago, 1935. Gottschalk's four volume work is by far the best source for Lafayette's activities in the American Revolution and this essay has drawn heavily on it.

——, *Lafayette Joins the American Army*. Chicago, 1937.

——, *Lafayette and the Close of the American Revolution*. Chicago, 1942.

——, *Letters of Lafayette to Washington*. New York, 1944. The preface to this volume carries an incisive essay on the relations between the two men.

——, *Lafayette Between the American and French Revolution, 1783–1789*. Chicago, 1950.

Loth, David, *The People's General*. New York, 1951. Emphasizes the personal aspects of Lafayette's life.

Nolan, J. Bennett, *Lafayette in America Day by Day*. Baltimore, 1934. A compilation of Lafayette's movements in America.

Sedgwick, Henry D., *Lafayette*. Indianapolis, 1928. More of a character study.

Tower, Charlemagne, *The Marquis de La Fayette in the American Revolution*. Philadelphia, 1895. An older work that is still interesting and reliable.

Henry Knox:

AMERICAN ARTILLERIST

———•———

NORTH CALLAHAN

New York University

ONE of the most impressive developments in the Continental army was the creation of the artillery arm. Not even in existence at the beginning of the war, this branch of the service grew to a point where big guns became the decisive factor in the York-town campaign. A portly but energetic young officer named Henry Knox was the person primarily responsible for this amaz-ing expansion. Inside of six years, Knox rose from a civilian book-seller in Boston to become the youngest American major general in the army.

"Henry Knox," Washington Irving once observed, "was one of those providential characters which spring up in emergencies as if formed by and for the occasion." He was born on July 25, 1750, in Boston, a collateral descendant of the famous Scottish reformer, John Knox. Before reaching his teens, he was forced to drop out of school to support his mother, who had been de-serted by her husband. Knox started working in a local book-store—an occupation he found interesting because it gave him time to read and to satisfy his inquiring mind. He was present at the Boston Massacre and tried, without success, to restrain the British from firing into the mob. As a result of this episode among others, he became committed to the patriot cause.

Love knows no loyalties, however, and Knox soon was attracted to Lucy Flucker, the plump daughter of a prominent Tory. Thomas Flucker, the royal secretary to the Massachusetts colony, cared neither for the politics nor social station of his daughter's suitor. It was Lucy who finally resolved the matter. She embraced the patriot cause, married Knox in 1774, and fled from Boston the following year, never to see her parents again.

Knox cut a fine figure as a man and no doubt it was his military bearing that first caught Lucy's eye. He was already inclined to that stoutness for which he was well-known in later life. But his six-foot-plus frame with its broad shoulders always seemed to carry its great weight with such verve that one almost forgot he was fat. His merry, handsome face set off by sharp though genial gray eyes, gave him an air of sociability that delighted all he met. In fact, before the war his English-educated patrons made a habit of meeting their friends in Knox's bookstore because of the fine companionship and stimulating conversation the proprietor provided.

When Knox offered his services to Washington in the summer of 1775, the newly appointed commander-in-chief received him with greater cordiality than he had accorded to most New Englanders entering the army. Washington was impressed because he learned the young bookseller had read widely about British theories on the use of artillery. Knox already had put some of his ideas to the test with the Boston militia. Consequently, Washington was favorably disposed when John Adams suggested that Knox be given the rank of colonel and made chief of the Continental army artillery. There was only one slight problem—the army had little or no artillery to command.

Knox then proposed a plan that was to earn him his first fame —a trek to Ticonderoga to bring back some captured artillery with which to blast the British out of Boston. Washington quickly agreed and directed Knox to go after the guns. Before leaving Cambridge, Knox expressed his contempt for the British artillerymen who had fired over one hundred rounds at the Americans at close range. "And did what?" Knox asked sarcastically. "Why scraped a man's face with the splinters of a rail fence . . . nor am I afraid they will hit me, unless directed by the hand of Providence." [1]

Upon reaching Ticonderoga in December, 1775, Knox quickly surveyed the captured artillery and found that many of the guns were too worn for more use. He sorted out some three score usable pieces, ranging from 4-pound to 24-pound guns, as well as a number of howitzers and mortars. Altogether the guns weighed more than 120,000 pounds and they had to be hauled almost 300 miles through the snow and ice.

Rounding up a small task force of soldiers, hired civilians, horses and oxen, Knox started back to Massachusetts with a long caravan of 42 sledges, bearing 59 fieldpieces. Hauling the heavy cannon was hard, back-breaking work, but with shouting drivers cracking whips the column slowly inched its way across the frozen countryside. The work was not only difficult but dangerous. To prevent runaway sledges from crashing downhill upon the men in front, drag chains and poles were thrust under the runners, and check ropes were fastened around the trees along the way to hold back the heavy cargo. As an early January thaw set in, some of the big guns broke through the ice on the rivers and lakes. But the "drowned cannon" were laboriously recovered in almost every case. Making its way along the Hudson and then turning eastward through the Berkshires, the column finally emerged from the mountains entering upon an old Indian trail running across Massachusetts. Upon reaching Springfield, however, the snow was almost gone and Knox could proceed no farther. Fortunately the weather turned cold again and as the ground froze the column lurched on toward Cambridge.

By early February, Knox completed his journey and delivered to Washington a "noble train of artillery." It is a feat at which soldiers and engineers still marvel. Washington promptly placed the cannon atop Dorchester Heights where they could fire down upon the British troops, forcing General Howe to evacuate Boston. There was rejoicing in the streets as the American army triumphantly trooped in. As befitted the important part he played in driving the British out of Boston, Knox rode beside Washington at the head of the army. The occasion was not without its humor. As the procession passed by the celebrated, punning Tory clergyman Mather Byles, he was heard to exclaim loudly on seeing the portly artilleryman: "I never saw a (Kn)ox fatter in my life!"

From the outset of the war, Knox was forced to struggle along with a collection of ill-assorted cannon of various caliber. Besides captured British cannon, he had French fieldpieces and some guns cast in crude American foundries. At no time during the war was Knox able to achieve uniformity in the Continental army's artillery. The cannon also used different types of ammunition; some fired solid cast-iron shot, others grapeshot, still others canister. Guns varied so in size that ammunition usually was not interchangeable. Despite these difficulties, Knox put together a formidable force and rightfully deserves his reputation as "father of the American Army Artillery."

When the scene of fighting shifted to New York in the spring of 1776, Knox participated in the preparations to fortify Manhattan Island. Following a careful reconnaissance, he reported to Washington that there were 120 light and heavy cannon mounted and ready for action in and around New York City. About 1,200 artillerymen would be needed to man these guns, but Knox's own regiment numbered only 520. He recommended, therefore, that additional men be drafted from other units to make up the difference. Under the supervision of the commander-in-chief, Knox also helped to fortify Fort Washington, which lay on the east bank of the Hudson a short distance above the city.

Although there were rumors for some time that General Howe had left Halifax and was sailing toward New York, Lucy Knox was determined to be with her husband. She travelled down from Connecticut and joined him in New York City. One bright morning in early July as they were seated at breakfast, the young couple looked up to see a huge British fleet sailing toward them down the Narrows between Staten Island and Long Island,

on a fair wind and rapid tide. As Knox wrote to his brother
William:

> . . . one could scarcely conceive the distress and anxiety Lucy then
> had. The city in an uproar, the alarm guns firing, the troops repair-
> ing to their posts, and everything in the height of bustle, I not at
> liberty to attend her, as my country calls loudest. My God, may I
> never experience the like feelings again! They were too much; but
> I found a way to disguise them, for I scolded like a fury at her for
> not having gone before.[2]

After scolding Lucy, he sent her packing back to New England.

Knox, along with other American officers, was stunned at the
size of the British armada sent to seize New York. Besides a powerful British fleet, there were more than 150 transports and
10,000 men. After landing on Staten Island, Howe began a rapid
military buildup, massing more than 32,000 men before he was
through. New York harbor swarmed with masts as men-of-war
and transports kept shuttling in troops. It was the largest expeditionary force ever seen in American waters. To oppose this
invasion, the Americans had about 20,000 troops, many of whom
were untrained and poorly armed.

The first indication of impending disaster came when British
ships sailed boldly up the Hudson and East rivers in defiance of
the patriot batteries. Knox reported that his cannon opened fire
on two or three vessels moving up the Hudson, but they kept so
close to the Jersey shore as to be out of reach of his short-range
guns. In fact, Knox lost six men as the result of the bombardment. His crude cannon were apt to burst upon firing, maiming
or killing the gun crews. In this instance, defective Continental
cannon caused more casualties than did the fire from British
ships.

General Howe began his campaign for capturing New York
City by landing a large force on the western tip of Long Island.
After defeating the patriots in the Battle of Long Island in late
August, the British began preparing for an amphibious attack on
the lower end of Manhattan Island in mid-September. Washing-
ton, rather than risk being trapped in the city, started his troops

moving toward the hilly terrain on upper Manhattan. But before the retreat was completed, the British struck. Landing one-third of the way up the island, Howe threatened to cut off a large section of the American army still straggling out of the city. Knox was among those in the winding, sweating column as it made its way up the island. All day the column was in danger of being caught, but as night fell the weary soldiers finally slogged safely into the American camp on Harlem Heights. Almost the last man to arrive was Knox, who was welcomed joyously by all, for he had been previously reported as captured.[3] "My constant fatigue and application to the business of my extensive department has been such," he wrote his brother, "[that] I have not had my clothes off anights for more than 40 days."[4]

After some sharp skirmishes on Harlem Heights in mid-September, the British and American armies settled down to a stalemate because each felt the position of the other was impregnable. During this lull in the fighting, Knox was busy on other matters. Having seen how totally unprepared the patriots were to wage war, he had been thinking for some time about the founding of a military academy to teach the theories of warfare. When a Congressional committee set out to explore the idea of an academy, John Adams, who knew of Knox's interest, asked him to submit a plan for such an institution. Taking advantage of this opportunity to call attention to the needs of his own corps, Knox modestly titled the plan "Hints for the Improvement of the Artillery of the United States," and included therein his specific suggestions for a military academy.[5]

Knox's plan first recommended the establishment of a number of laboratories for making artillery materiel. To be certain that these manufacturing centers would be beyond the reach of the enemy, they were to be located in parts of the country far removed from the fighting. The laboratories were to be furnished with raw materials for making cannon carriages, ammunition, and wagons and to contain foundries for casting cannon, mortars, and howitzers.

Besides producing equipment, Knox urged that artillery officers be trained at an academy where the "whole theory and practice of fortifications and gunnery should be taught." He recommended that such an academy be modeled along the same lines as the military school at Woolwich, England. Unless immediate steps were taken to make the military service sufficiently attractive, the armed forces would suffer from lack of leaders. Not only academies but every form of encouragement should be offered to attract qualified men. "As the army now stands," he stated, "it is only a receptacle for ragamuffins." Despite the costs involved, Congress should set up academies or else the war would be lost, Knox concluded. Thus he helped to give birth to the idea of the United States Military Academy at West Point. Although the Academy did not come into being until 1802, its pedigree in part can be traced back to Knox's proposal.

Knox was busily engaged also in changing the army's concepts on the use of artillery. He attacked the old idea of employing only heavy artillery and of placing emphasis on cannon primarily for siege operations. His trek from Ticonderoga had convinced him that artillery could be made to keep pace with marching regiments. He placed great stress on building and improving gun carriages to provide greater mobility for the cannon with Washington's army. In the next two major battles in which Knox was involved—the Battles of Trenton and Princeton—his idea paid off handsomely.

On a stormy Christmas night in 1776, Washington decided to cross the Delaware River to deliver a surprise attack upon the isolated Hessian garrison at Trenton. From the very start of the campaign, it was assumed that cannon were to play an important role in the assault. The most critical part of the entire operation came when Knox began to ferry his heavy fieldpieces across the ice-choked river with the help of Colonel John Glover's regiment of rugged Marblehead fishermen.

Knox seemed to be everywhere. Pacing nervously along the river's edge, he supervised the entire ferrying operation. His ringing bass voice was put to use as a kind of modern walkie-talkie as he shouted instructions to Glover's boat crews in their trips to and fro. For a time it appeared that the floating masses of ice might obstruct their passage, but as Knox observed later, ". . . perseverance accomplished what at first seemed impossible."

About 2,400 men were ferried across the river along with Knox's 18 pieces of field artillery. Such a heavy proportion of guns to men was almost unheard of in eighteenth-century warfare. Usually two or three cannon were employed per 1,000 foot soldiers. Washington's task force had three times the normal number. There were two sound reasons for this preponderance of fieldpieces. First, artillery was considered the army's wet-weather weapon because muskets in that day could be fired only when completely dry. Realizing December weather might bring storms that would render his men's muskets unusable, Washington was relying heavily on his artillery. Secondly, bringing along an abnormally large number of guns was as much a psychological as a military move. Knox's gunners were known to have high morale and could be depended upon to stand and fight. They would make their presence known with their booming cannon and thereby help to stiffen the resolve of the infantry.[6]

Once across the Delaware, the troops marched throughout the night in good order toward the small village of Trenton. As wet snow started to fall, Knox's guns took on an increased importance. A violent sleet storm developed and began blowing upon the backs of the trudging Continentals. But snow flew into the faces of the Hessian sentries and they failed to see the American soldiers emerging out of the early morning air until it was too late. During the fighting that followed, the shoulder weapons of both sides were largely useless because of wet firing pans. It was the artillery that bore the brunt of the battle.

Knox was able to move some of his batteries into position at the head of the two main streets—King and Queen streets—which almost ran together at the head of the village. By controlling this crucial location, his gunners were able to dominate the fighting. As enemy soldiers came stumbling sleepily out of their houses into the street, Knox's cannon cut them down. The Hes-

sian cannon were only able to fire a few rounds before they were
knocked out of action.

At the other end of the village, the story was much the same.
The only escape route out of the village lay over the Assunpink
Bridge and American artillery soon commanded the strategic
spot. One artillery sergeant drew a graphic picture of what happened:

> We had our cannon placed before a bridge. . . . The enemy came on
> in solid columns . . . then by given signal, we all fired together. . . .
> The enemy retreated. . . . Our whole artillery was again discharged
> at them—they retreated again and formed. . . . We loaded with
> canister shot, and let them come nearer. We fired altogether again
> and such destruction it made, you cannot conceive—the bridge
> looked red as blood, with their killed and wounded and their red
> coats. The enemy beat a retreat. . . .[7]

Within an hour the battle was over and a brilliant victory
won. Knox bragged of his exploits to Lucy, but his pride was justified. His cannon had played a crucial role in the American
success. He was unaware at the time he had been promoted to
brigadier general of the artillery on December 27, 1776. The
Continental Congress had rewarded him even before they
learned of the remarkable contributions he and his gunners had
made at Trenton.

After both armies had maneuvered for about a week, the British general, Cornwallis, advanced upon Trenton where Washington had drawn up his army. Knox's gunners saved the army from
what might have been a disastrous defeat in this so-called "Second Battle of Trenton" on January 2, 1777. It took the entire
force of Continental artillery to throw back the British attack
across the Assunpink Creek after the enemy had taken most of
Trenton. Knox's massed artillery fire probably was the heaviest
ever delivered on any American battlefield up to that time.[8]

Knox's artillerymen barely had time to catch their breath before they plunged into the Battle of Princeton. On January 3,
the night after the second Trenton battle, Washington slipped

quietly around Cornwallis' army and engaged some British reinforcements on their way to Cornwallis. For a fleeting moment, the fate of American independence hung in the balance as the patriot vanguard was routed and the Continental army was on the verge of defeat. Then Knox's gunners came to the rescue by holding back the British attack, thereby giving Washington's forces a chance to rally. The tide of battle turned and the Americans went on to win overwhelmingly.

Washington withdrew his tired troops from the field and soon took up quarters at Morristown, New Jersey, for the remainder of the winter. The cessation of hostilities during the winter months gave the American commander a chance to bolster his military strength, and he sent Knox back to Massachusetts to oversee the casting of cannon and production of gunpowder. Knox was overjoyed at the assignment because it gave him an opportunity to see his beloved Lucy. The sturdy horse he rode to Boston was not spared. Once back in his home state, Knox scurried about trying to round up supplies. He wrote Washington that in his judgment Springfield, Massachusetts, was the best place in all the four New England states for a cannon factory. Washington thereupon issued the necessary orders and the Springfield arsenal of the United States Army remains there to this day.

Upon his return to the army at Morristown, Knox was involved in an event that rocked the army's high command. One of the problems Washington had to face was that of finding places in the Continental army for foreign officers who secured military commissions from American diplomats stationed in Europe. Silas Deane, who was representing this country in France, for example, sent over one Philippe du Coudray who held a rank somewhat higher than that of an American brigadier general. Du Coudray, an arrogant troublemaker, was soon styling himself as the new "commander-in-chief of the Continental Artillery" and hinted he had a contract with Deane making him chief of the artillery arm. Washington was alarmed and quickly wrote to Congress in Knox's defense. He praised Knox as a valuable officer with sound judgment, clear conception, and one who was widely read in military matters. If he were superseded, said Washington, the artillery would be "convulsed and unhinged," for it was Knox who had placed this part of the army on firm footing. The letter was one of the most glowing Washington ever wrote on behalf of one of his generals.

But such high praise was not enough. Du Coudray showed his commission from Deane which revealed that he was to become general of the artillery and ordnance with the rank of major general, and Congress took the matter under advisement. Knox promptly wrote to Congress asking that he be retired if Du Coudray were placed in command. Because Du Coudray's commission would affect their seniority, Generals Greene and Sullivan wrote similar letters to Congress. Members of Congress resented these blunt letters which disregarded the normal channels of communication, but after some delay they agreed to let Knox remain on as head of the artillery. Du Coudray was given another command and shortly thereafter lost his life in an accident.

Knox's next major campaign against the British took place in the fall of 1777, when General Howe sought to take the American capital, Philadelphia. By September 11, the two armies which had been marching toward one another made contact and the Battle of Brandywine was on. While Lord Cornwallis led a wide flanking movement to strike the main blow on the American right, the Germans under General von Knyphausen attacked the center at Chad's Ford. Although the patriots suffered a defeat, Knox's artillerymen gave an unusually good account of themselves. Washington reported to Congress that his artillery delivered its fire with better aim than did the British batteries. He had personally gone among Knox's guns while the battle was in progress and was pleased with what he observed. At times during the fighting the British overran American artillery positions, but most of the gunners stayed by their cannon until shot down or forcibly removed from their stations. When the British reported they had captured "five French brass guns, three Hessian and three American pieces," it gave some indication of the motley collection of cannon Knox had to depend upon during the early years of the war.

"My dear girl will be happy to hear of her Harry's safety," wrote Knox to his wife, "for, my Lucy, Heaven who is our guide has protected him in the day of battle." He described the battle as "the most severe action that has been fought this war," and boasted, "My corps did me great honor." Nor was Knox alone in his pride. One newspaper noted that "The regiment of artillery, with their general, behaved with their usual coolness and intrepidity. Some of them could scarce be prevailed on to quit their guns, even when surrounded by the enemy and forsaken by our infantry." [9]

For a young man only twenty-seven years of age, Knox had demonstrated remarkable powers of military organization and administration. By choosing his officers carefully, he had built up an efficient arm that was second to none in Washington's army. His gunners possessed an *esprit de corps* that was truly unusual. Few American generals had been able to accomplish so much with so little in such a brief space of time.[10]

After Howe captured Philadelphia, Washington brought on another engagement by attacking the British main camp at Germantown on October 4. During this battle there occurred an episode that was to be one of the low points in Knox's army career. In the initial stages of the fighting, the Americans had the British on the run and victory seemed within their grasp. But Colonel Thomas Musgrave with some British infantry barricaded themselves inside a large stone structure known as the Chew House which lay directly in the path of the advancing Americans and resisted all attempts to root them out. From the second story of the house, Musgrave's men poured a hail of fire upon the vanguard of patriot troops and finally forced them to take cover. The American attack rolled to a halt and Washington considered the situation so serious that he held a staff conference on the battlefield. Some generals were all for leaving a regiment behind to immobilize the garrison inside the house and for pushing on. Knox thought differently. In his study of mili-

tary classics in his Boston bookstore he had read that while penetrating an enemy's country, you must never leave an occupied
castle to your rear. Washington, always respectful of Knox's
military knowledge, agreed with him. An officer carrying a
white flag was sent out to demand surrender, but Musgrave's men
fired and killed him.

Knox then threw his artillery in a circle around the building.
His cannon pounded away, blowing in the front door, smashing
windows, and piercing the roof. But the house was built with
thick stone walls which resisted the battering by cannon balls.
Here was a situation which military books failed to cover. Knox's
guns opened up again, but they failed once more. After repeated
barrages, the Chew House stood rugged and unyielding. This
delay, among other factors, turned victory into defeat. In his
report to Congress, however, Washington blamed the early
morning fog that confused his troops for the defeat more than
the Chew House incident.[11]

With the coming of cold weather, campaigning ceased and
Washington's army headed for its winter quarters at Valley
Forge. As soon as he had established the artillery park in camp,
Knox set out for Boston once again to round up supplies and
men. But he found prices in and around his native city so high
that he hesitated to place orders for supplies. Moreover, many
civilians were reluctant to work for the government. Knox informed Washington that wages were so high in New England
that the artificers at the Springfield arsenal whose contracts were
expiring spurned the thirty dollars a month plus clothing and
rations he offered them. "As the necessity is so great," he wrote,
"I shall be obliged to offer them, besides the above pay and clothing, one-half ration and a jill or half pint of rum per day." [12]
Knox found that recruiting also was difficult despite the bounties
being offered.

Upon his return to Valley Forge, Knox decided that Lucy
should come to stay with him at camp. Martha Washington, Mrs.
Greene, and Lady Stirling were already there and with Lucy's
arrival the drab routine of army life would be brightened a bit.

Lucy quickly became a social leader and her lively if sometimes meddlesome disposition and boundless energy almost matched that of her husband. Both were jovial people and Nathanael Greene commented that the Knoxes were "a perfect married couple."

But there was always business amidst the social pleasures. Washington was soon asking his generals whether the patriots should attack the British in Philadelphia. Knox was ready with his answer. Once again he turned to military books for his solution to the problem. Quoting from *Mes Rêveries*, written by Maurice Saxe, marshal of France in the early eighteenth century, Knox advised against an attack. The English historian, George Trevelyan, commenting on the soundness of Knox's views a century later wrote: "Henry Knox, the best artilleryman and almost best tactician in the Confederacy, pronounced such an attack on Philadelphia impossible." [13]

When the British gave signs that they were evacuating Philadelphia in mid-June, Washington again called a council of war to decide what to do. Some generals favored bringing on an engagement. Knox believed "it would be the most criminal madness to hazard a general action at this time." Why fight for the city, Knox asked, when it soon would be abandoned and turned over to the Americans anyway? How apt this question was may be judged by the fact that on the very day Knox asked it—June 18, 1778—the British left Philadelphia. Once the British army was on the move toward New York, Washington started after them in eager pursuit. Upon overtaking the enemy near Monmouth Court House early on June 28, Washington attacked. The training Knox had given his artillerymen during the long months at Valley Forge began paying dividends. His gunners were so mobile with their cannon that they were able to shift their artillery support to different units as needed in quick order. On the battlefield Knox's cannon were directly under the command of his brigade adjutant, Chevalier de Plessis.

Knox himself dashed about the battlefield, reconnoitering the enemy here and directing the movement of guns there. The artillery was on both flanks of the main action and performed magnificently. Henry Dearborn wrote later that "the briskest cannonade occured on both sides . . . the finest music I ever heard." Knox's leadership was so conspicuous that he was singled out for special mention. "In the hard-fought contest of Monmouth," wrote one army surgeon, "no officer was more distinguished than General Knox. In the front of the battle, he was seen animating the soldiers and directing the thunder of their cannon. His skill and bravery were so conspicuous that he received the particular approbation of the commander-in-chief in the general orders issued on the day succeeding the battle."

Monmouth was to be the last major battle of the war in the North. During the months that followed, Knox spent most of his time training his troops. In the winter of 1779, while at Pluckemin, New Jersey, he established what might be termed a forerunner of the United States Military Academy. Knox, in fact, called it "the academy" and used the camp to instruct military personnel. The physical arrangement was appropriate, the big guns being arranged in a neat row, huts for the personnel in an opposite line, while in the center was located a large building, wider and taller than the others. From an elevated platform in the main room in this building, Knox gave military lessons on gunnery, tactics, and related subjects. His corps was in better shape than ever before; but how much better it had become could be judged by the decisive role his artillery played at the Yorktown campaign in the fall of 1781.

Yorktown turned out to be the American artillery's sternest test because the campaign developed into a full-scale siege operation. Lord Cornwallis was bottled up on the Yorktown peninsula between the Franco–American forces on land and De Grasse's fleet on the water. Siege guns were placed into position to fire into the British camp and Knox issued precise orders on the procedures to be followed. One field officer was to be appointed each day to command in the trenches for each 24-hour period. He was to see that the guns were well-directed and to report the number of shots fired and the apparent effect on the enemy's works. Ricochet firing of shot and ball was to be employed. By this method, cannon balls bounced along the ground taking off the arms and legs of enemy soldiers. Only battalion officers were to level pieces. Strict silence was to be maintained at all times and sentries in sandbag observation posts were to shout a warning of any artillery fire from the British lines.

With his preparations completed by the afternoon of October 9, Knox opened up on Cornwallis' position. The first shots were said to have crashed into the house where British staff officers were gathered for mess, killing Commissary General Perkins and wounding three of his companions. The combined artillery fire from French and American cannon was devastating. Houses came tumbling down, cluttering the streets of Yorktown with debris. The ricochet firing that Knox had ordered sent cannon balls bounding along the ground filling the British camp with mangled soldiers. As one enemy soldier reported:

> One could not avoid the horribly many cannon balls either inside or outside the city. . . . Many men were badly injured and mortally wounded by the fragments of bombs which exploded partly in the air and partly on the ground, their arms and legs severed or themselves struck dead. . . . One saw men lying nearly everywhere who were mortally wounded.[14]

With his artillery so destructive at distances of 800 to 1,200 yards, Washington hastened to open a second siege line in order to achieve even better results at closer range. Work on the new line began on the night of October 11, and continued for three days as Knox hauled his guns forward. The second siege line was completed and despite a British night attack to spike some of the guns, the cannon were soon delivering a withering fire. One American officer observed:

> It is astonishing with what accuracy an experienced gunner will make his calculations, that a shell fall within a few feet of a given point, and burst at the precise time, though at a great distance . . . The whole peninsula trembles under the incessant thunder of our infernal machines.[15]

The American fire throughout the campaign was, indeed, very accurate. Lord Cornwallis himself was almost hit by a cannon ball and at one point had to seek refuge under a cliff. British ships in the harbor were pinpointed, struck, and started burning. The emotional and expressive Lafayette was watching the fire of the American guns one day and turned to Major Samuel Shaw, aide to Knox, to say, "You fire better than the French." Shaw secretly agreed but diplomatically made a polite remonstrance to the Frenchman. "Upon my honor, I speak the truth!" cried Lafayette. "And the progress of your artillery is regarded by everyone as one of the wonders of the Revolution." [16]

The enemy's works were tumbling into ruins. Not a gun could be fired in reply, for the British artillerymen could not approach their cannon because of the murderous fire from the second siege line. At ten o'clock on the morning of October 17, the fighting came to an end. Cornwallis decided to surrender. Knox wrote exultantly to Lucy two days later:

> A glorious moment for America! This day Lord Cornwallis and his army march out and pile their arms in the face of our victorious army. They will have the same honors as the garrison at Charleston, that is, they will not be allowed to unfurl their colors *or play Yankee Doodle.* [17]

Both friend and foe alike praised Knox's artillery at Yorktown. As one observer noted, "The English marveled no less at the extraordinary progress of the American artillery and at the capacity and instructions of the officers." [18] The crowning tribute to Knox was Washington's comment in his report to Congress that "His genius supplied the deficit of means." [19] The commander-in-chief recommended Knox for a promotion to major general in November and he shortly became the youngest American general to hold that rank in the Continental army. One of Washington's last official acts in the army was to designate Knox to succeed him as commander.

When it came time for Washington to take leave of his officers, he met with them at the picturesque Fraunces Tavern near the Battery on the southern tip of Manhattan Island. The usually composed and reserved commander-in-chief entered the room with deep emotion showing in his face. "I cannot come to each of you," he said brokenly. "But I shall feel obliged if each of you shall come and take me by the hand."

Henry Knox being nearest to him was the first to come forward, and fittingly so. He was the one senior officer who in eight years of faithful service had never given Washington a moment's worry and had remained completely devoted. When the tender-hearted Knox, his own eyes brimming with tears, took Washington's hand, the commander-in-chief was so overcome he threw his arms around him and wept.

Knox went on to serve as Secretary of War under the Confederation government. In this capacity he set forth a memorable plan for a national militia which set a precedent for our peacetime military training for over a century and a half. Some of his ideas are still expressed in our National Selective Service manuals to this day. Immediately after the war, Knox also helped to form the fraternal organization of Continental army officers called the Society of the Cincinnati. Named after the famous farmer-general Cincinnatus, who left his plow in Roman times to lead his countrymen to military victory, the Society soon became a controversial one in American affairs. Although ostensibly formed to perpetuate wartime friendships, the organization briefly played a political role that many considered dangerously antidemocratic.

Knox, a strong Federalist, personally took part in many of the major political events of the postwar period. As Secretary of War, he was instrumental in helping to suppress Shays' Rebellion in Massachusetts in 1786–87. Disappointed in the weaknesses of the Confederation government, Knox submitted a "rude sketch" for a stronger central government to Washington even before the latter attended the Constitutional Convention in Philadelphia in 1787. While the convention was in session, Knox's friend, Rufus King, kept him posted on the proceedings. Once the Federal Constitution was written, Knox became one of its staunchest supporters and helped to get the document ratified in Massachusetts.

When Washington was elected President he named Knox Secretary of War, and the two men collaborated as well on governmental affairs as they had on military matters. Knox proved quite competent at his post. He negotiated a series of treaties with southern Indian tribes, urged the establishment of a strong navy, and sought to build a chain of coastal fortifications for the country's defense. After six years in the cabinet, he retired to private life in 1794.

His remaining years were spent near Thomaston, Maine, where he settled on a huge estate inherited by his wife. Here he lived in an imposing mansion called "Montpelier," living in baronial splendor, and carrying on business affairs in land speculation, ship-building, lumbering, and brick-making. From time to time he sat on the Massachusetts General Court and served on several important state commissions. When war with France threatened in 1798, he was appointed a major general by President John Adams. He then had a falling out with General Washington, who had been called out of retirement, over the question of rank. Fortunately, the two old friends patched up their differences before Washington died in 1799. Knox himself died unexpectedly seven years later at the age of fifty-six as the result of swallowing a chicken bone.

Of all Washington's generals, Knox was, without doubt, the most faithful. Only a youth in his mid-twenties when he first reported for military duty, Knox quickly became one of Washington's most loyal friends and trusted advisers. He was probably closer personally to Washington as commander-in-chief and President than any other man. One of the qualities that appealed most strongly to Washington was Knox's great optimism. Like the commander-in-chief, his courage never flagged even during the darkest days of the Revolution. By his able administration of the artillery he created a formidable branch of service in the Continental army and contributed greatly to the winning of America's independence.

FOOTNOTES

1. North Callahan, *Henry Knox: General Washington's General* (New York, 1958), p. 37.
2. Knox to William Knox, July 11, 1776, Knox Papers, Massachusetts Historical Society; hereinafter, Mass. Hist. Soc.
3. Extract of anonymous "Letter from Harlem," September 16, 1776, *American Archives*, Peter Force, ed., 4th series, II, 352.
4. Callahan, *op. cit.*, p. 70.
5. Knox to William Knox, September 23, 1776, Knox Papers, Mass. Hist. Soc.
6. Jac Weller, "Guns of Destiny: Field Artillery in the Trenton–Princeton Campaign 25 December 1776 to 3 January 1777," *Military Affairs*, XX (Spring, 1956), 7–8.
7. Callahan, *op. cit.*, p. 88.
8. Weller, *op. cit.*, p. 2.
9. *Independent Chronicle*, October 2, 1777.
10. Weller, *op. cit.*, p. 12.
11. Callahan, *op. cit.*, p. 122.
12. *Ibid.*, p. 137.
13. George O. Trevelyan, *American Revolution* (London, 1909–14), IV, 305.
14. Callahan, *op. cit.*, p. 185.
15. *Ibid.*, p. 187.
16. Shaw to Knox, April 15, 1792, Knox Papers, Mass. Hist. Soc.
17. Callahan, *op. cit.*, p. 189.
18. Marquis de Chastellux, *Travels in North America in the Years 1780, 1781 and 1782* (London, 1787), I, 150.
19. Washington to President of Congress, October 31, 1781, in John C. Fitzpatrick, ed., *The Writings of George Washington* (Washington, D.C., 1931–44), XXIII, 308.

BIBLIOGRAPHY

Allis, Frederick S., Jr., ed., *William Bingham's Maine Lands 1790–1820. Publications of the Colonial Society of Massachusetts, Collections,* XXXVI–XXXVII. Boston, 1954. Of special interest for Knox's speculations in Maine lands.

Becker, John, *The Sexagenary.* Albany, 1833. Contains considerable information regarding Knox's trek from Ticonderoga.

Billias, George A., *General John Glover and His Marblehead Mariners.*

New York, 1960. Shows the importance of Knox's role at the Battle of Trenton.

Brooks, Noah, *Henry Knox: A Soldier of the Revolution.* New York, 1900. An older work on Knox's life, but still valuable for some of the letters quoted therein.

Callahan, North, *Henry Knox: General Washington's General.* New York, 1958. The most recent biography of Knox's career.

Drake, Francis S., *Life and Correspondence of Henry Knox.* Boston, 1873. Valuable for the Knox letters it contains.

Ford, Worthington C., "Henry Knox—Bookseller." *Massachusetts Historical Society Proceedings,* VI (Boston, 1927–28), 227–303. An interesting account of Knox's prewar occupation.

Starrett, Lewis F., *General Henry Knox; His Family, His Manor, His Manor House, and His Guests.* Rockland, Maine, 1902.

Weller, Jac, "Guns of Destiny: Field Artillery in the Trenton–Princeton Campaign 25 December 1776 to 3 January 1777." *Military Affairs,* XX (Spring, 1956), 1–15. Contains a brief but accurate survey of the field artillery used by both armies in this and other campaigns.

Whitcomb, Joseph W., *Memoir of General Henry Knox of Thomaston, Maine.* Bangor, 1890. Contains the eulogy delivered at Knox's funeral and a copy of his will.

Anthony Wayne:

MILITARY ROMANTICIST

HUGH F. RANKIN

Tulane University

ANTHONY WAYNE was an anachronism in the eighteenth century. A knight errant riding forth to do great and noble deeds, he was five hundred years too late to don shining armor. His reckless courage, dash, and daring in the Revolutionary War were reminiscent of a romanticism found back in the days of chivalry.

In the sturdy stone house built by his grandfather at Waynesborough, Pennsylvania, Anthony was born January 1, 1745, the son of the brusque Isaac and the gentle Elizabeth Iddings Wayne. Sent to his uncle Gilbert Wayne's school, young Anthony's interest lagged except when the reading concerned military matters. The fancies of his nephew led the harassed uncle to complain to Anthony's father:

> What he may be best qualified for I know not. He may perhaps make a soldier. He has already distracted the brains of two-thirds of the boys under my charge by rehearsals of battles, sieges, etc. During noon, in place of the usual games of amusement, he has the boys employed in throwing up redoubts, skirmishing, etc.[1]

Eventually Isaac sent his volatile son off to the Academy at Philadelphia, where the youth became something of a dandy and a frequenter of taverns. Still, Anthony absorbed enough knowledge of mathematics to establish himself as a moderately successful surveyor at East Town in Chester County, Pennsylvania. In the spring of 1765, when he was twenty, he began courting a slim blonde girl of sixteen, Mary "Polly" Penrose, whose parents were disturbed by the uneasy reputation of her suitor. Anthony and Mary were persuaded to postpone marriage until his future was more certain.

It was during this same year that Wayne was employed by a Philadelphia syndicate (which included Benjamin Franklin) to survey the 200,000 acres they hoped to acquire in Nova Scotia. Working swiftly through the autumn, the lovesick youth returned to Pennsylvania in late December to press his suit with Mary. A promising future softened family resistance, and on March 25, 1766, Anthony carried her off as his bride to Waynesborough.

Later that spring he went back to Nova Scotia, but rising tensions between the mother country and her colonies caused the syndicate to lose interest in land speculation. Anthony returned to Waynesborough; he cultivated his farm and built a thriving tannery upon it. As he prospered, his family grew larger. In 1768, there was a daughter, Margaretta, and four years later, a son, Isaac.

By 1774, Anthony had fallen heir to his father's fortune. He was now quite successful—enough so that he had already taken on the swagger which he affected the rest of his life. Although only of medium height, he appeared taller because of his commanding presence. His handsome features were so clear-cut they seemed almost chiseled from stone and his dark hair, aquiline nose, and penetrating brown eyes added to his good looks. His personality bordered on the quixotic, for he was vain, impulsive, and given to the use of hyperbole. But he had great qualities of leadership and was most popular in the community where he lived.

With his educational background, natural talents, and attractive personal characteristics, Wayne soon emerged as a leader of the patriot cause. He was elected chairman of the Chester County Committee of Safety in 1774 and headed the local committee chosen to carry out the provisions of the boycott on British goods proposed by the First Continental Congress. In January, 1775, he represented his community in Pennsylvania's Provincial Congress, arguing the virtues of greater efforts for home manufactures. Yet he never allowed politics to overshadow his periodic exercises with the militia.

Although the ranks of the local regiments filled very quickly after the outbreak of war, Wayne was not commissioned colonel of the Fourth Battalion of the Pennsylvania line until January 3, 1776. When his command was ordered to join Washington around New York, he complained that at least one-half were armed with little more than "damned tomahawks." His Pennsylvanians had encamped on Long Island only a short time before orders came to relieve the sagging Canadian expedition. The American efforts to take Quebec had suffered a severe setback in December, 1775. Brigadier General Richard Montgomery had fallen victim to British bullets and Benedict Arnold had retreated to Montreal with the small force that had managed to escape capture.

Under Washington's mandate that the Quebec "misfortune must be repaired," [2] the first objective became the reportedly lightly-held post of Trois Rivières, halfway down the St. Lawrence between Montreal and Quebec. Wayne was ordered to serve under General William Maxwell along with Arthur St. Clair and William Irvine. Disembarking from their bateaux some three miles above the town at three in the morning of June 8, 1776, the Americans were discovered and fired upon by enemy vessels in the river. Led astray by their guide, the troops were soon lost and floundering belly-deep in the midst of "the most Horrid swamp that ever man set foot in."

It was nearly eight in the morning when Wayne and his 200 men broke into the clearing before the town, only to discover that redcoated regulars were driving down upon them. Wayne's muddy troops sent the enemy reeling back with a well-directed volley. British light artillery was brought up and this, added to the fire from boats on the river, swept the field clean of invaders.

A second British force was set ashore upstream to cut off the retreating Americans. The swamp offered the only route of escape. Other fugitives staggered in, their faces puffed from the "stings of Musketoes of a monstrous size and inumerable numbers." Rallying as many of his disorganized soldiers as possible, Wayne, limping from a "Slight touch in my Right leg," led them at last to safety across the New York border. There was more than a trace of egotism in Wayne's letter to Franklin, "I believe it will be Universally allowed that Col. [William] Allen & myself have saved the Army in Canada."

Even in the retreat down Lake Champlain, the dandy in Wayne showed itself when he ordered that a barber be appointed for every company and prescribed punishments for those soldiers who appeared shaggy or dirty. As he explained to General Washington:

> I have an insuperable bias in favour of an elegant uniform and a soldierly appearance, so much so that I would rather risk my life and reputation at the head of the same men in an attack, clothed and appointed as I could wish, merely with bayonets and a single charge of ammunition, than to take them as they appear in common with sixty rounds of cartridges. It may be a false idea, but I cannot help cherishing it.

Wayne was made commandant at Ticonderoga, the key fortress on the lakes in northern New York, in the fall of 1776 and readied his troops for what he grandly called "Death or Glory." But he had earlier lamented to his Polly that "Fortune has heretofore been a fickle Goddess to us—and like some other females changed for the first new face she saw." Sectionalism was rampant in the ranks. The Pennsylvanians had little use for the "damn'd Yankees," as they termed the New Englanders, and there was one mild riot involving some gunfire when the "leveling principle" of the northern troops became too much for the more class-conscious Pennsylvanians.

The discipline and uniformity so ardently desired by their colonel seemed remote for the Pennsylvanians. One teamster noted: "The vices of insubordination, gambling & rioting marked their battalion, and we ourselves had great trouble with them." Conditions inside Ticonderoga were such that it was hard to boost morale. Wayne dubbed the fortress a "Golgotha" and felt that if God had any hand in its being, "it was surely done in the dark; it is one confused jumble of stones, without order, beauty or profit." During the winter, the men within its walls shivered with cold. There was little food, and clothing fell into rags. The British were expected to come pouring down the lake with warmer weather. Discontent became vocal and Wayne's men began calling him a "tyrant." One company of infantrymen maintained their enlistments had expired and were driven back as the angry colonel thrust a pistol into the chest of the sergeant leading the malcontents; when there were increasing whispers of mutiny, the ringleader was publicly slapped across the cheek and sent to Albany for court-martial.[3]

On February 21, 1777, Wayne was promoted to brigadier general, and two months later received instructions to rejoin Washington's army at Morristown. But sad news from home took some of the edge off the joy of impending combat. His farm was being badly managed in Wayne's absence; no provisions had been made to educate his children while he was away; and politics in Pennsylvania were in a "sickly state." War, however, had become too fascinating a game to abandon, and his domestic concerns were drowned in a torrent of flowery words as he assured his harried Polly that he was indispensable to the army and elaborated upon the "pristine Lustre" of the "Blessings of Liberty."

When General Howe, in June, 1777, began the evacuation of British posts in New Jersey, Nathanael Greene's division was ordered to harass them on their march. After numerous delays and frustrations, only the troops led by Wayne and Daniel Morgan managed to reach the area, on June 22, in time to be of any service. They advanced on the British redoubts on the left bank of the Raritan and, in general, according to Washington, "behaved in a manner that does them great honor."[4] Writing to a friend, Wayne proudly exulted: "This Howe who was to March through America at the head of 5000 men had his coat much Dirtied, his Horses taken off, and himself badly Bruis'd for having the presumption at the head of 700 British Troops to face 500 Penns'as." Wayne was inclined to make too much of his small success. When Polly wrote pleading letters asking that he come home to handle pressing problems, he justified his reluctance to request leave with the assertion that he was doing the work of three general officers and was "peremptorily forbid by His Excellency to leave the Army." He had, indeed, entered upon a new phase of his career, for he began serving as a division commander with Washington's main army.

When finally it became evident that Howe's objective was Philadelphia, Washington decided to make his stand on the east bank of the Brandywine. Wayne, enthusiastically citing Caesar and Marshal Saxe, proposed that he lead a surprise attack against the marching enemy and perhaps throw them into "Confusion, Disorder or Retreat." The commander-in-chief, however, was in no mood to gratify Wayne's whims and stationed the spirited Pennsylvanian at Chad's Ford—the logical spot where the stream might be crossed. For an officer of limited combat experience Wayne did well, throwing a series of light, jabbing probes against Knyphausen's Hessians to keep them off balance. His defense of the ford was later termed "most conspicuous" by Henry Lee. Only after a sizable segment of the army had been outflanked by Cornwallis and a general retreat had been ordered, did Wayne and Maxwell fall away from their positions under the full fury of enemy artillery and musketry.[5] It is not unreasonable to suppose that Wayne's tenacious resistance at Chad's Ford may have helped to save Washington's army from envelopment.

Wayne's new-found fame was followed by one of the more shameful episodes in his career. As Washington withdrew from the Brandywine, Wayne's detachment of 1,500 men and four fieldpieces was sent to the neighborhood of Warren's Tavern near Paoli, close to Wayne's own home and only three miles from the left flank of the enemy. There, in the skirt of a thick wood, they lay awaiting a British move. When and if Howe marched, the Americans might fall upon his rearguard and baggage train. Wayne's position was not a well-kept secret, but he could see little reason for alarm and reported that the "enemy are very quiet, washing and cooking." In fact, he considered them ripe for a "fatal blow" and dispatches to Washington urged, "for God's sake push on as fast as possible." [6]

The British struck even as Wayne dreamed of victory. Major General Charles Grey, leading a detachment whose arms had their charges drawn or flints removed, slipped silently through the night of September 20–21, 1777. Some time after nine o'clock, a Mr. Jones, "an Old Gent'n" of the neighborhood, came into the American encampment with the information that the British had planned a surprise assault. Additional videttes and pickets were thrown out, but when nothing happened Wayne ordered Major Francis Nicholas "with some degree of anger to go to bed—for having made a mistake."

At about eleven o'clock that night, the British burst upon the camp from out of the shadows and caught the Pennsylvanians as they were crawling out of their blankets groggy with sleep. Wayne declared later that he had stationed his troops in some semblance of order, but neither the British narratives nor American casualties bear out this assertion. Major John André implied that the surprise was complete, while a fellow officer referred to the so-called "Paoli Massacre" as "a dreadful scene of havoc," marked by "shrieks, groans, shouting, imprecations, deprecations, the clashing of swords and bayonets." Not a shot was fired by the disciplined British regulars and they depended exclusively upon their bayonets. The American artillery was brought off with some difficulty, but eight supply wagons were lost to the enemy. Estimates of casualties were indefinite, ranging all the way from Howe's 370 to Elias Boudinot's 25 or 30. Historians have generally agreed that Wayne's losses were about 150, while those of the British seem to have been no more than 10. [7]

Thus did Anthony Wayne suffer a deflation of ego, personally more damaging than his military defeat. Although he was exonerated by a court of inquiry, the persistent accusations of Colonel Richard Humpton of the Eleventh Pennsylvania "that he had timely notice of the enemy's intention to attack" and had done nothing, led Wayne to demand a court-martial. He was acquitted "with the highest honor." [8] Physically worn out by this ordeal, Wayne began to entertain serious doubts as to whether he should continue in service. Yet wounded vanity demanded that he vindicate himself. As the two armies maneuvered, Wayne bombarded Washington with proposals that he be allowed to lead a flank attack upon the enemy.

He was soon to have his revenge. At the Battle of Germantown, on October 4, 1777, Wayne went charging into the British lines like a whirlwind. In the early morning hours, British officers were startled from their sleep by ringing cries of "Have at the bloodhounds, revenge Wayne's affair!" [9] Revenge must have been sweet. Wayne's men killed some British soldiers even after they had thrown down their arms and offered to surrender, but the Pennsylvanian only noted piously: "Our people Remembering the Action of the Night of the 20th of Sep'r . . . pushed on with their Bayonets—and took Ample Vengeance for that Nights Work. Our Officers Exerted themselves to save many of the poor wretches who were Crying for Mercy—but to little purpose; the Rage and fury of the Soldiers were not to be Restrained for some time—at least not until great numbers of the Enemy fell by our Bayonets."

From the patriot point of view, the Battle of Germantown was one long string of mistakes. Some of the blame must fall upon Washington, whose orders were so confusing that even the guides lost their way. The battle plan, classic in conception, was based on four pincer columns which, marching through the night, were to converge upon the British lines from different directions. At sunrise Wayne's troops, in Sullivan's division, drove the British before them with bayonets, but many units soon became separated in the dense morning fog. Wayne, hearing artillery and musketry to his rear, thought Sullivan was in trouble and turned back. A dim and distant line of men was faintly outlined through the mist. Both sides fired. Both were Americans, although Wayne later claimed that the other group was dressed in red coats. The battle which had begun with such great promise quickly came to a disastrous end. Nathanael Greene furnished cover for the subsequent retreat, which was described as beyond all "powers of description: sadness and consternation expressed in every countenance."

The troops wandering through the fog and fired on by Wayne's men had been under the command of Adam Stephen. Stephen, who was to be accused of drinking heavily that day, argued that Wayne's troops had brought on the exchange of shots when they fired on a British group who were coming forward to surrender. Stephen, however, was later found guilty of "Unoffercerlike conduct" and "drunkenness" and dismissed from the service.[10] Had Wayne been able to pursue his initial assault without interruption, he might well have pierced the British center and won the battle out of hand.

The fog, insisted Wayne, had been responsible for the defeat that had flirted with victory—a victory which he declared "in all Human probability would have put an end to the American War." He scarcely mentioned Washington's willingness to listen to those officers who protested leaving "a castle in our rear" when a detachment of the enemy sought refuge within the sturdy stone walls of the Chew House. Nor would he admit that even after two years of war there was still such a woeful lack of experience that officers found it necessary to quote from military textbooks when making tactical decisions.

One of the American positions that had withstood the enemy assault near Philadelphia was Fort Mifflin—a bastion located on Mud Island below the city, which denied the British passage farther up the river. Wayne, continually searching for military immortality, pleaded that he be allowed to lead a relief expedition to the fort. Instead, Washington called a council of war, a practice Wayne felt "was the surest way to do nothing." When Fort

Mifflin fell in mid-November, Wayne still urged the commander-in-chief to take the field: "You will not be in a Worse Situation, nor your Arms in less Credit if you should meet with a Misfortune than if you were to Remain Inactive." If nothing else, he argued, constant action should be maintained against the enemy's outposts. In the end no action was taken, and it was said that Wayne was the one who suggested Valley Forge as winter quarters because of its proximity to the enemy.

Perhaps it was the pain of being ignored or the growing tradition of defeat surrounding Washington that finally led Wayne to nurture doubts as to the ability of the commander-in-chief. After Gates's victory at Saratoga, Wayne wrote that "whether I shall remain longer in the service than this Campaign depends on Circumstances—there are certain Generals—as *Lee—Gates—Mifflin* &cᵃ. who will point out by their Conduct the line which I shall follow. . . ." Washington, on the other hand, had bungled his opportunities at the Battles of Brandywine and Germantown, and Wayne complained "if our Worthy General will but follow his own good Judgment without listning too some Council. . . ." [11] Being headstrong and bold himself, Wayne wanted Washington to assert more vigorous leadership.

Wayne was disenchanted too with the vaunted riflemen by whose efforts so many had expected to win the war. He expounded to a friend on a theme that had been preying on his mind for over a year:

> I don't like rifles—I would almost as soon face an Enemy with a good Musket and Bayonet without ammunition—as with ammunition without a Bayonet for altho' there are not many Instances of bloody bayonets yet I am confident that one bayonet keeps off an Other—and for the Want of which the Chief of the Defeats we have met with ought in a great measure to be Attributed—the Enemy knowing the Defenseless State of our Riflemen rush on— they fly mix with or pass thro' the other Troops and Communicate fear that is ever incident to a retiring Corps—this Would not be the Case if the Riflemen had bayonets—but it would be still better if good muskets and bayonets were put into the hands of good

Marksmen and Rifles entirely laid aside—for my own part I never
Wish to see one—at least Without a Bayonet.

With the days growing warmer, Wayne was sent into New
Jersey to round up some cattle for feeding the army. It was a
task he considered beneath his dignity as a soldier. But the scattered contacts and skirmishes he had with the enemy fired his
ambition to a point where he again began bombarding Washington with suggestions for striking at the British.

By June, 1778, it became known that Sir Henry Clinton had
replaced General William Howe as commander-in-chief of the
British army, and the bustle in Philadelphia suggested an evacuation of the city. When Clinton's army and extensive baggage
train stretched itself into a slow crawl across New Jersey, Washington promptly called a council of war—a council characterized
by such caution on the part of his generals that Alexander Hamilton sarcastically noted it "would have done honor to the most
honorable body of midwives, and to them only." [12] Wayne along
with General John Cadwalader urged an immediate attack on
the premise that it would be impossible to overcome the enemy
once they reached New York. Even if Clinton did gain the advantage, they argued, he would be unable to pursue the American
army because of his baggage train. An attack by Washington,
however, would make it appear that the enemy was fleeing before him.[13] Charles Lee wavered as to whether he would accept
the command of the vanguard in an attack upon the baggage
train, an attack he was convinced would be futile, but he finally
assumed command of the advance corps in what came to be
called the Battle of Monmouth.

Even as they marched, Alexander Hamilton reported back
that "General Wayne's detachment is almost starving and seems
both unwilling and unable to march farther till they are supplied." [14] Yet Wayne bullied his troops forward and after
contact was made, Washington, despite the reluctance of his
council, decided to attack in force. On the morning of June 28,
1778, Lee appeared to be maneuvering his troops aimlessly in the

vicinity of the Monmouth Court House with "no plan of attack."
Wayne's troops bore the brunt of the fierce fighting that followed
until, in the confusion and amidst a flurry of contradictory orders, Lee ordered a retreat.

Washington appeared on the scene and after some hot words
with Lee took command of the situation. The commander-in-
chief rallied the retiring troops and instantly ordered a new line
formed on Wayne's men, who had taken up a position in an
orchard at the edge of a road between two hills. Three times the
British came rushing along the low ground hoping to drive
through Wayne. Each time they were driven back with heavy
casualties as Wayne held his fire until the last minute. When
the British formed for a fourth assault with a body of troops so
large as to outflank both ends of his position, Wayne withdrew
in good order inside the main lines of the American army. Wayne
was satisfied; he had met and bested the flower of the British
army. "Among them are Numbers of the Richest blood of England," he wrote. "Tell the Phil'a ladies," he added sarcastically,
"that the heavenly, sweet, pretty red Coats—the accomplished
Gent'm of the Guards and Grenudiers have humbled themselves
on the plains of Monmouth." At Monmouth, Wayne had found
at last the glory that had eluded him so long.

Charles Lee, smarting under a reprimand from Washington,
began a vicious tirade against the commander-in-chief. Because
of his disrespect toward Washington and formal charges of misconduct on the battlefield by Wayne and General Charles Scott,
Lee was court-martialed. Wayne and Scott became important
witnesses for the prosecution.

Lee, fighting for his military reputation, railed against false
intelligence and, in part, blamed his difficulties on "the temerity,
folly and contempt of orders of General Wain. . . ." Wayne, on
the other hand, testified that Lee was dilatory in both decisions
and actions upon the battlefield. In the opinion of some historians, politics was the prime factor in Lee's conviction; his
biographer concluded that "the court-martial sacrificed Lee be-

cause of partisan passions in the army and a belief that the public welfare should override all other considerations." [15]

Lee was his own greatest enemy; he wrote and talked too much. His tart remarks brought a challenge from Von Steuben and a duel with John Laurens, aide-de-camp to Washington. While Lee was recovering from the slight wound received in the Laurens duel, Wayne, in early January, 1779, demanded satisfaction for Lee's strictures upon his conduct at Monmouth and the "ungenerous tho' free Manner in which you Affect to treat my Opinion & military Character. . . ." [16] When Lee explained that he was only defending his own reputation and that no personal affront or animosity was intended, Wayne was satisfied and dropped the idea of a duel.

Wayne had likewise suffered a blow to his pride—a blow that may have made him sensitive enough to challenge Lee. The gradual decline in numbers had made it necessary to reorganize the Pennsylvania line. Some of his enemies gained the upper hand in his state and Wayne, a brigadier general, was replaced by Major General Arthur St. Clair. His bitterness was compounded by humiliation, being "superseded at this late hour by a man in whose conduct and candor I have no confidence hurts me not a little." Wayne's sense of personal injury became so great that he "therefore determined to return to domestic life, & leave the blustering field of Mars to the possession of Gentlemen of more worth."

He was not to sulk for long. When an elite corps of Continental light infantry was formed, made up of veterans who were picked from the regular regiments on the basis of youth, agility, and daring, Wayne intrigued for the command. Of special interest to him was the fact that these select troops were to be rigorously drilled in the use of the bayonet. Wayne wanted the command so badly, he threatened to resign unless awarded the post. Daniel Morgan was another contender for the command. The very day that Wayne's appointment was announced in June, 1779, Morgan submitted his resignation and went home, "deeply affected with this Injury done my reputation." [17]

Wayne's popularity among the Pennsylvania troops became

evident when large numbers expressed a desire to follow him into the light infantry. One and a half battalions of Pennsylvania troops were included in the 2,000 soldiers who were planned for this new command, "preferable to any in the army." It was with these elite troops that Wayne was to tread the paths to glory.

Wayne was eager to commit the new corps to combat as soon as possible. "I believe that sanguine God is rather thirsty for human gore," he wrote grandly. Stony Point, the British strongpoint below West Point on the Hudson was selected as his objective. Serving as the southern gate to the Hudson Highlands, this position was of great strategic and economic significance. To Wayne it was much more. Stony Point was to furnish him with final retribution for Paoli. He had learned much from that night of misery and was determined to repay the enemy in kind by relying upon the bayonet as his weapon of victory in storming the garrison. For two days prior to the assault, it is said, American patrols killed every dog along the route of approach, and all communications with Wayne's men were halted to preserve secrecy. After dark on the night of July 15, 1779, the march began. One account stated that a soldier who refused to believe that a post could be taken with empty weapons stepped from the ranks to load his piece and was immediately run through by his captain.[18]

A man of Anthony Wayne's temperament would have considered himself negligent of the demands of posterity had he not composed words for the ages. To his friend Sharp Delany he wrote as one who felt death's chill breath, expressing the fear that his wife would die of grief, and requesting that Delany educate his children. After berating "the parsimony and neglect of Congress," he added the flourish, "I am called to Sup, but where to breakfast, either within the enemy's lines in triumph or in the other World!"

Approaching silently in two columns, with a third unit under Henry Lee demonstrating in front of the post, Wayne's men began their assault about a half-hour past midnight. A bullet crease along his skull allowed Wayne to indulge his flair for the dramatic. Crying out that the wound was fatal, Wayne asked that he be carried inside the fortress walls to die. His soldiers gave a shout, charged up the slope of Stony Point bearing their commander on their shoulders, and swept over the crest of the ramparts.

In less than a half-hour, the entire fort had been overrun. It was a feat that Nathanael Greene said would "for ever immortalize Gen. Wayne, as it would do honor to the first general in Europe." The light infantry, despite the large number of Pennsylvanians within the ranks, displayed a quality of mercy that led one British naval officer to comment: ". . . they showed at this moment a generosity and clemency which during the course of the rebellion had no parallel." As one American officer explained, ". . . the usage of arms justifying, and the *lex talionis* demanding, a carnage, yet that humanity, that amiable weakness, which has ever distinguished Americans, prevailed." [19] Over 500 prisoners, 15 cannon, and a quantity of valuable military stores had been taken.

Although Stony Point was abandoned after the victory, the legend of Anthony Wayne is based on this triumph. His first dispatch to Washington, though brief, boasted, "This fort & Garrison with Coln. Johnson are our's. Our Officers & Men behaved like men who are determined to be free." The conquest, said Washington, "will have a good effect upon the minds of the people, give our troops greater confidence in themselves and depress the spirits of the enemy proportionately." [20] Even British accounts conceded that "considered in all its parts and difficulties, it would have done honor to the most veteran soldiers." And, unbeknownst to Washington, the time the British consumed in reoccupying and rebuilding Stony Point, forced Clinton to abandon plans for a new offensive. [21]

In the opinion of certain of his officers, the glory of the day had not been properly shared by Wayne. Replying to Lieutenant Colonel Isaac Sherman's "You have not arrived beyond the regions of censure," Wayne penned an angry "I put up with no man's Insults." But the grousing soon disappeared, possibly because of the breakup of the light infantry.

Success has a way of healing old wounds, and Stony Point was instrumental in mending the breach between Wayne and Charles Lee. Insisting that he had "no intent in paying court to any individual," Lee lauded the conqueror of Stony Point as "a brave officer, and an honest man," and referred to his recent success as "not only the most brilliant, in my opinion, through the whole course of this war, on either side, but that it is the most brilliant I am acquainted with in history. . . ." The vaulting ambition of Anthony Wayne would not allow him to overlook such "encomiums." His reply was a bouquet of similar strain, most appreciative of Lee's sentiments "because they come from a Gentleman of the first experience—whose military abilities stand high in this age of the World." [22]

Although the light infantry had proved its worth, Washington decided to break up the corps after Congress had detached one of the most serviceable regiments for other duty. In December, 1779, with his former officers expressing "that confidence essentially necessary to ensure success in military operations," Wayne retired to Waynesborough. There he battled boredom until May 18, 1780, when he received Washington's "I shall be happy to see you in camp again, and hope you will, without hesitation, resume your command in the Penn'a line."

Once back in the army, Wayne was put to work harassing some of the outlying British posts along the lower Hudson and in New Jersey. One objective Washington ordered him to attack was the enemy position at Bull's Ferry at Bergen, four miles north of Hoboken. This strong blockhouse, "Garrisoned by the Refugees & a wretched banditti of Robbers horse thieves &c" not only sheltered woodcutters for the British army and protected the cattle in the area, but served as a repository for the booty taken by local Tory raiders. Wayne, leading the First and Second Pennsylvania Regiments, attacked the blockhouse during the night of July 21, 1780. For an hour, light artillery pounded the log walls without effect. Then, with the enemy rushing forward reinforcements, there was a charge through the abatis to the stockade wall. This rash act which Wayne attributed to the "enthusiastic bravery of all ranks of officers and men," resulted in 65 casualties.[23] The attack ended in a stalemate and all Wayne succeeded in doing was to burn a few boats and drive off some cattle before he withdrew.

The failure to repeat the conquest of Stony Point stimulated a bit of notoriety that Wayne did not relish. Major John André, Clinton's adjutant general who fancied himself a poet, composed a frothy rhyme called "The Cow Chace." The poem, ridiculing Wayne, ended with these oft-quoted lines:

> And now I've closed my epic strain,
> I tremble as I show it,
> Lest this same warrier-drover Wayne
> Should ever catch the poet.

The last canto, ironically, was published the same day that André was captured at Tarrytown and held as a spy for assisting Benedict Arnold. Although some biographers claimed that Wayne did not gain the prefix "Mad" until after the war or certainly no earlier than the summer of 1781, it appears that the nickname was already associated with him. One line in "The Cow Chace" referred to "mad Anthony's fierce eye."

There was considerable unrest and discontent in Wayne's command during the summer of 1780. A dispute arose over the command of a new corps of light infantry that was to be created from the ranks of the Pennsylvania line. Faced with a rash of resignations, Wayne resorted to his entire repertoire of rhetorical grandiloquence by appealing to the friendship, honor, and patriotism of his officers. His address ended on this stirring note: "For God's sake, be yourselves—and as a band of Brothers—rise superior to every Injury—whether real or imaginary—at least for this Campaign which probably will produce a Conviction to the World—that America owes her freedom to the temporary sacrifice you now make." Fortunately the plan to organize the new corps was abandoned and the problem resolved itself.

When Benedict Arnold attempted to deliver West Point to the enemy in September, 1780, Wayne's quick move to that post prevented a British occupation. Leaving his tents standing at Tappan on the Hudson at two in the morning, he raced his Pennsylvanians northward to Haverstraw—a distance of sixteen miles—in less than four hours. Washington thought the feat "fabulous" and received Wayne "like a God," exclaiming "All is safe, and I again am happy." Once West Point was secure, Wayne bitterly denounced the traitor Arnold, claiming "that honor & true Virtue were Strangers to his Soul . . . he never possessed either fortitude or personal bravery—he was naturally a Coward, and never went in the way of Danger but when Stimulated by Liquor even to Intoxication. . . ."

But Wayne was soon to discover that Benedict Arnold was not alone in his dissatisfaction with conditions in the Continental army. In December, 1780, there was a great deal of grumbling in the Pennsylvania line. Wayne's soldiers were unhappy for a variety of reasons—their clothing consisted of tattered rags, the food was poor, there was no rum, and no one had seen "a paper dollar in the way of pay for near *twelve months*." By mid-December, Wayne was warning Joseph Reed, president of the Pennsylvana Executive Council, that the British were aware of this restlessness and were circulating tracts among the troops urging them to desert. He was beginning, Wayne said, to fear the "Ides of Jan[uar]y." [24] There were complaints also that those who enlisted "for three years or during the war" were being held in service longer than three years—the term that the troops interpreted as the limit of their obligations. Tempers were brought to a boil when it was discovered that new recruits were being offered an enlistment bonus of twenty-five dollars, "hard money," while veteran troops remained unpaid.

New Year's Day, 1781, dawned bright and clear, but the fine day proved a false omen for the events that followed. With his troops encamped at Mount Kemble near Morristown, Wayne had established his headquarters east of the bivouac in the house of the staunch loyalist Peter Kemble. There he spent the day with

his field officers discussing the new "arrangement of the Line."
As a New Year's treat each soldier had been issued a half-pint of
spirits and those who had money purchased more at local taverns.
Officers in the camp found their pleasure in "an elegant regimental dinner and entertainment." About eight in the evening,
a few huzzas rose from the Eleventh Regiment area. Within an
hour all was quiet again and the outburst attributed to an over-
indulgence in strong drink. Around ten o'clock a general huz-
zaing began to roll from one side of the camp to the other.
Lieutenant Enos Reeves dashed onto the parade "and found
numbers in small groups whispering and busily running up and
down the line." A musket fired, and a skyrocket split the night.
It was mutiny!

Wayne galloped in with several officers. Colonel Richard Butler joined him in a futile haranguing of the troops. Three of the
more energetic officers already had been wounded, one fatally.
The mutineers insisted they had been wronged in their pay and
other matters and demanded a hearing with their state officials.
Wayne argued that he would endeavor to remedy their grievances. The reply was that their dispute was not with him and
could be settled only by the Congress. When Wayne persisted in
standing in their path, a volley whistled over his head. In a melo-
dramatic gesture, Wayne threw open his tunic and shouted: "If
you mean to kill me, shoot me at once—here's my breast." The
mutineers replied that they had no intention to harm any officer,
"two or three individuals excepted."

Part of the Fourth Regiment was paraded and ordered to
charge the malcontents. They refused. Around two in the morning, formed in platoons and with drums throbbing and fifes
squealing, the Pennsylvania line marched out of camp. Wayne
made his stand at the Chatham–Princeton crossroads, some say
with pistols drawn, determined to dissuade them should they turn
left in a mass desertion to the British. They answered him with
assurances that their march was to the Congress at Philadelphia,
and should the enemy sally forth to seek advantage from their
defection they would turn back to fight. "If that is your senti-

ments," said Wayne, "I'll not leave you, and if you won't allow me to march in your front, I'll follow in your rear." It was later reported that he not only offered them advice, but also forwarded provisions in order to prevent any depredations upon private property.[25]

True to their word, the mutineers not only made no attempt to reach the enemy but turned over two British emissaries to be hanged as spies. Their appeals were forwarded to Congress as they halted at Princeton for an answer. Lafayette and Arthur St. Clair rode out to negotiate, but they were requested to leave. The insurgents declared that they would deal only with Wayne, Walter Stewart, and Richard Butler, or the Congress.

In Philadelphia there was a near-panic. Some even suggested that the Congress flee the city. Joseph Reed went with a committee from Congress to start negotiations. The committee remained at Princeton while Reed, Wayne, Stewart, and Butler opened discussions with the sergeants at Trenton. A settlement was finally reached calling for payment of all arrears in pay plus depreciation, and the issuance of all articles of clothing to which the soldiers were entitled. Any soldier who had enlisted on an option of three years' service or the war's duration could be discharged at the end of three years. In the absence of documentary proof, a man's oath was to be considered sufficient.[26]

By January 29, 1781, nearly 1,250 men had been discharged from the Pennsylvania line—a large number swearing falsely they had been in the service for three years. On February 20, 1781, the Congress resolved that all Continental troops from Pennsylvania to Georgia were to be included in the Southern army. Without consulting Washington, Congress ordered the Pennsylvania line to the South as soon as it could be rebuilt. Wayne was confident he could raise his command to its old strength, but Washington commented, "I fancy he rather overrates the matter."

In the days that followed, matters went from bad to worse. Perhaps the mutiny had rubbed tempers that were already raw, for not only did Alexander Hamilton resign in a huff from

Washington's staff, but there are indications that Wayne had a tiff with the general and was nursing a bruised ego. Nevertheless he spent much of his time lobbying with the Pennsylvania Executive Council and the Continental Congress. However, he soon reported sadly, "They all present me that Gorgon Head, an empty treasury." [27] The Council did pardon some convicts on condition that they enlist in the line, and some of those soldiers recently discharged re-enlisted to receive the bonus.

When Wayne arrived at York, Pennsylvania, on May 19, he found what he termed a "little well appointed army." Inclement weather caused a three-day delay in his plans to march for Lafayette's army in Virginia. Then it happened once again—mutiny!

This time the discontent seems to have arisen from wages paid in the "Ideal money" of Pennsylvania, worth about one-seventh as much as specie. It was not a full-scale revolt, and varying reports confuse the events. Six soldiers were charged with such crimes "as exciting mutiny as far as in his power," for "mutinous expressions such as asserting that if any officer dared touch him he would shoot him," while one soldier, who later claimed he was drunk at the time, shouted in the hearing of the officer of the day, "God damn the officers, the buggers." Of the six mutineers, Wayne pardoned two, while the remaining four were executed by firing squad in "a most painful scene." And, according to one account, "The Line marched the next day southward, mute as fish." [28]

By June 10, 1781, Wayne's Pennsylvanians, almost 800 strong, were with Lafayette in Virginia. One observer described their elegant appearance to his wife in these words:

> They were a splendid and formidable corps. If the laurels which they win bear any proportion to the plumes they are adorned with, the heroes of antiquity will soon sink into oblivion. Were I a native of Laputa, with the assistance of a quadrant I might possibly calculate the altitude of that which nods over the brow of their General. Their military pride promises much, for the first step to make a good soldier is to entertain a consciousness of personal superiority;

and this consciousness is said to prevail in the breasts of these men, even to the meanest private in the ranks.[29]

Despite the Pennsylvanians and their magnificent plumes, Lafayette's army was too weak to do little more than dance away before Lord Cornwallis. On June 26, there was a skirmish at Spencer's Ordinary, but it ended only in a tangle of crackling musketry and plunging horses.

Finally at Green Spring, near Jamestown, on Friday, July 6, 1781, Anthony Wayne "pick'd a Quarrel [with] the British. . . ." Ostensibly, Cornwallis had ferried most of his troops across the James River; actually only the baggage and a mounted detachment were on the far side. Wayne assumed he was attacking the rearguard when he sent forward several hundred riflemen to harass the British while the Pennsylvanians advanced across a morass. Resistance by Banastre Tarleton's legion screened the major force of the enemy from view. When Lafayette threw in the Pennsylvanians still held in reserve, Cornwallis sallied forth with his entire army. What had been a supposed rearguard action turned into a full-scale battle.

Wayne, fearing to give the order to retreat lest it become a rout, impulsively ordered a bayonet charge. A heavy discharge of musketry and grapeshot brought it to an abrupt halt 200 yards from the enemy. Cornwallis could not but take this bold advance as a presage of a much more formidable attack. He hesitated and took up a defensive position waiting for the main blow to fall. For the next quarter-hour, as darkness began falling, the fighting grew fierce. Two British regiments, the Seventy-sixth and Eightieth, reported they gave the Pennsylvanians "a trimming" and claimed that they would have captured the whole corps had there been a little more daylight. Eventually Lafayette rode forward and ordered a retreat. Newspapers boasted of "Wayne, with a handful of Pennsylvanians, frightening the whole of Cornwallis' army of 'undaunted Britons.' " Others were less laudatory. Dr. Robert Wharry was even bitter: "I make no doubt, but you have heard of the Brush we had with the whole British Army; I was brought to bed with a Disappointment, another blockhouse affair—Madness—Mad A————y, by G—— I never knew such a piece of work heard of—about eight hundred troups opposed to five or six thousand Veterans upon their own ground." Ebenezer Wild commented, "General Wayne, being anxious to perform wonders! attacked the whole British Army with about 1000 men." French military censure was milder with General Rochambeau referring to Wayne as a *"brave homme, mais très ardent."* Even Wayne's friends voiced some apprehension as Nathanael Greene wrote of Lafayette's "military ardor, which no doubt is heated by the fire of the Modern hero, who by the by is an excellent officer. . . ." [30]

As Cornwallis maneuvered through the Virginia tidewater before fortifying the little village of Yorktown, Wayne's troops relaxed. Some even began to pay court to the Virginia belles. Wayne narrowly missed death when a befuddled sentry fired into the darkness wounding him in the thigh. The injury healed enough for Wayne to realize his "hope to participate in the glory attending the capture of Lord Cornwallis and his marauding army."

The Yorktown siege was dull in comparison with the actions that had gone before. Brigaded with Virginia troops in Steuben's division, Wayne found few opportunities to distinguish himself. When two redoubts were overrun in the most spectacular action of the siege, the Pennsylvanians remained in reserve. But in the colorful Steuben, Wayne found a kindred soul. After the completion of the second siege parallel, Wayne and Steuben were in the trenches together when a British cannon ball fell near by. The baron fell flat as Wayne tripped and sprawled across him. "I always knew you were a brave man," said the amused German, "but I did not know that you were so perfect in every point of duty: you cover your general's retreat in the best possible manner." [31]

Wayne believed, and undoubtedly hoped, that Cornwallis would not surrender nearly 6,000 troops without a "severe sortie." He was still awaiting such action when a chamade was beat on October 17, calling for a parley. The only compensation was that Wayne's troops were in the trenches when terms were requested. After the capitulation, Cornwallis was besieged with so many invitations that he was forced to decline Wayne's request to come to dinner.

On November 1, 1781, the Pennsylvania line, with St. Clair as major general and Wayne as brigadier, marched to South Carolina to reinforce Greene's Southern army. Henry Lee recorded his impressions of this "Irish" unit which could well be interpreted as a reflection of Wayne's personality:

> Bold and daring they were impatient and refractory; and would always prefer an appeal to the bayonet, to a toilsome march. Restless under the want of food and whiskey; adverse to absence from their baggage; and attached to the pleasure of the table; Wayne and his brigade were more encumbered with wagons than any equal portion of the army. The general and his soldiers were singularly fitted for close and stubborn action, hand to hand, in the centre of the army. . . ." [32]

After a leisurely march, the Pennsylvanians joined Greene on January 4, 1782. Within a short time Wayne was detached with 170 inexperienced men—and as many militia as could be persuaded to take the field—into Georgia. Taking post at Ebenezer, twenty-five miles above Savannah, he was soon sending dispatches to Greene, begging for some of his Pennsylvanians "who have fought and bled with me during my campaigns."

On February 19, he decoyed a large party of Indians into a trap, capturing the provisions they were taking to the enemy in Savannah. He sent the Indians back to their tribes, telling them that Savannah would soon fall to the Americans and that they had best remain neutral for the duration of the war. On May 21, the Savannah garrison under Colonel Thomas Brown made a sortie. Acting on the maxim that "the success of a night attack depends more on the prowess of the men than their numbers," Wayne marched four miles in the darkness across a narrow causeway through a swamp. A sudden charge, and Brown's force of cavalry, infantry, and Indians were sent fleeing into the night.

Three nights later some of the more defiant of the Creek Indians, led by the intrepid Guristersijo, turned the tables by surprising Wayne's camp. After the first recoil, Wayne rallied his troops and a sudden charge not only threw the savages into the swamp, but left Guristersijo among the slain. At daylight the British sallied out in support, but were driven back by a vigorous counterattack. "Our trophies," bragged Wayne, "are an elegant standard, 107 horses with a number of packs, arms &c. and more horses are hourly secured and brought in."

When the British evacuated Savannah on July 11, 1782, Greene wrote, "Georgia is ours, and Wayne has acquitted himself with great honor." [33] There was even a note of pride in Wayne's complaint:

> The duty done by us in Georgia was more difficult than that imposed upon the children of Israel. They had only to make bricks without straw, but we have had provisions, forage, and almost every other apparatus of war to procure without money; boats, bridges, &c. to build without materials except those taken from the stumps, and what was most difficult of all, to make Whigs out of Tories.

In August, 1782, after his return to South Carolina, Wayne fell victim to the same fever that was ravaging the rest of the Pennsylvania line. He doctored himself in the usual manner with "Frequent emetics & constant application of the Peruvian bark." While recovering, he managed to negotiate a treaty with the Creeks and Cherokees that helped to bring greater peace in Georgia.

On December 14, 1782, when Charleston was evacuated, Greene granted Wayne the privilege of leading the American troops into the city. The subsequent period of marking time until the formal peace was anticlimatic—winning independence was more exciting than the realization. In response to rumors that he was contemplating a future life on the plantation given him by the grateful citizens of Georgia, his fellow Pennsylvanian, Benjamin Rush, urged him to "Come and let the name of Wayne descend to posterity in your native State."

Wayne did return to Pennsylvania, having been promoted, by brevet, to major general. Still in poor health, he was elected, in 1783, to the Council of Censors, a watchdog organization whose duties were to determine if the provisions of the Pennsylvania Constitution of 1776 were being carried out. In 1784 and 1785, he was elected to the Assembly from Chester County, and vainly attempted to mollify retaliatory actions taken against the loyalists of the state.

By 1786, his financial problems had become critical. He sojourned south in an effort to make his Georgia plantation pay. Down the river was the plantation of Nathanael Greene, and when his general died in June, 1786, Wayne was at his bedside, distressed "because I have seen a great and good man die." [34]

Debt became an intolerable burden and Wayne took it as a personal insult when his creditors attempted to collect their money. Back in Philadelphia he became a member of the Pennsylvania Convention that ratified the Federal Constitution, but he returned to Georgia in 1788 in an attempt to bring some order out of the chaotic conditions on his plantation. He was bored, and proved to be an indifferent planter: "God, how tired I am of being buried in a damned rice swamp. I want a more active scene!" Overwhelmed with self-pity, he quoted the following lines from "The Old Soldier" to his wife:

> Ungrateful country! when the danger's o'er,
> Your bravest sons cold charity implore.
> Ah! heave for me a sympathetic sigh
> And wipe the falling tear from sorrow's eye.

The plantation was sold to satisfy his creditors, but his popularity was such that he became president of the Georgia Society of the Cincinnati. After a spirited campaign, he was elected a member of the House of Representatives from Georgia in 1791. He served only from March 4, 1791, to March 21, however, as his defeated opponent protested so loudly and presented such damaging evidence of fraud that the election was voided.

After Generals Josiah Harmar and Arthur St. Clair suffered

defeats by the Indians in the Northwest Territory, President Washington weighed the merits of his old officers as possible successors to the western command. Seemingly against his better judgment, Washington appointed Wayne to the post. Confirmation was not easily obtained, for too many in the Senate remembered that he was a business failure and a repudiated congressman. But Washington prevailed. Created a major general, "Mad Anthony" built an army around the riflemen of the frontier. Although this was a different type of warfare, Wayne still stressed the musket and the bayonet as the "most formidable weapons." Despite factions created among the officer corps by his subordinate, Brigadier General James Wilkinson, Wayne still managed to win a brilliant victory against the Indians in the Battle of Fallen Timbers in the summer of 1794. His triumph was gained through a volley and a charge with the bayonet. A year later, he was able to dictate the terms of the Treaty of Greenville that opened up the Northwest for settlement to a land-hungry people.

Because his victory brought an end to Indian resistance and gave additional stability to the government, Wayne easily overcame the charges of James Wilkinson, who spoke of him as "a liar, a drunkard, a Fool, the associate of the lowest order of Society, and the companion of their vices . . . my rancorous enemy, a Coward, a Hypocrite, and the contempt of every man of sense and virtue." Wayne's popularity was so great that he was able to dismiss such carping as "the idle Phantom of a disturbed imagination." [35] Indeed, in view of Wilkinson's subsequent duplicity in selling out to the Spanish for gold, his description of Wayne might easily have been applied to himself.

Upon Wayne's return to Philadelphia, he received the one thing he had sought and fought for all his life—adulation as a military hero. John Adams was to report one gathering: "General Wayne was there in glory. The man's feelings must be worth a guinea a minute." There was even talk that Wayne would become Secretary of War, although there were those who feared "we should be reduced to a State of insolvency" should he be appointed.[36]

But Wayne was worn out at fifty-one. When Jay's Treaty called for the evacuation of British posts in the Northwest, he hurried westward again. Upon his taking possession of Detroit, Congressman William Vans Murray mused, "Wayne! ah could we both have but seen W's Entre into Detroit! when he pranced over the Barbacon." Wayne soon busied himself with the inspection of posts. All the while he suspected his old enemy Wilkinson of intrigue with the Spanish, but never was able to furnish proof. It was to be 150 years before documents in the archives of Madrid would establish Wilkinson's treacherous intrigues with the Spanish governor of Louisiana. At Presque Isle, Wayne's health broke under what was termed "a severe fit of gout." [37] On the evening of December 15, 1796, Anthony Wayne suffered the indignity of dying in bed.

"Mad Anthony" seems particularly appropriate for the man. Proud, quick-tempered, impetuous, and even arrogant, he was consumed by a hero complex. His flaming and often uncontrolled temper revealed openly his passionate likes and dislikes. His entire life was a parade, with even a strut in his correspondence. Yet he was a useful man to have around during a rebellion, for his patriotism made him an inspiring leader on the battlefield. Homer surely had such a man in mind when he wrote, "Men grow tired of sleep, love, singing and dancing sooner than of war."

His comrade-in-arms came closest to describing Wayne's true character. Henry Lee, whose own temperament was not unlike Wayne's, said, "General Wayne had a constitutional attachment to the sword, and this cast of character had acquired strength from indulgence, as well as the native temper of the troops he commanded." [38] And George Washington, when searching his memories for a general in the Northwest, was more perceptive than is sometimes realized. Wayne, he noted, was "More active & enterprising than Judicious & cautious. No economist it is feared: —open to flattery—vain—easily imposed upon and liable to be drawn into scrapes. Too indulgent . . . to his Officers and men— Whether sober—or a little addicted to the bottle, I know not." Yet, Washington concluded, ". . . under a full view of *all* circumstances, he appeared most eligible. . . . G.W. [General Wayne] has many good points as an officer, and it is to be hoped that time, reflection, good advice, and above all a due sense of the importance of the trust which is committed to him, will correct his foibles, or cast a shade over them." [39] At places like Monmouth Court House, Stony Point, and Fallen Timbers, Anthony Wayne had more than met the "trust" committed to him, leaving behind a record of service that is hard to equal in America's military history.

FOOTNOTES

1. Charles J. Stillé, *Major-General Anthony Wayne and the Pennsylvania Line in the Continental Army* (Philadelphia, 1893), p. 6. All quotations in this essay are from Stillé's *Wayne* unless otherwise noted.

2. John C. Fitzpatrick, ed., *The Writings of George Washington, from the Original Manuscript Sources, 1745–1799*, 39 vols. (Washington, 1931–44), V, 78–79. Hereinafter cited as Washington, *Writings*.

3. Peter Force, ed., *American Archives*, 5th series, 3 vols. (Washington, 1848–53), I, 130; C. H. Jones, *History of the Campaign for the Conquest of Canada* (Philadelphia, 1882), pp. 122–23; "Memoirs of Brigadier-General John Lacey, of Pennsylvania," *Pennsylvania Magazine of History and Biography*, XXV, No. 4 (1901), 513.

4. Washington, *Writings*, VIII, 282, 292.

5. Henry Lee, *Memoirs of the War in the Southern Department of the United States*, Robert E. Lee, ed. (New York, 1870), p. 89. Hereinafter cited as Lee, *Memoirs*; James McMichael, "Diary of James McMichael of the Pennsylvania Line, 1776–1778," *Pennsylvania Magazine of History and Biography*, XVI (1892), 150.

6. William B. Reed, *Life and Correspondence of Joseph Reed*, 2 vols. (Philadelphia, 1847), I, 312–13. Hereinafter cited as Reed, *Reed*.

7. John André, *Major André's Journal*, Henry Cabot Lodge, ed., 2 vols. (Boston, 1903), I, 94; J. Smith Futhey, *Paoli Massacre* (West Chester, Pa., 1877), pp. 47–48; Benson J. Lossing, *Pictorial Field Book of the Revolution*, 2 vols. (New York, 1852), II, 370.

8. Washington, *Writings*, IX, 352, 361, 421, 422, 491.

9. "Extract from the Diary of General Hunter, originally printed in the *Historical Record of the 52d Regiment*," *Historical Magazine*, IV (1860), 346–47.

10. Washington, *Writings*, IX, 436.
11. Wayne quoted in Broadus Mitchell, *Alexander Hamilton: Youth to Maturity* (New York, 1957), p. 135.
12. *Lee Papers, New York Historical Society Collections*, 4 vols. (1871–74), II, 468.
13. John Richard Alden, *General Charles Lee: Traitor or Patriot* (Baton Rouge, 1951), p. 205.
14. *Lee Papers*, II, 420.
15. Alden, *op. cit.*, p. 242.
16. *Lee Papers*, III, 291.
17. Don Higginbotham, *Daniel Morgan: Revolutionary Rifleman* (Chapel Hill, 1961), pp. 95–97.
18. William Abbatt, ed., *Memoirs of Major-General William Heath, By Himself* (New York, 1901), p. 193.
19. Josiah Quincy, ed., *The Journals of Major Samuel Shaw, the First American Consul at Canton* (Boston, 1847), p. 63.
20. Washington, *Writings*, XV, 451.
21. *Annual Register for 1779* (London, 1779), p. 193; Douglas S. Freeman, *George Washington: A Biography*, 7 vols. (New York, 1948–57), V, 140.
22. *Lee Papers*, III, 357, 375–76.
23. Jared Sparks, ed., *Correspondence of the American Revolution*, 4 vols. (Boston, 1853), III, 39–40.
24. Reed, *Reed*, II, 315–17.
25. "Extracts from the Letter-Books of Lieutenant Enos Reeves, of the Pennsylvania Line," *Pennsylvania Magazine of History and Biography*, XXI, No. 1 (1897), 72–74; *Journals of Major Samuel Shaw*, pp. 85–86.
26. Edmund C. Burnett, ed., *Letters of the Members of the Continental Congress*, 8 vols. (Washington, 1921–36), V, 514–41.
27. Washington, *Writings*, XXI, 145–46, 173; Wayne quoted in Carl Van Doren, *Mutiny in January* (New York, 1943), p. 233.
28. Van Doren, *op. cit.*, pp. 233–36, 251.
29. St. George Tucker to his wife, June 24, 1781, *Magazine of American History*, VII (September, 1881), 204.
30. Cornwallis to Leslie, July 8, 1781, Cornwallis Papers (Public Record Office, London, 30/11/88); "Letters to Dr. Robert Beatty," *Pennsylvania Magazine of History and Biography*, LIV, No. 2 (1930), 160; Ebenezer Wild, "Journal of Ebenezer Wild," *Massachusetts Historical Society Proceedings*, 2nd series, VI (Boston, 1891), 144; Frank Moore, *Diary of the Revolution*, 2 vols. (New York, 1860), II, 450; Comte de Rochambeau, *Mémoires Militaires, Historiques et Politiques*, 2 vols. (Paris, 1831), I, 284; Greene

quoted in Bernard C. Steiner, *The Life and Correspondence of James McHenry* (Cleveland, 1907), p. 38. Hereinafter cited as Steiner, *McHenry*.

31. Friedrich Kapp, *The Life of Frederick William Von Steuben, Major General in the Revolutionary Army* (New York, 1859), p. 457.

32. Lee, *Memoirs*, p. 420.

33. Greene quoted in Reed, *Reed*, II, 471.

34. George Washington Greene, *The Life of Nathanael Greene, Major-General in the Army of the Revolution*, 3 vols. (New York, 1871), III, 534.

35. Anthony Wayne quoted in James Ripley Jacobs, *The Beginnings of the U. S. Army, 1783–1812* (Princeton, 1947), p. 190.

36. John Adams to his wife, February 12, 1796, *Pennsylvania Magazine of History and Biography*, XXI, No. 1 (1897), 33; Steiner, *McHenry*, p. 165.

37. James Craig to James McHenry, December 9, 1796, *Pennsylvania Magazine of History and Biography*, XV, No. 2 (1891), 247–48.

38. Lee, *Memoirs*, p. 420.

39. "Washington's Opinion of General Officers," *Magazine of American History*, III (1879), 82–83.

BIBLIOGRAPHY

Boyd, Thomas, *Mad Anthony Wayne*. New York, 1929. This biography though colorfully written contains the flavor of fiction.

Moore, F N., *Life and Services of General Anthony Wayne*. Philadelphia, 1845. One of the earliest attempts at a Wayne biography and now largely superseded.

Pratt, Fletcher, *Eleven Generals*. New York, 1949. Contains a most interesting chapter on Wayne.

Preston, John H., *A Gentleman Rebel: The Exploits of Anthony Wayne*. New York, 1930. Written in flamboyant phraseology and probably contains fabrications of colorful events.

Spears, John R., *Anthony Wayne*. New York, 1903. A short standard account of Wayne's life.

Stillé, Charles J., *Major-General Anthony Wayne and the Pennsylvania Line in the Continental Army*. Philadelphia, 1893. The best over-all study of the man. Despite his tone of rampant patriotism, Stillé made careful transcriptions of Wayne's letters, and his book contains much that is useful for any student of the Revolutionary War.

Wildes, Harry E., *Anthony Wayne: Troubleshooter of the Revolution*. New York, 1941. Wildes added little that was not known about Wayne other than a suggestion of a love affair with Mary Vining.

Daniel Morgan:

GUERRILLA FIGHTER

———•••———

DON HIGGINBOTHAM

Louisiana State University

NEARLY a century and a half ago Karl von Clausewitz, the Prussian military theorist, wrote that when war is mainly carried on by an armed citizenry rather than by professionals, "warfare introduces a means of defense peculiar to itself." Whenever men with little or no formal training in combat play a key role in dislodging an invader, they usually resort to tactics that reflect their immediate, local experience. The Revolutionary War in many ways was that kind of struggle. True, American military efforts sometimes followed the Old World pattern in the coastal areas: certain generals such as Lee and Gates had been trained in the British army, and native American commanders like Knox and Greene had read professional military treatises published in Europe. But by their frequent use of thin skirmish lines, highly mobile forces, night marches, winter campaigns, and hit-and-run tactics, the Americans revealed New World fighting methods alien to the conventional eighteenth-century practice.

Today, actions of this nature are called guerrilla or partisan warfare. The guerrilla—in the American Revolution, or in the mountains of Yugoslavia in World War II, or in the jungles of Southeast Asia in the 1960's—has attempted to confuse, harass, and destroy by methods his opponent does not understand. In the war for independence, such activity was most prevalent in the backwoods, and the American general who achieved the greatest success as a guerrilla fighter was a Virginia frontiersman named Daniel Morgan.[1]

Much of Morgan's early life is shrouded in mystery. His parents, farming people, were apparently Welsh immigrants living in New Jersey at the time of Morgan's birth, about 1735. At seventeen, after a quarrel with his father, Daniel fled to the frontier—a common practice among the restless, high-spirited youths of that day. By the spring of 1753, he was in Winchester, Virginia, a remote western settlement and the seat of Frederick County.

His awkward speech, coarse manners, and homespun clothing were not handicaps to the newcomer, who was to make his home in Frederick County. The English, Scotch-Irish, and German inhabitants of the county and surrounding area known as the Valley of Virginia were simple people. Life was hard with its exacting demands for survival—cutting timber, rooting stumps, planting crops, and erecting houses. Such a life sharpened the self-reliance of the settler and put a premium on initiative. Here law and order meant little when it prevented rough frontiersmen from getting the necessities of life, be they land, liquor, or women. If one can believe the tales of pious Moravian missionaries, scarcely a hardier breed of men existed than those on the fringes of western Virginia. Compounding the frontier disorder was the threat of Indian assaults as Valley men encroached on the redman's hunting lands in the Ohio country.

For Morgan, the alarms and excursions of war began in 1755. By that time, the French had started moving forces south from Canada to make good their King's claim to the Ohio Valley. Morgan, a teamster, secured employment from Major General Edward Braddock, sent from England to repulse the French tide. At Fort Cumberland, Maryland, Morgan and his fellow Virginia wagoners exasperated imperious British officers by their drinking, brawling, and lusty flirtations with Indian women. Once, when a redcoat reprimanded Morgan, the fiery young teamster knocked the man down—an offense which brought a drum-head court-martial sentence of several hundred lashes.

If, as Morgan claimed, he retained consciousness throughout the ordeal, it was a tribute to his superb physique. Standing six feet tall, with broad shoulders and massive arms, he was certainly capable of enduring great pain. Even so, he bore the scars from that beating the rest of his life, and with them he carried a firm conviction that the lash was a brutal, inhumane form of punishment. It was a kind of discipline he subsequently refused to use as an officer in the American army.[2]

Morgan learned still another lesson from the campaign when Braddock suffered his catastrophic defeat near the Monongahela River in southeastern Pennsylvania. Braddock's vain attempt to maintain line fire and regular formations against his French and Indian assailants, fighting from behind trees, bushes, and rocks, proved that European military methods were often futile in a wilderness setting. Later in the French and Indian War, Morgan served with the Virginia rangers. Once he was shot through the mouth and narrowly escaped death when he eluded capture by the Indians.

The years following "the French War" were carefree and roistering ones for Daniel Morgan. He was constantly in trouble with the law either for brawling in taverns or for not paying his liquor bills and card debts. But by 1763, when Morgan formed a common-law union with sixteen-year-old Abigail Curry, his conduct underwent a marked change. He settled down, purchased a farm, acquired some slaves, and began enjoying a more prosperous and peaceful existence. His changed way of life soon gained him the respect of the more important members of his rural community. The justices of the peace appointed him to several minor administrative posts, and in 1771 he was made captain in the militia.

Captain Morgan saw strenuous duty in 1774 when the white man's intrusions into the Ohio Valley set off another Indian conflict known as Lord Dunmore's War. He was a member of a special expedition under Major Angus McDonald which marched into the Ohio homeland of the Shawnee Indians, destroying crops and burning villages. Afterward Morgan participated in a similar mission that razed the lands of the Mingo, allies of the Shawnee. This campaign was among the last in Virginia's victorious war against the redman.

By the eve of the Revolution, the forty-year-old Morgan had been tested and tempered as a frontier fighter. The Indians, all unwittingly, had schooled him and countless others in the ways of wilderness warfare.[3] He had become proficient with the scalping knife and tomahawk, in addition to the so-called Kentucky rifle, a long, slender weapon designed by German gunsmiths. In the field he wore Indian leggings and moccasins and a hunting shirt, dyed the brownish color of a dry leaf. When the war clouds, hanging over the colonies since Parliament's passage of the "Intolerable Acts," finally burst at Lexington and Concord, Morgan found new opportunities to practice his military skills.

In June, 1775, the Second Continental Congress resolved that ten companies of light infantry be raised, including two from Virginia. The legislators were not thinking of the traditional European light infantry of the eighteenth century. They desired, said Richard Henry Lee, men who were known for their "amazing hardihood" gained through "living so long in the woods." Such veteran Indian fighters and hunters could travel far without provisions. They could perform remarkable feats with the rifle, allegedly hitting targets 200 yards away, whereas musketmen were ineffective at only half that distance. As snipers and woods-fighters, they could assault enemy supply trains, disrupt communications, and harass enemy armies as they marched into the interior.

Morgan, with his physical stamina, his experience in Indian warfare, and his knowledge of the rifle, was as well prepared to lead frontier light infantry as any colonial American. He was selected to head one of the Virginia companies authorized by Congress, and the rest of his Revolutionary War assignments, save one, involved light infantry. After recruiting ninety-six men, Morgan raced to Washington's camp outside Boston in amazing time, covering the 600 miles from Frederick County, Virginia, to Cambridge in three weeks.[4] Morgan may well have been acquainted with Washington before their meeting at Cambridge, for both Virginians had served with Braddock. In any event, the commander-in-chief took a genuine interest in the riflemen, for they were the first troops to come from his own colony. Washington, moreover, had spent much time in Frederick County and had once represented the region in the Virginia Assembly.

When the commander-in-chief organized an army under Colonel Benedict Arnold to invade Canada by way of Maine, three rifle companies, including Morgan's, were selected as part of the expedition. From the beginning, Arnold considered Morgan a valuable officer and appointed him to command all the riflemen. After plunging into the tangled Maine forests, Morgan led the forward units, while Arnold directed the bulk of the force composed of New England farmers and fishermen. As Arnold conceded later, no one did more to get the little army to the shores of the St. Lawrence—after traversing exhausting portages, rampaging streams, and deep swamps—than Daniel Morgan.

Stripped to the waist, attired in leggings and breech clout, Morgan toiled with his men as they cleared a rough trail for the troops behind them. Youthful Joseph Henry, a Pennsylvania rifleman, marveled at Morgan's strength and stamina. Henry's lone criticism was that the husky rifle captain demanded the same endurance from his men. On reaching the formidable Height of Land, which drops away toward the Canadian plain, Morgan insisted that his Virginians carry their heavy boats, for they would be needed on the north-flowing Chaudière and the St. Lawrence. The four-and-a-half-mile snow-covered trail crossed ravines and underbrush. Henry declared that Morgan's men had the flesh "worn from their shoulders, even to the bone." Yet Henry admitted that only by such exertions did Arnold's gallant little army finally emerge on the Plains of Abraham before Quebec in November, 1775, a distance of over 350 miles from the Maine coast. Henry, without disparaging Arnold's magnificent leadership, wrote that the individual, unforeseen, day-to-day problems were "left to the energy of Morgan's mind, and he conquered." [5]

Early in December, Arnold was joined by Brigadier General Richard Montgomery commanding a second army that had invaded Canada. Montgomery's troops had proceeded northward from Ticonderoga, taking British forts on the Sorel River and capturing Montreal, before descending the St. Lawrence to unite with Arnold. In planning the Quebec attack, Morgan, though only a captain, continued to play a more significant part than his rank would normally allow because he alone among Arnold's officers had seen important military service.

Since Governor Guy Carleton's combined force of British regulars and Canadian militia inside the walls of Quebec was double the 975 men of Montgomery and Arnold, the Americans needed both luck and the element of surprise to succeed. Their plan, to go into effect on the first stormy night, called for Arnold and Montgomery to attack from opposite directions. Both columns moving simultaneously were to strike against the Lower Town, a narrow strip along the river that was not as well protected as the rest of the city.

As snow whirled down in blinding intensity on the night of December 30, Arnold's men began their advance, with their commander and Morgan in the lead. One moment they were picking their way around the ice cakes thrown up by the river, the next they were scrambling out of the snowdrifts as they stumbled into the Lower Town. Sighting a barrier at the far end of the dark street, Arnold called for a frontal assault, since his only cannon had been abandoned in the deep snow. But a whirring musket ball tore into his leg, and he fell heavily to the ground. At this point, Arnold persuaded Morgan to take over. Arnold, the short, stocky apothecary from Connecticut, and Morgan, the tall ex-teamster from Virginia, came from different worlds, and on the wilderness trek and the Plains of Abraham they had had their differences. Yet as soldiers they had genuine respect for each other; both were brave, oblivious to personal danger, and, most important, both were leaders capable of arousing intense loyalty in their men.

Now all was up to Captain Morgan. Yelling for the rest to follow, he dashed toward the barrier. His performance in the moments that followed was one of the great personal deeds of the war. Setting a ladder against the barrier, Morgan scampered to the top. First a musket ball ripped through his hat, then a second creased his cheek. Falling backward into the snow, he lay there an instant, then he rose and bounded up and over the wall. Luckily he fell beneath a cannon which offered momentary protection from the thrusts of enemy bayonets. Riflemen, pouring over the wall, quickly overcame the opposition and saved him from harm.

Morgan had entered the Sault au Matelot, a narrow street where Arnold's division was to await Montgomery's force before the two would drive into the Upper Town. Finding no resistance, Morgan was convinced that the enemy was surprised and disorganized and that he should push on without waiting for Montgomery. But he soon discovered that Arnold's officers who outranked him disagreed. Although Morgan had assumed a colonel's command, he was still only a captain.

Even while the Americans stood quarreling in the streets, their attack was doomed to failure. Montgomery, after cutting a swath through two undefended palisades, had been shot down. His timorous subordinate, Lieutenant Colonel Donald Campbell, had beaten a hasty retreat. With Montgomery's troops out of the picture, Carleton dispatched units to the previously undefended barrier at the Upper Town end of the Sault au Matelot, while at the same time he sent a Captain Laws out the Palace Gate with instructions to hit Arnold's command from the rear.

Spotting the British activity at the second barrier, Arnold's field officers finally agreed to support Morgan and asked him to serve as their leader. Morgan, accompanied by Lieutenants Heth, Humphreys, and Steele, planted ladders and went up the wall; but they did not go over. A synchronized volley hurled them back. From upper-story windows on the British side of the barrier, musket flashes lit up the cold, gray dawn. Morgan, his stentorian voice sounding above the wind and musketry, rallied the Americans for repeated tries at the barrier—two, three, four, and more—all without success. He seemed to be everywhere, dashing here and there, now carrying a wounded comrade to shelter, now calling for still another assault at the wall. Morgan, declared one of his riflemen, was "brave to temerity," a sentiment echoed by another who wrote in his journal that "Betwixt every peal the awful voice of Morgan is heard, whose gigantic stature and terrible appearance carries dismay among the foe wherever he comes." [6]

As the British brought up an artillery piece, Morgan pulled his men back down the street toward the first barrier, hoping desperately that Montgomery would appear. At that point Laws's flanking unit from the Palace Gate swung into the street. The Americans were hemmed in front and rear—"caught as it were in a trap," wrote Carleton. Morgan begged to lead an attempt to fight their way out, an appeal Arnold's subordinates refused to heed. The Americans threw down their arms. Shouting, raging, tears streaming down his leathery cheeks, Morgan braced his back against a building and pulled out his sword. Which of the redcoat scum would try and take his sword, he yelled. When they threatened to shoot him, he told them to go ahead. At last, sighting a priest in the milling throng, he handed the astonished cleric his sword; at least no British "scoundrel" would take "it out of my hands." [7]

Morgan's anguish must have deepened when he later learned he had been accurate about the confusion among the British during the initial stages of the battle. A British officer, Major Henry Caldwell, declared that had Arnold's column pushed on, as Morgan had urged, the city might possibly have fallen. As it was, approximately 100 Americans were killed and wounded and 400 captured, compared to Carleton's loss of only 20.

Morgan and his fellow prisoners passed long months of confinement, until August, 1776, when Carleton released the Americans on condition they would not fight again until formally exchanged for Britons in Washington's hands. Though the labors of Montgomery, Arnold, and Morgan had failed to wrest Canada from the Crown, Morgan's role in the ill-fated Quebec venture brought him well-deserved recognition. Once he reached the American lines, he was promoted to colonel and slated for an important command.

In June, 1777, Washington gave Morgan a special corps of light infantry composed of 500 picked Continentals—men from the western counties of Maryland, Pennsylvania, and Virginia. Officially known as the rangers, more commonly called Morgan's riflemen, this unit compiled a spectacular record, scarcely excelled by any regiment in the Continental army. Outfitted with hunting shirts and rifles, these men included such celebrated backwoods fighters as Timothy Murphy, who during the Revolutionary War reputedly killed forty redmen and scalped twenty. The commander-in-chief considered Morgan's force a psychological as well as military weapon; they could serve to unnerve British soldiers who fancied all New World inhabitants as barbarians. In his first assignment, Morgan dressed his men in Indian garb and war paint before skirmishing with General Howe's forward units near New Brunswick, New Jersey. Let them shout and whoop, Washington added slyly; ". . . it would have very good consequences." [8]

Valuable as the riflemen were to Washington in the summer of 1777, as he and Howe engaged in a game of cat-and-mouse in the Jerseys, Washington agreed to a Congressional request that Morgan's unit be sent to upper New York. Morgan was to assist the American Northern army, then feebly contesting the southward drive from Canada of General John Burgoyne's Anglo–German army, supported by Tories and Indians. Just as Burgoyne's Indians had intimidated the New Yorkers with their scalping knives and hatchets, so Washington felt the same methods, if employed by Morgan's men, would demoralize the British and their allies. Horatio Gates, recently appointed commander of the Northern army, even hoped an American hatchet might find its way into Burgoyne's skull.

"Gentleman Johnny," the gay, wine-loving, playwright-soldier, kept his scalp but lost his military reputation. Later he frankly admitted Morgan's part in his undoing. Burgoyne, advancing through the red and gold of the autumn wilderness, had already overextended his supply lines from Canada. A force of British and Indians under Colonel St. Leger that was to drive from Oswego eastward along the Mohawk Valley to meet Burgoyne and Clinton at Albany, had been defeated near Oriskany. And one of his flanking parties already had been repulsed by a body of patriot irregulars at Bennington. But his situation deteriorated even further because of harassment from Morgan's forest-wise riflemen. They so terrorized his redskin scouts that not one could be brought within the sound of a rifle shot—a fact which seems to explain why the British moved to within three miles of Gates's encampment at Bemis Heights on September 18, 1777, without having any specific idea of the American general's whereabouts.

Even so, Burgoyne groped forward for an attack on the morrow. Gates, entrenched on Bemis Heights, held his main force inside his fortifications, but he wisely sent Morgan's riflemen into the woods in front of his lines to retard the enemy's progress. As a tactician, Morgan was best at woods-fighting. Here, as was customary with Morgan, he grouped his men in thin skirmish lines, which could be shifted about in the rough terrain more easily than the bulky British linear formations. He instructed his sharpshooters to concentrate their aim at enemy officers. Later Morgan received criticism for encouraging this practice, for a kind of gentlemen's agreement existed in European wars to spare opposing leaders. But as an Indian fighter, Morgan had concluded there was nothing chivalrous about war: it was ugly business, with one's chances of victory enhanced by crippling an opponent in any way possible, not by observing time-honored rules and customs.

Having deployed his riflemen, Morgan took a position slightly to the rear of his main skirmish line: there, in his favorite battle station, he could obtain reports easily and keep contact with the greater part of his men. But when his advance parties collided with Burgoyne's pickets, the Americans in front broke ranks as the enemy pickets fell back. Morgan then blew his familiar "turkey-call," a shrill gobble, and his men gathered around him. By this time, Burgoyne was aware of Morgan's presence in the woods. In a clearing 350 yards long, known as Freeman's Farm, Burgoyne had drawn up his center column which was widely separated from the supporting columns to his left and right. Morgan, while arranging his men in the foliage just beyond the clearing, was joined by Continental regiments sent out by Benedict Arnold, who directed the left wing of Gates's army.

Shortly after one o'clock in the afternoon, Morgan's corps, with the aid of Arnold's Continentals, opened a brisk fire that compelled the British to withdraw into a pine grove to the north. But when the Continentals attempted to occupy the farmyard, they were swept back by an enemy bayonet charge. The riflemen, whose weapons were not equipped to carry bayonets, seem to have stayed behind cover throughout the afternoon. Climbing trees, Morgan's marksmen took a heavy toll in officers and artillerymen. They were likewise "sedulous" in hitting the Tories, a "misfortune" that "accelerated their estrangement from our cause," as one redcoat sergeant put it.[9]

Though neither side could gain a decisive advantage in the bloody clearing, Burgoyne's losses were staggering. As daylight faded into dusk, Burgoyne's center was rescued by German reinforcements from his left column. The sulphurous smoke wafted upward and the din of firearms died away. Morgan and the Continental officers retired to their own lines. They had halted the enemy, inflicting 600 casualties upon Burgoyne as opposed to 320 of their own. Accounts by British participants reveal Morgan's corps as the most successful American unit engaged that day.

Gates, awaiting another thrust by Burgoyne, declined a request by Washington to return Morgan's riflemen. He wrote that "your Excellency would not wish me to part with the corps the army of General Burgoyne are most afraid of."[10] That Morgan's woodsmen continued to plague the British general is evident from his remark that not a night between September 20 and October 7 passed without harassment. For this reason, plus the arrival of chilly weather and a shortage of supplies, Burgoyne tried a second time to crush Gates in order to complete the British scheme of reaching Albany and eventually driving a wedge between New England and the states to the south.

When Burgoyne advanced toward the American left on October 7, Morgan, "with his usual sagacity," suggested that he assail the British right flank while a second American force—under General Enoch Poor—burst out on Burgoyne's left flank. Gates accepted the idea, which Colonel James Wilkinson called "the best . . . that could be devised." [11] Morgan and Poor, striking almost simultaneously, rolled up the enemy flanks. Hastily Burgoyne regrouped his command, which then occupied the middle of a wheat field. As Morgan and Poor pressed against Burgoyne's center, held mainly by German General Riedesel and his blue-coated Brunswickers, the Americans received the welcome assistance of Arnold, leading General Ebenezer Learned's brigade.

Arnold, who had quarreled with Gates and had been subsequently confined to camp, dashed onto the field without permission. He is said to have shouted that he was going to help Morgan. Though Morgan and Arnold pushed the enemy back, the Brunswickers fought stubbornly. When British General Simon Fraser rode forward with reinforcements, Morgan called on rifleman Timothy Murphy, who shot down the brave Scotsman.[12] Now Burgoyne's troops gave up the field and withdrew into the fortifications they had erected in the previous few weeks.

Not content with partial victory, the Americans smashed against the redoubts on the enemy's right and center, and overran the extreme right redoubt garrisoned by Colonel Heinrich von Breymann's Germans. As in the first battle, darkness called a halt to the contest. Even so, the end was in sight for Burgoyne, who capitulated to Gates on October 17, after an unsuccessful attempt to flee northward.[13]

Historians have spilled much ink in arguments over which of

the American leaders—Gates, Arnold, or Morgan—deserves the greatest credit for Burgoyne's humiliation. In fact, all had a significant hand in the outcome. Gates, though cautious in committing his entire army against Burgoyne, was wise: with fall approaching and the British on rough, unfamiliar terrain, he permitted Burgoyne to wear down his forces by fruitless probes. The credit for leadership in the field belongs to Arnold and Morgan. Following the engagement of October 7, the short, ruddy-faced Gates embraced the rifleman, saying, "Morgan, you have done wonders"; while in his battle report to Congress Gates wrote that "too much praise cannot be given to the Corps commanded by Col. Morgan." [14]

Washington, meanwhile, had suffered reversals at the Battles of Brandywine and Germantown and had sorely missed Morgan's riflemen. Their services were "essential" to the army in the dreary days of late 1777. When Washington's tattered legions retired to Valley Forge to take up winter quarters, Morgan's men were among them. Indeed, upon their return that fall and during the following year, Washington made frequent use of Morgan's corps—at Whitemarsh, Valley Forge, and Monmouth. Throughout this period Morgan kept advocating the importance of cavalry to act in conjunction with his light troops and stressed the need for militia and partisan forces to co-ordinate their guerrilla activities with his own command. In view of his performance in the Canadian and Saratoga campaigns, Morgan now considered himself the foremost authority in the Continental army on the use of mobile forces.

Morgan found the year 1779 to be the most trying period of his military career. His famous rifle regiment, most of its companies having previously been detached to the West for Indian fighting, was disbanded. His next permanent assignment was the colonelcy of a Virginia infantry regiment, hardly an invigorating post for an ambitious man whose laurels were no doubt greater than those of any colonel in the army. Restless and sensitive, Morgan soon learned that a large light infantry unit had been formed, and he was obsessed with the idea of leading it.

When he found the command had gone to Anthony Wayne, he resolved to present Congress his resignation. Though Wayne was an able officer and held the rank of brigadier general, Morgan had had more experience with light troops.[15]

Morgan was deeply disappointed that Washington had not supported his candidacy for the command. Only recently he had been one of the general's staunchest defenders at the time of the Conway Cabal, an alleged plot by politicians and officers to remove Washington from supreme command.[16] When Morgan confronted Washington, the latter was not disposed to show him more than moderate sympathy, nor did he offer his unhappy rifle officer any compensation such as a recommendation for promotion in rank. The fact that Morgan, like Washington, was a Virginian did him no good, for Washington bent over backward to avoid charges of being partial to men from his own state. Nevertheless, in a letter of introduction for Morgan addressed to the president of Congress, the commander-in-chief wrote that Morgan was "a very valuable officer" who had "distinguished himself upon several occasions." In Philadelphia, the congressmen agreed that Morgan had been "Neglected, but not intentionally." Nothing, however, was done in his behalf. Contrary to what historians have often written, he did not resign but accepted an "honorable furlough" until a more promising position became available.[17]

Proud and indignant but not wrathful, Morgan journeyed back to western Virginia, where he stayed for nearly a year. It was not a happy interlude, for Morgan was one of those hearty breed of men who fails to find satisfaction in "the sweets of domestic life." He was, as a contemporary is reputed to have said, "exactly fitted for the toils and pomp of war." Then, in 1780, Morgan received a letter from Horatio Gates, newly appointed commander of the Southern army. Gates had requested Morgan to head a regiment similar to the rifle unit which had performed so admirably against Burgoyne. Indeed, it seemed that the guerrilla warfare in which Morgan excelled was the only American hope of slowing the British invasion of the American southland, for during 1779 and 1780, British forces had overrun Georgia and much of South Carolina.

In the South, a land of innumerable rivers and creeks, intersected by swamps and forests, Morgan and other guerrilla fighters could be invaluable. Morgan fairly leaped at this opportunity, particularly since Gates trusted him and recognized his abilities. Aware of Morgan's concern over previous neglect, Gates promised to urge Congress to promote the frontiersman to brigadier general. Unfortunately, however, Morgan had experienced such a painful and crippling attack of sciatica, an ailment contracted earlier in the war, that he was unable to reach Gates's headquarters in North Carolina until mid-September. By then, Gates had been decisively beaten by Lord Cornwallis at the Battle of Camden, when Gates's militia, forming the American left wing, had fled without fighting, leaving the exposed Continentals to be chewed up by British regulars.[18]

Because of the Camden debacle, Morgan received a light corps much smaller than he had expected. During the dismal fall of 1780, when patriot prospects in the South were at their lowest ebb, Morgan labored with little success to make his light corps equal or superior to its British counterpart, Colonel Banastre Tarleton's Tory legion. Unlike most British units in the South, the legion specialized in mobility—especially slashing, head-on assaults that were not only effective but often brutally conceived. Cornwallis had also kept Tarleton and the legion busy in beating back patriot guerrillas and in maintaining supply lines between British outposts in South Carolina. The British general told his short, chunky, twenty-six-year-old subordinate that he wished Tarleton were three men instead of one: "We can do no good without you."

Morgan, chafing at his idleness, got an opportunity for action in December of that year. Nathanael Greene, Gates's replacement as Southern commander, shared Morgan's enthusiasm for partisan-type operations. Even with a minuscule army, he intended to play the hit-and-run game against Cornwallis—the "old Fox," as Morgan called him. With his long overdue promotion now in hand, Brigadier General Daniel Morgan tramped into the South Carolina back country to sit on the enemy's left flank and rear. Greene, in the meantime, with the remainder of the Southern army advanced to Cheraw, South Carolina, to annoy the British right and front.

Morgan's sudden appearance in the hinterland unnerved Cornwallis. Rural patriots rallied to the standard, Tories deserted in droves, and Morgan's operations threatened the British post at Ninety-Six. His Lordship was not the only British military leader in the war to discover that rear areas could not be treated in the European sense—as free of enemy forces and simply as zones of communication. In the Revolutionary struggle, because of the activities of Morgan, Sumter, Pickens, Marion, and others, the front-behind-the-front became a theater of operations in its own right. Hence, before Cornwallis could launch his long-planned invasion of North Carolina and the upper South, Morgan would have to be eliminated. Cornwallis selected his best man, Tarleton, for the task.

Getting wind of Tarleton's approach, Morgan hastily fell back toward the North Carolina line. The guerrilla fighter has traditionally tried to avoid the challenge to positional combat in the open; his value lies in harassment, and often many of his men are unfamiliar with orthodox warfare. In Morgan's case, approximately half his force consisted of militia. But with Tarleton's Tory legion pursuing "like Bloodhounds" after prey, Morgan concluded that he would have to make a stand. He hoped to stop and fight somewhere beyond the Broad River in the rough terrain near Thicketty Mountain. But by the afternoon of January 16, 1781, Morgan became grimly aware that it was impossible to reach his destination. Tarleton was only a few miles behind. Even if he reached the Broad, a crossing would be difficult because of heavy rains and in the darkness Tarleton might surprise and destroy his corps.

Morgan prepared, therefore, to do battle on the west side of the Broad, at a place called the Cowpens—a grazing area well known to Carolina farmers. Historians have been fascinated by

Morgan's choice of ground. Both Morgan and Tarleton later admitted that the Cowpens, with its gently sloping ridge sparsely covered with oak and hickory, offered no protection for the American flanks. Morgan explained that he did not want his militia to have swamps or underbrush nearby for fear they would flee at the appearance of Tarleton's dragoons: with no shelter available they would be compelled to stand and fight. But this observation was made with the benefit of hindsight. Morgan probably had no alternative except the Cowpens because night was approaching.[19]

There is no higher quality of generalship than the ability to dominate a situation, no matter how difficult; bad as his situation was, Morgan resolved to make the best of it. He had utmost faith that he could devise a battle plan that would combine the particular talents of his militiamen and Continentals. Instead of entrusting his poorly trained militia with part of the main line of defense (as Gates had so foolishly done at Camden), Morgan proposed to make the most of the sharpshooting abilities of the frontier militiamen, without forcing them to stand for long in open combat. Placing his Continentals—under Colonel John E. Howard—at the crest of the elevation, he would deploy the bulk of the militia—commanded by Colonel Andrew Pickens—150 yards in advance of the regulars. Well in front of Pickens' line, however, he would station a small body of frontier riflemen in a skirmish line. The plan called for the riflemen and militia to fire one or two well-aimed volleys, then retire to the rear of Howard's troops, where they were to be re-formed and held in reserve.

The scheme was sound only if Morgan could infuse spirit and confidence in the men. Here, again, his qualities as a dynamic leader were of the utmost importance. In the darkness, moving from one campfire to another, he talked and joked with the men about the prospect of beating Tarleton. The "Old Wagoner" would crack his whip over "Ban" Tarleton, he cried, provided they would help him. Victory would bring them glory, and at home the old folks would praise them and the girls would kiss them. As the men crowded about, slapping each other on the back, and betting on the number of legionnaires they would bag, Major Thomas Young "was more perfectly convinced of General Morgan's qualifications to command militia than ever . . . before. . . ." [20]

At dawn, after a sleepless night, Morgan repeated his rounds, reminding them of Saratoga, Monmouth, Paoli, and Brandywine; reminding them, too, that this day they could make their own contribution to "liberty's cause." Morgan and other officers like him led the American soldier to believe he had a personal stake in the war; quite often this encouraged him to hold his own against the better-trained redcoat or German who performed merely for pay and in response to orders. Though battlefield oratory was not uncommon in the patriot army, seldom did it bring more striking results than at the Cowpens. [21]

When the battle began at seven in the morning, the air was crisp and clear. To Tarleton, the riflemen and militia along the American front must have looked like easy prey, reminding him of his conquest at Camden. As the British advanced, the riflemen emptied fifteen saddles. Pickens' line followed with a blast that shook the green-jacketed legion. That was all for the militia. They filed off to the left and passed around the end of Morgan's main line—all the while under the protection of Morgan's small but effective cavalry commanded by Colonel William Washington. Tarleton's troops took the irregulars' withdrawal for panic-stricken flight. Again surging forward, they were brought up short, this time by Howard's line of Continentals. During the next few minutes the opposing forces dueled at point-blank range. Howard's veterans gave the enemy a "well-directed and incessant fire," Morgan later reported. Tarleton agreed: "The fire on both sides was well supported and produced much slaughter."

The climactic phase of the struggle saw the Americans capitalizing on luck and Morgan's quick thinking. Because of mistaken orders, Howard's line began a slow retrograde movement. Tarleton's men, sensing victory, broke ranks to pursue their foe. Morgan, seeing that the Continentals had maintained their own good order, called for a sudden volley. Taken unawares, the line of red and green staggered. Howard now called for a bayonet charge. Morgan, almost simultaneously, threw the re-formed militia against the unsuspecting British left and at the same time sent Washington's cavalry smashing down on Tarleton's right. Morgan had achieved a double envelopment, one of the most difficult maneuvers. The legion was thrown into a "panic," admitted Tarleton, who fled with a handful of officers and horsemen. As Morgan informed a friend, "I was desirous to have a stroke at Tarleton—my wishes are gratified," and "[I] have given him a devil of a whipping, a more compleat victory never was obtained." He had "entirely Broke up Tarleton's Legion," the "flower" of Cornwallis' army; British losses in men amounted to 110 killed and 702 captured as against Morgan's 12 killed and 60 wounded.[22]

Though Cowpens was one of the tactical masterpieces of the war, Morgan's success would have gone for naught if Cornwallis had overtaken his corps and released the Cowpens prisoners. Aware of this danger, Morgan hastily retreated into central North Carolina. That he made good his escape, with prisoners encumbering his withdrawal and many of his own men barefoot and nearly naked, across the swollen Catawba and Yadkin rivers, was as remarkable as his crushing defeat of Tarleton. The British were scarcely a stone's throw away when Morgan reached Guilford Court House, where he united with Greene's wing of the Southern army, which had headed northward to assist against Cornwallis.

For all practical purposes, Morgan's direct participation in the war was at an end. Dampness and exposure had so aggravated his sciatica that he was compelled to return to Virginia to recover his health. Yet Morgan, whose performance had vindicated Greene's bold strategy of dividing the Southern army in the face of a superior foe, was to exert further influence. On his way homeward he wrote Greene to resort to the tactics used at Cowpens in the event of a full-scale encounter. Greene followed Morgan's advice in the Battle of Guilford Court House; and though the British emerged victorious, the action was a costly one for Cornwallis. "Great generals are scarce," Greene assured his former subordinate; "there are few Morgan's to be found." [23]

The spring and summer months of 1781 were agonizing for Morgan, who exploded in helpless frustration in writing his friends. To be sure, the war in the South became high drama, with Greene mopping up South Carolina and Georgia, and Cornwallis opening a major theater in Virginia. Morgan briefly took the field with Lafayette in Virginia, but his sciatic condition caused a sudden return home. He came so close to death, he reported, that he "literally peeped . . . into the other world." If the end must come, the Old Wagoner preferred to die "more gloriously" in combat.[24] But he realized he was too late; Washington's rapid move into Virginia had spelled Cornwallis' doom.

Morgan had lost none of his respect for Washington in spite of their earlier differences. In the numerous references to Washington in Morgan's papers, there is not the slightest intimation of criticism or doubt of the commander-in-chief. To Morgan, Washington was the sustaining force of the Revolution; without him the cause would collapse. Morgan's steadfast loyalty was all the more remarkable because the rifleman must have known that Washington had criticized him for leaving the service because of dissatisfaction over rank and command. Uncertain of Washington's feeling toward him at this time, and aware of his superior's consuming duties on the Virginia peninsula, Morgan was clearly hesitant about writing to the commander-in-chief. But, as he apologetically explained in a lengthy letter, "the feelings of my heart will not permit me to be silent. . . ." It had been his "particular fate" never to have served directly under Washington in an important contest, "a misfortune I have ever sincerely lamented." Nothing on earth would have given Morgan more pleasure than to have performed in the Yorktown campaign "under your excellency's eye, to have shared the danger, and let me add, the glory too." [25] Washington was touched and replied in a generous vein. Morgan, he wrote, breathed "the Spirit and Ardor of a Veteran Soldier, who, tho impaired in the Service of his Country, yet retains the Sentiments of a Soldier in the firmest Degree." [26]

The two generals had seen little of one another during the war and each had fought in his own fashion. While Washington, the commander-in-chief, had directed operations along the eastern seaboard of the Middle States, Morgan, the guerrilla, had found his duties in the mountainous hinterland. Washington, like Morgan, had begun his military career as a frontier soldier in the French and Indian War. If in the Revolution the commander-in-chief was confronted with the more complex problems of maneuvering large forces and fighting pitched battles somewhat along the lines of European engagements, he nevertheless retained his respect for the partisan operations of Morgan and others like him. Though never intimate, their exchange of letters shows that the Virginia aristocrat had developed a genuine admiration for the Virginia farmer.

What was the value of Morgan's kind of guerrilla warfare in the Revolution? It goes without saying that it was highly successful when the British left the coastal plains and plunged into the interior, a region largely unsuited to European combat and inhabited by men who fought according to their own rules. In fact, Clausewitz might have given our struggle for independence as his prime example when he wrote that rarely indeed are orthodox forces ever successful against guerrillas. Partisans, however, seldom bring about total victory in war. Though they may weaken the enemy and make him increasingly vulnerable, the final blow is generally delivered by large, well-organized armies, working in smooth harmony. In this case, French and American forces in co-operation with the French fleet trapped Cornwallis at Yorktown and hammered him into submission.

Morgan, of course, would have been out of his element at Yorktown: the partisan leader generally has little understanding of grand strategy or the administration of large divisions. Fortunately, Morgan never was thrust into a position beyond his training or talents, as were Lincoln, Putnam, and a number of other Revolutionary generals. Morgan was admirably suited for every command he held.[27]

Retirement posed difficulties for the military hero. Though up to his "Head and ears" managing a grist mill and speculating in western lands during the postwar years, Morgan manifested a restlessness, a longing to "Keep a loose foot." Despite a new home, a more comfortable way of life, and greater respectability in the Valley of Virginia, the old soldier still craved excitement. Memories of his illustrious past weighed heavily upon him, and he felt he was growing "very rusty." Morgan, whose prose did not rival that of "pope, Voltiere or Shakespear," corresponded frequently with his "old swords," former army friends, and a number of them visited the Morgan home—"Saratoga."

In the 1790's, Morgan's letters turned from Revolutionary reminiscences to the subject of political combat. An ardent Federalist and supporter of President Washington's policies, Morgan was convinced that the Jeffersonian Republicans were trying to destroy the Constitution, "the Envy and wonder of the surrounding world." The Whisky Rebellion, an outburst against the Federalists' excise tax, brought Morgan into the field once more in 1794, as the commander of a Virginia militia detachment. Though Morgan felt "as Hearty as I ever was" and could "undergo the fatigues of two or three campaigns," he won no new laurels; the whisky rebels in Pennsylvania capitulated without firing a shot.

If the Republicans would not meet him on the field of battle in Pennsylvania, Morgan would assault them in the halls of Congress. In 1797, he ran on the Federalist ticket and won a seat in the House of Representatives. He served a single term, and on one occasion threatened to call out his Virginia militiamen against the "seditious" Jeffersonians within his own state.

Advancing age, complicated by years of sciatica and eventually crippling arthritis, had reduced his mighty frame to near helplessness, but mentally he remained alert. Nothing could have been more in character with the colorful old veteran than a remark to his physician shortly before his death on July 6, 1802:

"Doctor," said the general, "if I could be the man I was when I was twenty-one years of age, I would be willing to be stripped stark naked on the top of Allegheny Mountain, to run for my life with a pack of dogs at my heels." [28]

Mighty of spirit, independent of mind, resourceful and self-reliant, a man who rose from humble immigrant stock to military fame, modest wealth, and national political office, Morgan symbolized Crèvecoeur's image of the American—a wholly "new" man.

FOOTNOTES

1. Though the nucleus of this essay is derived from my *Daniel Morgan: Revolutionary Rifleman* (Chapel Hill, 1961), I have placed greater emphasis on the guerrilla theme here than I did in the biography. I have benefited especially from the increasing interest of historians in guerrilla warfare, a trend that doubtless reflects our desire to gain a fuller understanding of the partisan-type operations carried on in South Vietnam and other so-called backward areas of Asia and Africa.

2. [Joseph Graham], "A Recollection of the American Revolutionary War," *Virginia Historical Register*, VI (1853), 211; "Notes from . . . Benjamin Berry . . . in Relation to General Daniel Morgan," Ludwell–Lee Papers, Virginia Historical Society; James Graham, *The Life of General Daniel Morgan* . . . (New York, 1856), pp. 29–30, contains an account of the whipping that is not completely accurate.

3. See John K. Mahon, "Anglo-American Methods of Indian Warfare, 1676–1794," *Mississippi Valley Historical Review*, XLV (September, 1958), 254–75, which discusses the strengths and weaknesses of colonial tactics and strategy on the frontier.

4. Franklin B. Dexter, ed., *The Literary Diary of Ezra Stiles* (New York, 1901), I, 601.

5. Journal of Joseph Henry, in Kenneth Roberts, ed., *March to Quebec* (New York, 1938), pp. 329, 335–36.

6. Journals of Henry and George Morison, in *ibid.*, pp. 378, 537–38.

7. Graham, *Morgan*, pp. 102–03.

8. For the formation of the rifle corps, see John C. Fitzpatrick, ed., *The Writings of George Washington* (Washington, D.C., 1931–44), VI, 128 and VIII, 236–37, 246; hereinafter, Washington,

Writings; "Orderly Book of Major William Heth," *Virginia Historical Society Proceedings 1891,* X, 332–76.

9. R. Lamb, *Memoirs of His Own Life* (Dublin, 1809), p. 199.

10. Jared Sparks, ed., *Correspondence of the Revolution* (Boston, 1853), I, 437.

11. James Wilkinson, *Memoirs of My Own Times* (Philadelphia, 1816), I, 268.

12. Morgan told the story of Fraser's death to a British officer. [Graham], "A Recollection of the American Revolutionary War," p. 210. It also appears in William L. Stone, *Burgoyne's Campaign and St. Leger's Expedition* (Albany, 1877), pp. 324–25.

13. Only recently another British account of the campaign has come to light: S. Sydney Bradford, ed., "Lord Francis Napier's Journal of the Burgoyne Campaign," *Maryland Historical Magazine,* LVII (December, 1962), 285–333.

14. Gates to John Hancock, October 12, 1777, Papers of the Continental Congress, No. 154, I, 272, National Archives.

15. For evaluations of the rifle and light infantry, see the articles by John W. Wright: "The Rifle in the American Revolution," *American Historical Review,* XXIX (January, 1924), 293–99; "The Corps of Light Infantry in the Continental Army," *ibid.,* XXXI (April, 1926), 454–61.

16. Higginbotham, *Morgan,* pp. 82–84.

17. Washington, *Writings,* XV, 342; Morgan to William Woodford, July 22, 1779, Chicago Historical Society.

18. I have found no sound evidence to support the old story—still repeated—that Gates tried to draw Morgan into a plot against Washington after Saratoga, that Gates failed to accord Morgan full recognition for his part in Burgoyne's defeat, and that consequently Morgan initially refused to assist Gates in the South. To be sure, Gates and Morgan had an excellent relationship in 1780.

19. Henry "Light-Horse Harry" Lee maintained that Morgan turned on Tarleton and fought in an "irritation of temper." *Memoirs of the War in the Southern Department . . .* (Philadelphia, 1812), I, 253–54. Lee's view has received little support.

20. Joseph Johnson, *Traditions and Reminiscences Chiefly of the American Revolution in the South* (Charleston, 1851), p. 449.

21. Higginbotham, *Morgan,* pp. 95, 136, 211.

22. The most detailed account of this battle is by Hugh F. Rankin, "Cowpens: Prelude to Yorktown," *North Carolina Historical Review,* XXXI (July, 1954), 336–69. A number of Morgan's letters written during the Southern campaign are printed in Graham,

Morgan. Morgan's graphic description of the outcome at Cowpens is in a long letter to William Snickers, dated January 26, 1781, now in the Gates Papers, New York Historical Society.

23. Graham, *Morgan,* p. 395.
24. Morgan to Richard Butler, January 17, 1782, Lyman C. Draper Papers, 27CC69, State Historical Society of Wisconsin.
25. Graham, *Morgan,* p. 399.
26. Washington, *Writings,* XXIII, 174.
27. Several valuable articles point out the importance of American guerrilla warfare in the South: Eric Robson, "British Light Infantry in the Eighteenth Century: the Effect of American Conditions," *Army Quarterly,* LXII, No. 2 (1950), 209–22; Robert C. Pugh, "The Revolutionary Militia in the Southern Campaigns, 1780– 1781," *William and Mary Quarterly,* 3rd series, XIV (April, 1957), 154–75; Jac Weller, "The Irregular War in the South," *Military Affairs,* XXIV (Fall, 1960), 124–36.
28. David H. Conrad, "Early History of Winchester," *Winchester, Va., Historical Society Annual Papers* (1931), I, 172.

BIBLIOGRAPHY

Bass, Robert D., *The Green Dragoon: The Lives of Banastre Tarleton and Mary Robinson.* New York, 1957. Contains a wealth of recently unearthed material on Tarleton's American service and his subsequent mistress Mary Robinson, a London socialite.

Blacker, I. R., ed., *Irregulars, Partisans, Guerrillas: Great Stories from Rogers' Rangers to the Haganah.* New York, 1954. Provides a valuable introduction to this subject.

Callahan, North, *Daniel Morgan: Ranger of the Revolution.* New York, 1961. Takes a life-and-times approach.

Graham, James, *The Life of General Daniel Morgan of the Virginia Line of the Army of the United States.* New York, 1856. Still retains a large number of letters printed in full.

Hart, Freeman H., *The Valley of Virginia in the American Revolution.* Chapel Hill, 1942. Offers a sound and readable description of frontier Virginia in Morgan's formative years.

Higginbotham, Don, *Daniel Morgan: Revolutionary Rifleman.* Chapel Hill, 1961. Stresses the uniqueness of American eighteenth-century warfare.

Nickerson, Hoffman, *The Turning Point of the Revolution.* Boston, 1928. Continues to be the standard work on the Saratoga campaign.

Robson, Eric, *The American Revolution in its Political and Military Aspects*. London, 1955. Emphasizes the importance of New World conditions and American fighting methods in bringing about British defeat.

Smith, Justin H., *Our Struggle for the Fourteenth Colony*, 2 vols. New York, 1907. Presents an exhaustive account of the campaigns of Montgomery and Arnold against Canada.

Volume II
GEORGE
WASHINGTON'S
OPPONENTS
British Generals and Admirals in the
American Revolution

Preface

THIS BOOK is a collection of interpretive essays covering some of the most important generals and admirals who served on the British side during the American War of Independence. One purpose of the volume is to present the findings of recent scholarship. Few reliable biographies about such men were available before the 1940's. Since that time, however, two definitive studies have appeared—John R. Alden's account of General Thomas Gage and William B. Willcox's Bancroft Prize-winning work on General Henry Clinton. Piers Mackesy's book, *The War for America, 1775–1783,* moreover, devoted much attention to an analysis of the character and capabilities of numerous high-ranking officers. British cabinet members as well as commanders in the field have been subjected to closer scrutiny in the last few years. Recent writings on the leaders in London—Bradley D. Bargar's study of William Legge, Earl of Dartmouth, as American secretary; Gerald S. Brown's monograph on Lord George Germain as American secretary from 1775 to 1778; Alan Valentine's biographies of Lords North and Germain; and George Martelli's life of John Montagu, Earl of Sandwich, as first lord of the Admiralty—have told us more about the war effort mounted by the mother country. Much of this latest scholarship on Britain's statesmen was revisionist in nature and has necessitated a reevaluation of her military leaders.

A second aim of this book is to view the Revolutionary War in a broader perspective than has been done in the past. The authors have tried at times to remove military history from the narrow confines of battles and campaigns, and to discuss the war instead in terms of the complex problems of strategy, logistics, and civil-military relations facing the British. In this same vein, the writers have often explored the degree to which military decisions for the North American theater of operations were dictated by political considerations.

This book, conceived as a companion volume to *George Washington's Generals,* admittedly has certain inherent limitations in its organization. Because of restrictions of space, only a few of the major British generals and admirals are discussed; the editor alone bears the responsibility for the selection. The essays, moreover, concentrate solely upon an officer's military career during the Revolutionary War in the American theater of operations. Thus, Admiral Howe's triumphs in European waters in 1782 and the careers of General Cornwallis and Admiral Hood in subsequent wars are not dealt with. Also, primary attention is focused upon naval affairs in the North Atlantic; very little has been said about important campaigns in Caribbean waters. Finally, there is some unavoidable repetition in these essays because many of the generals and admirals under discussion participated in the same military operation.

The contributors to this volume are all scholars who have written previously in the area of military history. Although they may disagree in many of their judgments, as editor I have let their conclusions stand unchanged in the best interests of scholarship.

I should like to express my thanks to many individuals who gave me a helping hand. To my contributors, I am obligated for their part in this book. My major thanks in this regard must be reserved for Professor William B. Willcox of the University of Michigan, who not only contributed two selections but kindly consented to review and comment on the other essays. To my fellow historians—Dean Milton M. Klein of the State University of New York at Fredonia, Dr. Clifford K. Shipton, former Director of the American Antiquarian Society, and Professor Gerald N. Grob of Clark University—I am indebted for reading parts of the manuscript. To my graduate students—Lawrence Kazura and Mrs. Barbara Rosenkrantz—I am grateful for certain insights into the character of General Burgoyne. And to my wife, Joyce Baldwin Billias, I am beholden once again; she helped me on this book, provided inspiration during the task, and, as always, contributed to my happiness.

The book is dedicated to an old friend, Herbert J. Bass, whose personal and professional qualities I have admired for many years.

G.A.B.

Introduction

To WHAT extent did the quality of British military leadership affect the outcome of the Revolutionary War in America? The war was *lost*, some scholars insist, because British commanders on land and sea were guilty of incompetent leadership—bungling their assignments, resorting to outmoded strategy and tactics, and demonstrating a lack of desire for an all-out victory on many occasions. The war was *won*, other historians argue, because Washington and his colleagues exercised superior generalship—adopting sounder strategy, applying shrewder tactics, and motivating their men with a greater desire to win. Almost two centuries have passed since the fighting began, but the debate regarding the relative importance of British military leadership goes on.

The answer may be supplied, in part, by studying those generals and admirals who conducted operations in North America. Of course, such an answer can only be a partial one. Viewed in the broadest possible setting, it is clear that the outcome of this war was profoundly influenced by nonmilitary factors—diplomatic, economic, and constitutional considerations—over which these men had no control. Even if the conflict is evaluated strictly in military terms, any judgment on the performance of British commanders is complicated by other circumstances. The Revolutionary War was only one part of a world-wide struggle in which Britain was involved from 1775 to 1783. The depth of that involvement is sometimes overlooked: hostilities with France, Spain, and Holland as well as America; threats of invasion of England itself; struggles to maintain control of the seas and the Channel; attacks upon Canada, the West Indies, and Gibraltar; the war in India; and popular unrest in Ireland and other parts of the realm. It was little wonder, then, that the Ministry relegated the war in America to a position of secondary importance at certain stages. The demands of the army and navy in this theater of operations often had to be balanced against those needs in other parts of the globe; and not infrequently the requests of British commanders in America for men and materials were given a lower priority. Finally, many of the major strategic decisions were made by cabinet ministers in London rather than by men in the field.

The assessment of any British general or admiral must take into account the period of the war during which he was in command. For this purpose, the Revolutionary War may be conveniently divided into two phases—the periods before and after France's entry into the war. In the first phase—the colonial phase from 1775 to 1778—Britain faced two major problems: the military struggle with the American colonies abroad and the political struggle at home. Despite her military and naval supremacy throughout the first phase, Britain's commanders were unable to deal a decisive blow in America. Political divisions on the domestic scene between those who backed a policy of coercion toward the American colonies and those who favored a policy of conciliation also made it more difficult to carry on the war. During the second phase—the international phase from 1778 to 1783—Britain's problems grew even more acute. Military leaders now could count on a stronger united front in the homeland because France and Spain, her traditional foes, had come into the war. But Britain was forced to cope with this coalition of enemies on the continent and to fight a global war. From 1778 on, British armies and fleets in the American theater had to conduct their operations under the constant threat of enemy sea power. Between the first and second phases, the character of the war was completely altered.

When fighting first broke out, British commanders in America appeared to possess an overwhelming military superiority. All the advantages, it seemed, were on their side. They could depend upon a professional army—a well-equipped, experienced, and disciplined force; a navy that outnumbered American ships of war by one hundred to one; financial resources which would permit the hiring of foreign troops to supplement the regular army; the cooperation of American loyalists who formed a significant portion of the colonial populace; and a bureaucracy in Britain to provide a system of command.

But as the war wore on, many disadvantages became apparent and certain advantages decreased or disappeared. Two of the most decisive disadvantages were geographical in nature—the vastness of America and the width of the Atlantic. Invading British armies found it impossible to conquer or occupy the far reaches of the North American continent. The three-thousand-mile supply line from Britain to America proved cumbersome and costly. Another disadvantage was the military assistance America increasingly received from her ally, France. Many of Britain's earlier advantages, moreover, were sharply diminished with the passage of time. The army was undermanned and given greater responsibilities as the war spread to other parts of the world. The navy—Britain's most powerful military machine—was forced to stretch its resources thin, as France, Spain, and Holland sent out hostile fleets to attack the home island and parts of the empire. The system of public finance was found to be weak and Britain soon faced a mounting war debt. Proper strategic management of the war became impossible, in part, because lines of communication were slow and undependable. And British generals proved reluctant or unable to mobilize the loyalists into an effective fighting force. Viewing the many obstacles the British had to overcome, certain historians have concluded that the surprising thing about the Revolutionary War is not that the Americans won, but that they did not win more easily.

The first British military man to grapple with the problem of rebellion was Thomas Gage—commander-in-chief of the army in America in 1775. Gage was more than a military figure, however; he played a dual role as a kind of proconsul as well as general. Both in his capacity as imperial statesman and commander-in-chief, he appears to have lacked the perception necessary to cope with the crisis facing him. Despite almost two decades of service in America, he completely misjudged the temper of the people. From the point of view of the British government, he was an alarmist about the large number of troops that would be needed for coercion and his warnings were ignored. His judgment on matters of military strategy was likewise faulty. He believed that Boston was the major source of unrest; if the city could be isolated and subdued the discontent would lessen. Only after the march on Concord and the battle of Bunker Hill did he begin to show a growing awareness of the complexities involved in dealing with the uprising.

Sir William Howe—who replaced Gage in the fall of 1775—was, perhaps, the British commander-in-chief who had the best chance of crushing the rebellion. In 1776 the mother country mounted a war effort of unprecedented proportions; Howe could count upon a 34,000-man army—the greatest expeditionary force ever assembled by Britain to that time—and the support of a vast naval armada—one of the largest fleet of warships ever seen in North American waters. A methodical and experienced soldier, he proceeded to show his superiority as a tactician over Washington by defeating the American general in battles at Brooklyn, Brandywine, and Germantown. But Howe had fatal flaws as a field commander. His strategy was not based upon any clear-cut conception of how the war might be won; he preferred a war of posts and maneuver rather than a ruthless and single-minded pursuit of the Continental army. Howe clung stubbornly to conventional eighteenth-century methods of warfare and tended to maneuver for position, to occupy strategic points, and to avoid battles except when success was certain. Above all, he was ultracautious and argued that the British army in America was a national resource to be hoarded and kept intact at almost all costs rather than risked in aggressive engagements.

Howe's successor, Sir Henry Clinton, proved something of a paradox as commander-in-chief during his four years from 1778 to 1782. While serving as Howe's subordinate from 1776 to 1778, Clinton showed great promise in his sure grasp of strategy, penchant for sound planning, and competence in field operations. Once he became commander-in-chief, however, he grew as cautious and hesitant as Howe. Much of his time was spent in drafting plans that were rarely carried out. His inability to cooperate with his colleagues—both generals and admirals—produced what has been called a paralysis of command: he and Cornwallis were temperamentally unsuited to work with one another and each tended to frustrate the other's plans; and Clinton's incapacity to collaborate with Admiral Arbuthnot made it impossible to conduct joint operations against Newport in the summer of 1780. There may well be, as his biographer has suggested, a psychological explanation for Clinton's behavior—a pathological incapacity on his part to use or share authority. Although Clinton succeeded in winning the greatest single British victory of the war—the capture of General Benjamin Lincoln's army at Charleston in 1780—it was his ironic fate also to be in over-all command of the British forces in America when Cornwallis met defeat at Yorktown.

The last commander-in-chief in America during the war—Sir Guy Carleton—was, in many ways, the most controversial. Serving as governor of Quebec at the outbreak of the war, Carleton helped to shape the future course of the conflict by keeping Canada loyal during the American invasion in 1775–76. But he has been both praised and criticized for the proclamation issued early in 1776 in which he offered to pardon Americans taken as prisoners. Carleton was seeking, no doubt, to counter the growing movement toward independence with a policy of kindness and conciliation. Historians have also taken sides on the dispute between Lord George Germain—secretary of state for the American colonies—and Carleton regarding the latter's failure to pursue more aggressively the Americans retreating from Canada during the summer and fall of 1776. When Carleton was appointed to succeed Clinton in 1782, it was too late to change the outcome of the conflict on the continent; having lost two armies at Saratoga and Yorktown the British had given up hope of recovering America by military means.

Of all the British generals who held high command, none has been ridiculed more than John Burgoyne. Pictured by some historians as a playboy who drank and danced his way to defeat, Burgoyne was actually a hard-driving, courageous commander consumed with ambition for fame, high rank, and honor. Burgoyne had more ability than most scholars credit him with; he was a superb leader of men, recognized the role of ideology in the Revolutionary War, and proved flexible enough to adapt his tactics to American conditions. But he was also hasty and seemed devoid of a sound sense of strategy. He should not bear the entire blame for the disaster which befell him at Saratoga in 1777—it should be shared with Germain and Howe—but Burgoyne's bold attempt to fight his way to Albany more or less on his own was reckless and unrealistic. Hoping to gain great glory by reaching his objective, he never seems to have given thought to the questions of broad strategy he would face after arriving at Albany—exploiting his victory, supplying his army, and dealing with Gates' force. When he lost his gamble, Burgoyne changed the course of history; the loss of his army was destined to bring France into the war.

Lord Cornwallis, like Burgoyne, showed more boldness than most British generals. Serving as Howe's subordinate in the north during the early years of the war, he proved to be aggressive, resourceful, and capable in a series of important battles. As a commander in the field, he courted danger but was as decisive as he was daring. After a brief leave of absence, he returned to America in 1778 to become Clinton's second in command. When personal differences arose between the two men, they were compounded by the fact that Cornwallis held a dormant commission as commander-in-chief in the event of Clinton's resignation or death.

Cornwallis, placed in command of a British army in the summer of 1780, set out to secure the southern colonies for the mother country and to exploit the imagined strength of the loyalists in that region. Although his force of 2,200 men was outnumbered by almost 3,000 Americans facing him at Camden,

South Carolina, in August, 1780, he inflicted a crushing defeat upon Horatio Gates' army. After much maneuvering, during which his subordinates suffered defeats at King's Mountain and Cowpens, Cornwallis met the Continental army led by General Nathanael Greene at Guilford Court House, North Carolina, in March, 1781. In a bloody battle in which he was once again outnumbered, Cornwallis won the field. But he did so at a tremendous cost—nearly one-fourth of his small army. The anticipated uprising of large loyalist forces in the Carolinas had failed to occur and Cornwallis found his victories to be barren ones because of the surprising resilience of the American forces. He thereupon made a fateful decision to march his army to Virginia to join the British troops already stationed there. Trapped at Yorktown by superior French and American forces on land and sea, Cornwallis surrendered his army on October 19, 1781, ending the last major land campaign on the North American continent.

At the same time that Britain sought to subjugate America with land armies, she also employed her mightiest military weapon—the navy. Undisputed control in North American waters for the first three years of the conflict presented her with an opportunity to win the war primarily by the application of sea power. By strangling American trade with a tight blockade clamped upon colonial seaports, it is conceivable that Britain could have brought about the collapse of the rebellion before France entered the war. Such a solution, of course, would have been predicated upon two conditions: a clear understanding of the problem on the part of the British Ministry so that a major strategic decision would have been made to concentrate upon a full-scale effort to impose a close blockade; and a solid commitment of ships and other resources required to exploit to the fullest this form of naval warfare. Throughout the first phase of the war, neither of these conditions was met.

The Ministry was guilty of muddled thinking in framing its broad strategy of war from 1775 to 1778. Although cabinet members dimly perceived the possibilities of applying sea power and subordinated military operations on land to the needs of a blockade up to 1777, they never saw the problem with sufficient clarity to adopt such a strategy of naval warfare as a clear-cut policy. Too often, British strategy and planning constituted a series of *ad hoc* responses to meet particular military situations in America or to cope with domestic political considerations in England. As a result, the British never undertook a consistent policy to station fleets in America with systematic plans for blockading all major colonial ports, attacking American privateers and commercial vessels, and destroying dock facilities with periodic raids.

The resources of the Royal Navy, it is true, were rather limited at the outbreak of the Revolutionary War. After Britain's victory over France in the Seven Years' War, the navy entered upon a period of decline as the service reverted to peacetime footing. Ships were decommissioned, junior officers discharged in droves, and naval recruits sharply cut in numbers. Between the two wars, the navy continued to decline both in strength and efficiency. The result was that when fighting began in 1775, Admiral Samuel Graves—commander-in-chief on the North American station—did not have enough ships on hand to cow the colonists. But even when more ships and sailors were sent to America in the next two years, the idea of exerting pressure at sea by a tight blockade was never fully exploited. Inhibited by the Ministry which failed to think through clearly the problem of an over-all war strategy, limited in the number of ships and men that could be raised and deployed in the American theater of operations, saddled with the burden of supporting the army in major land operations, and commanded by admirals who would not or could not adopt a vigorous policy, the navy was never able to impose a really successful blockade during the first phase of the war.

While the British navy was undergoing a decline after the Seven Years' War, the French navy was being rebuilt and improved. By the time of the Revolutionary War, France possessed a naval force that could challenge Britain's supremacy of the seas. The initiative in naval warfare in North America after 1778, therefore, frequently passed over to the French.

Whether or not the British had sufficient ships to impose a close blockade on the French fleet in European waters in 1778 is a matter of controversy among historians. At any rate, developments in the next two years diminished the possibility of employing such a strategy. By 1780 two other principal naval powers—Spain and Holland—were at war with Britain. When a coalition of neutral countries hostile to Britain—the League of Armed Neutrality—was formed in 1780, the presence of yet another potential enemy force restricted even further the efforts of the Royal Navy. The British Ministry during these years found itself incapable of matching the size of the naval forces France and Spain sent into the English Channel or countering all of the enemy fleets that appeared in the Caribbean and Mediterranean. French squadrons often sailed unopposed in American waters where the Royal Navy lost its superiority at least once a year from 1778 to 1781. Under these conditions, the capture of a beleaguered British army—such as that which occurred at Yorktown—became almost inevitable.

Although the surrender of Cornwallis' army practically ended the fighting in North America, the war continued elsewhere. Throughout 1781 the British had suffered a series of setbacks in the Caribbean as Tobago, St. Kitts, Nevis and Montserrat fell to the enemy. Having lost the war on the continent, they appeared to be well on their way to losing it in the West Indies. But in a brilliant naval victory near Martinique in April, 1782, Admirals Rodney and Hood helped to restore the balance. This triumph went far toward retrieving the British position in the West Indies and was, in fact, the last major battle in the waters of the New World.

Of the naval leaders appointed to the post of commander-in-chief on the North American station, Admiral Richard Howe, named in February, 1776, was perhaps the first to possess the necessary resources to conduct meaningful operations against the colonists. The Admiralty ordered him to prosecute the war

vigorously with the 73 warships and 13,000 seamen that were
to be under his command. He was authorized to deal with the
Americans only in the event of a surrender, but after he joined
his brother—General William Howe—at New York in July,
1776, he set about to promote a reconciliation instead.

The admiral appeared determined to use the olive branch as
well as the sword. He first approached the Continental Congress
to discuss a peace proposal in September, 1776—after the American defeat on Long Island. When Congress indicated its unwillingness to negotiate, Howe, with his brother, issued a proclamation in November appealing to the people to lay down their
arms. Throughout the second half of 1776, he apparently
adopted a deliberate policy toward the Americans: to make a
show of strength, to exert limited use of force, and then to make
repeated overtures of peace. But General Washington's victories
at Trenton and Princeton around the end of the year revived
America's expectations of victory and dashed Howe's hopes for
reconciliation.

Howe's naval policy underwent several changes in the course
of 1777 and 1778. Seeing little prospect of negotiating a peace
and having little taste for exerting overwhelming military force,
he adopted halfhearted measures in 1777. Although Howe applied a blockade, he never fully exploited its possibilities. Firstly,
he was unwilling to carry the war into colonial ports where
American shipping might be more easily destroyed. Secondly, he
committed much of his force to supporting the army in land
operations and thereby limited the number of vessels available
for blockade duty. Once the French entered the war, however,
Howe's attitude altered completely. He showed great gallantry in
preparing to fight d'Estaing's superior fleet at New York and off
Newport in the summer of 1778—even though these impending
battles never took place. After conducting a successful defensive
naval strategy, Howe returned to England in September, 1778.

Howe's successors proved to be either mediocrities or incom-
petents. The Royal Navy was in the doldrums by the time of the
Revolutionary War because it lacked great leaders as well as

sound ships. Many gifted admirals who served in the Seven Years' War had died or retired, and some senior British officers still on active service refused to accept command in America for political reasons. Lord Sandwich—first lord of the Admiralty—had few outstanding men to choose from and those he picked often proved to be singularly bad selections. General Henry Clinton aptly characterized his naval colleagues as a pack of "old women."

Three of the long list of admirals who followed Howe in North America—James Gambier, Marriot Arbuthnot, and Thomas Graves—illustrate how poor naval leadership was throughout most of the war. Although not all were appointed to the position of commander-in-chief, delays in naming and replacing admirals to that post frequently enabled subordinates to assume responsibility on the station. Gambier—who held command during part of the winter and spring of 1778–79—was probably the sorriest of the lot. Timid and indecisive, Gambier found himself in a position that called for qualities of leadership he did not possess; he returned to England without accomplishing a great deal. Arbuthnot, on the other hand, worsened the friction already existing between the two services to a point where it was impossible for the army and navy to cooperate on joint operations during 1780. Matters became so bad that Clinton sent an ultimatum to the Ministry declaring that either he or his colleague must go. As a result, Arbuthnot was recalled. Thomas Graves, an uninspired tactician, fought an undramatic but crucial battle with the French fleet under Admiral de Grasse off the Virginia Capes in September, 1781. When the British fleet was driven off and the French were left in command of the sea near Yorktown, the fate of Cornwallis' army was sealed.

The admirals who served mostly in West Indies waters—in contrast to many who held command off the coast of North America—were often competent, if not talented, men. Sir George Rodney, one of the more able and energetic officers, had had a highly successful career in the Seven Years' War before being offered command of the fleet on the Leeward Islands station late in 1779. It is possible that Rodney missed his first opportunity to defeat the French fleet in February, 1781, because part of his squadron was engaged in gathering booty from St. Eustatius—the rich island in the Dutch West Indies. But he gained a decisive victory over de Grasse in the battle of the Saints off Martinique on April 12, 1782. Partly owing to luck, he was at considerably greater strength than his opponent and made the most of his advantage. Certain of his contemporaries and some historians argued, however, that Rodney might have exploited his advantage even more.

Sir Samuel Hood, who worked mainly with Rodney in the West Indies, was a brilliant officer; but the full range of his capabilities may never be known because he was a subordinate so much of the time. His ability to anticipate enemy intentions, to analyze strategic situations, and to make moves with decisiveness marked him as a man of great potential. But the fortunes of war never favored him with an outstanding victory. The final outcome of two engagements in which he was involved—the battles of the Virginia Capes and of the Saints—might well have been different if he had been in full command.

Although the Royal Navy had at least three outstanding admirals in the Revolutionary War—Howe, Rodney, and Hood—the service failed to produce final victory as it had in the past. Why? In part, because naval commanders in America had to cope with many complex problems not of their own making. The government's neglect of the navy between two wars resulted in too few ships and too few seamen to carry out too many missions. The Ministry's failure to plan decisively for the American theater during the first phase of the war left admirals in a quandary as to what strategy they should follow. Once France entered the war, demands for naval resources from other theaters of war resulted in a lower priority as North America was downgraded to a subordinate theater. The Ministry's failure in 1778 to blockade the home ports of France—though it is by no means certain that Britain had the necessary naval superiority to employ such a strategy in that year or thereafter—exposed British naval commanders to an annual foray of French fleets in American waters and enabled French commanders to seize the initiative quite often. But British admirals must also share much of the blame for the war's outcome. They evaded for the most part the hard thinking that was required to formulate a successful naval strategy and merely drifted instead into a course of action that led to a series of expedient but haphazard moves. Some admirals, like Howe, adopted halfhearted measures and refused to prosecute the war vigorously. Friction between the services also blunted the effective use of the naval arm at times. And in certain situations—such as the battle of the Virginia Capes—British commanders showed themselves unwilling to take risks against an equal or slightly superior French fleet at the crucial moment. In short, the admirals failed to make the most of the means at their disposal—particularly during the first phase of the war.

This last comment applies to British generals as well as admirals—but to a lesser degree. The chances of winning the war by waging land campaigns were slimmer than those of ending the conflict by a strategy of naval warfare during the first few years. But opportunities did present themselves to generals to put down the rebellion—to Gage at Bunker Hill in 1775; to Howe on Long Island in 1776; and to Howe and Burgoyne along the Hudson River Valley in 1777, if they had coordinated their campaigns. Why did these men fail? The generals, like the admirals, faced problems over which they had no control: the British government's failure to frame a consistent war strategy and to adhere to it; the Ministry's refusal to recognize that even more troops were required to conquer an entire continent; and Britain's system of command which was so complicated and inefficient as to create misunderstandings between the leaders in London and the men in the field.

British generals, nevertheless, must bear part of the blame, even when allowances are made for such matters. In carrying out their campaigns, many of them tended to be too traditional and to cling too closely to the military orthodoxies of the day. Howe after the battle of Long Island in 1776, for example, was more interested in maneuvering into position to occupy New York City than in capturing Washington's army. Waging warfare along conventional eighteenth-century lines which called for the conservation of forces, battlefield commanders were often too cautious in committing their troops in aggressive engagements or campaigns. Two generals—Burgoyne and Cornwallis—went to the other extreme, on occasion, and ran bold risks; but they gambled with their armies on unlikely objectives and lost. Although commanders in the field were granted considerable latitude by Germain in conducting operations, none of them produced a battle plan which would have assured Britain of total victory. There was no military genius in their midst—no Marlborough or Wellington—who could come up with a successful strategy before 1778; a strategy to suppress a colonial rebellion in a vast country where a people, not a professional army, was under arms.

To return, then, to the original question: to what extent did the quality of British military leadership affect the outcome of the Revolutionary War in America? From this brief survey of generals and admirals which has concentrated perforce upon their errors in strategy and tactics, it might be tempting to conclude that the war's outcome was determined primarily by British mistakes. But such a view runs the risk of giving rise to a new myth: that between bungling British commanders and foreign aid from France, the American army had little or nothing to do with the winning of the war, and that the non-military and quasi-military factors mentioned in this introduction were of small consequence.

The fact of the matter is, British miscalculations alone would not necessarily have led to defeat: the American high command had to capitalize on these mistakes if they were to have any meaning. Much more important than British blunders themselves was the ability of the Americans to exploit these errors—especially during the first phase of the war. However much Howe erred in separating his army from that of Burgoyne in

1777, for example, it would have come to nothing unless American commanders perceived this flaw in strategy and acted upon it. By taking advantage of such mistakes, the American army was able to survive and to gain time—time to develop from an amateur into a professional fighting force, and to secure the foreign aid from France which brought final victory. By preventing the British from winning the war before 1778, the Americans made possible ultimate military success, and, in this sense, the Revolutionary War may be called an American victory rather than a British defeat.

GEORGE ATHAN BILLIAS

Clark University

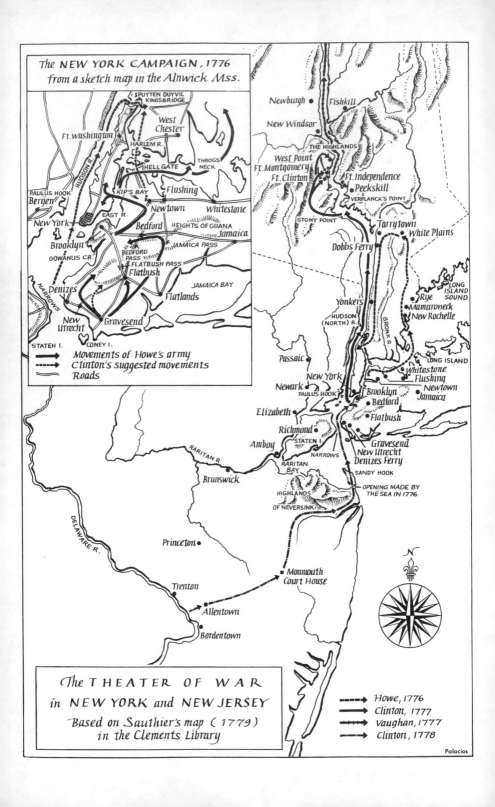

The NEW YORK CAMPAIGN, 1776
from a sketch map in the Alnwick Mss.

SPUYTEN DUYVIL
KINGSBRIDGE

West Chester

Ft. Washington

HARLEM R.

THROGS NECK

HELL GATE

PAULUS HOOK
Bergen

HUDSON R.

KIP'S BAY

Flushing

EAST R.

Newtown

Whitestone

New York

Bedford

HEIGHTS OF GUANA

Jamaica

Brooklyn

JAMAICA PASS

GOWANUS CR.

BEDFORD PASS

JAMAICA BAY

FLATBUSH PASS

Flatbush

NARROWS

Denizes

Flatlands

New Utrecht

Gravesend

STATEN I.

CONEY I.

→ Movements of Howe's army
⇢ Clinton's suggested movements
〰 Roads

Newburgh ●   Fishkill

New Windsor

THE HIGHLANDS

West Point
Ft. Montgomery
Ft. Clinton

Ft. Independence
● Peekskill

VERPLANCK'S POINT

STONY POINT

Tarrytown   White Plains

Dobbs Ferry

Yonkers

LONG ISLAND SOUND

Rye
Mamaroneck
New Rochelle

HUDSON (NORTH) R.

BRONX R.

LONG ISLAND

Passaic ●

New York

Whitestone
Flushing

Newark   Brooklyn
PAULUS HOOK   Bedford   Newtown
Jamaica

Elizabeth   Flatbush

Richmond ●

STATEN I.

Amboy   NARROWS

Gravesend
New Utrecht
Denizes Ferry

Sandy Hook

RARITAN R.

RARITAN BAY

OPENING MADE BY
THE SEA IN 1776

Brunswick

HIGHLANDS

OF NEVERSINK

DELAWARE R.

Princeton ●

N

Monmouth
Court House

Trenton ●

Allentown ●

Bordentown ●

The THEATER OF WAR
in NEW YORK and NEW JERSEY
Based on Sauthier's map (1779)
in the Clements Library

⇢ Howe, 1776
→ Clinton, 1777
⇢ Vaughan, 1777
→ Clinton, 1778

Palacios

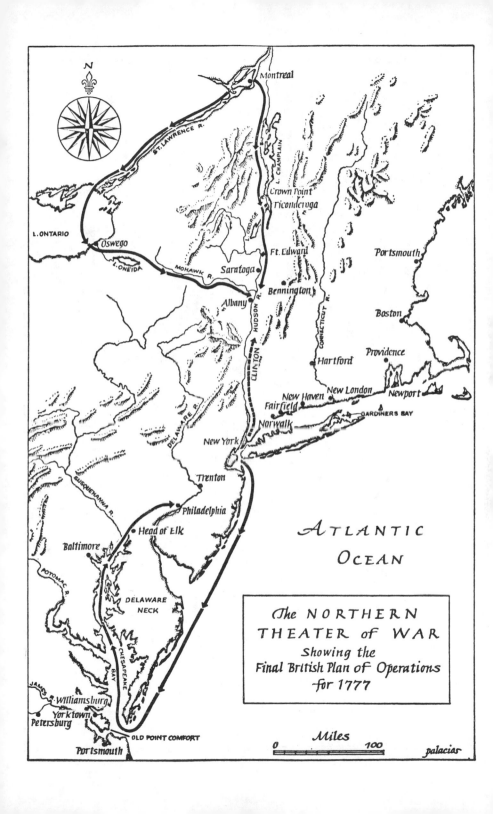

N

St. Lawrence R.

Montreal

L. Ontario

Oswego

L. Oneida

Mohawk R.

L. Champlain

L. George

Crown Point

Ticonderoga

Ft. Edward

Saratoga

Bennington

Albany

Hudson R.

Connecticut R.

Portsmouth

Boston

Hartford

Providence

New Haven

New London

Newport

Fairfield

Gardiners Bay

Norwalk

New York

Delaware R.

Susquehanna R.

Trenton

Philadelphia

Head of Elk

Baltimore

Potomac R.

Delaware Neck

Chesapeake Bay

James

Williamsburg

Yorktown

Petersburg

Old Point Comfort

Portsmouth

ATLANTIC OCEAN

The NORTHERN
THEATER of WAR
Showing the
Final British Plan of Operations
for 1777

Miles

0   100

palacias

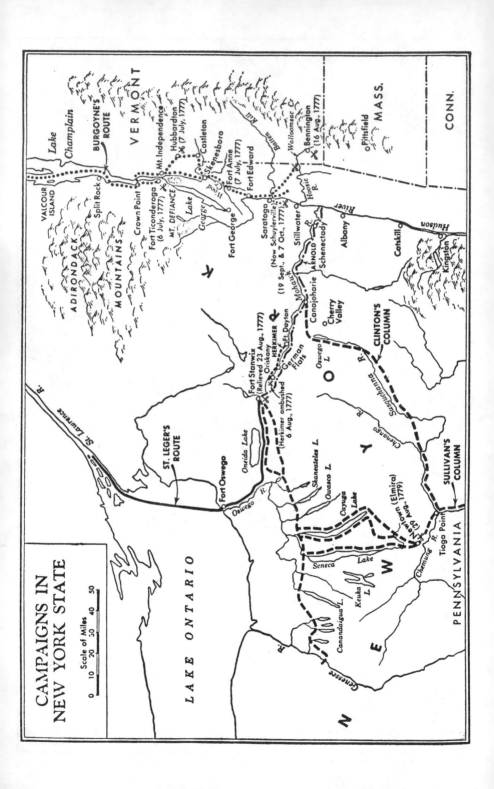

CAMPAIGNS IN NEW YORK STATE

Scale of Miles
0 10 20 30 40 50

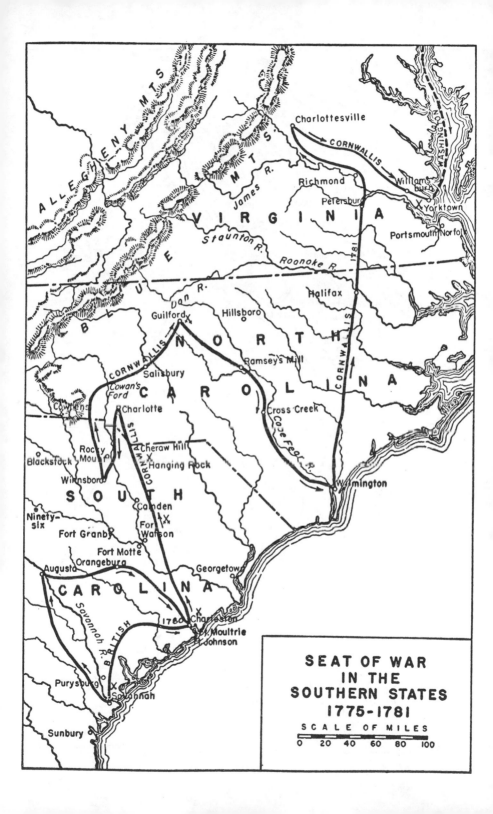

SEAT OF WAR
IN THE
SOUTHERN STATES
1775-1781
SCALE OF MILES
0   20   40   60   80   100

L. MICHIGAN
L. HURON
L. ONTARIO
L. ERIE

Boston
ROCHAMBEAU
New York
Newport
WASHINGTON AND
ROCHAMBEAU
Philadelphia

OHIO R.

Charlottesville
Richmond
Petersburg
York-
town
Guilford
CAPE FEAR R.
Charlotte
Winnsboro
Camden
CORNWALLIS
Wilmington
Charleston
Savannah

GRAVES & HOOD
DE BARRAS
HOOD
DE GRASSE

N

ATLANTIC OCEAN

FLORIDA

GULF OF
MEXICO

HOOD

BAHAMA
ISLANDS

DE GRASSE

CUBA

HAITI
JAMAICA
SANTO
DOMINGO

The CAMPAIGN
of 1781

palacios

Miles
0   300

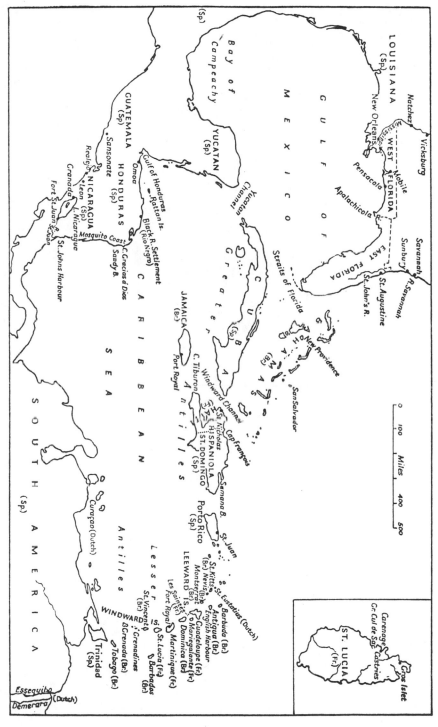

THE CARIBBEAN AND CENTRAL AMERICA

GEORGE WASHINGTON'S OPPONENTS

British Generals and Admirals in the
American Revolution

Thomas Gage:

WEAK LINK OF EMPIRE

—•—

JOHN SHY

University of Michigan

THOMAS GAGE, as commander-in-chief of the British army in North America in 1775, was trapped by historical forces he could neither control nor avoid. But his frantic efforts to elude the trap, if unsuccessful, were not inconsequential. He could not have prevented the American Revolution, but he could, and did, give its beginning a particular shape. The Revolutionary War began on land, under ambiguous circumstances, at the heart of rebel strength, in an area that could only be a dead end for British strategy, and with a series of humiliating setbacks for His Majesty's arms. In the years that followed, British policy could never quite shake free of this bad beginning—never again was the range of strategic and political choice as wide as it had been in 1775. There were others who must share the blame with Gage, but he more than anyone else might have made a different beginning. His personality and previous military experience suggest why he did not.

Thomas Gage was the second son of a noble family known primarily for its lack of distinction and its reluctance to give up Catholicism. His father, the first Viscount Gage, pursued an erratic course in British politics. Thomas' mother had a reputation for sexual promiscuity, while his brother's outstanding trait seems to have been absent-mindedness. His sister married into

3

a Catholic family, and both of his parents, after living as nominal Anglicans, appear to have returned to the Catholic Church at the end of their lives. Great wealth entered the family only when Thomas' brother, who was the eldest, married a Jewish heiress. But long before that event, Thomas had to find his own way.

The Church, the law, the army—these were the paths open to younger sons of nobility in eighteenth-century England, and so, after eight years at Westminster School, young Thomas set out on a military career. In getting a commission, he naturally had the help of his brother William, the future Lord Gage, who just as naturally would soon enter the House of Commons from the borough of Seaford, Sussex, one of whose seats was in the Gage family pocket. For fifteen years, Gage's military career was not unusual in any way: service in Flanders against the French, in North Britain against the Jacobites; a captain at twenty-three, a lieutenant colonel at just past thirty, both ranks acquired of course by the purchase of a vacant commission. As an officer with good "connexions," however, he was expected to serve some time at headquarters: "For a man who intends to be military nothing so pretty as an aide de camp in service with an intelligent general," was the advice of Jeffrey Amherst, later conqueror of Canada, to his younger brother.[1] Accordingly Gage served on the staff—in "the family" was the phrase—of the Earl of Albemarle, father of his school friends at Westminster, the Keppels.

In 1755, he told an historian many years later, some American land speculators, among them George Washington, interrupted the typical pattern of Gage's military career, and incidentally started a world war.[2] But the British government at the time decided that the troubles of the governor of Virginia and his land-hungry cronies were caused by French aggression in the Ohio Valley. Neither version was more than half true. The cabinet nevertheless took drastic action: it ordered British regulars to defend American territory and colonists, something rarely done in the past. The 44th, Gage's regiment, and the 48th, both stationed in Ireland, received orders to embark for Alexandria, Virginia, under the command of Major General Edward Braddock, who carried a commission as commander-in-chief for North America.

"My honest friend Gage is to be of the Ohio party," wrote James Wolfe when he heard the news of Braddock's expedition. It is interesting to learn that Wolfe, already known in the army as an exceptionally zealous and able officer, thought well of Gage.[3] But the Braddock campaign against the French at the forks of the Ohio turned into a disaster. Crippled at the start by problems of supply, Braddock lost the advantage that either a rapid march or methodical approach might have offered. When, after more than two hundred miles of marching, his column ran into ambush almost within sight of its objective, the French had had ample time to bring up reinforcements. The British force, on the other hand, was hungry and its march formation cluttered with wagons, cattle, and pack horses. Only a 300-man advance party was in position to prevent surprise and to protect the main body while it deployed, but the advance party failed. It collapsed at first contact, transmitted its panic to the entire force, and its commander, Lieutenant Colonel Thomas Gage, could do nothing to stop the ensuing rout.

Modern historians have criticized Gage on several grounds—failing to occupy the high ground near the line of march, leaving behind a pair of light cannon that might have turned the tide, even fleeing the battlefield—but all such criticism is captious, and some is merely uninformed, for no one criticized him at the time.[4] The French force, though outnumbered by the whole British column, simply overwhelmed the advance party. Surprise, fear, inexperience in forest warfare, and a faulty tactical arrangement of the main body did the rest. It was not a battle, but a massacre.

Gage "distinguish'd himself by Encouraging the men as much as he Could," according to an anonymous eyewitness, and had "several narrow escapes."[5] But if he had minor wounds to prove his bravery, and in justice deserved little blame for the debacle, Gage had shown no special talent for leadership in combat. His own account of the battle puts all blame on the rank and file, which he certainly knew was an exaggeration. He had hardly reported the death of his colonel before he was asking for promotion to the vacancy. His assertion that he was the senior lieutenant colonel on the field, and that Braddock, "had he lived a few days longer," would have given him the regiment, hit a sour note even for the eighteenth century.[6] He did not get the colonelcy.

With Braddock's defeat, the British government found that the small expedition was becoming a full-scale war, and Thomas Gage found that his military education in America was going to last more than a season. New commanders with new regiments came over with new plans; Gage and the 44th moved north toward Canada in keeping with those plans. British North America spent all of 1756 trying to reorganize its military effort, and Gage soon learned how low regular troops could sink under the primitive conditions of the frontier: he had seen a mutinous detachment of the 51st "in a filthy condition covered with vermin, . . . legs mortified thro dirt cold and want of change." [7] His own regiment was not much better: "The [44th] Regt is in Rags," wrote Lord Loudoun, the new commander-in-chief, but added that "they look like Soldiers" because "Lt Col Gage is a good Officer and keeps up Discipline Strictly." [8] In 1757, he was a member of the amphibious expedition that never quite reached its objective—the fortress of Louisbourg on Cape Breton Island. He did, however, manage to avoid the epidemic of backbiting and recriminations that infected the officer corps after the abortive campaign that summer which saw the fall of Fort William Henry and the slaughter of some of its garrison by Indians.

During the following winter, Gage moved toward the colonelcy that had eluded him in 1755. All British officers with experience in America recognized the value of provincial rangers, armed woodsmen who were somewhat more dependable than Indians and more skillful than either British regulars or American militia in the techniques of forest warfare. Rangers were vital elements in gathering intelligence and in screening the army when it was in camp or on the move. But rangers were expensive because of their high rate of pay, they were unmilitary in dress and deportment, and, during the illness of their leader Robert Rogers, they had become unruly, even mutinous. Gage apparently saw his chance, and offered to raise a regiment of light infantry that could, in time, obviate the need for rangers.

It was a good idea, and often has been noted as a landmark in the history of the British army. There is little to suggest, however, that Gage was leading his British comrades toward a full acceptance of the lessons of Braddock's defeat. Gage raised his light infantry regiment, the 80th, and it served in 1758 alongside rangers and Indians in the unsuccessful campaign against Ticonderoga. But Gage himself, for some reason, hardly appears in the record. The 80th was parceled out among the three brigades of regulars, while Gage was an acting brigadier general and became second in command after the death of Lord Howe. But Gage seems to have done nothing to help the unfortunate General Abercromby avoid or retrieve his errors of judgment, which included a frontal attack without artillery support on a strongly fortified position. It is difficult to resist an impression that Gage had finally got his regiment, and was content. He improved his situation still more when at the end of the summer he hurried away from the sick and defeated army to marry Margaret Kemble, daughter of a wealthy New Jersey family.

His position as brigadier general became permanent in 1759, and that year he got his first independent command. Amherst, Abercromby's successor, sent Gage to take over the siege of Fort Niagara. Once the fort had fallen, Gage was to move against the French post of La Galette at the head of the St. Lawrence. While Wolfe attacked Quebec, and Amherst led his army down Lake Champlain toward Montreal, Gage was expected to exert pressure on Canada from the West. As in 1755, Gage, if he did not fail, at best failed to succeed.

He had excuses: the failure of the quartermaster at Albany to support him properly, the unexpected size of the French garrison at La Galette, and the attrition of his own force. But Amherst and especially Wolfe badly needed a diversionary attack, even if it were repulsed, and the commander-in-chief refused to accept the excuses. Gage had not carried out his orders, and "may not have such an opportunity [again] as long as he lives," was Amherst's judgment. "They have found out difficulties where there are none." [9] In the final campaign of the war on the continent in 1760, when Amherst accepted the surrender of Canada, he had Brigadier General Gage bringing up the rear.

Perhaps the rear was the right place for a general officer whose record indicated that running a regiment—making men look like soldiers and keeping strict discipline, as Loudoun had put it—was about the ceiling of his military abilities. In the rear he could keep the supplies moving forward and the reserve forces in good order, ready for the commander's call. In the rear he could avoid the need to make quick decisions under pressure. There were some, though, who thought that Gage was not inept as a commander, only unlucky. Dr. Richard Huck, a highly intelligent surgeon on the headquarters staff, believed that Gage had received impossible orders and then been blamed when he could not execute them. "Gage is certainly none of the Sons of Fortune," Huck wrote to his old chief, Loudoun, and his epigram seems an apt description of Gage's entire wartime record, from Braddock's field to Bunker Hill. But even Huck reported that, according to French prisoners, the situation in Canada had been so desperate that two or three more days of pressure on La Galette would have brought collapse, and the doctor conceded that Gage perhaps had too much "Nonchalance" for his own good. [10]

In reviewing Gage's early military career in America, the record that he would carry into the opening battles of the Revolution, one is struck by how little combat experience he had had in six years. Twice he had been involved in an approach march through broken, unfriendly country: once with Braddock in 1755, and again near Ticonderoga in 1758. On both occasions he had seen a British army surprised. The result in 1755 had been panic and slaughter; in 1758, confusion, disorganization, and moderately heavy casualities. He had also taken part in an unsuccessful infantry assault on an entrenched position, at Ticonderoga in 1758, at a cost to the attackers of one quarter of their force. The following year at Niagara, just a few weeks before he arrived to take command of the siege, a relief column of French regulars had smashed itself against an entrenched position in a small-scale repetition of the Ticonderoga attack; Gage must have seen the ground and heard the action described in detail.[11] Two surprise marches, two bloody infantry assaults— these made up his personal fund of tactical experience in American warfare before 1775.

The war ended for Gage in 1760. He did not go campaigning in the West Indies during 1761–62; instead, he served as military governor of Montreal, where combat experience was less important than some other qualities like intelligence, patience, honesty, and tact. Gage was a good governor, and became popular among people who had recently been his enemies. The "nonchalance" of which Dr. Huck had complained was an asset under peacetime conditions; a relaxed, understanding approach was what post-war Canada required.

But Montreal was cold and primitive, and, when peace came early in 1763, there was little to keep him there, or anywhere else for that matter, on active service. He held the rank of major general, and had become colonel of a senior regiment that would not be disbanded, as was the 80th, in the peacetime reduction of the army. Further promotion seemed unlikely. Few colonels actually served with their regiments, but merely enjoyed the honor and the emoluments. Gage could have done likewise, pleading perhaps that the climate of Canada was ruining his health, and have retired to Sussex or even New Jersey.

The Indian uprising of 1763 changed all such thoughts, which clearly Gage had been entertaining. The commander-in-chief, Sir Jeffrey Amherst, had grossly underestimated the Indian problem after the war. For years the Indians had complained of traders who cheated them with rum and short weights, but now, with countervailing French power eliminated, they increasingly feared Anglo-American migration onto their hunting grounds. The war had taught Amherst to have utter contempt for Indians; he refused to listen to the pleas of Sir William Johnson, the Indian superintendent, and instead cut off their supply of ammunition and relied on small garrisons of regulars scattered through the West to hold them down by force. It was a stupid policy. The Indian uprising had been brewing for several years and may have been unavoidable, but when it broke out Amherst seemed the obvious culprit and was recalled. Thomas Gage took his place.

As the new commander-in-chief moved into his headquarters at New York, he faced two related problems: pacifying the northern Indian tribes, and managing a peacetime army scattered over a half-continent. For the first task he had the plans already developed by Amherst, the reinforcement by provincial troops which had been requested, and two able and experienced subordinates—John Bradstreet and Henry Bouquet. Bradstreet and Bouquet, with mixed forces of British regulars and American volunteers, moved westward from Albany and Pittsburgh, respectively, against little resistance. Gage, as he had been instructed, left the negotiation of peace to Sir William Johnson, whose stock with the British government had risen upon the fall of Amherst. The campaign of 1764 was arduous, but it was almost bloodless because the Indians had failed to destroy the garrisons at Detroit, Niagara, and Fort Pitt in 1763, and their small resources were nearly exhausted. Gage was able to put down the uprising more easily than expected.

The Indian problem did not disappear, however, with the end of the uprising. In fact, preventing another costly Indian war became more than ever a major concern to those responsible for British colonial policy, and the regular garrison in America figured prominently in their plans.

Prior to the French and Indian War, Britain had kept few regular troops in the colonies: several regiments to watch over a hostile population in Nova Scotia, and several more to curb slave insurrections in the West Indies. But, with the exception of a few undermanned companies in New York and South Carolina, the mainland colonies were completely dependent on their own militia for defense.[12] This arrangement seemed to break down in 1755, and Braddock's defeat brought thousands of regulars to America. At the end of the war it was decided to keep fifteen regiments on the mainland—three in Nova Scotia, four in Canada, four in Florida and along the Gulf coast, and the remaining four dispersed among the middle Atlantic seaboard, the Great Lakes, the Carolina and Georgia backcountry, and the Illinois side of the Mississippi. Gage was to command this army of about six thousand men, stretched across a thousand miles of wilderness.

The presence of a regular garrison led directly to the British attempt to raise a revenue in the colonies, but even now the mission of this military force is not altogether clear. Defense, properly speaking, was not a major consideration. The French population of Canada, and the relative emptiness of Florida and the trans-Appalachian region, demanded a garrison for those areas. It was hoped that military posts in the backcountry could keep frontiersmen off Indian lands and bring some order to the fur trade, thus allaying the grievances that had led to the Indian uprising of 1763. New York City, New Jersey, and Philadelphia were convenient places for the rest and recuperation of units en route to other stations; these units would also be available, if needed, to act against smugglers. Finally, there was a vaguely expressed fear that troops might be useful to keep unruly Americans "in due subordination." No one, on the other hand, thought that a few thousand regulars could protect the whole frontier from another Indian attack, and everyone knew that sea power was the principal defense against France or Spain.[13]

Specifically, Gage was told to conciliate the Indians by:

1. "Restraining all unjust Settlement, and fraudulent Purchase of their Lands,

and

    2. "Suppressing all unfair Practices in the free and open Trade to
       be carried on with them at the several [military] Posts,"
and to assist the customs officers in
    3. "The effectual Suppression of Contraband Trade in America." [14]

Privately Gage was warned of the general opinion within the
government "that the Indians have of late Years been too much
neglected, and that the . . . present Hostilities, have been in great
Measure owing to an apparent Contempt of their Consequence." [15] The message was unmistakable.

What thus appears on the surface to be a reasonable attempt
to improve the administration of the empire soon gave rise to a
set of complicated, interlocking problems that were difficult
even to state clearly, much less solve. Gage himself was one of
the sponsors of the new plan to placate the Indians through protection of their lands and regulation of the fur trade, but he
gradually came to understand that enormous obstacles stood in
the way. Frontier settlers and fur traders easily avoided the few
small garrisons in the back country, and when Gage tried to
restrict their movements he often found himself caught between
rival pressure groups. His legal authority against civilians was
virtually nil, and colonial governors hesitated to cooperate with
the army against their own subjects, especially when they were
associated with land companies or commercial firms. Army post
commanders themselves could not be relied upon to refuse bribes
or to refrain from abusing Indians, nor could their behavior be
controlled or checked easily when they were hundreds of miles
from headquarters. Although the British government continued
to fear the financial and political cost of another Indian war,
Gage and a few well-informed officials in London were beginning to realize that the army could do little to prevent it.

By the end of 1765, civil disorders along the seaboard seemed
to pose a more pressing problem for the army than the danger
of Indian uprisings on the frontier. During the riots over the
Stamp Act in the autumn, no governor dared to call for military
assistance, apparently because the troops nearby were too few to
be employed effectively against the mobs in Boston, New York,

Philadelphia, and Charleston. Gage began moving troops eastward, but was abruptly stopped when the Rockingham government decided to repeal the Stamp Act at the end of the year. Obviously the mission of the army in America was changing, but no one in an official position dared to articulate the change.

Confusion on the British political scene exacerbated the situation, making it difficult to adopt or pursue any coherent policy for the colonies or for the army in America. This confusion was only incidentally a result of trouble over American affairs. It was caused primarily by the successive political impact of the great but unorthodox war leader, William Pitt, of a new young king, George III, who was equally unorthodox in his view of politics, and by the collapse of a coalition that had ruled England for most of the century. The resultant bitterness among political leaders, coupled with severe economic distress in the postwar period, produced an instability at the cabinet level that is reminiscent of the Fourth French Republic.

From the American point of view, a "hard" Grenville Ministry was succeeded in 1765 by a "soft" Rockingham government, which in turn was followed in 1766 by a coalition with Pitt at its head. Nominally "soft," this coalition steadily hardened in its approach to the American problem, becoming the "hardest" of them all when reorganized by Lord North in 1770. But Gage's immediate superior was the secretary of state for the southern department, and the succession of men in that office did not quite conform to the general pattern of political change. The Earl of Shelburne, who served from 1766 to early 1768, was believed to be liberal in his approach to American grievances; the Earl of Hillsborough, who took the new office of secretary of state for the American colonies and served until mid-1772, was notoriously conservative. But Hillsborough was followed by the pious Earl of Dartmouth, North's step-brother, a man thought to be even more sympathetic than Shelburne toward America. More important than any of these dubious labels was the fact that, for a variety of reasons, no colonial secretary after the war held a strong position either in the cabinet or in the House of Commons. Under these circumstances, American questions were buffeted by the rapidly shifting wind of politics. No question was more exposed to those winds than that of the colonial army, which was draining over £400,000 from the Treasury every year.

Gage responded to this instability with caution. During the past decade, British governments had dealt harshly with military commanders who had made mistakes: Admiral Byng had been shot, the Duke of Cumberland disgraced, three commanders in America sacked in three years, Lord George Germain (who would direct the war against the colonies after 1775) court-martialed, and Amherst recalled. When Shelburne asked Gage for his opinion on desirable policies for the Indians, the unsettled West, and the American army, Gage sent back a long report full of information, but almost devoid of opinions that might later be used against him if things went badly. He knew that the historic antipathy in Britain toward a standing army would encourage a shaky government to make him the scapegoat if his advice turned out wrong.

Gage had opinions, however, and the men closest to him played on those opinions, drawing him toward a more active role in colonial affairs. A hint of what was in his mind came during the war when he wrote to his brother of the need to change the constitutions of Pennsylvania and Maryland. Sir William Johnson won Gage's official support for the plan to regulate the fur trade. And Lieutenant Colonel James Robertson, Gage's principal staff officer and a Scot whose view of American disorder was unusually narrow, persuaded him in early 1765 to propose an Act of Parliament that would legalize the quartering of soldiers in private houses. The Ministry, under pressure from the agents in London of the colonial governments, revised the bill to allow quartering only in vacant buildings and existing barracks, though at colonial expense. Even as modified, the Quartering Act was a chronic source of trouble between Britain and her colonies.

More than anyone else, the secretary at war, Lord Barrington, worked on and with Gage to help shape American policy. The office of secretary at war was a secondary administrative post that constitutionally had nothing to do with either policy-making or the American colonies. Yet Barrington, who was at once a political hack and a charmingly honest fish in a sea of courtly hypocrisy, enjoyed the personal confidence of the king, serving him in the War Office from 1765 to 1778. Barrington had given up higher political ambitions, and the security of his position was due to a genuine zeal for the welfare of the army. Frequent visits to the royal closet on minor matters of military business gave Barrington an access to the king that even cabinet officers must have envied. It also gave Gage, one of Barrington's oldest friends, a line to the center of power if he cared or dared to use it.

In 1766, Barrington drafted a memorandum in which he proposed withdrawal of the army from the western posts and the middle Atlantic seaboard, and its concentration in Canada, Nova Scotia, and Florida. The West was to become a vast Indian reservation—"a desert," Barrington ignorantly called it—where no white settlement would be permitted to stir up another war. Withdrawal of troops from the West would facilitate their removal from the East, where there would no longer be any need for the Quartering Act. He appealed to the king and the army staff with the argument that a concentrated army would be better disciplined and better trained; he appealed to the cabinet with the prospect of eliminating the heavy cost of supplying troops in many remote garrisons. A few regiments, he suggested, might even be brought back to the British Isles.

Barrington showed his memorandum to Shelburne and Pitt (newly created Earl of Chatham), and sent a copy to Gage. At first Barrington thought that Chatham and Shelburne liked the plan, but he soon learned that his proposal to make the West "a desert" was drawing serious opposition to the plan as a whole. All those with an interest in western colonization or land speculation, including the postmaster general for America, Benjamin Franklin, were lobbying against it. General Amherst, who had returned to a position of influence on colonial and military questions when the Chatham government came to power, criticized Barrington's suggestion that small garrisons in the West (where Amherst had first put them) were useless against Indian uprisings. Amherst had never really understood what had gone wrong in 1763, and he never would, but his opinion carried weight. Shelburne vacillated. Chatham, meanwhile, fell ill and lost his effectiveness as a political leader. Thus, when the question of the cost of keeping the army in the American West came before the House of Commons, the leaderless cabinet divided. Parliament thereupon passed a new set of measures to raise a revenue in America—the Townshend Acts of 1767.

Barrington had expected that at least Gage would support him. For the most part, Gage did. But he objected to one key feature of Barrington's plan—the proposal to remove troops from the seaboard. Barrington had argued that troops in the colonial port cities were of little use, because by law only a civil magistrate could employ them against a mob, and few magistrates, however loyal they might be to the Crown, had shown themselves willing to take this extreme step. Withdrawal of troops would remove an irritant and serve as a conciliatory gesture, Barrington reasoned, but they could quickly return from their bases to the North and South in case of a real rebellion. Gage disagreed. With more troops on the spot, he reasoned, magistrates would act more vigorously. Halifax, Quebec, Montreal, and St. Augustine were too far away for prompt action in the event of serious trouble. It is possible, and what is known of Mrs. Gage makes it rather likely, that Gage also did not want to move his headquarters away from the temperate, civilized atmosphere of New York City; he had already served one bleak tour in Canada, and had read enough dispatches relating the horrors of Florida to know what awaited the Gages at St. Augustine. Barrington deferred to firsthand knowledge of his friend Gage for the time being, but the secretary at war never gave up the hope of removing all regular soldiers from those colonies that had resisted taxation.

Whatever their disagreement over deployment of troops in the

East, Gage and Barrington were as one on the need to get as many troops as possible out of the West—the soldiers stationed there were expensive, of no apparent use, and suffering from poor morale and inadequate supervision. The two men also agreed that the government ought to take a firm line toward American disorder. Both were ready to make minor gestures of conciliation, but they were unwilling to compromise on the basic issues of taxation, sovereignty, and obedience to law. In a fascinating private exchange of letters over the years, they alternately prayed for the government to stand firm and condemned its pusillanimity when it did not. In 1768, when another old friend of theirs, the Earl of Hillsborough, became secretary of state for the American colonies, their prayers and complaints stood in a fair way to be answered.

Hillsborough began by blocking Shelburne's plan for three new colonies in the West, and then gave Gage permission to reduce some of the western garrisons. Barrington was disappointed that withdrawal was only partial—troops remained in Illinois and at Fort Pitt for the time being, and there was no sign of the three Great Lakes posts (Niagara, Detroit, and Michilimackinac) being given up. But Hillsborough as secretary of state would suffer the political consequences in case his orders and an Indian war happened to coincide, and so he was moving cautiously. Hillsborough was aware that he had already incurred the enmity of influential Englishmen and Americans who were interested in western colonization by his resistance to their plans; they would not miss a chance to attack him if he made a mistake. He next used a minor fracas at Boston in March, 1768, as an excuse to order a regiment there, where troops had not been since the Seven Years' War. But before Gage received the letter, a real mob had run the customs officials out of town when they tried to seize John Hancock's sloop *Liberty* for smuggling, and Hillsborough told Gage to rush more troops to Boston.

Gage himself, confident as never before in the support of his two colleagues, dropped the mask of caution. "Quash this Spirit at a Blow," he wrote privately to Barrington, "without too much

regard to the Expence and it will prove oeconomy in the End."
Later, in an official dispatch to Hillsborough, he stepped well
outside the limits of his military duties: "I know of nothing
that can so effectually quell the Spirit of Sedition . . . as Speedy,
vigorous, and unanimous Measures taken in England to suppress it." Earlier he had warned Barrington: "If the Principles
of Moderation and Forbearance are again Adopted . . . there
will be an End to these Provinces as British Colonies." [16] For
once even the Parliamentary Opposition, frightened by a series
of riots in London and throughout the country during the year,
seemed ready to acquiesce in "vigorous measures." By November,
four regiments and part of a fifth had assembled at Boston; the
crisis had come.

But nothing happened. Boston leaders kept the town quiet
while the troops landed, and subsequent reports received in
England, including one from Gage, who had paid a visit to
Boston, suggested to the government that the *Liberty* riot might
have been provoked and then exaggerated by royal officials in
Boston. At home, the government found itself deeply involved
in another crisis, unrelated to America, over the election of the
radical leader, John Wilkes, to the House of Commons. The
Opposition was taking heart, and the Ministry was losing its
zeal for a crackdown at this time in Massachusetts. Only Hillsborough continued the fight, pushing for a set of meaures similar to those adopted five years later. He would have altered the
Massachusetts charter, bringing the province more directly
under royal control, and military enforcement was implicit in
such a step. But even the king had lost interest by February,
1769, and Parliament disposed of the matter by passing eight
fiery, ineffectual resolutions.

Gage thus had almost a third of his army in Boston to no
apparent purpose. During the year that followed, he had a
chance to learn a little more about the dynamics of a revolution.
Bostonians found ways to harass the customs officers and the
troops without breaking any laws. Magistrates, who were as
afraid of not being supported by a fickle Ministry as they were

of retaliation from their neighbors, refused to call for military aid. Gage, when he saw that troops were worse than useless, wanted to use the discretion Hillsborough had given him to withdraw them, but the Massachusetts governor, fearful of agreeing to any step that might be wrong, demurred. Two regiments remained in Boston during the next winter, 1769–70. With no one—the Ministry, the governor, or Gage—able to make a decision, and with Bostonians growing in their determination to get soldiers out of their town, it was only a matter of time before an incident like the "Massacre" of March 5, 1770, took place. Under the direct threat of a massive uprising in the countryside on March 6, one regiment departed and the other moved to Castle Island in the harbor.

Gage, Barrington, and Hillsborough were sobered if not discouraged. Yet the experience left their belief unshaken that something drastic would have to be done about Boston; if anything, their belief was strengthened, because they could charge past failures to weakness in the government. Never in the next few years do they seem to have considered seriously whether military coercion was really feasible.

Gage had his hands full during 1771–72 merely administering an army that was slowly deteriorating under the pressure of its American environment. Though regiments rotated across the Atlantic every four years or so, the chronic shortage of recruits forced Gage to permit men who wanted to stay in the colonies for some reason to transfer out of departing regiments. There proved to be hundreds of such men. Likewise, those officers most willing to remain at their posts in the colonies were the ones who had acquired American wives or American land or both, like Gage. The army gradually became a domesticated core of aging officers and men who were themselves virtually Americans, joined by a growing proportion of raw young subalterns (many of them sons of officers) and recruits (some illegally enlisted in America itself).

Away from the middle Atlantic coast, living conditions were unusually bad, even for an eighteenth-century army, and they were not getting any better. Gage had won respect from the government for his honesty and ability to cut costs, but human misery paid the price for part of his reputation. Being stationed at a post like Niagara was unpleasant to begin with, but it became unbearable when the roof was leaking, the bedding was filthy and falling apart, and the commander-in-chief asked for further information before agreeing to any expenditures. In the 1760's Gage had emphasized tactical training—marksmanship, for example—but little was heard of training in the early 1770's; sheer survival was task enough.

In 1772, Hillsborough fell from power when he refused to agree to a new colony in the Ohio Valley. Many speculators had merged to form this "Vandalia" project, as it was called, and they had managed to purchase a good deal of support even within the Privy Council. The whole affair was "an Infamous Jobb in every part of it," according to an undersecretary of state in a letter to Hillsborough's successor.[17] Gage was convinced that a western colony would mean an expensive and distracting war with the Indians, and he took up the fight that Hillsborough had lost. Barrington was now showing the king parts of his private correspondence with Gage, and the two friends worked together to delay royal approval of Vandalia until Gage could come home on leave. When he arrived in the summer of 1773, he succeeded in quietly getting the colony quashed, despite the powerful interests behind it.[18]

It is difficult to assess Gage's position with the government accurately at this crucial point in his career. His ability to block the Vandalia scheme suggests that he stood well with the king himself. But close association with the deposed Hillsborough and the fairly unpopular Barrington did not help him in the cabinet. Gage wrote in late 1773 from London to an old comrade, Lieutenant Colonel James Abercromby, who in turn reported as follows: "I am told General Gage is to go back to America. It seems they have offered him nothing on this side, and paid him but little attention."[19] It appears that Gage was seeking a better or an easier office—a major governorship or a sinecure. The adjutant general, Edward Harvey, added another dimension to Abercromby's report: "Gage is come Home, it was thought not to Return, but the whisper now is, that M-d-m [Mrs. Gage] likes her Native Country better than Britain." There is evidence that the government had considered, even before he returned to England, replacing both Gage as commander-in-chief and Thomas Hutchinson as governor of Massachusetts with a single officer—Robert Monckton, a British general who had won great popularity in America during the last war.[20]

There is no clue as to whether the government was dissatisfied with Gage, or Gage had given the government some hint of being dissatisfied with his job. Despite his harsh private views on American resistance to British policy, Gage had been able to maintain an image of moderation within the colonies. Perhaps the strain of dissimulating toward Americans, of managing an army stretched over unmanageable distances, and of dealing with an erratic government, were proving too much for him. Five years before, an officer visiting headquarters, in writing to his commander in Florida, noted that Gage was so affected by his failure to get a clear statement of military policy from the government that "he is not the same Man he was when you left [New] York." [21] A reasonable guess is that Gage was indeed sick of his job, had thought seriously of giving it up, but changed his mind when Margaret Kemble Gage began longing for what they had left behind in New York and New Jersey.

Whatever the truth about Gage's motives and position, his situation changed abruptly in early 1774 when news of the destruction of the tea in Boston harbor reached London. Within a week Gage had had an interview with George III, and the king's report to Lord North is worth quoting at length:

> Since You left me this day, I have seen Lieutenant General Gage, who came to express his readiness though so lately come from America to return at a day's notice if the conduct of the Colonies should induce the directing coercive measures, his language was very consonant to his Character of an honest determined Man; he says they will be Lyons, whilst we are Lambs but if we take the

resolute part they will undoubtedly prove very meek; he thinks the four Regiments intended to Relieve as many Regiments in America if sent to Boston are sufficient to prevent any disturbance; I wish You would see him and hear his ideas as to the mode of compelling Boston to submit to whatever may be thought necessary.[22]

Years later, in reply to the question of an historian, Gage recollected that he had said something quite different:

The General [Gage referring to himself] not long from his command by leave, and still holding it, made no objection to return to his duty, but was averse to taking the Government of the Massachusetts Bay. He desired at length that a much larger force than four weak regiments might be sent out, and the Town of Boston declared in rebellion, without which his hands would be tied up.[23]

About the same time, James Paterson, who had been a colonel in 1775 and became a major general in the American war, told Frederick Haldimand, who had been one of Gage's brigadier generals, that "he was present when the general told the King (speaking of Boston) that he had sufficient troops to bring these people to reason." [24] The presumption must be that Gage, who had been gradually becoming more outspoken in his opinions on America, made promises to the king that both men would live to regret.

For Gage, regret may have begun as soon as he stepped out of the royal closet. He had promised to ram the policy of the government down American throats before he (or anyone else) even knew what that policy would be. Anxiously he sought to strengthen his legal position by asking the cabinet if he could use troops against civilian disorder. As commander-in-chief, he had no power to do so, and when made governor, he was constitutionally required to seek the advice of his Council. The cabinet, with some equivocation, said that he could.[25]

So far as is known, Gage played no part in drafting those "Coercive Acts" of the spring of 1774, which closed the port of Boston, made the Council of Massachusetts appointive, and curbed the power of town meetings. He certainly had a hand in new laws for the trial of accused persons outside the province, and for the quartering of soldiers wherever they were needed; both were intended to prevent some of the problems the army had had previously with juries and quarters in Boston. It is also likely that he supported the Quebec Act, which among other things provided for a clear legal authority in the trans-Appalachian West.

When Gage had departed New York in 1773, the mayor and Council had tendered him the freedom of the city and a flowery address. When he returned to America a year later, Boston welcomed him with dignity and even a touch of warmth. As one intelligent Bostonian reported, Gage was proclaimed governor "amid the acclamations of the people. He express'd himself as sensible of the unwelcome errand he came upon, but as a servant of the Crown, he was obliged to see the [Port] Act put in execution: but would do all in his power to serve us." At an "elegant entertainment" afterward at Faneuil Hall, Gage toasted the prosperity of Boston.[26] Since he had intervened to prevent bloodshed during the Stamp Act riots at New York in 1765, Gage had been surprisingly popular in the colonies. He had run his army with evident care and common sense, avoiding disputes whenever possible, and he had behaved himself with tact and sobriety. Late in 1774, Dr. Joseph Warren, a leader of the Boston radicals, still considered Gage as "a man of honest, upright principles" who would work for "a just and honourable settlement."[27] Americans looked to him as their last hope for some reasonable solution of the tea controversy, while his own government believed that he was the man who could bring Boston to its knees without a civil war. He could not possibly satisfy both at once, and he was doomed to satisfy neither.

His first dispatches home were fairly optimistic. With the help of the navy, he had closed Boston port, and had shifted the capital to Salem. There was little that rebellious spirits could do about a blockade, and they were less daring as regiment after regiment moved into Massachusetts. But with the announcement of the Massachusetts Government Act, which virtually annulled the charter of the province, effective August 1, the situation began to change. On September 7, the British government heard from Gage that trouble was likely; by October 1 it was learned that trouble had occurred—the new Crown-appointed members of the Council had been terrorized into resignation, courts had been closed by mobs in the interior of the province, and "Civil Government is near its End . . . Conciliating, Moderation, Reasoning is over, Nothing can be done but by forceable Means." Gage complained that his troops were too few, and he promised to "avoid any bloody Crisis as long as possible" while "His Majesty will in the mean Time Judge what is best to be done." [28] The government, believing that it had already decided "what is best to be done" when it sent Gage to Boston, was apparently thunderstruck; it took sixteen days to write an answer to his letter.

Even more incredible, Gage did not send off his next dispatch for another three weeks. As autumn storms lengthened the time-distance between Boston and London, the government heard nothing from him until November 18. Throughout this seven-week interval Gage's stock had been dropping; it dropped lower still when the government read his next bundle of dispatches. He reported that all the northern colonies were supporting Boston to a degree "beyond the Conception of most People, and foreseen by none. The Disease was believed to have been confined to the Town of Boston . . . But now it's so universal there is no knowing where to apply a Remedy." Only the conquest of New England would be effective. To accomplish this end, he proposed, in a private and round-about way, suspending the Coercive Acts, withdrawing all troops, blockading the coast, and returning only after a much larger army, including German mercenaries, had been raised. From that time on, the government stopped listening to Thomas Gage.[29]

Gage seems not to have realized what was happening to his reputation at home. Toward the end of October he was reading warm praise in a private letter from Secretary of State Dartmouth for his prudent conduct under "the nice and delicate circumstances" which existed in Massachusetts.[30] But that letter had crossed those dispatches of his own that would cause his supporters in the government to lose faith in him. As early as September they had been irritated by the infrequency of his letters and their lack of detailed information. By December, both of the undersecretaries of state for the colonies, men who had supported the hard Hillsborough line toward colonial disorder, were writing to Dartmouth of Gage's "timidity and weakness," and the "Inactivity and Irresolution of his Conduct," which "astonished and alarmed" everyone because it seemed "devoid of both sense and spirit." [31] Even his friend, the tactful and cautious ex-governor of Massachusetts, Thomas Hutchinson, warned him that his proposal to suspend the Acts and to raise German mercenaries had not been well received.[32] Only Barrington continued to write encouragingly.

The government went on listening to messages from America, if not to those of Gage. When he had decided in late August that the next move was up to the king and his ministers, he had withdrawn himself and his army to the Boston peninsula and had begun buttoning up for the winter. Boston had a population of less than 20,000 and it was now occupied by over 3,000 officers and men who had come to police the whole province. Little imagination is required to see what was likely to happen. The townspeople were angry and afraid, the army—especially its officer corps—was bored and humiliated, and everyone was tense and crowded. Gage, as governor, was determined to prevent trouble. If trouble came despite his efforts, he was determined that he, his army, and the home government would not be caught on the wrong side of any dispute or incident. He negotiated an agreement with a committee of the town in which he promised to keep his troops on a tight rein and to listen sympathetically to all complaints concerning their behavior. He kept his promise to Boston, but it cost him the morale of his men and confidence of his officers.

Not all the officers attacked Gage; there were a few who understood his predicament. But there were many more who sent home disparaging comments about their general. Young John Barker of the 4th Foot, for example, was an immature officer who might have criticized any commander under whom he served, but Barker's complaints of "Tommy" who favored the Yankees over his own soldiers were the sort of news from Boston that had made Gage's timidity a subject of coffee-house gossip in London by the end of the year.[33] Far more weighty with the government, however, was a letter like the one from Lieutenant Colonel James Abercromby, a respected officer who had served with Gage during the last war and who had been sent to Boston especially to serve on his staff. Soon after Gage withdrew to the Boston peninsula, Abercromby wrote that "he likes his Colonel [that is, Gage] as a gentleman, but would never employ him on a forlorn hope." [34] Even Bostonians knew that his army was calling Gage *"Old Woman."* [35]

In eighteenth-century England, where a small aristocracy both ruled the country and officered the army, such complaints struck resonant chords. For those at the highest levels of government, policy and honor were becoming hopelessly confused with one another. The honor of the army, virtually penned up inside Boston by fear of a rabble that had proved its cowardice and indiscipline during the last war, was at issue; thus, by extension, the honor of the king (commander-in-chief of the army), of the nobility (whose sons led it), and even of the "nation" (which the army represented in the eyes of the world), were involved. Though the Boston crisis required the most careful calculations of power and interest, the king seemed more upset by the shameful rate of desertion from his regiments in Boston than by the prospect of war; reportedly he wept on General William Howe's shoulder when they heard how fast soldiers were running off into the Massachusetts countryside. By the end of 1774, there was no more calculating of the evidence at Whitehall, Westminster, or St. James. The king had told Lord North, "Blows must decide"; the government had ceased to think—it was merely reacting.[36]

Only a few men in the government had both the knowledge

and the self-control to realize that Gage was right, however unpleasant the realization might be. Barrington and the adjutant
general, Edward Harvey, believed him when he said that Americans would fight rather than submit. They understood also how
nearly impossible it would be for Britain to carry on a land war
across an ocean against an armed population. Both men thought
that pacification had to be achieved by naval blockade. At
Boston itself, Frederick Haldimand, a capable Swiss officer and
a veteran of the last war in America who had served as Gage's
second in command, was not impressed by those who dismissed
the colonial militia as a rabble in arms. "The Americans," Haldimand noted, "would be less dangerous if they had a regular
army." [37] A later generation of Americans, learning lessons of
their own about revolutionary wars, can readily understand
what Haldimand meant.

But the government had already made up its mind. Gage
would have to be superseded, though the king was unwilling
to recall him in disgrace. General William Howe would go out
to Boston, nominally as second in command, but all would
understand that Howe was to be the "acting officer." [38] Howe
would take with him as lieutenants Henry Clinton and John
Burgoyne. While Howe, Clinton, and Burgoyne were gathering
together their baggage and the reinforcements they would take
with them, Gage himself should do something to salvage the
situation. Dartmouth accordingly signed a long, secret letter
which first rejected Gage's appreciation of the situation and
his proposals for action, and then ordered him to go out into
the countryside and arrest the leaders of the Massachusetts Provincial Congress. In case there was any doubt about what the
government expected of him, Barrington also wrote to say that
he was organizing a hospital for the army in America "on a
large scale." [39]

The actions at Lexington and Concord, like that at Bunker
Hill, have been exhaustively studied, but they raise more questions about Gage than have ever been answered. He had known
in February that spring would bring some positive order from

the government, and that the order would probably mean war. Through an excellent spy system, he also knew what was going on in the countryside, that the Americans were training troops and gathering supplies at Concord, Worcester, and elsewhere. By early April, he had begun to get unofficial news of the measures adopted by the British government. At the same time, one of his spies informed him that the Provincial Congress had been greatly alarmed by the recent march of a brigade of British regulars out of Boston. A committee of the Congress had reported its opinion "that should any body of troops, with Artillery and Baggage, march out of Boston, the Country should instantly be alarmed and called together to oppose their March, to the last extremity." Towns around Boston had petitioned Congress to the same effect. Gage had seen the militia rise on several previous false alarms, and he had no reason to think these words were an empty threat.[40]

Gage had already started preparations for an offensive move into the countryside when he received the secret orders from Dartmouth on April 14. The Massachusetts leaders were as well informed about his preparations as he was about their activities, so there was little mystery on either side. More obscure is the question of why Gage organized the expedition as he did. He must have known that the colonists would resist if he marched to destroy their munitions or arrest their leaders, yet his plans suggest that he counted on avoiding hostilities. He knew the sort of broken terrain his troops would be marching through, and he could not have forgotten the difficulties it posed for a column of regulars, but there is no hint that he was seriously concerned about tactical problems. He sent an improvised brigade made up of 21 grenadier and light infantry companies— the elite troops drawn from each regiment, about 800 men. Every man carried one day's ration but no knapsack. No artillery or baggage accompanied the column. Its commander was the senior field officer on duty, "a very fat heavy Man," seconded by a major of Marines. One can only guess that Gage hoped to make up in speed of movement what such a force lacked in weight and cohesion. Its mission was to destroy the American supplies at Concord and return to Boston, 32 miles round trip.

There was a brief skirmish at Lexington, ten miles out, a fight at Concord, and a running battle all the way home in which the British suffered over 250 casualties. In what seems to have been an afterthought, Gage ordered a brigade to set out with two light artillery pieces ten hours later in support of the first column. The grenadiers and light infantry probably would have been wiped out except for meeting this relief force with its cannon near Lexington on the journey back. Numerous details of the whole operation—its conception, the security measures surrounding it, and its execution—indicate that either Gage did not really believe the militia would fight (which would have contradicted what he had been telling the government), or he did not do even a routinely competent job of planning and supervision. As far as the historian can tell, he had learned nothing from the last war about ambush and tactical marches in America.

Although Gage was henceforth literally besieged in Boston by thousands of New England militia, he obviously continued to hope that Lexington and Concord were not the beginning of a civil war but only an incident that might somehow be smoothed over. He disarmed the people of Boston, and severely restricted civilian movement over Boston neck, but he did not declare martial law. There was talk, at least, of conciliatory measures in both London and Philadelphia, and Gage did not want to jeopardize even a slim chance for peace. Admiral Samuel Graves, who commanded the small fleet in Boston harbor, wanted Gage to seize and fortify Charlestown and Dorchester peninsulas which, like Boston, commanded part of the harbor from their heights and were connected to the mainland by narrow, easily defended causeways. But Gage refused. He was convinced that his army of 4,000 effectives was too weak. Moreover, he was unwilling to begin offensive operations before all political remedies were exhausted. Nor did Graves himself employ the navy on offensive missions. In the end, both men suffered from criticism for their inactivity.

With the arrival of Howe, Clinton, and Burgoyne in late May, Gage, though still commander-in-chief, all but disappears in a fog of collective responsibility. How he finally came to declare martial law on June 12 is unknown, but it is certain that Burgoyne wrote the bombastic proclamation. In a leisurely manner, the generals began to plot how they might pursue Graves' sound proposal to occupy Charlestown and Dorchester, clearly a necessity if Boston were to remain tenable. But they do not seem to have spent much time discussing broader questions of strategy, such as why an army should be in Boston at all. Gage had asked for help from Governor Guy Carleton of Canada, and he had authorized Lieutenant Colonel Allen Maclean to raise a corps of Scottish Highland immigrants in the Carolina back country; otherwise the commander-in-chief waited for reinforcements, further orders, and the next American move.

That move came, of course, with the appearance of fortifications one morning in mid-June on a spur of Bunker's Hill, on Charlestown peninsula. General Clinton wanted to cut off the American forces by landing behind them on Charlestown Neck, but his colleagues decided that the militia should be taught a different kind of lesson. Some insight into the mind of the British council of war, which decided to make a frontal assault, can be gained from a letter written by Burgoyne two months after the ensuing battle:

> I believe in most states of the world as well as in our own, the respect, and control, and subordination of government . . . depends in a great measure upon the idea that trained troops are invincible against any numbers or any position of undisciplined rabble; and this idea was a little in suspense since the 19th of April.[41]

In short, the attack at Bunker Hill, which cost the British over 1,000 casualties, was to be understood on psychological rather than tactical grounds.

Once again, as at Lexington and Concord, neither the plan nor its execution does Gage any credit, though not all the blame can justly be laid to him alone. But, as at Lexington and Concord, he seems to have learned nothing from his own previous military experience. The unsuccessful assaults at Ticonderoga in 1758 and at Niagara in 1759 were basically similar to the situation at Bunker Hill in 1775, with one exception: at Bunker Hill the *militia* stood behind the fieldworks. Gage apparently thought that the one difference made all the difference, for his post-mortem lament to Barrington shows that he finally understood:

> These People Shew a Spirit and Conduct against us, they never shewed against the French, and every body had Judged of them from their former Appearance, and behaviour . . . which has led many into great mistakes.

And, at last, he had begun to grasp the strategic problem as well:

> We are here, to use a common expression, taking the Bull by the horns, Attacking the Enemy in their Strong parts, I wish this Cursed place was burned . . . its the worst place to act Offensively from, or defencively. I think if this Army was in New York, that we should find many friends, and be able to raise Forces in that Province on the side of Government.[42]

Boston was a trap; New York was the key. But by then everyone saw it (Howe had seen it as early as June 12), and it was too late to move the army until 1776. Gage could only wait gracefully for his recall, which arrived in September.

Thomas Gage lived 12 more years, to the age of 67, never doing or saying anything to attract special notice. He made few excuses and blamed no colleagues, which is remarkable among disgraced leaders in any age. Equally remarkable was the agreement among his contemporaries in their estimate of him. Burgoyne had begun a tortuous description of his chief with the following words:

> I have a most sincere value for his private character which is replete with virtues and with talents. That it is not of a cast for the situation in which he is placed I allow; and hence many, tho' far from all, of our misfortunes.

Major James Wemyss, on the other hand, wrote incautiously, but he said the same thing about Gage:

> Of moderate abilities, but altogether deficient in military knowledge. Timid and undecided in every path of duty, was unfit to command at a time of resistance, and approaching Rebellion to the Mother Country.

Almost every other estimate of Gage points in the same direction: pleasant, honest, sober; a little dull; cautious, even timid at times; no talent at all for making war.[43]

Despite his comparatively simple personality, and the contemporary consensus about him, it is difficult to reach a satisfactory judgment on Gage's role in the outbreak of the American Revolution. Without the revolution smoldering beneath him, he would have been the ideal peacetime military administrator. Before 1774, he was generally liked and respected, both by his troops and by the colonists. He had gone far to keep the army, as such, from being an important grievance to Americans. Unlike some other British officials in the colonies, Gage never played with a high hand, nor was there ever a sign of scandal in his conduct of business. Finally, he was tied to America by marriage, property, and length of service on this side of the Atlantic.

His administrative record is balanced by his combat record. Americans could count themselves fortunate to have been opposed in the beginning by a general with so little ability as a fighter. Perhaps, as has been said about other British leaders in the Revolutionary War, he had no heart for the fight against fellow Englishmen. Or perhaps, as Dr. Huck had said, Gage was unlucky—"none of the Sons of Fortune." But chance ought to have given even an unlucky man, provided he had a modicum of skill, some small success in the course of two years.

Gage the military administrator and Gage the combat leader were, however, incidental to his third role—Gage the imperial statesman.[44] Nothing in his commission as commander-in-chief required that he play such a role, and a great deal in his personality indicated that he would not, but circumstances thrust him into the part. His particular interest in finding a policy for the trans-Appalachian West, and his strong personal ties to Barrington and Hillsborough, tended to erode his self-protective reserve. The king's special concern with the army offered Gage a better chance to be heard, and the coincidence of his presence in London with the Boston Tea Party brought all circumstances to a focus. Gage encouraged the king and his government to make him the last major link between Britain and America.

Unfortunately, Gage was a weak link: his understanding of the situation in the colonies was surprisingly feeble. There were those who thought that Gage, despite almost twenty years' service in America, had permitted a few personal associates to insulate him against the facts of colonial life. Whatever the explanation, his poor understanding of the problem was responsible for the government's resting its policy on a false premise: that the main obstacle to the use of military force in America was legal, not practical; that Britain actually could coerce the colonists whenever it decided to pass the necessary laws. The ministers managed to slight the fact that Americans, unlike Englishmen or Irishmen or Scots, were armed. In playing his political role, Gage did not remind them early or forcibly enough to make them reconsider. Only at the end did he himself see the great difficulty of coercing thousands of armed men, and even then, through another kind of weakness, he failed to make himself heard.

This other weakness, weakness of temperament rather than of understanding, led him to support a second false premise of British policy: that Boston was the source of revolutionary infection, and that Boston could be isolated. He must have known better as early as 1769, when New York and South Carolina gave Massachusetts vigorous support against military occupation. But he also must have been temperamentally unable to tell Barrington, or Hillsborough, or the king, anything except what they wanted to hear and he wanted to believe—until it was too late.

The obverse effect of temperamental weakness was the kindly

face he presented to the colonists themselves. Even as he arrived at Boston to enforce the Coercive Acts, he exuded easygoing charm and gave Americans a feeling that he, and the government he represented, would never push matters to civil war. A Boston radical read the smiling face and solicitous manner as weakness in the man and in the government behind him. It is only fair to admit that Gage was indeed unlucky, that he was caught up by forces no one could direct or deflect. But it is also fair to conclude that he was a modest force in his own right, and that his impact served to increase miscalculation by both sides.

FOOTNOTES

1. Quoted in John C. Long, *Lord Jeffrey Amherst, a Soldier of the King* (New York, 1933), p. 41. The information on Gage's family and early life comes from John R. Alden, *General Gage in America* (Baton Rouge, 1948), a sound study that is the only full biography of Gage.
2. Massachusetts Historical Society, *Collections*, 4th series, IV (Boston, 1858), pp. 369–70, in reply to the queries of the historian George Chalmers.
3. October 17, 1754, quoted in Robert Wright, *The Life of Major-General James Wolfe* (London, 1864), p. 293.
4. And it was not for lack of contemporary criticism of the conduct of the campaign in general, because invective flew after the battle. The principal sources are Winthrop Sargent, ed., *The History of an Expedition Against Fort DuQuesne in 1755* (Memoirs of the Historical Society of Pennsylvania, vol. V, Philadelphia, 1855); Stanley M. Pargellis, ed., *Military Affairs in North America, 1748–1765: Selected Documents from the Cumberland Papers in Windsor Castle* (New York, 1936), pp. 77–132, hereafter *Military Affairs;* and Charles Hamilton, ed., *Braddock's Defeat* (Norman, Oklahoma, 1959). A case of modern, uninformed criticism is in the editorial note by Hamilton, pp. xvi–xvii, which is not supported by any contemporary account. The most interesting analysis is by Pargellis, "Braddock's Defeat," *American Historical Review*, XLI (1936), pp. 253–69, though I cannot agree with all of his opinions, and the fullest account is in Lee McCardell, *Ill-*

Starred General: Braddock of the Coldstream Guards (Pittsburgh, 1958).

5. July 25, 1755, Pargellis, *Military Affairs*, p. 117.

6. Gage to the Earl of Albemarle, July 24, 1755, in Thomas Keppel, *The Life of Augustus, Viscount Keppel* (London, 1842), I, pp. 213–18.

7. Gage to Major Craven, June 19, 1759 (copy), LO 6114, Loudoun Papers, Henry L. Huntington Library and Art Gallery, San Marino, California, hereafter Huntington Library.

8. To the Duke of Cumberland, October 2, 1756, Pargellis, *Military Affairs*, p. 235.

9. J. Clarence Webster, ed., *The Journal of Jeffrey Amherst* (Toronto, 1931), p. 171.

10. Huck to Loudoun, December 3, 1759, LO 6153, Loudoun Papers, Huntington Library. Huck may have been grinding some ax in this letter for Loudoun's benefit, but I doubt it.

11. The fullest account of these battles is in Lawrence H. Gipson, *The Great War for the Empire: the Victorious Years, 1758–1760* (*The British Empire Before the American Revolution*, vol. X; New York, 1949).

12. The introduction to Stanley M. Pargellis, *Lord Loudoun in North America* (New Haven, 1933), is an excellent discussion of defense policy before 1755.

13. A good discussion of the rationale for an American garrison is in Bernhard Knollenberg, *Origin of the American Revolution: 1759–1766* (New York, 1960), pp. 27–28, 87–98, though he is wrong in his contention that the Indian problem had little to do with the decision.

14. Secretary of State Halifax to Amherst (received by Gage), October 11, 1763, Clarence E. Carter, ed., *The Correspondence of General Thomas Gage . . . 1763–1775* (New Haven, 1931–33), II, pp. 2–3, hereafter *Gage Correspondence*.

15. Halifax to Gage, "Private," January 14, 1764, *ibid.*, p. 10.

16. Gage to Barrington, June 28, 1768, "Private," *Gage Correspondence*, II, pp. 479–80; Gage to Hillsborough, September 26, 1768, *ibid.*, I, p. 197.

17. John Pownall to the Earl of Dartmouth, September 22, 1773, Dartmouth Papers, I (2), nr. 882, William Salt Library, Stafford, England, hereafter Salt Library.

18. Alden, *Gage*, p. 149; and John Armstrong to George Washington, December 24, 1773, Stanislaus M. Hamilton, ed., *Letters to Wash-*

ington and Accompanying Papers (Boston and New York, 1898–1902), IV, pp. 290–91.

19. Abercromby to Loudoun, December 2, 1773, LO 6447, Loudoun Papers, Huntington Library; Harvey to Governor Johnstone of Minorca, September 21, 1773, War Office Papers 3/23, pp. 126–27, British Public Record Office, London. I have repunctuated and expanded abbreviations in these sentences for clarity.

20. James Grant to [James Wemyss], June 14, 1773, Wedderburn Papers, I, p. 38. William L. Clements Library, Ann Arbor, Michigan, hereafter Clements Library.

21. Captain J. Marsh to Brigadier Haldimand, January 22, 1768, British Museum Additional Manuscripts 21728, London.

22. King to North, February 4, 1774, Sir John W. Fortescue, ed., *The Correspondence of King George the Third* (London, 1927–28), III, nr. 1379, hereafter *Correspondence of George III*.

23. Massachusetts Historical Society *Collections*, 4th series, IV (Boston, 1858), p. 371, in reply to the queries of the historian George Chalmers.

24. "Private Diary of Gen. Haldimand," Douglas Brymner, *Report on Canadian Archives, 1889* (Ottawa, 1890), p. 129.

25. Cabinet minutes, April 7, 1774, Dartmouth Papers, II, p. 883, Salt Library.

26. John Andrews to William Barrell, May 18, 1774, Massachusetts Historical Society, *Proceedings*, VIII (Boston, 1866), p. 328.

27. Warren to Josiah Quincy, Jr., November 21, 1774, Josiah Quincy, *Memoir of the Life of Josiah Quincy, Junior* (Boston, 1875), pp. 178–79.

28. Gage to Dartmouth, September 2, 1774, *Gage Correspondence*, I, p. 371. I have rearranged the order of sentences slightly.

29. Gage to Dartmouth, September 25, 1774, two letters, one of them private, *ibid.*, pp. 275–77. His specific proposals were made in a private letter to Thomas Hutchinson, which he asked Dartmouth to peruse.

30. Dartmouth to Gage, "Private," August 23, 1774, *ibid.*, II, pp. 171–72. Gage received the letter October 28.

31. William Knox to John Pownall, September 13, 1774, Knox Papers, II, nr. 17, Clements Library; Knox to Dartmouth, November 15, 1774, and Pownall to Dartmouth, December [16], 1774, Dartmouth Papers, II, nrs. 994 and 1022, Salt Library.

32. Hutchinson to Gage, November 19, 1774, Gage Papers, Clements Library.

33. Barker's diary is printed in the *Atlantic Monthly*, XXXIX (1877), pp. 389–401, 544–54.
34. Peter O. Hutchinson, ed., *The Diary and Letters of . . . Thomas Hutchinson* (Boston, 1883–86), I, p. 232.
35. John Andrews to William Barrell, March 18, 1775, Massachusetts Historical Society, *Proceedings*, VIII (Boston, 1866), p. 401.
36. Horace Walpole, *Journal of the Reign of George the Third*, ed. John Doran (London, 1859), p. 445; King to North, *Correspondence of George III*, III, nr. 1556.
37. Quoted in Allen French, "General Haldimand in Boston," Massachusetts Historical Society, *Proceedings*, LXVI (Boston, 1942), p. 91.
38. Major Philip Skene to Lord North, January 23, 1775, Dartmouth Papers, II, nr. 1116, Salt Library.
39. Dartmouth to Gage, "Secret," January 27, 1775, *Gage Correspondence*, II, pp. 179–83. The circumstances surrounding this letter are discussed in John R. Alden, "Why the March to Concord?" *American Historical Review*, XLIX (1944), pp. 446–54. Barrington's private letter, February 3, 1775, is in the Gage Papers, Clements Library.
40. "Intelligence" received April 3, 1775, Gage Papers, Clements Library.
41. Burgoyne to Lord George Germain, August 20, 1775, Germain Papers, Clements Library.
42. Gage to Barrington, "Private," June 26, 1775, *Gage Correspondence*, II, pp. 686–87. I do not agree with Alden, *Gage*, p. 254, that Gage understood the importance of New York *before* the battle of Bunker Hill.
43. Burgoyne to Lord George Germain, August 20, 1775, Germain Papers, Clements Library; Wemyss quoted in Allen French, *The Day of Lexington and Concord* (Boston, 1925), p. 61.
44. I am indebted to Professor Howard H. Peckham, director of the Clements Library, where he has lived many years with Gage, for the suggestion that Gage's crucial role was political.

BIBLIOGRAPHY

Alden, John R. *General Gage in America: Being Principally a History of His Role in the American Revolution*. Baton Rouge, 1948. This is the only biography. The present essay is indebted to its scholarship, but does not completely share its sympathy with the subject.
Carter, Clarence E. (ed.). *The Correspondence of General Thomas*

Gage. 2 vols. New Haven, 1931–33. Basic published sources for Gage's career.

Donoughue, Bernard. *British Politics and the American Revolution: The Path to War, 1773–1775.* London, 1964. An excellent, thorough study, accurately described by its title.

French, Allen. *The First Year of the American Revolution.* Boston and New York, 1934. An outstanding work of scholarship and historical understanding that was the last of a series of works by the author on 1775.

Gipson, Lawrence H. *The British Empire Before the American Revolution.* 13 vols. to date. Caldwell, Idaho, and New York, 1936—. A monument of historiography that provides detailed accounts of the campaigns, 1755–60, and of problems of the empire after the war.

Ketchum, Richard M. *The Battle for Bunker Hill.* Garden City, 1962. A reliable, well-written narrative that owes a great deal to French's work.

Knollenberg, Bernhard. *The Origin of the American Revolution: 1759–1766.* New York, 1960. An argumentative, thoroughly researched book that has some provocative things to say about the army.

Pargellis, Stanley M. *Lord Loudoun in America.* New Haven, 1933. Provides an understanding account of British defense problems to 1757 and of the army that Gage would soon command.

Tourtellot, Arthur B. *William Diamond's Drum.* New York, 1959. Republished in paperback as *Lexington and Concord*, it is, like Ketchum, an excellent popularization that draws heavily on French.

Sir William Howe:

CONVENTIONAL STRATEGIST

MALDWYN A. JONES

University of Manchester, England

SIR WILLIAM HOWE, one of the Revolution's most controversial military figures, remains so down to this day. He was, perhaps, the only British commander-in-chief with a real chance to crush the American rebellion. Why did he fail to do so? Why did he let slip a succession of seemingly easy opportunities to destroy Washington's army? Was he more concerned with reconciliation than with reconquest? Did his political responsibilities as peacemaker interfere with his military obligations as general? These questions, raised by his contemporaries, have divided historians ever since and make the problem of evaluating Howe's record a perplexing one.

It is not difficult to see why Howe's lack of success chagrined and disquieted the loyal subjects of George III. During the first three years of the war Britain mounted a truly prodigious effort on both land and sea. Howe was provided with a military force which seemed more than adequate to restore royal authority in the colonies. It represented the greatest army Britain had ever sent overseas and was infinitely superior to anything that the Americans could put in the field. The British fleet enjoyed complete mastery of the sea and kept lines of communication open at all times. Yet in three successive campaigns this formidable military machine failed either to inflict a decisive defeat on the

Continental army or to recover more than a tiny portion of enemy territory. Small wonder, then, that in the dark days after Saratoga, Englishmen confessed they were at a loss to understand how "such an army, so well appointed, served by so large a train of artillery, and attended by so numerous a fleet, could fail of success against a divided people, destitute of Officers, Soldiers, Magazines, fortified towns, ships of war, or any apparent resources." [1]

Many Englishmen, feeling that the Saratoga defeat was a national humiliation, eagerly cast about for a scapegoat. Some blamed Burgoyne, others Lord George Germain, but a considerable number placed the responsibility squarely on Howe's shoulders. The same was true of American loyalists. "It is a unanimous sentiment here," wrote a disgruntled New Yorker in December, 1777, "that our misfortunes this campaign have arisen, not so much from the genius and valour of the rebels, as from the misconduct of a certain person." [2] Howe, the writer went on, had made many mistakes in earlier campaigns, but these seemed trivial compared to the "gross and mortifying blunders" committed in 1777. Either the general had never looked at a map of America or, if he had done so, he had not understood it. Otherwise, how could he have chosen the campaign in Pennsylvania while Burgoyne was attempting to link up with him on the Hudson? By making Philadelphia his main objective in 1777, Howe had abandoned Burgoyne to his fate.

After Howe's recall in the spring of 1778 such indictments against him lengthened steadily. He returned to London to face criticism, not merely for his supposed miscalculation in the Saratoga campaign but for his entire conduct during his three years in America. In Parliament and the press he was accused, among other things, of having conducted the war with no clear appreciation of strategic realities; of having moved his army backward and forward to no apparent purpose, "as if valour consisted in a military jig"; of having shown undue tenderness to the rebels; and of having failed to make proper use of the loyalists.[3] Besides having abandoned Burgoyne, he had failed to take advantage of his opportunities to smash Washington's army. Even the Americans, declared Howe's critics, recognized that their salvation was due to his excessive caution and procrastination. To many it seemed that Howe had prolonged the war deliberately, either for his own financial advantage, or because he was "wedded to a system of politics that favoured the rebellion." [4]

Howe resented such attacks all the more keenly because Lord North's government made little effort to defend him. Indeed, many believed that the more pungent criticisms of the general were inspired by a member of the government, Lord George Germain.[5] To vindicate himself Howe in 1779 demanded a parliamentary inquiry into his conduct of the war. He seized the opportunity not only to answer his critics but to bring charges of his own. He claimed that to have pursued Washington with greater vigor would have exposed his army to grave dangers; that the loyalists, being a minority in America, would not have aided his cause greatly; and that the government had failed to send him the reinforcements required for the task at hand.[6]

The inquiry led nowhere. Producing nothing but a flood of charges and countercharges, it became little more than a verbal duel between Howe and Germain. Each man claimed he was making no allegations against the other, but was concerned only with defending his honor. The fact of the matter was that the investigation became enmeshed in a factional struggle between the administration and those opposition critics like Fox and Barré who opposed the war. With the entry of Spain into the conflict, the inquiry petered out in June, 1779, and the committee never even rendered a report.

Thus Howe's generalship remained an enigma for historians to puzzle over. Scholars have been no more able to agree on a solution than the inquiry of 1779. Some have attributed Howe's lack of success simply to incompetence—to that "monotonous mediocrity" about which his subordinate, Charles Stedman, complained in his early history of the war.[7] According to such historians, Howe was by nature slow, unimaginative and excessively cautious.[8] Others have suggested that indolence and self-indulgence left him disinclined for active military operations.[9] Still others have endorsed the contemporary charge that Howe's failure resulted from his sympathy with the American cause.[10]

But Howe has not gone undefended. Some scholars have asserted that Sir William had real grounds for complaining that he was not adequately supported by George III's ministers, especially Lord George Germain.[11] Howe's champions have also stressed the difficulties of his task.[12] Indeed, certain historians have argued that, in the long run, Howe's generalship was of little consequence in deciding the outcome of the Revolution. The scales were heavily weighted against Great Britain from the start, they claim, and there was little hope of holding the populous and distant American colonies. Howe's inadequacy amounted, therefore, to no more than that he failed to achieve the impossible.[13]

There are grounds, however, for believing that George III and Germain may have been right—at least until Saratoga—in their conviction that the rebellion could be subdued by force of arms. The triumph of independence movements is not inevitable, as subsequent events in American history were to show. Between 1861 and 1865 the Southern Confederacy was to learn that an embryonic nation could be destroyed on the battlefield. That the Confederacy was finally obliged to surrender to superior force suggests that a similar outcome might not have been impossible during the Revolutionary struggle nearly ninety years earlier. If British commanders had waged war on the colonists as remorselessly as Grant and Sherman did on the Confederates, or if Washington's army had been as decisively defeated in 1776 or 1777 as Lee's was in 1865, patriot morale in all probability would have been shattered as completely as the final campaigns of the Civil War demoralized the South.

If this assumption is correct, then Howe's military failures were neither unimportant nor irrelevant. Howe was the key figure in the first crucial stages of the Revolutionary War, while it was still a domestic rebellion and before France intervened and changed the character of the contest. For the first three years, Britain was spared those distractions that later made it necessary to deploy her strength against other foes and in distant parts of the world. General Howe thus had advantages denied to his successors. That he failed to capitalize on them, that in so doing he allowed the rebellion precious time to take root, was probably the decisive factor in the outcome of the struggle.

Howe was born in 1729, the third son of the second Viscount Howe and of his wife, Mary Sophia, the daughter of Baroness Kielmansegge, who had been a mistress of George I. All three Howe brothers were destined for prominent careers in military service—a fact their enemies often attributed, perhaps unfairly, to the family connection with the house of Hanover. Certainly William's early career showed no evidence of royal favor. In 1746, at the age of seventeen, he joined the army as a cornet in the light dragoons of the Duke of Cumberland. Promoted to lieutenant the following year, he served in Flanders in 1747–48 with the British force sent to oppose Marshal Saxe. After the war he served for several years in the 20th Foot with James Wolfe, with whom he became close friends.

Howe's acquaintance with America did not begin with the Revolution. During the French and Indian War he spent several years in the colonies, and served under Wolfe in the conquest of Canada. At the siege of Louisbourg in 1758 he commanded a regiment and won Wolfe's warm commendation. The following year he distinguished himself by leading the light infantry who first scaled the Heights of Abraham and thereby facilitated the capture of Quebec. In 1760 he commanded a brigade in the Montreal expedition. Returning to Europe, Howe took part in the siege of Belle Isle off the French coast, and then served as adjutant general of the army which captured Havana from Spain in 1762.

By the close of the war Howe had compiled a splendid record and his star was clearly in the ascendant. He added further to his reputation in the early 1770's by introducing a new system of light drill in the army. With the idea of increasing infantry mobility Howe, now a major general, organized lightly equipped companies drawn from the line regiments and trained them to move rapidly. The innovation was an instant success and led to light companies being introduced into all line regiments.

In the period between the two wars opportunities for active service were scarce, and Howe's only military employment was in the purely nominal position of governor of the Isle of Wight. He followed also a political career and represented the town of Nottingham in the House of Commons, being first elected in 1758 to succeed his brother George, who had been killed at Ticonderoga. There was nothing unusual about military men serving in Parliament at that time. In the general election of 1761 no fewer than sixty-four army officers were elected.[14] Besides Howe they included two other men who were to hold important commands during the Revolutionary War—John Burgoyne and Charles Cornwallis. But, unlike Burgoyne, Howe was not an active politician. He entered politics no doubt because, as Lord Chesterfield remarked in 1741, it "was the known way to military preferment." [15] At all events Howe apparently played no part in the prolonged controversy over colonial taxation prior to the war.

There is every indication, however, that Howe held the Americans in high regard. In part this stemmed from his service in America. But even more it sprang from the friendly relationship that had developed between his brother George and the colonists. George Howe—the third Viscount Howe—had been one of the few British officers to welcome personal contact with Americans, and during the French and Indian War had gained the affection of the colonial troops who had served under him. When he fell at Ticonderoga there was genuine grief in the colonies, and the Massachusetts Assembly erected a monument in his honor in Westminster Abbey. The surviving Howe brothers appreciated this gesture and it created for them a sentimental attachment to Americans that they found difficult to break.

When a policy of coercion against Massachusetts was adopted by Parliament, General Howe opposed it. During the winter of 1774–75 he informed his Nottingham constituents that he would not accept an American command, if it were offered him.[16] But in February, 1775, he changed his mind. Among his Nottingham constituents were many who were notoriously pro-American, and one was so disturbed that he wrote to Howe asking for an explanation.

Howe's reply was not entirely convincing. He was going to America, he declared, because he had been ordered to do so. Refusal would have meant that he would incur "the odious name of backwardness to serve my country in distress." "A man's private feelings," he added, "ought to give way to the service of the public at all times." [17] This view was not shared by other prominent military men who faced the same dilemma. General Amherst and Admiral Keppel, for example, both refused to command against the Americans, while other officers resigned their commissions rather than take part in a war they found distasteful. Howe evidently had fewer scruples about serving against the colonists. If he had felt an initial twinge of conscience about the matter, he was not prepared to sacrifice his military career to his feelings. Indeed, if Burgoyne is to be believed, Howe actively sought the chief command in America.

Troyer Anderson, Howe's most ardent advocate in modern times, argues that there was no inconsistency in the general's behavior at this time. Howe, he says, believed his task would be primarily one of negotiation, and his willingness to serve in the colonies did not imply that he was willing to wage war on the Americans.[18] While it is true that Howe and his brother Richard, Admiral Lord Howe, were subsequently appointed in 1776 to a commission empowering them to negotiate with the rebels, there is no evidence that they thought their mandate was political rather than military. Along with most other Englishmen, General Howe believed that the great bulk of the colonists were still loyal to George III and that the insurgents, being an insignificant minority, would not present a serious military problem.

Although he may have hoped for some formula to remove colonial grievances, he seems to have gone to America prepared to use force to restore the authority of the Crown.

Certainly it was Howe's qualities as a soldier which weighed most with the Ministry in deciding to send him to America. Major Philip Skene in reporting to Lord North in January, 1775, that Howe was prepared to serve under Gage, declared that he had served with Howe in many difficult situations and had found him to be "unsurpassed in activity, bravery and experience, and beloved by the troops." [19] Germain, a few months later, gave the Ministry's reasons for choosing Howe. No one, wrote the American secretary in June, 1775,[20] understood the peculiarities of American campaigning better than Howe, who in the French and Indian War "Had command of the light troops and . . . will, I am persuaded, teach the present army to be as formidable as that he formerly acted with." Germain went on to say that the conduct of the coming war required "more than common ability [for] the distance from the seat of Government necessarily [left] much to the discretion and resources of the general." General Gage, for all his good qualities, found himself "in a situation of too great importance for his talents," and rarely ventured to take a single step beyond the letter of his instructions. Dissatisfied with Gage, Germain believed that in Howe he had a general not only experienced in tactics but capable of acting on his own initiative.

Despite the misgivings about Gage, he remained for the moment as commander-in-chief. But to rouse him into taking more vigorous action Howe and two other major generals, Clinton and Burgoyne, were sent to Boston in the spring of 1775. Within a few days of their arrival on May 25, Gage decided to take the offensive and occupy the Charlestown peninsula. Forestalled in this intention by the American militia, Gage instructed Howe to make a landing at the tip of the peninsula and to lead an assault on the American entrenchments. In the ensuing battle— known to posterity as Bunker Hill—the Americans were ultimately driven from the peninsula, but at a terrible cost. Over one thousand of Howe's men, 40 per cent of his entire force, were either killed or wounded. In his own words, it was a "success . . . too dearly bought." [21]

Howe has often been blamed for Bunker Hill. But in two important respects he does not deserve censure. The decision to concentrate upon a frontal assault—rather than land in the American rear at Charlestown Neck—was one in which Howe probably concurred, but final responsibility rested with Gage, who was the ranking officer. Secondly, there seems to be little substance in the charge that Howe failed to pursue the Americans during their retreat to the mainland. His force suffered so heavily in gaining the peninsula that it was in no condition to take up further pursuit.

Yet Howe cannot be excused altogether. Defective as the British plan was, it might have been executed without such heavy losses by a more energetic and resourceful general. For the attackers, speed of movement was essential because the Americans were using every moment to strengthen their defenses. But Howe saw no need for haste. Confident that the rebel militia would scatter before an assault by regulars, he wasted precious time and did not land his men on the peninsula until the afternoon.[22] He erred also in ordering an advance in line instead of in column—a decision which exposed a better target to the defenders. Observers agreed that Howe behaved with exemplary courage on the battlefield and rallied his men at a critical point of the attack.[23] But his tactics, resulting from what one of his subordinates termed his "absurd and destructive confidence," contributed not a little to the slaughter.[24]

Whether Howe's experience at Bunker Hill colored his subsequent generalship has been much debated. It may well have. His account of that "unhappy day," as he called it, spoke of his horror at losing so many brave men.[25] The battle left a deep impression and for the remainder of the war he shrank from frontal assaults whenever possible.

After succeeding Gage as commander-in-chief, Howe received orders in early November, 1775, to abandon Boston and move the army to New York. But owing to the lateness of the season and to lack of transports, Howe decided instead to spend the winter in Boston. There he remained until March 17, 1776, when Washington's seizure of Dorchester Heights made the city untenable. Howe thereupon withdrew his army to Halifax.

Howe's inactivity during the siege of Boston is difficult to understand. His own explanation, which his modern defenders have endorsed, was that nothing decisive could be accomplished in Boston. The Americans outnumbered him and were strongly fortified; any attempt to storm their lines might have led to another Bunker Hill. He complained also that his army lacked the supplies and transport necessary for offensive operations.[26] The most that could have been attempted, according to his apologists, was a large-scale raid, but even that might have ended as disastrously as the Concord expedition. Far better, therefore, to wait until 1776 when reinforcements would arrive and New York would offer a more promising base of operations.[27]

There is no denying that Howe had serious problems during the winter of 1775–76. But that does not excuse him, for his opponent was, perhaps, even worse off. The Continental army was disorganized and undisciplined, and desperately short of powder and artillery. Worst of all, it threatened to disband itself, when enlistments expired on the last day of 1775.[28] Washington, driven to despair by "such a dearth of public spirit, and such want of virtue" as he saw around him, was apprehensive lest the British take advantage of his difficulties and attack him. "Our situation," he wrote in November, "is truly alarming; and of this General Howe is well apprized, it being the common topic of conversation . . . [in] Boston. . . ." [29] That this critical period passed without any offensive action by the British was an immense relief to Washington. But at the same time, he was puzzled. "Search the vast volumes of history through," he wrote in January, 1776, "and I must question whether a case similar to ours is to be found; to wit, to maintain a post against the flower of the British troops for six months together . . . and at the end of them to have one army disbanded and another to raise within the same distance of a reinforced enemy." [30]

Washington's astonishment is understandable. Even if Howe was incapable of carrying out a major offensive, he should have made harassing attacks upon the besiegers, if only to retain the initiative. That he failed to do so has sometimes been attributed to the attachment he formed for Mrs. Joshua Loring, and to his love of gambling. But Howe's dissipation was probably more a result than a cause of his military inactivity. His disinclination to set his troops in motion at this time in reality can be traced to another source, namely, the limitations imposed by his military education. Like most soldiers reared in the formalized military tradition of the eighteenth century, Howe closed his mind to the possibility of winter campaigns. With the first frosts, he put aside all thoughts of soldiering until spring. The fact that the Americans did not share this attitude was shown when Arnold assaulted the fortress of Quebec in a blinding snowstorm in December, 1775. It was to be demonstrated still more strikingly a year later by Washington's daring riposte at Trenton. But Howe proved incapable of learning anything from the Americans. Hence he remained passive during the winters of 1776 and 1777, hibernating snugly in New York and Philadelphia respectively, and ignoring the existence of Washington's shivering army barely a day's march away.

Howe revealed his true character in his first few months as commander-in-chief. His flair for improvisation—demonstrated earlier in his organization of the light infantry—gave way to a timid adherence to accepted practices. The boldness he had shown on the Heights of Abraham and at Bunker Hill were replaced by a policy of caution. Howe's frame of mind boded ill for Britain's hopes of reconquering America; once the chief responsibility was his, Howe became oppressed by the magnitude of his task and had doubts about his ability to carry it to a successful conclusion. The American army, he informed Dartmouth in January, 1776, was not "by any means to be despised, having in it many European soldiers, and all or most of the young men of spirit in the country." To defeat the Americans large reinforcements would be required. If these were not forth-

coming, Howe concluded, it might be "better policy to withdraw entirely from the delinquent provinces, and leave the colonists to war with each other for sovereignty." [31]

For a man newly appointed to put down the rebellion, this
was an astonishing statement. On the strength of a single encounter with the rebels, and six months before the Declaration
of Independence, Howe was prepared to contemplate a complete
withdrawal from America. Nothing could better illustrate his
bankruptcy of mind than this gloomy prognostication. Howe
seems to have expected the mere presence of a sizable British
force in America to bring about a collapse of the rebellion.
When that hope was shattered, he was no longer sure how to
proceed. He could have understood much better a purely military problem, but a situation in which he had both to conquer
and to pacify appears to have made him uncertain what measure
of coercion was to be used. It is true that there were occasional
moments when his confidence returned, as in April, 1776, when
he wrote to Germain of his hopes of bringing Washington to
a decisive action at New York, an action "than which nothing
is more to be desired or sought by us, as the most effective means
to terminate this expensive war." [32] But such optimism was
short-lived. As the war dragged on, his doubts multiplied. Small
wonder that his operations, instead of reflecting a sense of urgency, were characterized by hesitancy and delay.

Howe's decision, on abandoning Boston in March, 1776, to
go to Halifax instead of New York was a correct one. He had
little alternative. The reinforcements promised him had not yet
arrived and his army was in no condition to attack New York.
The winter in Boston proved to be a trying one and the troops
required a period of rest and reorganization. Howe in particular
wanted an opportunity to exercise them in line—"a very material part of discipline," as he later remarked, "in which we were
defective until that time." [33]

Nor was the delay in opening the 1776 campaign entirely
Howe's fault. His timetable, already disarranged by his forced

withdrawal from Boston, was thrown further into disarray by the difficulty of obtaining supplies at Halifax and by Germain's instructions to postpone the expedition against New York until reinforcements had arrived from England. But even after landing on Staten Island in early July, Howe waited nearly two months before moving against the Americans on Long Island.

Howe's dilatoriness has been explained by his alleged desire to attempt a reconciliation before resorting to further bloodshed. But his peacemaking efforts in July do not appear to have interfered much with his military plans. The determining factor was Howe's unwillingness to begin operations until he received reinforcements from England and from the expedition against South Carolina. The last of these reinforcements did not reach him until mid-August, a circumstance to which he later pointed as proof that he could not possibly have started his campaign earlier.[34]

The validity of his argument depends on whether Germain's instructions to await reinforcements before commencing operations were so binding as to deprive Howe of freedom of action. The inescapable conclusion is that they were not. The Ministry had given Howe full discretionary powers to crush the rebellion and, in view of his distance from London, did not expect him to carry out particular instructions if local circumstances or his own judgment suggested otherwise.[35] Proof that Howe understood the situation perfectly lies in his earlier decision to remain in Boston during the winter of 1775–76 despite instructions to the contrary.

Howe's failure to attack sooner in New York was a serious mistake. Even without the expected reinforcements, he enjoyed a substantial margin of superiority over Washington. Had he attacked at once he might have captured New York City with even less difficulty than he subsequently experienced. While he delayed, the Americans improved their defenses: fortifications were strengthened, arms and ammunition poured in, and Washington imposed some semblance of discipline on his army.[36] Washington's force, moreover, was joined by local militia, and by the time Howe belatedly began operations he was facing the largest number of Americans to be gathered in one army during the entire war.

The weather provided Howe with another excuse for doing little that summer. During the Parliamentary inquiry of 1779, Howe reported that "from the violent heat of the weather, little active service could have been done, and . . . such service would probably have been attended with much sickness to the troops." [37] Having earlier rejected American winters as too cold for campaigning, Howe now complained the summers were too hot. Here was additional proof of his tendency to exaggerate his difficulties and his readiness to submit to circumstances.

Slow though he was to begin operations, Howe could exhibit considerable skill in planning and executing military maneuvers of a conventional and uncomplicated nature. His handling of the battle of Long Island showed him at his best. Landing his army in the vicinity of the Narrows under the cover of the fleet, Howe exposed the American left by a flanking march which, timed to the minute, resulted in the rout of the enemy. This victory, greeted in Britain as a sure sign that the rebellion would shortly be over, raised Howe's reputation to its peak. Germain paid Howe a high compliment by describing the battle as "the first Military Operation with which no fault could be found in the planning of it, nor in the Conduct of any Officers to whom you entrusted the Command." [38] George III rewarded Howe by conferring a knighthood upon him and showed concern that the general was too fond of exposing himself to fire. He ought to consider, the king told Germain, "how much the Publick would suffer by the loss of a General, who had gained the Affection of his Troops, and the Confidence of the Country." [39]

Yet Long Island was not the complete British victory it might have been. Had Howe taken the advice of Clinton and others to continue the pursuit and storm the American entrenchments, there is little doubt that the entire American force on Long Island would have been annihilated. But he halted the attack short of the American lines, observing that "the Troops had for that day done handsomely enough." [40]

Howe was bitterly assailed for this decision during the Parliamentary inquiry. His critics fastened upon his own admission, made within a week of the battle, that "had the Troops been permitted to go on . . . they would have carried the Redoubts." [41] Confronted with this statement three years later, Howe swallowed his words and claimed that storming would not have produced the destruction of the rebel army.[42]

It is, of course, true that only half the American army of 20,000 was stationed on Long Island. But to have destroyed or captured this substantial force personally led by Washington would have dealt the Americans an irreparable blow. Had such a stroke been followed by a prompt landing on the northern part of Manhattan, the war would no doubt have been over.

Howe's defense of his conduct at Long Island goes far to explain his failures in the Revolutionary War. It provides also a revealing comment upon the military system that produced him. He declared in 1779:

> The most essential duty I had to perform was not wantonly to commit his majesty's troops where the object was inadequate. I knew well that any considerable loss sustained by the army could not speedily, nor easily, be repaired. In this instance . . . to have permitted the attack in question would have been inconsiderate, and even criminal. The loss of 1000 or perhaps 1500 British troops, in carrying those lines, would have been but ill repaid by double that number of the enemy, even could it have been supposed they would have suffered in this proportion.[43]

Howe's sentiments were characteristic of British—indeed of European—military thought in the eighteenth century. The army was recognized as the product of a great national effort. It took several years of intensive training to instruct soldiers in the complicated maneuvers required in the warfare of the period. It took equally long to amass the necessary weapons and equipment. The cost of raising and maintaining military forces imposed such a severe strain on the limited resources of the government that the army came to be regarded as a species of national wealth. It had to be husbanded accordingly. To lose an army in battle was an almost irretrievable disaster; for this reason it was more important for a general to preserve his own force than to defeat that of the enemy.[44]

The precepts on which Howe's military education were based posed a serious handicap in a war which, by its very nature, required bold offensive action if it were to be won. It is true that some of Howe's subordinates, notably Clinton, who had received the same education, urged a bolder course on Howe at Long Island. But these generals did so knowing that Howe, and not they, would bear ultimate responsiblity for the army's safety. It was significant that once Clinton became commander-in-chief, he became as cautious as Howe.[45] The truth was that Howe's military upbringing made it difficult for him to act otherwise than he did. If that consideration is given due weight, the allegation that Sir William, out of sympathy for the Americans, deliberately withheld the *coup de grâce* at Long Island so as to permit the enemy to retire in safety to Manhattan, can be seen for the absurdity it is.

Howe's critics can nevertheless be pardoned for continuing to suspect his intentions. His dawdling in the weeks after the battle of Long Island seemed to suggest that he was not serious about his efforts to end the rebellion. Having bestirred himself sufficiently to take possession of New York on September 15, he left Washington undisturbed on Harlem Heights for nearly a month. Despite the fact that the American army was again on the verge of dissolution and was too weak to attack him, Sir William went to elaborate lengths to fortify his newly won base. Indeed, he had already concluded that there was "not the smallest prospect of finishing the contest this campaign," and had turned his thoughts to 1777.[46]

There was no justification for so gloomy a view. The military situation still offered Howe splendid opportunities for striking a decisive blow. As long as Washington remained at Harlem Heights, the American army was in a highly precarious position: British landings in Westchester, if followed up quickly, could sever his lines of retreat to the mainland. But Howe's amphibious operations against Westchester, tardily begun on October 12, aimed not at trapping Washington but only at maneuvering him out of Manhattan Island. After landing his troops behind the American lines at Throg's Neck in the East River, Howe remained inactive for several days. According to his own account, he was anxious to secure his supply lines before penetrating inland. To have struck out at once from Throg's Neck, he claimed later, would have been "an imprudent measure, as it could not have been executed without much unnecessary risk." [47]

Yet if Howe had acted promptly to seize the exit from the Neck, and had then moved inland, Washington could not have escaped encirclement. As it was, Sir William's hesitation permitted the patriot army to slip away to White Plains. Though he achieved his object of forcing the Americans out of their entrenchments, Howe failed to take full advantage of the situation. [48]

At White Plains, Howe repeated his performance at the Battle of Long Island. Having carried an American outpost on Chatterton Hill, he declined a further assault on the enemy lines. Thus, in the eyes of many observers, he let slip one more opportunity of inflicting mortal injury. As at Long Island, he excused himself by claiming there was no reason to suppose that the forcing of the lines would have led to the destruction of the enemy: Washington, he said, would simply have withdrawn to another defensive position. [49]

The final phase of the 1776 campaign virtually settled the outcome of the war. The reduction of Fort Washington in mid-November presented Howe with a fresh and unexpected opportunity. The way was open for an advance into New Jersey and, if vigorously pursued, this might have carried the British into Philadelphia. Washington's army, weakened by desertion and dispirited by defeat, could not have halted a British offensive.

Indeed, Howe might have intercepted the American army as it straggled across the Delaware.

Yet this opportunity too was squandered. Howe's rigidity of mind prevented him from seeing how vital a rapid advance on Philadelphia was at this stage. In light of the changed situation, he might have recast his strategy. He had planned, as a preliminary to the 1777 campaign, to send an expedition to take Newport, Rhode Island. But once there was a prospect of annihilating Washington's army in New Jersey and of capturing Philadelphia, Newport ceased to have strategic significance. Clinton, who had been named to command the Newport expedition, quickly grasped that what was needed was a concentration of force to the south. He proposed that the troops intended for Newport should be landed instead on the New Jersey shore to cooperate with Cornwallis, who was in pursuit of Washington. As another alternative, Clinton urged that they be transported by sea to the Delaware to chase Congress out of Philadelphia.[50] But Howe rejected both suggestions. He insisted on sending the expedition to Newport as planned.

The decision was a grievous mistake. But it was not necessarily a fatal one; Cornwallis still had twice as many troops as Washington. At the time the American army retreated across the Delaware, its situation was desperate. "With a little enterprise and industry," Washington wrote later, it would have been a simple matter for the British "to dissipate the remaining force which still kept alive our expiring opposition."[51]

But enterprise and industry were qualities Sir William Howe lacked most. Even with so rich a prize within his grasp he made no attempt to hasten the pace of pursuit. He ordered Cornwallis not to go beyond New Brunswick until reinforcements arrived, and when the Americans retreated across the Delaware he called off the pursuit for lack of boats with which to cross the river.

His action was a characteristic one—an expression of the caution which had now become second nature. Had Howe been determined to continue as far as Philadelphia, the river barrier at the Delaware might have been surmounted. He could either have built boats from the lumber that lay near at hand or brought small craft down from New York. But Howe felt the campaign had gone on long enough.[52] At the end of November, he decided to defer further operations until spring and went into winter quarters.

The consequences of his decision were not long in coming. Taking swift advantage of the unexpected respite, Washington revived American hopes with two stunning victories at Trenton and Princeton. Howe had been aware of the risk involved in extending his outposts to Trenton. But he believed the disposition of his troops was justified by the need to give protection to the New Jersey loyalists and the fact that the American army appeared too weak to strike a counterblow.[53] In fact, Howe was less to blame for the Trenton setback than his subordinates who failed to erect redoubts as he had ordered. But the fact remains that had the pursuit across New Jersey been conducted with greater vigor, Washington would have had neither the strength nor the opportunity to counterattack.

The 1776 campaign, in retrospect, proved to be the turning point of the war. No other British general was presented with such a succession of opportunities for ending the struggle as Howe had in the summer and fall of that year. Time and again sluggishness and timidity prevented him from taking chances. When Howe turned his back on the Delaware, he decided the fate of the Revolution.

British strategy in the campaign of 1777 was equally defective. It was aimed at the conquest of territory instead of the destruction of Washington's army. Moreover, the moves of the British armies were ill-planned. Howe's invasion of Pennsylvania and Burgoyne's descent from Canada were conceived as two entirely separate operations and no attempt was made to coordinate them. It was little wonder that British arms met with disaster at Saratoga.

Howe cannot bear the entire blame for the Saratoga defeat. He had nothing to do with the planning of the Canadian expedition; it was worked out in London by Burgoyne and Germain. Nor was it Howe's responsibility to coordinate his own offensive with that of Burgoyne. The trouble here was a faulty command structure. It had been decided early in the war to have two independent commands in North America, one under Howe for the American colonies, the other under Carleton for Canada. The relationship between the two theaters was never defined, so that each commander was dependent for information upon the other and upon what he learned from Germain. If anyone was responsible for coordination, it was Germain.

During the planning of the 1777 campaign, however, Germain failed to discharge this responsibility. It was not that he neglected to inform Howe of Burgoyne's movements; the old story of a forgotten dispatch, unsent through Lord George's indolence, need no longer be taken seriously.[54] It was rather that Germain failed to insist upon Howe's completing operations in Pennsylvania in time to return to the support of Burgoyne. Indeed, the need for such a precaution did not occur to Germain until it was too late.

Thus when Howe left New York for the Chesapeake, his mind was focused almost entirely upon reaching Philadelphia. He was aware of the impending invasion from Canada, but he had no reason to suppose that a northward advance in strength up the Hudson was expected of him. Nor did Burgoyne count upon such a move. He was confident when he set out from Canada that he could reach Albany without Howe's help. It was only after his surrender that Burgoyne complained of lack of cooperation.

These facts, however, do not absolve Howe altogether of blame for Saratoga. His critics may have been wrong when they accused him of willfully sacrificing Burgoyne. But what he did was almost as bad. By moving away from the strategic center, he deprived himself of the opportunity of influencing events. To embark on a seaborne invasion of Pennsylvania without making clear provision for a junction with Burgoyne was to act as though the Canadian command did not exist.

Howe's part in the chain of events that led to Saratoga reveals his limitations as a strategist. Between November, 1776, and April, 1777, Howe sent Germain three separate plans that varied greatly. The first envisaged an attack on Boston from Rhode Island by one army and an advance up the Hudson by another. Within a month of sending this plan to London, and prior to his receiving a reply, he drew up a second one that was radically different. This proposal envisaged a double offensive against Philadelphia: the main force to proceed overland across New Jersey and a smaller contingent to go by sea. No sooner had Germain given his approval to this second scheme than Howe produced a third—the one he actually put into practice. The advance across New Jersey was abandoned and the entire army was to be taken to Philadelphia by sea instead.[55]

Whatever the respective merits of these plans considered individually, the fact that they succeeded each other so rapidly is a commentary on the shallowness of Howe's strategic thinking. No general with a clear appreciation of the task confronting him could have shifted so abruptly from one set of strategic ideas to another. Indeed, it was irresponsible on Howe's part to bombard Germain with a succession of divergent proposals over so short a period of time. When every packet from New York carried fresh proposals from the commander-in-chief, the American secretary could hardly be expected to coordinate operations effectively.

During Parliament's inquiry Howe spent a good deal of time defending his decision to campaign in Pennsylvania instead of going up the Hudson to assist Burgoyne. He produced plausible arguments. The Canadian army, he asserted, was thought to be fully capable of looking after itself. Had he gone up the Hudson, he would have been accused of wasting the campaign and of attempting to steal some of Burgoyne's thunder. In any event an attack on Philadelphia was, in his opinion, the most effectual diversion that could be made to help Burgoyne. Washington was obliged to defend the American capital and this precluded his marching up to the Hudson. Moreover, an attack on Philadelphia was the best way of bringing Washington to battle.[56]

But Howe's arguments had serious weaknesses. It was only

after the Saratoga surrender that he began to think of the Pennsylvania campaign as a diversionary move in Burgoyne's favor. Nor could he have been certain at the time that Washington would decide to defend Philadelphia in preference to marching northward. Indeed, during the six weeks he spent on the voyage to the Chesapeake, Howe was out of touch with Washington's army and was powerless to influence its movements. Had the American commander been better equipped to exploit his advantage of interior lines, he might have intervened decisively against Burgoyne during Howe's absence at sea and then have marched south with his army and that of Gates in time to repulse the British invasion of Pennsylvania.[57]

Howe's fundamental error was not that he chose to invade Pennsylvania, but rather that he failed to do so overland. Had he advanced on his objective across New Jersey, as the second of his plans proposed, he would have been justified in his claim that he was helping Burgoyne. He would also have been in position to double back instantly if Washington had threatened either New York City or Burgoyne's army. When asked during Parliament's inquiry why he had not proceeded overland, Howe could only offer the same puerile excuse he had used to explain his failure to capture Philadelphia in 1776: he lacked "sufficient means" to cross so large a river as the Delaware and therefore "judged the difficulties and the risk too great." [58]

Howe conducted the whole campaign of 1777 with all the deliberation for which he was now notorious. He began the year by neglecting to take advantage of Washington's weakness at Morristown. After the American army had doubled its size during the spring, Howe wasted precious time in a series of half-hearted attempts to induce Washington to do battle.[59] Thus the summer was far advanced before the Pennsylvania expedition even got under way. Keeping his troops on board transports for two weeks in New York harbor, Howe finally set sail for Philadelphia on July 23.

His progress by sea was painfully slow. The armada first of all put in at Delaware Bay, probably to allow Howe to find out whether Washington had moved toward Albany. Learning that he had not, and finding the Delaware heavily fortified, Howe abandoned his plans for a landing and put out to sea again. Owing to contrary winds three more weeks elapsed before he sailed into the Chesapeake and disembarked his army at Head of Elk. Defeating Washington at the Battle of Brandywine on September 11, Howe tarried another two weeks before occupying Philadelphia. It thus took him more than two months to reach an objective only one hundred miles away from his New York base.

At Brandywine, Howe repeated the tactics he had employed so successfully at Long Island. Once more he skillfully executed a flanking movement which obliged the American army to retreat in disorder. However, he again halted the attack at a time when, had he pressed on, he might have turned the American retreat into a rout.

Sir William fought his last major battle when Washington's surprise attack caught him off guard at Germantown in early October. Contrary to his usual policy, Howe relaxed his vigilance once Philadelphia was captured and failed to order entrenchments built. He felt that to do so might be taken by Washington as a sign of weakness. When the battle began the British were in danger of defeat, but the American attack miscarried and Washington's men finally retired in confusion.

Germantown destroyed what little remained of Howe's military reputation. It did not add much to Washington's either. In fact, the inadequacies of the rival commanders were such that neither seemed capable of winning a decisive victory. An anonymous correspondent of a London newspaper aptly summed up the battle in these words: "Any other General in the world than General Howe would have beaten General Washington, and any other General in the world than General Washington would have beaten General Howe." [60]

Soon after hearing the news of Saratoga, Howe requested that he be allowed to resign his command. He gave two reasons for stepping down: the government had failed to support him adequately, and his recommendations had been consistently ignored. But Howe had other motives for resigning. He correctly antici- pated that he would be blamed for Burgoyne's defeat and he was anxious to return to London so as to answer his critics. After spending a final winter of inactivity in Philadelphia, Howe learned his resignation had been accepted and he was free to go home. On the eve of his departure a mock tournament, known as the Mischianza, was staged in his honor. It was de- scribed by one eyewitness as "the most splendid entertain- ment . . . ever given by an army to their General," [61] and this absurd spectacle demonstrated, if nothing else, that Sir William had not lost the regard of his officers.

Howe sailed from Philadelphia for England on May 25, 1778, three years to the day since his arrival in Boston aboard the *Cerberus*. The years had been ones of frustration, disappoint- ment and lost opportunities. To the very end Howe believed that the fault did not lie with him. But some contemporaries disagreed. In the papers of Sir Henry Clinton is the following anonymous and acid comment:

> Had Sir William fortified the hills around Boston he could not have been disgracefully driven from it; had he pursued his victory at Long Island he had ended the rebellion; had he landed above the lines at New York not a man could have escaped him; had he co- operated with the Northern Army he had saved it, or had he gone to Philadelphia by land he had ruined Mr. Washington and his forces; but, as he did none of these things, had he gone to the D . . . l before he was sent to America, it had been the saving of infamy to himself and indelible dishonour to his country.[62]

The inconclusiveness of Parliament's inquiry left Howe a haunted and an aggrieved man. His critics shared his feelings of dissatisfaction, and they kept up their pamphlet attacks upon him for more than a year. The most bitter and persistent of his adversaries was the loyalist refugee, Joseph Galloway, whose attacks stung Howe in 1780 into publishing a lengthy re- joinder.[63]

About this same time, Howe suffered a political setback when he lost the seat in Parliament he had occupied for more than twenty years. His Nottingham constituents were deeply divided by the American war. The noncomformist members of the corporation were strongly pro-American; their opponents were no less anxious to stamp out the rebellion. Howe's participation in the war cost him the support of both groups, and he was defeated in the general election of 1780.[64]

But Sir William's military career had not yet run its course. Although rejected by the electorate and unpopular with the Ministry, Howe still managed to retain the favor of George III. When North was replaced by Rockingham in 1782, Howe was made lieutenant general of ordinance. Had the Nootka Sound dispute with Spain in 1789 led to war, he would have commanded the so-called "Spanish armament." By the time war broke out with France in 1793, he was considered for active service abroad, but remained at home to command first the northern, and then the eastern, military districts of England. It was not until 1803 that he finally retired from the army. In 1799, on the death of his brother Richard, he became Viscount Howe. He had been appointed governor of Berwick-on-Tweed in 1795, and in 1805 he became governor of Plymouth, where he died nine years later at the age of eighty-five.

The crushing of the American rebellion was a task bristling with difficulty. But it was not an impossible one for a country with such a preponderance of military force as Great Britain possessed. How it could be achieved was to be demonstrated a century later when the British faced a similar problem in South Africa. Just as the Boers were first crushed and then persuaded to accept the continuance of British rule, so might a defeated America have been brought, at least for the time being, to abandon its aspirations to independence. But the first requirement was military victory and this a gifted soldier might have won. Contrary to what has often been asserted, the cards were not stacked against the British from the start; the trouble was that they were dealt to a general who was not qualified to play an admittedly difficult hand.

Sir William Howe's deficiencies as a general are obvious enough. His movements were incredibly slow and ponderous; his tactics were timorous, unimaginative, and predictable; and his strategy was based on no clear conception of how the war was to be won. His plans, accordingly, lacked not only inspiration but even coherence.

But Howe's failings, though easy enough to catalog, are difficult to account for. To some contemporaries, the explanation lay in his weaknesses of character. Charles Lee, who spent several months in Sir William's company in 1777 as a prisoner of war, subsequently painted this unflattering picture of his host.

> He is naturally good-humour'd, and complacent, but illiterate and indolent to the last degree, unless as an executive Soldier, in which capacity He is all fire and activity, brave and cool as Julius Caesar. His understanding is . . . rather good than otherwise, but was totally confounded and stupefy'd by the immensity of the task impos'd upon him. He shut his eyes, fought his battles, drank his bottle, had his little Whore, advised with his Counsellors, receiv'd his orders from North and Germain . . . took Galloway's advice, shut his eyes [and] fought again. . . .[65]

This portrait of Howe contains some element of truth. There can be no doubt that he had an easygoing, even a lethargic, disposition. But he was neither a fool nor a libertine. An experienced and competent soldier, he had no need to lean on others for advice; indeed, it might have been better for him if he had done so. Fond though he was of pleasure, he does not appear to have pursued it to the neglect of his duties.

But if Lee was wrong perhaps in suggesting that Howe's moral shortcomings were responsible for his lack of military success, he was surely right to depict him as a man of average abilities placed in a situation which called for something more. This assessment was confirmed by one of Howe's subordinate officers, Allen Maclean, who wrote in 1777:

It would not be unjust to say that General Howe is a very honest man, and I believe a very disinterested one. Brave he certainly is and would make a very good executive officer under another's command, but he is not by any means equal to C. in C. . . .[66]

To the embittered group of loyalist refugees who spent the war years in England and became some of Howe's sternest critics, the issue was not Sir William's alleged incompetence but his reluctance to exploit his victories. It seemed to them that after each of the major battles of 1776–77—Long Island, White Plains, Brandywine and Germantown—Howe could have destroyed the Continental army if he had wanted to.[67] Howe, in Galloway's words, "succeeded as far as he chose"; but because of Sir William's delusion that the empire might be saved by conciliation, he had chosen to prolong the war.

These unsubstantiated charges are almost certainly false. Sympathetic though Howe may have been to the rebels at the outset, his sense of duty as a soldier and his loyalty to the Crown would have precluded his showing them undue tenderness. One must accept his statement that he never permitted the hope of reconciliation to color his military thinking.

That Howe failed to strike relentlessly and unremittingly at Washington's army was a consequence of the philosophy of war he had imbibed during his military education. In the course of the inquiry in 1779, he summed up that philosophy in one tortuous but revealing sentence:

> As my opinion has always been, that the defeat of the rebel regular army is the surest road to peace, I invariably pursued the most probable means of forcing its Commander to action under circumstances the least hazardous to the royal army; for even a victory, attended by a heavy loss of men on our part, would have given a fatal check to the progress of the war, and might have proved irreparable.[68]

In short, Howe would seek a battle only when he could be sure that the engagement would leave his army virtually intact. This was because the army was, in Howe's own words, "the stock upon which the national force in America must in future be grafted." [69] Given such an attitude, the wonder is not that Howe so rarely took the initiative against Washington, but that he took it at all.

There is some reason, therefore, to doubt Howe's assertion that he always considered the Continental army to be his primary objective. Many of his strategic dispositions were directed, not toward bringing Washington to battle, but toward occupying territory. His strategic planning was based on the assumption that the civilian population could be cowed into submission by an overwhelming display of force.

This assumption was most clearly demonstrated in Howe's original plan for 1777—a plan he abandoned when the large reinforcements he required for its execution were not forthcoming. It called for 10,000 men to operate against Boston, and 10,000 more to move up the Hudson to facilitate Burgoyne's approach. Washington's army, meanwhile, was to be held in check by an additional force of 8,000 men which was to make feints against Philadelphia. In the fall there was to be an advance into Pennsylvania, followed by winter operations in Virginia, the Carolinas, and Georgia. These operations, Howe wrote in November, 1776, "would strike such terror through the country that little resistance would be made to the progress of His Majesty's arms." [70] The main function of the British army, as Howe conceived it, was to make a demonstration over a wide area in order to encourage the loyalists and to persuade the rebels of the futility of further resistance. Washington's army entered hardly at all into these calculations: it was simply to be prevented from interfering with the triumphant march of the British. [71]

There was nothing eccentric or sinister in such an approach. It was all of a piece with Howe's conventional military ideas. In proposing to march his soldiers through the length and breadth of the colonies in preference to attacking the Continental army, Howe was simply conforming to the widely held belief that campaigns were not necessarily won by fighting battles. "Battles," wrote one of his contemporaries, "have ever been the last resource of good Generals. . . . The fighting of a battle only because the enemy is near, or from having no other plan of offence, is a direful way of making war." [72] The proper method of proceeding was to maneuver for position, to occupy strategic points, to avoid engagements except when success was certain, and above all to preserve the army intact.

This method was appropriate enough for the limited wars of eighteenth-century Europe, but it was useless in the struggle for America. The Revolutionary War was not a war about territorial boundaries or dynastic rivalries; it was a war of ideology, and could be won by Britain only by a decisive victory on the battlefield. Even if Howe had come to recognize the need for this kind of warfare, he would have been inhibited by his professional training from practicing it as commander-in-chief. It was one thing for Howe as a young colonel to lead a daring exploit to the top of the Heights of Abraham; it was quite another for him as a middle-aged general to risk losing the only army his country could raise. Faced with a situation that demanded boldness, ruthlessness, and imagination, Howe could only take refuge in a military orthodoxy that was irrelevant to his needs.

FOOTNOTES

1. [Anon.], *A View of the Evidence relative to the Conduct of the American War. . .* , 2nd ed. (London, 1779), p. 127.
2. *Ibid.*, p. 86.
3. *Ibid.*, pp. 7, 138.
4. *Ibid.*, p. 129.
5. Worthington C. Ford, "Parliament and the Howes," Massachusetts Historical Society, *Proceedings*, XLIV (November, 1910), pp. 120–43.
6. *The Narrative of Lieut. Gen. Sir William Howe . . . relative to his Conduct . . . in North America*, 2nd ed. (London, 1780).
7. Charles Stedman, *The History of the origin, progress and termination of the American war* (London, 1794), I, p. 398.
8. John R. Alden, *The American Revolution, 1775–1783* (New York and London, 1954), p. 127.
9. Charles F. Adams, "Cavalry in the War of Independence," Massa-

chusetts Historical Society, *Proceedings,* XLIII (April–June, 1910), p. 580.

10. Bellamy Partridge has alleged—though without producing any evidence to substantiate the charge—that Howe's failure on several occasions to press home his advantage against the enemy was directly attributed to his friendly feelings toward the Americans and to his hopes for a reconciliation. See Partridge, *Sir Billy Howe* (London and New York, 1933), pp. 98–99, 101–03, 148–51, 168, 241–42.

11. The famous historian of the British army, Sir John W. Fortescue, who was always ready to blame politicians rather than generals, exculpated Howe on these grounds. See John W. Fortescue, *A History of the British Army,* 13 vols. (London, 1899–1930), III, pp. 174–75, 204, 208, 397–98.

12. Howe's most persuasive modern advocate has been Troyer S. Anderson. In *The Command of the Howe Brothers during the American Revolution* (New York and London, 1936), Anderson noted that Howe had to act as military commander and as peacemaker simultaneously; that he was beset by immense logistical problems because all supplies had to be sent from England; that he had to conduct operations over vast distances; and that he found fewer loyalists prepared to make personal sacrifices for George III than ministers in England believed. According to Anderson, Howe's caution and avoidance of risks were due to the precariousness of his position. Because British losses could not speedily be replaced, Howe felt bound to conduct operations with prudence in order to minimize the chances of a serious defeat.

13. This argument was, in effect, that of Fox, Burke, and Chatham, who believed from the first that the colonies could not be recovered by force. The same thesis appears in the works of Whig historians, notably in George O. Trevelyan's *History of the American Revolution,* 2 vols. (London, 1899–1903).

14. Lewis B. Namier, *The Structure of Politics at the Accession of George III* (London, 1929), pp. 32–33.

15. Quoted in *ibid.,* p. 31.

16. Anderson, *op. cit.,* p. 48.

17. *Ibid.,* p. 49.

18. *Ibid.,* p. 50.

19. Skene to North, January 23, 1775, Historical Manuscripts Commission, *Dartmouth MSS.,* II, p. 262.

20. Germain to Suffolk, June 16 or 17, 1775, Historical Manuscripts Commission, *Stopford-Sackville MSS.,* II, p. 2.

21. John W. Fortescue, ed., *Correspondence of King George III*, 6 vols. (London, 1927–28), III, pp. 220–24.
22. Alden, *The American Revolution*, pp. 38–39. For a detailed account of the battle, see Allen French, *The First Year of the American Revolution*, (Boston, 1934), pp. 211–67.
23. Sydney G. Fisher, *The Struggle for American Independence*, 2 vols. (Philadelphia and London, 1908), I, pp. 337–39.
24. *Detail and Conduct of the American War*, p. 13, quoted in Henry S. Commager and Richard B. Morris, eds., *The Spirit of 'Seventy-Six* (Indianapolis and New York, 1958), I, p. 135.
25. Fortescue, *Correspondence of King George III*, III, p. 220–24.
26. Anderson, *op. cit.*, pp. 108 ff.
27. *Ibid.*, pp. 88–90, 97.
28. John C. Miller, *The Triumph of Freedom, 1775–1783* (Boston, 1948), pp. 80–84.
29. Washington to the President of Congress, November 28, 1775, John C. Fitzpatrick, ed., *The Writings of George Washington* (Washington, D.C., 1931–1944), IV, p. 122.
30. Washington to Joseph Reed, January 4, 1776, *ibid.*, IV, p. 211.
31. Howe to Dartmouth, January 16, 1776, C.O. 5/94, pp. 65–74, quoted in Anderson, *op. cit.*, p. 117.
32. Howe to Germain, April 25, 1776, C.O. 5/93, pp. 277–84, quoted in Anderson, *op. cit.*, p. 121.
33. Howe, *Narrative*, p. 4.
34. *Ibid.*, pp. 47–48.
35. Eric Robson, *The American Revolution, 1763–1783* (London, 1955), p. 140. Howe later admitted that he had had a free hand, and made no complaint of interference from London. See Howe, *Narrative*, p. 46.
36. Fisher, *op. cit.*, I, pp. 484, 490–91.
37. Howe, *Narrative*, p. 4.
38. Quoted in Miller, *op. cit.*, p. 125 fn.
39. *Ibid.*
40. *Ibid.*, p. 124.
41. Quoted in *ibid.*, p. 124.
42. Howe, *Narrative*, pp. 4–5.
43. *Ibid.*, p. 5.
44. Eric Robson, "The Armed Forces and the Art of War," in J. O. Lindsay, ed., *The New Cambridge Modern History*, VII, pp. 163 ff.
45. William B. Willcox, *Portrait of a General: Sir Henry Clinton in the War of Independence* (New York, 1964), pp. 494–96.
46. Quoted in Fisher, *op. cit.*, I, p. 522.

47. Howe, *Narrative*, p. 6.
48. Fisher, *op. cit.*, I, pp. 524–25.
49. Howe, *Narrative*, pp. 6–7.
50. William B. Willcox, ed., *The American Rebellion: Sir Henry Clinton's Narrative of his Campaigns, 1775–1782* (New Haven, 1954), pp. xxiii, 55.
51. Circular to the States, October 18, 1780, Fitzpatrick, *Writings of Washington*, XX, p. 206.
52. Fisher, *op. cit.*, I, pp. 537–38.
53. Howe, *Narrative*, pp. 7–9.
54. Willcox, *Portrait of a General*, pp. 143 ff; Anderson, *op. cit.*, pp. 213 ff; Piers Mackesy, *The War for America, 1775–1783* (London and Cambridge, Mass., 1964), pp. 117–18.
55. Anderson, *op. cit.*, pp. 214–22; Howe, *Narrative*, pp. 9–13.
56. Howe, *Narrative*, pp. 16–21.
57. Charles Francis Adams, Jr., "The Campaign of 1777," in Massachusetts Historical Society, *Proceedings*, XLIV (October, 1910), p. 30.
58. Howe, *Narrative*, p. 16.
59. Fisher, *op. cit.*, II, pp. 11–13.
60. *The Gentleman's Magazine*, XLVIII (August, 1778), p. 368, quoted in Martin Kallich and Andrew MacLeish, *The American Revolution Through British Eyes* (Evanston, Illinois, and New York, 1962), p. 113.
61. *Annual Register for 1778*, pp. 267–70, quoted in Commager and Morris, *op. cit.*, I, pp. 657–60.
62. Quoted in Alan Valentine, *Lord George Germain* (Oxford, 1962), pp. 259–60.
63. Worthington C. Ford, "Parliament and the Howes," Massachusetts Historical Society, *Proceedings*, XLIV (November, 1910), pp. 120–43.
64. Ian Christie, *The End of North's Ministry* (London, 1958), p. 145.
65. Lee to Benjamin Rush, June 4, 1778, *Lee Papers, Collections of the New York Historical Society for the Year 1872*, p. 398.
66. Allen Maclean to Alexander Cummings, February 19, 1777, quoted in E. Stuart Wortley, *A Prime Minister and his Son* (London, 1925), pp. 105–06.
67. William H. Nelson, *The American Tory* (Oxford, 1961), pp. 134 ff.
68. Howe, *Narrative*, p. 19.
69. Quoted in Robson, *op. cit.*, p. 109.

70. Howe to Germain, November 30, 1776, C.O. 5/93, quoted in Anderson, *op. cit.*, pp. 214–15.
71. Anderson, *op. cit.*, p. 215.
72. Major Thomas Bell, *A Short Essay on Military First Principles* (London, 1770), quoted in Robson, *The American Revolution, 1763–1783*, p. 99.

BIBLIOGRAPHY

Alden, John R. *The American Revolution, 1775–1783*. New York, 1954. Concludes that Howe lacked ability and being unimaginative merely followed traditional British military practices and procedures.

Anderson, Troyer S. *Command of the Howe Brothers during the American Revolution*. New York, 1936. The most recent reliable study of the Howe brothers, and concentrating more on the general than the admiral. Anderson is sympathetic to General Howe, claiming that his dilemma arose from the fact that he had to function as a military commander and as peacemaker at one and the same time.

Brown, Gerald S. *The American Secretary: The Colonial Policy of Lord George Germain, 1775–1778*. Ann Arbor, 1963. Casts new light on the relationship between General Howe and Lord Germain. The book dismisses the idea of a "pigeon holed dispatch" which Germain reputedly failed to send that would have ordered Howe to lead his army up the Hudson.

Fisher, Sydney G. *The Struggle for American Independence*. 2 vols. Philadelphia and London, 1908. A diatribe against Howe, suggesting that the Whig general may have wished to deprive the Ministry and Burgoyne of a victory at Saratoga.

Ford, Worthington C. "Parliament and the Howes," Massachusetts Historical Society, *Proceedings*, XLIV (October, 1910), pp. 120–143. Serves as the best guide to the materials in the confrontation between General Howe and Parliamentary leaders.

Fortescue, Hon. John W. *A History of the British Army*. 13 vols. in 20. London, 1899–1930. Tends to excuse General Howe and to place the blame for Britain's defeat on the Parliamentary leaders.

Howe, Sir William. *The Narrative of Lt. Gen. Sir William Howe in a Committee of the House of Commons on 29th April 1779, Relative to His Conduct During His Late Command of the King's Troops in North America, to Which Are Added Some Observations upon a Pamphlet Entitled Letters to a Nobleman*. London, 1780. This is Howe's own defense of his conduct.

Partridge, Bellamy. *Sir Billy Howe.* London, 1932. A popularized biography that is often unreliable and undocumented.

Mackesy, Piers. *The War for America, 1775–1783.* Cambridge, Mass., 1964. Tends to be very critical of Howe's generalship.

Robson, Eric. *The American Revolution, 1763–1783.* London, 1955. A perceptive evaluation of General Howe, showing that he adapted well to American conditions in his use of tactics but often showed a lack of imagination.

Willcox, William B. *Portrait of a General: Sir Henry Clinton in the War of Independence.* New York, 1964. Demonstrates that Howe was often unwilling to accept sound suggestions on strategy from his subordinate, General Clinton.

Sir Henry Clinton:

PARALYSIS OF COMMAND

———•-•-•———

University of Michigan

SIR HENRY CLINTON stands out in a number of ways from his military and naval colleagues in the War of Independence. He served longer than any of them, for two and a half years as second in command to Howe and for four years as commander-in-chief; between 1775 and 1782 his tour of duty was interrupted only once, by a two-month leave in England. He alone, among the officers of high rank, wrote a full account of his campaigns; he spent years in compiling it, and it was virtually ready for the publisher by the time he died in 1795. He also left behind him an enormous mass of official and private papers, in which he reveals himself more fully in his own words than almost any other general of the eighteenth century.[1] He was not a winning person; his friends were few and his enemies legion. Neither was he a great general. He was a better one than most of his critics averred, and would have been better still if his talents had had free scope; but he was the victim of both external circumstances and his own inner uncertainties. He did not fail sensationally, like Burgoyne and Cornwallis, or put his hand on victory and let it slip through his fingers, like Howe in 1776. His failure was slower and more subtle, and punctuated by successes; but in the end it was just as important in determining the outcome of the war.

Clinton was an aristocrat by birth and a New Yorker by up-bringing. He was the first cousin, protégé, and for a time the heir presumptive of the second Duke of Newcastle-under-Lyme, who came as near to being a political nonentity as a duke could in an age when title and influence went hand in hand. Clinton's father and the duke's uncle was Admiral George Clinton, the governor of New York during King George's War. The admiral was a fussy and ineffectual man, who received his governorship largely because he was incompetent to command a fleet; he had, however, like most of his aristocratic contemporaries, great skill in finding and pulling every string that might lead to a lucrative plum. Young Henry stayed with his father in America, mostly on Manhattan, until 1749, when at the age of nineteen he left for England. His connections there brought him promotion in the army; and during the Seven Years' War he was sent to Germany, became an aide-de-camp to Prince Charles of Bruns-wick, and made a name for himself by his gallantry in action. When he was ordered to Boston to strengthen the hand of Gen-eral Gage in 1775, in company with William Howe and Bur-goyne, Clinton was a middle-aged major general of forty-five, who had never had a command and had not seen active service for many years.

On the voyage to Massachusetts he was thrown (literally as well as figuratively, for the weather was rough) with Howe and Burgoyne, and their acquaintance slowly ripened. They were an interesting trio, destined to be closely linked for the next two years but far apart in character and background. Burgoyne was eight years older than Clinton, Howe one year; their seniority in the army, however, was determined by the dates of their pro-motions, and here the order was Howe first, then Clinton, then Burgoyne. Clinton differed markedly from both his shipmates. He lacked their self-assurance and the ease of manner that at-tracted friends; for he was, as he said of himself at the time, "a shy bitch." He did not have their natural gift for command and was never, as they were, popular with the army. But he had compensating advantages. His mind was keen and worked smoothly, with none of Howe's intellectual torpor; and his judgment was not warped, like Burgoyne's, by a gambler's recklessness. As a planner he was superior to them both. If generalship had involved no more than planning, he would have been the outstanding member of what Gentleman Johnny, with his taste for the orotund phrase, called their "triumvirate of reputation."

The professional backgrounds of the three during the Seven Years' War were as diverse as their personalities. Howe's principal service had been in America under Wolfe. Burgoyne, whose military career had been delayed by a runaway marriage, had redeemed himself late in the war by a distinguished record against the Spaniards in Portugal. Only Clinton, of the three, had served in the German campaigns; and the veterans of that hard school tended to look down upon officers who had had their military education anywhere else. Clinton rarely mentioned his training, but colleagues who did not share it either sensed in him or imputed to him a superiority that annoyed them. Although he would never have been popular at headquarters in any case, because he lacked the gift of popularity, it seems to have been this antipathy to the German school that at critical moments tipped the scales against him.

The three generals, when they landed at Boston in May, found everything at sixes and sevens. Lexington and Concord had brought on an investment of the city, and the garrison was in a state of nerves bordering on panic; "the rebels are seen in the air carrying cannon and mortars on their shoulders." If General Gage had been going to start a war, Clinton complained, he should have started it by striking a first blow, at Concord, that was sudden and severe. "Alas, it was the last—but to us!" [2] The three newcomers agreed that the British position had to be enlarged; and Clinton was particularly active in reconnoitering the enemy defenses, forming ideas for attack, and then pushing them at Gage. But, before any plan could be acted upon, the Americans suddenly occupied and fortified Charlestown Neck;

and the attempt to dislodge them brought on the battle of Bunker Hill.

The problem that faced Gage was simple. The Americans on the neck, which communicated with the mainland by a narrow isthmus, could readily be attacked from the bay; if they were thus taken in the rear, their fortifications would be useless and their retreat would be cut off. Clinton proposed that the main army should attack their front, while he landed with a detachment near the isthmus. The importance of his landing might have seemed self-evident; it would have unhinged the whole enemy position. But the commander-in-chief ignored him. "Mr. Gage," he commented later, ". . . would not take any opinion of others, particularly of a man bred up in the German school, which that of America affects to despise." [3] Howe consequently led the direct frontal assault, unsupported on the isthmus, and lost almost half his force in casualties.

This was Clinton's initiation to his role as a subordinate, and it was a foretaste of much that was to come. He had presented an eminently sensible idea, which promised to secure possession of the neck at minimum cost *and*, in the process, to surround and destroy the enemy; this would have been the kind of blow that Gage had failed to strike at Concord. Clinton may have been tactless in approaching his chief, although on that point there is no direct evidence. In any case his plan was turned down out of hand, and for an alternative that was patently inferior on its merits and that proved to be disastrous in its result. The episode is puzzling.

The next phase of Clinton's career was significant for the future in a different way. In the autumn he became second to Howe, who took the command on Gage's recall; and in the following January the new commander-in-chief detached him on an expedition to the southern colonies. The government planned to send a large reinforcement from Britain to meet the expedition in early spring at the Cape Fear River, in North Carolina, to raise the loyalists of the south and permit them to reestablish royal authority; command would be shared by Clinton and the naval commandant of the reinforcements, Sir Peter Parker. In March, Clinton reached the Cape Fear, where he waited idly for two months while his small force almost starved. In early May, Parker arrived at last, and after considerable discussion he and Clinton decided to attack Sullivan's Island, which guarded the entrance to the port of Charleston. The general landed his troops on an island adjacent to Sullivan's, thinking that they could wade to it across a small inlet—which turned out to be seven feet deep. The army was helpless to co-operate with the navy. Parker eventually went ahead on his own, bombarded the fort on Sullivan's, and was ignominiously repulsed. The two commanders thereupon threw in the sponge and sailed for the north.

This fiasco reveals Clinton at his rock-bottom worst. He had no valid reason for attacking Sullivan's in the first place, because he could never have held it if he had captured it. His landing, based on no reconnaissance worth the name, brought his troops to the wrong island and turned them into mere spectators. This was bad enough; what was worse, in its implications for the years ahead, was that he made no real effort to collaborate with Parker. The two services went their separate ways, and for months afterward the two chiefs quarreled about what had happened. They might have agreed to share the blame and keep quiet; instead each tried to fix responsibility on the other, and Clinton was far the more pertinacious of the two. In the process of wrangling he acquired an ineradicable sense of grievance. It spilled over onto the new secretary of state for the American colonies, Lord George Germain, who he believed was supporting Parker against the army; and the principal purpose of Clinton's returning to England in the following year was to secure redress from the minister.

But a great deal happened between grievance and redress. At the end of July, 1776, the battered expedition from South Carolina joined General Howe and his brother, Lord Howe, for the opening of the New York campaign; and Clinton resumed his former position of second in command. He also resumed his habit of offering advice, with which he bombarded his chief throughout the campaign. Only one of his suggestions was accepted, the design for the battle of Long Island. Headquarters grumbled and sniffed at this plan "as savoring too much of the German school," but finally, reluctantly, decided to try it.[4] Clinton used his favorite maneuver, envelopment, by leading the main attack in a wide circuit around the Americans' left wing, so that he was behind their center before the real fighting began. The result was the most brilliant tactical triumph that the British scored in the field during the war.

Triumph might have been expected to give weight to Clinton's future suggestions, but it did nothing of the sort. In the rest of the campaign he argued over and over again for using other forms of envelopment to destroy Washington's army—enveloping Manhattan while the Americans were still on it, by way of the Hudson or the East River to the Harlem; enveloping their army later as it retreated across New Jersey, either by seizing Philadelphia in its rear or attacking its flank from the Jersey coast. All these plans were turned down. Instead Howe, in slow and stately fashion, maneuvered the enemy out of Manhattan to White Plains, out of White Plains to the New Jersey side of the Hudson, out of New Jersey into Pennsylvania; and there the campaign ended. It had produced great but not decisive gains. Washington's army was still in existence and, as he soon proved, capable of striking back.

Clinton and his chief had contrasting views of what the operations around New York ought to achieve, and the contrast reveals their different styles of generalship. Howe's focus was territory, Manhattan and its environs; and he used military means to clear the enemy out of that area at the smallest possible cost to himself in killed and wounded. This was a policy of minimum risk, which by precluding the chance of heavy losses precluded the hope of a quick decision. Clinton's focus was the enemy army. He wanted to encompass its destruction, not merely drive it back; and for that purpose he wanted to exploit to the full the mobility that the British derived from controlling

Photograph of painting. Courtesy of William L. Clements Library, University of Michigan.

THOMAS GAGE

From an engraving by Rogers.
Courtesy of William L. Clements Library, University of Michigan.

SIR WILLIAM HOWE

Engraving by Ritchie.
Courtesy of William L. Clements Library, University of Michigan.

SIR HENRY CLINTON

SIR GUY CARLETON

JOHN BURGOYNE

Photograph of painting.
Courtesy of National Portrait Gallery, London.

CHARLES LORD CORNWALLIS

From the painting by John Singleton Copley.
Courtesy of National Maritime Museum, Greenwich, England.

RICHARD LORD HOWE

By Bartolozzi after Northcote. Courtesy of National Maritime Museum, Greenwich, England.

THOMAS GRAVES

By Hodges after Rising. Courtesy of National Maritime Museum, Greenwich, England.

MARRIOT ARBUTHNOT

Painting by Northcote. Courtesy of National Maritime Museum, Greenwich, England.

SIR SAMUEL HOOD

Painting by Mosiner. Courtesy of National Maritime Museum, Greenwich, England.

SIR GEORGE RODNEY

the water. All his plans for envelopment, except the one that was adopted on Long Island, involved the fleet; and the amphibious operations that he proposed may have been as unwelcome to Lord Howe as to his brother.[5] In any case they were never tried. Washington extricated himself from the trap into which he had blundered, and at the turn of the year the battles of Trenton and Princeton showed how far his army was from being defeated.

By then Clinton was far away. In the late autumn of 1776 he had occupied Rhode Island, which Lord Howe wanted as a naval base and his brother, now Sir William, was determined to give him; and in the following January Clinton secured permission to go home on leave. He hoped to stay there. He was still nursing his grievance against Germain over Sullivan's Island, and the recent campaign had confirmed his resolve never again to serve under Howe. A knighthood, however, solaced the grievance and weakened the resolve. Clinton was also given to understand that he might have command of the invasion from Canada that Burgoyne had mapped out and that was then in preparation; but this suggestion, much as it appealed to him, he turned down out of deference to Burgoyne. Germain promised to support, the king refused to let Clinton resign, and his friends persuaded him that all might yet be well. In early May, 1777, the newly dubbed and still reluctant Sir Henry sailed from Plymouth to resume his post.

He arrived in July, to find that Howe was about to take his army by sea against Philadelphia, so that the commander-in-chief could be of no help to the invasion from the north, and that Clinton was to be left as garrison commander at New York. Sir Henry was appalled. In his opinion the southern move would imperil Manhattan, Burgoyne's Canadian army, and the whole war effort. The New York garrison would be condemned to what Clinton called "a damned starved defensive"; and Howe's approaching Philadelphia from the south, by way of the Delaware or Chesapeake, would permit Washington to abandon Pennsylvania and bring the whole weight of his army against Manhattan. Burgoyne's troops, once they reached the upper Hudson and lost their supply lines to Canada, would have to depend on river communication with New York, which could not be secured unless Howe's entire force were on hand to break through the barrier of forts that the Americans had erected in the Highlands near West Point. The move to Pennsylvania would jeopardize the war effort by making a quick, decisive victory impossible. Philadelphia was not important enough for the Americans so that Washington would be forced to fight for it; this was one of the few points on which Clinton and Howe agreed. Once the British occupied the city, furthermore, most of their army would be pinned down in garrison duty, and could not return to win the war on the Hudson. The only way to win, Sir Henry argued, was to move northward from New York at once and in full force. If Howe and Burgoyne cooperated in the neighborhood of the Highlands, they might draw the Americans into battle and destroy them, or cut off New England from the middle colonies. In either way the rebellion might be crushed before winter set in.

The logic of this argument was unanswerable, and Howe made no real attempt to answer it. For weeks the two generals talked at cross purposes, until at last they decided that "by some cursed fatality we could never draw together." [6] The trouble, however, was not in their stars but in their characters. Under his genial surface Howe was as stubborn as a mule (*entêté*, Gage had called him); in a less genial way so was Clinton. Almost from the start of their service together Sir William had been exposed to an unrelenting flow of advice from his junior. It had sometimes in the past turned out to be sounder than his own opinion, and he seems to have wondered at moments whether it could be in this case. But he could scarcely derogate from his position by saying so. He was too deeply committed to Pennsylvania to let himself be overruled by a subordinate, no matter how good the logic. The government had approved his plan, he said; he could not change it now even if he would. On July 23 he sailed for the south.

By the end of the summer Burgoyne was clearly in trouble.

Although Clinton did not know where Washington's troops were (Howe had not bothered to tell him that they had been committed to the defense of Philadelphia), he decided that the crisis in the north justified some risk to Manhattan; and in early October he moved against the Highlands. It was the nearest approach to a gamble that he ever made, and his reasons for making it were cogent. He had no hope of opening the Hudson and keeping it open with his small force; his aims were less ambitious and more realistic—to take pressure off Burgoyne and to demonstrate to Howe that the barrier could be broken. Sir Henry carried out the attack in masterly fashion, and within three days had captured the two key forts and possessed the Highlands. At that moment came word from Burgoyne that he was in desperate straits, and Clinton responded at once by detaching half his force up river on an equally desperate attempt at rescue. On the day that his ships reached their farthest point, some forty-five miles below Albany, Burgoyne surrendered. Sir Henry had done what he could by speed and skill, and in the process had won a neat little victory. But its fruits, like the larger fruits of Howe's Pennsylvania campaign, were lost at Saratoga.

That blow shattered the government's plans for winning the war, and forced a drastic review of strategy. As autumn wore on into winter in London, the news from Paris grew more and more ominous; and it was clear to the Ministry that Britain, if France intervened, could not go on fighting as she had. It was much less clear to Howe in Philadelphia. All he proposed was opening an offensive in the south, for which he would need ten thousand more troops, or sitting still for a year to see what happened—suggestions that were scarcely calculated to galvanize an apprehensive government. After prolonged debate the cabinet decided that Sir William must go, and then tackled the question of who should succeed him. Lord Amherst declined. Sir Guy Carleton detested Germain and vice versa; they could not serve together, and jettisoning the minister was too high a price to pay for finding a commander-in-chief. Someone, in a moment of madness, suggested Prince Ferdinand of Brunswick, Frederick the Great's chief lieutenant in the Seven Years' War. The list of those who deserved sober consideration, however, was extremely small; and Clinton was at the head of it. Lord North distrusted him, because of his constant complaints and attempts to resign; but the administration had no feasible alternative. On February 4, *faute de mieux*, Sir Henry was appointed.

The circumstances of his receiving the command influenced his tenure of it. He had no firm backing in the political world of London. Newcastle, his only patron, was singularly ineffective; Sir Henry's friends in the House of Commons were few and far between, and such support as he had from leaders of the Opposition was for their purposes rather than his. The king kept sending him kind messages, but did not have the partiality for him that he had shown earlier for Burgoyne and showed later for Cornwallis. The prime minister looked on him askance. Lord Sandwich, as spokesman for the navy, was cool toward a man as talented as Clinton in quarreling with naval officers; and Germain, after the Sullivan's Island affair, could not be expected to be his wholehearted champion. Sir Henry's position in America was no stronger than at home. He lacked Burgoyne's and Corwallis' magnetism, and the geniality that made Howe popular. Perhaps inevitably, after his long dissension with Sir William, Clinton had disparaging critics even among his own entourage; and his capacity for feuding increased their numbers. Within a year of taking the command he was aware that "I am hated—nay, detested—in this army." [7]

Success was his only way to gain support from the government and the army, but here two major factors militated against him. One was the gulf that developed between Britain's military ambition and her attenuated resources for waging war in America. She refused to do what Adam Smith, in concluding *The Wealth of Nations* in 1776, had warned that she might have to do, "accommodate her views and designs to the real mediocrity of her circumstances"; instead she reached for conquests that were beyond her grasp. The other factor was Clinton's inability to cooperate with the colleagues to whom he was yoked. The pattern of conduct that he had first revealed on Sullivan's Island became more pronounced as his responsibilities increased, until in the last year and a half of campaigning his friction with the two men on whom he chiefly depended for success brought about a slow but inexorable paralysis of command.

Sir Henry was promoted at a moment when the government was ready, if need be, to surrender the whole area of rebellion. His instructions in March, 1778, ordered him to evacuate Philadelphia and authorized him, in an emergency, to abandon New York and Rhode Island as well and fall back on Halifax, Nova Scotia. Simultaneously the Carlisle Peace Commission was sent to offer the colonies the substance of independence without the name, and to keep open the possibility that even the name might be formally recognized.[8] Whitehall, in short, was ready to conclude the American war on almost any terms it could get, including military withdrawal and political capitulation on every point worth fighting for.

The reason for this retreat is obvious. French intervention shifted the focus of the struggle from the American theater to the West Indies, which for Britain had far more economic importance than the mainland. The only hope of success in the West Indies lay in withdrawing troops from Clinton, because no other forces were available; he would therefore have to retrench if he did not evacuate. Retrenchment, furthermore, was required by the altered naval situation. French sea power, once it was thrown into the scales, jeopardized British supply lines to America and lateral communications along the coast. To mitigate the danger from this new quarter Sir Henry's army, spread out from the Delaware to Narragansett Bay, had to be consolidated. He was consequently ordered to begin his command by abandoning Pennsylvania, and simultaneously to detach roughly one-third of his troops to the Caribbean; and for the next four years he never was given more than driblets of reinforcements.[9] He complained that he was being willfully neglected, which was a half-truth. The neglect was not willful, but it was only too real.

He was forced to pull in his horns at just the moment when the Americans were extending theirs. The French alliance was an enormous stimulus to their self-confidence—a much greater one, in fact, than was justified by anything that France did for them until the summer of Yorktown. They had other reasons for believing in themselves. They had survived the loss of New York, Newport, and Philadelphia; their cause had proved to have no geographical center without which they could not exist. Their militia had stood up to the redcoats and Germans in the wilderness around Saratoga, where for the first time European regulars had blundered their way to disaster. Washington had learned to be a general since the dark days of 1776, and his prestige had grown accordingly; during the recent winter at Valley Forge, furthermore, he had fashioned an army that was more effective than anything Howe had met, as Clinton soon discovered at Monmouth Court House. Thus Sir Henry had a depleted force with which to meet opponents who were stronger than before, and the Royal Navy could no longer guarantee his communications and supplies.

The British government under these circumstances might have been expected to follow a consistently defensive policy in America. But it did not. Once Clinton and Lord Howe had succeeded, by the skin of their teeth, in holding out against d'Estaing in the campaign of 1778, Whitehall began to recover from the shock of French intervention and to forget how narrowly defeat had been averted. The mood in official circles became more cheerful, and Germain reverted to the old idea of a move against South Carolina. His reason was an unconquerable hope that somewhere, if only the British could find them, were thousands upon thousands of loyalists ready to rise en masse as soon as the king's troops appeared, and to take over their own defense while the regulars passed on to new conquests. If the hope were well founded, even Clinton's small army could produce great results. The experiment had already been made in Rhode Island, on the upper Hudson, around New York, in New Jersey and Pennsylvania; everywhere it had failed. But the minister was an incorrigible optimist, whose power of wishful thinking drew strength from any one—hopeful exiles in London, colonial governors—who told him what he wanted to hear. He urged Clinton on to the south. In the autumn of 1779, Sir Henry fell in with the idea. His detachments had already safeguarded Florida and secured Georgia; he had just failed, in the summer of 1779, to achieve anything decisive in the north against Washington, and may have been eager for new fields to conquer. On the day after Christmas he and Admiral Arbuthnot, his new naval colleague, sailed for South Carolina.

In the spring of 1780, Clinton invested Charleston, using just the kind of envelopment that he had urged upon Howe at New York, and captured the city and the American army of over 5,000 men that defended it. This was the most resounding British victory of the war. It was also the most dangerous. Sir Henry now had two bases, New York and Charleston, that depended upon Britain for their supplies and were in communication with each other across hundreds of miles of water. He had committed himself to dispersing his exiguous forces along the seaboard, and soon had to disperse them even further by establishing a post on the Chesapeake. Command of the sea was more vital than ever, and he quickly discovered that it was more precarious than ever; for a French fleet and army established a base on the New England coast. His whole position was endangered, but by then he could not turn back from the road on which he had started.

Why Clinton started on it, apparently with little thought for the risks that might be involved, is hard to understand. No one in the army recognized more clearly than he did the overriding importance of sea power, or was more realistic about its effects upon land operations. He knew that the navy gave British troops their mobility, what Washington called their "canvas wings." Sir Henry also knew that their mobility on land was limited because they were tethered to the coast, from which alone they could be supplied. Their existence depended on naval predominance, and in full knowledge of this fact the commander-in-chief moved to South Carolina.

If he did not weigh at the start the risks he was running, he soon became aware of them. His awareness is revealed not only in his reiterated pleas to the government, from the fall of Charleston to the eve of Yorktown, for an adequate supporting fleet, but also in his idea of the way in which the southern campaign would develop. When he returned to New York in June, 1780, and left that campaign to Earl Cornwallis, his second in command, Clinton expected the earl to extend his conquests methodically northward, keeping in touch with the sea, holding onto gains already made, and above all never endangering the safety of his base at Charleston. Sir Henry meanwhile would detach troops from New York to establish a post on the Chesapeake, partly to assist the earl's operations to the southward, partly to provide a base for the navy, and partly to furnish the loyalists of the area with a secure refuge. Once North Carolina was firmly in Cornwallis' hands and he was able to send part of his troops to Virginia, Clinton hoped to cooperate with him in a two-pronged attack on Pennsylvania, from the upper Chesapeake and from New York. This was the design for a war of attrition, and it had much to be said for it.

One of its major virtues was that it would utilize the loyalists in the only way that Sir Henry considered feasible. Cornwallis, to judge by his subsequent conduct, shared Germain's illusion that loyalists with any initiative could stand by themselves without support from the regulars. Clinton disagreed. Throughout the war he frequently expressed his conviction that the loyalists could be expected to lend their assistance only when they were assured of lasting protection. Once they were led to declare themselves by the appearance of British troops, those troops had to remain. Too often the military had departed, leaving the civilians to their fate and thereby discouraging others from following their example. Such a betrayal, to Clinton's mind, was stupid as well as immoral, because it cut off the roots of loyalist support. If, on the other hand, the friends of Britain felt themselves secure, they would in time be extremely useful, as militia for home defense and for guarding supply lines; and the regulars would then be released to continue their advance. But the process could not be hurried and, once begun, should never be reversed.

Clinton's plan for the south was designed to do two things: to give the loyalists the maximum chance to show what they could do, and to make the maximum use of the regulars at his command. If reinforcements came from England—always a large *if*—they would help to accelerate the advance, but it would not depend upon them. Extending conquest northward through the Carolina lowlands would keep the army in touch with the sea, so that the navy could safeguard supplies and, if worst came to worst, could evacuate the troops. This strategy was unlikely to yield quick or dramatic results. But it might yield significant ones, always provided that Cornwallis would collaborate and that Whitehall would be patient.

At this stage of the war Clinton was a gradualist. Although he never entirely lost hope of drawing the enemy into one final, decisive battle, he did not put much stock in the possibility; the days when he had been intent on a bold envelopment, a blow at the heart, were over. Part of the reason was in him: he became more cautious as soon as he had sole responsibility. Another part of the reason was in his circumstances: he did not have the means to strike at the enemy's heart. His only chance was to build up his position cumulatively, step by step, until it became so strong that the Americans either lost the will to continue the conflict, or grew desperate enough to fight him on terms of his own choosing.

Before the British had more than begun this gradual build-up in the south, however, they were confronted by a situation in the north that required a quite different strategy. A substantial French armament suddenly materialized, in the form of a fleet under the Chevalier de Ternay and an army under the Comte de Rochambeau; this force was bound for Rhode Island, from which the British garrison had been withdrawn in the previous year. When the enemy landed there in July, 1780, they posed a threat that could not be countered by slow and systematic advance, but only by fast action. The crisis demanded an energy and resolution that Clinton no longer possessed. He had once known how to cope with a sudden demand on him, as in the Highlands in 1777; and before that he had often urged on Gage and Howe the daring course that his intelligence told him was the right one. Now, when his intelligence told him the same thing, he did not respond.

Why he did not is a matter of speculation. He was coming to distrust his naval colleague, Admiral Arbuthnot; but that in itself is an inadequate explanation. Sir Henry could have done far more than he did—could have gone to the fleet that was cruising off Rhode Island, could have observed the enemy position for himself, could have tried to persuade his colleague to take some kind of action. Instead he allowed the precious weeks to pass in letter-writing, as if his will to act had drained away. He became a spectator, as he had during his first independent command four years before in South Carolina. "This business . . . does not crush me," he had written then, "but [is] rather too much merely to steady me." [10] In the summer of 1780 he again was not crushed, but neither was he steady enough to push through to his objective.

When he and Arbuthnot failed to dislodge the French that summer, they imperiled British operations in the south. De Ternay's squadron, which was thenceforth blockaded in Narragansett Bay, might at any time break through the blockade, disrupt communications, and even join the Americans to attack and destroy a British army that depended on the sea. The threat of such an attack increased as Cornwallis moved northward, within closer range of Rhode Island and of Washington's forces. The situation, therefore, required the British army and navy to work hand in glove with each other; yet by the end of the summer of 1780 cooperation between them was out of the question. Clinton detested Arbuthnot too much to have any dealings with him, and could never predict what his colleague would do on his own. Either the admiral must be removed, Sir Henry told the government, or he himself would resign.

The situation also required the two army chiefs to work in

close harmony, and whether they could do so remained to be seen. During the siege of Charleston, Clinton had come to distrust Cornwallis, who held a dormant commission to succeed him and was quite ready to do so. For a time during the siege the earl, supposing that Whitehall would grant one of his chief's periodic demands to resign, had behaved almost as if the command were already his. Sir Henry was profoundly ambivalent about wanting to be recalled, but not at all so about Cornwallis' eagerness to fill his shoes, or about the army's patent delight at the prospect. The earl's conduct was intolerable to his chief, who concluded that the man was a Machiavellian schemer. Sir Henry, when he was forced to return to New York and leave his subordinate to an autonomous command in the south, carried with him distrust and suspicion; and absence did not make his heart grow fonder.

The two men had more than personal reasons for friction; they were poles apart in their views of the war. Cornwallis either never understood or chose to ignore his chief's ideas, and Clinton took less pains than he should have to make them clear. The earl was a man of action. He wanted victories, not a slow, methodical advance up the coast; and he was convinced that the only way to solidify his hold on South Carolina was to destroy the American forces between him and the Chesapeake. He was so intent upon the enemy that he paid scant attention to the other two factors in his situation, of which Clinton was intensely aware— the need to bring out the loyalists and the need to keep in touch with the navy. These two factors were interrelated: an army out of communication with the sea was chronically short of supplies; it could not remain stationary long enough to encourage the loyalists to show themselves, but had to move on in search of food. The earl rejected the invasion route along the coast that Clinton had suggested, as too fever-ridden to be safe for his troops, and chose to advance by way of the North Carolina piedmont. There, far from the sea, he found neither supplies nor loyalists, but only the elusive army of Nathanael Greene.

Cornwallis retreated once from North Carolina, after a detachment was wiped out at King's Mountain, but was back by the beginning of 1781. After a second detachment was defeated at Cowpens he refused to retreat again; he threw caution to the winds, destroyed most of his baggage, and advanced. Greene was more than a match for him, and gained even in defeat. At Guilford Court House, in March, Cornwallis won "that sort of victory which ruins an army." [11] All the battle netted him was casualties, and he was by now as short of men as he was of supplies. With the wreck of his force he retreated to Wilmington, on the Cape Fear, and there pondered where he would go next.

Clinton meanwhile was totally ignorant of what was happening, for his subordinate sent him no word. All he knew was that the earl had requested a post on the Chesapeake, which was thoroughly in accord with his own ideas. In December, 1780, Sir Henry had sent an expedition under his new American brigadier general, Benedict Arnold, to seize Portsmouth, Virginia; and in the following March Major General William Phillips superseded Arnold and brought substantial reinforcements. In April, Cornwallis informed headquarters that he was at Wilmington. A month later, before Sir Henry could communicate with him, came the staggering news that the earl had marched to the Chesapeake and joined Phillips' army. He had thereby ruined Clinton's whole concept of the southern campaign.

Cornwallis had begun to undermine this concept months before in North Carolina, by his fast-moving invasion that gained nothing solid. He had lost all chance of loyalist support, and therefore of progressive occupation; but he had at least kept his army between the enemy and his base. Now he had thrown away even that advantage. Once he was on the Chesapeake he was out of touch with South Carolina, which Greene was free to attack and did. The whole position that the British had built up in the south during the past year began to crumble. Cornwallis believed, for reasons he never explained, that Virginia must immediately become the focus of the war; to make it so he was willing to imperil Charleston and, if necessary, to abandon New York.

To Clinton this idea was midsummer madness. He knew that

tidewater Virginia, which was as fever-ridden as the Carolina coast, was a death trap for an army during the hot months; in May, General Phillips had died of fever. The Chesapeake, furthermore, was wide open to an enemy fleet; if the British lost command of the bay for even forty-eight hours, Clinton remarked, their operations would be crippled. These two dangers, from climate and from French sea power, made Sir Henry adamant against a large-scale summer campaign on the shores of the Chesapeake.

When Cornwallis brought his army there, he converted Virginia into a major theater of war against the wishes of his chief, but not against the wishes of the government. Germain had long been harping on the importance of the bay, and had recently made clear that he and the earl thought alike, whatever Clinton might think. The commander-in-chief's caution was no longer popular in Whitehall, where his energetic subordinate looked like the coming man; and the minister took no pains to conceal this change of attitude. He hoped to jolt Clinton into greater activity, or into resigning; but he misjudged his man. Sir Henry still expected, so he said, to resign at any moment unless a new naval chief were appointed; and he jumped to the conclusion that Cornwallis had come north in expectation of taking over the command. But giving it to him was another matter. His unauthorized move to Virginia, which in his chief's eyes amounted to insubordination, was one that Clinton expected the government to support. Germain and Cornwallis were in league to oust him, Sir Henry concluded; and his reaction was defiant. He refused to budge.

His obvious alternative to resigning was to bring Cornwallis to heel. This he might have done in either of two ways. He might have gone to Virginia to assess the situation, and then decided for himself and forced the earl's compliance; or he might have sent explicit orders from New York. He did neither. He thought of visiting the Chesapeake, but decided against it on the implausible ground that New York would not be safe in his absence; and during the whole summer he sent Cornwallis only one categorical order. For the rest he sent him suggestions and requests, interlarded with criticism of his previous conduct, almost as if he had no more control over the earl than over the navy. This bifurcation of authority within the army had the effect, which Clinton might have anticipated, of ruining his plans.

He knew what he wanted. The navy was eager for a base on the Chesapeake, and neither Arnold nor Phillips had found a suitable one; Cornwallis must locate the best available site and fortify it promptly. For this purpose he could not conceivably need his entire complement, Sir Henry believed, and would be able to return a substantial proportion to New York. It would be welcome there. The French and Americans were known to be planning a concentration of forces, backed by de Grasse's fleet from the West Indies; and Clinton was convinced that their objective was Manhattan. If he could draw reinforcements from the Chesapeake, he would both decrease the dangerous commitment there that Cornwallis had forced upon him, and strengthen his own defenses against the siege that he expected.

For months he tried, with no success whatever, to get Cornwallis to detach some troops. His first request arrived in late June when the earl was approaching Yorktown, which he had finally decided was the best base he could find. He misinterpreted the request as a demand that took precedence over establishing a base at all; he did not, he protested, have enough men to do both. In high dudgeon he marched to Portsmouth to embark the regiments asked for, and prepared to abandon the Chesapeake entirely. Clinton was aghast; he wanted the base even more than the reinforcements. For once he sent an explicit order—to return to Yorktown, fortify it, and keep whatever men were needed. He went on trying to get some of them, but he had vitiated his own efforts by permitting Cornwallis to retain such force as he thought necessary. Not a man was sent.

The long-run effect of this imbroglio was disastrous. The earl wasted a month in marching to Portsmouth and then back again, so that he did not start fortifying his position at Yorktown and Gloucester until the beginning of August. When he was besieged there in late September, consequently, his works were incomplete; and he could not hold out in them long enough for the attempted rescue from New York.[12] Far more important, by retaining his entire force he preserved the Chesapeake as the focus of the war. He had hoped to concentrate enough troops there for final victory; instead he kept enough for final defeat.

He cannot be blamed for keeping them, because he was authorized to do so if they were needed for establishing a base, and he was the proper judge of need. Whether Clinton was to blame for insisting on a base is another question. The insistence stemmed from his plans for the future. He had long intended to make the Chesapeake a major theater as soon as the Carolinas were subdued; he still intended, after Cornwallis reached the bay, to conduct important operations there in the autumn. Those operations would depend on water-borne supplies and therefore on naval control, for which the prerequisite, as the navy kept pointing out, was a safe anchorage for ships of the line. But was the need for such a base immediate and important enough to justify risking troops in the sickly season, especially when de Grasse was expected on the coast? This question Clinton and Admiral Graves, who replaced Arbuthnot in early July, never seem to have considered, any more than they did the risk in again attacking Rhode Island.[13] Throughout the summer they remained consistently blind to what might happen, in Virginia or in Narragansett Bay, if the French West Indian fleet gained even a temporary predominance.

But, whatever Clinton's share of responsibility for the ensuing disaster, Cornwallis' share was greater. After failing to establish control of North Carolina the earl moved to Virginia entirely on his own responsibility, and once he arrived there he wasted precious time; even when he did belatedly start to fortify his position he showed little sense of urgency. When the French fleet arrived he did nothing, but waited passively for the trap to close upon him. He shifted the focus of the war to the Chesapeake on his own initiative, in short, and then the initiative evaporated.

His shortcomings are worth emphasis because Clinton was subsequently saddled with all the blame. Cornwallis went home months before Sir Henry did, and arrived when North's government was on its last legs and desperately hunting for scapegoats. The earl was not an attractive one, partly because he had powerful connections and was on hand to use them, and partly because he had a warm welcome at court. His simple explanation of the surrender, that he had been ordered to hold his post at all cost and had been promised succor that did not come, gained wide credence; it put the whole onus on Clinton, and there it remained. The earl went on to a new and more successful career in India. Sir Henry, forced into retirement, did not receive even the routine honors that were usually accorded to commanders-in-chief when they were laid on what he called "the shelf of oblivion." Posterity benefited from his bitter sense of injustice, which turned him to compiling the record of his services that was to be his *Apologia pro Bello Suo*. But writing did not expunge his bitterness or clear his name.

Injustice was done him, for in considerable measure he was the victim of circumstance. He came to the command at a time when British resources in America were at their lowest ebb, and he never thereafter received a fraction of the support that his predecessor had had. His first campaign began with a retreat and ended with a defensive at New York and Rhode Island, in which he and Lord Howe preserved everything that the government had hoped they would and more than it had feared they might. His second campaign, in 1779, came to nothing because the meager reinforcements on which he had counted did not arrive in time. His third, in South Carolina, was the only one that developed according to plan; and it was a complete success. The surrender of Charleston in May, 1780, was the zenith of his career; thereafter his fortunes declined. The decline was only in part his fault. To work hand in glove with Arbuthnot would have taxed the patient finesse of a Marlborough; and even the great duke, if he had been in Clinton's place, could scarcely have worked hand in glove with Cornwallis, who was not only hundreds of miles away in the Carolinas but was touchy, headstrong, and egged on by his own government. No one in North America, in the summer of 1781, could have influenced the series of miscalculations in the Caribbean that left Admiral Graves so much inferior to de Grasse; and no general could have prevented Graves' subsequent defeat. Yorktown was not the product of any one man's incompetence, but the collapse of a slipshod system.

Although Clinton as commander-in-chief was the victim of that system, he might have used it to better effect than he did. If he lacked the force for sensational achievements, he also failed, except in the Charleston campaign, to obtain maximum results with the force that he had. "Generals gain at least as much honor by their able management of small armies," Germain told him in 1779, "as when they act with a superiority that commands success." [14] A generation later, in the early phase of the Peninsular War, Wellington demonstrated the truth of this comment; but Clinton was no Wellington. In three summers, from 1779 to 1781, Sir Henry had opportunities to gain honor by able management. In every case he *planned*, laboriously, meticulously, almost lovingly, and then fell back upon inaction. Of course he had reasons not to act; any general has. But the ones that he gave are not sufficient to explain his passivity.

Take for example his failure to attack the French on Rhode Island in 1780, and grant him his point that Arbuthnot was an infuriatingly inert colleague. Clinton ought to have known him well enough to realize that the one way *not* to get a decision out of him was by badgering from a distance, "amusing me with his situation," as the admiral put it, ". . . and aide-de-camps dancing backwards and forwards." [15] The old man was easily confused, and confusion bred annoyance. In trying to reach him through formal letters and dancing aides-de-camp Sir Henry was ensuring failure. But he preferred those methods to direct involvement, to using his own eyes and tongue, and never tried until too late to meet the admiral in the flesh.

This shying away from personal confrontation is typical of Clinton. At Sullivan's Island he and Sir Peter Parker almost never met, but carried on their business—as they later carried on their quarrel—by letter. As second in command, Clinton's peculiar relationship with Howe permitted him many face-to-face discussions with his chief, some of them extremely heated; yet even to Howe, on Long Island, he submitted his battle plan in writing and through an intermediary. As commander-in-chief Sir Henry was even more averse to disagreeable meetings. In the summer of 1781 he should have gone to the Chesapeake, as he should have gone to Rhode Island the summer before, to feel out the situation for himself; but again he fell back on letters. Even if he had been a forthright and pellucid correspondent, he would have had trouble in concerting plans in that way; and he was far from pellucid. His letter-writing style was formal, involved, and sometimes ambiguous, as he discovered in asking Cornwallis for reinforcements. Clinton knew that the earl had misread him (intentionally, he suspected), and the knowledge gave him all the more incentive for an interview, which he evaded on a flimsy excuse. The reason for these repeated evasions seems to have been in the character of the man.

Sir Henry, the "shy bitch," insulated himself from the men around him. He was able to be surprisingly open with a few, usually his juniors; but sooner or later he quarreled with most of them. Among the senior officers in America he had only one lasting friend, General Phillips. All the others he kept at a distance, and they did not know what he was thinking; "the commander-in-chief lives so retired that his secrets seldom take air." [16] His colleagues reacted by calling him proud, but pride and diffidence are two sides of the same coin. He was not enough at ease with himself to be at ease with his peers. He did not like to confront them, particularly one of them, like Arbuthnot or Cornwallis, in whom he sensed hostility yet with whom he had to work. The reason may have been that he did not trust his assertiveness in the give and take of conversation, and preferred a letter because he could fashion it to his purposes without interruption. He needed to impose order upon his dealings with his colleagues, according to this hypothesis, and found the written word more orderly than the spoken. "The tongue can no man tame."

A similar hypothesis may explain his passion for planning. He almost never relied upon the inspiration of the moment, but was continually drawing up on paper his ideas of what he could or should do. He had a sound analytic intelligence; and the ideas, when written down, looked good. Yet he seems to have cared more about formulating a plan than about implementing it, as if the plan itself met his problem without any need for acting. In his last two years at headquarters the hours that he spent at his desk writing, often far into the night, must have greatly exceeded the hours that he spent in the field. Burning the midnight oil, or rather the midnight candle, apparently gave him a sense of ordering, regulating, and somehow mastering whatever difficulty he had to face. A case in point is his design for attacking Rhode Island in the summer of 1781. He spared no effort to work out the plan in detail—forges for heating shot, ammunition for the cannon that he expected to capture from the French—and made no commensurate effort to see that it was carried out. He knew that time was short, because de Grasse might appear at any moment; yet when Admiral Graves postponed all action for weeks Clinton did not lift a finger to dissuade him.[17] The plan existed; by existing, his conduct implies, it took care of the matter.

Such an implication would of course have infuriated him; but he did realize that his plans were seldom executed, and that he was consequently blamed for inaction. He wanted to avoid the blame by finding explanations outside himself, as any man would; his need to find them was abnormally intense, however, because he would not admit to any slight share of responsibility. Others were blameworthy, not he; hence his almost incredible proclivity for quarrels and accusations. Before he was through he had a long list of the guilty men and the charges against them. Germain had not supported him properly and had interfered with his plans for the Chesapeake. Sandwich had neglected the American station. Parker had caused the failure at Sullivan's Island, Arbuthnot at Rhode Island, Rodney and above all Cornwallis at Yorktown. None of these men was completely innocent, but that is not why Clinton went on accusing them for the rest of his life. They turned his bitter criticism outward, away from himself.

Where and to what extent was he open to criticism? Little can be said against him as a military thinker, for here he was at his best; his ideas were not brilliant, but they were eminently sound. He understood the relationship of geography and sea power to all land operations, and he had a realistic view of the loyalists and of how they could and could not be utilized. He frequently showed his strategic acumen. In 1776 he contended that Washington's army was the focal point of the rebellion, and in 1777 that the Highlands, not Pennsylvania, were the key to the war; he cannot be proved right in either contention, but he had a better argument for both than Howe had for his strategy. As a leader of troops in the field Sir Henry won more praise than censure. He showed his skill in planning and executing the battle of Long Island, in attacking the Highland forts, in his retreat across New Jersey in 1778, and at Charleston two years later. On the other side of the ledger was one lamentable failure, at Sullivan's Island, but this was the exception. When he acted, by and large, he acted successfully. He almost never showed the boldness that elicits, if successful, wild acclaim from the public and from historians; but boldness in itself is no military virtue. Burgoyne displayed it after Bennington in marching to Saratoga, Cornwallis after Guilford in marching to the Chesapeake. Clinton's record is better, not worse, because it contains no such resolute blunder.

The principal charges against him arise from his inaction at moments when he himself recognized the opportunity to act. All those moments were after he became commander-in-chief.

Only one was when he was virtually his own master, in the wasted summer of 1779; the others were when he was trying to concert action with Arbuthnot or Graves or Cornwallis. With those colleagues his task was not easy, but even with them a more determined and self-confident man might have had some degree of success. Sir Henry had none. From the fall of Charleston to the fall of Yorktown he moved from one frustration to another; he watched, as if in a paralysis of will, as his plans were vitiated and his power to command evaporated, until in the final weeks before the catastrophe he was reduced to being what he had been years before at Sullivan's Island, a spectator of the navy's failure.

The end of a man's career has an element of pathos, especially when he does not know that the end is at hand. Four days before he sailed, as he thought, to gamble his army and his life on rescuing Cornwallis at Yorktown, Sir Henry wrote to say good-by to his sisters-in-law, the only family that he had; and his letter was at moments unconsciously symbolic. He had settled his affairs, paid his servants, and made his will, he told them; for "I guard as much as possible against everything." The time had come to close; "I have got to the end of my paper, my candle, and my eyes. I therefore, dearest sisters, take my leave, and after two hours' midnight writing . . . go to rest." [18]

FOOTNOTES

1. His memoirs remained unpublished until I edited them a decade ago (*The American Rebellion: Sir Henry Clinton's Narrative of His Campaigns, 1775–1782, with an Appendix of Original Documents;* Yale historical publications, manuscripts and edited texts, XXI; New Haven, 1954). His papers, which fill almost 300 volumes in the Clements Library of the University of Michigan, are the principal source of my biography, *Portrait of a General: Sir Henry Clinton in the War of Independence,* New York, 1964. Most of what follows is drawn from this study, and the footnote citations below refer to the biography.
2. *Ibid.,* p. 45.

3. *Ibid.*, p. 48.
4. *Ibid.*, p. 105.
5. The navy certainly scotched one of them. In September, just before the landing on Manhattan, Clinton suggested that he should take a detachment by the East River to the mouth of the Harlem, to cut off the enemy's retreat. This scheme was turned down because it would have brought the troop-laden boats nearer to the tide rips of Hell Gate than the naval officers thought safe. *Ibid.*, p. 109.
6. *Ibid.*, p. 160.
7. *Ibid.*, p. 279.
8. Mackesy strongly implies that the British government would have conceded independence if the war could have been ended on that basis (Piers Mackesy, *The War for America, 1775–1783*; Cambridge, Mass., 1964; pp. 187–89). I contend that the king would not agree to this final concession (Willcox, *op. cit.*, pp. 219–20). If the Americans demanded it—in fact they refused to negotiate at all —the commissioners were instructed to refer the demand back to London, which does not mean that it would have been accepted there. The king, I believe, did not intend to go beyond the terms authorized by Parliament; in case they were rejected, he seems to have envisaged military evacuation of the colonies and a continued naval war against their commerce. See his correspondence cited in Mackesy and, for the attitude of the government when the Commission left England, Charles R. Ritcheson, *British Politics and the American Revolution* (Norman, Okla., 1954), pp. 266–67.
9. In the four years after Saratoga the army at New York, by Sir Henry's computation, received 4,700 men as reinforcements from home, and lost 19,200: 6,000 in Burgoyne's surrender and 13,200 in detachments to Canada, Florida, Georgia, and the West Indies. The total depletion was therefore 14,500. Clinton memorandum filed at the end of September, 1781, Clinton Papers, Clements Library.
10. Willcox, *op. cit.*, p. 68. For the unsuccessful attempt on Rhode Island, and the resultant breakdown of collaboration between the two services, see *ibid.*, pp. 323–337.
11. The remark of General Phillips, Willcox, *op. cit.*, p. 384.
12. *Ibid.*, p. 426.
13. *Ibid.*, pp. 419–420.
14. *Ibid.*, p. 316.
15. *Ibid.*, p. 335.
16. Chief Justice William Smith in 1779, Historical Manuscripts Commission, *Fifteenth Report* (London, 1897), App., pt. VI, p. 432.
17. Willcox, *op. cit.*, p. 423. Even this brief survey of Sir Henry's char-

acter is enough, I hope, to make clear that he showed strong neurotic tendencies. These I have examined with a psychotherapist, and our tentative conclusions are embodied in the final chapter of *Portrait of a General*.

18. To Elizabeth and Martha Carter, October 15, 1781, Clinton Papers, Clements Library.

BIBLIOGRAPHY

Clinton, Henry. *The American Rebellion: Sir Henry Clinton's Narrative of His Campaigns, 1775–1782, with an Appendix of Original Documents*, William B. Willcox, ed., Yale historical publications, manuscripts and edited texts, XXI. New Haven, 1954. Sir Henry's apologia, for all its bias, is invaluable for understanding his role in the war; and he also goes into considerable detail about campaigns, during his command-in-chief, in which he was not a participant. With a few exceptions he is scrupulously accurate in citing evidence and in imputing to himself the views that he actually held at the time. Most of the exceptions are pointed out in the editorial notes, and the few that I have found since are mentioned in my biography.

Mackesy, Piers. *The War for America, 1775–1783*. Cambridge, Mass., 1964. See comment in the bibliography of "Arbuthnot, Gambier, and Graves: 'Old Women' of the Navy."

Stevens, Benjamin F., ed. *The Campaign in Virginia, 1781: an Exact Reprint of Six Rare Pamphlets on the Clinton-Cornwallis Controversy*. 2 vols., London, 1888. The standard source for the British side of the military campaign after the fall of Charleston. It contains chronological correspondence, primarily between Clinton and Cornwallis, and the dreary polemics of the pamphlet war that broke out between them after Yorktown.

Stuart-Wortley, the Hon. Mrs. E. *A Prime Minister and His Son, from the Correspondence of the 3rd Earl of Bute and of Lt.-General the Hon. Sir Charles Stuart, K. B.* London, 1925. Young Stuart was for a short time one of Clinton's confidants at headquarters in New York, and his letters are filled with comments—largely uncharitable —on the commander-in-chief and his entourage. Neither his views nor his facts are reliable, but they make good reading. Although he had an annoyingly high opinion of himself, his subsequent career bore it out.

Van Doren, Carl. *Secret History of the American Revolution*. New York, 1941. The focus of the book is the Arnold conspiracy; but it also contains a great deal of information, drawn largely from the Clinton Papers, on Sir Henry's negotiations with other Americans and the workings of the British intelligence system in general.

Ward, Christopher. *The War of the Revolution*, John R. Alden, ed. 2 vols., New York, 1952. The fullest modern account of military operations in the war, with much less attention to the naval side. Thickets of detail often obstruct the narrative, and emphasis is badly apportioned between minor and major campaigns. The work is, nevertheless, the most authoritative in the field.

Willcox, William B. *Portrait of a General: Sir Henry Clinton in the War of Independence.* New York, 1964. See comment in the bibliography of "Arbuthnot, Gambier, and Graves: 'Old Women' of the Navy."

Sir Guy Carleton:

SOLDIER-STATESMAN

PAUL H. SMITH

University of Florida

GUY CARLETON, governor and captain-general of Quebec at the outbreak of the American rebellion, was the only one of George Washington's high-ranking opponents whose official career in America successfully survived the War of Independence. Applauded for his defense of Quebec against American attack in 1775–76, but passed over for John Burgoyne when command of the 1777 "northern" invasion was assigned, Carleton resigned in pique prior to the debacle at Saratoga and escaped virtually unscathed from the recriminations that followed that event. Hopelessly at odds with Lord George Germain, the secretary of state for American affairs, he then spent more than three quiet years in England until the collapse of North's administration brought the more pacific Rockingham Ministry to power in the spring of 1782. When Carleton returned to America, it was as commander-in-chief to negotiate the reconciliation of the colonies. Though disappointed in that enterprise, he managed the subsequent British evacuation from the now independent United States with great competence and compassionately directed the flight of thousands of loyalists to their new homes in Canada. After a second interlude in England, he capped his distinguished career with a second term as governor of Canada—from 1786 to 1796—during the formative period of the second British Empire when difficult adjustments were required because of the sudden intrusion of exiled loyalists upon the dominant French-Canadian society. Thus, Carleton's career in North America was a dual one as soldier and statesman.

As an imperial statesman, Guy Carleton (Sir Guy after 1776, and finally Lord Dorchester after 1786) has an undeniable claim to eminence. But his career as a military commander during the War of Independence is curiously ambiguous. Though a soldier by profession, and the senior officer in America after Gage returned to England in November, 1775, he never commanded a sizable army in a significant or major battle. His military reputation rests almost entirely upon two modest—though meaningful—achievements: the repulse of an American force which attacked the formidable walled city of Quebec on December 31, 1775, and the defeat on Lake Champlain of a small enemy flotilla commanded by Benedict Arnold in October, 1776. Upon several other important occasions his conduct was equivocal at best. He responded ineffectively to the initial enemy thrusts into Canada in 1775, losing control of the approaches to the St. Lawrence Valley, and, when the tide turned after massive British reinforcements arrived in the spring of 1776, thrice permitted a weak and disorganized enemy to escape his superior army. The contrast between his reputation as a soldier-statesman and his actual achievements in the field is striking. The disparity suggests that his military career has not attracted the critical attention that has been focused upon his fellow British generals.

The little that is known of the early life of this puzzling man is quickly told. He was born in 1724, of Scotch-Irish stock, the third son of Christopher Carleton, a landowner of County Down, Ireland. When Guy was fourteen his father died, and his mother, of County Donegal, married a second time. His stepfather, the Reverend Thomas Skelton, apparently arranged for Guy's education and had an important share in molding Carleton's character; but Skelton's influence can only be surmised. Commissioned an ensign in 1742, the young officer advanced slowly for a decade, and then attained the rank of lieutenant colonel after the outbreak of the Seven Years' War. Apparently befriended by James Wolfe, who was three years his junior, new vistas opened to Carleton as Wolfe secured for him an appointment as quartermaster general to the army charged with the capture of Quebec in 1759. Before the war was over, Carleton saw action in Canada, in Europe, and against the Spanish at Havana. In the course of combat, he was wounded three times. Little more than this is known of Carleton until he was appointed lieutenant governor of Quebec in 1766, for upon his own instructions Carleton's widow faithfully burned the entire collection of his personal papers after his death in 1808.[1]

Carleton's return to Quebec in September, 1766, as successor to Governor James Murray launched him on a long career closely bound up with the future of British rule in North America. He inherited from Murray a difficult situation that put his talents as a statesman to a stern test—his lot being to fit an old French and Catholic colony into an English and Protestant empire. Though many officials believed that Canada could be treated like any other British colony, Carleton boldly attacked that widely held assumption. "This country must, to the end of time, be peopled by the Canadian race, who have already taken such firm root, and got to so great a height, that any new stock transplanted will be totally hid and imperceptible amongst them, except in the towns of Quebec and Montreal." In seeking to give substance to this insight, Carleton led officials in London to accept the assumptions that were woven into the Quebec Act in 1774. From these assumptions there developed the finest flower of the empire—the concept of a larger "British" liberty of non-English people to retain their own distinctive character.

It was quite another matter, however, to nurse such a policy to fruition because there were elements in Canada inimical to it. Before he completed his first administration in 1778 (he was formally promoted to the governorship in January, 1768), the ties of empire were strained to near the breaking point. Carleton was limited from the outset by the conditions prevailing in the colony at the time it passed to the British and by the policies and experiences of his predecessor. Although it was imperative that the Canadians not remain a sullen and hostile people, the small yet important English-speaking mercantile minority that settled in the towns of Quebec and Montreal after the British occupied Canada had interests which conflicted with the vast majority of persons of another race, language, and religion. To administer a government satisfactory to all these groups would have confounded Solomon. Nor was it likely that Britain could extend justice to her "new subjects" without giving added offense to her "old subjects" to the southward who were already restive under the economic policies of George Grenville. Finally, the demands for tax relief in the mother country, the depressed condition of the fur trade, and the continued restlessness of the natives in the western areas of Canada, made it obvious that Carleton's position as governor would be a difficult one.

It was unfortunate, moreover, that many of Carleton's earliest recommendations for assuring Canada's military security were ignored, while some of his errors survived to plague him and belatedly bore bitter fruit in the internecine conflict that developed. Concerned with the threat to imperial authority posed by the colonies' hostile reaction to the Stamp Act, Carleton as early as 1767 laid out a prescription for permanently attaching Canada to the empire. Militarily, the defenses of Quebec and Montreal would have to be rebuilt.[2] Since Quebec and New York were the keys to British control over the colonies, the line connecting them would have to be kept strongly fortified. He repeatedly urged restoration of the defenses of Ticonderoga, and his worst fears were realized when the fort became the first British position to fall to the rebels when war broke out.[3]

His political views were much more complex. Although he was supported by some members of the British minority who were well disposed toward the Canadians, his program was a direct challenge to the "English party," which previously had balked at Murray's decision to postpone election of a legislative assembly. Convinced that the colony could not be governed without the services of the Canadian leaders, Carleton wished to restore at least French civil law, give legal force to the tithe, and maintain the seignorial system. Canadians, he believed, should be appointed to governmental posts of secondary importance. There should be no elected assembly, as no viable government could truly represent the various elements in Canada. Legislative power should be reposed in the governor and an appointive council. When the substance of this policy was incorporated into the Quebec Act, the principal Canadian leaders—especially the higher clergy who were the most influential representatives of the Canadian community—rallied to Carleton's support. His benevolent despotism fulfilled their aspirations, although they continued to fear the augmented personal power placed in his hands.

In contrast to his broad policy views on Canada's future, Carleton's administrative conduct and exercise of executive power was arbitrary and narrow. Unwilling to implement his policies with the generosity that marked their conception, he needlessly antagonized important persons who experienced the sting of his whip and learned to fear his methods. Carleton brought to Quebec in 1766 a preconceived hostility to Murray's supporters. He had heard only one side of the troubles that had led to Murray's return and hence had a contempt for the English mercantile minority. Above all, he distrusted them because of their eagerness to pursue profits at the expense of the welfare of the Canadians. Furthermore, his autocratic temper led him to brook no interference with his will, and he soon set out to eliminate from the government those whom he distrusted. At the outset he excluded certain Council members from the regular meetings of that body, and when challenged struck down his opponents and misrepresented their action in his reports to London.[4] In the course of his long administration in Canada he unjustly managed the virtual political destruction of a lieutenant governor, a chief justice, and a judge of the Court of Common Pleas; eliminated the Council as a check on his executive authority; and prevented any really free discussion of his decisions. In the words of one leading authority, "he had a mean temper, and would stop at nothing to cover up his mistakes." [5] A man so sensitive to criticism and exposed to possible censure in case of an unexpected investigation would be extremely vulnerable if agents of sedition from outside the province arrived to foment discontent and encourage rebellion.

Carleton's first administration in Canada was interrupted by his return to England in August, 1770. He was originally granted leave to settle personal affairs, but four years elapsed before he returned to Quebec. During the long interval he had ample opportunity to expound his views on Canadian questions, and though months dragged into years before he finally saw his recommendations safely through Parliament, the Quebec Act, which received the king's assent in June, 1774, embodied most of the essential features he desired. His return to Canada that fall was therefore a happy one.

Carleton had reason to be happy on personal as well as political grounds. On his return, he was accompanied by a newly acquired wife and two children. During his unexpectedly prolonged visit in England he had, at the age of forty-seven, married Lady Maria Howard, the eighteen-year-old daughter of the Earl of Effingham. Her presence in Quebec added a charming new dimension to his social life, and her partiality for things French, a reflection of her education at Versailles, perhaps reinforced Carleton's optimism about Canada's future under the Quebec Act.

But if he hoped to find repose in Quebec he was rudely disappointed. While his ship was still at sea, the first Continental Congress was convening at Philadelphia and the crisis was deepening. General Thomas Gage in Boston, alarmed over Massachusetts' response to the Coercive Acts, penned a letter calling on Carleton for reinforcements from Canada. Less than 24 hours after Carleton set foot in Canada, Gage's letter of September 4, 1774, was handed to him. Transports for the 10th and 52nd regiments, which comprised half the entire Canadian garrison, he learned, had already been dispatched to Quebec. Moreover, he was requested to report on the prospects for raising "a body of Canadians & Indians" for future use in conjunction with the king's forces in Massachusetts should resort to force become necessary.[6]

Carleton's response to Gage was an optimistic one.[7] In fact, during the following winter his reports to both Dartmouth, the American secretary, and Gage, his immediate superior officer until Carleton was placed on independent command in September, 1775, betrayed no real sense of alarm. Even when some months passed and the Americans became more intransigent, Carleton was slow to reappraise his position. His four-year absence soon proved to be a serious handicap. Nursing dubious conceptions of Canadian society from the outset, and out of touch with the events of 1770–74, Carleton obviously was not master of the Canadian situation after his return. He gradually lost the initiative which the Quebec Act should have placed in his hands. His enthusiasm about the future effect of the Quebec Act, strengthened by those in high positions around him, blinded him to immediate conditions and dangerously prolonged the illusions nursed by Dartmouth and Gage concerning the faithfulness of most colonists. Such illusions were the very stuff of the American Revolution.

Knowing that his policy had secured him the support of the clergy and the seigniors, Carleton hoped to make Quebec a secure base from which to launch any attack required against the colonies in rebellion. Encouraged by the response of those who applauded the Quebec Act, he imagined that a Canadian militia manned by docile habitants could secure the province from invasion. He did not recognize, or refused to believe, that the bulk of the habitants sullenly acquiesced in the recent restoration of ancient clerical and seignorial privileges directed against their liberties, and accepted British occupation with a measured loyalty that bordered on passive resistance. Considering the degree to which he was out of touch with the bulk of the population, it was to be expected that Carleton would be disappointed at their response when the American invasion in May, 1775, shattered Quebec's calm. Despite exhortations from the pulpit and the urgings of the seigniors, the habitants simply refused to take up arms. When not merely indifferent, they occasionally joined the invading Americans. Because the Americans had little to offer the habitants, and harbored deep-seated religious prejudices against them, the number of Canadians who openly deserted their leaders was not large. But even their prudent neutrality was fatal to Carleton's plans, and it very nearly enabled the Americans to prevail in the province.

Carleton gradually awakened to the flaws in his earlier assumptions as reports reached him that the Americans were already among his people spreading sedition and threatening waverers who refused to throw in their lot with the insurgents. As a result, he revived a scheme for arming the Canadians that previously had been ignored. As the habitants could not be trusted to throw back an invasion, and even the gentry did not "relish commanding a bare Militia," Carleton renewed his request for the establishment of a "Canadian" regiment. Regular commissions in the army, he hoped, would revive the zeal of the seigniors and bestir them to take up the defense of their country. Creation of a "Canadian" regiment would not only "restore them to a significance they have nearly lost," but it would rectify a wrong done them in 1764 when those who had volunteered for service against Pontiac's warriors were dismissed "without gratuity or recompence . . . tho they all expected half pay." [8] Only by placing a "Canadian" regiment on the establishment could Britain allay the fears of the seigniors that they might again be ignored at the close of the present disorders.

In this instance Carleton had accurately diagnosed the situation and recommended a suitable remedy. But he should have anticipated that his recommendation would be ignored. Placing a new regiment on the establishment would be expensive, and it would jeopardize vested interests throughout the entire British officer corps. The government normally augmented the army by enlarging old regiments—a procedure that minimized the irregularities and abuse of seniority that often attended creation of new ones—and it could hardly be expected to approve a regiment to be officered by French Catholics. Military convention and the prejudices of the ruling officer class had long thwarted similar efforts to organize regular "provincial" regiments even among Britain's "old subjects." Carleton was unrealistic in his hopes of receiving preferential treatment for his supporters from the British establishment.

Additional troubles were just around the corner. At the approach of the first of May, 1775, the day the Quebec Act was to take effect, Carleton returned momentarily to his civil duties. He had to face the rising opposition of the English-speaking mercantile minority who feared the consequences of enforcement of the new act. The North Ministry, anticipating their concern, had already taken steps to protect them against injuries that full restoration of French civil law would inflict. But Carleton decided to ignore the Ministry's recommendations. In flagrant disregard of these orders—which directed him to consult the Council on legislation to preserve the right to habeas corpus and English law for civil suits in which a natural-born subject was a party—Carleton kept his royal instructions secret.[9] The effect on Britons in Canada was disastrous for the security of the province. Disappointed with the home government's apparent callousness and exasperated at their obvious betrayal, dozens of them now sought recourse in rebellion. They welcomed revolutionists from the south and aided in spreading sedition among the credulous habitants. Thus when Canada was invaded, Carleton quickly found himself occupied on two "fronts": fighting agents of revolution from without and engaged in a double game on the political front from within.

The day of reckoning came in mid-May. Hearing of the American capture of the British-held forts at Ticonderoga and Crown Point on Lake Champlain, Carleton took what limited measures he could. When a rebel force under Benedict Arnold appeared at St. Johns a few days after the forts fell, the security of the settlements of the upper St. Lawrence Valley seemed shattered. Carleton sent all the available troops in the province, plus a few Canadian volunteers, to the area. Almost immediately he abandoned Quebec and left for Montreal, which he reached the 26th day of May. St. Johns became the object of all his attention and work on implementing the new government stopped. Troops arriving from distant points took up positions in the fort at St. Johns. Ship carpenters and supplies were also ordered in to begin construction of armed vessels adequate to clear the rebels from the river and the lake above. St. Johns on the Richelieu controlled both the funnel through which rebel troops could pour into the valley and the road west to Montreal just fifteen miles away. Arnold's men had abandoned the fort almost immediately after capturing it, but had taken away with them a sloop and a well-armed schooner which gave them control of the entire waterway from St. Johns to Ticonderoga.[10]

In Montreal, Carleton found himself facing other problems. Although he had all summer to prepare against a full-scale invasion, his efforts came to very little. The English merchants at Montreal offered him almost no support and indulged instead in intrigue and treason. Small bands of American troops reappeared through the woods from time to time and intimidated the inhabitants of the valley who otherwise might have been persuaded to join the king's troops. Carleton simply had too few regulars to defend against an invading force of any significance, and the Canadians would not voluntarily risk their lives in behalf of British sovereignty. In a desperate effort to revive the militia, Carleton proclaimed martial law on June 9, 1775, but he foolishly continued to rely upon the seigniors and old French army officers to rouse the habitants.[11] His proclamation produced meager results; it succeeded only in further irritating the habitants, and stirring up the English merchants who viewed the measure with suspicion as another act of arbitrary government.

There was one major alternative in raising a military force which Carleton refused to consider. He might have been able to rally upwards of 2,000 Indians—a number far greater than that needed to check any invasion the rebels could launch—but he rejected proposals to turn them loose. Curiously enough, how-

ever, his policy of not employing Indians produced some unexpected results. Carleton's ambiguous letters to Dartmouth and
Gage on this matter failed to change the minds of these military
planners about using Indians in future operations. They continued to base their beliefs upon optimistic reports from Indian
Superintendent Guy Johnson, who claimed that redskins could
be hurled against rebel invaders. Carleton, on the other hand,
had refused to state openly his opposition to using the Indians,
choosing instead, somewhat deviously, to complain of their un-
dependability, and to hint that Johnson was unable to mobilize
them at the proper moment.[12] Thus, he left the implication that
Indians might be available for future use. The rub was that officials in England were accurately informed of the Indian forces
available, and instead of preparing to send Carleton reinforcements at once—having swallowed also Carleton's confident predictions of Canadian loyalty—they expected him to reinforce
Gage's army in New England and to make a diversion along
the northern frontier to relieve the pressure on Boston.

With so much confusion swirling about, it was little wonder
that Carleton was left to his own inadequate resources. Few
officials were able to recognize the dimensions of the struggle
that was about to engulf them, and Carleton was no exception.
Furthermore, at the beginning of the American rebellion all
shared the great illusions of their day: the assumed loyalty of
most Americans, the incapacity of the rebels to fight, and the
invincibility of the redcoats. Government by instruction in
America contained the seeds of its own failure. It was left to
chance to determine whether the harvest would yield thirteen or
fourteen provinces.

Fortune finally smiled on Guy Carleton. Although he suffered
many defeats, he was ultimately able to spin out the campaign
until he was saved by the elements. The Americans, novices at
organizing large-scale warfare, were only able to plan a modest
invasion of Canada. Congress wasted valuable time during the
summer before coming to a resolution to invade Canada, and
it was hesitant to launch an offensive that might slam the door

to a peaceful reconciliation. Once the invasion was approved, moreover, Generals Philip Schuyler and Richard Montgomery consumed weeks struggling with shortages of money and supplies, provincial jealousies, and inadequately trained troops, before they were ready for a second assault on St. Johns. Carleton in the meantime returned to the seat of government in Quebec to convene his first Legislative Council under the Quebec Act, trusting the St. Johns garrison to withstand any initial blow the rebels might deliver.[13]

On September 4, Montgomery's men camped on Isle-aux-Noix in the river just twelve miles from St. Johns. Although two initial attempts on the post were beaten off, the fort was finally invested on September 17. Since nearly four-fifths of all regulars in the area were inside the walls—or at Chambly a few miles down river where Major Stopford commanded 80 men—the Americans were now free to roam that triangle of land formed by the St. Lawrence and the Richelieu, exhorting the Canadians to arms in defense of liberty. Carleton learned to his chagrin, upon hurrying back to Montreal on September 7, that several hundred Canadians had joined the rebels. When most of the Indians under Johnson's command, who had been disappointed with months of inactivity, slipped away into the forests after St. Johns was invested, Carleton's last real hope for saving Montreal was virtually extinguished.

Carleton nevertheless had nearly six weeks to play out his hand, and twice during that interval he found cause for hope. The first opportunity given him to check the tide resulted from a foolhardy, poorly planned assault on Montreal—the only one attempted during the period—commanded by the brave but blustering Ethan Allen. Encouraged by several dissident Montreal merchants led by Thomas Walker—who nursed ancient grievances against the governor—Allen became convinced that Montreal could be taken by a *coup de main*. Thus on September 24 he crossed the river at Long Point at the head of 110 men, expecting the city to be delivered to him on command. Having got wind of the scheme, however, Carleton had a force three times the size of Allen's under Major Carden ready to greet them. Within a few hours the British were able to capture 36 of the attacking force, including their embarrassed leader. Taking heart momentarily, Carleton acknowledged with guarded optimism that "our victory has had good effect." [14] Two-thirds of Allen's rebels, he estimated, were Canadians "who expected to march in without opposition." He hoped, no doubt, that the lesson would be taken to heart and that other Canadians who had joined the Americans might recover their senses.

In mid-October, however, a fatal blow was struck that apparently caught Carleton unawares. Disappointed with the progress against St. Johns, Montgomery was persuaded by James Livingston to turn his attention to the fort at Chambly scarcely ten miles down river. The post was defended by fewer than 100 men under the command of Major Stopford and was known to be stocked with a large quantity of valuable stores. Under the cover of darkness a few cannon placed in bateaux were easily floated by St. Johns undetected and brought to bear against the thin stone walls that offered feeble protection to the garrison at Chambly. The result was more satisfying than Montgomery ever could have dreamed. On October 18, Major Stopford surrendered at the first cannonading and delivered up not only his troops but all his supplies, which he neglected to have his men throw over the walls into the river. For their troubles the Americans were paid handsomely with 124 barrels of gunpowder, over 6,000 cartridges, 150 stand of arms, and 238 barrels of provisions. While the major's concern for his men was commendable, his delivery of everything in the fort was patently inexcusable. Carleton apparently knew little about the man's character or judgment and had overlooked an important detail in permitting such a quantity of stores to remain so poorly protected. Although Carleton never censured Stopford, he surely saw that disaster had struck. Perhaps he thought it would be well if the issue could be forgotten without a searching investigation that might cause him some embarrassment.

Although the loss was immediately made known to the St.

Johns garrison because Montgomery hoped to use the victory to undermine the morale of the defenders there, the commander, Major Preston, ignored the incident and continued to hope for relief. Preston noted, however, he "had not a syllable of intelligence from Genl Carleton . . . from the first day of the blockade." [15] Facing mounting criticism from several leading seigniors as Preston's position became progressively more desperate, Carleton finally decided upon making an attack. Lieutenant Colonel Allen Maclean, who had been authorized to raise a regiment of "provincials" from among the Highland Emigrants who had settled in America after the Treaty of Paris, was called up from Quebec for the assault. Carleton, with a few regulars and a mixed force of Canadians and Indians, planned to cross from Montreal and join Maclean as he moved up from Sorel. As matters turned out, however, Seth Warner and his Green Mountain Boys were prepared on the eastern bank of the river and beat off Carleton's boats before they could effect a landing. Maclean, encountering a superior force, turned back to the safety of his boats and wisely decided to make the protection of Quebec his primary object. Finding the French-Canadian militiamen deserting fast and his remaining Indians slinking away, Carleton finally gave up the idea of a relief expedition on October 30. Three days later, Preston reported to Montgomery his readiness to negotiate an end to the 55-day siege. On November 3, the surviving defenders laid down their arms. During the preceding two months more than 700 men had been lost or taken prisoner in the unsuccessful effort to halt the American invasion. The entire region was now devoid of any means of further defense.

On November 5, Carleton reported the surrender of St. Johns to Dartmouth and took advantage of the occasion to analyze the reasons for his inability to check the American advance.[16] At the root of each point he listed lay a common answer—"want of hands." He had lost the race in constructing vessels "to dispute the passage of Lake Champlain" because ship carpenters were not available. Entrenchments adequate to protect Chambly and St. Johns could not be constructed and manned because of "the corruption and stupid baseness of the Canadian peasantry." When St. Johns was put under siege the Indians had left and the militia deserted. He was now prepared to abandon Montreal as soon as attacked because "the lower orders will not act, and there are not means to defend the place."

With such a dismal record, Carleton was even apprehensive about defending Quebec. The military defenses of the capital were ill-prepared and he now knew that an American force under Benedict Arnold was marching on Quebec from Maine via the Chaudière. Carleton, anxious to make his way back to the government seat, waited only for the loading of his vessels and a breeze before making off for the capital.

But what ought to have been a routine trip downstream quickly turned into a perilous adventure. It was to cost him dearly and exposed his unfortunate tendency to underestimate the enemy and to overlook ordinary, though vital, details. By November 10 all the powder and supplies that could be carried away were loaded on 11 small vessels that had been collected at Montreal. The following day, with the 130 men and officers who yet remained under his command, Carleton stepped on board to catch a fair wind to Quebec. But his force was delayed first by a sand bar and then by a change of wind before they reached Sorel. When he reached the mouth of the Richelieu, Carleton was surprised to find his way blocked by a floating battery and cannon placed on shore by the resourceful Americans. He had not expected Montgomery to undertake anything below Montreal until that city had been secured, but by the time his fleet approached Sorel, troops under James Easton and John Brown had been working hard there for a week.[17] Barred from landing by an enemy detachment hurrying down from Montreal, and finding escape past the American batteries impossible, Carleton was in desperate straits. His pilots were mutinous, and the commander of the powder ship made it known that he would surrender before risking a fatal bombardment. Although Carleton himself succeeded in slipping by the American artillery in a whale boat on the night of November 16,

Montgomery had the satisfaction of capturing the entire fleet with the last remnant of redcoats who had been brought up in September to oppose his advance. After having been delayed eleven weeks by Carleton's small force, nothing now lay between Montgomery and Quebec. He had put Carleton to a challenging test and had found him a worthy but far from ingenious opponent.

The next great challenge to Carleton's leadership, which he met more successfully, had already begun when he arrived in Quebec on November 19. Although he had escaped Montgomery's troops, Carleton appeared for a time to have merely exchanged one trap for another. The capital to which he returned was already a beleaguered city. Benedict Arnold had arrived at Quebec two weeks earlier at the head of 600 men after an incredibly difficult march across the northern wilderness from Maine. Within a few days after Carleton's arrival, Arnold was joined by Montgomery. Together the American commanders were able to muster about 1,000 effectives, little more than half the number of men available to Carleton. But the rebels retained the advantages of mobility and surprise and they posed a serious threat to the city.

Carleton's qualities in this trying situation showed to their best advantage. His calm and aristocratic bearing awakened confidence in his subordinates and his tireless energy aroused the fainthearted. Expelling all able-bodied men who refused to bear arms and cracking down hard on malingerers, he appreciably lessened the threat of sedition within the walls and reduced the strain on his supplies. A new fighting spirit, clearly derived from his presence, was aroused among his troops. Within a few days, the work on the fortifications begun by Maclean was almost completed and the defenders were organized for round-the-clock duty. Sleeping fully dressed for nights on end to be ready for an assault, Carleton was well prepared to put the Americans to a stiff test if they elected to defy the elements and attempt to storm his defenses.[18]

As the end of the year approached, Montgomery and Arnold

came to a desperate decision. Facing the dismal prospect of a long winter siege, concerned over an outbreak of smallpox, and worried about the impending expiration of the terms of enlistment of their men, they decided to launch an attack on the first night that there was a storm. To succeed, the Americans were counting on the element of surprise. They needed as well a large measure of luck, for in the game they elected to play they were working against long odds.

When the assault came, in the predawn hours of the last day of the year, Carleton was equal to the occasion. He was certain an attack was pending from reports of deserters and was prepared. Since he expected a diversion against the Lower Town while an attack was delivered against the landward walls—perhaps at Cape Diamond Bastion or St. John's Gate—Carleton maintained a command post at the Récollect monastery where he could be contacted by couriers from his scattered defenders and quickly send men where they were most needed. He was wrong about the details of the plan—for Montgomery and Arnold were personally leading converging columns in a main attack against Lower Town—but his error in this regard made little difference. Montgomery was killed instantly when trying to penetrate the Près-de-Ville barricade, and Arnold took a ball in the leg trying to enter the walls from the opposite direction. Livingston's feint against the landward walls did not distract Carleton long enough to permit Arnold's men—now under Daniel Morgan's command—to carry the second barrier after they entered Lower Town. Montgomery's men, on the other hand, failed to press on after the fall of their leader. Although he was surprised when Maclean reported the breakthrough of Morgan's men, Carleton was able to send Major Caldwell with reinforcements in time to check their advance. As the darkness lifted, Carleton also ordered a detachment out through Palace Gate to take Morgan's men by surprise from the rear. Four hundred exhausted and nearly leaderless rebels were rounded up, and half that number nursing wounds escaped back to the American camp. Carleton buried nearly a hundred of their fallen comrades. He counted fewer than one-tenth as many casualties among his own men, and concluded that the victory was as nearly perfect as could have been desired.[19] Although the siege was maintained until May, 1776, by the remnant of the American force, Carleton's defense against the assault had been an able one.

During the winter of Carleton's confinement in Quebec, the North Ministry began to respond more vigorously to the requirements of the war in America. In comparison to the opening moves of the war that had taken on something of the appearance of a series of "midnight" sieges, 1776 was to see the delivery of a grand offensive. General William Howe replaced Gage in command in Boston, and a determined Lord George Germain was appointed to succeed the gentle Dartmouth in the American Department. Simultaneously a strategy of reconquest had begun to crystallize and was already beginning to take form when Germain took office.[20] Howe was ordered to transfer from Boston to the more useful base at New York in order to prepare for a spring offensive. Reinforcements were readied for Canada. Moreover, seven regiments had been dispatched to Carolina for a winter campaign against the southern colonies. Howe was to have the reinforcements he requested for delivering the main blow at New York, and a 10,000-man striking force was to be sent to the St. Lawrence for an advance from Canada.

Of all this, however, Carleton knew nothing. Cut off from the outside world in early November, he received no word about these preparations until May 10, 1776. Indeed, though he had been established in an independent command when Gage returned to London, he gave little thought to his military role within the over-all perspective of the 1776 campaign.[21] As governor of Quebec he was preoccupied with re-establishing order in his own province, clearing the rebels from the St. Lawrence, implementing the Quebec Act, restoring the Canadians to a sense of duty to their sovereign, and, in general, vindicating his Canadian policy. Carleton only faintly grasped the idea that a sizable force was about to be placed in his hands and that he was expected to deliver a decisive blow to the rebels on the frontiers of New York. Whether he was overconfident that Howe would overwhelm the enemy in New York on his own or underestimated the Americans, he refused generally to concern himself with the larger problems of suppressing the rebellion in the other colonies. His experience of a decade had been that of a provincial governor, and he continued to perform as a provincial governor.

Uninformed of the details of the strategy of reconquest, and conditioned by his civil responsibilities and a winter of confinement to assume that the burden of crushing the revolt would be left to others, Carleton was not quite equal to the challenge placed before him. Yet it was understandable that his response betrayed no real sense of urgency. During the few weeks after reinforcements arrived in the spring it was extremely difficult for him to form an adequate image of the size and capabilities of the army available to him at any particular moment. His reinforcements were dispatched from no fewer than five different points over a period of several weeks and consequently the bulk of them straggled into the St. Lawrence intermittently between early May and the middle of June. Similarly, he had difficulty gauging the strength of the American forces contesting his advance back up river—intelligence reports reached him that the enemy numbered from 5,000 to 25,000 men. Since Carleton had already experienced several bitter failures because of faulty intelligence in 1775, he became inclined toward an uncharacteristic caution. And finally, Carleton was extremely irritated with the appointment of Germain. He believed, because of the court-martial that had pronounced judgment on Germain's conduct at the battle of Minden in 1759, that the new secretary was unfit to hold any important public office. The contempt with which Carleton regarded Germain therefore ruled out the possibility that any genuine understanding might prevail between the governor and the secretary of state. This animus left a bitter legacy and was to cost Britain dearly in 1777.[22]

Despite Carleton's hesitancy, the 1776 campaign opened auspiciously for him. The desperate siege before Quebec that was maintained by the Americans throughout the winter broke up with the appearance of the first British relief ship on May 6. Carleton immediately sent 900 men marching out of Quebec and across the Plains of Abraham, but they found only a disordered abandoned American camp. Since he had received only token reinforcements as yet, Carleton made no further attempt to pursue the retreating Americans. Even after General Burgoyne arrived in Quebec on June 1 with full instructions for the 1776 campaign, Carleton took no energetic action. Instead he paused to supervise elaborate preparations for the advance up the St. Lawrence against Montreal and St. Johns, as day after day additional British transports and warships arrived. Not the least of his concerns was the need to re-establish his communications across the Canadian countryside to learn what he could of the enemy's retreat.

Fearing that the rebels were still strong enough to threaten his exposed moving columns should he drop his guard, Carleton prepared to establish and organize his forces at Three Rivers before advancing upon Sorel and Montreal. His caution apparently was warranted. On June 8, General Sullivan with about 2,000 men dropped down from Sorel, crossed the St. Lawrence, and struck the redcoats collecting at Three Rivers. Ignorant of the British strength and disposition, and delayed from delivering a surprise blow at the critical moment because of the treachery of his guide, Sullivan was completely routed by the vastly superior force he encountered. The American general thus found himself on the north side of the river and all but cut off from his main army by the British forces controlling the waterway. Had Carleton been disposed to give chase, or had he fully realized the predicament the rebels were in, he might have smashed Sullivan's force in short order. But other matters were uppermost in his mind. Lacking precise knowledge of the situation, he permitted his "deluded" foe to escape, hoping the Americans might return home convinced of the benevolence of British rule and of the futility of trying to resist British regulars.[23] His thinking along these lines was perhaps natural when serving as a statesman of the empire, but it was odd conduct for a military commander.

Rather than attempting to follow up his unexpected victory over Sullivan by pressing the pursuit and improvising to meet changing conditions, Carleton chose to proceed with his original plan. Brigadier General Fraser, placed in command of a strong column, was directed to march up the north shore of the St. Lawrence for Montreal to cut off one avenue of retreat. General Burgoyne with 4,000 men was ordered to move against the main body of Americans withdrawing toward St. Johns from Sorel. Carleton himself set off with the remaining troops on board ship for Montreal. He intended to advance from that point on the St. Lawrence overland to cut off the Americans at St. Johns before they could escape southward. To ensure that the enemy would not elude the trap, Burgoyne was cautioned to advance slowly, lest the Americans flee too rapidly. This would enable Carleton to move into position. But Carleton had failed to reckon with two factors—the wind, which delayed his advance up river from Sorel, and the energy of the Americans, who learned of the British approach in time to effect a hasty retreat. Burgoyne, as a result, was denied a deserved victory by a very narrow margin. Just as Burgoyne's advance guard rushed into St. Johns, the last boatloads of Arnold's men rowed out of sight toward Lake Champlain.[24] By moving ponderously and with such measured speed, Carleton had clearly demonstrated that he did not have the instincts of a skilled military commander.

Although St. Johns was his, the governor now found that he had to fight for control of the lakes before he could make the force of his numbers felt against the rebels to the southward. Having foreseen the need of vessels for just this occasion, he had long ago requested that boats, naval stores, and artificers be sent out with his relief. But shortages of materials and skilled labor, coupled with Howe's more urgent need for landing craft at New York, had made it impossible for the government to meet his request.[25] A few small gunboats capable of mounting one gun each and flat-bottomed boats for carrying troops were sent, but they hardly met his requirements.

Carleton had no choice, then, but to set his men to building vessels capable of wresting control of Lake Champlain from the Americans. In the meantime, he returned to Quebec to address himself to the problems of the province. During the long pause in the fighting that followed, he was again plunged into the oft-delayed task of organizing the Canadian government. Simultaneously, however, he had the pleasure of learning that for his successful defense of Quebec he had been knighted by a grateful king.

The task of constructing a fleet dragged on throughout the summer and was pursued with little sense of urgency. The Americans meanwhile were left virtually unmolested, and Carleton did almost nothing to reconnoiter the enemy positions. Although the American situation at Ticonderoga was often desperate and the leading officers there were for a time divided on the wisdom of contesting passage of the lake, Carleton made no significant move to ascertain the enemy's ability to defend the forts at the southern end of Lake Champlain. Early in September, when he learned of the unexpected strength of the rebel armament on the lake, he belatedly decided to have the *Inflexible*—a square-rigged three-master mounting eighteen guns—dismantled, dragged up from Chambly to St. Johns, and reassembled. His decision to do so was correct, for the *Inflexible* provided the margin by which Carleton would dominate the lake, but the project was a herculean one that consumed an additional 28 crucial days.

By the time Carleton sailed from Isle-aux-Noix on October 4 and began to search for the American flotilla under Benedict Arnold which was to dispute his passage, the season for campaigning was drawing rapidly to an end. Proceeding slowly and keeping a sharp watch, Carleton spotted the enemy vessels on the eleventh. They were anchored advantageously between Valcour Island and the west shore of the lake where he would be forced to attack them from the leeward. The battle that followed, decisive as it was, was a very unequal match.[26] Although the Americans fought heroically, Carleton's men performed skillfully and the British naval force had guns capable of discharging double the weight thrown out by the enemy. Arnold's flotilla suffered a disastrous defeat. Prolonging the inevitable, Arnold maneuvered his battered force past the British under cover of fog and darkness and momentarily escaped southward. But two days later, Carleton finished off the American fleet within sight of Crown Point. Watching his advance, the American troops on shore put the Crown Point fort to the torch and marched off to Ticonderoga, leaving the British to take possession of the smoldering ruins the following morning, undisputed masters of the lake.

Carleton now faced the most crucial decision of his military career—whether to attempt to drive the Americans from Ticonderoga at once or withdraw for the winter and resume the attack in the spring. Maintaining a large garrison deep in the wilderness exposed to enemy harassment during a northern winter involved risks that even a less careful commander would have hesitated to take. Considering Carleton's prudence, the advanced season, and the hazards to which his army would be exposed in winter quarters on the lake, the decision was perhaps inevitable. After surveying the outer works of the fortress, Carleton feared that General Gates, now in command of the northern army, had done his work too well to attempt a challenge so late in the year. The vigor with which Arnold and Gates had already moved to slow his advance suggested that Ticonderoga would be difficult to storm, and too little time remained to carry out a protracted siege. Following a cautious thrust at the American defenses on October 27, Carleton ordered a more vigorous probe on the twenty-ninth, which confirmed his worst suspicions. He promptly ordered a withdrawal.[27] A few hours later, preparations were also underway for the evacuation of Crown Point.

Within two weeks Carleton was back in Quebec immersed in his work as governor of the province. Although he did not know it at the time, his days of active campaigning against American armies were at an end. From this point on in his career, he was to be a statesman rather than soldier.

During the winter, Carleton could reflect pleasantly on the changes he had wrought in Quebec's situation, and on the honor bestowed upon him for his tenacious defense of the city—the red ribbon of a Knight of the Bath—but surely little else gave him comfort. He knew he had failed to destroy the American army thrown against him, and the lake forts remained in enemy hands. Moreover, when meetings of the Legislative Council were resumed in the spring he found himself in the unaccustomed presence of men who dared to question his recommendations. Before long he was embroiled in controversy over alleged irregularities in his administration.[28] Thus, when he received letters from Germain questioning his management of the 1776 campaign coupled with news that General John Burgoyne would be given command of the northern army for the 1777 offensive, the implied criticisms were more than Sir Guy could stand. His letters of May 20th and 22nd to Germain, written in whatever passion he permitted himself, were surely two of the most vitriolic ever penned by a British officer to a secretary of state.[29] Even the king took note of them, remarking that "Carleton was highly wrong in permitting his pen to convey such asperity to a Secretary of State." [30]

Although the quarrel between the two men ostensibly flared up as a consequence of Germain's criticism of Carleton's conduct in 1776, the dispute actually arose from an accumulation of disappointments which Sir Guy had encountered since his return to America in 1774.[31] Despite his early confident predictions, the Quebec Act had not won the active support of the Canadians. Neither his military victories nor his humane treatment of prisoners had brought the rebels to their senses. He had been criticized for dividing his army into brigades and ignoring eligible senior officers in filling the new positions he had created. Several of his civil appointments had been questioned or vetoed.[32] And his use of the Council had drawn him into political squabbles which eventually led him to a painful confrontation with the chief justice of Quebec. Germain, no less frustrated by the outcome of the 1776 campaign and already stung by offensive letters from Carleton, had reacted to the withdrawal from Lake Champlain by binding Carleton to inflexible orders—orders which left Carleton little future discretionary control over troops in Canada and which could only be construed as a want of confidence.

Carleton's reaction, intemperate as it was, is not at all surprising. Germain, whipping boy of the Ministry and architect of Britain's aggressive military plans, was an easy mark for his attack. No individual was responsible for all the delays and shortages that had contributed to the failures of British arms in 1776, but the secretary of state was the person most vulnerable to criticism. He was not inclined to be charitable toward his commanders in America. Believing that Carleton had mismanaged the defense of Canada in 1775, he had begrudged him the red ribbon in recognition of his preservation of Quebec. And from the time he received Carleton's first insulting letters in mid-1776 he had intrigued to have him recalled from Canada. Their reaction to one another after 1777 was the struggle of two offended prima donnas. Certainly neither man was entirely free of guilt nor merited the full abuse they heaped upon one another. But since Carleton launched the attack and resorted to false charges and devious accusations, his surely was the greater offense.

Nevertheless, Carleton did not permit the dispute with Germain to hamper preparations for Burgoyne's invasion of New York. Carleton rose momentarily above his pique and contributed importantly, as only he could do, to place the resources of Canada at the disposal of Burgoyne's army. Indeed, the zeal he displayed in behalf of the expedition was later explicitly acknowledged by Burgoyne in a speech before Parliament. Despite the decisive consequences of his failure to capture and retain control of Lake Champlain in 1776, Carleton's conduct in 1777 was clearly not directly responsible for the British defeat at Saratoga.

Yet his usefulness in Canada, he felt, was at an end. In an explosive letter on June 27, 1777, he finally released his remaining pent-up feelings against Germain and formally requested permission to return to England. Since his letter of resignation was written in the aftermath of an unpleasant political encounter with one of the most respected members of his Council, it is probable that he had more than the secretary of state's criticisms on his mind. His shafts were aimed unmistakably at Germain, however, and could not help but have the intended effect. Every line bore the mark of Carleton's bitterness.[33]

> [As] . . . all the marks of your Lordship's displeasure affect not me but the King's service and the tranquillity of his people, I flatter myself I shall obtain his royal permission to return home this fall, the more so that from your first entrance into office, you began to prepare the minds of all men for this event, wisely foreseeing that under your Lordship's administration it must certainly come to pass, and for my own part I do not think it just that the private enmity of the King's servants should add to the disturbances of his reign. For these reasons I shall embark with great satisfaction, still entertaining hopes and ardent wishes that after my departure you may adopt measures tending to promote the safety and tranquillity of this unfortunate Province; at least, that the dignity of the Crown may not appear beneath your Lordship's concern.

Although a successor was immediately named to replace him, Carleton remained in Canada until the summer of 1778. Bad weather intervened to delay the changing of the Canadian command, forcing him to remain yet another winter in Quebec, and extending his term of office in the province to nearly twelve years. He had filled a taxing post, demanding a wide range of talents, during some exceedingly difficult years, and though he was returning under something of a cloud all who knew his record still regarded him as one of Britain's foremost statesmen. Few questioned the results of his command in America at that time, for attention in 1778 was drawn to Saratoga and the entry

of France into the war; the grosser details of his conduct of
government in Canada were as yet undisclosed.[34]

Within a few months after his return, Carleton had settled
down to the leisurely routine of a Hampshire country gentleman. But he was not destined for early retirement. With the
passage of time, his name was frequently mentioned in connection
with a possible new assignment in America. Yet there were obstacles to be overcome. As long as Germain remained in office,
Carleton's appointment was out of the question. And he apparently nursed such a grievance against the commander-in-
chief (Jeffrey Amherst) that George III was once led to remark that "Sir Guy Carleton dislikes Ld. Amherst so much that
it is not very easy to employ him." [35]

But by the time of the Yorktown disaster, over three years
had elapsed since Carleton's departure from Canada, and Britain
had nearly exhausted her supply of eligible generals. When
Germain was jettisoned in February, 1782, in a last-minute political move to save the North Ministry, the way was cleared
for Carleton's selection as Sir Henry Clinton's successor as commander-in-chief in America. All that had to be decided was the
precise nature of the powers that were to be conferred upon
the new commander. On his part, Sir Guy ardently hoped to
negotiate a reconciliation of the American colonies. On March
26, 1782, he was formally notified that in addition to his military appointment he had been designated, along with Admiral
Digby, commissioner "for restoring peace and granting pardon
to the revolted provinces in America." [36]

Much to his subsequent regret, Carleton had unwittingly
stepped back onto the stage of history in the midst of a mo-
mentous political crisis.[37] During his last days in England, the
Opposition in Parliament had gained momentum, and barely
forty-eight hours after he received his appointment the Rockingham Ministry took office. Despite all the king could do—for
he kept insisting that he would sanction only "a change in men"
—the occasion became one for sweeping changes. The result has
been labeled a "political massacre"; and in the aftermath, those

in office were "shot by platoons." In order to carry out the
wishes of the new Ministry to liquidate the war with America
and to make peace, Carleton was pointedly notified, on the eve
of his departure, that "the first object of your attention must
be to provide for withdrawing the Garrison . . . from New
York and its dependencies to Halifax." Similar arrangements
were to be made for Charleston, Savannah, and St. Augustine.[38]
With a few strokes of the pen, Carleton's dreams of a reconciliation were shattered beyond repair.

The news must have hurt Carleton deeply. As he made the
voyage to America, the parallel between the position he was now
in and that of the Carlisle Commission in 1778 could not have
escaped his attention. If he were to conduct any negotiations at
all, it would be from a position of obvious weakness. Although
the Ministry had not formally recognized the independence of
the colonies, he now believed with others that a giant step had
been taken in the headlong plunge toward the dissolution of
the whole empire.

Nevertheless, Carleton put on a good face as he stepped ashore
at New York in the first week in May, 1782. He was determined
to make the best of a bad situation. Within a few days, he was
hard at work trying to find out what might yet be done to save
his mission from failure. In a play for time, he made polite overtures to Washington while he wrote reports to London that he
had reason to believe the colonies might acknowledge allegiance
to the king, if they were given control over the management of
their internal affairs.[39] He proposed also that he evacuate the
southern ports first and bring their garrisons to New York—
where their presence might strengthen his hand with Congress—
claiming that adequate tonnage was not available for the immediate evacuation of New York. Finally, to complete his
scheme, he audaciously diverted to New York reinforcements
intended for Halifax.[40] For a time he must honestly have believed that he could so augment the strength of the New York
garrison that he might bring the Americans to the bargaining
table, despite the drift of the Ministry on another course. His-

torians, surprisingly enough, have never noted Carleton's interesting attempt to challenge the Ministry's policy at this stage.[41]

It was all in vain. To open the way for serious negotiations with the American commissioners in Paris, the Ministry already had made concessions that Carleton interpreted as tantamount to a recognition of independence. He learned of these concessions on July 31. Two weeks later he decided to request the king's permission to resign, for he had accepted the American command only to promote a reconciliation.[42] Moreover, recent reports from his American informants were less favorable than previous ones. The "rulers of the provinces" had not yet shown the least disposition to take "pacific measures," and it was all too obvious that "every artifice" was being employed to inflame the passions and mislead the understanding of the public.[43] Thwarted in a noble enterprise by misguided leaders bent on sacrificing American interests to France, and feeling victimized by ministers at home once again, he wanted to wash his hands of the whole affair. Only fourteen weeks had passed since his arrival in New York.

But it was not to be. Tedious communications and a late change in British strategy designed to exploit Rodney's stunning naval victory in West Indies waters in April, 1782, delayed acceptance of Carleton's request until January 1, 1783. Ironically enough, the orders directing Carleton to embark for Barbados to take on new duties after he had completed the evacuation of New York were dispatched from London the very day Sir Guy had written for permission to resign.[44] Since the Ministry now planned a new West Indian campaign, it was at first assumed that Carleton would withdraw his request to resign once he received his new instructions. Another exchange of letters was required in October, 1782, before the Ministry learned that he was firm in his intention to leave. Apparently not even the prospect of a new offensive could reconcile Carleton to the government, and General Charles Grey was finally appointed to relieve him.

The change of command, however, never took place, and in

consequence the greatest opportunity of Carleton's career now opened to him. Sent to New York on a difficult mission, and stranded there by a quirk of fate, he soon found a new cause worthy of his commitment—the protection of the refugee American loyalists. New York, the site of some of the most heart-rending scenes during the closing months of the war, provided Carleton a unique vantage point from which to survey the ruins of the Old British Empire and to catch a glimpse of a new one. He helped to evacuate all loyalists who desired to remain under His Majesty's protection, and used every resource at his command to secure them new homes. These refugees, he believed, would form the nucleus of a regenerated empire which Carleton hoped to salvage from the American wreck.

When the last refugees had been evacuated, Carleton sailed for London, where plans were matured to consolidate the remaining North American provinces under a single government.[45] Within a short time, he reluctantly abandoned the idea of retirement for the prospect of returning to Canada as governor-general of British North America. But he failed to secure the broad powers that would have made him an American viceroy. The government, perhaps in response to Carleton's previous authoritarian rule in Quebec, was reluctant to place such authority in the hands of one agent so far removed from direct control. Though created Baron Dorchester in 1786 and returned to Canada as governor and commander-in-chief of several provinces jointly, he was consistently thwarted in his final efforts at imperial consolidation. He later made only minor contributions to the Constitutional Act of 1791, which against his will divided a great imperial domain into Upper and Lower Canada. Characteristically, he ended his days in America wrangling with the United States over British control of the Northwest posts and arguing with Canadian officials whom he could not bend to his decisions. Rebuked by the home government for inflammatory conduct against the United States at a time when John Jay was on his mission to London in 1794 to settle the Anglo-American dispute, Carleton for the third and last time in his life offered his resignation. He returned to England finally in the summer of 1796, and spent the last twelve years of his life in retirement on his country estates.

In the strict sense that he had not achieved what had been expected of him and had made inadequate use of the resources placed at his disposal, Guy Carleton's military command was a failure. But to stop the evaluation of his military career at that point is to miss much of the significance of his role in America. Carleton's generalship can no more be separated from his governorship than one can study the war with the colonies independently from the war between England and France. He must be judged, if judged fairly, in the context of the operation of the British imperial system and eighteenth-century provincial government as well as in the light of his military record.[46]

There was a certain logic in his conduct, which if not always excusable, is certainly explicable. Although a general by profession, he became an active military leader by force of circumstance, and made the transition from peacetime provincial governor to wartime commander with difficulty. His experience of nearly a decade led him at the outset to view the Revolution primarily as a political rather than a military matter, and long after the government had decided to apply a military solution to the problem Carleton was still preoccupied with provincial political issues. The result was to blunt the ministerial program of coercion. He was not, of course, entirely wrong in his assumptions, but at times he arrogated to himself choices that were not his to make.

An autocrat, suspicious of the motives of others and often devious in his methods, Carleton was frequently at odds with his superiors. In part, the conflicts must be charged to ample defects of character. He had a strong tendency to self-righteousness, and too little sense of his fallibility. His self-confidence often betrayed him into arrogance, and his independence of will into insubordination. Yet who could rule Canada for a dozen years, cut off from the outside world six months of each twelve, without developing such defects? Governors of Quebec were expected to exhibit many of Carleton's qualities. His orders almost always reserved to him options that only he could judge at the scene of action. If in the end the empire suffered because of the character of her officials, such abuses were inevitable.

As a military commander, Carleton had obvious shortcomings. His was not an agile mind; he did not respond quickly to changing conditions, and too often seemed content merely to meet the most immediate threat, leaving greater initiative to others. He responded unenthusiastically to Gage's earliest calls for a military diversion on the frontier and consistently looked first to the defense of his own province. When the American command was divided after Gage returned to England, Carleton never quite fully grasped the fact that his responsibilities for checking the rebellion transcended provincial boundaries. Charged with more than any man could handle, busy vindicating his Canadian policies, and forced to grapple with "seditious" merchants and "stupid" habitants, he probably never adequately identified the real enemy.

Yet Canada itself was "saved." Although there were some in Britain who hoped that Carleton might have helped to save the other provinces as well, many believed that he had done enough. He had not, of course, and as a result of this contradiction Carleton will always remain a controversial figure.

Any assessment of Carleton as a military man has similar contradictions. His critics, on the one hand, have argued that he virtually "threw away" resounding victories that were within his grasp, without adequately considering whether *any* defeat administered to an American army within the borders of Canada would have had a decisive effect beyond its boundaries.[47] Carleton's military responsibilities beyond the frontier of the province of Quebec were never clear, but this ambiguity cannot be laid entirely to the governor. His apologists have generally been even less helpful, for too often they have absolved Carleton of almost every failure. Uncritically attributing his defeats simply to incompetence in London,[48] they have ignored much of the reality of eighteenth-century warfare. Moreover, they go much too far in claiming that Carleton was indispensable after Yorktown, and that in this last crisis Britain was forced to seek "the master-hand of Carleton . . . for no government could have done without him." [49]

To numerous loyalist exiles, particularly those "British Canadians" who sought to make a new life for themselves as neighbors of the French already in Canada, Carleton was a statesman without peer. If ever they and the "French Canadians" were to be reconciled to a life together within a single state, their leader had to combine the vision that produced the Quebec Act with the humanity that marked the British treatment of the loyalists. Thus, with the passage of time Carleton easily became a legend. For many he became a hero in Canada comparable perhaps to Parson Weems' Washington, but such myth-making could only be achieved by neglecting critical contemporary accounts. In the popular imagination he was easily contrasted with a bumbling Germain, and serious students, noting the dearth of surviving Carleton manuscripts, shied away from any evaluation of him until the past generation. Perhaps enough never will be known of him to remove the shell of legend from the kernel of truth that lies inside. But those who would understand Carleton's role in the War of American Independence must attempt to see both the man and the legend.

FOOTNOTES

1. The bare details of his early life can be found most conveniently in Arthur G. Bradley, *Sir Guy Carleton (Lord Dorchester)*, (3d ed.; Toronto, 1966); and William Wood, *The Father of British Canada: A Chronicle of Carleton* (Toronto, 1916).
2. Carleton to Shelburne, November 25, 1767. Adam Shortt and Arthur G. Doughty, eds., *Documents Relating to the Constitutional History of Canada, 1759–1791*, 2 vols. (Ottawa, 1907), I, pp. 196–99.
3. Carleton to Gage, February 15, 1767, Gage Papers, Clements Li-

brary, Ann Arbor, Michigan. Hereafter, all Gage Papers cited are in Clements Library.

4. William Smith, "The Struggle over the Laws of Canada, 1763–1783," *Canadian Historical Review*, I (1920), pp. 166–86; and Alfred L. Burt, "Sir Guy Carleton and His First Council," *ibid.*, IV (1923), pp. 321–32.

5. Alfred L. Burt, *Guy Carleton, Lord Dorchester, 1724–1808*, Canadian Historical Association, Historical Booklet No. 5 (Rev. ed.; Ottawa, 1964), p. 3.

6. Gage to Carleton, September 4, 1774, Gage Papers.

7. Carleton to Gage, September 20, 1774, *ibid.*

8. Carleton to Gage, February 4, 1775, "secret," *ibid.*

9. Smith, "The Struggle over the Laws of Canada," pp. 173–76.

10. The fullest accounts of these events and the operations that follow are Justin H. Smith, *Our Struggle for the Fourteenth Colony*, 2 vols. (New York & London, 1907), I, pp. 304–491; and Allen French, *The First Year of the American Revolution* (Boston, 1934), pp. 376–442.

11. Peter Force, ed., *American Archives*, Fourth Series (Washington, 1837–53), II, p. 940; Alfred L. Burt, *The Old Province of Quebec* (Minneapolis & Toronto, 1933), p. 213.

12. The extensive correspondence bearing on this problem is conveniently summarized in "Extracts from records of Indian affairs under Colonel Guy Johnson during 1775," Germain Papers, Clements Library. It can be followed more laboriously through Carleton's correspondence with Dartmouth, "Q" series, Volume XI, pp. 152–271, Public Archives of Canada (Ottawa), and with Gage, in the volumes for February 4, 1775–September 29, 1775, Gage Papers.

13. Carleton to Gage, July 27, 1775, Gage Papers; and Carleton to Dartmouth, August 14, 1775, "Q," XI, pp. 222–25.

14. Carleton to Dartmouth, October 25, 1775, *ibid.*, pp. 268–69.

15. "Papers Relating to the Surrender of Fort St. Johns and Fort Chambly," *Report of the Work of the Public Archives for the years 1914 and 1915*, (Ottawa, 1916), Sessional Paper 29a, App. B, p. 25.

16. Carleton to Dartmouth, November 5, 1775, *Report on Canadian Archives, 1890* (Ottawa, 1890), pp. 65–66.

17. Smith, *Struggle for the Fourteenth Colony*, I, pp. 487–88.

18. *Ibid.*, II, pp. 76–110.

19. In addition to Smith, *ibid.*, pp. 111–47, see also French, *The First Year of the American Revolution*, pp. 595–620; Christopher Ward,

The War of the Revolution, John R. Alden, ed., 2 vols. (New York, 1952), I, pp. 181–95; and Carleton to Germain, May 14, 1776, "Q," XII, pp. 7–10.

20. For an authoritative discussion of the "strategy of reconquest," see Piers Mackesy's splendid work, *The War for America, 1775–1783* (Cambridge, Mass., 1964), pp. 56–61. From our present perspective, the vigor and energy that went into the organization of the 1776 campaign appear as something of an illusion, but no assessment of British strategy can ignore the very real achievements of the North Ministry in this work. No one could have foreseen that neither Howe nor Carleton would be able to strike the rebels a mortal blow with the great armies about to be placed at their command.

21. Since Carleton was the senior officer in America when Gage left Boston, the American command was divided at that time to enable Carleton to remain in Quebec to deal with that province and "the frontiers bordering thereupon," while Howe was left in command of all forces operating in the remaining colonies. Dartmouth to Gage, August 2, 1775, Gage Papers; and Dartmouth to Carleton, August 2, 1775, "Q," XI, pp. 198–99. The fact of Carleton's seniority over Howe was also at the root of another important matter, the appointment of Burgoyne to command the northern army in 1777. It was always assumed that Carleton would supersede Howe should their armies be united, and Burgoyne was eventually given command to avoid this embarrassing possibility. But Carleton by chance failed to learn the reasons for the decision until nearly nine months had elapsed after it had been made, and he preferred to believe that the appointment was a form of censure. The episode therefore contributed importantly to his estrangement from Germain. Germain to Carleton, August 22, 1776, "Q," XII, pp. 88–90, and March 26, 1777, Historical Manuscripts Commission, *Report on the Manuscripts of Mrs. Stopford-Sackville, of Drayton House, Northamptonshire,* 2 vols. (London, 1904–10), II, pp. 60–63; John W. Fortescue, ed., *Correspondence of King George III,* 6 vols. (London, 1927–28), III, Nos. 1630, 1685.

22. Gerald S. Brown, *The American Secretary: The Colonial Policy of Lord George Germain, 1775–1778* (Ann Arbor, 1963), pp. 6–16, 83–85, 89–93, 103; Alfred L. Burt, "The Quarrel between Germain and Carleton: An Inverted Story," *Canadian Historical Review,* XI (September, 1930), pp. 202–22.

23. Similarly, when Carleton later took time to explain to Germain his policy of releasing prisoners, he emphasized the need "to con-

vince all His Majesty's unhappy subjects, that the King's mercy and Benevolence were still open to them." Britain could only "turn the scale," he believed, by exhibiting "valor and good conduct in action, with humanity and friendly treatment to those who are subdued and at our mercy." Carleton to Germain, August 10, 1776, "Q," XII, p. 135. See also his letter to Howe of August 8, 1776, quoted in Bradley, *Sir Guy Carleton,* p. 139.

24. Carleton to Germain, June 20, 1776, "Q," XII, pp. 64–67. For an interesting contemporary picture reflecting a sense of the confusion and disorder that marked the army's activities during the spring and summer of 1776, see the journal of Lt. William Digby, "Some Account of the American War between Great Britain and her Colonies," in James P. Baxter, *The British Invasion from the North* (Albany, 1887), pp. 104–77.

25. Mackesy, *The War for America,* pp. 94–95.

26. There is considerable literature upon the subject, for the control of the lake was rightly considered crucial to the outcome of the War of Independence. See, for example, Alfred T. Mahan, *Major Operations of the Navies in the War of Independence* (Boston, 1913), pp. 13–26; Gardner W. Allen, *A Naval History of the American Revolution,* 2 vols. (Boston, 1913), I, pp. 163–79; and Ward, *The War of the Revolution,* I, chapter 35.

27. The fullest recent account dealing with Carleton's career in 1776 is Perry Eugene Leroy, "Sir Guy Carleton as a Military Leader during the American Invasion and Repulse in Canada, 1775–1776," (unpublished Ph.D. dissertation, Ohio State University, 1960). For the decision to withdraw from Lake Champlain, see pp. 472–81, and for the staggering logistical problems that faced Carleton, pp. 542–47. For a contemporary view of Carleton's "very unaccountable conduct" during this period, see Historical Manuscripts Commission, *Report on the Manuscripts of the Late Reginald Hastings,* 4 vols. (London, 1928–41), III, p. 189.

28. Smith, "The Struggle over the Laws of Canada," pp. 177–78.

29. Germain to Carleton, March 26, 1777, *Manuscripts of Mrs. Stopford-Sackville,* II, pp. 60–63; and Carleton to Germain, May 20 and 22, 1777, "Q," XIII, pp. 111–20, 156–59.

30. *Correspondence of George III,* IV, No. 2202. George III was equally disturbed with Germain's performance during the dispute between the two men, noting "the malevolence of his mind." *Ibid.*

31. The dispute has been treated at length by Alfred L. Burt, "The Quarrel between Germain and Carleton: An Inverted Story." For an interesting discussion of Burgoyne's contribution to the quarrel

and the influence of the dispute on the selection of a commander for the 1777 invasion of New York, see William B. Willcox, *Portrait of a General: Sir Henry Clinton in the War of Independence* (New York, 1964), pp. 133–34.

32. Since Carleton by chance received no fewer than fourteen letters from Germain on May 6, 1777, dated August 22, 1776, March 24 and 26, 1777, an accumulation of Germain's criticisms fell upon him as a single blow. See "Q," XII, pp. 84–93, and "Q," XIII, pp. 73–98.

33. Carleton to Germain, June 27, 1777, *Report on Canadian Archives, 1890*, pp. 88–89.

34. Lord North, for example, believed him to be "so much of a soldier, and so little of a politician, such a resolute, honest man, and such a faithful and dutiful subject," that he wished another command was available for him. North to George III, August 30, 1779, *Correspondence of George III*, IV, No. 2753. And of his professional qualities even Germain retained a high opinion throughout the war. See Germain to William Knox, July 13 and November 11, 1782, Historical Manuscripts Commission, *Report on Manuscripts in Various Collections*, 8 vols. (London, 1901–14), VI, pp. 186, 189.

35. *Correspondence of George III*, IV, No. 2754.

36. Welbore Ellis to Carleton, March 26, 1782, British Headquarters' Papers, No. 4302. New York Public Library. Hereafter N.Y.P.L.

37. Mackesy, *The War for America*, pp. 466–74.

38. Orders of April 4, 1782, Colonial Office Papers, Series 5, vol. 106, pp. 1–13. Library of Congress.

39. Carleton to Shelburne, May 12, 1782, *ibid.*, p. 41. For the place of Carleton's mission in the policy of Secretary of State Shelburne, see Vincent T. Harlow, *The Founding of the Second British Empire, 1763–1793* (London, 1952), pp. 263–68.

40. Carleton to Shelburne, May 24, and June 18, 1782, C.O. 5: 106, pp. 50–51, 267–68. Library of Congress.

41. Though it would be unfair to charge that Carleton upon his arrival deliberately hatched a plan to challenge the Ministry, it is nevertheless clear enough that so long as he thought he still had the chance he seized every opportunity available to play the role of an American viceroy. The day after he decided to resign, he wrote the following explanation of his recent acts. "My intentions were to have assembled here the troops from the southward, with the years' reinforcement from Europe; had this measure taken place, it would have given some security till an evacuation became pos-

sible; *it would have added some weight too to any negotiation here,* had such been thought advisable; in every circumstance *it must have commanded a respect which we have no claim to in our present situation.* Carleton to Shelburne, August 15, 1782, *ibid.,* pp. 332–33. Italics mine.

42. See Carleton to Haldimand, August 3, 1782, British Headquarters' Papers, No. 5203, N.Y.P.L.; and Carleton to Shelburne, August 14, 1782, *ibid.,* No. 5292.

43. Carleton to Shelburne, June 18, 1782, C.O. 5: 106, p. 269. Library of Congress.

44. Townshend to Carleton, August 14, 1782, *ibid.,* pp. 291–306.

45. Leslie F. S. Upton, *The Diary and Selected Papers of Chief Justice William Smith, 1784–1793,* 2 vols. (Toronto, 1963), I, pp. xxxiv–xxxvii.

46. For an analysis of the complex interaction between political and military factors that shaped British policy before the Revolution, see John Shy's admirable recent study, *Toward Lexington: The Role of the British Army in the Coming of the American Revolution* (Princeton, 1965), especially pp. 418–24.

47. Burt, *Guy Carleton, Lord Dorchester, 1724–1808,* p. 9.

48. Bradley, *Sir Guy Carleton (Lord Dorchester),* pp. 165–70.

49. Wood, *The Father of British Canada,* p. 164.

BIBLIOGRAPHY

Bradley, Arthur G. *Sir Guy Carleton (Lord Dorchester).* Toronto, 1907. A readable study, first published in the Makers of Canada Series, sympathetically portraying Carleton as one of the greatest proconsuls of the empire, but innocent of any real appreciation of the actualities of his administrations. Should be read only in the revised editions (1926, 1966), for which Alfred L. Burt furnished numerous critical appendices.

Burt, Alfred L. *Guy Carleton, Lord Dorchester, 1724–1808.* Ottawa, 1964. A brief summation by the leading Carleton authority, erring seriously only in his estimate of Carleton's conduct in New York in 1782.

————. *The Old Province of Quebec.* Minneapolis & Toronto, 1933. The indispensable work on the subject of the forces working upon Carleton. Mild reservations to Burt's judgments have been registered in Michel Brunet's brief *French Canada and the Early Decades of British Rule, 1760–1791* (Ottawa, 1963).

French, Allen. *The First Year of the American Revolution*. Boston, 1934. A good detailed account of the American invasion of Canada and the assault on Quebec.

Mackesy, Piers. *The War for America, 1775–1783*. Cambridge, Mass., 1964. The best comprehensive study of the British conduct of the war. Accurately depicts the place of Canada in the opening phases of the war, and shrewdly assesses Carleton's qualities as governor and commander in the field.

Smith, Justin H. *Our Struggle for the Fourteenth Colony*. 2 vols. New York, 1907. An older reliable work containing the most detailed descriptions of military operations in Canada before 1777.

Wood, William. *The Father of British Canada: A Chronicle of Carleton*. Toronto, 1916. A popular survey, drawing heavily upon Bradley's work.

Wrong, George M. *Canada and the American Revolution*. Toronto, 1935. A useful study assessing broadly Carleton's conduct and the impact of the Revolution on the development of Canada.

John Burgoyne:

AMBITIOUS GENERAL

GEORGE ATHAN BILLIAS

Clark University

OF THE British generals in the American Revolution, none has been ridiculed more than John Burgoyne. Perhaps this was so because no other British military leader lent himself so readily to caricature. Certain of his contemporaries pictured Burgoyne as a playboy general—a card-playing, wine-loving *bon vivant* who had a winning way with women in the boudoir but a losing style on the battlefield; a buffoon in uniform who bungled his assignments badly; and a dilettante who pursued three careers— those of soldier, politician, and playwright—and mastered none. Such a conception of Burgoyne was based upon hostile sources of the period—the *Parliamentary Debates* in which Lord George Germain vilified him, the memoirs of Baroness von Riedesel, and the journals of Horace Walpole. The baroness, who accompanied Burgoyne's army to Saratoga, was responsible for one of the brilliant but bitter portraits left for posterity: Burgoyne liked a "jolly time," she wrote, and spent "half the night singing and drinking and amusing himself in the company of the wife of a commissary, who was his mistress, and, like himself, liked champagne." [1] More touches were added by Horace Walpole, the English author, who dubbed him "General Swagger" and "Julius Caesar Burgonius," and complained of his boasts to cross America in "a hop, step and jump." [2] But this characterization of

142

Burgoyne is misleading. While revealing some of his personality traits, it discloses little regarding his military capabilities. To understand Burgoyne's qualities as a general, one must look beyond his moral foibles as a man.

Many military historians and biographers writing about Burgoyne in later years often perpetuated much the same conception of the man as that held by his less friendly contemporaries; hence, the widespread use of the nickname, "Gentleman Johnny." Picturing him as an eighteenth-century gentleman-general, these writers drew conclusions about his military ability based upon this crude stereotype. Even when fighting in the forests of upper New York, they noted, he insisted upon the social amenities of an English drawing room—silver plate, fine wines, and female companions. Burgoyne's need for creature comforts in the wilderness, they went on, caused him to swell the size of his baggage train and slowed down the advance of his invading army. This weakness, coupled with his ignorance of conditions in America and his incompetence as a commander, led to his downfall at Saratoga. Those historians who projected the myth of the Revolutionary War as a struggle between two sets of generals—bumbling British aristocrats versus shrewd American citizen-soldiers—often used Burgoyne as their British example.

Like most stereotypes, this picture of Burgoyne as a gentleman-general had some truth to it. He was, after all, a member of the English ruling class, one accustomed to holding and wielding power throughout most of his life. As a military man, he was the product of a system in which family, "connexions," and wealth played a greater role in securing promotions than did merit. Functioning within this system, Burgoyne became as adept in the politics of the English military establishment as any of his fellow officers. If he differed in this respect from his colleagues, it was only because he was brighter, bolder, and often more open and direct in the manner in which he solicited patronage and position. In his personal as well as professional life, Burgoyne acted out the role of aristocrat; he drank, gambled, and pursued women as did other members of English high society.

But there was much more to Burgoyne than the stereotype suggests. His flamboyant style of life, in fact, concealed a complicated personality; both as a human being and soldier, he presents something of an enigma. He was, on the one hand, an appealing person to many; one with "a thousand good qualities," as Charles Lee put it.[3] Tall, graceful, and handsome, his charm and magnetism attracted men and women alike. Far from being a gay playboy, however, Burgoyne was a bleaker, tougher, and more driven individual than most historians realize. Throughout his life he displayed a ruthless egoism and constant compulsion to prove himself in whatever he attempted. A military man of considerable talent, he was romantic enough to have visions of gaining a great reputation as a general. His towering ambition and passion for fame explain, in large part, his restless energy as an army commander, his tendency to draw attention to himself, and his willingness to take risks on the battlefield.

Burgoyne's ideas on military matters likewise show that he was not the shallow person pictured by many writers. His views regarding the psychological basis for much of the military discipline of his day were striking. Such an understanding of disciplinary psychology helped him to evaluate foreign armies and to formulate his concept of leadership in the British army. His recognition of the role of ideology in the Revolutionary War enabled him to view the conflict in terms different than those of his fellow generals. And he demonstrated some degree of flexibility in changing his tactics to deal with an enemy who resorted to what he considered unorthodox methods of fighting.

Burgoyne, moreover, must be seen in broader perspective than that of a military man. With his extraordinary variety of talents, he was a perceptive critic as well as a participant in the events of the period. As a politician and playwright, Burgoyne showed the ability of standing apart from those English institutions of which he was a member and of viewing them in a critical light. The opinions he expressed in politics and literature did not always square with the stereotyped portrait presented by historians.

The circumstances of Burgoyne's birth—bearing as they do the breath of scandal—provide a possible insight into his aggressive drive for recognition in his military career. Presumably his father was Captain John Burgoyne, a baronet's son who squandered his wife's fortune and died a debtor; his mother, who reportedly gave birth on February 4, 1722, was the daughter of an English merchant.[4] Horace Walpole spread the story, however, that Burgoyne was illegitimate—the bastard offspring of Lord Bingley, chancellor of the Exchequer under Queen Anne and treasurer of the household at the time of his death in 1731. Walpole's remarks might be dismissed as malicious gossip were it not for the terms of Bingley's will. After providing for his wife, legitimate daughter, and an illegitimate daughter, Bingley left an annuity of £400 and two houses to Burgoyne's mother with the stipulation that her husband was to have no claim to the legacy. Bingley stipulated further that, if his legitimate daughter had no children and his illegitimate daughter no male heirs, his remaining property was to pass to John Burgoyne, "(which godson, I desire take [my name] . . . if my estate comes to him) for the rest of his natural life."[5] When a legitimate heir was born, Burgoyne lost his claim to the Bingley fortune. Whether he was illegitimate or merely Bingley's godson will never be known, but reports circulating during his lifetime regarding his parentage may have troubled Burgoyne and accentuated his desire to achieve distinction.

Burgoyne's runaway marriage at the age of twenty suggests not only a headstrong young man but one who was also a social climber. He eloped with Lady Charlotte Stanley—the daughter of the Earl of Derby and sister of his closest friend and former classmate at the Westminster School, Lord Strange. Running off with a woman of means was generally frowned upon in aristocratic circles, but Burgoyne was by no means unique in this respect. The practice became so commonplace that Parliament passed an act in 1753 to prevent such clandestine marriages. The bride's father, disapproving of the match, supposedly cut off the couple from any financial support for several years. Burgoyne's marriage into the great Stanley family, however, provided him with the necessary "connexion" with which to gain entry into the English power structure.

For his career, Burgoyne chose soldiering—one of the paths of preferment open to sons of the nobility. The fact that his father, several relatives, and his own son became army officers indicates that soldiering was in the family tradition. Burgoyne may have held an officer's commission prior to his marriage, but his rapid purchase of commissions after his elopement suggests that his bride brought a dowry with her despite parental objections to the match. The year after his marriage—1744—he was made a cornet in the 1st Royal Dragoons; in 1745 he purchased, in rapid succession, a lieutenant's and then a captain's commission.[6]

Burgoyne's army career, like that of so many British officers, was often interrupted for long periods. Having expensive tastes, he incurred huge debts which forced him to sell his commission in 1751 in order to pay off part of his bills. He fled to France to escape his unsatisfied creditors and lived on the continent for five years in self-imposed exile.[7] Being a man of a lively and inquiring mind, he put his time to good use; he mastered the French language and literature, studied the contemporary political scene, and learned much about conditions in the continental armies. Exactly how he settled his debts so that he might return to England is not known, but there is a strong suspicion that his father-in-law, the Earl of Derby, had become reconciled to the runaway match and changed his mind about helping his married daughter.

Burgoyne re-entered the British army in 1756, but apparently did so only because he was promised rapid promotion. After complaining to a friend about serving under officers he had formerly commanded, Burgoyne hinted that he could not long endure such an experience "had I not good assurances that I should not remain long a captain." [8] These "assurances" coupled with his purchase of a captaincy in the 11th Dragoons provide further evidence that the Derby family influence and fortune were being employed in Burgoyne's behalf. His prospects for a promising military career brightened even more when Britain and France went to war in mid-1756.

In the Seven Years' War, Burgoyne distinguished himself by a series of daring exploits. After participating in the coastal raids against Cherbourg and St. Malo, he was commissioned a lieutenant colonel in 1759 and ordered to raise a regiment of light cavalry. The 16th Dragoons bore so much the imprint of their dashing commander that they became known as "Burgoyne's Light Horse." Placed in command of an Anglo-Portuguese brigade of which his regiment was a part, Burgoyne sailed off to Portugal in the spring of 1762 to fight against the French and Spanish. His bold use of cavalry as an offensive striking arm soon earned him a reputation. Storming the town of Valencia with cavalry alone, Burgoyne surprised and destroyed an entire Spanish regiment in the summer campaign. He distinguished himself a second time by directing a raid of cavalry and grenadiers against the Spanish camp near Villa Velha in the fall. Although this stunning little victory over a superior force was actually carried out by his subordinate, Charles Lee, Burgoyne was given credit for planning the attack. Count William von der Lippe, the brilliant German general commanding the Portuguese army, sent glowing reports of Burgoyne's achievements to the British government and recommended him as an "excellent officer" and one "extremely worthy of his Majesty's remembrance." [9]

During this period, however, Burgoyne did not depend solely upon his military exploits to gain promotions; he resorted also to family influence, powerful friends, and personal effrontery. In a day when place-hunting was common, Burgoyne pushed his claims for higher command more ruthlessly than usual and without regard for the unwritten rules which normally governed politics within the English military establishment. Just how greedy he was in grasping for higher rank and personal privileges may be seen in two episodes. The first took place in 1759 when Burgoyne wrote to Viscount Barrington, the secretary at war, demanding a chaplain and hautboys for his regiment. Barrington refused the request, insinuating that it was an unseemly one from a man "who was [only] a captain a year and a half ago." Burgoyne, he noted, had became one of the youngest lieutenant colonels in the service "after a series of favors of which the army does not furnish a precedent." Barrington took exception also to the insolent tone of Burgoyne's request. It was, he wrote, "the least courtly letter ever written by an officer to a Secretary at War." Angrily, Barrington went on: "You threaten me with the House of Commons. . . . This is not the way to influence me." [10] Burgoyne employed similar strong-arm tactics when he was refused a promotion in the spring of 1762. Writing to Charles Townshend, the new secretary at war, Burgoyne complained that his failure to be promoted was not only a personal disappointment but could be construed as a slight against his patron and brother-in-law, Lord Strange. Such threats apparently proved effective; he was promoted to colonel that fall "out of regard to Lord Strange and your own merit." [11]

On the basis of his combat experience, Burgoyne emerged from the war with some firmly held military ideas. For one thing, he became a confirmed cavalryman—one who tended to look upon his dragoons as mounted light infantry which could be employed either in hard-hitting surprise raids, skirmishing, or reconnaissance. According to Burgoyne, it was the Seven Years' War which demonstrated the tremendous potential of the cavalry; prior to the war this branch of the service had long been neglected because generals neither understood nor were prepared to use it.[12] In retrospect, Burgoyne's experience with the cavalry in this war may have set the pattern for what he was to do in the Revolution. He learned that boldness, swiftness of movement, and surprise attacks could bring military success.[13]

Besides the cavalry, Burgoyne showed a keen appreciation for the uses of artillery. In this matter he may well have been reflecting the views of Count von der Lippe, his remarkable commander-in-chief in the Portuguese campaign. The count, one of the great military minds of the eighteenth century, gained his reputation in part as a teacher of two famed German generals, Gneisenau and Scharnhost, and he may have been Burgoyne's mentor as well. Although both men were about the same age, von der Lippe was already a veteran of almost twenty years of uninterrupted combat. Before being called to command the army in Portugal, the count had served as master general of the artillery under Prince Ferdinand of Brunswick. Thomas Carlyle called von der Lippe "the best artillery officer in the world," and Burgoyne's penchant for employing that branch of the service in America may well be traced back to his European experiences.[14]

Burgoyne also held certain views regarding the common soldier which were hardly typical of the military men of his day. His ideas on the subject may best be seen in two documents: the report he prepared comparing European armies in 1766 after a tour of the continent; and a treatise he wrote for his regimental officers in 1759. His assessment of the Prussian, French, and Austrian military systems showed him to be a shrewd student of disciplinary psychology. To Burgoyne the soldiers in the army of each country reflected faithfully the national character of its people: the Prussian military system being based upon blind obedience; the French upon appeals to love of king and country, and the Austrian representing a composite of the Prussian and French systems. Viewing the troops in terms of such archetypes, Burgoyne believed that the military methods used to recruit and train soldiers in each of these countries should be related to these same elements of national character. Since one-third of the Prussian army was made up of foreigners, appeals could not be made to national spirit or to love of king and country; hence, the Prussian system relied primarily upon rigid discipline, fear of punishment, and impressive appearance while on parade. French soldiers, on the other hand, responded best to sentimentality—appeals to their pride, honor, and glory.[15]

For the British army, Burgoyne recommended a middle-of-the road approach between these two extremes—"the [Prussian] one . . . *of training men like spaniels by stick;* the other after the French, *of substituting the point of honor in place of severity.*" [16] In his regimental treatise, Burgoyne stressed the role of reason in dealing with British troops. The British soldier, according to Burgoyne, was distinguished by education and a concern for his fellow creature which developed in him the faculties of reason and sensitivity. Soldiers should be treated as "thinking beings;" officers should appeal to their reason, spirit of nationalism, and sense of personal loyalty and comradeship. Since British soldiers were drawn from the dregs of society, Burgoyne's view was obviously a highly idealized one. But the impact of Enlightenment ideas on Burgoyne's military thought is striking.

When Burgoyne became an army commander in America he seems to have followed the philosophy he had expressed. He had a genuine affection and respect for his soldiers and was always thoughtful of their needs as his general orders show. As a result, Burgoyne was beloved by his men. William Digby, one of his subalterns in the Saratoga campaign, called him "the soldiers friend" and analyzed the reasons for his success: Burgoyne's winning manner and impressive appearance made him a hero in the eyes of the private soldier and he was "idolized by the army"; his orders seemed to assume subordination rather than to enforce it; and he always made soldier-like conduct appear honorable and worthy of emulation while slackness was characterized as "odious and unmanly." Burgoyne, Digby concluded, was well aware that "the most sanguine expectations a general can have of success, must proceed from the spirit of the troops under his command." [17]

Burgoyne's military ideas represented but a single facet of his broader outlook on the nature of man and society in general. He was, in this sense, a conventional eighteenth-century English gentleman—one who considered himself a citizen of the most enlightened and liberty-loving of all nations. Conditioned

by the society in which he lived and the ideas current at the
time, Burgoyne believed in an orderly and rational world. In
his eyes man's best hope for achieving a reasonable and rational
society lay in the British constitution—the greatest instrument of
government ever devised. His political and military careers, then,
were of a piece and seemingly dedicated to the same common
objective—the defense of the British constitution and English
liberties as he understood them.

It was not uncommon for military men to serve in Parliament,
for the British army was not yet a professional service offering
lifetime employment. Officers, once commissioned, remained on
the army list (unless they resigned or were discharged for misconduct) even though they were simultaneously engaged in other
pursuits. Many men from good families combined a career of
soldier and politician, and, more often than not, used their political positions to further their service careers. In Burgoyne's
case, his parliamentary career for over 31 years played an important part in his rise within the military hierarchy.

Lacking family political connections by birth, Burgoyne was
forced to find some other means of entering Parliament. A
friend and fellow officer in his regiment, Sir William Peere Williams, generously came to his support. Williams, having bought
a number of burgages at Midhurst in 1760, offered to bring him
into the House of Commons in 1761.[18] As a result, Burgoyne
was returned unopposed and was the Midhurst M.P. for the next
seven years. But in the election of 1768, Burgoyne entered the
contest for the Preston borough in the electoral interests of the
Derby family. After one of the most fiercely contested elections
of the century, he was seated on petition. The following year
Burgoyne was brought to trial for attempting to incite violence
during the past election and admitted going to the polling place
with a military guard and a loaded pistol in each hand.[19] After
escaping imprisonment and paying a stiff fine of £1,000, Burgoyne went on to represent Preston from 1768 until the day he
died.

Throughout his parliamentary career prior to the Revolutionary War, Burgoyne showed a consuming interest in three major matters—opportunities for military promotions, questions concerning the army, and controversies between the colonies and mother country. His promotions after the Seven Years' War came mainly as the result of family influence, royal favor, and good fortune. Political manipulation by the powerful Derby family, the great expense to which he had gone in the 1768 election, and the fact that his dragoons were among the regiments the king prized most, soon raised Burgoyne to a position as court favorite. In 1769 he was rewarded by being appointed governor of Fort William, a lucrative sinecure rarely granted to an officer below the rank of general. Three years later, he was made a major general. Some measure of his rapid rise may be seen by comparing his military career at this stage with that of Sir William Howe. Although Howe was born into a more prominent family and had seen more combat service, both men were promoted to major general at about the same time.

Burgoyne claimed that his political maxim in Parliament was "to assist [the] government in my general line of conduct," but this aim did not prevent him from showing occasional flashes of political independence when issues arose concerning the army. In at least three episodes between 1768 and 1774, he spoke out or voted against the court when the employment of army units was at stake.[20] One such break with the court came during the East India Company scandal. Burgoyne was appointed chairman of an investigating committee to inquire into the affairs of that organization in 1772 and promptly introduced a resolution to prevent the military forces in India from being used by company officials for private rather than public purposes.[21] Although he was not altogether successful in getting his views accepted, Burgoyne acted independently of the government in this matter; his speeches hint of an ideology quite different from that which one might expect of a military man in Parliament who had to depend upon the king's favor for rewards and advancement.

When it came to questions concerning the American colonies, however, Burgoyne generally supported the government. He favored the Stamp Act, for example, and made a speech in support of the Declaratory Act during the crisis of the mid-1760's. In keeping with his ideas on the British constitution, he could not understand why the Americans were unhappy under the just and orderly government provided by the mother country. His conception of the British empire was that of a family—Britain, as the kind parent, exercising a benevolent authority over her children, the colonies.

Burgoyne believed that Britain had been too lenient and forbearing toward the colonies in the past. Speaking on a motion to repeal the tax on tea in April, 1774, he said: "I look upon America to be our child, which I think we have already spoiled by too much indulgence." On the question of American independence, he declared himself ready "to resist that proposition, and to contend, at any future time, against such independence." But like most Britishers, Burgoyne had a blind spot on this issue: he could not bring himself to believe that the colonists might resort to force to resolve the matter. He relied upon reason to prevail in imperial relations. His April speech made clear his position on the colonial crisis: he "wished," he said, "to see America convinced by persuasion rather than the sword." [22]

When the North Ministry proposed to take military measures in America, however, Burgoyne delivered a speech in support of the government in February, 1775. "Sir, in foreign war, the conscience of the quarrel belongs to the state alone. . . . In civil discord . . . I believe a consideration of the cause will find its way to the breast of every conscientious man. . . . Is there a man in England (I am confident there is not an officer or soldier in the King's service) who does not think the parliamentary rights of Great Britain a cause to fight for, to bleed and die for? . . . The reason of the nation has been long convinced; the trial now only is whether we have spirit to support our conviction." The speech made a great impression and Burgoyne observed: "I spoke from my heart and to that cause I impute its success." [23]

As a general, parliamentarian, and son-in-law of one of England's wealthiest peers, Burgoyne was accustomed to moving in the best social circles. He cut an imposing figure in the glittering high life of London, and his reputation as a wit, man of fashion, and connoisseur of good wines was well known. A member of many London clubs, he numbered among his friends some of the most famous artists of his time—Sir Joshua Reynolds, who painted his portrait, and David Garrick, the Shakespearian actor. His compulsion to shine in whatever company he found himself soon led him to seek recognition in literary circles as a playwright.

Burgoyne showed more than a little talent as a dramatist. In 1774 he wrote a play, *Maid of the Oaks,* in celebration of the marriage of his wife's nephew. The play, a witty commentary on the importance of class and status in English society, was brought out by Garrick at Drury Lane in 1775. After his return to England from America, Burgoyne resumed writing plays and scored his greatest success with *The Heiress* in 1785. Even the hostile Horace Walpole confessed that this play was "the best modern comedy." [24]

In his plays Burgoyne demonstrated a spontaneous wit combined with a lively commentary on English social customs. Although the plots were typical of the elaborate fabrications popular in that day, the dialogue was replete with pointed characterizations that revealed an awareness of the difference between social artifice and reality. His works show that while Burgoyne was a member of English high society, he could view that society from without—criticizing and even mocking it in an effort to reform it.

Certain other aspects of Burgoyne's social life brought to light the same grasping qualities in his make-up that were evidenced in his military career. Along with other members of the aristocracy, he was swept up in the general craze for gambling that seized British society in the mid-eighteenth century. Burgoyne soon proved to be expert; he became known as a "fortunate gamester" who drew a "splendid subsistence" from card playing.[25] But his methods left something to be desired. "Junius," an anonymous essayist who wrote a series of satirical sketches on leading figures of the day, hinted that Burgoyne was not above "taking his stand at gaming-table, and watching with the soberest attention for a fair opportunity of engaging a drunken young Nobleman at Picquet." [26]

"Junius" observed one other outstanding characteristic in Burgoyne's personality: "No man," he noted, "is more tender of his reputation." Terms like "reputation," "honor," and "fame" held a high place in the lexicon of eighteenth-century Englishmen and in their code of social values. To Burgoyne, whose birth was neither celebrated nor free from the suggestion of scandal, such words held an even greater significance. Although he poked fun at English society in his plays, he was more anxious than most men to succeed and to be accepted within it. He had, therefore, an extreme sensitivity to any slights or aspersions cast upon him. "If the wretch, Junius, is now lurking here in any corner of the House," Burgoyne declared in Parliament, "[I] would tell him to his face that he was an assassin, a liar, and a coward." [27]

Burgoyne's appointment to an American command in February, 1775, thrust him abruptly back into active military life With the crisis deepening in the colonies during the winter, George III decided to dispatch three major generals—Howe, Clinton, and Burgoyne—to Boston to assist Thomas Gage, commander-in-chief of the British army in North America. Burgoyne, curiously enough, did not view his appointment with favor at first. When tendered the offer in January, he seemed unwilling to accept. The reason for his reluctance was obvious: he was the junior general of the three. Burgoyne agreed to go, but only after being told that he had been named by George III himself.[28]

His attitude changed once he realized America would open up new opportunities for advancement. He was soon busily exploring the possibility of becoming governor of New York. Tryon, the incumbent, was in England; Colden, the lieutenant governor, was aged and failing in health; and the British government was planning to send a body of troops to New York City. After politicking furiously, Burgoyne discovered that General Howe had been promised the proposed post. George III confessed later that he felt Burgoyne could "best manage any negotiation" required of a New York commander.[29]

Undaunted by this failure, Burgoyne tried a different tack. Before leaving for America, he solicited the king's permission to return to England by the end of the year. Ostensibly his request was based on two grounds: first, that certain private matters would require his attention; and secondly that there would be value in a personal report to the king about American affairs. His real purpose for returning, however, was to make certain he would figure in any future appointments of importance. The king approved the request, though Burgoyne was not informed at the time.

Burgoyne sailed with Howe and Clinton in what he called "a triumvirate of reputation" on April 20—the day after the Americans drove British troops back to Boston from Lexington and Concord. Arthur Lee, Congress' confidential diplomatic agent in London, wrote a letter at about the same time describing the trio. In Lee's opinion, Burgoyne would be the most dangerous to deal with.

> The first [Howe] is an honorable man, respected in the Army, & trained in the late American War. He goes reluctantly.
> The second [Clinton] is a man of very fair character. He served all the late War in Germany. His abilities, tho not brilliant, are yet respectable.
> General Burgoyne is of a very different character. A man of dark designs deep dissimulations, desperate fortunes, & abandond of principles. He is closely connected with the Bedford Party in this Country. No Banditti were ever bent on blood & spoil, & on more desperate principles than this Bedford Party. . . . They are as ready to sacrifice this Country as America to the arbitrary views of a tory, tyrannical Court. Among the worst of their Party is Gl. Burgoyne. You will see his character well drawn in the Letters of Junius. . . . To finish his character of dissimulation tho an abandond & notorious Gambler & engaged in every scene abhorrent

from true religion & virtue, he has always effected to be exemplary
in religious Worship. . . . You will judge however from what I
have said, that he is a dangerous character; & therefore be on your
guard. If he is solicitous to commune with you, it will be to betray
you.[30]

Burgoyne had barely landed in Boston in late May before he
began complaining about his insignificant role in American affairs. His position, he wrote Lord North on June 14, was "too
humble" to enable him to contribute in a meaningful way "to
his Majesty's service in the military line in America." [31] Even
as a lowly lieutenant colonel, he had led more troops than the
number now under his immediate command. Burgoyne's claim
that his talents were not being used properly was to be a chronic
complaint until he secured a separate command in America.

Ambitious to play a more important part, Burgoyne proposed
a scheme for settling the American crisis by peaceful means. He
requested dismissal from the army and authorization for a rov-
ing commission to visit those colonies where there was no fighting in order to sound out American sentiment for a possible
compromise. Burgoyne asked that he not be charged with any
direct proposal from the British government nor authorized to
treat with the Americans in any official capacity. Instead, he
would deal with the Americans as an individual member of
Parliament, "a friend of human nature," and a "sincere well
wisher to the united interests of the two countries." [32] His proposal was rejected, but it was significant from two points of
view: it showed his self-assurance in proposing a solution after
being in America only a few weeks, and it indicated his conviction that negotiation and compromise were preferable to war
and bloodshed at this stage.

Burgoyne's hope of settling the issue by other than military
means could be seen also in the proclamation he framed in General Gage's name.[33] When the home government suggested that
a proclamation be published indicating the policy Britain proposed to adopt in Massachusetts, Gage, feeling inferior as a pen-
man to Burgoyne, turned to the playwright-soldier for assist-

ance. The proclamation, issued on June 12, imposed martial law on Massachusetts but promised pardons to all who would lay down their arms—except for political leaders like Sam Adams and John Hancock. Its tone, however, was intemperate; Burgoyne denounced the "infatuated multitude" who "with a preposterous parade . . . affected to hold the [British] Army besieged." [34] Because of its bombastic language, the proclamation aroused ridicule rather than alarm. Some Americans jokingly proposed that a counterproclamation be published pardoning certain British generals, admirals, and government officials.

Historians, for the most part, have criticized Burgoyne's proclamation, calling it "foolish," "sounding brass," and a "pompous, high-flown, inaccurate and silly production." [35] But Burgoyne, as a writer, was rarely careless in his use of words—his plays reveal a tight control of language, and his private correspondence shows he resorted to crude verbiage only when such usage seemed necessary for emphasis. Read in its proper context, the language of the proclamation was not at all inappropriate. The document was an attempt at psychological warfare—a propaganda piece aimed at frightening Americans into submission with words rather than bullets. Burgoyne was convinced that if the rebel forces in and around Boston were dispersed, Americans elsewhere were not likely to offer any drawn-out resistance.

Five days after the proclamation appeared, American patriots called Burgoyne's bluff when the British resorted to military force in the battle of Bunker Hill. Although British redcoats captured their main objective, the redoubt on Breed's Hill, they did so at tremendous cost—losing 1,054 killed and wounded out of 2,200 men engaged. Burgoyne did not participate in the fight because, as he wrote, "the inferiority of my station as the youngest Major-General on the staff, left me almost a useless spectator." But what he saw raised his respect for the fighting ability of the Americans. "The defence was well conceived and obstinately maintained," he reported. "[T]he retreat was no flight; it was even covered with bravery and military skill." Burgoyne was shocked, on the other hand, by the behavior of the British soldiers; they showed a lack of discipline and hesitated in the midst of their attack.[36]

Bunker Hill resulted in some changes in Burgoyne's thinking regarding the American rebellion. Evaluating the situation soon after the battle, he viewed the rebellion in broad terms as both a political and military problem. His long letter to Lord Rochford, member of the cabinet, suggested that two long-range alternatives were open to Britain: to make the greatest political concessions possible to America, or to wage an all-out war. If the mother country adopted halfway measures between these two "disagreeable extremes," he predicted they would only produce "much fruitless expense, great loss of blood, and a series of disappointments." [37]

Burgoyne's suggestion that the issue be settled by political means has escaped the attention of most historians. One reason for this was Burgoyne himself. Confessing that his judgment was limited by his army position, Burgoyne confined most of his remarks to military matters. Nevertheless, his comment to Rochford regarding political concessions to the colonies must be taken seriously: "Should it be thought more expedient to the nation, and reconcilable to its honor, to relinquish the claims in question, I doubt not the wisdom of those councils of which your Lordship is so distinguished a part, will propose such relinquishment as will be at once effectual." [38]

If America was to be subdued by force, on the other hand, Burgoyne warned there was little prospect of a speedy victory unless important military steps were undertaken immediately. It was readily apparent to him that the soldiers available from Great Britain and Ireland would be insufficient for the enormous task at hand. Burgoyne recommended, therefore, that three armies be raised to wage war on America: a huge army of foreign mercenaries striking up the Hudson; a second army composed of trained British troops and Canadians invading from the north; and a large levy of Indians and Negroes to cooperate with detachments of British regulars in overawing the southern colonies. With such formidable allies on land and the Royal

Navy patrolling the entire coast, Burgoyne speculated that the British might conquer the Americans in a single campaign.

Since such long-range measures would take time to implement, Burgoyne proposed also a plan for the current campaign. With four regiments of reinforcements reportedly on the way, the British army would be in a position to launch an offensive. Burgoyne saw no sense in attacking the strongly entrenched American posts surrounding Boston with so small an army—a successful assault would only win one line of entrenchments or a hill, leaving more entrenchments and hills to be taken without any substantial gain in military advantage. Instead he suggested two steps: the continued occupation of Boston and a war of expedition to the southward. Placing part of the British army on shipboard, he proposed attacks upon parts of Rhode Island, Connecticut, and New York to test the strength and temper of the rebels in these colonies. Burgoyne was still hopeful of regaining New York for the British if sent to that province with an independent command.

Besides these immediate military moves, Burgoyne pressed for what might be called psychological warfare measures. He was quicker than his colleagues in grasping the implications of the revolutionary idea that the British were fighting a people in arms rather than a professional army. He suggested, for example, that Gage release the prisoners taken at Bunker Hill because such an act of mercy might make a great impression upon the Americans. "You have been deluded," the prisoners should be told. "[R]eturn to your homes in peace; it is your duty to God and your country to undeceive your neighbors." [39] Aware that at bottom the war was a war of ideology, Burgoyne asked also that the most able men in England frame a proclamation urging the Americans to lay down their arms; such a proclamation was to be issued prior to carrying out the military expeditions he had proposed. Few of Burgoyne's ideas regarding long-range policies, plans for a 1775 campaign, or psychological warfare methods were adopted by the government; but the proposals showed his understanding of strategy, comprehension of the magnitude of effort required to reconquer America, and insight into the true nature of the war.

After the battle of Bunker Hill, Burgoyne revealed also just what his relations with his fellow generals would be; he was consistently to undermine those with whom he was competing for higher command. He began criticizing Gage almost from the moment he landed in America. His estimate of the commander-in-chief in the letter to Lord Rochford was clever, indeed; it provided some small measure of praise, but suggested at the same time that Gage's abilities were limited and that a more talented man was needed for the job. "I hope I shall not be thought to disparage my general and my friend in pronouncing him unequal to his situation, when I add that I think it one in which Caesar might have failed." [40] Reading between the lines the implication was clear: since Caesar was unavailable, Burgoyne might do instead. Such backbiting, of course, was common among British senior officers; Howe and Clinton wrote similar letters about Gage. But Burgoyne seems to have handled this technique more effectively than his colleagues and for this reason earned their fear and dislike in some instances.

During the remainder of his stay in Boston in 1775, Burgoyne did little except propose plans and write letters. Much of what he had to say he had said before. In August he advocated two possible courses of action: either remove the army from Boston to New York, or dispatch an expedition to Rhode Island. [41] But his commander-in-chief ignored both plans. Burgoyne thereupon became more critical, calling Gage "an officer totally unsuited for command," and the man responsible for "many of the misfortunes the King's arms have suffered." His estimate of the Americans, on the other hand, remained high: "The rebels though undisciplined are expert in the use of firearms, and led by some very able men." [42]

Throughout this same period, Burgoyne seized every opportunity to use his pen as a propaganda weapon. In June and July he exchanged letters with Charles Lee, his former fellow officer who had been appointed general in the Continental army, hoping to bribe or wean him away from the Americans. When General Washington complained in August about the ill-treatment of American prisoners, Burgoyne carried on an exchange of correspondence in Gage's behalf. Toward the close of the year, he turned to playwriting and prepared a prologue and epilogue for the tragedy of *Zara* that was performed at Faneuil Hall.[43] In his lines, Burgoyne called upon the conquering British to be merciful and the rebellious Americans to return to the fold. By this time, however, the army had gone into winter quarters and he was able to return to England in December in accordance with his agreement with the king.

Burgoyne's foresight in insisting upon a return to England soon became apparent. During the early spring of 1776, the British government was engaged in planning military operations for the coming year and appointing the appropriate army commanders. Burgoyne, a veritable johnny-on-the-spot, was strategically situated for voicing his opinions and pushing his claims for higher command. His presence in England early in 1776 and during the same period in 1777, was partially responsible for his success two years in a row in superseding men who outranked him.

When called upon to submit his views regarding military operations for 1776, Burgoyne, some time in the first three months of the year, produced an interesting paper entitled, "Reflections upon the War in America." His major proposal called for an invasion of New York from Canada. Burgoyne mistakenly believed that Quebec had fallen to the enemy; but he was certain that the navy could push past the city to land a British army that could drive south from the St. Lawrence. He pointed out at the same time the possibility of a joint expedition—one army marching south while another moved north out of New York City—to make a juncture at some central location. Burgoyne, in short, was proposing in broad outline the strategy attempted in the campaigns of 1776 and 1777. He was, however, by no means the only one thinking along such lines.

Burgoyne's paper was equally important for revealing the

flexibility of his military ideas. He arrived in America a confirmed cavalryman, but gradually changed his views because of the geography of the country and its mode of warfare. The Americans, Burgoyne predicted, would not risk a general combat, or a pitched battle, or even stand to fight at all, except in entrenchments such as those found outside of Boston. Accustomed to working with shovels and axes, they would throw up earthworks with surprising speed, and fight behind them with great skill:

> Composed as the American army is, together with the strength of the country, full of woods, swamps, stone walls, and other enclosures and hiding places, it may be said of it that every private man will in action be his own general, who will turn every tree and bush into a temporary fortress, from whence, when he hath fired his shot with all the deliberation, coolness, and certainty which hidden safety inspires, he will skip as it were to the next, and so on for a long time. . . .

What then, was the solution? To dislodge the Americans either with cannon fire or an attack by light infantry. Heavy cannon and howitzers could destroy such defenses. Light infantry units —made up of fast moving men who carried less equipment— would possess the necessary mobility to outflank entrenched positions. Burgoyne was to stick fast to these ideas: in his paper he proposed that "light infantry in greater numbers than one company per regiment" be added throughout the British army; and in his operations in America he was to rely heavily upon cannon.[44]

When the campaign plan for 1776 was finally adopted and commanders picked for the respective armies, Burgoyne emerged with a key role. The campaign called for a two-pronged invasion of America: the main army landing in New York and pushing north up the Hudson, while a smaller but substantial army was to reinforce Quebec and then sweep south from Canada down through the Lake Champlain-Hudson River corridor. It was hoped this dual offensive would either force Washington's army to stand and fight or make the Americans abandon the Hudson River line and thereby expose New England to an attack from the west. Plans were also made for a small expeditionary force to sail against the southern colonies, but it was to return north in time to participate in the invasion of New York. Lord George Germain, the colonial secretary, had little difficulty in choosing his top commanders: General Howe, now commander-in-chief in America, was named to head the main army; and General Carleton was placed in charge of the one in Canada. Originally, plans called for Clinton, who outranked Burgoyne, to become Carleton's second-in-command. But Clinton had already sailed with the expeditionary force to the south, and Burgoyne was picked instead.

Burgoyne left for Canada in early April, but he did so with a heavy heart. His wife was so ill that he despaired of ever seeing her alive again. After landing in America, he poured out his grief to Clinton, who was himself a widower. Calling Lady Charlotte "that truest friend, amiable companion, tenderest, best of women and of wives," Burgoyne declared he had been ready to sacrifice both ambition and fortune to avoid the coming campaign to remain at her side. But, he went on to say, his sense of duty to his king, his country, and profession enabled him to control his private feelings. While asking for Clinton's sympathy, Burgoyne protested—perhaps too much—that his position as Carleton's second-in-command had been "unsought for." [45]

In the midst of the campaign, Burgoyne learned of Lady Charlotte's death. Overcome with grief, he described himself as "an unconnected Cypher in the world—The partner lost which made prosperity an object of solicitude—Interest, ambition, the animation of life is over." All that remained, he wrote, was "professional honor"; it was better to be "finished in a professional grave" than waste away to a slow death of old age.[46] Burgoyne apparently meant what he said; at the second battle of Saratoga, a year later, he deliberately courted death at the head of his troops to retain some semblance of professional honor prior to his impending surrender.

Burgoyne found himself facing professional as well as personal problems during the campaign. His relations with Carleton followed much the same pattern as those with Gage the year before. Anxious to prove himself and to gain some share of glory, Burgoyne made a series of proposals to his superior only to find them rejected. Disenchantment soon set in. He became restless, increasingly critical of his chief's dilatory tactics, and soon was undermining Carleton's position as he had Gage's earlier.

Carleton, aided by heavy reinforcements of British regulars and German mercenaries, raised the siege of Quebec and launched a counteroffensive during the summer months of 1776. Driving a dispirited American army before him, he advanced south almost to the head of Lake Champlain. Here both armies halted and began constructing fleets to contest for command of the lake— the key to all strategy. Rather than allow the entire British force to remain idle during this period, Burgoyne proposed a bold plan. He would lead a detachment across Lake Ontario and thence move east by way of Oswego, Fort Stanwix, and the Mohawk to meet Carleton at the junction of that river and the Hudson. Such a move, he noted, would raise a "powerful diversion," enabling Carleton's army to move south down the lake and Howe's army north up the Hudson. The plan, though approved in principle, was never put into operation because of a lack of supplies.

The proposal itself, however, was important from two points of view. Burgoyne's idea for a diversion down the Mohawk served as the basis for St. Leger's expedition from that direction in 1777. Of even greater significance was Burgoyne's remark regarding the ultimate destination of Carleton's army: "I cannot suppose any General," he wrote, "would have remained at Ticonderoga, Fort Edward or any other post above the junction of the Mohawk and Hudson Rivers." His reasoning here helps to explain, in part, Burgoyne's determined drive to reach Albany— located near the junction of these two rivers—with an army of his own the following year.[47] His attention was focused not on the enemy's army but upon Albany as a territorial objective.

When Carleton was finally ready to sail down Lake Champlain in early October, Burgoyne came up with a second suggestion. He proposed that a corps of the army accompany the naval force to exploit any military opportunity that might develop. Carleton, after some indecision, rejected this plan too. Instead he proceeded down the lake in command of his naval force, leaving the army behind. Writing of Carleton's rejection to General Clinton, Burgoyne resorted to his usual technique of denigrating his superiors with a combination of praise and blame:

> I should be unjust to General Carleton, if I denied that odd and misplaced as his part may appear at the Head of the naval department only, he has reasons to justify that proceeding. They would carry me too far, nor is the occasion proper to open them to you now.[48]

After Carleton had smashed the American fleet on Lake Champlain, occupied Crown Point, and advanced on Ticonderoga, Burgoyne's ideas regarding a future course of action differed even more sharply with those of his superior. He acquiesced in Carleton's decision not to attack Ticonderoga, but only because he assumed that Crown Point would be held through the winter. Before retreating to Crown Point, however, Burgoyne indicated that he would have surrounded the Americans in Ticonderoga, "felt their pulse" in a probing action, and attempted to cut off their lines of communication to the south. Since none of these ideas were seriously considered and the army was going into winter quarters, Burgoyne felt free to leave the field and to begin his trip back to England.

Shortly after leaving the army, Burgoyne was astonished to learn that Carleton had abandoned Crown Point. "I think this step puts us in danger . . . of losing the fruits of our summer's labor & autumn victory," he wrote bitterly. Burgoyne had suggested that a brigade be left behind to hold the post, and since all the buildings had been burned, that huts be hastily constructed to house the men. But Carleton, guided by the advice of his "dull, formal, methodical fat engineers," had been persuaded that Crown Point could not be held. Commenting on this decision Burgoyne observed:

> I must honor Carleton's abilities & judgement, I have lived with him upon the best terms & bear him friendship—I am therefore doubly hurt that he had taken a step in which I can be no otherwise serviceable to him than by silence.[49]

Burgoyne's "silence" lasted only as long as it took him to cross the Atlantic. Rushing to Germain on December 10—the day after he landed in England—Burgoyne criticized Carleton by emphasizing that he had been strongly opposed to giving up Crown Point. Before leaving Canada, Burgoyne had expressed unhappiness over his status in "a secondary station in a secondary command"; now he proceeded to do everything in his power to correct that situation. Despite his protestations at a later date that he had not intrigued to supplant Carleton, and the false impression given by Burgoyne's biographer of his complete faithfulness to his superior, Burgoyne's actions in writing to Clinton and speaking to Germain belie such an interpretation.[50]

With the Ministry dissatisfied over the disappointing results in the Canadian campaign, Germain at odds with Carleton, and the king expressing the need for a "more enterprizing Commander" for the northern army, Burgoyne loomed as a likely candidate.[51] His ambition was fired further when he learned that Germain had sent a dispatch during the previous summer ordering Carleton back to Quebec and giving Burgoyne command of the army. The order, issued to prevent a clash of jurisdiction between Carleton and Howe in the event of a juncture between the two armies, had never been carried out; the vessel bearing the dispatch had been forced to turn back because of bad weather.

When Burgoyne submitted an important memorandum in February, 1777, containing suggestions for conducting the war, his chances of succeeding Carleton improved markedly. The origins of this memorandum provide additional proof that Burgoyne was angling for the Canadian command. Prior to Burgoyne's departure from Canada, Carleton had discussed his own views regarding the 1777 campaign and set down his thoughts in a letter. When Burgoyne was leaving for England, Carleton instructed him to frame a memorandum incorporating these ideas and to present it to the government. Burgoyne did as instructed and submitted a short and rather sketchy résumé. He then followed it up with a memorandum of his own which was much more impressive, forceful, and complete. In late February, Burgoyne drew up still another document entitled, "Thoughts for Conducting the War from the Side of Canada," elaborating more fully his views regarding the coming campaign. Burgoyne's last memorandum in large part was responsible for his being selected over Carleton and Clinton to command the army in Canada.[52]

His paper contained three possible courses of action for the Canadian army, and the government adopted one. This operational plan revived Burgoyne's proposal of a year before calling for the main army to advance south from Montreal to the upper Hudson at the same time a small diversionary force was working its way east down the Mohawk River Valley to link up at Albany. Historians in the past believed that Burgoyne was solely responsible for the general conception of the 1777 campaign. The scheme, in reality, was an old and familiar one for many of its more important features had already been suggested by others.[53]

The purpose behind Burgoyne's plan has likewise been a matter of historical dispute. Scholars long assumed that the *immediate* objective of the 1777 campaign called for a convergence of not two but three forces at Albany—Burgoyne's northern army at Montreal, St. Leger's expedition down the Mohawk, and Howe's southern army moving north from New York City up the Hudson. It was assumed further that the main aim of the campaign was to seal off New England from the rest of the colonies and therefore that Howe had strict orders to advance up the Hudson to effect a juncture with Burgoyne. Some recent historians have demonstrated, however, that the British may have viewed Burgoyne's northern invasion as an attempt to draw Washington's attention away from Howe's offensive in the south against Philadelphia as well as a move to form a juncture between the northern and southern armies. The two moves— Burgoyne's toward Albany and Howe's against Philadelphia— were not considered incompatible; the British believed confidently that both objectives could be achieved. Although the juncture of Burgoyne and Howe remained an essential part of the plan—it was to be an ultimate, not an immediate, goal of the campaign.[54]

Burgoyne's own ideas in his paper, "Thoughts," regarding the purpose of the campaign were ambiguous. His paper, on the one hand, showed that Burgoyne was well aware at the outset that Howe's main army might turn south rather than proceed north up the Hudson to join him. On the other hand, a key sentence implied that Burgoyne was counting upon Howe's cooperation to some degree: "These ideas are formed upon the supposition, that it be the sole purpose of the Canadian campaign to effect a junction with General Howe," he wrote, "or after cooperating so far as to get possession of Albany and open the communication to New York, to remain upon the Hudson River and thereby enable that general to act with his whole force to the southward." [55] Although this statement can be interpreted several ways, it strongly suggests that Burgoyne believed that even if Howe intended to go to Pennsylvania he was expected to make some move to help the northern army establish itself at Albany. Such an interpretation did not mean, however, that Burgoyne expected Howe to meet him in Albany immediately, or that the entire southern army was to be committed on the Hudson—any detachment of forces or diversionary attack which permitted the northern army to reach Albany would do. The statement implied also that once he reached Albany, Burgoyne expected his army to sustain itself, to keep open the communications to New York, and to act independently while Howe campaigned to the south.[56]

If Burgoyne's views on strategy were vague in his paper, he

was extremely perceptive in anticipating the problems he would
encounter on his march toward Albany. He predicted accurately
that he would meet no naval opposition on Lake Champlain such
as Arnold's fleet had provided in 1776. Nor did he expect to
encounter the enemy in great force until he reached Ticonderoga
—another assumption in which he was correct. He forecast
rightly what the Americans would do to oppose his advance
south by either of the two alternate routes, Lake George and
Skenesborough—he expected them to maintain a strong naval
force on Lake George and to block the trail from Skenesborough
to Albany by felling trees and destroying bridges. Finally, he
singled out the supply problem as "one of the most important
operations of the campaign, because it is upon that which most
of the rest will depend." [57] Although he anticipated many of his
problems, Burgoyne, as will be seen, underestimated the difficulties he would encounter in trying to overcome them.

To carry out his invasion, Burgoyne requested that the northern army be supplied with a sizable force. At least 8,000 regulars,
2,000 Canadians, and more than 1,000 Indians would be required. With characteristic care, Burgoyne named in great detail
the British regiments he wanted and recommended that the
German mercenaries assigned him come with their "grenadiers,
light infantry, and dragoons complete." He requested also ample
artillery because he expected the Americans to fortify strong
ground in various places. Because he expected a problem of
adequate transportation on both water and land, Burgoyne asked
for a corps of watermen, some hatchet men, and other work-
men. If such a force were supplied him and adequate preparations made, Burgoyne predicted that Ticonderoga might be taken
"early in the summer." [58]

Burgoyne's general conception of the invasion was approved
by Germain, but with some changes. For one thing, Burgoyne
was told that the total of 8,000 trained troops would be reduced
to 7,000. Nothing was said about Howe's coming north to meet
him. Most important of all, Burgoyne's orders called for him "to
force his way to Albany," and there to place himself and his

troops under Howe's command. It was implied, however, that until Burgoyne came under Howe's orders he was to act on his own "as exigencies may require." These two phrases gave rise to a conflict in interpretation. Had Burgoyne been given a narrow peremptory command to proceed to Albany regardless of the costs? Or had he been granted discretionary power that permitted some latitude of action? After his defeat at Saratoga, Burgoyne was to fall back upon a narrow interpretation of his orders. But before the campaign, he did not complain about his orders being inflexible. In fact, he seemed reasonably satisfied with the final outcome of the government's approval of his plan. "Being called upon at home for my opinion of the war on this side," he wrote, "I gave it freely; the material parts of it have been adopted by the Cabinet." [59]

At about the same time that Germain passed upon Burgoyne's plan for invasion, he likewise approved Howe's campaign against Pennsylvania. Howe made it clear in December, 1776, that any move he might make up the Hudson would depend upon two conditions—whether he received reinforcements, and whether he completed his own campaign in time to return north to help Burgoyne. Since Germain did not send the requested reinforcements and yet approved Howe's plan, he has been blamed for agreeing to two seemingly incompatible campaigns.[60] But Burgoyne himself expressed no misgivings on this score at this stage —he too thought that both campaigns could be completed by the close of 1777.

Burgoyne's self-assurance, it should be emphasized, reflected the optimistic outlook of the British government as a whole regarding the outcome of the 1777 campaigns. The king and his ministers at Whitehall were in high hopes that the summer of 1777 would bring the rebellion to an end. Basing their plans upon the presumed weakness of the Americans and the supposed strength of the loyalists in both upper New York and Pennsylvania, British officials confidently prepared two major campaigns against widely separated objectives with the expectation that both would succeed. The result was a lack of careful planning;

relatively little effort was made to co-ordinate the moves of Burgoyne's army in the north with Howe's main force in the south. Despite the fact that Germain sent eight letters to Howe between March 3 and April 19, for example, he neglected to make clear in any of them the strategy upon which Burgoyne's campaign was based.[61]

Burgoyne's confidence that he could carry out his campaign to Albany with relatively little help was revealed again when he saw a letter from Howe to Carleton written in April, 1777— before the northern army had begun its invasion—expressing the limited degree of cooperation that might be expected from the southern army. First, there was the matter of timing: Howe indicated that in all probability he would be in Pennsylvania when the northern army launched its invasion and therefore would be unable "to communicate with . . . [Burgoyne] so soon as I could wish." Secondly, Howe stated that few, if any, troops from his army would be available to support Burgoyne. He could not spare a corps, Howe wrote, to act upon the Hudson at the beginning of Burgyone's campaign. However, he would leave behind sufficient forces in New York City to open the shipping lanes on the lower Hudson which were being obstructed by American forts in the Highlands. After accomplishing this mission, Howe said, such a corps might "afterwards act in favor of the northern army." This halfhearted promise of a few troops was as far as Howe would go. Despite the fact Burgoyne now knew that he could count on very little cooperation from Howe in the initial advance toward Albany, he was determined to press ahead on his invasion plans.[62]

The inherent inadequacies of the British system of command came to light with a major change in plans for the campaign of 1777. In April, Howe wrote Germain that he intended to carry out his invasion of Pennsylvania from New York by sea rather than a march overland. This change meant that the southern army would be on shipboard rather than being situated somewhere between Washington's force and the northern army. By undertaking his campaign so late—Howe's troops did not embark until July 23—and by carrying out his invasion by sea rather than land, Howe made virtually impossible any kind of meaningful cooperation with the northern army at a crucial time. Howe either honestly did not view the campaign of 1777 as a joint operation, or, finding himself unable to help Burgoyne, pretended to be unaware that some kind of cooperation was expected of him.

The reaction to this change in plans revealed the confusion and misunderstanding that existed in both government and military circles. In his reply to Howe, Germain urged, but failed to insist, that Howe complete his Pennsylvania campaign in time to return north to cooperate with Burgoyne.[63] The old story of the "pigeon-holed dispatch" that Germain reputedly failed to send to Howe specifically ordering him to come to the assistance of Burgoyne seems to be unsupported by any evidence. General Clinton, who had just returned from England, argued with Howe that the only chance of success lay in a move by the southern army up the Hudson instead of against Pennsylvania; but his arguments proved to no avail.[64] So far as Burgoyne was concerned, the fact that he learned about Howe's altered plans at a later date made little difference: he remained optimistic about reaching Albany on his own. While it is true that Burgoyne's overconfidence was a contributing factor in his downfall, Germain and Howe must bear part of the burden of defeat for failing to give him proper orders and information based upon their understanding of the 1777 campaign.

Burgoyne's invasion got under way from St. Johns on June 12. Under his command were over 7,000 regular infantry—about half of whom were German mercenaries. Both the British and German troops were of good quality and well led. In keeping with his ideas, Burgoyne brigaded the light infantry companies from the British regiments, some grenadier companies, and one regular British regiment to form his vanguard. He had, in addition, an impressive and powerful train of artillery—more than 138 cannon and about 600 artillerymen. But of the 3,000 Canadians and Indians expected, only 650 Canadians and loyalists

and 500 redmen came forward. Nor was Burgoyne provided
with adequate transport; only one-third of the horses promised
were available and the number of carts for the wagon train fell
far short of the estimated requirements. Despite the fact he had
not been supplied with precisely the forces and equipment he had
requested, Burgoyne issued an order early in the campaign that
read: "This army must not retreat." [65]

Although Burgoyne later blamed his failure partly upon the
lack of loyalist military support, he gave no indication at the
beginning of the invasion that he was counting on any significant assistance from irregulars. His main reliance would be on
regulars: provincial troops were to be used for purposes of
guerrilla tactics and psychological warfare. "I mean to employ
them particularly upon detachments for keeping the country in
awe and procuring cattle," he wrote. "Their real use I expect
will be great in the preservation of national troops; but the
impression which will be caused upon public opinion, should
the provincials be seen acting vigorously in the cause of the
King, will yet be more advantageous . . ." [66]

Burgoyne made much the same use of proclamations in New
York as he had in Boston in 1775. Believing in the power of the
written word and that the war was a struggle against a people
in arms rather than against an enemy army, he issued one proclamation addressed to the local inhabitants. British military
forces had been called forth at first to restore constitutional
government, he wrote, but now they were seeking to protect
the "general privileges of Mankind." American rebels had set
up "the compleatest form of Tyranny that ever God in his displeasure suffered . . . to be exercised over a . . . stubborn generation," and were responsible for "arbitrary imprisonment, con-
fiscation of property, [and] persecution and torture." Burgoyne
offered encouragement and employment to all who would participate in "the glorious task of redeeming their Countrymen
from Dungeons, and reestablishing the blessings of legal government." But for the rebels, "justice and wrath await them in
the field; and devastation, famine, and every concomitant

horror." One "horror" Burgoyne had in mind was the Indians in his army. He addressed another proclamation to his redskinned warriors calling upon them to "strike at the common enemies of Great Britain and America—disturbers of public order, peace, and happiness—destroyers of commerce, parricides of the State." [67] Although he forbade the Indians to shed blood except when engaged in combat, events proved that they were sadly averse to any military discipline.

In one important respect, Burgoyne approached the invasion with a different attitude than he had in earlier campaigns: he had sharply revised his high estimate of American military capabilities. When he arrived in Boston in 1775, he modified his expectations of a quick victory after seeing the Americans fight fiercely in the battle of Bunker Hill. In 1776 in his paper, "Reflections Upon the War in America," he continued to hold the enemy in high regard and warned that their militia would prove to be "respectable" opponents. But by 1777 these more realistic observations seemed to give way to the same unwarranted optimism of an imminent victory in that year held by the British government. This attitude was evident in the plans Burgoyne made for the invasion from Canada. When he took Ticonderoga with deceptive ease in early July, 1777, any careful appraisal of American capabilities seemed to vanish completely. "The manner of taking up the ground at Ticonderoga," he wrote, "convinces me that they have no men of military science." [68] He was so cocky at this point and so unconcerned for the safety of his army that he expressed regret his orders would not permit him to turn his troops toward New England so that he might conquer that region instead of continuing south in the direction of Albany.

One reason for Burgoyne's great optimism arose from his assumption that his march in northern New York would be made through a region essentially loyal to the king. He expected to meet little resistance in the countryside because large numbers of loyalists had already been recruited for the British army from that area. But it was soon apparent that Burgoyne had made a major miscalculation; he began encountering local opposition instead of local support. Two months before his surrender, Burgoyne recognized his error and confessed to Germain on August 20: "The great bulk of the country is undoubtedly with the Congress, in principle and zeal; and their measures are executed with secrecy and dispatch that are not to be equalled. Wherever the King's forces point, militia, to the amount of three or four thousand, assemble in twenty-four hours." Although he had begun to realize the depth to which Americans were committed to their cause, he still had faith that his army could overcome such odds.[69]

Despite a series of unexpected setbacks—the Bennington defeat on August 16 which cost him one-tenth of his army, and St. Leger's retreat toward Oswego on August 22 which canceled out any hope of help from that diversionary force—Burgoyne was determined to plunge ahead. He was fully aware of the dangers involved. His army was diminishing in numbers while the size of the enemy force in his front was growing daily; his communications to Canada were vulnerable to attacks from the militia on his flank and would cease to be safe once he crossed the Hudson; and his supply system had broken down to the point where he had to halt almost a month to collect provisions in order to proceed further. Why then did he advance? His explanation at this stage was that he had positive orders to "force a junction with Sir William Howe"; but this was probably an excuse to cover himself in the event he failed.[70]

His real reasons for refusing to retreat were twofold: personal ambition and professional honor. Burgoyne was simply too ambitious to turn back while his army was still intact and there remained some chance of success—no matter how slim that chance might be. Having clawed his way to an independent command, he was not about to let pass this opportunity to gain greater glory. Professional honor, moreover, compelled him to pursue his drive to Albany. What would his countrymen say if he stayed where he was? "My conduct would have been held indefensible," he wrote in a telling letter after his surrender, "by every class and distinction of men in government, in the army, and in the public." [71] Burgoyne, in fact, felt that the honor of the king's army was at stake in his campaign: he considered a retreat under any conditions an ignominious act and a sign of weakness. In a characteristic move, he refused to retreat from the Skenesborough route, where he was experiencing some difficulty moving cross-country, to start over again down the Lake George route because of "the general impressions which a retrograde movement is apt to make upon the minds of enemies and friends." [72]

But even more important in Burgoyne's decision to push ahead was his romantic faith in the superior fighting abilities of British soldiers coupled with a correspondingly low opinion of American troops. His confidence in British regulars was great, indeed. "Had all my troops been British," he declared to Howe after Saratoga, "I, in my conscience, believe I should have made my way through Mr. Gates's army." [73] Easy successes in the early stages of the campaign, on the other hand, had given him a false picture of American capabilities. "The spirit of the enemy in combat against regular British troops, had only been tried at Ticonderoga, at Huberton, at Skenesborough, and Fort Anne," and, he noted, "in all which places it had failed." [74] Remembering that such encounters were his first as an independent army commander, he was, no doubt, overly impressed with these initial experiences.

Only after his army had laid down their arms on October 17 did Burgoyne fully realize how much he had underestimated the Americans. He was allowed to inspect Gates' troops at close range and sent Germain this revealing statement:

> The standing corps which I have seen are disciplined: I do not hazard the term, but apply it to the great fundamental points of military institution, sobriety, subordination, regularity, and courage. The militia are inferior in method and movement, but not a jot less serviceable in woods. *My conjectures were very different after the affair of Ticonderoga; they were delusive, and it is a duty to the state to confess it.*[75]

If Burgoyne was willing to admit he was wrong in his appraisal of his opponents, another letter to Germain on October 20 showed that he had not yet grasped the full implications of the strategic problem. Rather than calling a council of war, he wrote, he had taken it upon himself to make the decision "to force a passage to Albany." Burgoyne in this phrase was revealing, once again, the single fixed idea in his mind. His eyes were set only upon Albany; to reach that objective, in his view, was tantamount to a major victory. But was it? He never seems to have looked beyond Albany—to the questions of what he would do once he got there, how his army would be supplied, or what measures he might take against Gates' army.[76] In leaving such large questions unanswered, Burgoyne showed he had not completely thought through his campaign on a strategic level. By committing his force solely to the idea of reaching Albany, and by being obsessed with the thought of seizing that objective at all costs, Burgoyne perhaps had surrendered his army miles before Saratoga.

Burgoyne capitulated under terms that he considered both honorable to himself and advantageous to England. The Saratoga Convention called for his army to be marched to Boston and shipped back to England with the understanding that the men were not to fight again in the war against the colonies. Since his troops could replace garrison forces abroad, thus releasing other men for service in America, Burgoyne boasted: "I have made a treaty that saves them to the State for the next campaign." Despite his satisfaction at having made the best of a bad situation, Burgoyne was anxious to return home to defend himself against the expected storm of criticism:

> [M]y honor and my life in great measure depends upon my return to England . . . . I think that the persons who are most bound to vindicate me will be the first to attack my reputation, those for whom I cheerfully undertook a forlorn hope, and who would have crushed me had I remained inactive, I expect to find my accusers for rashness.[77]

Having obtained permission to give his parole, he arrived in England in May, 1778, ready to place the blame on anybody but himself. He had not yet decided upon the line of defense he would take, but as he cast about for a scapegoat his fellow general, Howe, seemed to be the most likely victim. Burgoyne quickly discovered, however, that the nature of his defense was destined to be political rather than military and that any hope of restoring his reputation lay in shifting his traditional allegiance from the court party to the Opposition. Thomas Hutchinson, the former governor of Massachusetts, described in his *Diary* why Burgoyne changed his mind: "It is said that when Burg[oyne] arrived, Charles F[ox] asked him his plan?—To charge Howe with leaving him to be sacrificed [Burgoyne answered] 'If that's y[ou]r plan we must forsake you: we are determined to support H[owe].' The next news—that [the] Ministry is chargeable; and his [Burgoyne's] speech in the H[ouse], and his new publication, are conformable to this account." [78] In short, Burgoyne discovered he could not count on Fox's support if he planned to attack one of the generals the Opposition hoped to use to embarrass the Ministry. When in late May Burgoyne demanded a Parliamentary inquiry to defend his conduct in the campaign and was refused, he clearly aligned himself with the Opposition. [79]

The Parliamentary inquiry into Burgoyne's conduct begun in May, 1779, was thoroughly political in nature and shed no new light upon the military reasons for the failure of the 1777 campaign. It was, in fact, part of a much larger political maneuver in which the generals—both Burgoyne and Howe having inquiries in 1779—combined with the Opposition politicians to embarrass the Ministry. [80] Germain, on his part, tried to shift the blame for the campaign to Burgoyne. Burgoyne's defense was, of course, that the disaster resulted from the inflexibility of his orders from Germain, leaving him no choice but to force his way to Albany regardless of the consequences. The findings of the inquiry were inconclusive and Burgoyne became a bitter man.

He persisted in provoking the Ministry and kept asking for a court-martial to review his conduct in the campaign. His request was denied, but political retaliation against him was prompt. In September, 1779, he was told that his failure to return to his army in America was considered by the king "as a neglect of duty, and a disobedience of orders."[81] Burgoyne defended himself in a long letter, closing with a demand for a court-martial to clear his name, and offering to resign his appointments to the American staff, his regiment, and the governorship of Fort William.[82] Such steps would leave him only his pay as lieutenant general, the rank to which he had been promoted in 1777. His resignation was quickly accepted and resulted in a considerable financial sacrifice of about £3500 a year.[83]

Having broken with the court party, Burgoyne began acting more and more in concert with the Opposition. Charles Fox insisted that Burgoyne had been used badly and the general's reputation within the ranks of the Opposition became that of a martyr whose defeat was due to the deficiencies of the Ministry. At the urging of Burke and Rockingham, Burgoyne published in 1780 his account of the campaign in which he repeated his old argument concerning his orders, claimed his army was one-half the size he demanded, and insisted that his force was poorly supported.[84]

With the fall of the North Ministry, Burgoyne's fortunes revived briefly as his friend Rockingham returned to power. In 1782 he was made commander-in-chief in Ireland and secured an appointment as colonel of the 4th Regiment. When the subsequent coalition Ministry fell, however, Burgoyne resigned his post as commander-in-chief in 1784. Denouncing the new Pitt administration as unconstitutional, Burgoyne used a familiar weapon, his pen, to ridicule his political opponents and wrote part of the vicious "Westminster Guide." From this point on, Burgoyne withdrew more and more from politics and devoted himself to literary and social affairs. He died on August 4, 1792, after having fathered four children by Susan Caulfield, an actress whom he had taken as his mistress about 1780.

It might be said of Burgoyne that he has been condemned by historians for allowing himself to be defeated in a situation which admitted of nothing but defeat. Too much has been made of the tactical reasons for the capture of his army—the size of his baggage train, his supposed dawdling after taking Fort Ticonderoga, his choice of the Skenesborough route over that of Lake George, and his move in crossing over to the west bank of the Hudson. The causes of the failure of the Saratoga campaign were strategic rather than tactical; the greatest mistakes were made in the planning in London rather than the fighting in upper New York—though Burgoyne himself participated, of course, in the planning. Given the misunderstanding that existed between Burgoyne, Howe, and Germain, the lack of careful planning and co-ordination, the unwarranted optimism about ending the war in 1777, and the mistaken assumptions concerning loyalist support in America, the collapse of the northern campaign might well have been predicted.

The question of his Saratoga defeat aside, what else might be said about Burgoyne's generalship? One of his outstanding characteristics as a commander was his boldness. As Carleton's second-in-command in 1776, he proved aggressive: he almost trapped the retreating Americans at St. Johns on the Richelieu River, called upon Carleton to test the Ticonderoga defenses, and urged the occupation of Crown Point to provide a suitable jumping-off point for an invasion the following spring. Burgoyne was equally bold as commanding general in 1777 when he continued marching toward Saratoga after his plan had received two major setbacks—St. Leger's retreat and the Bennington defeat. But boldness in war is not always a virtue; indeed, there is reason to believe that the Americans counted on this trait in Burgoyne. A month after the fall of Ticonderoga, Washington's adjutant general commented: "Burgoyne is supposed to have ability, but be too sanguine and precipitate, and puffed up with vanity;

which failings, we hope may lead him into traps that may undo
him." [85] Just before the second battle at Saratoga, General Gates
shrewdly anticipated Burgoyne's move and sized up his opponent
as an "old gamester" whose "despair may dictate him to risque
all upon one throw." [86]

Burgoyne also gave evidence of greater understanding of the
complexities of the war than some other generals such as Gage
and Howe. He quickly came to the conclusion that the Revolutionary War was a different kind of war—a war of ideology and
waged against a countryside under arms rather than against a
professional army—and hence one which required different
methods. Recognizing that the war was a battle for men's minds,
Burgoyne insisted initially on seeking a solution by political as
well as military means. For similar reasons, he persisted in issuing
proclamations to persuade Americans to lay down their arms
and looked upon the presence of loyalists within his army as
important because they provided tangible evidence that many
Americans still sided with the king.

By the same token, Burgoyne was ready to resort to psychological warfare when applying military force. Burgoyne believed
that when British troops were employed in battle it should be
for psychological as well as tactical reasons: to drive home the
lesson that regular troops would always prove superior to untrained men in combat. He discussed the battle of Bunker Hill in
precisely these terms:

> [The] event . . . effaces the stain of the 19th of April, and will,
> I hope, stand a testimony and record in America of the superiority
> of regular troops over those of any other description. . . .
>
> In this point of view the action is honourable in itself; and what-
> ever measures his Majesty's councils may now pursue, it must be of
> important assistance by the impression it will make, not only on
> America, but universally, upon public opinion. It may be wise
> policy to support this impression to the utmost, both in writing and
> discourse . . .[87]

This insistence upon maintaining the impression of British military superiority explains why Burgoyne refused to allow his
army to retreat except under desperate circumstances.

Burgoyne's use of certain allies and weapons must be viewed within the same context as a form of psychological warfare. He advocated using Indians primarily for the psychological impact they would have upon the enemy. As early as the summer of 1775, he noted, "the rebels are more alarmed at the report of engaging the Indians than at any other measure. And I humbly think this letter alone [General Charles Lee's letter] shows the expediency of diligently preparing and employing that engine." [88] His employment of cannon likewise was based, in part, on the premise that artillery would appear "extremely formidable" to raw American troops who were unused to such weapons.

In his tactics, Burgoyne showed some ability to adapt to American conditions and to the different kind of opposition that he faced in the Continental army and militia. His emphasis upon the use of light infantry was a direct response to the use Americans made of entrenchments and the techniques of guerrilla warfare they employed in wooded country. Even more important was Burgoyne's willingness to learn from the Americans and to adopt their tactics. In his standing orders issued during the Saratoga campaign, Burgoyne called upon his own officers to fortify and entrench their positions wherever possible by "Felling Trees with their Points outward, barricading Churches and Houses, [and] Breastworks of Earth and Timber." Such measures were necessary, Burgoyne noted, because "the Enemy, infinitely inferior to the King's Troops in open space and hardy Combat, is well fitted by disposition and practice for the Stratagems and Enterprises of little War." Burgoyne also paid the Americans the compliment of emulation when he formed a body of sharpshooters in his army similar to Daniel Morgan's corps of riflemen just before the battles at Saratoga.[89]

But if Burgoyne showed considerable boldness, an insight into the true nature of the war, and a certain flexibility in his tactics, one major flaw in his generalship arose from his failure to free himself more completely from the military orthodoxies of his day. Although he perceived dimly that the war might be won or settled by resorting to rather unorthodox military methods, Burgoyne tended to think in traditional terms when he suggested solutions. Most of his suggestions in the first year of the war were predicated on two assumptions: that the American military forces, although able and respectable opponents, were unlikely to offer any long and drawn-out resistance; and that the mass of the population would be duly impressed by a sufficient show of strength on the part of the British army. He continued to cast about, therefore, for some form of political adjustment that would obviate the need for anything more than a show of force. After 1775, however, he seems to have shifted to a more traditional view and called for more men and more material to exert greater military pressure.

Burgoyne remained rather optimistic about Britain's chance for success during the first two and one-half years of the war. His optimism rested mainly on two premises. First, his lifelong belief as a professional soldier that trained troops were inevitably bound to win out over untrained forces. Secondly, his skepticism regarding the strength of the revolutionary movement. Burgoyne initially took the position that the supporters of the American cause were dominated by a few despotic figures, and that these leaders were subject to bribery. "[T]here was hardly a leading man among the rebels, in council, or in the field, but at the proper time, and by proper management, might have been bought," he wrote in 1775.[90] That Burgoyne was deadly serious about this idea was made evident when he suggested that General Charles Lee, a former British officer, might be bribed and persuaded to come over to the cause of the king.[91] Only during the late stages of the Saratoga campaign did Burgoyne begin to recognize the degree to which American soldiers were committed to their cause. "The panic of the rebel troops is confined, and of short duration," he wrote after his surrender, "the enthusiasm is extensive and permanent." [92]

When it came to ideas of strategy, Burgoyne seems to have been similarly hidebound by military orthodoxy. Many of his suggestions on strategy were aimed at seizing a specific geographical objective—such as Albany—rather than capturing one of the American armies. Such ideas, of course, were in keeping with the traditional military thought of the day. Nor did he appear to understand the connection between logistics and sea power. He seems to have been unaware that the lifeline of every British army, including his own, rested upon its communication with the sea.[93] Generally speaking, many of his strategic ideas were shallow and self-centered; he was often angling for the very command he proposed be sent.

Burgoyne showed a similar reluctance to break completely with many of the European methods while fighting in America. Like most officers schooled in the art of European warfare, he tended to place greater reliance upon the bayonet than the bullet and favored the bayonet charge over the close-order volley. During the Saratoga campaign, he exhorted his officers to impress their men with the use of the bayonet:

> Men of half their bodily strength, and even Cowards may be their match in firing; but the onset of Bayonets in the hands of the Valiant is irresistible. The Enemy, convinced of this truth, place their whole dependence in Entrenchments and Rifle pieces. It will be our Glory and preservation to storm where possible.[94]

The purpose of such tactics was obvious: to teach the rebels the superiority of trained troops and show them the military consequences of their defiance of the king.

A second major flaw in his generalship—besides his fear of straying too far from orthodox military practices—was Burgoyne's overpowering ambition. Too much has been made of his tendency to resort to intrigue to gain a higher command; in this he was no different than his fellow generals. It was in allowing his ambition to color his military judgment that Burgoyne showed his greatest weakness. His desire to reap fame resulted in an excessive optimism that often blinded him to a realistic assessment of his chances. Such overconfidence sometimes led directly to miscalculation.

In summary, Burgoyne was hardly the stereotyped figure of the English gentleman-general as usually represented. Living in a transitional period of great military, political, and social changes, he appears to have been acutely aware of contemporary developments and attempted to adjust to them accordingly. Militarily, his recognition of the Revolutionary War as an unorthodox war that could not be settled by the usual means brought forth some suggestions on his part for a political solution, changes in tactics, and a greater emphasis upon a show of force to impress the insurgent population. Politically, Burgoyne showed he was cognizant of the changes underway when he began speaking of the Americans as a "nation" rather than "rebellious subjects" while the war was still going on, and by declaring his support of American independence as early as 1778.[95] Had he been able to curb his ambition, to break more completely with his European past, and to be more innovative and less traditional in his professional outlook, Burgoyne might have made the War of Independence—in a military sense—a truly revolutionary war.

FOOTNOTES

1. Marvin L. Brown, Jr., ed., *Baroness von Riedesel and the American Revolution* (Chapel Hill, 1965), pp. 55–56.

2. Horace Walpole to Countess of Upper Ossory, August 8, 1777; Horace Walpole to same, August 24, 1777; and Horace Walpole to same, November 13, 1777, in W. S. Lewis, *et al.*, ed., *Horace Walpole's Correspondence* (New Haven, 1955), XXXI, pp. 368–71, 372–76, and 397–99; hereafter, *Walpole's Correspondence* since all Walpole letters will be cited from the Yale edition of Walpole's correspondence.

3. Charles Lee to Miss Sidney Lee, [?] 1782, *Lee Papers*, New York Historical Society *Collections*, 1871–74, IV, p. 12; hereafter referred to as *Lee Papers*.

4. Lewis Namier and John Brooke, eds., *History of Parliament: House of Commons 1754–1790* (New York, 1964), II, p. 141; hereafter Namier and Brooke, *History of Parliament*. The discrepancy concerning the date of Burgoyne's birth is discussed in Edward B. de Fonblanque, *Political and Military Episodes . . . Derived from the Life and Correspondence of the Rt. Hon. John Burgoyne* (London, 1876), pp. 4–8.

5. Lord Bingley's Will, June 27, 1729, cited in *Walpole's Correspondence*, XXVIII, p. 336.

6. Namier and Brooke, II, *op. cit.*, p. 142.

7. *Ibid.*

8. Burgoyne to George Warde, November 23, 1757, in Fonblanque, *op. cit.*, p. 11.

9. Fonblanque, *op. cit.*, p. 46.

10. Viscount Barrington to Burgoyne, October 27, 1759, Shute Barrington, *The Political Life of William Wildman, Viscount Barrington* (London, 1815), pp. 55–62.

11. Lord Bute to Burgoyne, November 2, 1762, Fonblanque, *op. cit.*, p. 49.

12. Fonblanque, *op. cit.*, p. 79.

13. *Ibid.*, p. 14.

14. *Ibid.*, p. 32.

15. *Ibid.*, pp. 15–20 and 62–82.

16. George O. Trevelyan, *The American Revolution* (4 vols. London, 1913), IV, p. 75.

17. James Phinney Baxter, ed., *The British Invasion from the North: The Campaigns of Generals Carleton and Burgoyne from Canada, 1776–1777 with the Journal of Lieutenant William Digby* (Albany, 1887), p. 157; hereafter Baxter, *Digby's Journal*.

18. Namier and Brooke, *op. cit.*, II, p. 142 and III, p. 645.

19. *Ibid.*, II, p. 142. To be fair to Burgoyne, it should be noted that the "corporation mob" in Preston was likewise armed.

20. Fonblanque, *op. cit.*, p. 124; John Debrett, *History, Debates, and Proceedings of both Houses of Parliament of Great Britain from the Year 1743 to the Year 1774* (7 vols. London, 1792), VI, pp. 10–13; VI, p. 444; and VII, pp. 175–76.

21. Debrett, *op. cit.*, VI, p. 79.

22. *Ibid.*, VII, p. 175–76. Burgoyne had a reputation as a pompous speaker. In the course of his speech on April 19, 1774, members of the House of Commons became bored and the remark passed that Burgoyne "belonged rather to the heavy than the light horse." Burgoyne, considerably embarrassed, promptly sat down.

23. *The Parliamentary Register* or, *History of the Proceedings and Debates of the House of Commons . . . During the First Session of the Fourteenth Parliament* (London, 1779), I, p. 252; Fonblanque, *op. cit.*, p. 130.

24. Walpole to Lady of Upper Ossory, June 14, 1787, *Walpole's Correspondence*, XXXIII, p. 563.

25. Walpole to Mason, October 5, 1777, *Walpole's Correspondence*,

XXVIII, p. 336; and Nathaniel W. Wraxall, *Historical Memoirs of My Own Time* (2 vols. London, 1815), II, p. 50.

26. Fonblanque, *op. cit.*, p. 90.
27. *Ibid.*, p. 91.
28. *Ibid.*, pp. 120–21.
29. George III to Lord North, April 11, 1775, in John W. Fortescue, ed., *Correspondence of George III*, (6 vols. London, 1927–28) III, p. 202; hereinafter *Correspondence of George III*.

30. [Arthur] Lee to John Dickinson, April 25, 1775, Dickinson Papers, pp. 25–28, Library Company of Philadelphia.
31. Burgoyne to Lord [North], June 14, 1775, Historical Manuscripts Commission, *Tenth Report* (London, 1887) app., pt. VI, p. 8.
32. *Ibid.* Burgoyne proposed his plan for conciliation and requested official leave from America on the very same day, Allen French, *First Year of the Revolution*, p. 204 fn.
33. Lord George Germain to General Irwin, July 26, 1775, in Historical Manuscripts Commission, *Report on the Manuscripts of Mrs. Stopford-Sackville* . . . (London, 1904–10), I, p. 136.
34. Proclamation, June 14, 1775, in Peter Force, ed., *American Archives*, 4th Series, II, pp. 968–69.
35. Fonblanque, *op. cit.*, p. 136; French, *op. cit.*, p. 202; and John Alden, *General Gage in America*, p. 264.
36. Burgoyne to Lord Rochford, June [?], 1775, in Fonblanque, *op. cit.*, pp. 142–54. This may be the letter abstracted in *Correspondence of George III*, III, p. 224 and, if so, is dated June 25.
37. *Ibid.*
38. *Ibid.*
39. *Ibid.*
40. *Ibid.*
41. Fonblanque, *op. cit.*, p. 190.
42. Burgoyne to Germain, August 20, 1775, in Historical Manuscripts Commission, *Report on the Manuscripts of Mrs. Stopford-Sackville*, II, pp. 6–8.
43. French, *op. cit.*, p. 537.
44. "Reflections upon the War in America," 1776 [?], is abstracted in Fonblanque, *op. cit.*, pp. 208–10. The fact that Burgoyne assumed that Quebec had fallen places the date of the paper probably in January or February of that year. Burgoyne in a separate memorandum suggested also that the number of light dragoons in America be increased for purposes of greater mobility. Burgoyne to Germain, January 4, 1776, in Historical Manuscripts Commission, *Report on the Manuscripts of Mrs. Stopford-Sackville*, I, pp. 383–84.

45. Burgoyne to Clinton, July 7, 1776, in Clinton Papers, William L. Clements Library, Ann Arbor, Michigan.
46. Burgoyne to Clinton, November 7, 1776, in Clinton Papers, William L. Clements Library, Ann Arbor, Michigan.
47. *Ibid.*
48. *Ibid.*
49. *Ibid.*
50. Germain to the king, December 10, 1776, *Correspondence of George III*, III, 1936; Burgoyne to Clinton, November 7, 1776, in Clinton Papers, William L. Clements Library, Ann Arbor, Michigan. Fonblanque, *op. cit.*, pp. 225–28.
51. King to Lord North, December 13, 1776, *Correspondence of George III*, III, 1938.
52. General S. Brown: The American Secretary (Ann Arbor, 1963), pp. 92–97.
53. *Ibid.*, p. 99.
54. *Ibid.*, 93–107.
55. See "Thoughts for Conducting the War from the Side of Canada," in Hoffman Nickerson, *Turning Point of the Revolution* (Boston, 1928), pp. 83–89.
56. Piers Mackesy, *The War for America, 1775–1783* (Cambridge, 1964), p. 115; William B. Willcox, *Portrait of a General: Sir Henry Clinton in the War of Independence* (New York, 1964), pp. 146–47.
57. Nickerson, *op. cit.*, p. 85.
58. *Ibid.*, pp. 83–89.
59. Burgoyne to Fraser, May 6, 1777, quoted in Eric Robson, *The American Revolution, 1763–1783* (New York, 1955), p. 139.
60. Brown, *American Secretary*, pp. 107–16.
61. Paul H. Smith, *Loyalists and Redcoats* (Durham, N.C., 1964), p. 51; William B. Willcox, "Too Many Cooks: British Planning Before Saratoga," *Journal of British Studies*, II (November, 1962), p. 66.
62. Howe to Carleton, April 5, 1777, Historical Manuscripts Commission, *Report on the Manuscripts of Mrs. Stopford-Sackville*, II, pp. 65–66.
63. Brown, *American Secretary*, p. 115.
64. Willcox, *Portrait of a General*, pp. 153–68.
65. Fonblanque, *op. cit.*, p. 245.
66. Burgoyne to Germain, July 11, 1777, in John Burgoyne, *State of the Expedition* (London, 1780), app., p. xxxvii.
67. Fonblanque, *op. cit.*, pp. 489–92.
68. Burgoyne to General Harvey, July 11, 1777, Fonblanque, *op. cit.*, p. 247.

69. Burgoyne to Germain, August 20, 1777, Burgoyne, *State of the Expedition*, app., p. xlvi; Smith, *op. cit.*, pp. 51–55.
70. Burgoyne to Germain, October 20, 1777, Burgoyne, *State of the Expedition*, xcvii.
71. *Ibid.*
72. Fonblanque, *op. cit.*, p. 264.
73. Burgoyne to Howe, October 20, 1777, in Historical Manuscripts Commission, *Report on American Manuscripts in the Royal Institution of Great Britain* (London, 1904), I, p. 140.
74. Burgoyne to Germain, October 20, 1777, in Burgoyne, *State of the Expedition*, app., pp. xcvi–xcviii.
75. *Ibid.*, italics are mine.
76. Willcox, *Portrait of a General*, pp. 147 and 153.
77. Burgoyne to Howe, October 20, 1777, Historical Manuscripts Commission, *Report on American Manuscripts in the Royal Institution of Great Britain*, I, p. 140.
78. Peter O. Hutchinson, ed., *Diary and Letters of His Excellency Thomas Hutchinson* (London, 1886), II, p. 210.
79. Namier and Brooke, *History of Parliament*, II, p. 144.
80. Brown, *American Secretary*, pp. 135–36.
81. Jenkinson to Burgoyne, September 24, 1779, *Annual Register*, xxii (1779), pp. 304–05.
82. Burgoyne to Jenkinson, October 9, 1779, *Annual Register*, xxii (1779), pp. 305–08.
83. Namier and Brooke, *History of Parliament*, II, p. 145.
84. This was his *State of the Expedition from Canada.*
85. Timothy Pickering to Mrs. Pickering, August 2, 1777, in Octavius Pickering, *Life of Timothy Pickering* (Boston, 1867), I, p. 150.
86. Horatio Rogers, ed., *Hadden's Journal and Orderly Books* (Albany, 1884), p. lxxxiv.
87. Burgoyne to Lord Rochford, June [?], 1775, in Fonblanque, *op. cit.*, p. 146.
88. Burgoyne to North, June–July [?], 1775, in Fonblanque, *op. cit.*, p. 178; and Burgoyne, *State of the Expedition*, p. 15.
89. E. B. O'Callaghan, ed., *Orderly Book of Lieutenant General John Burgoyne* (Albany, 1890), pp. 2–3, 91.
90. Burgoyne to Lord Rochford, June [?], 1775, in Fonblanque, *op. cit.*, p. 150.
91. Burgoyne to Lord North, [?], 1775, in Fonblanque, *op. cit.*, pp. 176–77.
92. Burgoyne to Germain, October 20, 1777, in Burgoyne, *State of the Expedition*, p. xcviii.

93. Willcox, *Portrait of a General*, p. 45.
94. E. B. O'Callaghan, *op. cit.*, p. 3.
95. *The Parliamentary Register* or, *History of the Proceedings and Debates of the Fourth Session of the House of Commons of the Fourteenth Parliament of Great Britain* (London, 1778), IX, p. 258.

BIBLIOGRAPHY

Brown, Gerald S. *The American Secretary: The Colonial Policy of Lord George Germain, 1775–1778.* Ann Arbor, 1963. The fullest discussion, by far, of the planning of the Saratoga campaign and concludes that Germain gave Burgoyne great latitude in the instructions about whether he should proceed to Albany.

Burgoyne [John], Lieutenant-General. *A State of the Expedition from Canada as Laid Before the House of Commons by Lieutenant-General Burgoyne.* London, 1780. Burgoyne's own defense of his conduct of the Saratoga campaign and indispensable for an understanding of the man.

Clark, Jane. "Responsibility for the Failure of the Burgoyne Campaign," *American Historical Review*, XXXV (April, 1930), pp. 543–559. An important article which inspired a major revision about the purpose of the Saratoga campaign as being an effort to drive a wedge between the New England colonies and those areas further south.

Fonblanque, Edward B. de. *Political and Military Episodes . . . Derived From the Life and Correspondence of the Right Hon. John Burgoyne.* London, 1786. The classic apologia for Burgoyne.

Hudleston, Francis J. *Gentleman Johnny Burgoyne.* Indianapolis, 1927. A popularized biography in the pro-Burgoyne tradition, and one in which the line between history and romance is often a thin one.

Nickerson, Hoffman. *The Turning Point of the Revolution, Or Burgoyne in America.* Boston and New York, 1928. Still the most complete and authoritative treatment of the Saratoga campaign, and quite critical of Burgoyne. Must be supplemented, however, by the recent work of Willcox and Brown about the planning of the campaign.

Stone, William L. *The Campaign of Lieut. Gen. John Burgoyne and the Expedition of Lieut. Col. Barry St. Leger.* Albany, 1877. Contains much material about the campaign that cannot be found elsewhere, but often does not document key points.

Willcox, William B. "Too Many Cooks: British Planning Before Saratoga," *Journal of British Studies*, II (November, 1962), pp. 56–90.

A brilliant article that concludes the most fundamental errors were made not so much in the execution as in the planning of the Saratoga campaign.

———. *Portrait of a General: Sir Henry Clinton in the War of Independence.* New York, 1964. Focuses more on the execution of the Saratoga campaign than the article above and concludes that General Clinton did all that could be expected of him in coming to the assistance of Burgoyne.

Charles Lord Cornwallis:

STUDY IN FRUSTRATION

HUGH F. RANKIN

Tulane University

MEASURED in terms of his military experience, Charles, Earl Cornwallis, should have been the outstanding British general in the American Revolution. Educated at Eton, tutored by a Prussian officer, and trained at the military academy in Turin, his knowledge of strategy and tactics encompassed a far greater scope than that of the average British officer. His formal education in martial matters was broadened by a lengthy career in active service. He was not quite eighteen when he secured a commission in the First, or Grenadier Guards in 1758; he purchased a captaincy in the 85th Foot a year later; was promoted to lieutenant colonel of the 12th Foot in 1761; and became colonel of his own regiment, the 33rd, in 1766. As a young officer he was battle-tested at Minden, Kirch Donkern, Wilhemstadt, and Lutterburg. He was commended on several occasions for his gallant conduct upon the battlefield. But neither training nor experience guarantees military greatness and Cornwallis was destined to go down in history as the general whose defeat made possible American independence.[1]

Cornwallis' rapid rise in military and political circles was as much the result of a distinguished ancestry as of his inherent talents. Born into a noble family, he was appointed aide-de-camp to the king in 1765, lord of the bedchamber that same year, chief justice of Eye in 1766, and constable of the Tower in 1770. In 1760, he entered the House of Commons as Lord Brome, representing the family borough of Eye. Upon the death of his father and his succession to the earldom in 1762, Cornwallis took his seat in the House of Lords. He was neither particularly active nor original in politics, however, usually voting with the faction controlled by Lord Shelburne. In this latter connection he was alleged to have opposed taxing the American colonies. When Shelburne left office, Cornwallis resigned his positions as lord of the bedchamber and chief justice of Eye. From this time on, he devoted more attention to military affairs than to political activity.

When the rebellion in America broke out in 1775, the earl was in Ireland with his regiment. With his military ambition piqued by rumors of an expedition to the southern colonies, Cornwallis indicated to the Ministry his willingness to serve in America. Lord North was pleased: "his example will give credit & spirit to our proceedings against America. The Ardor of the Nation in this cause has not hitherto arisen to the pitch one could wish, & it certainly should be encouraged whenever it appears." [2] As his reward, Cornwallis was given the command of the force to be dispatched from Ireland to make a junction with Henry Clinton in the Cape Fear River of North Carolina. He was to serve as second-in-command to Clinton, who expressed his pleasure at the prospect of a reunion with "my friend Lord Cornwallis." [3]

The witty, charming and frail Jemima, who married Cornwallis in 1768 and bore him a son and a daughter, protested her husband's eagerness to serve overseas. She enlisted the influence of her husband's uncle, the Archbishop of Canterbury, in a vain effort to have the orders revoked. Yet the earl, who obviously loved his wife, refused to listen to her pleadings and appeared determined to seek those laurels that the American war seemed to promise.

The expedition was beset with delays and disappointments. Not until February 12, 1776, some four months after the campaign had been ordered, did the first transports sail from Cork. Contrary winds and turbulent seas delayed the passage and the fleet did not assemble in the vicinity of Cape Fear until late May. By that time it was too late to be of aid to the North Carolina loyalists who had been decisively defeated in the battle of Moore's Creek Bridge. Rather than leading his command into battle, the earl's first military duty was exercising his troops on the hot sands beneath the towering pines and leading them on several small raids to burn the homes of prominent Carolina rebels.[4]

Cornwallis' first exposure to actual combat in the colonies— the expedition against Charleston in June, 1776—proved to be an equally frustrating experience. In the subsequent attack on that city, he and Clinton could only stand by helplessly, isolated by an inlet too deep for the ground troops to ford, as Parker's fleet received a mauling from the makeshift fort on Sullivan's Island. With the collapse of the southern campaign, Cornwallis sailed north to join the main army in New York.

His arrival under Howe's command clarified his standing among the generals of the army. Earlier, Cornwallis had been promised the post of second-in command in Carleton's army in Canada. But Burgoyne returned to England at the end of 1775 and managed to secure that position. Both Henry Clinton and Hugh, Earl Percy, were senior to Cornwallis in Howe's army and the earl had to be content with the command of the reserve.

Despite this seemingly minor post, Cornwallis managed to gain a share of the glory at the battle of Long Island on August 22, 1776. His reserve supported Clinton's flanking movement through Jamaica Pass and on August 27 the earl personally led his troops in a spirited charge along the Cowanus Road. Several observers noted that both Clinton and Cornwallis exposed themselves to enemy fire with almost reckless abandon. Victory came so easily that Cornwallis was led to believe the war would soon be over and that he was "bless'd with the Prospect of being soon restored to my Family."[5]

After the action on Long Island, Cornwallis was involved in several engagements around New York—often as Clinton's sub-

ordinate. He was active in the landing at Kip's Bay and maintained a position on the right flank at White Plains. When Fort
Washington was overrun, his astute disposition of troops sealed
the rebel escape route. After White Plains there was a breach
in the seemingly cordial relations between Cornwallis and Clinton when Cornwallis repeated to Howe Clinton's peevish criticisms of the commanding general. In this betrayal of confidence
lay the embers of a smoldering feud that was to break out later
in a heated controversy.[6]

Cornwallis received his first independent command on November 19, 1776, when he was sent across the Hudson to reduce
Fort Lee on the Jersey shore. His mission was accomplished with
ridiculous ease. As the rebels fled before him, Cornwallis took
up pursuit. But he was restrained by Howe's orders and could
move no farther south than the Raritan. Cornwallis was forced
to cool his heels five days while Howe made his leisurely way
down from New York to inspect the situation personally.[7] By
the time pursuit was resumed, Washington had put the Delaware
River between his force and the British army.

With the army going into winter quarters, Howe granted
Cornwallis leave to return to England to be with his ailing wife.
The war, it was felt, was nearly over. Cornwallis was to return
in the spring, if there was need of another campaign. Just as he
was preparing to embark, however, grim news of the Trenton
disaster arrived. His leave canceled, Cornwallis rode 50 miles
through a frigid night to assume command of the Jersey force.
After overcoming some difficulty in gathering scattered troops
and artillery, he arrived at Trenton late in the afternoon of
January 2, 1777, to find Washington encamped on the far side
of Assunpink Creek.

Cornwallis' decision to wait until the following morning to
launch his attack was to be subjected to critical review in later
years. His choice at the time, however, made sense. Although his
troops were superior to the rebels, they were weary, rain-soaked,
and badly in need of rest. The Americans, moreover, wherever
protected by good terrain, had always been able to give a good

account of themselves. Cornwallis in the meantime so posted his force that it was impossible for Washington to recross the Delaware. The earl's greatest mistake was in allowing his intelligence to break down. Sounds of activity and the sight of blazing fires on the far side of the Assunpink lulled him into such a state of complacency that no patrols were ordered out. While the British slept the night away, Washington marched through the darkness to attack the post at Princeton. Despite the tendency of many British officers to praise Washington for his deft maneuver, Cornwallis, in covering his own blunder, dismissed it as a last defiant gasp. In any future move by Washington, he declared, "the march alone will destroy his army." [8]

It was not until the early morning of April 12, 1777, that Cornwallis again took the field against the Americans. He marched out of Brunswick to attack what were termed "the most miserably looking creatures that ever bore the Name of Soldiers, covered with nothing but Rags and Vermin" at Bound Brook under Benjamin Lincoln. Once again, he gained an easy conquest. The rebels, discovering themselves encircled, ran "off in their shirts." Despite the insignificance of the engagement, the affair was blown up out of proportion in dispatches and did much to puff Cornwallis' reputation. His shrewd maneuvers around Quibbletown in enticing Washington out of a strong position in the hills to "act according to circumstances," added additional luster to the earl's fame.[9]

Although his actions in New Jersey were neither large-scale nor brilliant, Cornwallis had demonstrated that he was a field commander of considerable ability. He had lost little prestige as a result of his humiliating experience at Trenton. General Howe, for reasons of his own, may have wished to elevate Cornwallis above Clinton (who was in England at the time) in the minds of those at Whitehall, for he constantly commended the earl's actions. Indeed, Cornwallis was praised so lavishly that Lord George Germain wrote Howe that he was fortunate to have serving under him "an Officer, in whose Zeal, Vigilance, and active Courage you can so safely confide." [10]

An opportunity for additional glory became possible when Cornwallis was selected as second-in-command on Howe's expedition against Philadelphia. When Washington chose to make his stand at Chad's Ford on the Brandywine, and the Hessian general, Knyphausen, directed a feint toward that crossing, Cornwallis led the flanking movement that resulted in ultimate victory. Near Birmingham Meeting House, despite the favorable position of the rebels under John Sullivan, the earl directed the bayonet charge that forced the enemy from their lines. Had he been given a free hand to push his advantage, Cornwallis might well have made Brandywine the long-sought decisive defeat of Washington. But Howe followed his usual dilatory tactics and consolidated his gains very slowly.[11].

Perhaps it was because of his actions in battle that Cornwallis was permitted to assume the role of conquering hero in leading a detachment of the army into Philadelphia on September 26, "amidst the acclamations of some thousands of the inhabitants mostly women and children." [12] Not only did Cornwallis supervise the fortification of the city, but he directed the drive against the Delaware forts that blocked the entry of British vessels into Philadelphia. When Washington attacked Howe at Germantown in October, Cornwallis wisely refused to allow himself to be distracted by the diversionary militia force sent to amuse him and rushed fresh battalions to the scene of the primary action. Cornwallis added to his laurels when he stormed Fort Mercer at Red Bank in November, forcing the Americans to evacuate that post.

Cold weather brought an end to formal campaigning and Cornwallis now reapplied for the leave he had been forced to give up a year earlier. When measured by the yardstick of reputation, the delay had been fortunate; for the most part, fortune had smiled upon his efforts. In his first 18 months in America, the earl had distinguished himself in subordinate roles and proved he was an able and colorful field commander. On December 16, 1777, he sailed for home aboard the *Brilliant*.

England provided few opportunities for relaxation. His wife's health had steadily declined. He kept the political fences mended by an occasional appearance in the House of Lords. The Ministry subjected him to a rather heavy grilling about Howe's operations and attempted to wring from him a statement fixing the responsibility for Burgoyne's defeat at Saratoga on Howe. But Cornwallis appeared reluctant to criticize his commanding officer—especially one who had sought to favor his fortunes.[13]

Moreover, Cornwallis' previous optimism had been tempered by now by the continuing resistance offered by the Americans. His true feelings perhaps were best sensed by Lady Jemima, who wrote, "I am really so bilious as to think our army in America, Fleets everywhere, Possessions in the West Indies, &c., &c., &c., will be frittered away and destroyed in another Twelve months." [14]

Some of his contemporaries suggested that Cornwallis' answers to the questions put to him were too critical of the Ministry and that he was reprimanded accordingly. Horace Walpole, for example, observed that the earl was rather summarily ordered back to America "with little civility." [15] But the facts do not substantiate this assertion. When Howe was relieved of his command and Clinton elevated to commanding general, Cornwallis was issued a dormant commission as commanding "General in Our Army in America only," which was "not to take place, but in case of a contingency in order to secure you in such case the chief Command over the foreign Generals, [and] is not to be made public if this contingency does not happen." [16]

Upon his return, Cornwallis was not at all pleased with the way things were going in America. There was little future in any army that was obviously going on the defensive—or so it seemed on the basis of Clinton's instructions from the Ministry. On the day the British army evacuated Philadelphia, Cornwallis wrote a letter to Germain requesting permission to return to England as quickly as possible. Germain's ultimate refusal was based on the grounds that Cornwallis' dormant commission made it necessary that he remain with Clinton, in the event of the latter's death or incapacity.[17]

Both Clinton and Cornwallis were unhappy with the lack of

discipline and the "indecent, ungovernable impetuosity" among the officers in the army. The situation took on a more serious tone when, on the march from Philadelphia to New York, it became apparent that Washington would seize the first opportunity to strike at the long column winding its way across New Jersey. Clinton posted the earl with 2,000 of the "elite of the army" to cover the rear guard, and supported Cornwallis with another 4,000 troops under his personal command. It was Cornwallis' division that counterattacked under the burning sun on the plains of Monmouth.[18]

The glory of the day—if glory it may be termed—seemed to belong to Clinton, who "appeared at the head of our left wing accompanied by Lord Cornwallis, crying out 'Charge, Grenadiers, never heed forming!' " Cornwallis shared the embarrassment of other officers "at seeing the Commander of an Army galloping like a Newmarket jockey at the head of a wing of Grenadiers." [19] The same criticism, however, might well have been leveled against Cornwallis as Clinton; he reacted much the same way in the course of the battle.

In New York, the earl established himself in a fine country house on Long Island, and, as under Howe, acted as Clinton's field commander. With Clinton's force weakened by orders to dispatch troops to the West Indies, the commander-in-chief confined his army to routine operations. Cornwallis soon grew bored with this duty that seemed to have no other purpose than to protect foragers.[20] As his wife's health grew increasingly worse, Cornwallis became even more restless and was finally permitted to return to England in November, 1778.

For Clinton's aide, Captain William Sutherland, Cornwallis' return occasioned no great sorrow; "Lord Cornwallis is gone home to cock his eye in the House of Lords, insipid good natured Lord & the worst officer (but in personal courage) under the Crown." [21] Nevertheless, Clinton and Cornwallis seemingly enjoyed cordial relations. Cornwallis promised while in England to look in on Clinton's motherless children. Clinton, on his part, seemed willing to stake his reputation on the earl's report to the Ministry, "where his Knowledge of this Country and of our Circumstances may during this Season be as Serviceable as I have found his Experience and Activity during the Campaign." [22]

After his arrival in England, Cornwallis seemed to have second thoughts about remaining in service and resigned his commission. His wife's death in February, 1779, however, led him to change his mind once again and he offered to return to America. But by the time he advanced his services, Germain had already dispatched a dormant commission to General John Vaughan. Perhaps Germain had been piqued by the earl's recent testimony in the House of Commons; certainly he was reluctant to recall Vaughan's commission, stating that "If the King and Lord Amherst like this new arrangement it must be their measure not mine. . . ." But Lord Cornwallis went over Germain's head and carried his offer of service to the Court, and "His Majesty was graciously pleased to accept." [23]

Cornwallis returned to America, in part, because he could no longer tolerate England. To his brother, William, he explained: "I am now returning to America, not with view of conquest & ambition, nothing brilliant can be expected in that quarter; but I find this country quite unsupportable to me. I must shift the scene. I have many friends in the American Army. I love that Army, & flatter myself that I am not quite indifferent to them: I hope Sr. H. Clinton will stay, my returning to him is likely to induce him to do so. If he insists on coming away, of course I cannot decline taking the command, & must make the best of it, & I trust that good intentions & plain dealing will carry me through." [24]

There was more to his returning to America than mere restlessness. Sir Henry was periodically offering his resignation and the path to the post of commander-in-chief seemed clear for Cornwallis. Still he preferred not to show his hand, and played his cards in a disingenuous fashion. On April 4, 1779, he assured Clinton that he would not have offered his services if it meant "consenting to take command in case you should persist in coming home." [25]

When the earl landed in New York on July 21, 1779, Clinton appeared genuinely happy to see him. In fact, Clinton looked upon Cornwallis' return as an opportunity to resign his command. "I flattered myself that every objection to my request of being released from my very arduous and unpleasant situation must now cease," he wrote years later, "since His Majesty had upon the spot an officer of rank and experience upon whom to confer the command of his army." [26] Clinton's request for relief, however, went unanswered for seven months.

During the second Charleston campaign that took place in 1780, Clinton took Cornwallis more into his confidence, discussing every move with him on the grounds that his own strategy should be clear to his successor should the request for resignation be honored. Although on the surface he remained a dutiful subordinate, a tone of arrogance began to creep into the earl's letters. Even Clinton noticed, after the rumors spread that Cornwallis was to succeed him, that the earl was "regarded by a majority of the officers as actually possessed of the command: and so certain did his Lordship himself be of it that he made no scruples to declare he would assume it as soon as my leave should arrive, let the siege of Charleston be ever so advanced at the time." [27] So much had Cornwallis assumed the pose of a commanding general that a denial of Clinton's request for relief could bring only humiliation.

During the initial stages of the siege, Clinton received word that the king had denied his request for relief. Cornwallis immediately seemed to withdraw into a shell of self-pity as a result of his acute embarrassment. His subsequent behavior suggests that he blamed Clinton for his troubles. Within a week he requested that he not be consulted on future planning as, Clinton explained, "he feared he was a clog upon me, that I gave way too much to his opinion." [28] To Sir Henry's credit, he made an attempt to work matters out between himself and his sulking subordinate. Cornwallis merely took the occasion to deny that he was fomenting discord among the officers of the army, although he admitted suggesting to them several irregularities on the part of the commanding general. Cornwallis likewise counterattacked by accusing Clinton of not complying with all of the king's instructions.[29]

The dispute between the two generals abated temporarily when Cornwallis requested a separate command and was dispatched up the Cooper River to block the American escape route from Charleston. Yet Clinton feared to allow his second-in-command to range too far and soon began to "repent that I sent him. He will play me false, I fear; or at least Ross will." [30] Captain Alexander Ross, Cornwallis' friend, aide, and alter ego, was beginning to play a sinister role in widening the breach between the two generals. Despite the growing antagonism, when Clinton considered storming Charleston Cornwallis requested that he be allowed to share the glory of the day, reasoning that "perhaps you may think that on an occasion of this sort you cannot have too many officers," and concluding with "it is my hearty wish to attend you on that occasion." [31] But the city fell before such a massive assault became necessary.

Following the surrender of Charleston, the ill-feeling between the two men continued in churlish silence. Indeed, on the day after the capitulation, Cornwallis wrote Lord Amherst complaining that since Clinton had "now come to a resolution to remain in this country, my services here must necessarily be of less consequence." [32] Cornwallis requested duty in any part of the empire where there was action and Clinton did not command.

Although he seemed to hold Clinton personally responsible for his plight, past prejudices were quickly forgotten when Cornwallis learned that he was to be left in command of the southern army when Clinton returned to New York. In fact, there were even some indications of cordiality toward the commander-in-chief. When Clinton requested that Cornwallis move toward Camden to block the retreat of those troops who had been marching to the relief of Charleston, the maneuver was executed with alacrity. This move resulted in the slaughter of Buford's Virginians and the capture of Andrew Williamson and around 300 rebels. With this success, Cornwallis confidently reported to

Clinton that all resistance in South Carolina had been eliminated.[33] Clinton sailed for New York on June 8, 1780, convinced that "we may have gained the two Carolinas in Charles Town." [34]

With Clinton's departure, Cornwallis seemed intent on making himself popular with the troops, even if it meant a decline in discipline. The affection for him was reflected in the observation that "His army is a family, he is the father. There are no Parties, no Competitiones." [35] Banastre Tarleton was allowed to remount his British Legion on so many South Carolina horses that one loyalist newspaper boasted: "Colonel Tarleton took so great a number of exceeding fine horses, as enabled him to produce 400 as well mounted and well appointed cavalry, as would do him credit *en revue* at Wimbleton." [36] Soldiers were permitted to plunder at will. Looting was so widespread that crusty old Admiral Arbuthnot, no saint himself, had felt compelled earlier to protest "that this province with common prudence will submit & esteem it happiness to enjoy that freedom they once possessed if Lord Cornwallis can restrain their rapacity, etc." [37]

Despite his popularity with the troops, Cornwallis was a lonely man. He began to turn to a quartet of young officers in his quest for companionship: Nisbet Balfour, commandant at Ninety Six; Banastre Tarleton, of the British Legion; Francis, Lord Rawdon, who commanded the Volunteers of Ireland, a provincial unit; and Alexander Ross. To Balfour he issued an invitation to familiarity, "I beg you will continue to mention your opinion freely to me, without the Assistance of my Friends, I could never get through this arduous task. . . ." [38] His letters to this select group held a tone of cordiality that was conspicuously absent in his correspondence with other military men.

There was one officer under his command—Major Patrick Ferguson—whom Cornwallis did not cultivate. Ferguson, probably one of the most brilliant young officers in the British army, had been issued his commission as inspector of militia by Clinton and was charged with organizing loyalists in the back country: a Clinton appointee could hardly hope to find favor in Cornwallis' eyes. The general constantly threw obstacles in the major's path under the pretense that Clinton's instructions were too imprecise. Nisbet Balfour, who had warned Clinton not to appoint Ferguson, did not like the man. Balfour had disparaged the major with "Ferguson and his Militia . . . [have] great matters in view, and I find it impossible to trust him out of my sight, he seems to me, to want, to carry the war into N. Carolina himself at once." [39] In his reply to this observation, Cornwallis confided, "Entre nous, I am afraid of his getting to the frontier of N. Carolina & playing us some cursed trick." [40] Balfour, with the full approval of Cornwallis, kept Ferguson occupied with busy work rather than fully utilizing his talents to counteract the guerrilla raids and plunderings of the loyalists by that bold partisan, Thomas Sumter. And so it was that military politics and petty jealousies cost Cornwallis the services of an officer whose abilities might have eased the problems of the back country.

As early as June 30, Cornwallis was reporting to Clinton that victories in several skirmishes had "put an end to all resistance in South Carolina." Yet when Clinton wanted to detach troops from South Carolina to bolster his own operations, Cornwallis painted a grave and exaggerated picture of local conditions. [41] The more troops he retained, the greater his chance would be of gaining that glory that had eluded him at Charleston.

Despite the activities of guerrilla bands led by Thomas Sumter, Francis Marion, and Andrew Pickens, the British control of South Carolina was not seriously threatened until General Horatio Gates, the hero of Saratoga, commissioned by the Continental Congress to lead an army south to challenge Cornwallis, arrived on the scene. When Gates, with a motley collection of Continentals and militia, began to march against the British outpost at Camden, Cornwallis set out to meet him with about 2,400 men. Attack, Cornwallis felt, was the best defense. With the rebel army encamped only 14 miles away and "seeing little to lose by a defeat, & much to gain by a Victory," Cornwallis set out on the evening of August 15, determined to fall upon

Gates' force in a surprise attack at daybreak. After a chance encounter with the enemy around two o'clock in the morning, the earl was surprised the following morning when the American general "persisted in his resolution to fight." The bravery and discipline of the British regulars, and their effective use of the bayonet in the blue haze of fog and burned powder, burst the "Gates bubble" in less than an hour. With one stroke Cornwallis destroyed the effectiveness of the southern army of the rebels and they, with Gates leading the way, streamed from the field in terror and confusion.[42]

Cornwallis' victory was so overwhelming that he sent word to the North Carolina loyalists to arm themselves immediately, to seize all rebel leaders, military stores, and to pursue the refugees from Gates' shattered army. At the same time, he promised to "march without Loss of time to their Support." So infectious was his confidence that one military surgeon boasted, "We shall in a few days take another Stripe off by reduction of a Neighbouring Province." [43]

Curiously enough, Cornwallis reported his victory to the government and to Clinton in strikingly different terms. His dispatch to Germain was more detailed, more cheerful in outlook, and stressing the possibilities of success in future operations. The report to Clinton, on the other hand, emphasized the large number of sick troops in his command. The latter letter appeared to be written with a view of convincing the commanding general of the necessity of a diversionary expedition into the Chesapeake area to take some of the pressure off of Cornwallis' North Carolina venture.[44]

The Camden victory made Cornwallis overly optimistic and colored his reasoning. Despite the rising tide of partisan activities and hit-and-run raids by Francis Marion, the earl seemed to think that these actions were of little consequence in light of the victory over Gates and Tarleton's overwhelming defeat of Sumter at Fishing Creek. Cornwallis had long suspected certain political leaders of fanning the "flame of Rebellion," but had resisted the temptation of taking them into custody lest the action "might be considered rather as an act of Fear than of Justice." After Camden, or so Cornwallis claimed, evidence that a number of prominent South Carolinians had broken their paroles was discovered among Gates' captured papers. Twenty-nine citizens, among them Lieutenant Governor Christopher Gadsden, were sent to St. Augustine for confinement. To all protests Cornwallis would answer merely that the measures had been adopted from "motives of policy." [45] This stroke, he seemed to feel, restored South Carolina to a state of subjugation.

Cornwallis was anxious to acquire new laurels in North Carolina despite "the Insolence & Perfidy of our Enemys and the Timidity of our Friends" in South Carolina. The victories in South Carolina, he believed, would awe the rebels of North Carolina into submission. Yet he must keep on the move, he told Clinton, for if the army retired behind the fortifications of Charleston both Carolinas would soon be lost. [46] Ambition had colored his reason to the point of recklessness.

His plans called for a detachment under Major James Craig to take Wilmington, giving the British control of the Cape Fear River and a supply route into the interior. Ferguson's militia were to be thrown out on the left flank as protection from attack by the back-country people. Cornwallis still did not trust Ferguson or his "miserable naked Corps" of militia, "whom he says he is sure he can depend on for doing their duty & fighting well, but I am sorry to say his own experience as well as that of every officer is totally against him." [47] On September 8, 1780, despite the obvious growing unrest in South Carolina, Cornwallis began a slow, almost leisurely, march northward. His advance was hampered by the agues and fevers that beset his troops as well as by the harrying activities of rebel partisan bands. On September 25 he bivouacked in Charlotte to rest his men and to investigate the reports that great bodies of militia were turning out to oppose his march. [48]

Out in the west, Ferguson had met with some success in several skirmishes with the "Back Water Plunderers." As the aroused frontiersmen, under Charles McDowell, Isaac Shelby,

Benjamin Cleveland, John Sevier, and William Campbell, began to gather against him, Ferguson's dispatches reflected an increasingly dangerous situation. He requested that Tarleton's Legion be sent out to cover him as he fell back toward the main army, and a note of urgency crept into his "Something must be done soon." [49] Cornwallis refused to take Ferguson seriously, but finally sent out a battalion of the 71st Regiment to make a junction with Ferguson on the banks of the Catawba River. Within three days, alarmed at the reports of rebel militia gathering around him in the neighborhood of Charlotte, Cornwallis recalled this relief force. He explained this move to Ferguson with the statement, "I now consider you Perfectly safe." [50] By the time this dispatch was written, Patrick Ferguson had no need of reinforcements—he had been killed the day before when the backwoodsmen had wiped out his force at King's Mountain.

With his flank exposed and fearful of the enemy militia, anxious for the health of his own troops, and himself abed with a "feverish Cold," Cornwallis pulled back into South Carolina. There were, however, other reasons for this withdrawal. Because of the low spirits of the loyalists after Ferguson's defeat, it was feared that the "Over Mountain Men" would grow bold enough to attack the frontier forts in South Carolina, especially Ninety Six. Moreover, there were persistent rumors that Gates had collected a new army and once again was marching south. In the face of these considerations, Cornwallis weakened his own command by dispatching reinforcements to Ninety Six and Camden. [51]

Clinton had earlier sent Major General Alexander Leslie into the Chesapeake area to act "in favor of Lord Cornwallis." From his camp at Winnsboro between the Broad and Catawba rivers, Cornwallis sent word to Leslie to abandon his operations in Virginia and to sail to South Carolina as reinforcements for his own army. By late November, with both himself and his army healthy again, Cornwallis was almost exuberant as he boasted, "for the numbers there never was so fine an Army. . . ." [52]

Cornwallis now had to match wits with a new rebel general, for Nathanael Greene had been sent south to relieve Gates. Despite the growing activity in back country South Carolina, Cornwallis was impatient to resume his invasion of North Carolina. When Greene split his force and sent Daniel Morgan into the Broad River region, posing a threat to Ninety Six, Cornwallis unsuccessfully attempted to persuade the Indians to divert the attention of the enemy by attacks upon frontier settlements.[53]

Although he was in a situation that could grow dangerous, many of Cornwallis' letters brimmed with confidence. Tarleton was sent to take care of Morgan at about the same time Benedict Arnold was dispatched by Clinton to replace Leslie in the Chesapeake. With this disposition of troops Cornwallis was predicting to Lord Rawdon that "we may make a great change in the Southern Colonies in the next few months." [54] But there was a different cast to his dispatches to Clinton on January 6, 1781; he reported a "constant alarm" in South Carolina. Cornwallis appeared to be of two minds, for in this same letter he declared he was beginning his march into North Carolina. He had no intention of moving, however, until three basic conditions had been met: Leslie's reinforcements had joined him, Tarleton had disposed of Morgan, and a base had been firmly established at Wilmington.[55] In all these plans, Cornwallis left little margin for unexpected developments.

No one anticipated what came to pass at the Cowpens battle. Heavy rains prevented Tarleton's suggestion that the main army be stationed so as to cut off any possible retreat by Morgan. Tarleton's dispatches, written with the flourish of a conqueror, assured his commander that he would crush Morgan just as soon as the rebel force could be made to stand and fight. Cornwallis was encamped at the confluence of Turkey Creek and Broad River, some thirty miles from Winnsboro, when he first received reports of Tarleton's defeat at the Cowpens. Tarleton himself did not come into camp until the following morning, January 18, 1781. A rebel prisoner of war was to write in later years that the general was leaning forward on his sword as Tarleton made his report. In his fury, Cornwallis pressed forward with such strength that the weapon broke beneath him; he swore loudly that he would free Tarleton's men who had been taken prisoner by Morgan, no matter what the cost.[56]

The earl's pride had been hurt at so "extremely unexpected" a defeat that "almost broke my heart." He seemed to take it as a personal affront that Morgan should dare inflict disaster upon one of his young protégés. There was also the possibility that Tarleton's defeat might be interpreted at Whitehall as evidence of the earl's inadequacies. After Leslie arrived on the morning of January 18, and another day was spent collecting the fugitives from Cowpens, Cornwallis set forth in search of Morgan. When intelligence reached him that Morgan had retreated northward the same day of the battle, Cornwallis took up the pursuit. In a note of self-pity, he wrote, "I was never more surrounded with difficulty and distress, but practice in the school of adversity has strengthened me." [57]

By the time he reached Ramsour's Mill in North Carolina, it was reported that Morgan had already crossed the Catawba River. Despite the possibility that Greene might attack the British outposts in South Carolina, and the increasing improbability of catching Morgan, Cornwallis decided to press the pursuit, rationalizing, "I see definite danger in proceeding, but certain ruin in retreating," for to adopt "defensive measures would be the certain ruin to the affairs of Britain in the Southern Colonies." [58] When Greene was reported marching northward to make a junction with Morgan, time became a vital factor. Much of the mobility of Cornwallis' army had been destroyed with the defeat of Tarleton's light troops at Cowpens, but the earl resolved to burn the majority of his wagons and excess baggage to enable his force to move with greater speed.[59]

The pursuit through North Carolina resembled more a game of hare and hounds than a military operation. Greene constantly outwitted Cornwallis, beginning at the Yadkin River where he gathered up all available boats and forced the British to detour upstream to passable fords. Then, too, the earl had a penchant for accepting faulty intelligence. When word was received that the lower fords of the Dan River were impassable, Cornwallis had his men discard their packs and marched swiftly to intercept Greene on the upper reaches of the Dan. Frustration was compounded when he discovered that he had been led away from the main American army by a detachment commanded by Otho Williams and that Greene had safely crossed the lower fords into Virginia. Cornwallis thereupon turned back into North Carolina.[60]

Hillsborough, supposedly a center of loyalist activity, was reached on February 20, 1781. Two days later, the king's standard was raised to the accompaniment of a twenty-one-gun salute. A proclamation invited all friends of government to aid in "the re-establishment of good order and constitutional government." Despite the claims of loyalist newspapers that loyalists were flocking into the village, few actually joined the British force.[61]

Those who came in expressed their resentment that so little had been done to aid them since the beginning of the war. Others had grown wary because of the miscarriage of British plans in the past. Persecutions by the rebels had broken the spirits of some, while still others openly voiced the opinion that the British army was spread too thin to offer effective protection.[62] Inasmuch as relief for the loyalists had been one of the primary objectives of the North Carolina campaign, their poor response lent an air of failure to the enterprise.

Cornwallis was happy to leave Hillsborough. The massacre of a loyalist force under Dr. John Pyle by Henry Lee and Andrew Pickens, coupled with Tarleton's impetuous charge against another group of the king's friends marching in to join the British, dampened all enthusiasm for the forces of the Crown. Greene, meanwhile, had been reinforced in Virginia, and had recrossed the Dan. Although his troops were ragged and nearly barefoot, Cornwallis began to move slowly toward Cross Creek where supplies might be brought up the Cape Fear from Wilmington. After a brief skirmish with Greene's forces at Wetzel's

Mill, he encamped at New Garden Meeting House. There, on March 14, he learned that the American general was moving in his direction. Hoping to revive loyalist interest by an impressive show of British strength, the earl began a move to bring Greene to a decisive action.[63]

It was a foolish decision; the British army simply was in no condition to fight. Although outnumbered by approximately 4,400 to 1,490 troops, Cornwallis himself was inclined to discount the difference between the two forces because the majority of Greene's army was composed of militia. As at Camden, the very fact that he moved against such odds revealed his contempt for the poorly trained and supposedly undisciplined American militiamen. His ego needed a victory at this point, no matter what the odds. Apparently he had decided that a defeat of Greene would cancel the humiliations suffered at Cowpens and during the race to the Dan. Information about the terrain proved inaccurate, and on March 15 he found Greene's army stationed at Guilford Court House in a rather formidable position—three battle lines judiciously positioned on steep and wooded ground. Despite these unfavorable conditions, Cornwallis decided to do battle, relying, perhaps, too much on the use of the bayonet which was to prove ineffective in some of the more thickly wooded areas. It was a grubby, vague kind of combat, the broken terrain leading to gaps in the battle lines and the isolation of some units. Still the earl kept driving his troops ahead and was forced to commit his reserves much earlier than he had planned.[64]

During the battle, Cornwallis was foolhardy in his personal bravery. He was slightly wounded, but refused to allow his name to be placed on the casualty list. Two horses were killed beneath him. When the Guards were thrown into retreat, the general ordered a charge of grape fired through the British ranks at the pursuing enemy—a desperate measure, but an effective one.[65] Cornwallis was to claim a "compleat Victory" at Guilford Court House, but one is inclined to agree with the statement in the *Annual Register* that proclaimed the battle to be "productive of all the consequences of defeat." [66] And one young officer, after boasting of gaining the field of battle, added rather wist-fully, "I must own, without any brilliant advantage arising from it." [67]

After announcing his victory in a pompous declaration, Corn-wallis marched for Cross Creek. Greene pursued him as far as Ramsey's Mill on Deep River before turning back into South Carolina, hoping to lure the British general away from North Carolina and Virginia. Finding the supply situation at Cross Creek impossible, Cornwallis moved down to Wilmington. By this time, his letters had taken on a tone of desperation. They were filled with excuses for past misadventures, explored the possibilities for future action, and complained that he was "quite tired of marching about the Country in Quest of Adventure." [68]

Although he had agreed with Clinton that Charleston should be held at all costs, it was at Wilmington that the earl permitted his imagination to get out of hand. He decided that an offensive war should be carried into Virginia, seeking the ever-elusive decisive victory over the Americans. The main focus of the war, he now decided, should be the Chesapeake, even if it meant abandoning New York.[69] By moving into that area, he seemed to think, he might force Clinton into abandoning some of his own plans.

With his army but a shadow of its former strength, Corn-wallis was in desperate need of reinforcements. Since January 15, he had lost 1,501 men from a total of 3,224.[70] On April 24, 1781, therefore, the earl wrote General Phillips that he was marching to the Chesapeake to assume command of the British troops in that area. He was almost certain, as were a number of other officers, that Greene was returning to South Carolina for another strike at Camden, but Cornwallis felt himself too weak to return to the state.[71] Marching toward Virginia in an almost aimless fashion in late April, Cornwallis allowed his army to plunder so much that he alienated the countryside and the Brit-ish gained a reputation therein for "Cruelty & inhumanity." Somewhere along the way he lost another 300 men from his command.[72]

Cornwallis finally made a junction with Phillips' army on May 20 at Petersburg and discovered that Phillips had died three days earlier of a "teazing indisposition." His small force, added to the troops on the ground and subsequent reinforcements, soon brought Cornwallis' strength up to 7,500 men. Once he assumed the command, however, Cornwallis seemed unable to come up with a definite plan of action. He was worried about a possible junction of the forces of Lafayette and Anthony Wayne, which might well present a formidable obstacle to any operations he might undertake. At the same time, he was apprehensive lest he become the objective of a French fleet reported sailing from Rhode Island.[73]

Clinton was equally concerned for Cornwallis' army. He warned his lordship that "in carrying on operations in the Chesapeake . . . they can be no longer secure than whilst we are superior at Sea." Although there was an air of reproach in Clinton's letter relative to Cornwallis leaving South Carolina, he still allowed the earl a great leeway and freedom of action in his planning of future operations.[74]

Past misfortunes weighed heavily on his mind, yet Cornwallis seemed determined not to accept any blame for them. In dispatches to Clinton he argued that if an offensive war was intended, Virginia was the logical place to wage that war; it was the one region in the south where Americans had so much at stake and the subjection of that state would isolate the areas to the southward.

Most of the remaining days in May were spent in attempting to bring Lafayette to a decisive action. Failing to accomplish this purpose, Cornwallis turned his attention to the destruction of rebel stores. Although his raiding parties met with some success, the earl appeared to feel that such successes were of little consequence. When Lafayette was reinforced, first by Wayne and then by von Steuben, Cornwallis fell back toward the coast and on June 19 established himself at Williamsburg. By late June, with his confidence shattered, the general was writing Clinton requesting that he be allowed to return to South Carolina. Perhaps it was a creeping sense of failure that allowed Cornwallis to let himself be caught up in such an emotional rip tide; he now seemed to harbor an almost overwhelming compulsion to return to South Carolina and Camden, the scene of his greatest triumph.[75]

As the American force gained strength and Clinton requested 2,000 troops to help defend New York against a rumored assault, it appeared as though Cornwallis would have to go on the defensive. But he wanted no part of defensive operations: the idea of returning to Charleston had now become an obsession with him. As a result, the feud between Cornwallis and Clinton fell into the realm of the petty, and their letters became filled with thinly veiled sarcasm and vindictiveness as the two generals argued about future strategy.

In July, Cornwallis finally decided to return to Portsmouth from whence he planned to detach troops to Clinton, throw in the sponge, and, if possible, return to Charleston. It was this move, coupled with the capriciousness of Anthony Wayne, that allowed him to salvage a bit of pride. Wayne attacked the British force as it was preparing to cross the James River at Jamestown. Cornwallis, allowing Wayne to think that he was attacking the rear guard, then attacked with his primary force. Had not darkness fallen, the earl might have inflicted a near disastrous defeat upon the Americans rather than a mere "trimming."[76]

The exultation of having bested the enemy was lessened when Cornwallis learned that General Alexander Leslie had been ordered to South Carolina rather than himself. He grew bitter and morose. Still he felt that he might persuade Clinton to send him back to Charleston and was soon writing friends that "it is not improbable that I shall soon be with you in S. Carolina."[77]

His future moves, however, were determined by the commander-in-chief. Clinton had no intention of allowing Cornwallis to return to Charleston to sulk. Dispatches received from Clinton on July 20 instructed Cornwallis not to detach troops to New York but instead to prepare to hold Old Point Comfort on Hampton Roads "at all Events." Admiral Thomas Graves, commanding the British fleet in North American waters, had concluded that he needed a southern anchorage for the great ships of the fleet during the freezing months. A position on the Chesapeake would likewise provide shelter for ships of the line from which they could protect seaborne commerce between New York and Charleston. In a like manner, French ships would be prevented from using the bay as a base. Then, too, such a stronghold might well become a rallying point for the loyalists of the area, although Clinton never intended that the Chesapeake should become a major operational region at that time. Cornwallis had, in early July, suggested Yorktown as a means of securing Point Comfort from land attack.[78]

The business of going upon the defensive and the possibility of doing garrison duty irritated Cornwallis. He appeared to view these developments almost as a reprimand and as a means of removing him from active duty. Certainly he seemed to leave that impression among the officers; as one wrote, "His Lordship, who has performed Wonders & done more than all the Generals thats been in America. . . ." [79] And to Lord Rawdon, Cornwallis whimpered, "that the C[ommander] is determined to throw all blame on me & to disapprove of all I have done, & that nothing but the consciousness of my going home in apparent disgust would eventually hurt our Affairs in this Country could possibly induce me to remain." [80]

But the responsibility for selecting a defensive position had fallen on Cornwallis' shoulders and duty dictated that he follow the wishes of his commanding officer. Engineers were sent to examine Point Comfort and on July 25, Lieutenant Alexander Sutherland submitted his report, followed by a similar document signed by the "Captains of the Navy." Their conclusion was that a post on Point Comfort "must be attended with many inconveniences." The channel in Hampton Roads was so wide that enemy vessels could sail past beyond artillery range; for those same reasons the post could offer no protection to British naval vessels against a superior enemy fleet. Moreover, the cost of maintaining a post on Point Comfort would be prohibitive. There is the suggestion, however, that these reports reflected opinions previously expressed by Lord Cornwallis. The earl, interpreting instructions originally issued to General Phillips, decided to fortify instead the little village of Yorktown as a protected anchorage for the fleet.[81]

Work on fortifications at Yorktown was underway by the first of August, but there was little sense of urgency. The weather, Cornwallis felt, was too warm for his men to engage in heavy labor and he regarded lightly those rumors that reported that a French fleet would soon be operating in the area. The earl resorted to a labor force of "Hundreds of wretched Negroes, that are dying by scores every day." [82]

Cornwallis, by this time, had assembled a military force of more than 8,400 soldiers to man the works, including about 5,000 British regulars, 1,800 Hessians, and 1,500 loyalists. When Clinton suggested that since he had fortified only the one post, perhaps now he could spare some of his troops for the defense of New York, Cornwallis insisted that he needed every man. Despite the size of the army, however, he did not consider his position a strong one. Now that he had occupied the place, Cornwallis had changed his mind as to the value of Yorktown and concluded the site was "after all I fear not very strong." [83]

By the end of August, rumor became reality and work on the fortifications was pushed with frantic haste. A French ship of the line could be seen lying off the mouth of the York, while reports from Point Comfort stated that between 30 and 40 French vessels were within the Virginia Capes. On September 2, the French began landing troops on Jamestown Island on the far side of the peninsula formed by the James and York rivers.[84]

Intelligence soon reported the combined forces of Washington and Rochambeau marching southward toward Virginia. Matters were further complicated when, on September 5, Comte de Grasse sailed out from the Capes and made contact with the British fleet under Admiral Thomas Graves. In the ensuing battle, the French admiral managed to damage the outnumbered British fleet to the extent that one observer noted that "To explain it to one who was not there requires a considerable explanation." Another officer wrote, "It appears that the English were second Best," and Graves' ships were mauled so badly that his fleet was forced to return to New York for repairs.[85]

Clinton promised aid by sea, but Cornwallis warned that help must come soon or "you must be prepared to hear the worst." Once Admiral Robert Digby's expected naval reinforcements arrived and repairs could be made to Graves' squadron, Clinton promised, the British naval force would sail for Virginia. They would leave New York, he added, no later than October 5th.[86]

Cornwallis' disposition, ironically enough, improved as the military situation worsened. There was an almost exuberant note to his dispatches when the Franco-American forces marched down from Williamsburg to lay siege to Yorktown. As the enemy advanced, the earl pulled in his defenses, abandoning all of his outer redoubts except those located on critical sites. Not only did this allow Washington to begin his siege parallels much nearer the British works, but it massed Cornwallis' men within the town in such numbers as to subject them to saturation bombardment. Nevertheless, his dispatches to Clinton held such confident statements as "I have ventured these last two days to look General Washington's whole force in the position outside my works, & I have the pleasure to assure Your Excellency that there was but one Wish throughout the whole Army, which was, that the Enemy would advance." [87]

The earl's general orders bristled with bravado. His men were assured of their security by exaggerated reports that the enemy were inferior in numbers to the British, that they had no heavy siege artillery, and that the French had come only to procure tobacco and would sail away within two weeks. Cornwallis' soldiers, however, remained unconvinced; a number of them felt they were in "a very bad situation." [88] As enemy batteries began their "awful music," the troops were forced to flee their tents, British ships in the river were set afire by hot shot, and a substantial number of soldiers and sailors deserted. While the houses of Yorktown crumbled into rubble under the intense bombardment, the townspeople crowded down to the river's edge to escape the iron hail. Cornwallis himself was forced to seek shelter in "a kind of grotto . . . where he lives underground." [89] The allied cannonade was so incessant that Captain Samuel Graham of the 77th Regiment complained that the British could scarce fire a shot in return with their "fascines, stockage platforms, and earth, with guns and gun carriages, being pounded together in a mass." [90]

The possibility of ultimate defeat became apparent when word was received on October 10 that Clinton's relief expedition could not possibly sail within the next two days. When the Americans and French, during the nights of October 14th and 15th, overran redoubts nine and ten near the river, allowing them to complete their second parallel, a note of despair crept into Cornwallis' correspondence: "The Safety of this Place is so precarious, that I cannot recommend that the Fleet & Army should run great risque in endeavoring to save us." [91]

Nevertheless, Cornwallis refused to admit defeat until he had exhausted every measure. Early in the morning of October 16, he sent out Major Robert Abercromby in a desperate sally which reached the enemy lines, spiked the guns of a French battery, and ended in savage fighting. The following night he made an attempt to break out of the trap by ferrying his troops across the York to Gloucester Point. Cornwallis had hoped to land within the works commanded there by Tarleton and to fight his way back to New York. A sudden squall frustrated the operation.[92]

On the morning of October 17, 1781, Cornwallis went down into the hornwork, and, after staring at the enemy lines for some time, sent a flag across requesting a 24-hour cessation of hostilities. In the subsequent negotiations, Cornwallis vainly attempted to persuade Washington to grant him the same terms that Burgoyne had wrung from Gates at Saratoga. Washington paid scant heed to such proposals and insisted instead that the conditions be the same as those granted the Americans at Charleston. On October 19, 1781, while Cornwallis pleaded illness, Brigadier General Charles O'Hara led the 6,000 troops out of the town to lay down their arms.[93]

The day after the surrender Cornwallis occupied himself in writing a long dispatch to Clinton, attempting to shift blame from his shoulders. "I never saw this post in a very favourable light . . ." he wrote. "Nothing but the hopes of relief would have induced me to attempt its defence. . . ." [94] His comments assumed the nature of a general accusation, but it dealt in such vague generalities that Clinton was able to demolish most of the arguments by citing specific examples to the contrary.

Allowed his parole, Cornwallis returned to New York in mid-November. His conversations with Clinton began amicably enough, but relations soon grew strained. As each of the two generals sought to absolve himself of the responsibility for Yorktown, they allowed their discussions to lapse into petty quarrels with minor incidents becoming major considerations. Clinton brought up Cornwallis' letter of October 20 in which the earl had vowed that he had never liked Yorktown, that he never would have attempted to hold the place had he not been promised aid, and that the village had not been properly fortified because he had only 400 entrenching tools.

Clinton was quick to seize upon obvious errors, pointing out that the report of Cornwallis' engineer on August 23 had listed as many as 992 entrenching tools and that even then the earl had only requested an additional 500. Because Clinton felt "that some people here suppose there are passages in that letter which Convey an Idea, that you had been compelled by my orders to take the post of York tho' it was not of your preference," he requested "a more formal avowal of your Sentiments. . . ." [95] But Cornwallis was not about to admit anything that might damage him in the future. Although refusing to retract his earlier statements, Cornwallis did admit that his October 20th letter had been written "under great Agitation of mind and in a great hurry, being constantly interrupted by numbers of people coming upon business or ceremony. . . ." [96]

By the time Cornwallis sailed for England in January, 1782,

he had already achieved a distinct advantage over Clinton. At home he was received more as a conquering hero than a defeated general. The government had received and published, without comment, his letter of October 20, thereby adding to the impression that Cornwallis had been made a sacrifice to Clinton's stubbornness. Unsolicited aid to Cornwallis' cause came from Benedict Arnold, who was also writing letters critical of Clinton. As a result there was little resentment against the earl. The king, in fact, went so far as to applaud Cornwallis' patriotism.[97]

Knowing himself to be at a disadvantage, Clinton promptly began publishing pamphlets, inaugurating a controversy that boiled for the next two years. Cornwallis and his supporters remained discreetly quiet, thus creating the impression that there was really little to be explained. When the earl did answer, his arguments were presented with the concise logic of a lawyer's brief. Clinton, on the other hand, seemed compelled to follow the dictates of a sensitive and tortured spirit; the earl became his *bête noire*, a haunting symbol of his own failure in America.

Cornwallis likewise had the advantage of powerful political allies. Lord Shelburne, with whom Cornwallis was "upon a very friendly foot," rose in political influence as the Rockingham Whigs returned to power with the resignation of Lord North. Even prior to the news of the Yorktown defeat, Rockingham had been suggesting that Cornwallis was a victim of circumstance and if, by some miracle, there was a British victory, that victory would only delay "our final Extirpation in America."[98] Then, too, Cornwallis had the advantage of family connection with a naval hero, for his brother William had recently behaved admirably in the action off St. Kitts.[99]

America was the preface and the training ground for the glory that Cornwallis was to gain later in his military exploits in India. In the early stages of the war he performed well in subordinate roles, although he appeared more fond of issuing orders than of receiving them. In fact, he was not above placing a superior officer in an unfavorable light when it suited his purposes or might elevate him in the minds of those who could provide future favors. But in pursuing such practices, Cornwallis was merely adopting traditions already established by other generals in the British army.

Cornwallis, in practice, was a better battlefield commander than a planner of grand strategy. Administrative duties bored him; Alexander Leslie was to note that Cornwallis never "had time to settle anything. . . ." [100] As the commanding general in the south, he attempted to curry too much favor from young subordinates and too often he listened too closely to their opinions without weighing the consequences. And in valuing their prejudiced opinions, Cornwallis allowed himself to distrust Patrick Ferguson before that talented young officer had an opportunity to prove himself in the field. When his young protégés made mistakes, he struggled to find excuses for them. Although the defeat at the Cowpens was largely a result of Tarleton's impetuosity and carelessness, Cornwallis not only salved his subordinate's feelings by placing the blame on the "total misbehaviour of the troops," but recommended him for promotion.[101]

He failed, moreover, to exercise proper discipline over the loyalists. Cornwallis allowed them to plunder friend and foe alike, and, like other British commanders, assigned them to menial roles in the over-all scheme of things. Not only did he permit the loyalists, but his army, to plunder almost at will—a practice that alienated many rebels who might have returned to the royal fold. One of the primary objectives of the campaign in North Carolina had been to arouse the loyalists, yet he marched away and left them at the mercy of the rebels. In fact, he left that state in worse condition than he found it, for loyalism became unpopular after his departure.

Among Cornwallis' failings as a tactician was his impetuosity. His pursuit of Morgan seems to have been dictated more by injured pride than by reason, especially since the British position in South Carolina had not been fully consolidated. His impulsive pursuit of Morgan and Greene through strange terrain in a season when streams were certain to be swollen by winter rains was gallant, but hardly in keeping with sound military tradition. The destruction of his baggage and supplies at Ramsour's Mill at a time of the year when foraging possibilities were not good seemed to lack foresight. Even though he sacrificed supplies for speed, he did not seem to have realized that his pace would be regulated by the presence of a train of artillery. Moreover, he should have sent the large number of camp followers and Negroes accompanying the army back to South Carolina. Not only did they slow the march and complicate the supply situation, but they systematically plundered both loyalists and rebels alike, thereby adding to a growing list of potential enemies.

In the boldness of his pursuit, Cornwallis pushed too far with too little. Like most of the military men of his day he must have been familiar with Frederick the Great's *Instructions,* which ran: "In pushing too far into the enemy's country you weaken yourself . . . it is necessary always to proceed within the rules: to advance, to establish yourself solidly, to advance again . . . always within reach of . . . your resources." [102] His complete disregard of such maxims made his march seem like a boat plowing through the water, pushing aside a bow wave that almost immediately closed in behind the stern. He appeared in great haste, seemingly determined to rush on to one victory after another, as if fearful that the luster of his reputation might fade. Joseph Reed succinctly summed up Cornwallis' North Carolina campaign:

> like a desolating meteor he has passed, carrying destruction and distress to individuals—his army walked through the country, daily adding to the number of its enemies, and leaving their few friends exposed to every punishment for ill-timed and ill-placed confidence. [103]

Following his Pyrrhic victory at Guilford Court House, Cornwallis seemed consumed with a fear of failure. Too often he abandoned caution as he sought to remove the tarnish from his reputation. When he marched into Virginia, he did so without specific orders and against the wishes of his commander-in-chief; he thereby deliberately isolated himself from British strength and the primary British command post at New York.

Perhaps the greatest weakness throughout the southern campaign was Cornwallis' ill-concealed contempt of Sir Henry Clinton. The dispute over Yorktown was, in reality, the climax to an antagonism that had been growing in intensity for several years. When Clinton's request for relief from his American duties was refused by the Ministry, Cornwallis appeared to consider this as a personal affront by his commander-in-chief. From this moment on there was a steadily widening breach between the two men. Cornwallis directed his irritation at Clinton and considered the latter as the source of all his disappointments.

When he was left in command of the southern army, the earl seized upon this as an independent command, virtually free of Clinton's direction. While his dispatches to Germain fairly bubbled with enthusiasm, those to Clinton were drab and too often loaded with complaints. He made elaborate excuses for not honoring Clinton's requests to detach troops, refusing to so weaken his own force as to prohibit extensive operations. Clinton, as commanding general, was often too tolerant of his subordinate. A careful reading of his correspondence could suggest that Cornwallis selected Yorktown as a means of exhibiting his superior military acumen and of embarrassing Clinton. After the fall of Charleston, there is the underlying theme in Cornwallis' letters that Clinton could do nothing right.

The earl's complaints that he had been unable to fortify Yorktown properly cannot be justified. His construction of the works there, up to the time that the French fleet actually appeared, were conducted in an almost leisurely fashion. He seemed to fear that in pushing his men too much, he would lose his popularity with his army. If examined in detail, the major blame for the defeat at Yorktown might be placed upon the navy. Yet, in retrospect, the greatest fault should fall upon the shoulders of Lord Cornwallis; for it was not Yorktown that was the critical factor, but his rash decisions made along the way that led to disaster in the little village on the banks of the York.

Charles, Earl Cornwallis, had seen the American war as an opportunity to achieve greatness, but instead he met constant frustration and his ambitions were unfulfilled. It was this frustration that led him into an inconsistent pattern of behavior. At times, his boldness led to success, while his timidity, such as hastily withdrawing support from Ferguson when there were rumors that the militia were gathering, led to disaster. The blame for King's Mountain, therefore, should be borne by Cornwallis as much as by Ferguson.

Perhaps Cornwallis' major weakness, ironically enough, was his excellent military background. He seemed to feel that his superior abilities were never fully utilized in the field. When he was finally thrust into a position of authority, his frustration was compounded by the relatively untrained American generals, who, with the exception of Horatio Gates, proved to be his equals. Unlike some British generals, his troop dispositions in battle were more in the classic textbook tradition when the situation called for a more fluid arrangement. Not once in the battles in which he commanded an army did he utilize the flanking movements that had proved so successful for Howe, and in which Cornwallis had taken part. He used the same basic battlefield formation at both Camden and at Guilford Court House. At Camden, on an open field, he was successful; at Guilford, in rough and wooded terrain, his losses were so great that his claim of victory was merely academic. In later and more mature years he subordinated his ambition to reason and found in India that success that had so constantly eluded him in America.

FOOTNOTES

1. H. Morse Stevens, "Cornwallis," *Dictionary of National Biography* (London, 1921–22), IV, pp. 1159–66; Charles Ross, ed., *Correspondence of Charles, First Marquis Cornwallis*, (London, 1859), I, pp. 1–43. Hereafter cited as Ross, *Correspondence Cornwallis*.
2. Sir John W. Fortescue, ed., *The Correspondence of King George the Third from 1760 to December 1783*, (London, 1928), III, pp. 294–95.
3. William B. Willcox, *Portrait of a General: Sir Henry Clinton in the War of Independence* (New York, 1964), p. 86.
4. Historical Manuscripts Commission, *Report on the Manuscripts*

of the Late Reginald Rawdon Hastings, Esq., (London, 1934), III, pp. 172–73.

5. Willcox, *Portrait of a General,* p. 108 fn., Cornwallis to Elizabeth, Dowager Cornwallis, September 2, 1776, Admiral Sir William Cornwallis Papers, COR/57, National Maritime Museum, Greenwich, England. Any sympathies that Cornwallis may once have held for the Americans seemed to dissipate in the heat of combat. He wrote his mother that "these unhappy people have been kept in utter darkness by the Tyranny of their wicked leaders & are astonished to hear how little is required of them by Great Britain."

6. Sir Henry Clinton, *The American Rebellion,* William B. Willcox, ed. (New Haven, 1954), p. 65 fn.

7. Archibald Robertson, *His Diaries and Sketches in America, 1762–80,* Harry Miller Lydenberg, ed. (New York, 1930), pp. 113–15.

8. Cornwallis to Germain, January 8, 1777, Germain Papers, William L. Clements Library, University of Michigan, Ann Arbor, Michigan; Thomas Dowdeswell to Rockingham, January 16, 1777, Rockingham Papers, R1–1706, Sheffield City Library, Sheffield, England.

9. New York *Mercury,* April 20, 1777; John Shuttleworth to ———. April 18, 1777, Spencer Stanhope of Cannon Hall (Cannon Hall Muniments, 60578), Sheffield City Library, Sheffield, England.

10. Germain to Howe, March 3, 1777, Secret Dispatch Book, Germain Papers, William L. Clements Library.

11. "Before and After the Battle of Brandywine, Extracts from the Journal of Sergeant Thomas Sullivan of H. M. Forty-Ninth Regiment of Foot," *Pennsylvania Magazine of History and Biography,* XXXI (1907), pp. 413–18.

12. John Montresor, "The Montresor Journals," Gideon D. Scull, ed., in the New York Historical Society *Collections* for 1881 (New York, 1882), p. 464.

13. Remarks on Lord Cornwallis' Evidence, Germain Papers, William L. Clements Library.

14. Lady Jemima Cornwallis to William Cornwallis, September 3, 1778, Admiral Sir William Cornwallis Papers, COR/57, National Maritime Museum.

15. Archibald Francis Steuart, ed., *The Last Journals of Horace Walpole during the Reign of George III from 1771–1783,* II, (New York and London, 1910), p. 161.

16. Germain to Cornwallis, April 12, 1778, Cornwallis Papers, PRO 30/11/60, Public Record Office, London, England.

17. Ross, *Correspondence Cornwallis,* I, pp. 33–34.

18. Clinton, *American Rebellion*, pp. 92–94, 98 fn.
19. Walter H. Wilkins, *Some British Soldiers in America* (London, 1914), pp. 257–61.
20. Lady Jemima Cornwallis to William Cornwallis, September 14, 1778, Admiral Sir William Cornwallis Papers, COR/57, National Maritime Museum; Clinton, *American Rebellion*, p. 104.
21. William Sutherland to Dugald Gilchrist, January 17, 1778, Gilchrist of Opisdale Muniments, Scottish Record Office, Edinburgh, Scotland.
22. Willcox, *Portrait of a General*, p. 255 fn., Clinton to Germain, April 11, 1778, Germain Papers, William L. Clements Library.
23. Historical Manuscripts Commission, *Report on the Manuscripts in Various Collections*, (London, 1901), VI, p. 157. Tradition maintains that the Lady Jemima died of a broken heart occasioned by the absence of her husband. Her death should not suggest such romantic connotations, for although she did love her lord passionately, she had earlier described herself "as yellow as an orange" suggesting a disease of the liver rather than of the heart. Lady Jemima Cornwallis to William Cornwallis, September 14, 1778, Admiral Sir William Cornwallis Papers, COR/57, National Maritime Museum.
24. Cornwallis to William Cornwallis, May 5, 1779, Admiral Sir William Cornwallis Papers, COR/57, National Maritime Museum.
25. Cornwallis to Clinton, April 4, 1779, Sir Henry Clinton Papers, William L. Clements Library.
26. Clinton, *American Rebellion*, p. 138.
27. *Ibid.*, pp. 160, 183; Willcox, *Portrait of a General*, p. 317.
28. Willcox, *Portrait of a General*, p. 318.
29. Clinton, *American Rebellion*, pp. 184–85.
30. *Ibid.*, p. 167 fn.
31. Cornwallis to Clinton, May 7, 1780, Cornwallis Papers, PRO 30/11/73.
32. Cornwallis to Amherst, May 13, 1780, Cornwallis Papers, PRO 30/11/100.
33. Cornwallis to Clinton, May 30, 1780, Cornwallis Papers, PRO 30/11/73.
34. Clinton to Sir Charles Thompson, June 10, 1780, Hotham Collection, DDHO 4/2, East Riding County Record Office, Beverley, Yorkshire, England.
35. James Franklin Jameson, ed., "Letters of Robert Biddulph, 1779–1783," *American Historical Review*, XXIX (October, 1923), pp. 96–97.
36. New York *Royal Gazette*, June 7, 1780.

37. Arbuthnot to Germain, April 20, 1780, Germain Papers, William L. Clements Library. Yet Arbuthnot later expressed the wish to "remain with Lord Cornwallis, who is well qualified." Arbuthnot to Germain, May 31, 1780, Germain Papers, William L. Clements Library.

38. Cornwallis to Balfour, June 11, 1790, Cornwallis Papers, PRO 30/11/87.

39. Balfour to Cornwallis, June 27, 1780, Cornwallis Papers, PRO 30/11/2; Willcox, Portrait of a General, p. 321.

40. Cornwallis to Balfour, July 3, 1780, Cornwallis Papers, PRO 30/11/78.

41. Benjamin F. Stevens, ed., The Campaign in Virginia, 1781: an Exact Reprint of Six Rare Pamphlets on the Clinton-Cornwallis Controversy, (London, 1888), I, p. 223.

42. Cornwallis to Germain, August 20–21, 1780, Cornwallis Papers, PRO 30/11/76.

43. John McNamara to Charles Mellish, August 22, 1780, Mellish Manuscripts 172–111, University of Nottingham, Nottingham, England.

44. Cornwallis to Clinton, August 23, 1780, Cornwallis Papers, PRO 30/11/79, Cornwallis to Arbuthnot, August 23, 1780, Cornwallis Papers, PRO 30/11/79.

45. Cornwallis to Clinton, September 30, 1780, Cornwallis Papers, PRO 30/11/72; Ross, Cornwallis Correspondence, I, p. 56; Mabel L. Weber, ed., "Josiah Smith's Diary, 1780–1781," The South Carolina Historical and Genealogical Magazine, XXII (January, 1932), pp. 2–5; David Ramsay, The History of the American Revolution, (London, 1793), II, p. 171.

46. Cornwallis to Clinton, August 6, 1780, Clinton Papers, William L. Clements Library; Cornwallis to Alured Clarke, September 5, 1780, Cornwallis Papers, PRO 30/11/80.

47. Cornwallis to Clinton, August 29, 1790, Cornwallis Papers, PRO 30/11/72; Cornwallis to Rawdon, August 29, 1780, Cornwallis Papers, PRO 30/11/79.

48. Cornwallis to Balfour, September 13, 1780, Cornwallis to Archibald MacArthur, September 29, 1780, Cornwallis Papers, PRO 30/11/80.

49. Ferguson to Cornwallis, October 5, 1780, Cornwallis Papers, PRO 30/11/3.

50. Cornwallis to Ferguson, October 8, 1780, Cornwallis Papers, PRO 30/11/81.

51. Cornwallis to Balfour, October 10, 1780, Cornwallis Papers, PRO

30/11/81; Rawdon to Clinton, October 20, 1780, Cornwallis Papers, PRO 30/11/3; Cornwallis to Tarleton, November 8, 1780, Cornwallis Papers, PRO 30/11/82.

52. Cornwallis to Leslie, November 21, 1780, Cornwallis to Balfour, November 29, 1780, Cornwallis Papers, PRO 30/11/82.

53. Cornwallis to Clinton, December 29, 1780, Cornwallis Papers, PRO 30/11/72.

54. Cornwallis to Rawdon, December 30, 1780, Cornwallis Papers, PRO 30/11/83.

55. Cornwallis to Clinton, January 6, 1781, Cornwallis Papers, PRO 30/11/72; Cornwallis to Balfour, January 12, 1781, Cornwallis Papers, PRO 30/11/84.

56. Roderick Mackenzie, *Strictures on Lt. Col. Tarleton's History* "*Of the Campaigns of 1780 and 1781, in the Southern Provinces of North America*," (London, 1787), pp. 102–03; "Memoir of Joseph McJunkin of Union," *The Magnolia or Southern Appalachian*, II (January, 1843), pp. 30–40.

57. Cornwallis to Germain, January 18, 1781, Cornwallis Papers, PRO 30/11/76; Cornwallis to Rawdon, January 21, 1781, Cornwallis Papers, PRO 30/11/84.

58. Cornwallis to Rawdon, January 25, 29, 1781, Cornwallis Papers, PRO 30/11/84.

59. Cornwallis to Germain, March 17, 1781, Cornwallis Papers, PRO 30/11/76. A. R. Newsome, ed., "A British Orderly Book," *North Carolina Historical Review*, IX (July, 1932), pp. 284–85.

60. Cornwallis to Germain, March 17, 1781, Cornwallis Papers, PRO 30/11/76.

61. Charleston, S.C. *Royal Gazette*, March 14, 1781.

62. Cornwallis to Germain, March 17, 1781, Cornwallis Papers, PRO 30/11/76; Cornwallis to Sir James Wright and other members of the Board of Agents for the American Loyalists, March 8, 1783, Cornwallis Papers, PRO 30/11/103.

63. Cornwallis to Germain, March 17, 1781, Cornwallis Papers, PRO 30/11/76.

64. *Ibid.*, Field Return of Troops Under the Command of Lieut. General Cornwallis in Action at Guilford, March 15, 1781, Cornwallis Papers, PRO 30/11/103.

65. Ross, *Correspondence Cornwallis*, I, p. 86; *Annual Register for 1781*, p. 69; Banastre Tarleton, *Campaigns of 1780 and 1781 in the Southern Provinces of North America* (Dublin, 1787), p. 275.

66. *Annual Register for 1781*, p. 71.

67. Francis Dundas to Robert Dundas, April 3, 1781, Laing Manuscripts, II, p. 500, University of Edinburgh, Edinburgh, Scotland.

68. Cornwallis to Germain, April 18, 1781, Cornwallis Papers, PRO 30/11/76; Cornwallis to William Phillips, April 10, 1781, Cornwallis to Amherst, April 18, 1781, Cornwallis Papers, PRO 30/11/85.

69. *Ibid.*

70. State of the Troops that marched with the Army under the Command of Lieut. General Earl Cornwallis, April 1, 1781, Cornwallis Papers, PRO 30/11/5.

71. Cornwallis to Phillips, May 8, 1781, Cornwallis Papers, PRO 30/11/86; James Hadden to Charles Mellish, May 11, 1781, Mellish Manuscripts, pp. 172–211, University of Nottingham.

72. David Mason to Littleberry Mason, May 13, 1781, Cornwallis Papers, PRO 30/11/105; State of the Troops that marched with the Army under the Command of Lieut. Genl. Earl Cornwallis, May 1, 1781, Cornwallis Papers, PRO 30/11/103.

73. Phillips to Cornwallis, May 6, 1781, Cornwallis Papers, PRO 30/11/70; Cornwallis to Clinton, May 20, 1781, Cornwallis to Clinton, May 26, 1781, Cornwallis Papers, PRO 30/11/74.

74. Clinton to Cornwallis, May 29, 1781, Cornwallis Papers, PRO 30/11/68.

75. Stevens, *The Campaign in Virginia, 1781*, II, p. 37.

76. Cornwallis to Clinton, July 8, 1781, Cornwallis Papers, PRO 30/11/74.

77. Cornwallis to Alexander Stewart, July 16, 1781, Cornwallis Papers, PRO 30/11/88.

78. Clinton to Cornwallis, July 8, 1781, Clinton to Cornwallis, July 11, 1781, Cornwallis Papers, PRO 30/11/68; Graves to Cornwallis, July 12, 1781, Cornwallis Papers, PRO 30/11/88.

79. Ralph Dundas to James Dundas, July 22, 1781, Dundas of Ochtertyre Muniments, No. 57, Scottish Record Office.

80. Cornwallis to Rawdon, July 23, 1781, Cornwallis Papers, PRO 30/11/74.

81. Alexander Sutherland to Cornwallis, July 25, 1781, captains of the navy to Cornwallis, July 26, 1781, Cornwallis Papers, PRO 30/11/74.

82. Charles O'Hara to Cornwallis, August 5, 1781, Cornwallis Papers, PRO 30/11/70.

83. State of the Troops under Lord Cornwallis at Yorktown, August 15, 1781, Cornwallis Papers, PRO 30/11/70; Cornwallis to Clinton, August 16, 1781, Cornwallis Papers, PRO 30/11/74; Corn-

wallis to Leslie, August 27, 1781, Cornwallis Papers, PRO 30/11/89.

84. Cornwallis to Clinton, August 31, 1781, Cornwallis to Clinton, September 2, 1781, Cornwallis Papers, PRO 30/11/74.

85. John Allen to Captain Sherwood, October 20, 1781, Haldimand Papers, British Museum, Additional Manuscripts 21835.

86. Clinton to Cornwallis, September 24, 1781, Cornwallis Papers, PRO 30/11/68.

87. Cornwallis to Clinton, September 29, 1781, Cornwallis Papers, PRO 30/11/74.

88. Stephen Popp, "Journal, 1777–1783," *Pennsylvania Magazine of History and Biography*, XXVI (1902), p. 41.

89. Edward M. Riley, ed., "St. George Tucker's Journal of the Siege of Yorktown, 1781," *William and Mary Quarterly*, 3rd series, V (July, 1948), pp. 386–87.

90. Samuel Graham, "An English Officer's Account of His Services in America, 1779–1781," *Historical Magazine*, IX (August, 1865), p. 248.

91. Cornwallis to Clinton, October 15, 1781, Cornwallis Papers, PRO 30/11/74.

92. Cornwallis to Clinton, October 20, 1781, Cornwallis Papers, PRO 30/11/74.

93. Ralph Dundas to James Dundas, November 6, 1781, Dundas of Ochtertyre Muniments, No. 57, Scottish Record Office; Return of the Killed, Wounded & Missing of the following Corps from the 28th Septr. to the 19th October 1781, Cornwallis Papers, PRO 30/11/103.

94. Cornwallis to Clinton, October 20, 1781, Cornwallis Papers, PRO 30/11/74.

95. Clinton to Cornwallis, November 30, 1781, Cornwallis Papers, PRO 30/11/68.

96. Cornwallis to Clinton, December 2, 1781, Cornwallis Papers, PRO 30/11/74.

97. Willcox, *Portrait of a General*, p. 456; Elizabeth, Dowager Countess Cornwallis, to William Cornwallis, April 2, 1782, Admiral Sir William Cornwallis Papers, COR/58, National Maritime Museum.

98. Rockingham to Portland, November 19, 1781, Rockingham Manuscripts, R1–1767, Sheffield City Library.

99. Cornwallis to William Cornwallis, May 1, 1782, Admiral Sir William Cornwallis Papers, COR/58, National Maritime Museum.

100. Leslie to Earl of Levin, December 6, 1781, Levin and Melville Muniments, Section IX, p. 512, Scottish Record Office.
101. Tarleton, *Campaigns of 1780 and 1781 in the Southern Provinces of North America*, p. 222.
102. [Frederick the Great], *Military Instructions, written by the King of Prussia, for the Generals of his Army; being his Majesty's own Commentaries on his former Campaigns. Together with short Instructions for the use of his light troops. . . . Translated by an Officer* (London, 1762), pp. 12–13.
103. William B. Reed, *Life and Correspondence of Joseph Reed*, (Philadelphia, 1847), II, p. 296.

BIBLIOGRAPHY

Bass, Robert D. *The Green Dragoon: The Lives of Banastre Tarleton and Mary Robinson*. New York, 1957. Contains new materials on Tarleton in America.

Ross, Charles, ed. *The Correspondence of Charles, First Marquis Cornwallis*. 3 vols. London, 1859. Although the emphasis is on Cornwallis' later career, the more significant letters relating to America are included. The introduction contains a useful life of the general.

Smith, Paul H. *Loyalists and Redcoats: A Study in British Revolutionary Policy*. Chapel Hill, 1964. An excellent analysis of the failure of British loyalist policy.

Stevens, Benjamin F., ed. *The Campaign in Virginia, 1781: An Exact Reprint of Six Rare Pamphlets on the Clinton-Cornwallis Controversy*. 2 vols. London, 1888. Contains the more significant of the bitter exchange of charges and countercharges between the two generals.

Tarleton, Banastre. *A History of the Campaigns of 1780 and 1781 in the Southern Provinces of North America*. Dublin, 1787. Portrait of a self-styled hero during his campaigns with Cornwallis in the south.

Willcox, William B., ed. *The American Rebellion: Sir Henry Clinton's Narrative of His Campaigns, 1775–1782, with an Appendix of Original Documents*. New Haven, 1954. Sir Henry Clinton's defense of his American career.

Willcox, William B. *Portrait of a General: Sir Henry Clinton in the War of Independence*. New York, 1964. A brilliant biography of Clinton and an excellent analysis of the dispute with Cornwallis.

Richard Lord Howe:

ADMIRAL AS PEACEMAKER

IRA D. GRUBER

Rice University

WHEN the War of Independence began, Admiral Richard Lord
Howe ranked as one of Britain's best-known and most-respected
seamen. Although he had never commanded a fleet in wartime, Howe had a reputation for aggressive leadership and professional competence during his thirty-five years in the Royal
Navy. One officer serving at Boston in 1775 thought the colonists would soon accept the laws of Parliament if an army of
10,000 men were sent to New York, "accompanied by My Lord
Howe or some other Capital man in that Department with a
number of Frigates and small ships." Even Howe's opponents
acknowledged that he "was certainly a very respectable officer
and high in the Opinion of ye publick." [1] Sailors liked to remember how during the Seven Years' War he hunted remnants of
a French squadron among the rocks of Quiberon Bay, placed
his own ship against the fort on L'Ile d'Aix, and went ashore under fire to direct the evacuation of St. Cas. They were, moreover,
fully justified in celebrating his accomplishments as a student
of tactics and signaling; by 1778 he would renovate the whole
system of managing a fleet in battle, replacing a cumbersome
set of fighting instructions with a signal book that admitted far
more flexible maneuvering. [2] If not unusually intelligent, Howe
was justly respected as a bold commander, who knew his pro-

fession and cared for his men. "Give us Black Dick and we fear
nothing," echoed from the line at Spithead to the floor of the
House of Commons.[3]

Although Howe was proud of his record and ambitious to
distinguish himself further, he had no wish to do so by fighting
against British subjects in America. He viewed the rebellion as a
personal and a national tragedy and wished for nothing more
than a chance to promote a lasting reconciliation between the
mother country and her colonies. There was, perhaps, more than
sentiment and patriotism in his desire to become a peacemaker,
for Howe was ambitious enough to think of saving the empire
in terms of his personal glory. But, above all, the rebellion reminded him of his family's close ties with Massachusetts Bay.
The General Court of that colony had erected a monument to
his older brother who was killed at Ticonderoga during the
Seven Years' War. Remembering the gesture, Howe had offered
to mediate the imperial quarrel as early as Christmas of 1774.
He did not propose making significant constitutional concessions
to the colonists, but he thought that kind words delivered by the
right person would do much to settle the quarrel and suggested
that the government send him to America as a peace commissioner. The Ministry, putting its faith in coercive measures,
consistently rejected his offers until the autumn of 1775. By
that time the government was confident that it could break the
revolt by force of arms and agreed to employ him in accepting
colonial surrender. Howe, of course, wanted to do more than
dictate the terms of peace and immediately began asking for
authority to negotiate a settlement.[4]

While he was struggling without much success to increase
the scope of his commission, chance seemed to offer an alternative solution. On December 7, 1775, Sir Charles Saunders died,
vacating a sinecure worth more than £1200 per year. Lord
North, head of the Ministry, had promised this sinecure to
Howe but, forgetting his promise, agreed to award it to another
officer. When Howe discovered what had happened he threatened to resign from the navy. North certainly had no desire to

break with one of Britain's ablest officers and began searching for a suitable way to placate him. After a month of futile negotiations, Howe intimated that he would be willing to go to America as commander-in-chief as well as peace commissioner.[5] In so doing he probably reasoned that being commander-in-chief would strengthen his efforts in any negotiation. The king and all of the ministers, except the first lord of the Admiralty, welcomed Howe's offer. A majority of the Ministry, favoring a military solution to the rebellion, were glad to secure the services of such a distinguished officer and assumed that Howe would not allow his predeliction for peace to interfere with his conduct of the war. A minority, who still hoped for a negotiated settlement (among them Lord North), were delighted to have a commander-in-chief who was well known and popular in the colonies—a man who would do all that he could to preserve lives and restore imperial harmony. Outside the government, Howe's appointment to the American command was equally well received. The Morning Post, a newspaper that called for a vigorous repression of the rebels, reported that "no appointment ever gave more general satisfaction"; one of Lord Howe's friends described his nomination as "a most wise and popular measure"; and an inveterate placeman agreed that it was "in all lights a most happy event." [6]

Those ministers who selected Howe solely for his ability as an admiral had no illusions about his views on conciliation. They were, therefore, careful to see that his instructions for carrying on the war and making peace would not permit him to make concessions. Lord George Germain, who as colonial secretary had a large share of the responsibility for managing the war, was especially anxious to see that Howe would be narrowly bound. He tried at first to see if the peace commission might be abandoned altogether. When his efforts failed and when Howe refused to share his commission with someone of sterner views, Germain made sure that the commission would enable the admiral to do no more than receive colonial surrender. Until all congresses had been dissolved, royal officials restored, armed bodies disbanded, fortifications surrendered, and a local assembly had promised to obey the laws of Parliament, Howe could not undertake a negotiation. He might offer pardons, but until the rebels had fully surrendered he was not even to discuss a matter of such fundamental importance as taxation. Although Lord North had given Howe a plan for replacing Parliamentary taxation with colonial contributions for imperial defense, a plan under which the colonies would have granted an equivalent of not less than five or more than ten per cent of the sum voted annually by Parliament for the army, navy, and ordnance, he was to make no mention of the plan until the colonies had surrendered.[7]

Nor did the Ministry in drafting Howe's orders for carrying on the war leave much to his discretion. He was, first of all, to see that the Atlantic seaboard was tightly blockaded, thereby putting economic pressure on the rebels and denying them military supplies from Europe and the West Indies. In order that there might be no mistake about the way he was to deal with the colonists, the Admiralty gave him detailed recommendations for employing the 73 warships and 13,000 seamen that would initially make up the North American squadron. His cruisers were to provide asylum for royal officials and loyalists, retaliate against coastal towns that were in arms against the king, dismantle colonial merchantmen so that they might not be converted to ships of war, destroy all armed American vessels, clear the rivers of floating batteries and sunken obstructions, impress rebel seamen, and, whenever necessary, commandeer supplies. But Howe was not to confine his squadron to enforcing the blockade. He was also to cooperate with the British army in breaking the rebellion.[8] This cooperation promised to put a considerable burden on the fleet, for General William Howe, Lord Howe's brother who commanded the British army at Boston, planned to campaign about New York and in the Hudson River Valley (to isolate and starve New England and, if possible, to bring the Continental army to a decisive action).[9] Whatever Admiral Howe's views on reconciling the colonies, he could not have mistaken the government's desire for a vigorous prosecution of the war.

But when Admiral Howe joined his brother at New York in July of 1776, he promptly deviated from his instructions. Instead of waiting until the rebels had surrendered to open a negotiation, he at once attempted to discuss an end to the war. Although he arrived just after Congress had declared the colonies independent and although his brother doubted that the Americans would retreat before the Continental army had surrendered, Howe was determined to see if the rebels would respond to an offer of reconciliation. He began by issuing a proclamation that announced his appointment as peace commissioner with power to grant pardon and to declare at peace any area where constitutional government had been restored.[10] This done, he attempted to open a negotiation with General Washington. The American commander-in-chief at first refused to receive Admiral Howe's letters, saying they were improperly addressed; and when at last he agreed to meet with General Howe's adjutant, he said he understood the Howes were "only to grant pardons [and] that those who had committed no fault wanted no pardon." [11] For its part, Congress ordered Lord Howe's proclamation published "that the good people of these United States may be informed of what nature are the commissioners, and what the terms, with the expectation of which, the insidious court of Britain has endeavoured to amuse and disarm them." [12] Notwithstanding these rejoinders, the admiral made one last effort to avoid using force. In mid-August he tried to suggest, through an emissary, that he could offer a plan of fixed colonial contributions in place of taxation for revenue. Congress simply refused to reply. As one of Howe's juniors remarked, "It has long been too late for Negotiation, yet it is easy to be perceived, My Lord Howe came out with a different Idea. . . ." [13]

By mid-August, Lord Howe had come to accept the fact that force would have to be applied before the rebels would seriously think of making peace. But even his military decisions seemed to reflect a desire to spare as many lives as possible, to apply the least amount of force necessary to end the fighting. Indeed he had begun gathering a large part of his squadron at New York, leaving Charleston and the Chesapeake unguarded and only one frigate in the Delaware and two off Boston. He would, of course, have to keep a substantial number of ships with the army at New York, at least until the Americans had been driven from Long Island and Manhattan; but he should certainly have been able to spare more than one-tenth of his squadron for the blockade. Yet between mid-August and the first of December he rarely had more than seven or eight cruisers at sea, and none of these seems to have been engaged in retaliating against coastal towns or in dismantling potential warships.[14] The Americans, who were desperately short of military stores, took full advantage of the enormous gaps in the British blockade, importing before Christmas of 1776 more than 80 per cent of all the powder they consumed during the first two and one-half years of the war.[15] Considering Howe's desire for a reconciliation, his efforts to open a negotiation with the rebels, and the fact that he would soon instruct his captains to cultivate friendly relations with the colonists, his failure to establish an adequate blockade seems to have resulted from more than poor judgment.

Howe's arrival also appeared to affect his brother's conduct of the war. Until the admiral reached New York, General Howe had repeatedly declared that he not only desired a decisive encounter with the Continental army but also thought such an encounter essential for breaking the rebellion.[16] After his brother arrived, the general certainly seemed to abandon these views. Although the Continental army was divided between Manhattan and Long Island, and although British and American officers agreed that the British navy could have controlled the East River,[17] General Howe did not attempt to divide or trap his enemy. Instead, he planned to drive the Continental forces from Long Island, so that by placing his artillery on Brooklyn Heights he might also force them to give up New York City: he now preferred occupying territory to seeking a decisive victory. Nor did he deviate from his new design. After landing on Long

Island, he never asked more of the fleet than a diversion, and his brother never offered more. Even after the British army had driven the Americans into their lines at Brooklyn, trapping them against the East River, Lord Howe made no effort to block their line of retreat. When they fled across the river to Manhattan on August 29, at least one of the British captains was thoroughly disappointed: "had our Ships attacked the batteries [at Brooklyn], which we have been in constant Expectation of being ordered to do, not a Man could have escaped from Long Island." [18] General Howe had accomplished his first objective, but he had lost his finest chance for destroying the Continental army.

The Howes' performance during the remainder of the campaign of 1776, like that on Long Island, suggests that they were trying to end the rebellion with as little serious fighting as possible. Lord Howe had apparently convinced his brother that an overwhelming display of force might persuade the rebels to become once more contented and useful British subjects, whereas a series of crushing victories would leave the colonies desolated, hostile, and worthless to Britain. [19] Even before the rebels had fled from Long Island, the admiral was attempting to see if his brother's victory in the battle of Long Island had made the rebels more tractable. To this end he employed a captured American officer to tell Congress that he was empowered to discuss a permanent settlement and that he wished to confer before one side or the other was compelled to sue for peace. [20] Congress, firmly attached to its independence, wished only to discredit Howe and dispatched three delegates to do just that. After meeting with him on Staten Island, the Americans reported that he could only grant pardon and accept colonial surrender. [21] Frustrated once more, he was obliged to see what another application of force would do. When by landing on Manhattan above New York on September 15, the British had forced the rebels to give up the city without bringing on a major engagement, Lord Howe again paused to see if the colonists were ready for peace. Because Congress had demonstrated its unwillingness to negotiate, he now appealed directly to the colonists, inviting them to talk with the commissioners and suggesting that the king was disposed to grant considerable freedom to the colonial assemblies. So unsuccessful was this offer that he made no new overtures until the end of November.[22] By then the British had driven the Continental army away from New York with a succession of flanking maneuvers that were well calculated to win territory and avoid a decisive action. Only when the Americans refused to abandon Fort Washington did the British make a determined assault on the rebels.

Briefly in late November, it seemed that the Howes might have applied just the right amount of pressure to bring down the rebellion and produce a negotiated peace. After taking Fort Washington, the British had struck swiftly into New Jersey. The Continental army, demoralized by endless withdrawals and depleted by expiring enlistments, was no longer able to make a stand. On December 1, Washington decided to retire across the Delaware into Pennsylvania. At New York the British were elated to learn that Congress was losing its popularity, that loyalist strength was increasing, and that the Continental army was beset with internal quarrels. Many a redcoat began to think that the war would soon be over.[23] The Howes, hoping to exploit their advantage, issued a proclamation on November 30 that not only ordered the rebels to put down their arms and disband their congresses but also promised pardon to anyone who within sixty days would pledge his allegiance to King George III. If no important rebels accepted the offer of pardon, nearly 5,000 colonists did.[24] But before half the time for accepting pardon had expired, Washington managed to change the course of the war. On Christmas night he recrossed the Delaware to destroy a detachment of Hessians encamped at Trenton, and a week later fought a second successful action at Princeton. These two victories banished the illusion of British invincibility, restored American morale, and ended the Howes' hopes for a negotiated peace.[25] After Princeton the British army withdrew from western New Jersey to end a campaign that for Lord Howe and his brother had proved a great personal disappointment and for the

British government, a disaster. In their efforts to make the colonies useful and contented members of the empire, the Howes had lost a succession of opportunities to destroy the Continental army and, perhaps, the rebellion. Never again would the British government have so fair a prospect for a military decision.

After the British army had gone into winter quarters at New York and Rhode Island, Lord Howe at last concentrated on establishing a blockade. Although he ordered his ships to enforce the Prohibitory Act of 1775 and to take or destroy all armed colonial vessels, he recommended that his captains be lenient. They were to allow the rebels the "use of their ordinary Fishing-Craft or other means of providing for their daily Subsistence and Support, where the same does not seem liable to any material abuse" and to "encourage and cultivate all amicable correspondence with the said Inhabitants, to gain their good Will and Confidence, whilst they demean themselves in a peaceable and orderly manner. And to grant them every other Indulgence which the Limitations upon their Trade specified in the [Prohibitory] Act . . . will consistently admit: In order to conciliate their friendly Dispositions and to detach them from the Prejudice they have imbibed. . . ." Nor were the cruising ships to raid along the coast, lest such forays instruct the colonists in the art of defensive warfare.[26] In spite of these restrictions and the fact that there were not usually more than 20 cruisers at sea, the British blockade was far more successful during the first six months of 1777 than during any other comparable period of Howe's command. Between January 1 and June 30, 1777, the North American squadron took 277 prizes, an average of over 46 per month. During the first half of 1778, by contrast, the average was 35 per month, even though there were then more cruisers at sea.[27] But the blockade was not to be fully exploited. Lord Howe was unwilling to carry the war to colonial ports, where American ships might most easily have been destroyed; and he was all too willing to sacrifice the blockade whenever he might legitimately keep his fleet in attendance on the army.

While his cruisers spread out along the Atlantic coast from

Rhode Island and the Chesapeake, Howe remained at New York through the winter of 1776–77 searching for ways to reconcile the colonists. American victories at Trenton and Princeton together with adept political maneuvers—publishing accounts of British and Hessian atrocities, distributing supplies captured at Trenton among families that had been plundered by German mercenaries, and commanding all colonists who had accepted British pardon to renounce it or be considered enemies of the United States [28]—ensured the failure of the British proclamation of November 30. But in spite of all his disappointments, Lord Howe still hoped to open a negotiation with Congress. To this end he persuaded General Charles Lee, a high-ranking prisoner, to write to Congress, asking for an interview to discuss something of great consequence to himself and to America. Congress, agreeing that another negotiation could only impede its military efforts (it being "well known the conference with Lord Howe last summer had well nigh ruined our interest at the Court of France"), resolved to do all it could for Lee but refused to send a committee to meet with him.[29] It is little wonder that by April of 1777, Lord Howe declared he knew not "what were best to be done." [30] He had come to America to reunite the empire, but in nine months his efforts had earned him only rebukes from Congress and, as he would soon discover, the displeasure of his own government.

Up to February of 1777, most members of the North Ministry had been pleased with the progress of the war. Although the Howes were not acting with the vigor that the government desired, a succession of victories obscured the opportunities they had lost. But when on February 23 the *Bristol* reached England with news of Trenton and Princeton, the Ministry saw the need for enspiriting its commanders-in-chief. Approving Sir William's plans for invading Pennsylvania in 1777, Lord George Germain urged the Howes to raid the New England coasts, both to destroy rebel cruisers and to interrupt recruiting for the Continental army.[31] Above all, he recommended that they stop being lenient with the enemy: "I fear that you and Lord Howe will find it necessary to adopt such modes of carrying on the War, that the Rebels may be effectually distressed; so that through a lively Experience of Losses and Sufferings, they may be brought as soon as possible to a proper Sense of their Duty." [32] Scarcely had Germain completed his dispatches when on March 4 copies of Lord Howe's instructions for establishing a blockade arrived. What a striking contrast these instructions made with the secretary's recommendations. Both men proposed to end the rebellion: the admiral by cultivating "all amicable correspondence with the said Inhabitants" and granting them every indulgence "in order to conciliate their friendly Dispositions"; the secretary by bringing "a lively Experience of Losses and Sufferings" to the colonists. Yet in spite of Lord Howe's patent disregard for his orders the government was not prepared to do more than encourage him to change his methods. Because this was the first specific violation of his instructions and because he was a celebrated admiral with many powerful friends, Germain and Sandwich, first lord of the Admiralty, merely reproved him for showing too much generosity to the American fishermen and sent a Major Nisbet Balfour to call both the Howes to arms. [33]

Until the Ministry learned the result of Balfour's mission, it took no further measures to influence the Howes' conduct of the war. On July 10, however, Germain discovered that Balfour had failed: Lord Howe not only defended his leniency toward rebel seamen—saying that by allowing them to continue fishing he kept them from enlisting in the Continental army and navy —but he and his brother also refused to undertake raids against New England ports, because such raids would interfere with the "more important Operations of the Campaign." The Howes' arguments might well have stifled further criticism had they not arrived with news of a rebel sortie from New England in which four frigates and 14 smaller vessels had put to sea unopposed from Boston, Salem, and Marblehead on May 21. [34] The government needed no further proof that mistaken generosity was losing the war. Germain, determined to change the commanders-in-chief or their policy, applied irony in dealing with the Howes.

He was happy that the indulgence "shewn to the Inhabitants upon the Coast, in not depriving them of the means of Subsistence has had so good an Affect"; indeed, he continued, Lord Howe's blockade was so effective that American privateers were swarming about the British Isles. He hoped that the Howes might still undertake raids on New England and win the applause of their countrymen, who, if not strategists, would rejoice to see the bases of the privateers destroyed. Sandwich and the lords of the Admiralty, feeling no need for indirection, declared themselves "greatly astonished" that Admiral Howe had neglected to provide an adequate blockade for New England and that he had failed to send them intelligence of rebel preparations.[35]

Germain and Sandwich would have been even more distressed had they known precisely what the Howes were doing with the campaign of 1777. Lord Howe, seeing no prospect for bringing about a reconciliation and having little taste for prosecuting the war, seemed quite content to tie his ships to the British army for the duration of the campaign. General Howe, who intended to invade Pennsylvania by sea, seemed equally content to play out the campaign in elaborate maneuvers. While the fleet waited off Staten Island, the army expended the second half of June in a futile effort to bring Washington to a decisive action in New Jersey. Sir William wasted two weeks in abortive maneuvers and three more in preparing to sail from New York. Thus, the Howes did not reach the mouth of the Delaware until July 30. When the general then decided to go to Pennsylvania by way of the Chesapeake, he condemned his army to an additional three weeks at sea, delayed his arrival in Philadelphia by more than a month, and committed one-fifth of the North American squadron to a two-month cruise with his storeships. Although General Howe's extravagance affected the navy, Lord Howe seems to have been too demoralized to make an effective protest against the voyage to the Chesapeake.[36] Nor did the capture of Philadelphia restore his spirits. Pennsylvania was not, as the general had been told, teeming with loyalists;[37] and the brothers soon discovered that they would have great difficulty holding Philadelphia if they could not drive the rebels from their forts on the Delaware.

In fighting to open the Delaware the Howes were, for once, unencumbered by political aspirations. Yet because they failed to co-ordinate their efforts and because the Americans resisted with extraordinary determination, this was one of the least successful of their undertakings. When Lord Howe arrived off Chester on October 6, he discovered that the rebels were firmly in control of the passage to Philadelphia. By fortifying Mud Island at the confluence of the Delaware and Schuylkill rivers, placing a chain of sunken obstructions in the main channel between Mud Island and the New Jersey shore (where they had built a fort at Red Bank), and reinforcing the whole with a variety of floating batteries, fire ships, armed vessels, and galleys, the rebels effectively closed the river to all craft except boats of very shallow draft, which might still pass up the secondary channel between Mud Island and the Pennsylvania shore. To dislodge the Americans, the Howes planned a concerted attack. But when on October 22 the general's troops stormed the rebel fort at Red Bank before the admiral's ships were in position, the troops were repulsed and several British ships lost.[38] Profiting by this lesson, which they might well have learned at Long Island when the army attacked before the fleet was able to provide a diversion, the Howes finally took Mud Island by reserving their troops until gunfire from the fleet had destroyed the American works. All of their efforts had, however, consumed more than a month, and the Delaware was not open to Philadelphia until November 23, two months after the city had been captured.[39]

While the Howes struggled for control of the river, their differences with the government reached a crisis. On October 17, Lord Howe received Germain's ironic congratulations on the success of the blockade. He refused, temporarily at least, to be baited by the colonial secretary, saying he was pleased that his "conduct with respect to the inhabitants of the Sea Coasts on

this Continent, appear to have met with your Lordships approbation." [40] Sir William, for his part, did not possess such self-
restraint. Knowing that Burgoyne was in trouble, that he would
be blamed for failing to do more to assist him, and that the
capture of Philadelphia had been less decisive than he had hoped
—certainly not of sufficient importance to justify the loss of the
Canadian army—General Howe was ill-prepared to ignore Germain's irony. On October 22 he asked to be recalled, asserting
that as his recommendations were ignored he had lost the confidence of the government. He also went to some trouble to
detach himself from all responsibility for whatever had happened to Burgoyne.[41] A month later, after the Howes had had
an opportunity to discuss the consequences of Burgoyne's surrender, Lord Howe asked the Admiralty to name an officer to
replace him in case poor health should force him to resign. He
did not refer to the ministers' dispatches; nor did he do so until
early December, when he finally replied to the charge that he
had neglected the blockade of New England. The admiral then
admitted that the blockade was inadequate but argued that his
force was too small both to support the army and to contain
American privateers.[42] Although the government might well
have asked why he had waited so long to say that his squadron
was too small, the need for further debate had passed.

Burgoyne's surrender and the Howes' resignations forced the
Ministry to consider changes both in strategy and in commanders-in-chief. The loss of the Canadian army ended all plans
for occupying the Hudson River Valley; it impelled the Ministry
to concentrate on ending the rebellion through a blockade, a
series of raids on colonial ports, and land operations elsewhere.
When Burgoyne's defeat subsequently brought France into the
war, the British government subordinated raids against the
rebels to a retaliatory expedition against the French in the
West Indies.[43] But before this change in plan had taken place,
the British had also decided to change commanders. Although
the Howes' resignations were under consideration early in January, no final action was taken at that time. The brothers had

many powerful friends, including the king, and Germain and Sandwich had to be careful lest in removing the Howes they sacrifice their own political ambitions. By mid-February, however, Sir William had been ordered to give up his command to Sir Henry Clinton and Lord Howe told that he too might resign.[44] Because Clinton was in America, there was no further delay in relieving General Howe. The same was not true of his brother. Lord Howe had to wait for a successor, and while that successor was preparing to sail from England, France entered the war and the Ministry changed Howe's orders. He was told to retain his command until he had mounted an expedition against the French island of St. Lucia, sent troops to the Floridas, directed an evacuation of Philadelphia, destroyed a French squadron under La Motte Picquet that was reportedly bound for America, and sent reinforcements to the Channel fleet.[45]

Nor was the change in Howe's orders the only factor that would determine the length of his stay in America. Although La Motte Picquet promptly returned to Brest, the Ministry had scarcely concluded its secret dispatches of March 21 when it learned of a more powerful French squadron of 12 ships of the line and five frigates that was fitting at Toulon. This squadron, commanded by Count d'Estaing, was reportedly under orders to attack the British somewhere in North America or the West Indies. The king and Lord George Germain were anxious to intercept d'Estaing at Gibraltar but were dissuaded by Sandwich and the commander of the Channel fleet, who argued that such an undertaking would unduly expose the British Isles. Even though this decision made England more secure, it did nothing to protect British forces in America. When subsequent intelligence confirmed the earlier reports that d'Estaing was bound for America, the Ministry ordered Admiral Byron to reinforce Lord Howe with 13 ships of the line. But while contrary winds kept Byron in port, the Ministry, fearing an invasion of England, decided not to let him sail until it received confirmation that d'Estaing had gone to America. As a result of the Ministry's indecision, compounded by bad luck, Byron did not proceed to

New York until June 9, three weeks after d'Estaing had left the Mediterranean. Lord Howe would soon be able to thank his own government as well as the French navy for his summer's employment.[46]

While in London the ministers took counsel in their fears, at Philadelphia Howe was devoting the late spring of 1778 to preparations for giving up his command. On May 8 he received the Admiralty's instructions of March 21 together with the news that Admiral Gambier was appointed to succeed him. By then he was heartily tired of being commander-in-chief and anxious to carry out his orders and go home.[47] As he had heard nothing of La Motte Picquet, he began at once assembling his ships at Philadelphia to escort the expeditions ordered to St. Lucia and the Floridas. Unfortunately for his hopes of a speedy departure, the North American squadron was widely scattered in order to intercept increasing numbers of armed French blockade runners. Before he could assemble enough ships for the expedition to St. Lucia, Sir Henry Clinton decided not to make any detachments from the army until Philadelphia was abandoned.[48] While Sir Henry was making preparations to go to New York, Lord Howe learned that La Motte Picquet had returned to Brest; hence when finally he sailed from Philadelphia on June 18, he did so with the expectation that he would soon be rid of his command. As Gambier had already reached New York, and as there no longer seemed any danger of being interrupted by a French fleet, Howe could expect to resign his command as soon as he had dispatched the expeditions to St. Lucia and the Floridas and sent part of his squadron to England.[49]

But Howe's plans for returning home were soon superseded by the necessity of preserving his fleet from d'Estaing. Delayed by calms and frequent groundings, his fleet did not reach the mouth of the Delaware until June 28. On the following day as he sailed north along the Jersey shore, he first learned of the Toulon squadron. Germain's dispatches warned Howe of d'Estaing and told him that Admiral Byron was en route to Halifax with a reinforcement.[50] News of the French squadron forced

Howe to defer the projected expedition to St. Lucia as well as his plans for resigning the American command. Herding the transports and warships to New York and dispatching cruisers to find d'Estaing, he prepared to put to sea with his warships in an effort to join Byron and attack the French.[51] He had scarcely begun the necessary preparations when his cruisers announced d'Estaing's approach: on July 7 he learned that the Toulon squadron had reached Virginia on the fifth; and on July 8, that they had been at the mouth of the Delaware the day before. There was no time to put to sea; indeed the British ships were not in position to defend the channel at Sandy Hook when d'Estaing arrived on the afternoon of July 11.[52] Although Lord Howe had the advantage of position (he promptly arranged all his larger ships so that their guns commanded the bar at Sandy Hook), and although his ships were better manned and in better repair than those of his enemy, the French had a marked superiority in firepower. Two 80's, six 74's, three 64's, and five frigates were more than a match for six 64's, ten frigates, and an assortment of smaller vessels.[53] But at New York position was all-important, and on July 22, d'Estaing, concluding that the channel off Sandy Hook was too shallow and narrow for his heavy ships, took his force to join General John Sullivan in an attack on the British garrison at Rhode Island.[54]

Having parried d'Estaing at New York, Howe was now faced with the problem of preserving the British garrison at Rhode Island. Temporarily, at least, his squadron was so inferior to d'Estaing's that he could do no more than send a warning to Rhode Island, order his cruisers to keep a close watch on the French, and hope that Byron would soon reach New York. While he waited at Sandy Hook, his force grew stronger: one 50-gun frigate arrived from the West Indies, a 64 and a 50 came in from Halifax, and July 30 the first of Admiral Byron's ships, the *Centurion* of 74 guns, anchored at Sandy Hook. Reinforced by two ships of the line and two heavy frigates and having learned from the *Centurion* that Byron was bound for New York, Howe prepared to put to sea at once to relieve Rhode

Island, where his cruisers reported the French had gone.[55] Although he said publicly that he intended to attack d'Estaing, his close friends believed that he would try to lure the French from Rhode Island and avoid an action until he had been reinforced.[56] Whatever his plans, he was ready to sail on August 2 but, detained by contrary winds, did not reach Rhode Island until August 9, by which time the French had begun landing troops in support of a much-delayed American offensive. Even then Howe was in time to relieve the garrison without attacking d'Estaing. When he learned that his arrival had persuaded the French to re-embark their troops, he decided to lie off Block Island, watching d'Estaing and waiting for Byron.[57]

Howe did not have long to wait. On the morning of August 10 the French, having no desire to be caught at anchor by the combined forces of Howe and Byron, took advantage of a northeast wind to sail from Rhode Island. D'Estaing apparently hoped to destroy Howe's squadron before it was reinforced. For his part, Howe had no intention of fighting the French except on the most favorable terms; he had little to gain by engaging d'Estaing before Byron arrived. When, therefore, he saw the French putting to sea, he immediately cut his cables and sailed south, waiting for a change in the wind that would give him the weather gauge and permit him to use his fire ships to offset the enemy's heavy guns.[58] After twenty-four hours, there being little change in the wind or in the relative position of the two squadrons (north and south of each other, eight miles apart), Howe decided to maneuver for a more favorable position. At eight in the morning he brought his line of battle from southeast to south, at ten to southwest, at eleven-thirty to west, and at one-thirty to northwest. Instead of changing course to match the British and thereby keeping their position relative to the wind, the French chose to press after the sternmost of Howe's line, closing rapidly as they did but slipping from the north to the east and then to southeast of the British.[59] By late afternoon Howe had nearly weathered d'Estaing; indeed his adjutant judged that one more change of course would have done so.

But by that time the wind and sea had grown so violent that another change of course was impossible, and as darkness and flying spray enveloped the two squadrons, both admirals turned their attention to the weather.[60]

The storm, which continued unabated until the morning of August 14, damaged and dispersed both squadrons. In its aftermath the French reassembled 75 miles east of Cape May, while the British straggled to their rendezvous at Sandy Hook. Howe and Sir Henry Clinton, assuming that d'Estaing would return to Rhode Island, began planning an expedition to relieve the British garrison. But before Howe could put to sea, he learned that d'Estaing had returned to Rhode Island, gathered several frigates left behind on August 10, and sailed again. Because he knew that several of the largest French ships had been dismasted in the storm, Howe felt sure that d'Estaing had taken his ships to Boston to refit; indeed he was so sure that he sailed directly for Boston in an attempt to intercept the French and to exploit whatever damage the storm had done to their ships.[61] Although he made the passage to Boston in five days, he arrived on August 30, two days behind d'Estaing. Realizing that the enemy was unassailable in Nantasket Road and that they would be detained a considerable time by repairs, he put back to Rhode Island to see if he might help the garrison.[62] But again he was too late. By the time he reached Newport, Clinton had not only secured the town and island but also sent an expeditionary force to Buzzards Bay and Martha's Vineyard. After remaining a few days off Rhode Island, Howe returned to New York, where on September 11 he turned over his command to Admiral Gambier. The arrival of most of Byron's ships had at last given the British naval superiority in North America and provided Howe with an opportunity to resign.[63]

When he was sure that Byron himself was at Newport and that the incompetent Gambier would not be left to face the French alone, Howe sailed for England.

Lord Howe's service in America was, with one exception, disappointing both to the admiral and to the government. The source of their disappointment lay in the incompatibility of their aspirations. Howe went to America to promote a reconciliation, though he was bound by instructions that required colonial surrender. He soon discovered that Congress would not accept his meager terms, no matter how sweetly he entreated them to do so. But he had come to America to save an empire, to make the colonists happy and useful partners with the mother country. Destroying the Continental army, devastating the Atlantic ports, and ravaging the colonies might produce a military victory, but such a policy would never, he thought, render the colonies useful to Britain. Howe resorted, therefore, to the only plan that seemed likely to make the rebels accept his terms without jeopardizing a reconciliation: a show of strength, a limited use of force, and repeated overtures to the colonists. This plan, which often sacrificed military opportunities, might have succeeded had not Washington spoiled the Hessians' Christmas at Trenton. By April of 1777, however, it was clear that the rebels were not to be threatened or coaxed from their independence and that the British government would no longer tolerate Lord Howe's half-measures. Without prospect of negotiating peace or of receiving ministerial support for his efforts, Howe turned listlessly to transporting the British army to Philadelphia. Here his service in America might well have ended, if chance and d'Estaing had not conspired to prolong his stay. His last two months in America were unquestionably his most successful; still, two months of skillful defensive maneuvering were not enough to banish the disappointments and frustrations of two years. For the admiral and the British government, his experiment in peacemaking had been a failure—the least significant portion of his long and illustrious career.

FOOTNOTES

1. Robert Roberts to Sir Charles Thompson, Boston, August 14, 1775, Hotham Papers, HO/4/16, East Riding Record Office, Beverley, Yorkshire; Admiral Keppel to the Marquis of Rockingham,

January 5, 1776, Rockingham MSS, Wentworth Woodhouse Muniments, Sheffield City Library, Sheffield, Yorkshire.

2. Julian S. Corbett, *Signals and Instructions, 1776–94* (Publications of the Navy Records Society, vol. XXXV [London, 1908]), pp. 17, 33.

3. J. Almon, ed., *The Parliamentary Register . . . Proceedings and Debates of the House of Commons,* 83 vols. (London, 1775–1804), XII, p. 166.

4. For a more detailed account both of the ministers' attitudes toward the rebellion and of Lord Howe's relations with the government see Ira D. Gruber, "Lord Howe and Lord George Germain, British Politics and the Winning of American Independence," *William and Mary Quarterly,* 3d ser., XXII (1965), pp. 225–243.

5. Lord Hyde to Lord North, January 10 and 11, 1776, the Clarendon Deposit, Bodleian Library, Oxford University.

6. *The Morning Post and Daily Advertiser* (London), February 6, 1776; Sir Charles Thompson to [the Earl of Huntingdon], February 15, 1776, Hastings MSS, Henry E. Huntington Library, San Marino, California; Hans Stanley to [Andrew S. Hamond], March 27, 1776, Hamond MSS, Alderman Library, University of Virginia.

7. Instructions for the Howes, May 6, 1776, Colonial Office Papers, class 5, vol. 177, Public Record Office, London (cited hereafter as C.O. 5/vol. number); separate instructions for the commissioners, May 7, 1776, Great Britain, Historical Manuscripts Commission, *Sixth Report of the Royal Commission on Historical Manuscripts, Part I* (London, 1877), pp. 400–401.

8. Admiralty's instructions to Howe, May 4, 1776, and to Graves, July 6, 1775, Admiralty Papers, class 2, vol. 1332, Public Record Office, London (hereafter cited as Adm. 2/1332, etc.); Admiralty to Graves, August 31, September 14, October 23, October 15, and September 14, 1775, Adm. 2/100; Admiralty to Howe, May 4, 1776, Adm. 2/101. Abstract of monthly disposition, July 1, 1776, Adm. 8/52.

9. General Howe to the Earl of Dartmouth, October 9, 1775, C.O. 5/92; to Lord George Germain, April 25, 1776, C.O. 5/93; and to Germain, April 26, 1776, private, Hist. MSS Comm., *Report on the Manuscripts of Mrs. Stopford-Sackville . . . ,* 2 vols. (London, 1904–10), II, pp. 30–31.

10. Henry Strachey's journal, July 12, 1776, Hist. MSS Comm., *Sixth Report,* p. 402; Howe's proclamation of June 20, 1776, enclosed in Howe to Germain, August 11, 1776, C.O. 5/177; July 14, 1776, Edward H. Tatum, ed., *The American Journal of Ambrose*

Serle, Secretary to Lord Howe, 1776–1778 (San Marino, California, 1941), pp. 31–33.

11. July 14, 1776, Tatum, ed., *Journal of Serle*, pp. 32–33; George Washington to the president of Congress, July 14 and 22, 1776, John C. Fitzpatrick, ed., *The Writings of George Washington . . . 1745–1799*, 39 vols. (Washington, 1931–44), V, pp. 273–74, 321 fn–23 fn.

12. July 19, 1776, W. C. Ford, ed., *Journals of the Continental Congress, 1774–1789*, 34 vols. (Washington, 1904–37), V, p. 592.

13. Thomas, Lord Drummond to Howe, August 12, 1776, and Howe to Drummond, August 15, 1776, enclosed in Washington to the president of Congress, August 18, 1776, Peter Force, ed., *American Archives . . .* , 5th ser., 3 vols. (Washington, 1848–53), I, pp. 1025–27; August 22, 1776, Ford, ed., *Journals of Congress*, V, p. 696; quoting Andrew S. Hamond to [Hans Stanley], September 24, 1776, Hamond MSS, Alderman Library.

14. Disposition of North American squadron, August 13, 1776, enclosed in Lord Howe to Philip Stephens, August 14, 1776, disposition, September 18, enclosed in Howe to Stephens, September 18, and disposition, November 27, enclosed in Howe to Stephens, November 27, Adm. 1/487.

15. Orlando W. Stephenson, "The Supply of Gunpowder in 1776," *American Historical Review*, XXX (1925), pp. 272–80.

16. General Howe to Germain, April 25 and July 7, 1776, C.O. 5/93.

17. Collier's journal [c. September 1, 1776], 35 MS 0085, National Maritime Museum, Greenwich, England; Washington to the president of Congress, August 31, 1776, Fitzpatrick, ed., *Writings of Washington*, V, pp. 508–09.

18. General Howe to Germain, August 10, 1776, Germain Papers, William L. Clements Library, Ann Arbor, Michigan; to Germain, September 3, 1776, C.O. 5/93; and Lord Howe to Stephens, August 31, 1776, Adm. 1/487. Quoting Collier's journal [c. September 1, 1776], 35 MS 0085, National Maritime Museum.

19. Although General Howe had talked of destroying the Continental army as the best way of ending the rebellion, he was at the same time anxious to promote a reconciliation: Mrs. Howe "flatters herself his [General Howe's] advice will be a little attended to, and she knows he wishes to have a peace that is creditable to both." Lady Sarah Bunbury to Lady Susan O'Brien, August 21, 1775, the Countess of Ilchester and Lord Stavordale, eds., *The Life and Letters of Lady Sarah Lennox, 1745–1826*, 2 vols. (London, 1901), I, p. 244.

20. September 3, 1776, Ford, ed., *Journals of Congress*, V, pp. 730–31.

21. John Adams to Mrs. Adams, September 6, 1776, Edmund C. Burnett, ed., *Letters of Members of the Continental Congress*, 8 vols. (Washington, 1921–36), II, pp. 74–75; September 17, 1776, Ford, ed., *Journals of Congress*, V, pp. 765–66.

22. Proclamation of September 19, 1776, enclosed in the Howes to Germain, September 20, 1776, C.O. 5/177. Because there was no time limit for claiming pardon, the rebels fought until desperate and then asked for pardon. Lisburne to George Jackson, December 22, 1776, Additions to the Manuscripts, 34,187, British Museum.

23. October 1, 24, and 25, November 1, 10, and 11, December 8, Tatum, ed., *Journal of Serle*, pp. 117, 128, 130, 135, 138–39, 155–56; Lord Rawdon to the Earl of Huntingdon, November 28, 1776, Hist. MSS Comm., *Report on the Manuscripts of the Late Reginald Rawdon Hastings* (London, 1928—), III, 188.

24. Proclamation of November 30, 1776, enclosed in the Howes to Germain, November 30, 1776, C.O. 5/177; December 11, 1776, Tatum, ed., *Journal of Serle*, p. 157; the Howes to Germain, March 25, 1777, C.O. 5/177.

25. William Eddis to William Eden, July 23, 1777, C.O. 5/722: "Previous to the unhappy Affair at Trenton the general Disposition of the Colonies tended towards a Reconciliation with Great Britain on almost any terms . . . but the Surprise of the Hessian Post, however trifling it might have been thought in a regular War was attended with the most prejudicial Consequences to His Majesty's Arms. It gave Spirits to the Demagogues, recruited their Forces—and enabled their Leaders to magnify in the most exaggerating terms, the amazing Advantages that would arise from this unexpected Incident."

26. Howe to Sir Peter Parker, December 22, to Commodore Hotham, December 23, and to Hotham, secret, December 23, 1776, all enclosed in Howe to Stephens, January 15, 1777, Adm. 1/487.

27. Dispositions, January 15 and March 31, 1777, enclosed in Howe to Stephens, January 15 and March 31, 1777, Adm. 1/487. Lists of prizes in Howe to Stephens, March 31, 1777, Adm. 1/487, and in Howe to Stephens, October 24, 1777, October 23 and 30, 1778, Adm. 1/488. The one list that is now missing from the official correspondence may be found in the *London Chronicle* (London), July 12–15, 1777.

28. January 17, 1777, Tatum, ed., *Journal of Serle*, p. 156; Charles Stuart to the Earl of Bute, February 4, 1777, E. Stuart Wortley, ed., *A Prime Minister and His Son* . . . (London, 1925), p. 99; Wash-

ington's proclamation of January 25, 1777, enclosed in the Howes to Germain, March 25, 1777, C.O. 5/177.

29. February 21, 1777, Ford, ed., *Journals of Congress*, VII, pp. 140–41; Benjamin Rush to Robert Morris, February 22, 1777, Burnett, ed., *Letters of Members*, II, pp. 270–71.

30. April 17, 1777, Tatum, ed., *Journal of Serle*, pp. 212–13.

31. General Howe had been knighted for defeating the rebels on Long Island.

32. Germain to Sir William Howe, Nos. 4 and 5 of March 3, 1777, C.O. 5/94, quoting No. 4.

33. The Earl of Sandwich to Lord Howe, March 10, 1777, G. R. Barnes and J. H. Owen, eds., *The Private Papers of John, Earl of Sandwich, First Lord of the Admiralty, 1771–1782* (Publications of the Navy Records Society, vols. LXIX, LXXI, LXXV, and LXXVIII [London, 1932–38]), I, pp. 288–89; Germain to William Knox, June 11, 1777, Knox Papers, Clements; Lord Howe to Germain, May 31, 1777, Germain Papers, Clements.

34. Lord Howe to Germain, May 31, 1777, Germain Papers, Clements; Sir William Howe to Germain, June 3, 1777, C.O. 5/94; Lord Howe to Stephens, June 8, 1777, and intelligence from Captain Fielding enclosed in Howe to Stephens, June 8, 1777, Adm. 1/487; Stephens to Howe, August 20, 1777, Adm. 2/555.

35. Germain to Lord Howe and Germain to Sir William Howe, August 4, 1777, Germain Papers, Clements; Sandwich to Lord Howe, August 3, 1777, Barnes and Owen, eds., *Papers of Sandwich*, I, pp. 293–95; Stephens to Lord Howe, August 20, 1777, Adm. 2/555.

36. W. H. Moomaw, "The Denouement of General Howe's Campaign of 1777," *English Historical Review*, LXXIX (1964), p. 505.

37. Sir William Howe to Germain, November 30, 1777, C.O. 5/95.

38. Lord Howe to Stephens, October 25, 1777, Adm. 1/488; minutes of courts-martial for loss of *Augusta* and *Merlin*, November 26, 1777, Adm. 1/5308.

39. Lord Howe to Stephens, November 23, 1777, Adm. 1/488; November 23, 1777, Henry Cabot Lodge, ed., *André's Journal . . . June 1777 to November 1778 . . .*, 2 vols., (Boston, 1903), I, p. 121.

40. Lord Howe to Germain, October 18, 1777, Germain Papers, Clements.

41. Sir William Howe to Germain, October 22, 1777, C.O. 5/94.

42. Henry Duncan's journal, October 31, 1777, John Knox Laughton and W. G. Perrin, eds., *The Naval Miscellany* (Publications of the Navy Records Society, vols. XX, XL, LXIII [London, 1902–]),

I, p. 154; Lord Howe to Stephens, November 23 and December 10, 1777, Adm. 1/488.

43. Germain to Sir William Howe, February 18, 1778, and to Sir Henry Clinton, most secret, March 8, 1778; secret instructions to Clinton, March 21, 1778, all in C.O. 5/95. Secret instructions for Lord Howe, March 21, 1778, Adm. 2/1334.

44. Gruber, "Lord Howe and Lord George Germain," 242–43.

45. Secret instructions for Lord Howe, March 21, 1778, Adm. 2/1334.

46. Gerald Saxon Brown, *The American Secretary: the Colonial Policy of Lord George Germain, 1775–1778* (Ann Arbor, 1963), 149–73 gives a full and reliable account of the debate in the cabinet. For the idea that foul winds alone kept Byron from sailing between May 9 and May 13 see the King to Lord North, May 9, 1778, John W. Fortescue, ed., *The Correspondence of King George the Third from 1760 to December 1783*, 6 Vols. (London, 1927–28), IV, 138 and Sir Hugh Palliser to Sandwich, Spithead, May 12, 1778, Barnes and Owen, eds., *Papers of Sandwich*, II, 57–58.

47. Howe to Stephens, April 23 and May 9, 1778, Adm. 1/488.

48. Howe to Stephens, May 9, 1778, and disposition of American squadron, March 9, 1778, enclosed in Howe to Stephens, March 16, 1778, Adm. 1/488. Clinton to Germain May 23, 1778, C.O. 5/96.

49. Howe to Stephens June 10, 1778, Adm. 1/488.

50. Germain to Clinton, May 4, 1778, C.O. 5/95; Howe to Clinton, July 1, 1778 Clinton Papers, Clements; Howe to Stephens, July 6, 1778, Adm. 1/488.

51. Howe to Stephens, July 6, 1778, Adm. 1/488.

52. Howe to Clinton, July 8 and [July 8], 1778, Clinton Papers, Clements; Howe to Byron, July 8, 1778, in Howe to Stephens, July 11, 1778, Adm. 1/488; Duncan's journal, July 11, 1778, Laughton and Perrin, eds., *Naval Miscellany*, I, 159–60; captain's log *Eagle*, July 12, 1778, Adm. 51/293.

53. Captain John Montresor's sketch of Sandy Hook, showing the two fleets on July 22, 1778, G. D. Scull, ed., *The Montresor Journals* (Collections of the New York Historical Society for the Year 1881 [New York, 1882], opposite 505; list of d'Estaing's squadron bound with Admiralty's letter to Byron May 3, 1778, Adm. 2/1335; lists of Howe's and d'Estaing's squadrons in Germain Papers, Clements.

54. Alexander Hamilton to Washington, July 20, 1778, Harold C. Syrett and Jacob E. Cooke, eds., *The Papers of Alexander Hamilton* (New York, 1961-), I, 525–26.

55. Howe to Stephens, July 31, 1778, Adm. 1/488; Howe to Clinton, [July 30, 1778], Clinton Papers, Clements.

56. Sir William Howe to Henry Strachey, September 15, 1778, Strachey MSS, New York Public Library; George Mason, *The Life of Richard Earl Howe* (London, 1803), 43–44.

57. Captain Brisbane to Howe, August 9, 1778, enclosed in Howe to Stephens, August 17, 1778, and Howe to Stephens, August 17, 1778, Adm. 1/488.

58. Howe to Stephens, August 17, 1778, Adm. 1/488; Duncan's journal, August 10, 1778, Laughton and Perrin, eds., *Naval Miscellany*, I, 160.

59. Howe to Stephens, August 17, 1778, Adm. 1/488; Duncan's journal, August 11[–17], 1778, Laughton and Perrin, eds., *Naval Miscellany*, I, 162; captain's log *Nonsuch*, August 11–12, 1778, Adm. 51/64.

60. Duncan's journal, August 11[–17], 1778, Laughton and Perrin, eds., *Naval Miscellany*, I, 162; captain's log *Isis*, August 12, 1778, Adm. 51/484; d'Estaing to the secretary of the marine, November 5, 1778, Henri Doniol, *Histoire de la Participation de la France a l'Établissement des États-Unis D'Amérique*, 6 Vols. (Paris, 1884–92), III, 452.

61. Howe to Clinton, August 25, 1778, Clinton Papers, Clements; Howe to Stephens, August 25 and August 17, Howe to Fielding, September 2, 1778, enclosed in Howe to Stephens, October 25, 1778, all in Adm. 1/488.

62. Howe to Stephens, September 12, and Howe to Fielding, September 2, 1778, enclosed in Howe to Stephens, October 25, 1778, Adm. 1/488.

63. Howe to Byron, September 9, and to Gambier, September 11, 1778, enclosed in Howe to Stephens, October 25, 1778, Adm. 1/488.

BIBLIOGRAPHY

Anderson, Troyer Steele. *The Command of the Howe Brothers During the American Revolution*. New York, 1936. An imaginative study that is devoted mainly to Sir William Howe; it suffers, however, because Anderson relied too heavily on official correspondence and political pamphlets.

Barrow, Sir John. *The Life of Richard Earl Howe*. London, 1838. The only full life of Lord Howe. Not of much use to modern students of the Revolutionary War.

Brown, Gerald Saxon. *The American Secretary: The Colonial Policy of Lord George Germain, 1775–1778*. Ann Arbor, 1963. The best study of Germain, useful for following the development of British plans for the campaigns of 1777 and 1778.

Brown, Weldon A. *Empire or Independence, A Study in the Failure of Reconciliation, 1774–1783*. Baton Rouge, 1941. An examination of British peace efforts to 1778 that does little to show the relationship between Lord Howe's work as commissioner and as commander-in-chief.

Gruber, Ira D. "Lord Howe and Lord George Germain, British Politics and the Winning of American Independence," *William and Mary Quarterly*, 3d ser., XXII (1965), pp. 225–243. An attempt to relate British politics and political considerations to the conduct of the war in America.

Mahan, A. T. *The Major Operations of the Navies in the War of American Independence*. Boston, 1913. Still probably the best general study of the naval side of the American Revolution.

Mackesy, Piers. *The War for America, 1775–1783*. Cambridge, Mass., 1964. Puts British strategy in America into the context of a world war.

Willcox, William B. *Portrait of a General: Sir Henry Clinton in the War of Independence*. New York, 1964. The best biography of any British soldier, sailor, or statesman of the Revolutionary War.

Arbuthnot, Gambier, and Graves:

"OLD WOMEN" OF THE NAVY

———•••———

WILLIAM B. WILLCOX

University of Michigan

THE British navy during the War of Independence, according to a writer of a generation ago, was in adversity.[1] He might with almost equal truth have said that it was in stupidity. The great struggles that came before and after the Seven Years' War and the Wars of the French Revolution, gradually taught the British Admiralty and admirals their business: competent men rose to command, and in the long run sound policies won out over stupid ones. No such progress occurred between 1778 and 1782. The Channel fleet was in the hands of a succession of nonentities. In the West Indies only Rodney and Hood distinguished themselves; one was a hard fighter and poor strategist, and the other seldom had scope for his talents. On the American station, after Lord Howe had returned home in dudgeon from his successful defensive in 1778, his successors were what their harassed colleague in the army, Sir Henry Clinton, called "old women," who strutted and fretted their hour upon the stage and accomplished nothing positive. The first of them, Gambier, had little chance to do harm. But the negative accomplishments of his two successors, Arbuthnot and Graves, were of great value to the American cause. Arbuthnot helped to prepare, and Graves presided over, the defeat of the Royal Navy in the Yorktown campaign.

The question of why Britain was so badly served at sea throughout the war is unanswerable, like most such questions in history; but some factors are clear. One is as simple as it is unscientific: plain bad luck, in men and in events. The navy was in a trough between two periods of energetic leadership; Lord Anson was dead, Lord Hawke superannuated, and the leaders of the future, Cornwallis and Collingwood, Jervis and Nelson, were too young for major commands. The field was left to senior admirals who were for the most part mediocre, and their operations were plagued by mischance—by storms that scattered the reinforcement needed for success, by the capture or delay of crucial dispatches, by sickness that incapacitated a fleet or winds that held it back until a few hours after the enemy had escaped. "There is a great deal due to us from fortune," wrote Lord George Germain in the summer of 1778; "and I hope our luck will turn before we are quite ruined." [2] Three years later he was still waiting for the turn.

But luck turns, it may be argued, only for those who deserve it; Germain was ignoring Bacon's maxim that "the mould of a man's fortune is in his own hands." The administration of which Lord George was a part had its deserts, according to this argument, because it did not know how to mould the fortunes of war. The king had the will to win, and some flashes of strategic common sense, but little influence upon military policy. Lord North had neither the will nor the acumen to be a war leader, and knew that he was not one. Neither was Lord Amherst, who after 1778 was commander-in-chief of the army at home and a member of the cabinet; he buried himself in the details of his office, particularly of patronage, and left the war largely to his colleagues. [3] The chief responsibility, in consequence, devolved upon two men in the cabinet, and neither one was fitted to bear it.

Lord George Germain, the secretary of state for the American colonies, was as determined upon victory as his royal master, and was the chief architect of military policy. He was therefore con-

cerned perforce with naval affairs, because without the navy no
British army could function overseas. He had an intelligent grasp
of how sea power should be used, and did what he could to make
his views prevail; but for all his forcefulness he could not impose
them upon the Admiralty. There Lord Sandwich was autonomous. He and his service chiefs ruled the navy as their own preserve, and the first lord could vitiate even policies upon which
the rest of the cabinet agreed. On Sandwich, more than on any
other single man, depended the use to which British sea power
was put throughout the war. The first lord did not deserve all
the bad things said about him, at the time and since; nobody
could. He was an experienced and competent administrator,
much more competent than his enemies admitted. But he had
two fatal flaws: he could not pick a winning strategy or a fighting admiral.[4]

As a strategist Sandwich was the chief designer of a policy at
once defensive and supine, which almost lost the American war
in the spring of 1778, and was a main factor in losing it three and
a half years later. The crux of this strategy was detachment.
The Bourbon fleets were not contained by a blockade in home
waters, but left free to attack overseas wherever and whenever
they pleased; and their attacks were parried by detaching squadrons from the home fleet. Such a policy tempted fortune because
it rested upon hope—hope that the Admiralty could divine in
advance where the blow would fall, that the squadron detached
to follow would be equivalent in strength to the enemy, and
that it would reach the threatened point in time to be of use.
This was the way to lose a war, not to win it; and nowhere was
the danger of losing more apparent than in American waters. It
appeared in the first campaign against France in 1778, when
Byron's detachment from England did not arrive in time; it
appeared in 1779, when d'Estaing came north from the West
Indies with no covering British fleet; it appeared in 1780, when
Graves did not get out of Plymouth in time to join Arbuthnot
and intercept the French armament bound for Rhode Island.
Still the government did not learn. In the spring of 1781 it per-

mitted de Grasse to sail from Brest for the West Indies with twenty ships of the line, sent no equivalent British force to the Caribbean, and thereby set the stage for Yorktown.

The Admiralty failed not only to provide the naval strength needed at the points of danger, but also to ensure the efficiency of ships already there. A program for sheathing hulls with copper to prevent their fouling was begun in 1778; it more than doubled the length of time that men-of-war stayed in service between cleanings and greatly increased their speed, but was not pressed hard enough to be effective on any large scale. A proposal made in 1778 to improve the New York dockyard fell by the wayside, and every commandant in that port was hounded by the problem of refitting damaged ships. "Choice of difficulties," was Gambier's wail, "and scarcity of means!" [5]

Sandwich cannot be held accountable for all the mistakes of his department, but for the choice of flag officers he can be. All he asked of an admiral, apparently, was that he should not make trouble for the administration; ability to make trouble for the enemy seems to have been less important. During the years of the French war, while the first lord was entrusting the home fleet to a succession of timid old men, command on the American station passed from one incompetent to another. Lord Howe's replacement was Admiral Byron, who lived up to his nickname of "Foul Weather Jack" by arriving too late to help in the campaign of 1778, and then departed after a few months. The command devolved upon the senior officer on the station until the late summer of 1779, when Arbuthnot appeared as Byron's successor. Two years later, on Arbuthnot's recall, the same thing happened: the luckless Graves was left in charge during the worst crisis of the war because Arbuthnot's replacement, Admiral Digby, had not yet arrived; and when Digby did arrive he declined to serve until the crisis was over. After Howe, in other words, the three titular commanders-in-chief were Byron, Arbuthnot, and Digby, a sorry lot; and their delays in taking up the post left it for long periods to officers for whom Whitehall had never intended it. This was hardly what might be called an enlightened personnel policy.

The policy should have been discredited by the first experience of how it worked. When Byron finally reached New York in the autumn of 1778, he was authorized to pursue the French fleet if it sailed for the West Indies, as it did. He followed, and left the American station to the man who had been Howe's second in command, Rear Admiral James Gambier. This outcome was precisely what the government had tried to avoid by appointing Byron in the first place. Whitehall was convinced, with good reason, that Gambier was unfit for the command. He had botched his former job as commissioner of the Portsmouth Navy Yard, and had then been sent to America only because he was too well connected to be forced into retirement. The king, Germain, and North all had a low opinion of him. The prime minister was blunt: "I have seldom heard any seaman speak of Gambier as a good naval officer or as one who deserved to be trusted with any important command." [6] Sandwich gave no sign of disagreeing with this opinion, yet he expected Gambier to take over Howe's position both as commander-in-chief and as a member of the Carlisle Commission for negotiating peace; the first lord apparently considered American affairs subordinate to political convenience. Perhaps because of his resistance, it was November before Whitehall tried to redeem its error by ordering Gambier home; and the order did not take effect until the following April.[7]

From the moment he arrived at New York in the summer of 1778, Gambier was slighted. He had such a cold welcome from Lord Howe that he complained of being in Siberia. When his chief sailed off to rescue the British garrison on Rhode Island, leaving him to co-operate on Manhattan with the army commander, Sir Henry Clinton, Gambier had an attack of convulsions that alarmed the doctors, and an attack of nerves that must have alarmed Clinton even more. The admiral oscillated wildly between fright and determination. "Crippled and dying as I am," he wrote Sir Henry, "do you want aught in my power, say

but the word and you shall [have] it, even was it my last shirt."
"For God's sake tell me what I am to do about the Halifax and
Quebec applications. . . . Pray tell me what you wish to have
done." "What in God's name shall I do about transports, should
you find occasion to send for reinforcements? They tell me it's
impossible to procure them. I tell them at this time even impos-
sibility must be overcome. I will try at least." [8] The crisis passed,
Howe left, and Gambier continued to be slighted. He was not
named to the Carlisle Commission, and Clinton and the other
commissioners ignored him; he fumed at being "a mere laborious
fitting admiral, or rather superintendent of a port, . . . uncon-
sulted and in a manner uncommuned with in aught material."
But almost in the same breath he declared that Clinton "is spirited, liberal, and communicative, and has the service much at
heart. We have two good months more to operate in, and much
may be done and probably will." [9] Nothing was.

What the admiral had in mind were coastal raids to cripple
American trade. Clinton never had much enthusiasm for a policy
of "conflagration," as he called it; and the last trace of enthusiasm disappeared when he discovered how clumsy Gambier was
in handling the transportation of troops. Friction between the
services, which had been at a minimum in the days of the Howe
brothers, was generated by this issue and continued to plague
the war effort until the end. Sir Henry had a simple solution,
which was to give him control over all amphibious operations on
the coast. "After five campaigns in this country," he burst out
after a frustrating experience with Gambier, "commanding at
every embarcation, do or ought I not to know more than this
same Admiral, who is . . . in every respect a horrid performer?"
"*Entre nous* he is the most impracticable man I ever met with." [10]

Gambier seems to have been widely unpopular. The loyalist
chief justice of New York, William Smith, shared Clinton's
opinion of him for different reasons. Smith always observed what
was going on with a censorious eye, and he concluded that Gambier was an aging fop. "The Admiral is sixty-four [he was in
his mid-fifties] and affects the gaiety of thirty. He is the con-

tempt of the town, the army, and the navy, and the companion of . . . another old coxcomb, who appears in this season (as well as the Admiral) at church in a satin waistcoat. They do not respect their own years." "Gambier is a fool, who will sacrifice a good service to his vanity." Another observer commented, when the admiral finally left for home in the spring of 1779, that his departure aroused "the universal joy of all ranks and conditions. I believe no person was ever more generally detested by navy, army, and citizen than this penurious old reptile." [11]

Gambier arrived in England to find that his career was over. Even though Sandwich continued to express his support, the hapless admiral was denied the promotion that had been promised him, and was ordered to strike his flag while junior colleagues were still flying theirs. He concluded, understandably enough, that the cabinet disapproved his conduct in America; and his only answer was "I could do no more!" "My reward," he wrote Germain, "for every unremitting exertion of zeal, fidelity, and disinterested conduct [is] painful and heartfelt neglect and ostensibility of reprehension." He was not at home as a letter-writer, as this bombast suggests; and he urged Lord George to excuse inaccuracies "from an officer whose ship has been the only university he has been permitted to study at for upwards of forty years." [12] The tone of his letter is fussy, pompous, self-justifying, and also pitiable. He was a failure in the eyes of his contemporaries, and he seems to have struggled hard to keep from agreeing with them.

For a few months after Gambier's departure the American command devolved upon Sir George Collier, one of the rare naval officers who had a gift for collaborating with the army; and in those months something approaching harmony reigned between the services. Collier carried out a raid in the Chesapeake, and then thwarted an attack from Massachusetts against the loyalist colony on the Penobscot River in Maine. But these were the sum of his achievements, because in August Vice Admiral Marriot Arbuthnot arrived to supersede him. Clinton was disgruntled. He would have preferred Collier, or any one of a

number of names that he had suggested to friends in England
and that the Admiralty had ignored; he concluded that Sandwich neither knew nor cared about America. "I heartily wish
Lord Howe was at the head of the Admiralty. He knows how
the navy on this station and in this war ought to be conducted,
and he would direct accordingly." [13]

Sandwich's direction, as represented by the choice of Arbuthnot, was far worse than Sir Henry yet realized. The appointment
was a major blunder. It seems to have been made with almost no
discussion, and its very casualness suggests the first lord's indifference to "how the navy on this station and in this war ought to
be conducted." The American command had taxed Lord Howe's
resources to the utmost in the campaign of 1778, and it did not
belong in the hands of a man whose long career had brought
him almost to seventy without revealing any outstanding talent.
Arbuthnot had been commandant at Halifax in the early years
of the war, and had recently acted as a judge in the court-martial
of Admiral Keppel. Neither of these services qualified him for a
post that required both tact and vigor—tact to get on with
Clinton, who was by this time notorious as a difficult colleague,
and vigor to meet the perennial threat of French sea power. Any
government that knew its business would have subjected the
admiral's record to searching examination, and would then have
immured him in some harmless sinecure.

Arbuthnot had no tact at all. When he tried to be friendly,
it was in a wayward, blundering fashion that could not stand re-
buff; and when annoyed he either was waspish or wrapped himself in stiff punctilio. His vigor was never sustained: outbursts of
activity, often misdirected, were sandwiched between periods of
somnolence. He could fight the enemy when he had to, but his
tactical ideas resembled those of General Howe at Bunker Hill.
His strategic ideas were, to use the most kindly adjective, dim;
and his sense of the need to collaborate with the army was even
dimmer. Throughout his tenure of command he insisted that
the navy must retain its freedom of action, and nine times out
of ten he refused to act; then, instead of accepting responsibility,

he devoted much time and attention to shifting the blame for inaction onto others. He fawned on his superiors, Germain and Sandwich; he quarreled with his equals; he bullied his subordinates while he was being manipulated by them. He was a timid man, in short, who covered his timidity with blustering.

At first all went reasonably well between him and Clinton. The campaign of 1779 had been abortive, largely because the admiral had arrived late and with troops afflicted by a raging fever. But Arbuthnot and Sir Henry were at once plunged into a flurry of activity. First came news that d'Estaing, who had attacked New York and Rhode Island in 1778, was again in American waters. He was thought to be bound once more for Newport, and the British commanders-in-chief agreed to evacuate the garrison there. But Arbuthnot blew hot, then cold, and could not make up his mind to carry through the evacuation; instead he talked of taking his squadron to Halifax, in case that turned out to be the French objective. He did not understand Clinton's reasoning, or Clinton his; and misunderstanding bred suspicion. The two colleagues communicated for the most part through an intermediary, to whom each poured out helpless profanity about the other. Fortunately for them, d'Estaing did not appear; he had chosen to attack Georgia instead of Rhode Island, and was repulsed before Savannah. As the crisis waned at New York, and the evacuation of Newport was finally completed, relative calm returned to headquarters, and Clinton and Arbuthnot gradually and tentatively mended their relationship. But the first test of their ability to work together had not been heartening.

A much larger test came soon. During the winter the British moved to the south with a large fleet and army, and in the spring of 1780 started a major operation with the siege of Charleston. Clinton had chief responsibility for the siege, and Arbuthnot only a supporting role. But the admiral confirmed his colleague's distrust of him by refusing assistance when needed, by hanging back when he had promised to go ahead, and by hiding behind a smoke screen of words and friendly overtures.

Clinton, now thoroughly on his guard, chilled the overtures with icy politeness. "In appearance we were the best of friends," he wrote in his diary; "but I am sure he is false as hell, and shall behave in consequence." Arbuthnot gave up hope of thawing him, and was hard put to it to maintain a semblance of cordiality. "So many circumstances occur in the course of business that I submit to only for peace, that keeps my command of temper so continually upon the stretch," he confided to Germain, "that I am apprehensive I shall not be able much longer to possess philosophy sufficient." [14]

The summer of 1780 stretched the admiral's philosophy to the breaking point. In June, just after the surrender of Charleston, he and Clinton left for New York, because they had received word that a French army under the Comte de Rochambeau, convoyed by a fleet commanded by the Chevalier de Ternay, was bound for the New England coast. The French intended to establish for the first time a base of operations in America by seizing Rhode Island, as Clinton soon learned from his American correspondent, General Benedict Arnold. The British had three possible ways to frustrate this intention. Clinton might reoccupy Rhode Island before the enemy arrived; Arbuthnot might intercept and destroy de Ternay's armament at sea, while it was encumbered with transports; or the army and navy together might attack after Rochambeau's troops were ashore and before they had time to refortify the old British works around Newport. Either a naval battle or a *coup de main* while the French were landing offered hope of a signal victory. But both depended on getting accurate and prompt intelligence of the enemy's whereabouts, and responding with equal promptness; the all-important factor was timing.

Clinton proposed seizing Rhode Island ahead of the French. Arbuthnot refused. He was skeptical of Arnold's information (he had reason to be, considering its source) and preferred to wait for reinforcements that had been promised him. The Admiralty was using the same policy of detachment that had miscarried with Byron two years before. This time Rear Admiral

Graves, with six ships of the line, was racing de Ternay across the ocean, and was expected to arrive first because his vessels were copper-bottomed and therefore faster sailers than the enemy. If Graves appeared in time, and could be promptly refitted at New York, Arbuthnot would have such force that he would need only to find the French at sea in order to destroy them. He had good cause to wait.

His chance of victory was much better on his own than in conjunction with the army, because he could not work with Clinton and knew it. "The fellow," he said of Sir Henry, "is a vain, jealous fool!" [15] But the admiral could not act alone unless he found the enemy, and this he failed to do. On July 7 he heard that his scouting frigates had encountered de Ternay off Virginia two days before, only to lose him again. No watch whatever, apparently, was kept off Rhode Island. Eleven precious days passed before word arrived on the 18th, through army intelligence, that the enemy had landed there on the 10th. They were presumably busy entrenching themselves. The first and second possibilities, of anticipating the French and of intercepting them at sea, were now foreclosed; the only chance left was to strike before their position became impregnable.

Graves, meanwhile, had reached Sandy Hook on the 13th. Although he was subsequently accused of having delayed en route, he had in fact made one of the fastest crossings on record; and his squadron, except for having seven hundred men down with scurvy, was in fighting trim. Arbuthnot realized that every minute counted, and he showed the energy of which he was sporadically capable. He had prepared to refit Graves' ships outside the Hook, to save the delay of getting them across the bar and into the New York dockyard. The job was done in short order, and volunteers replaced the sick. On the 19th—a mere six days after Graves' arrival—the combined squadron sailed to reconnoiter the enemy. It was a remarkable performance.

It was also the last sign of vigor in Arbuthnot during the campaign. His initiative was never of long duration, and in this case it may have evaporated because he feared to cooperate with the "vain, jealous fool." But he certainly had the means of doing so. His fleet, one 98-gun ship of the line, four 74's, four 64's, two 50's, and a heavy frigate, was substantially superior to de Ternay's one 84, two 74's, four 64's, and five frigates; the old admiral should at least have been able to contain the enemy squadron while British troops landed, and so Clinton thought. He bombarded his colleague with detailed plans. They seem merely to have antagonized Arbuthnot, who was not given to systematic analysis and could not be forced into it. He paid scant attention to Sir Henry's ideas.

They came by letter, for the general was far away, waiting with his army on the Long Island coast. The admiral, cruising off Rhode Island, had to make whatever decisions were going to be made. Would he choose between Clinton's plans or advance an alternative suggestion? Would he determine the enemy's position and strength? Above all would he commit the navy to assist the landing? The answers to all these questions turned out to be no. Arbuthnot did not say a word about how the attack should be made. He disparaged the reports of officers whom Clinton sent to reconnoiter, and obtained no information himself; after more than a fortnight within sight of the French he protested that he had no idea of their dispositions, or of "pretending officially to know their strength." [16] The fleet could take care of de Ternay but render no other help, the admiral concluded; and the army should not come unless it were ready to attack on its own. He was washing his hands of responsibility, in short, and dumping the dirty water on his colleague.

The fleet thereupon withdrew for refitting to Gardiners Bay, some fifty miles from Newport on the eastern end of Long Island. Clinton's troops returned to New York, and the episode seemed to be over. But no. The admiral may have been uneasy about the supine role he had played, or been afflicted with one of his unpredictable attacks of optimism; in any case he proposed that Sir Henry meet him at Gardiners Bay to concert immediate action. Clinton at once agreed. He made the difficult journey overland, and arrived to find the anchorage deserted.

A casual note from Arbuthnot, dated the same morning, informed him that the French were reportedly putting to sea and that he had sailed to intercept them. Not so much as a boat had been left behind to keep communications open.

This incident reveals more than the admiral's flair for discourtesy; it also shows his strategic muddleheadedness. A few minutes of lucid thinking would have told him that if the French were leaving Newport (as in fact they were not) he had no reason to rush off in pursuit but had, on the contrary, every reason to wait for a discussion with his colleague. What were the enemy up to? If they were evacuating Rhode Island entirely, they must presumably mean to attack somewhere else; and measures to counter the blow ought to be arranged at once. If they were leaving their troops and taking only their fleet, they were offering a golden opportunity for a combined assault on their base. In either case a conference between the British commanders was of the first importance, but this idea does not seem to have crossed Arbuthnot's mind. All he saw was what was immediately before his eyes, a chance for the navy to act alone.

His departure on this wild-goose chase ended the last hope of collaboration between the two commanders-in-chief. Clinton sent an ultimatum to the cabinet: either he or his colleague must go. In deciding between them the government delayed unconscionably. Sandwich, loyal to his appointee, found one difficulty after another in removing him. Germain was ambivalent, torn between the desire to replace Clinton with a more energetic general and the fear that the commander-in-chief's resignation would have serious political repercussions.[17] Almost eleven months passed between the contretemps at Gardiners Bay and Arbuthnot's departure, and in that time cooperation between the two services reached its lowest point of the war.

The navy maintained a blockade of the French at Newport, but in the age of sail no blockade was proof against accidents of wind and weather. At any moment the blockaded ships might escape and disappear at sea. In the background there always lurked the danger that they might be released by, and added to, an enemy fleet from Europe or the West Indies. Arbuthnot's naval superiority had always been precarious, and now that he had failed to crush de Ternay it was more so. The army, to make matters worse, was more dependent upon the navy than ever. The British now had two widely separated bases, New York and Charleston, that were connected and supplied entirely by water; Clinton, moreover, was about to make a move that would further disperse his troops and place a contingent of them within striking range of de Ternay, so that its only protection would be Arbuthnot's guard on Narragansett Bay.

In the late summer of 1780, Lord Cornwallis, whom Clinton had left to command in the south, was about to advance into North Carolina. He asked Sir Henry to establish a post on the Chesapeake, to keep the Virginians occupied at home and to impede the movement of enemy troops and supplies southward, through the narrow corridor between the Alleghenies and the bay. In December, after an earlier attempt had failed, Clinton sent an expedition to occupy Portsmouth, Virginia. As commander he selected his new brigadier general, Benedict Arnold, who three months earlier had failed to deliver West Point and had fled to New York. Arnold showed his usual energy, but Portsmouth was a dangerous position. His fortifications were weak, and he was within reach of both Washington's army and the French squadron. Even if the Americans had not been thirsting for Arnold's blood, he would have been a tempting target. In January, 1781, the enemy began to concert an attack upon him from land and sea. The first effort failed because the Chevalier Destouches, who had succeeded to the naval command at Newport on de Ternay's death, sent only one ship of the line. The failure intoxicated Arbuthnot, even though he was in wretched health at the time. He began to plan euphorically, quite on his own, for moving troops to Virginia, conquering it, and perhaps forcing a junction with Cornwallis. When Clinton, baffled and alarmed, inquired what he had in mind, he abruptly dropped the whole idea.

At the beginning of March, the enemy's combined operation

against Arnold began in earnest. Destouches escaped from Narragansett Bay with his entire squadron and headed for the Capes of Virginia, and Arbuthnot set off in pursuit. The situation resembled, on a smaller scale, that which recurred six months later at the climax of the Yorktown campaign: an American army and a French fleet were bound for the Chesapeake to bottle up a British force; Clinton dared not send reinforcements from New York by the best route open to him, the sea, until he knew that the way was clear; and his naval colleague was trying to clear it by finding and defeating the French fleet. Arnold's life, and the existence of his corps, depended on the engagement that Arbuthnot was seeking.

The British line had recently been reduced, through damage wrought by a great storm, to one 98, three 74's, three 64's, and a 50, a force approximately equal to the French. Arbuthnot's ships, being copper-bottomed, were faster; and when the two fleets encountered each other off Cape Charles on March 16 the British were in the lead. They immediately went about to pursue the enemy, who put out to sea. After a time Destouches doubled back, and the two lines engaged. The French were to leeward, where they could use their lower batteries; the British, heeling before a heavy wind, could not use theirs without letting in the sea through the open gunports. The two vans battered each other and then drew apart, but Destouches brought the rest of his line past the damaged British ships and battered them again. The French then disappeared out to sea, having inflicted more harm than they had received. Arbuthnot's squadron was in no state to pursue, and he expected his opponent to return to the Chesapeake. He therefore made for the bay himself, and settled down in Lynnhaven Roads to nurse his battle wounds.

He had certainly not achieved a tactical victory. His method of engaging, line to line, had been the orthodox one to which the Royal Navy had adhered since the Duke of York's Fighting Instructions in the second Dutch War. A battle on this pattern was rarely conclusive when the two fleets were of equivalent strength and competently handled, because their cannonading usually did as much damage to one as to the other. In this case the French had inflicted more, partly because of their final man-euver and partly because, being to leeward, they had had greater firepower. Their behavior, according to a British observer, had been most unsporting: they had first put Arbuthnot's van to the disadvantage of having to close with them in order to make them fight, and had then mauled it, "the French having in this as well as in all other actions during this war constantly per-sisted in avoiding an engagement." [18] Destouches did not avoid one; he courted it in his own way, and Arbuthnot obliged.

But for once, whatever his tactical shortcomings, the British admiral showed strategic common sense. The point of overriding importance was to save Arnold, and this he did by anchoring in Lynnhaven Roads. When Destouches took to his heels, he threw away the advantage that he had gained by his tactical skill; for he did not have the force to dislodge the British once they were in the bay. His hope of a combined operation evap-orated, and he sailed back to Newport with nothing to show for his sortie. D'Estaing and now Destouches: for three years Bour-bon sea power had been ineffectual, and the promise that it had once held for the Americans seemed like a will-o'-the-wisp. *Dis aliter visum*. On the other side of the Atlantic, six days after the action off the Chesapeake, Admiral de Grasse put to sea from Brest with twenty sail of the line.

The crisis that de Grasse soon precipitated in North America might have fallen upon Arbuthnot, if he had performed better in the action of March 16. But the reports of the battle that reached London seem to have overcome even Sandwich's loyalty to him, and he was finally recalled. By the time this order reached New York at the end of June, his quarrel with Clinton had reached the point where no combined operations were pos-sible. The two men could not act alone and would not act to-gether, but all Sir Henry saw was that the navy would not act. "Our old Admiral has at last left us," he reported. "It was cruel to keep him here nine months after they had promised to remove him, and that at a time when the most active exertion of the fleet was necessary." [19] What would have happened if the two men had continued to be yoked for a few more weeks, while the campaign against Cornwallis was beginning to unroll, is an interesting speculation.

Arbuthnot was not at best an agreeable man or a talented admiral, but the situation into which he was thrown brought out the worst in him. William Smith, who knew him well, believed that "he may be humored into any useful service." [20] No one was on hand to humor him. He tried to make a confidant out of General Robertson, the governor of New York, and to use him as a go-between in dealing with Clinton (which only incensed Sir Henry the more); but Robertson was an aging, catty intriguer, who had no oil to pour on troubled waters. Neither had Clinton. Sir Henry was coldly suspicious of whatever suggestions Arbuthnot made, and confused and annoyed the old man by his own almost febrile planning. The admiral was forced, willy-nilly, to play a lone hand. He played it according to the rule book and to the best of his ability; but his best was inadequate.

The same was true of his successor, Thomas Graves, upon whom the command devolved on July 4. He had served well under Arbuthnot, and had had the good fortune to be rarely in his presence; his chief had left him in charge of the blockade and had chosen for himself the comforts of New York. Graves was courteous and hard-working, with none of his predecessor's irascibility and none of Gambier's flights of fancy. Although his letters give the impression of a colorless plodder, the new commander-in-chief won and retained Clinton's respect as few other admirals did. Whether he deserved it is another question.

Graves was as uninspired a tactician as Arbuthnot, and lacked the strategic foresight that his situation demanded. Perhaps he sensed his own shortcomings; certainly he gave no sign of welcoming the command. The Admiralty had not intended him to have it; although he was a relative and friend of Lord North, he was passed over for Admiral Digby, his junior and a protégé of Sandwich. Dut Digby was delayed in England till July, and did not arrive until late September.[21] In the months that Graves held his post he seemed to discharge its responsibilities with unruffled calm. Under his smooth surface, however, was a vein of timidity as strong as Arbuthnot's, although he showed it in different ways. He did not alternate between optimism and gloom, unconsidered action and lethargy; as a planner he was almost as systematic as Clinton. But he found one reason after another for not putting the important plans to the test. He acted twice, once by going on a cruise for which he had insufficient justification, once by attacking the French after his best chance of victory had passed. The rest of his brief command he spent in preparing for moves that were never made, while the British cause went down to defeat.

By the time Graves took charge at the beginning of July, British headquarters knew that Rochambeau's army had marched from Rhode Island to join Washington near New York. A new naval commandant, the Comte de Barras, who had arrived from France in May to supersede Destouches, had expected to retire to Boston as soon as the army left him; but he had not done so, and this the British also knew. The French ships were riding at anchor, protected by only a corporal's guard of regulars and militia, and farther up the bay at Providence was Rochambeau's siege train. The chance of attacking the enemy was brighter than it had been since their first landing a year before, and the incentive to attack was greater than ever. For Clinton and Graves had information that Admiral de Grasse, from the West Indies, planned to visit the American coast during the summer. Although they assumed that he would be followed by an equivalent British detachment, there was every likelihood that he would be able to lift the blockade of de Barras and add those ships to his fleet. The importance of destroying them before de Grasse arrived was self-evident.

But Graves behaved as if no threat from the West Indies existed. In mid-July, just after he had told the Admiralty that he would take shelter from de Grasse, he put to sea to hunt off

Boston Bay for a convoy of enemy supplies from France. This decision is hard to account for. It wasted precious weeks in which Newport might have been attacked. It removed Graves from his favorable position between de Barras and de Grasse, where he could get timely intelligence of what was happening and make his plans accordingly, and put him far to the east of the crucial area. It inflicted further strain on his ships, still suffering from their engagement off the Chesapeake, and put two of them out of action when, a few weeks later, he needed them the most. Apparently none of these considerations occurred to him. All he said about the effect of his cruise was that it would immobilize the enemy, "as they would be unable to guess at the intention of the squadron." [22] A more ridiculous argument is hard to imagine.

He continued, even after his return to New York on August 16, to belittle the menace from de Grasse. Three weeks earlier a sloop had brought the first definite word from Admiral Rodney, in the West Indies, that the French were coming and that a British fleet under Rear Admiral Sir Samuel Hood would follow them. By the 16th, Graves and Clinton had strong indications of what Rodney had not known; that de Grasse was bringing his entire line of battle. This was a formidable threat, regardless of what help Hood might bring; and even Arbuthnot had realized two months before that the help might not arrive in time. On August 19 the Franco-American army left the Hudson and began marching toward the Chesapeake, and in the next few days British intelligence agents bombarded headquarters with reports that a great French fleet was approaching the coast. Graves might have been expected to run for cover. Instead he pooh-poohed the danger, and went on calmly planning with Clinton an attack on de Barras' squadron. If the reports he was receiving had any truth in them, such an attack would be madness; for de Grasse might catch and overwhelm the attackers.

Graves may conceivably have understood the danger better than his letters suggest, and have had no real intention of implementing his plans. But in any case the Rhode Island scheme blinded him to another possibility, which was as obvious as it was promising. The naval problem that faced him had four elements: his own and de Barras' squadrons, of approximately equal strength, and the two great fleets under de Grasse and Hood, which supposedly would also be equal. The question was which two of these four, the French or the British, would join forces first. If the British did, they would have the choice of attacking one or the other of the separated enemy fleets; speed was what mattered, and the speediest junction could be achieved where Graves knew that Hood had been instructed to make his first landfall, the Capes of Virginia. Common sense might have dictated taking the New York squadron there immediately.[23] Instead Graves placidly whiled away his time in port.

On August 28 placidity ended. Hood arrived, and the same evening came word that de Barras had put to sea. Admiral Hood looked and behaved, said William Smith, like a stiff Yankee colonel. But he injected into the calm musings of the commanders-in-chief a new sense of urgency and pugnacity, a single-minded desire to be at the enemy. If he had not been junior and therefore subordinate to Graves, the whole campaign might have gone differently. Yet Hood did succeed in galvanizing his superior, and three days after his arrival the combined fleet set sail for the Chesapeake. The story of the previous spring was apparently being repeated. But this time the British admirals, although they did not know it, faced far heavier odds than Arbuthnot had.

De Grasse had brought twenty-eight ships of the line. He had left French commerce and possessions in the West Indies unprotected, a bold gamble that succeeded because Admiral Rodney did not dream that the enemy would dare take it. Hood brought fourteen of the line, and only five at New York were serviceable; Graves consequently sailed with nineteen. De Barras was at sea with eight.[24] He was convoying Rochambeau's siege grain from Providence and was bound for the Chesapeake, where de Grasse had arrived on August 31. The moment the two French contingents joined, they would outnumber Graves' fleet by almost two to one—odds to give pause to any British admiral.

Graves was happily ignorant of what faced him, for he had accepted Hood's assurance that their combined strength would be a match for whatever the enemy might bring. On September 5, when the British fleet raised the mouth of the Chesapeake, its commanders began to discover their error. French ships came out of the bay in staggering numbers; one by one the sails appeared, until twenty-four of the line were in sight. De Grasse had left four to guard his anchorage; with the remainder he intended to lure the British out to sea and away from de Barras, who would thus be able to enter the Chesapeake unmolested.

The battle of the Virginia Capes that followed—probably more important in its results than any other naval engagement of the eighteenth century—was a pedestrian affair. The two fleets approached each other as usual in parallel lines, the French to leeward; fighting opened between the two vans, and as soon as it became intense the French bore away. Graves did what he could to produce close action all along the line, but his signal flags betrayed him. Most of his captains, fresh from Rodney's quite different school of tactics in the West Indies, did not know their new commander's mind; and he had either not had the time or not taken the trouble to tell them how to interpret his flags. When he signaled to close, and also flew intermittently the signal to keep the line ahead, the result was confusion. Hood did not bring his rear division into the fight at all, and he was subsequently criticized as bitterly as he himself criticized his chief.[25] Who was to blame is not clear, but the result is. The engagement was tactically indecisive and therefore a defeat for Graves, because he needed to win and the French did not. All de Grasse needed was to be left in possession of the Chesapeake.

The battle in itself did not determine who would have possession. During the next week, while the two fleets were maneuvering at sea, Graves had the opportunity to slip by his opponent and enter the bay. Hood and others have censured him for not doing so, in order to paralyze the operations against Cornwallis as Arbuthnot had paralyzed those against Arnold. But the comparison, when examined, breaks down. If Graves had taken this gamble he might have destroyed de Barras' squadron, which slipped into the bay on September 10 carrying Rochambeau's precious siege train; the British would also have disrupted the water communications upon which the approaching enemy army was dependent. But Graves and Hood had left New York before that army had given proof that it was bound for the Chesapeake. Against the likelihood that it was, and that Cornwallis was consequently in grave jeopardy, Graves had to balance the risk to his fleet, upon which the whole British position in North America and Caribbean rested. Only a bold man, perhaps only a foolhardy one, would have dared to bottle up his ships while a superior French force was in the offing. Graves made for New York.

When he arrived there, on September 19, some hope still remained. He had established that there had been twenty-eight French sail of the line in the Chesapeake on the 5th, and assumed that de Barras' squadron had already joined and was included in this total. Graves had had to destroy one of his own ships after the action; but two that had been incapacitated by his cruise and left at New York were in service again, two more were expected from Jamaica, and Admiral Digby was bringing three from England. These increments would bring the British line to twenty-five, which would have a chance against the supposed twenty-eight of the French. On the 23rd, however, arrived crushing news: de Barras had joined *after* the battle, Cornwallis reported, and de Grasse now had thirty-six.

In the weeks that followed, the naval commanders at New York squirmed and twisted to get around the stark arithmetic of reality. They promised Cornwallis to try to rescue him, but postponed the date of sailing over and over again. The dockyard, they said, was to blame; and certainly the government's failure to improve its facilities three years before was one factor in the delay. Another, just as certainly, was the admirals themselves. They faced a staggering problem. To rescue Cornwallis they would have to enter the Chesapeake in the face of a superior

fleet that was presumably ready and waiting, would have to
fight their way past it to the vicinity of Yorktown, embark
the army, and then somehow fight their way out again. Could
this be done? Clinton for one knew his *Macbeth*; perhaps the
others did.

> If we should fail,—
>
>   We fail!
> But screw your courage to the sticking place,
> And we'll not fail.

Yet Macbeth, in failing, had lost only his life; the anxious members of the councils of war stood to lose more than that. If they
sacrificed the one and only British fleet on that side of the Atlantic, Britain might lose Halifax, New York, Charleston, the
West Indies, her whole position in the western hemisphere.
Against the possibility of saving Cornwallis' army, in other
words, had to be balanced the probability of imperial catastrophe.

Digby had arrived on September 24. Instead of assuming the
command for which he had been commissioned he left it to
Graves, perhaps understandably, and remained in the background
throughout the crisis. Such influence as he had was negative,
for he considered rescue as a desperate undertaking. The only
admiral who pressed for action at any cost was Hood, who
fumed at the delays and did all he could to overcome them. "He
detest[s] the want of exertion he discovers now, and fears the
fleet will get to the Chesapeake too late." [26] But Graves seemed
to be in no hurry, and on him the chief responsibility rested.
He was acting, said General Robertson, as if he thought of himself as already ruined; and as late as October 11 he reopened the
question of whether to go at all. "You have engaged under your
hand to go before," Hood answered, "and tomorrow is the
day." [27] But tomorrow was not: still another week elapsed before
the ships were ready. The very day that the fleet sailed from
Sandy Hook, October 19, Cornwallis surrendered.

On that day a lot of naval chickens came home to roost.
Graves had blundered through the summer, blundered in his one

battle, and then taken a month to refit his ships. Digby had remained a spectator while events ran their course. Rodney had made fatal miscalculations in the West Indies and had then sailed for home. Arbuthnot had failed to dislodge the French from Rhode Island. Only Gambier, for lack of opportunity, had contributed little or nothing to the long chain of events that led to Yorktown. All the others had some measure of responsibility, whether their sins were of omission or commission.

But in a larger sense they were sinned against as well as sinning, for they were victims of a government that did not know how to prosecute a war. Lord North's administration never came to grips with the question that faced it from the spring of 1778 on, of how Britain should allocate her resources between the various theaters of operation. Trying to hold onto everything, once France and Spain intervened, was a recipe for failure, as the king realized at the start. "If we are to be carrying on a land war against the rebels and against those two powers, it must be feeble in all parts and consequently unsuccessful." [28] Yet for the next three and a half years Britain attempted not only to suppress the rebellion and protect all that she had elsewhere, but to make new conquests from the Bourbon powers. On the wisdom of this strategy North's colleagues were divided; and the division was particularly marked between the two ministers, Germain and Sandwich, who were most concerned with the war in America. After an abortive attempt at disengagement there, through the Carlisle Peace Commission, military operations were renewed and extended when Germain, intent on victory, encouraged Clinton to attack the south. But the prerequisite for victory was naval predominance, and Sandwich continued to treat the American theater as subsidiary. "Let not thy right hand know what thy left hand doeth."

Sandwich's attitude was revealed in the men he chose or permitted to command on the American station. About Gambier he presumably had no more illusions than any one else, or he would not have cold-shouldered him on his recall; yet the order of recall was not sent until months after it should have been.

By then selecting Arbuthnot, the first lord showed either his indifference to what happened on the station or a desire to put Clinton in his place, or conceivably both; no admiral could have been better calculated to rouse Sir Henry's hackles, and rousing them paralyzed the war effort. Graves was scant improvement as a commander-in-chief, but here Sandwich had no responsibility except as he may have contributed to the delay in Digby's appointment. As for Digby himself, he had only the negative distinction of refusing to exercise command. When all is said and done, the first lord bears a heavy share of blame for the quality of the flag officers who held the American post after Lord Howe relinquished it. Not one of them knew how to plan a campaign or win a battle.

Sandwich, and his underlings at the Admiralty, had an even heavier share of blame for the way in which the policy of detachment worked. Whether the policy itself was necessary because Britain was weak, or whether she could have done more than she did to blockade the Bourbon powers at home, is a question that has long been debated and can never be settled. But, assuming that blockade was not feasible, detachments could succeed only if they were sent at the right moment. A reinforcement that left too late, like Byron's in 1778 or Digby's in 1781, was doubly wasted: it weakened the home fleet and did not affect the outcome of the crisis overseas. Some delays were of course inevitable; the eighteenth-century bureaucratic machine was cumbersome and slow, and no amount of energy at home could avail against unfavorable winds in the Atlantic. In most cases, however, energy would have helped; and the place where it was most needed was at the top. If Germain had had the authority and prestige of Pitt in the Seven Years' War, officials and dockyards might not have made their preparations at such a dilatory pace. But Lord George had little influence over the closed preserve of the navy, and Sandwich did not have his heart in America.

The first lord was obsessed with the defense of the British Isles. This obsession, even more than the shortcomings of the administrative machinery, weakened the whole policy of detachment, which required daring quite as much as efficiency. Every ship detached from the Channel fleet to meet a danger abroad increased the danger of invasion at home, and the second danger was what Sandwich consistently emphasized. His stress upon it appeared as early as the spring of 1778, when d'Estaing sailed from Toulon, and reappeared throughout the war. Germain took the opposite position, that victory overseas would justify some insecurity in the Channel; here again, however, he had no control over the navy. "I think we have little to fear at home," he complained in the spring of 1780, "but Lord Sandwich will not risk this country upon any account, so that I apprehend we shall have some misfortunes abroad. . . ." [29] Refusal of all risk at home precluded, as Lord George implied, effective support abroad.

The ingredients of Britain's naval disaster off the Chesapeake, in summary, had long been present. One was a lamentable choice of men for the command. Another was the habit of sending reinforcements that were too little and too late. A third, and the most important, was the strategy of trying to hold onto everything while reaching for new gains. At the start of the international war in 1778 the government decided that Britain did not have the naval strength to assume the offensive; hence the policy of concentration in home waters. But this policy was not consistently implemented, and became as the years went by no policy at all. Clinton was permitted to scatter his armies along the American seaboard, relying on a naval superiority that by the summer of 1781 no longer existed; for by then British power in the Caribbean, which had risen and fallen erratically, was no longer adequate for the defense of North America. Planning at the Admiralty had become a patchwork of expedients. The enemy concerted one brilliant blow, and the patchwork fell apart.

FOOTNOTES

1. William M. James, *The British Navy in Adversity: a Study of the War of Independence* (New York, 1926). This book is more descriptive than analytical; the best critical evaluation of the factors in Britain's naval defeat is still, in my opinion, the final chapter of

Alfred T. Mahan's classic, *The Influence of Sea Power upon History, 1660–1783* (24th ed., Boston, 1914), pp. 505–41.

2. Historical Manuscripts Commission, *Report on Manuscripts in Various Collections* (8 vols., London, 1901–14), VI, p. 145. This section of the report is a calendar of the papers of William Knox, Germain's secretary; the originals are in the Clements Library of the University of Michigan.

3. See Piers Mackesy, *The War for America, 1775–1783* (Cambridge, Mass., 1964), pp. 20–24, 180–81.

4. A recent biography of Sandwich attempts to defend him in the teeth of historical opinion: George Martelli, *Jemmy Twitcher: a Life of the Fourth Earl of Sandwich, 1718–1792* (London, 1962). The author treats incompetent admirals as a cross that the first lord had to bear, rather than one for which he was responsible, and claims that his calamitous strategy succeeded. For a more balanced view see Mackesy, *op. cit.*, especially pp. 165–68, 175–76, 204. 308–09, 442.

5. Gambier to Clinton, November 13, 1778, Clinton Papers, Clements Library. See also William B. Willcox, *Portrait of a General: Sir Henry Clinton in the War of Independence* (New York, 1964), p. 214 fn. 3; Willcox, "British Strategy in America, 1778," *Journal of Modern History,* XIX (June, 1947), p. 104 and fns. 13–14; Mackesy, *op. cit.*, pp. 156, 285, 356, 400. Much of the material that follows is drawn from my *Portrait of a General,* which I cite only to document direct quotations.

6. G. R. Barnes and J. H. Owen, eds., *The Private Papers of John, Earl of Sandwich, First Lord of the Admiralty, 1771–1782* (4 vols., [London], 1932–38; Navy Records Society Publications, LXIX, LXXI, LXXV, LXXVIII), II, p. 39; see also pp. 40–41.

7. *Ibid.*, II, pp. 292–93; Willcox, *Portrait of a General,* pp. 229, 254 fn. 2; Mackesy, *op. cit.*, p. 219, fn. 1.

8. To Clinton, Nos. 1 and 2, August 27, 1778, largely printed in Willcox, *Portrait of a General,* pp. 249–50.

9. Barnes and Owen, *op. cit.*, II, pp. 318, 314; see also pp. 293–301, 304–06, 308–10, 312–13, 315–19, and Gambier [to William Eden], December 24, 1778, Benjamin F. Stevens, ed., *Facsimiles of Manuscripts in European Archives Relating to America, 1773–1783* (25 vols., London, 1889–98), XII, No. 1232. Gambier's complaints flowed across the Atlantic in an endless stream: his force did not deserve the name; he was reduced to flying his flag in a storeship; he was desperately short of frigates, the whole fleet was in a shocking state, and the dockyards were bare of supplies for

refitting; the Americans had a formidable naval force at Boston
and were building in every harbor and inlet. If reinforcements did
not come by spring, in short, disaster threatened.

10. Willcox, *Portrait of a General*, pp. 271–72.

11. New York Public Library: William Smith, MS. Diary, entries of
    February 4 and 9, 1779; Isaac Ogden to Joseph Galloway, March 8,
    1779, Balch's Loyalist Letters, Bancroft Transcripts. For the Og-
    den reference I am indebted to my fellow contributor, Mr. Ira
    Gruber.

12. September 29, 1779, Public Record Office, C.O. 5/130/469–71,
    partly printed in Willcox, *Portrait of a General*, p. 274 fn. 6.

13. To the Duke of Newcastle, July 3, 1779, Clinton Papers, Clements
    Library. Howe was at the time under serious consideration for the
    Admiralty: Mackesy, *op. cit.*, pp. 244, 246.

14. Willcox, *Portrait of a General*, pp. 311, 319.

15. *Ibid.*, p. 325; see also pp. 308–09, 323–37.

16. *Ibid.*, p. 333 and the reference there to Clinton's memoirs (n. 8,
    AR). A year later the ineffable Commodore Johnstone behaved in
    the same way at the Cape of Good Hope; see Mackesy, *op. cit.*,
    p. 390.

17. Arbuthnot considered Germain his friend and benefactor, and ac-
    cording to rumor in New York, Lord George encouraged him to
    hold onto his post in order to force Sir Henry's resignation. Willcox,
    Portrait of a General, p. 400 and fn. 7; see also pp. 360–70.

18. G[eorge] Damer to Germain, March 26, 1781, Germain Papers,
    Clements Library, partly printed in Historical Manuscripts Com-
    mission, *Report on the Manuscripts of Mrs. Stopford-Sackville, of
    Drayton House, Northamptonshire* (2 vols., London, 1904–10),
    II, p. 207. See also Arbuthnot to Germain, March 21, 1781, Ger-
    main Papers, and Willcox, *Portrait of a General*, p. 376 and fn. 8.

19. Clinton [to William Eden], filed under July 4, 1781, Clinton
    Papers, Clements Library.

20. William Smith Diary, New York Public Library, entry of Decem-
    ber 17, 1780.

21. Mackesy, *op. cit.*, pp. 421, 452.

22. Willcox, *Portrait of a General*, p. 415.

23. Rodney later claimed, quite erroneously, that he had urged Graves
    to meet the reinforcement in the Chesapeake. *Ibid.*, p. 412; French
    E. Chadwick, ed., *The Graves Papers and Other Documents Relat-
    ing to the Naval Operations of the Yorktown Campaign, July to
    October, 1781* (Navy History Society Publications, VII; New
    York, 1916), p. 136, fn.

24. In March the French had captured the *Romulus,* a heavy British frigate, which they pressed into service in their line.

25. Graves expected the signal for close action to take precedence over that for line ahead, according to a recent writer, and was trying to order a slanting attack in line of bearing; his captains, however, had learned in the West Indies that the signal for line ahead overrode the other. He generously put no blame upon them, and explained to Clinton and to Sandwich that the indecisive result had been due to the signal book. But he never explained why he had not clarified his purpose in advance, as Nelson did before the battle of the Nile with captains whom he knew far better. See Richard W. Hale, Jr., "New Light on the Naval Side of Yorktown," Massachusetts Historical Society *Proceedings,* LXXI (for 1953–57; Boston, 1959), pp. 123–32; Willcox, *Portrait of a General,* p. 424, fn. 4; Mackesy, *op. cit.,* pp. 423–24.

26. William Smith Diary, New York Public Library, entry of October 10, 1781.

27. *Ibid.,* entry of October 13, 1781; see also Willcox, *Portrait of a General,* pp. 434, 436.

28. February, 1778, *ibid.,* p. 207. Sandwich said much the same thing. "We are upon the point of a war with France, and perhaps with Spain," he wrote in April, 1778; "an American war added thereto is, I fear, more than we are equal to." Barnes and Owen, *op. cit.,* II, p. 293.

29. Willcox, *Portrait of a General,* p. 214; for Sandwich's role in the naval crisis in the spring of 1778 see Gerald S. Brown, *The American Secretary: the Colonial Policy of Lord George Germain, 1775–1778* (Ann Arbor, 1963), pp. 154–70. "This country, with such numerous enemies, must be ruined unless what we want of strength is made up in activity and resolution," the king wrote Sandwich in 1781. "Caution has certainly made this war less brilliant than the former; and if that alone is to direct our operations . . . it is easy to tell we must be great losers." (Quoted by Mackesy, *op. cit.,* p. 399; see also his quotation of Middleton's views, p. 448.) The danger of a full-scale French invasion of England was real to contemporaries, particularly during the great scare of 1779; but by hindsight their fears seem wildly exaggerated. Vergennes had no such idea. The logistical problem alone would have been gargantuan; and the Franco-Spanish fleet, even if the Royal Navy had not existed, was in no condition to hold the Channel for the time that would have been required. See Mackesy, *op. cit.,* pp. 194, 279–97, 307–09, 514.

BIBLIOGRAPHY

Barnes, G. R., and Owen, J. H., eds. *The Private Papers of John, Earl of Sandwich, First Lord of the Admiralty, 1771–1782*, 4 vols., Navy Records Society Publications, LXIX, LXXI, LXXV, LXXVIII. London, 1932–38. The principal collection of source material on the making of naval policy during the war. The papers are arranged chronologically, and the later volumes contain a large number of letters to Sandwich from Gambier, Arbuthnot, and Graves.

Beatson, Robert. *Naval and Military Memoirs of Great Britain, from 1727–1783*, 2nd ed., 6 vols. London, 1804. A work published so soon after the War of Independence that it is almost a primary source. It contains a great deal of useful material, particularly about naval operations.

Chadwick, French E., ed. *The Graves Papers and Other Documents Relating to the Naval Operations of the Yorktown Campaign, July to October, 1781,* Navy History Society Publications, VII. New York, 1916. This and the Sandwich Papers are the two major collections of printed source material on the British side of the naval campaign of 1781, and the editor's introduction is extremely valuable for an understanding of Graves.

Clinton, Henry. *The American Rebellion: Sir Henry Clinton's Narrative of His Campaigns, 1775–1782, with an Appendix of Original Documents,* William B. Willcox, ed., Yale historical publications, manuscripts and edited texts, XXI. New Haven, 1954. The appendix contains some letters from Gambier and Graves and a large number from Arbuthnot, though often merely excerpts. In the text Sir Henry describes at length his quarrel with Arbuthnot, and the formal language only partly veils his bias and bitterness.

Clowes, William L., ed. *The Royal Navy: a History from the Earliest Times to the Present,* 7 vols. London, 1897–1903. Still the standard large-scale naval history. The chapters on the War of Independence are by Alfred T. Mahan, and are much more detailed than his *Influence of Sea Power*.

James, William M. *The British Navy in Adversity: A Study of the War of Independence*. New York, 1926. The only book specifically on the subject, and valuable as a survey of the campaigns rather than for its judgments upon them.

Mackesy, Piers. *The War for America, 1775–1783.* Cambridge, Mass., 1964. An excellent discussion of the British war effort in all its aspects, the product of thorough research and balanced judgment. The author is particularly skillful in relating broad governmental policies to specific operations, and in bringing out the administrative difficulties and the paucity of resources that underlay Britain's clumsy war-making.

Mahan, Alfred T. *The Influence of Sea Power upon History, 1660–1783*. 24th ed., Boston, 1914. Chapters IX through XIV deal with the War of Independence in various theaters. Much of the presentation has been rendered obsolete by later research, but the final chapter is still a stimulating critique of the strategy employed by both sides.

Willcox, William B. *Portrait of a General: Sir Henry Clinton in the War of Independence*. New York, 1964. A survey, with Clinton for its focus, of the whole American war, from which the bulk of the material for this article is drawn.

Sir Samuel Hood:

SUPERIOR SUBORDINATE

DANIEL A. BAUGH

Princeton University

FEW British admirals involved in the Revolutionary War managed to survive without a loss of reputation. Samuel Hood was
one of the few. Not that he became a naval hero: the fortunes of
war failed to favor him with a great victory. But his decisions
and actions in combat revealed the mind and spirit of a great
admiral. When Hood retired from active service, Horatio Nelson
judged him "the best officer, take him altogether, that England
has to boast of; equally great in all situations which an admiral
can be placed in." [1]

By temperament Hood was a man of action: "I never knew
good to come from procrastination." [2] His decisiveness arose
from a justifiable confidence he had in his professional knowledge and the great care with which he analyzed every strategic
situation. Hood always understood that the enemy's difficulties
might be greater than his own; this assumption freed him from
the fears that often paralyze a commander and render him
powerless to take bold action.

The vigor and clarity of Hood's thought were matched by
his plain, blunt manner of speaking. This behavior frequently
led to rough encounters with his superiors, but at the same time
inspired loyalty in his subordinates. Hood was also esteemed by
his colleagues because of an unselfish attitude toward his own

career. To a degree quite rare in the Royal Navy, Hood refused to allow self-interest to interfere with his country's interest. This dedication was so unusual at the time that one is led to wonder from whence it came.

Like Horatio Nelson, Samuel Hood was a clergyman's son. He was born on December 12, 1724, at Butleigh, Somersetshire. Although his father was the village vicar and the family respectable, Hood possessed neither the connections nor the wealth necessary for a promising naval career. Most officers who wound up at the top in the eighteenth-century navy—and Nelson was no exception—were closely related to some person of influence; the upper ranks were filled with sons and nephews of admirals, captains, leading politicians, naval officials, and, of course, landed aristocrats. Hood began his career in 1741 at the age of sixteen, when he and his brother, Alexander, went on board the *Romney* to serve under Captain Thomas Smith. Tradition has it that the Hood brothers were introduced accidentally to Captain Smith when he stayed the night at Butleigh vicarage while en route to Plymouth. But it is almost certain that the introduction came through the Grenville family instead. Smith knew the Grenvilles well; Thomas Grenville was his first lieutenant at the time, and James Grenville had recently become the chief landowner in Butleigh parish.[3]

Like hundreds of other aspiring young candidates who had had a remote introduction to a leading political family, Hood received negligible support from his connection. Although the Grenvilles were influential and immersed in the factional struggles within Parliament, they had other more important protégés to look after. Later on, when Hood had acquired some status in the service, the Grenville family might have welcomed him. But he was never destined to come within the family's orbit or to acquire the attitudes that such a move would have implied. That he did not do so must be credited, in part, to the influence of Captain Smith, his superior.

Smith, the illegitimate son of Sir Thomas Lyttelton, was in many ways an unusual officer. Well-educated, unaffected, generous, and honest, he made scarcely any enemies. Although Smith understood the importance of powerful friends and political connections, he rarely allowed such considerations to guide his behavior. He relied, instead, upon performing good and faithful service. Staying clear of factions, he managed, nevertheless, to find friends everywhere and eventually to rise to flag rank. This lesson was not lost on Samuel Hood. Although Hood was -not endowed with the easy manner and personal charm that had made Smith's course so easy, he followed a similar pattern in his own career.

At the outset, Hood needed help in the service. Unlike young men who could count on well-placed friends ashore to gain promotions for them, Hood was dependent on his mentor at sea. Under these circumstances, it was assumed that if Smith valued Hood, he would do his best to advance the young officer. And indeed, after serving out his required six years of apprenticeship at sea under Captains Smith, Thomas Grenville, and George Rodney, Hood was assigned to a squadron commanded by Smith and promptly promoted to lieutenant. His promotion came in 1746 and was not difficult to arrange because Britain was at war. Once peace came in 1748, however, Hood's prospects dimmed. The navy reverted to a peacetime footing and officers were discharged in droves.

Hood soon was cast ashore. In 1749 he married Susannah Linzee, the daughter of an important figure in Portsmouth politics. Married, and in his late twenties, he was understandably concerned about his future. Unless he could gain a promotion to captain and thus take post on the seniority list, a naval career would hardly prove worthwhile. There was no regular path of advancement from lieutenant to captain. To rise he would have to secure a command, and such an appointment would have to be made either by the Admiralty or by a commander-in-chief at sea (who had the power to fill vacancies). But in peacetime any employment was hard to get, let alone a post that would bring promotion.

Hood, however, was better off than most lieutenants. His education and manners were a cut above the average. More important, he had Smith's valuable support, and Smith, now an admiral, considered Hood "one of the foremost" of his protégés. Hood, in addition, was helped by his intimate connection with the Linzees of Portsmouth, who, though not to be ranked with the great families, could claim a modest measure of influence in the navy. Hood, therefore, did not remain unemployed for long. In 1753 he was assigned aboard a guardship in Portsmouth harbor. Although the post enabled him to be with his family and to serve with full instead of half pay, it was hardly a step toward professional advancement. He still yearned for a command and promotion.[4]

Hood thought for a time he might be assigned to the East Indies, but his first opportunity came from the other side of the world. The captain of the sloop *Jamaica* stationed at Charleston, South Carolina, was reported to be near death's door early in 1754. All in all there were enough possibilities for Hood to feel that at last he had "some chance of being a captain." Both his father-in-law and Smith were working hard in his behalf, and to strengthen his hand further Hood asked Sir Richard Lyttelton, who was very close to Lord Anson, the first lord, to "throw in a word." Despite the help of influential friends, Hood remained anxious. He feared, above all, that his connection with Portsmouth politics might do more harm than good and wrote to Smith: "All my friends here (as well as myself) are afraid his Lordship wants to put me off till after the election, and then will not do it unless Mr. Linzee will do everything he wants in regard to making aldermen. If so all will be over with me."[5] Political influence, Hood knew, could be a sword that cut two ways.

Whether Anson would have helped Hood will never be known. When Henry Pelham, the kingpin of the Ministry, died in the spring of 1754, Hood predicted that the resulting confusion might bring Smith's relations "more in play"; indeed, within three years the Pitts, Grenvilles, and Lytteltons were scattered throughout the top echelons of government.[6] One consequence of Pelham's death was the elevation of George Grenville to the treasurership of the navy, and shortly thereafter Hood received command of the *Jamaica*. Before the end of June, he said good-by to his wife ("my Susy") and sailed for America. "The parting was very severe," he wrote to Smith, "I did not think it would have affected me so much, but I find I love my sweet wench better than I thought for." [7]

Command of the *Jamaica* gave Hood the rank of master and commander, and he remained with the vessel for two years. In Charleston he was treated with great "civility and respect by all the best of the people" and admitted that if the assignment did not prove happy, it would be his own fault. Had peace continued, Hood hoped to bring his wife over, and wrote he would "then be happy indeed." But a war was brewing between the British and French in America, and Hood welcomed the coming conflict with enthusiasm and optimism.[8] Soon after war was officially declared, he received his promotion to captain. He took post on July 22, 1756, one month after his brother. Considering that peace had interrupted his career, Samuel had done quite well to rise to the rank of captain at the age of thirty-one.

Returning to England later in the year, Hood was eager for action. He wrote to Richard Grenville, now Lord Temple and head of the Admiralty Board, saying he was "no ways inclined to be idle" if a good command could be had. All he received at first, however, were temporary assignments. In the spring of 1757, he commanded three ships in rapid succession. In the third, the *Antelope*, he had an opportunity to demonstrate his ability. With considerable skill he drove the French frigate *Aquilon* ashore off the coast of Brittany, leaving her a total wreck. On this cruise, he also captured a small prize and a privateer. He fought so well that the Admiralty gave him a permanent command of the *Bideford*. Subsequently, he was promoted to the *Vestal*, a frigate of 32 guns. Once again he had occasion to distinguish himself. While en route to America in early 1759 the *Vestal* overtook a French frigate, the *Bellona*, also 32 guns, off Cape Finisterre, and after a three-hour battle forced her to surrender. Hood stayed with the *Vestal* for the rest of the war. After earning Rodney's praise for his conduct at the bombardment of Le Havre, he requested duty in the Mediterranean and spent three rather inactive years there.[9]

Although his benefactor, Admiral Thomas Smith, died in 1762, Samuel Hood hardly needed his help any more. He was well established, both socially and professionally. The same could be said of his brother. In 1758, Alexander married Maria West, a woman of position and wealth. It might be assumed that the 31-year-old Alexander took a 54-year-old bride for advancement rather than for love, but apparently such was not the case. Two years after the wedding, Lord Lyttelton reported: ". . . they live together like Celadon and Astraea in the first week of their marriage. He told me yesterday in a rapture that she was a *glorious girl*. Is not this a glorious proof of the power of Cupid? If a girl of fifty-six be loved at this rate, think what the charms of forty may do."

Alexander's marriage proved to be professionally valuable to Samuel. Maria West was intimate with the Lytteltons and also close to Hester (Grenville) Pitt, wife of the great William Pitt. The Pitts often stayed at Alexander Hood's house in London, and when their youngest son, James, chose a career at sea, he served part of his apprenticeship under Samuel.[10]

Samuel Hood was made commander-in-chief of the naval force in North American waters in 1767—an assignment that many captains had coveted. Although his base originally was to have been Halifax, rioting New Englanders forced him to spend a good bit of time at Boston in 1768 and 1769. His small force, ordinarily employed against smugglers, soon was called upon to transport troops to Boston. Hood himself was in favor of such coercive measures. In view of the colonial reaction to Parliament's revenue acts, he thought it "prudent and necessary" to be strong. Indeed, after the spirit of resistance spread to other colonies, he concluded that it had been a great error not to have shown more firmness in Boston right from the start. He abhorred the "rancorous and dangerous" revolutionary principles that were rapidly spreading among the Americans.[11]

The Admiralty's policy was to relieve commanders in time of peace every three years, and in 1770 Hood was replaced by Gambier. Before he relinquished his command, however, he raised one of his wife's brothers, John Linzee, to the rank of master and commander, and another, Robert Linzee, to captain.[12] Preferment for his relatives was about the only reward that Hood received from this tour of duty in American waters.

Returning to England, Hood enjoyed, once again, the comforts of guardship duty for a time. He established his household at Catherington, near Horndean, Hampshire, and traveled ten miles to work at Portsmouth. But in 1776 the years of inactivity came to an end. The Admiralty, in November, ordered the mobilization of all guardships, and Hood received orders to raise his ship, the *Courageux*, to full complement and to prepare for sea. Throughout most of the following year, he cruised in the Channel, protecting British merchantmen and trying to prevent French ships from carrying supplies to America. It was not an appropriate assignment for a 74-gun ship like the *Courageux*, but most of the frigates and sloops were employed elsewhere and the Admiralty had no other choice.[13]

By early 1778 it was fairly clear that war with France was imminent. Hood must have been aware of the possibility of a coming conflict and to have realized the great opportunities that war would bring to an officer of his rank. Nevertheless, on February 10, he discharged himself from the *Courageux*, resigned from sea service, and took up civilian employment as resident commissioner of the Royal Navy at Portsmouth Dockyard.[14]

Why did Hood leave the service at such a critical time? He later said he took the step not "from inclination," but "from a desire of giving accommodation to Government" in general and to Lord Sandwich in particular.[15] However, he probably had other personal reasons. His choice was between ambition and risk, on one hand, and ease and security, on the other. For the moment, he chose the latter. He was fifty-three, had fears for his health, and needed money. Moreover, the location of his civilian assignment was ideal. It is important to realize that Hood did not think he had irrevocably given up a career at sea; otherwise he might not have accepted the commissionership. Many officers in the past had taken up civilian employment in the navy and subsequently returned to active service without losing rank. Admittedly, it was risky to seek such employment in wartime, but Hood had not solicited the post he held. Moreover, although hostilities with the American colonists were underway, a major war involving European powers had not yet begun.[16]

As Britain prepared for such a war, Hood's thinking changed. The first months on his new job were marked by feverish activity as the navy plunged into full-scale mobilization. In May, the king himself visited Portsmouth Dockyard. "On quitting the carriage," George III wrote to his sons, "I instantly took every step necessary to quicken the sailing part of the fleet, and trust my directions will expedite the service." [17] The king's visit, no doubt, complicated Hood's administrative duties, but it carried also a reward. George III concluded that Hood was an officer who knew his business and granted him a baronetcy.

Hood now could not help looking at his career from a new perspective. He was Sir Samuel, an officer who was favorably noticed by the king. With a major war brewing, he indicated he was still available for sea service. "I think my Lord," he wrote to Lord North in June, 1778, "I may . . . say, that as an *officer* I stand fair & have good pretensions." At the same time, he took pains to avoid identifying himself with the Pitts and Grenvilles, who were members of the Opposition, and told North that not only in public business, but also "as a *private man*" he had "given great support" to the Ministry.[18]

Despite his change of heart, Hood was forced to stay on in the dockyard for the next two years. In the spring of 1780, he made another determined effort to get back to sea. The war had speeded up promotions, and Hood's name on the seniority list was reaching those who were close to being considered as rear admirals. Hood said he had "the mortification of seeing . . .

juniors placed in the road to glory and preferred to distinguished appointments." Writing to Lord Sandwich, he expressed his "very great desire of hoisting [his] flag and serving in the military line." [19] When his pleas got no results, Hood became impatient. He was irritated by the way he was being ignored by the first lord, but a friend told him that the king had good intentions toward him and advised Hood to be calm and to await further developments.[20] On September 16, 1780, a letter finally arrived from the Admiralty asking him whether—if there was a promotion of admirals—he would take his flag and go to the West Indies.[21] It was the chance of a lifetime, but surprisingly enough Hood turned it down.

Hood's excuse was ill health. His "stomack & Bowels" had given him some "very ugly" and alarming pains, and he claimed he had only a "short time" to live. Two days later, however, he wrote to Lord Sandwich that he was feeling much better, was eager to accept his flag, and hoped his offer had not come too late. And two days after that, on September 20, he reported that he was as "stout and well" as could be expected. All in all it had been a rather miraculous recovery.[22] In truth, to plead ill health was the conventional means by which officers refused assignments which they did not want or which were offered under circumstances they considered distasteful. To refuse on any other ground was to risk losing one's rank and half pay.

Why did Hood initially turn down an offer he plainly wanted? The evidence suggests that he was upset by Sandwich's handling of the Keppel-Palliser affair. The prejudiced manner in which the first lord dealt with the court-martial arising from Keppel's actions in the battle of Ushant cost the Royal Navy a number of fine officers who refused to serve. Samuel Hood came close to being one of them.

Unlike most of the discontented officers, who were shocked by the manner in which Sandwich used his powers as first lord to support Admiral Palliser, Hood was apparently upset by Sandwich's treatment of his brother. Alexander Hood had commanded the *Robust* in the battle of Ushant. Even before the court-martial, it was widely known that Alexander was partial to Palliser and "very adverse" to Admiral Keppel. When testimony revealed that Alexander Hood had altered his ship's log in such a way as to favor Palliser's case, the reaction was intense,[23] and he was *"sent to Coventry"* by his fellow officers.[24] He found himself, as his wife later remarked, "absolutely without support from any person whatever." [25] Even Sandwich abandoned him. The first lord had gone too far, and, eventually finding his position threatened, chose to wreck Palliser's career to save himself; it is not surprising, therefore, that he also turned his back on the unpopular Alexander Hood.[26]

Of Samuel Hood's private thoughts concerning his brother's conduct there is no record. It appears, however, that in his own deliberate way Samuel kept trying to help Alexander—even though his efforts were not always appreciated. Alexander in his bitterness over being denied preferment wanted Samuel to throw his influence at Portsmouth against the Admiralty and the government in the event of an election. But Samuel was not a man to plunge recklessly into opposition. There must be "some degree of consistency," he told his brother; Samuel had supported the Ministry in the past and must continue to do so. He agreed, nevertheless, to be "very strong and pointed" in discussing Alexander's position with those in power.[27]

Samuel's efforts in this regard were the most likely reason for his sudden change of mind in September, 1780. Alexander's name was slightly above Samuel's on the seniority list, and Samuel may have refused his flag on the assumption that his brother had been passed over for promotion. Either his assumption was incorrect or his letter did the trick, for the two brothers were promoted to rear admiral on the same date. Shortly thereafter Samuel hoisted his flag in the *Barfleur*, and by January, 1781, was in the West Indies with Admiral Sir George Rodney.

Because Hood was a junior flag officer during the American war, he performed nearly all his service as second-in-command. Like many other energetic men placed in a similar situation, he had trouble getting along with his superiors. His first commander-in-chief, however, would have been a challenge to any-one. Rodney, ambitious and temperamental, inspired little loyalty and was quick to suspect infidelity or hostility in others. Sand-wich promised Rodney that he would not send him a "factious person" as second-in-command. The immediate cause of Hood's assignment, in fact, arose from the inability of the Admiralty to find a suitable replacement for Rodney's previous second-in-command, Hyde Parker, who had resigned in anger when Rod-ney blamed the poor conduct of the battle of Martinique on his subordinates.[28] Hood was not factious and, indeed, had known Rodney since 1744 when he served under him as a midshipman. But the two men never were able to work out a compatible rela-tionship.

For one thing, they were of an entirely different temperament. Hood had an orderly mind; it was his habit to think things through and anticipate difficulties. He felt that a man in a position of responsibility should act according to some "rational well di-gested plan"; men with "no method" were useless. "What a misfortune it is," he wrote to his close friend, Sir Charles Middle-ton, "to have anything to do with men who are guided by whim and caprice, instead of common sense!" [29] In sizing up Rodney, Hood saw a man who admittedly had brilliance and imagina-tion, but no taste for orderly planning. His superior, Hood wrote, was a man whose manner of talking was "very extrava-gant and extraordinary, but without much meaning," and whose "unsteadiness" was such that he appeared to change his mind every hour. Rodney appeared to be "governed by whim and caprice, even in matters of the highest importance to the welfare of the State." "[He] requires a monitor constantly at his elbow, as much as a froward child." [30] Hood felt also that Rodney was vain and more concerned with the impression he was making than with winning the war.

One naval historian has claimed that Hood detested and hated Rodney.[31] This impression is not quite correct. It was rather that he mistrusted Rodney, and in this matter he was not alone.[32] Whatever Hood thought of Rodney, however, he was never insubordinate; he argued and grumbled, but did as he was ordered. Rodney, on his part, acknowledged that Hood was as competent to command a squadron as himself.[33]

In February, 1781, within a month after his arrival in the West Indies, Hood was in command of a squadron and charged with a major responsibility. His task was to intercept a French squadron that had been spotted in the Bay of Biscay and was presumed to be bound for Martinique with urgently needed supplies under convoy. Both Hood and Rodney realized the possible consequences of failure to intercept these ships: the approaching French squadron, when joined with the six vessels already at Martinique, might outnumber the British force. If so, the initiative in the Caribbean would pass to the enemy.

Hood felt that every available ship should immediately be pressed into service. Therefore, he urged Rodney to take over the command off Martinique and to bring together all the ships in the area. But Rodney was too busy counting the riches recently captured at St. Eustatius. Because, as Hood commented, "The Lures of St. Eustatius were so bewitching as not to be withstood by flesh and blood," [34] he held operational command off Martinique from February to April. But Hood held it without liberty to station his ships as he chose.

The prevailing wind blows toward the Lesser Antilles from the east or northeast with great consistency, and its effect is reinforced by a current which moves from east to west at one to two knots. Thus the line of approach of any fleet destined for Martinique was fairly predictable: the French could vary their landfall in order to avoid interception, but not to any great extent. What Hood could not predict with much confidence was the size of the French force and the time it would arrive. Weighing the situation, he decided that the best place for his fleet was to windward of Martinique. Initially he cruised about forty miles northeast of the island with his frigates spread out still farther to windward. By mid-March, however, it appeared that the original intelligence reports were false. Rodney thereupon ordered Hood to bring his squadron to leeward into the channel between Martinique and St. Lucia, and Hood reluctantly obeyed.

Rodney's change of plan was influenced by a number of considerations. He wanted to keep the six French warships at Martinique bottled up so that they could not threaten the rich convoy he was planning to send home from St. Eustatius. At the same time he wanted to blockade the island, which was known to be desperately in need of supplies. Moreover, when the arrival of the French squadron no longer seemed imminent, the problem of refreshing Hood's men and supplying his ships with water, victuals, and stores had to be faced; if his squadron cruised to leeward of Martinique the ships could be refreshed at St. Lucia one by one.

Hood tried hard to reverse his chief's decision. He considered the interception of the French squadron and its convoy to be of overwhelming importance. For this reason, he believed that the only sensible British station was to the windward side of the island. Against Rodney's view that the interception could be made from leeward, Hood argued: "Should an enemy's fleet attempt to get into Martinique, and the commander of it inclines to avoid a battle, nothing but a *skirmish* will probably happen, which, in its *consequences* may operate as a defeat to the British squadron, though not a ship is lost and the enemy suffer most." Hood, like Rodney, assumed that the original intelligence reports had been wrong, but he was sure that the French squadron would appear ultimately. His plan was to refresh his squadron at St. Lucia in a body—running the risk that the French would arrive in the interim—and then to return to the windward station. The French squadron, he estimated, would be "numerous, probably twenty," and he urged Rodney to send from St. Eustatius any ships that could be spared. But Rodney held Hood to leeward and refused to reinforce him.[35]

Hood's predictions turned out to be correct. Blockading Martinique exhausted his ships, for it proved impossible to refresh them adequately one by one. Scurvy increased alarmingly, and victuals and stores ran low. When the French squadron of 21 ships of the line, accompanying a large convoy, was sighted off the southeastern tip of the island, Hood's force was by no means in the best condition for combat.

Admiral de Grasse, who commanded the French force, cautiously anchored on the windward side of the island. Hood, having been alerted by his frigates, spent the night working his fleet up against the wind. On the morning of the 29th, the French squadron, formed in a line of battle, came around the southern end of the island, and shielded the merchant vessels, which kept near the shore. Hood took his 18 ships southward on a port tack, sailing as close to the wind as possible. The French rounded Diamond Rock heading north, while Hood tacked back and forth in a fruitless effort to close the distance. With the two fleets cannonading one another at long range, the French storeships gained the safety of Fort Royal harbor. At noon Hood gave up trying to move closer by tacking and brought his squadron to a standstill; as he wrote later: ". . . finding it impossible to get up to the enemy's fleet, I invited it to come to me." But de Grasse kept his distance.

When the contest was renewed the next day, the terms were no longer the same. Some of the British ships had been damaged and the French line now numbered 24 as the ships at Fort Royal joined de Grasse's fleet. Hood had to be wary. He attempted to take advantage of some capricious breezes to bring a portion of the French squadron to action, but at length decided the risks were too great and ran away to leeward. The French for a time gave chase, but in sailing before the wind they could not keep up with Hood's copper-bottomed ships.[36]

Hearing news of the French arrival, Rodney raced to join Hood, but it was too late. The initiative had passed to the French. While the British made repairs, took on supplies, and tried to refresh their crews at Antigua, the French launched expeditions against St. Lucia and Tobago. St. Lucia was saved by the fortunate arrival of three ships that had been cruising independently in the area. But Tobago was lost—largely because most of the

British squadron had to retire to Barbados to restore the health of the men who had cruised so long under Hood's command.[37]

At the end of May, with the hurricane season approaching, both sides began to prepare for the annual move to North American waters. De Grasse refitted at Martinique, went to Cap Français for a time, and then sailed on to North America. Rodney was directed by his orders to follow the French north with an equivalent force and to leave behind enough ships to defend the islands. Since Rodney had been told not to expect any reinforcements, he faced an impossible task. He correctly decided to leave the islands exposed; assigned two ships to convoy the homeward-bound trade; sent another to Jamaica for repairs; and selected a fourth to carry him home to England. The rest of the force, 14 of the line, he handed over to Hood with orders to proceed to North American waters. There was reason to think this diminished squadron, when joined with the ships at New York, would be sufficient to deal with de Grasse, for it was assumed that he would detach a substantial force to convoy home the French merchant vessels. But de Grasse left the French merchantmen sitting at Cap Français and took his full force, 28 ships of the line, to the American mainland.[38]

Hood sailed from the West Indies on August 10. His task was to locate de Grasse and, if possible, join with Admiral Graves in hopes of giving battle to one of the French squadrons—either de Grasse's or the one commanded by de Barras which lay in Narragansett Bay—before they managed to link forces. He made a good passage, and though he did not know it, beat de Grasse to the American coast. After looking into the Chesapeake and finding no sign of the French, he hurried on to New York, where he found Admiral Thomas Graves on August 28. Graves sent pilots to guide Hood's ships into the harbor for replenishing, but Hood was appalled at the thought of any such delay. He refused to enter the harbor, took a boat ashore, and in a conference persuaded his new commander-in-chief to put to sea immediately in search of the French.[39] Three days later, a British squadron of 19 ships of the line sailed for the Chesapeake, where on the morning of September 5 they found de Grasse coming out of the bay to meet them with 24. It was Hood's sense of urgency that brought the British squadron to the right place at the right time. The stage was set for the battle of the Virginia Capes.

The British had fewer ships, and most of their officers were not accustomed to working under Graves. Nevertheless, at the start of the battle the British enjoyed certain advantages. The wind was NNE on the starboard quarter as they bore down in line toward the bay entrance. They were coming upon an enemy hurriedly getting underway and struggling to form a line of battle. In fact, the van of the emerging French fleet was well ahead and to windward of the rest. It was this tactical situation that led Hood to comment after the battle that "the British fleet had a rich and most delightful harvest of glory presented to it, but omitted to gather it in more instances than one." Hood thought that at least three opportunities presented themselves for concentrating the full force of the squadron upon the exposed French van.[40] But such a thought never seems to have entered Graves' mind. As Graves neared the enemy van, instead of attacking he waited. In fact, Graves "brought to [stopped] in order to let the centre of the enemy's ships come abreast." [41]

What Graves had in mind was the standard form of eighteenth-century naval engagement: an exchange of broadsides with two lines of ships sailing parallel on the same course. His problem was a long-standing one for an attacking fleet—how to bring ships down close to the enemy without disordering the line or exposing the fleet to serious damage. There were two standard methods of attack. His line could slant down in column and each ship, upon reaching the proper distance for close engagement, could bear up parallel to the enemy. This method had the advantage of keeping the line tight and in good order; it was safer, moreover, because it afforded more certain mutual support. But this method had certain inherent disadvantages: the slowness with which the whole force was brought into action; and the possibility that the line might jam up if the leading ships lost

speed and maneuverability as a result of damage to their upper-
works, thus interrupting or halting the attack underway. The
other method was to signal a close engagement—that is to order
all ships to bear down simultaneously on the enemy line, each
seeking its opposite number. The advantage here was speed and
the certainty of bringing the whole force into action; the disadvantage being the possible confusion and disorder which might
lead to separation and losses.[42] Graves decided to attack in column. By 3:45 in the afternoon, however, it seemed that the distance was closing too slowly and he gave the signal for close engagement. In response to this signal the whole squadron should
have turned toward the enemy, but it did not. The reason was
that the signal for maintaining the line also continued to fly on
the flagship.

For the ships in the van, the simultaneous signaling of the line
of battle and close engagement caused no confusion. These vessels were close enough to the enemy to answer both signals, and,
by means of some minor maneuvering, they were soon hotly
engaged and taking considerable punishment. But for the ships
in the rear, under Hood's command, it was a different matter.
Their opposite numbers in the enemy fleet were at a great distance and it was almost impossible to single them out. Moreover,
the ships in the rear could not possibly come to close engagement
without temporarily disrupting the line of battle; for them, the
signals were contradictory. What should they do? Hood watched
the movements of Graves' flagship, the *London*, in the center
of the British line. Perhaps she would make clear, through maneuvering, the intentions which her ambiguous signals failed to
convey. But the *London*'s movements failed to provide him with
an answer. At first, she turned downwind to attack; but then
she bore up and opened fire at a range that could hardly be construed as close engagement. The *London* thereupon gave signals
for dressing up the line. These signals resulted from Graves'
anxiety to keep his van in good order, for it was under heavy
fire and beginning to bunch up. But Hood, who was in the rear,
assumed that the commander-in-chief was much more concerned

with the integrity of his line of battle than with close engagement. According to Hood, the signal for the line continued to
fly on the *London* until 5:25. When he saw it hauled down, he
moved his division closer and fired a few inconsequential shots
at long range. The French force at this point fell away to leeward and Hood did not pursue; he found his division was already to leeward of the *London*, which was apparently making
little effort to carry out her own signal to engage. At 6:30 both
fleets ceased firing and the battle was over.[43]

The fiasco of September 5, insofar as it was a matter of poor
execution rather than missed opportunities, arose from the failure
of Hood's division to take part in the action. The British were
outnumbered, their van had taken a beating, and yet seven ships
in the rear had scarcely fired a shot. For this failure, Graves,
Hood, and the inadequacies of the signaling system and fighting
instructions have all been blamed. The fighting instructions, it
is said, placed a fatal overemphasis on maintaining the line, and
therefore so did Graves and Hood. In all these criticisms, the assumption has been that nothing should have stood in the way of
bringing the entire squadron into a general engagement.

Hood's critics imply that he should have disobeyed the signal
to remain in line.[44] Hood, however, valued the power and safety
afforded by the line and thought that the battle could have
been fought effectively without disrupting it. Certainly he realized that his division should get into action. The question was:
Should it get into action at all costs? [45] As he saw it, the best
plan of attack for the inferior British force was to concentrate
a tightly formed line upon the French van. Being in the rear,
Hood had no way of encouraging such a plan through independent action. His only option—aside from staying in line as he
did—was to take his division down into the midst of the enemy
main body. But a decision to risk a showdown on such terms—
involving as it did the over-all strategic situation—was one
which a subordinate officer had no right to make. It could only
be made by the commander-in-chief, and Graves gave no indication of any desire to risk everything in order to come to grips

with the enemy; both the signals and the maneuverings of his flagship revealed caution and uncertainty.[46]

Naval historians, in retrospect, have felt that the risks should have been taken. The safety of Cornwallis' army depended on control of the Chesapeake; such control was bound to be contested by de Grasse; therefore, de Grasse should have been defeated before he was joined by de Barras. But these matters which seem obvious in hindsight, were not obvious to Hood and Graves. In fact, so far as de Barras was concerned, both admirals misunderstood the situation; they thought that de Barras had already joined de Grasse. The idea that de Grasse might bring all his ships to North America seemed so incredible that the British admirals were unable to realize he had done so even while fighting such a force. They did not learn the staggering truth until September 23, when word came from Cornwallis that the French fleet, then united in the Chesapeake, numbered 32 of the line.[47]

In respect to the other points, Hood showed himself to be far more perceptive than his superior. He understood the crucial necessity of controlling the Chesapeake. On September 10, when the British squadron lost touch with the French, Hood urged Graves to hurry back to the bay. But it was too late; de Grasse was already anchored there. Later, while the British squadron was refitting at New York, Hood was furious at the lack of any sense of urgency on the part of either Graves or General Clinton. Hood insisted that a rescue mission should be attempted at once. "*Desparate* cases require *bold* remedies," he wrote. But the refitting dragged on and his superiors decided to await the reinforcements coming out with Admiral Digby. The British relief expedition did not leave New York until October 17 and it arrived too late to be of any help. Cornwallis had already surrendered.[48]

With the close of the Yorktown campaign, Hood turned his attention to the coming operations in the West Indies. Realizing that the French squadron would initially outnumber the British, he pressed Admiral Digby, the new commander-in-chief in

North American waters, to lend him all of his ships of the line for the winter. Digby was reluctant. He probably feared he might not get the ships back in the spring, and thus lose some opportunities for prize money. Hood offered to share equally any prizes that he took while the ships remained with him. This generous offer—which reveals Hood's unusual readiness to place the national interest above his own—apparently worked, for Digby gave him the ships.[49]

Hood sailed for Barbados, surmising that the French would attack there first. He correctly anticipated the enemy's intentions, but the French were twice rebuffed by high winds. Hood realized that in order to defend Barbados he must expose the less valuable Leeward Islands. Thus, on January 14, when he learned that the French had been sighted off St. Kitts, he hurried to leeward. But by the time he arrived off St. Kitts, the only pocket of resistance left was the stronghold on Brimstone Hill on the northwest side of the island.

Hood had hoped to surprise the French squadron in the early morning at its anchorage in Basseterre Road. Unfortunately, two of his ships collided during the night and the resulting delay gave de Grasse time to weigh anchor and form a line of battle to leeward. Hood then decided to occupy Basseterre Road himself. As he told Middleton, "I thought I had a fair prospect of gaining the anchorage he left, and well knowing it was the only chance I had of saving the island, if it was to be saved, I pushed for it." [50] Perhaps his mind was still on what he thought might have been done for Cornwallis at Yorktown. Coming up from the south, he steered his line, which numbered 22 as opposed to 25 of the French, close to the lee shore of Nevis and St. Kitts. He gave every indication of preparing to engage, but when his leading ship was opposite Basseterre Road, he gave the signal to anchor. Each ship turned upwind and anchored in succession. It was a daring maneuver—since it involved deliberately masking part of his firepower and also exposing his ships to a raking from astern as they turned up to anchor—but Hood's execution was perfect and his move a brilliant success.

De Grasse was furious at being outwitted and the next day attempted to drive the British from their position. But the anchored ships were in tight formation and had springs out to their anchor cables which enabled them to aim their broadsides. De Grasse's superior force was driven off and suffered heavier losses than the British sustained.

Hood's flawless maneuvering, however, could not save St. Kitts. The besieged British garrison was ten miles from the fleet. The only hope was that Rodney—whom Hood had been "impatiently" expecting since mid-January—would arrive from England with enough reinforcements to drive off the French fleet and leave the enemy army high and dry.[51] With his victuals running low and his men falling ill, Hood held on, but his hopes were dashed on February 12 when the garrison on Brimstone Hill surrendered. Hood knew that it would only be a matter of time before the French army dragged its guns to a nearby shore, making the roadstead untenable. Yet waiting for him off shore was a French squadron now numbering 29 of the line. On the afternoon of the 14th, therefore, he assembled the captains of his squadron and outlined a plan. All the officers synchronized their watches and at eleven that night, without signal, the ships cut their cables and silently slipped away.[52] Thus the British fleet was saved to fight another day.

The effort at St. Kitts had not been entirely fruitless. Hood's presence detained the French and limited their conquests to St. Kitts and the neighboring islands of Nevis and Montserrat. By the end of February, 1782, the period of French supremacy was over as Rodney joined Hood and took over command. Rodney brought with him 12 ships of the line from England and five more were soon to arrive. De Grasse was also expecting reinforcements, but of the five ships sent to him, only two arrived.[53]

Despite the superior size of their force, things did not go well for the British at first. De Grasse, who was at Martinique, lay anxiously awaiting a convoy from France. Without it he could not carry out the projected Franco-Spanish assault on Jamaica. Hood and Rodney knew about the convoy and were bent on intercepting it. But they disagreed—as they had in a similar situation the previous year—on the best method for doing so. Once again, Hood's estimate of the situation proved to be the correct one.

Hood's plan was to divide the British fleet, which now numbered 36 ships of the line, sending half to cruise to windward of Point Salines, and the other half north, to windward of Guadeloupe. His reasoning was that even if the French escort numbered as many as 14 warships—which was highly unlikely—each British force would be sufficiently powerful to overcome the enemy. As for de Grasse, Hood doubted that the French admiral would venture out. If he did, the two British fleets, being to windward, could easily join in time to meet him. Rodney, on the other hand, was convinced that the French would make for Point Salines and refused to let Hood go further north. Hood argued: ". . . the commander of the French squadron must be a madman to think of coming in sight of St. Lucia, knowing, as he must, the force of the British fleet, which would naturally be upon the look out." [54] But Hood's arguments were to no avail.

The French convoy, with only three escorting warships, did in fact steer clear to the northward, made its landfall at Désirade (just to windward of Guadeloupe), and ran down safely between Marie Galante and Dominica to Martinique. Hood was beside himself when he learned the news: "How Sir George Rodney could bring himself to keep his whole force to guard one path, when half of it was fully equal to the service, and to leave another . . . without any guard at all, is matter of the utmost astonishment to me." [55]

De Grasse finally came out of Fort Royal on April 8 with the Jamaica expedition under convoy. His plan was to proceed to Cap Français along the islands, and, in the event of an attack, to send his transports into a friendly harbor. But the British caught up with him off Dominica. Both fleets were slowed down by calms in the lee of Dominica's mountains; this meant that as their vans worked clear to the north and picked up the sea breezes they became separated from the main forces. As a result, the

British van, Hood's division, was subjected to an assault by a superior French force on April 9. Hood might have been in serious trouble if de Grasse had thrown more ships against his force, for the becalmed British main body could not have come to his aid. But de Grasse's tactics were, for the moment, entirely defensive. After sending his transports into harbor at Guadeloupe, he tried to work up to windward and escape through the Saints passage. When, on the night of the 11th, a collision disabled one of his ships, de Grasse fell back to leeward in an attempt to shield the straggler, and that brought him within reach of the British.[56]

The fleets met at eight the next morning. While they were exchanging broadsides on opposite courses with the wind from the east, the breezes suddenly veered southward. De Grasse's ships, already sailing close to the wind, were forced to fall off toward the enemy; the French line became confused and gaps soon appeared in the formation. For the British, the situation was quite different; the wind had veered aft and they were thus given the choice of maintaining their line on its northerly heading or turning to starboard and knifing through the French line. As a gap opened in the French line opposite the *Formidable,* Rodney's flagship, he steered for it. In spite of the fact that the signal to engage from leeward flew from the *Formidable's* mast throughout the maneuver, she was followed by the ships in her wake.[57] Not only did these vessels follow, but the *Duke,* the next ship in front, cut through the French line, and Commodore Edmund Affleck in the *Bedford,* the sixth ship aft of the *Formidable,* seeing the flagship's maneuver, also cut through the French line. He was followed by Hood's entire division.

The consequences were staggering to the French. Their fleet was now divided into three ill-formed segments. The ships in the center segment, which contained de Grasse's flagship, the *Ville de Paris,* were unable to maneuver and wound up in a cluster. On each side the British sailed by in column, firing furiously. They could hardly miss.

When the British had passed through to windward, Rodney

signaled close engagement. Hood, like the others, worked feverishly to get back into the thick of the fight, but his division lay
nearest the lee of Dominica and could scarcely maneuver. Not
until late afternoon, when the battle was nearly over, did Hood
again approach the French. He saw the *Ville de Paris* give some
indications of challenging him. Having observed the punishment
she had been taking all afternoon, he guessed correctly that de
Grasse might be looking for a flag officer to whom to surrender,
so Hood steered his ship, the *Barfleur,* toward the French admiral.
The *Barfleur* was virtually undamaged, and her crew was fresh.
After ten minutes of withering fire, honor was satisfied and de
Grasse struck.[58] More men were killed on the *Ville de Paris* alone
than in the entire British fleet. The remaining French ships fled
in disorder downwind and five were captured.

Although Hood acknowledged the battle of April 12 to be a
great victory, he was by no means satisfied with the results.
Since the French were shattered and the British had many good
ships left after the clash, why had Rodney not led a vigorous
chase? Why was no attempt made to maintain contact with the
enemy during the night? The day after the battle Hood went
aboard the *Formidable* and begged Rodney to pursue the enemy.
Rodney said that he would, but did nothing. Hood was disgusted
and in a rage wrote to his friends:

> Sir George Rodney seems to be satisfied with having done enough
> as probably to save Jamaica and keep his popularity alive; but,
> good God! not to avail himself of the manifest advantage his most
> complete victory gave him is not to be thought of with any degree
> of temper. We might as easily have taken the whole of the French
> fleet . . . I find all this wasting of time here is to take the Ville de
> Paris to Jamaica with him. Such is the vanity of the man, he can
> talk of nothing else, and says he will hoist his flag on board her.
> Would to God she had sunk the instant she had yielded to the arms
> of his Majesty! We should then have had ten better ships in lieu of
> her.[59]

In the weeks that followed, Hood was like a man possessed; he
could not dismiss from his mind the golden opportunity that

had been lost and avidly collected every scrap of evidence that showed the vulnerability of the fleeing enemy squadron.[60]

The British fleet eventually went into Port Royal, Jamaica, to refit. Rodney pleaded illness and left to Hood the task of supervising the refitting. While Hood labored in the yard day and night, his disrespect for Rodney became greater than ever ("he is undoubtedly as well as I am"). Indeed, Hood took perverse pleasure in the fact that a broken leg excused him from attending a banquet given in Rodney's honor by the people of Jamaica. How could people celebrate—above all how could the commander-in-chief celebrate—as if Britain had won the war! Obviously, Hood was weary and sick at heart. The misfortunes of his country and the endless months of frustration he had suffered as second-in-command were eating away at his spirit.

Hood guessed that Rodney soon would be relieved by a senior admiral, and he pretended he did not care who it was. "[I] shall not repine if I am relieved also," he wrote Middleton.[61] In reality, he hungered for the West Indies command himself, but would not admit it. As matters turned out, he had to endure the additional frustration of serving under Rodney's replacement, Admiral Hugh Pigot.

The task of Pigot's squadron in the summer of 1782 was to search for a French squadron under the Marquis of Vaudreuil which was thought to have gone to the American mainland. Hood outlined for his new chief an imaginative plan of action, but to no avail.[62] While Hood worried over the possible courses of action open to Vaudreuil, Pigot calmly bore toward New York with some prizes in tow and refused to make any detachments to gather intelligence. "If he will risk nothing," Hood lamented, "and suffer himself to remain in ignorance of what is very material for him to know, he will do nothing but from the chapter of accidents." [63] Fortunately, Vaudreuil was also inactive: he was undertaking an extensive refit in Boston.

When Pigot sailed from New York in October for Barbados, he left Hood behind with 12 ships. Because the French and Spanish were thought to be planning an assault on Jamaica,

Hood's assignment was to intercept any squadrons—particularly Vaudreuil's—that might be bound for Cap Français or Havana. At last he was on his own. "If I am so fortunate as to get hold of Vaudreuil," he told Middleton, "I shall be satisfied of having lived to a good purpose." [64]

Hood laid his plans carefully. In December, 1782, he cruised off Hispaniola between Old Cape (Cabo Frances Viejo) and Monte Christi, with his frigates guarding the Bahamas passages. Too late he learned that Vaudreuil had been sighted off Puerto Rico, and Vaudreuil got through the Mona Passage before Hood could work upwind. Thinking that the Frenchman might run along the south coast of Hispaniola and either put into one of its western ports or try for Havana, Hood turned around and hurried downwind along the north coast in hopes of beating him to Cape Tiburon. By then it was February, and Hood had been at sea ten weeks; his water and victuals were running low; after a few days off Cape Tiburon, with no sign of Vaudreuil, he gave up and went to Port Royal.[65]

He could not help thinking that if Pigot had followed his suggestion and cruised off Puerto Rico, Vaudreuil would have been caught. But at the same time his own disappointment at failing to catch the Frenchman had mellowed him, and Hood acknowledged that his chief might have had "substantial reason" for doing what he did. Hood was obviously reflecting on his own conduct as much as Pigot's when he wrote: "When an officer does that which human prudence as well as sound judgment suggests, he ought to submit with becoming fortitude. There is no guarding against misfortune." [66] He did not know until later that he had tried to intercept an antagonist who was more interested in avoiding a fight than in gaining a strategic objective. Vaudreuil, judging his ships in no condition for battle, had gone south to Puerto Cabello.[67]

Although he sensed that peace was near, Hood would not quit. He hurried the refitting of his squadron, and the exhaustion of Port Royal's stores did not stop him: he cannibalized the worst of his ships to refit the rest. Early in March, 1783, he was at sea again. On the 21st he heard that the Spanish fleet had sailed from Havana, and "in high spirits" sought it out, envisioning "a glorious finish to the war." But before the Spanish were sighted the news reached him that the peace preliminaries had been signed.[68] The war was over before Hood could contribute a significant victory of his own.

Hood's reputation was destined to rest mainly upon his performance in the Revolutionary War. Because he had taken part in the great victory of the Saints, he became famous and was showered with honors. Popularity and honors of this sort may be the gift of fortune, but lasting fame must have a more enduring basis. Hood's reputation, in fact, was based upon his proven abilities and attitude toward service rather than his actions in any given battle. Appropriately enough, the Irish peerage he received was given to him not because of his slender role in the battle of the Saints but because of his consistently fine performance. George III insisted that if Rodney was to be rewarded, Hood should not go unnoticed. Some mark of approbation, the king thought, should be given a man who "has for the second time the misfortune of being superseded in the Command of a Fleet with which he has thrice proved victorious." [69]

What abilities had Hood demonstrated? Had he excelled in tactical maneuver? The king's phrase, "thrice proved victorious," obviously exaggerates Hood's achievements; he had little opportunity to show what sort of tactician he was. At the Virginia Capes and the Saints he was second-in-command and by no means in the thick of the fight. Off Martinique in April, 1781, when he had command, he was unable to draw the French into close engagement. Only at St. Kitts did he have the chance to act decisively, and there he moved with boldness and imagination. But aside from this there is little evidence that Hood was a brilliant tactician, unless one relies on the accounts he wrote— after the battles—of what his intentions had been.

As a strategist, however, Hood was unquestionably brilliant. Time and again he grasped the situation, or guessed correctly the enemy's intentions. He realized fully the necessity of concentrating every ship against de Grasse's squadron; of controlling the Chesapeake to protect Cornwallis; and of awaiting French convoys from Europe on the windward side of Martinique. Twice he suggested to Rodney what proved to be the correct procedures for intercepting the Martinique convoys. After the battle of the Saints he urged Rodney to pursue the defeated enemy, but Rodney demurred, arguing that the French had probably reassembled the bulk of their squadron. In fact, the French were scattered. When Hood was finally detached, after five days' delay, to go after them, he learned that a remnant of the French squadron had preceded him through the Mona Passage only the day before; even so he managed to capture four stragglers.[70] Evidence of these strategic insights lies in Hood's dispatches. There is no question of second guessing here. These dispatches contain analyses and plans that were either acted on at the time or urgently pressed on reluctant commanders-in-chief.

Hood's greatness as a strategist stemmed not only from his intelligence, but also from his character. If there was an enemy to defeat, he could think of nothing else, and fretted over every detail and contingency. Recognizing this trait in himself, he accepted it. Some men's minds, he wrote, "are full of anxiety, impatience, and apprehension, while others, under similar circumstances, are perfectly cool, tranquil, and indifferent. Mine is of the former cast." [71] It led him to argue violently with his superiors; he criticized them without reserve, and sometimes attributed their behavior to the worst of motives. When his advice was ignored, he poured his frustrations into letters to his friends. There was nothing furtive about his criticism: his superiors all knew his thoughts because he expressed them; in fact, he set down every important criticism in his official letters to the Admiralty.[72] When his friends advised him to quiet down, he answered that his views were already known throughout the fleet.[73] "My mind often tells me I express my thoughts too freely," he commented, "but I cannot help it." [74] His tactlessness

arose not from a backbiting disposition but from intense dedication and a deep sense of responsibility.

Obviously the will to win was deeply ingrained in Hood—yet
Britain was losing and all about him he saw officers who did not
seem to care. Toward the end of the war he wrote: "If officers
cannot be found that will make the glory of their King and
country to take place of every other consideration, there is no
salvation for us." [75] Hood himself lived by this dictum. He did
all he could to prevent prize money from influencing strategic
decisions. Believing that politics and commanding a fleet were
incompatible professions, he refused to become identified with
any faction. In 1782 the ministers in office, without his knowledge, nominated him for Westminster, the seat vacated by Rodney, but some friends withdrew his name. He considered this a
"lucky escape," and remarked: "I shall ever . . . steer clear, as
far as I am able, of all suspicion of being a party man; for if
once I show myself of that frame of mind . . . I must from that
moment expect to lose every degree of consideration in the line
of my profession. . . . I am vain enough to think that I am in
some small degree qualified . . . to fight the battles of my country
upon my own element, but acknowledge myself totally unfit
to fight the battles of a minister in a house of parliament; and
even if I had abilities equal to the task, I think it an employment derogatory to the true character of a sea officer." [76] Hood's
attitude was thoroughly professional; in his day it was admired
by many, but adopted by few.

In his later years Hood never abandoned his courageous and
energetic approach toward the service. He served on the Admiralty Board for seven years. After war broke out in 1793, he
was given the Mediterranean command and had the difficult
task of supervising the occupation of Toulon. Characteristically,
he quarreled in 1795 with the new first lord over the number of
ships he was to have, and was ordered to strike his flag; it was
the end of his career.[77] With retirement came a viscountcy in
1796. In 1805, at the age of eighty, Hood was seriously considered as a candidate for first lord of the Admiralty in Pitt's last

Ministry.[78] At eighty-five he still rode every day and had "no complaint but deafness." [79] At ninety he was "in good spirits, and full voice." [80] He died January 27, 1816, at ninety-one, and was buried in the old cemetery of Greenwich Hospital.[81]

FOOTNOTES

1. Quoted in Sir John K. Laughton, ed., *From Howard to Nelson: Twelve Sailors* (London, 1899), p. 394.
2. Sir John K. Laughton, ed., *Letters and Papers of Charles, Lord Barham* (Publications of the Navy Records Society, 3 vols., [London, 1907–11]), I, p. 228. Hereafter N.R.S.
3. The article on Hood in the *Dictionary of National Biography* (London, 1891), XXVII, pp. 263–79. Maud Wyndham, *Chronicles of the Eighteenth Century* (London, 1924), II, p. 84. I am grateful to the Rev. E. F. Synge, Vicar of Butleigh, for showing me the old parish rate book that makes James Grenville's standing in the parish clear.
4. On Hood's apprenticeship and relations with Thomas Smith see Wyndham, *Chronicles*, I, pp. 144–49, 166–72; II, pp. 60–65, 84–94, 96. See also Dorothy Hood, *The Admirals Hood* (London, 1942), pp. 11–14; Sir Richard Vesey Hamilton's biography of Hood in Laughton, *From Howard to Nelson*, pp. 361–64; and the articles on Hood and Smith in the *D.N.B.*
5. Wyndham, *Chronicles*, II, pp. 94–101.
6. *Ibid.*, II, p. 102. Thomas Smith, though of illegitimate birth, was fully accepted by his father's family, the Lytteltons; important in their own right, the Lytteltons were also intermarried with the Grenvilles, Temples, Wests, and Pitts.
7. *Ibid.*, II, pp. 102, 108.
8. *Ibid.*, II, pp. 103–06.
9. *D.N.B.*, "Hood"; *The Naval Chronicle*, II (1799), pp. 5–6.
10. Hood, *Admirals Hood*, pp. 24–25, 35–38; William S. Taylor and John H. Pringle, eds., *Correspondence of William Pitt, Earl of Chatham* (London, 1840), IV, pp. 233–36.
11. P.R.O. Adm. 1/483, March 28, November 22, 1768, February 27, June 4, July 10, 1769; Adm. 1/313, November 13, 1782; William J. Smith, ed., *The Grenville Papers* (London, 1852–53), IV, pp. 333–34, 377.

12. P.R.O. Adm. 1/483, May 5, September 17, September 18, 1768, April 8, April 28, 1769, May 27, August 22, November 6, 1770.
13. Hood, *Admirals Hood*, p. 33; P.R.O. Adm. 1/1902, Hood, November 28, 1776; Adm. 1/1903, Hood, February 5, February 22, March 15, July 27, August 10, September 25, December 20, 1777; G. R. Barnes and John H. Owen, eds., *The Private Papers of John, Earl of Sandwich* (N.R.S. [London, 1932–38]), I, pp. 201–05, 219–20, 242–44, 263–64, 334.
14. P.R.O. Adm. 1/1904, Hood, February 12, 1778.
15. *Sandwich Papers*, III, pp. 161–62; Hood, *Admirals Hood*, p. 46. Miss Hood has surmised that Sandwich was interested in putting Hood's professional knowledge and administrative ability to good use, but it is probable that Sandwich was also interested in gaining Hood's allegiance and that Hood was referring to "accommodation" of this sort. Any dockyard commissioner at Portsmouth was bound to have considerable influence in the town, and of course the appointment of Hood meant, in addition, the support of the Linzees for the Admiralty interest.
16. For the distinction between taking civil employment in peacetime and taking it in wartime, see the correspondence of Commissioner Laforey in *Barham Papers*, II, pp. 139–46. Laforey, searching for precedents, claimed that Hood had taken civil employment after the war "had spread to Europe," which, if one reckons from the actual declaration, was incorrect. The first lord of the Admiralty, ignoring the preliminary hostilities, ruled that Hood had taken civil employment in peacetime.
17. Arthur Aspinall, ed., *Correspondence of George, Prince of Wales 1770–1812* (London, 1963–67), I, p. 25.
18. Sir John W. Fortescue, ed., *The Correspondence of King George the Third* (London, 1927–28), IV, pp. 133, 170.
19. *Sandwich Papers*, III, p. 161.
20. See Fortescue, *Correspondence*, V, p. 52.
21. *Sandwich Papers*, III, p. 161.
22. *Ibid.*, III, p. 228; P.R.O. Adm. 1/1898, February 13, September 2, 1764. It is clear that Hood did not consider his physical defects to be as serious as he made them sound in his first letter; in his letter of the 20th he referred to his first letter as a "hasty reply" which he was anxious to revoke.
23. See Thomas Keppel, *The Life of Augustus Viscount Keppel* (London, 1842), II, pp. 112–15, 171–76; Fortescue, *Correspondence*, IV, pp. 225, 255.
24. Countess of Ilchester and Lord Stavordale, eds., *The Life and Letters*

of Lady Sarah Lennox, 1745–1826 (London, 1902), p. 290. This was Lady Lennox's impression; she sympathized with him and thought him an honest man.

25. *Sandwich Papers*, II, p. 199.

26. See Fortescue, *Correspondence*, IV, pp. 283–84; *Sandwich Papers*, II, pp. 193, 216, 274–76; J. H. Broomfield, "The Keppel-Palliser Affair, 1778–1779," *Mariner's Mirror*, XLVII (1961), pp. 202–03; William M. James, *The British Navy in Adversity* (London, 1926), pp. 139–40.

27. *Sandwich Papers*, II, pp. 237–41, 243–45; III, p. 60. Hood, *Admirals Hood*, pp. 48–49, 51, 54.

28. See Godfrey B. Mundy, *The Life and Correspondence of the late Admiral Lord Rodney* (London, 1830), I, p. 403; Alfred T. Mahan, *Major Operations of the Navies in the War of American Independence* (Boston, 1913), pp. 131–37; *Barham Papers*, I, pp. xlvii–xlviii, 53–55, 101–07.

29. David Hannay, ed., *Letters Written by Sir Samuel Hood* (N.R.S. [London, 1895]), p. 97; *Barham Papers*, I, pp. 198, 261.

30. *Ibid.*, I, pp. 157, 163; *Hood Letters*, pp. 18, 107.

31. It is possible that the rather extreme views put forward by David Hannay in his introduction to the *Hood Letters* (pp. x–xv) arose from his having recently completed a biography of Rodney.

32. See *Barham Papers*, I, pp. 62, 65; see also Rodney M. S. Pasley, *Private Sea Journals kept by Admiral Sir Thomas Pasley* (London, 1931), p. 259.

33. Mundy, *Rodney*, II, p. 163.

34. *Hood Letters*, pp. 21–23. Hannay transcribed "Lares" for what appears to be "Lures" in the original manuscript.

35. The letters exchanged by Hood and Rodney on this matter may be found in *Sandwich Papers*, IV, pp. 129, 155–61; *Hood Letters*, p. 15; Mundy, *Rodney*, II, pp. 55–70, 81–88. The fact that Mundy printed Hood's letter of April 1, in which Hood seemed satisfied with the number of ships he had, but not the letter of April 6, in which Hood wished for more, suggests that Mundy's editing may not be entirely trustworthy.

36. *Barham Papers*, I, pp. 109–16; James, *British Navy in Adversity*, pp. 258–61; Charles L. Lewis, *Admiral de Grasse* (Annapolis, 1945), pp. 106–10; Mahan, *Major Operations*, pp. 162–66.

37. *Barham Papers*, I, pp. 117–19; Mundy, *Rodney*, II, pp. 101–03, 120–37; James, *British Navy in Adversity*, pp. 261–62.

38. *Sandwich Papers*, IV, pp. 133–38; Piers Mackesy, *The War for America, 1775–1783* (London, 1964), pp. 418–20.

39. Mundy, *Rodney,* II, pp. 145–49; *Barham Papers,* I, pp. 121–22, 129–30; *Hood Letters,* p. 26.

40. *Sandwich Papers,* IV, pp. 189–91. It may be, as Prof. Charles L. Lewis has suggested (*Admiral de Grasse,* p. 162), that Hood "was exaggerating the possibilities of such an attack," but every account of the battle, including Lewis', indicates that it was probably the best thing to try.

41. *Sandwich Papers,* IV, p. 184. The words are from Graves' own log.

42. There was a third method, involving what was called "lasking." It was really a variation of the attack in column. Each ship, instead of aligning its heading with the line-of-battle axis, steered slightly upwind, thus allowing its broadside to fire with effect while permitting the wind to carry the ship down to closer range. Richard W. Hale, Jr., has suggested that the "lasking" approach was what Graves had in mind ("New Light on the Naval Side of Yorktown," Massachusetts Historical Society, *Proceedings,* LXXI [1959], pp. 124–32), but if it was, his failure to acquaint his subordinates with the manner in which he would signal seems, in view of its unusual nature, incredible.

43. *Sandwich Papers,* IV, pp. 181–91; Harold A. Larrabee, *Decision at the Chesapeake* (New York, 1964), pp. 184–210. How long the signal for maintaining the line continued to fly from the flagship was a disputed point after the battle.

44. French E. Chadwick, editor of the *Graves Papers,* Naval Hist. Soc. (New York, 1916), judged that Hood "did not do his duty," (VIII, p. lxxiii). Julian S. Corbett, in *Signals and Instructions , 1776–1794,* N.R.S. (London, 1908), suggested that if Hood had "acted with one-half of the spirit that Nelson showed at St. Vincent," the outcome would have been very different (p. 56). Admiral Robison (quoted by Larrabee, *Decision,* p. 276) wrote that Hood should have been court-martialed and would have been, like Palliser and Richard Lestock, had he not been a man of influence. This wild charge overlooks *inter alia* the facts that initially Palliser was not court-martialed, and that Lestock was *acquitted* in spite of the fact that Admiral Mathews (Battle of Toulon, 1744) had made clear his intentions by throwing his flagship into close engagement.

45. On this question see Mackesy, *War for America,* pp. 424, 456.

46. When Nelson performed his magnificent independent action at Cape St. Vincent in 1797 his commander-in-chief had already given every indication of throwing caution to the winds.

47. Larrabee, *Decision,* pp. 227–28.

48. *Ibid.*, pp. 211–35; *Sandwich Papers*, IV, pp. 191–93; *Hood Letters*, pp. 36–38.
49. *Sandwich Papers*, IV, pp. 195–204; *Hood Letters*, pp. 39–40, 48–54; *Barham Papers*, I, p. 126; Fortescue, *Correspondence*, V, p. 315.
50. *Barham Papers*, I, p. 143.
51. *Ibid.*, I, p. 147.
52. A full account of the St. Kitts operation may be found in Alfred T. Mahan, *Influence of Sea Power upon History* (New York, 1957), pp. 418–27.
53. See Mackesy, *War for America*, pp. 446–51, 457.
54. *Barham Papers*, I, pp. 149, 151–56; *Sandwich Papers*, IV, pp. 243–49.
55. *Barham Papers*, I, pp. 151–54.
56. Mahan, *Major Operations*, pp. 206–13; *Influence of Sea Power*, p. 433.
57. David Hannay, *Rodney* (London, 1903), p. 205.
58. *Barham Papers*, I, pp. 160–61.
59. *Ibid.*, I, pp. 161–65.
60. *Ibid.*, I, pp. 178, 181, 186–88, 207; *Hood Letters*, pp. 129–34.
61. *Barham Papers*, I, pp. 174–77, 184, 189–90, 194–200.
62. *Hood Letters*, pp. 140, 148; *Barham Papers*, I, pp. 203–05, 219.
63. *Hood Letters*, pp. 138–50; *Barham Papers*, I, p. 205.
64. *Ibid.*, I, pp. 214, 228–29.
65. *Ibid.*, I, pp. 230–49.
66. *Ibid.*, I, p. 247.
67. *Ibid.*, I, pp. 253, 262, 405–06.
68. *Ibid.*, I, pp. 252–55.
69. Fortescue, *Correspondence*, VI, pp. 33–36.
70. *Hood Letters*, pp. 133–34.
71. *Ibid.*, p. 145.
72. Hood's letters to Lord Sandwich (in *Sandwich Papers*) and those among the Admiralty in-letters at the Public Record Office (Adm. 1/313) contain most of the criticisms that are found in his private letters, printed in *Hood Letters* and *Barham Papers*.
73. Fortescue, *Correspondence*, VI, p. 210.
74. *Hood Letters*, pp. 149, 157.
75. *Ibid.*, pp. 142–43.
76. *Barham Papers*, I, pp. 249–50. See also Paget Toynbee, ed., *Letters of Horace Walpole* (Oxford, 1903–05), XII, p. 263. Hood's decision to stand for Westminster in 1784 may seem wholly inconsistent with this. In reality it was only partly so, for in 1782 he had been nominated by "the old gang" of politicians, whereas in 1784 he stood—he thought, and many others with him—as an opponent of

factions and parties and a supporter of the king and the reform ministry of young William Pitt.

77. Laughton, *From Howard to Nelson*, pp. 388–95.
78. *D.N.B.*, "Hood"; Historical Manuscripts Commission, *Fortescue (Dropmore) MSS.*, VII, pp. 256–57.
79. Francis Bickley, ed., *The Diaries of Sylvester Douglas* (London, 1928), II, p. 34.
80. H.M.C., *Fortescue (Dropmore) MSS.*, X, p. 350.
81. Hood, *Admirals Hood*, pp. 227–28.

BIBLIOGRAPHY

Barnes, G. R. and Owen, John H., eds. *The Private Papers of John, Earl of Sandwich, First Lord of the Admiralty, 1771–1782*, 4 vols., Navy Records Society Publications, LXIX, LXXI, LXXV, LXXVIII (London, 1932–38). The most important printed collection of letters concerning the British navy in the American Revolutionary War.

Hannay, David, ed. *Letters Written by Sir Samuel Hood (Viscount Hood) in 1781-2-3*. Navy Records Society Publications (London, 1895). Contains Hood's letters to George Jackson (Brit. Mus. Add. MS. 9343) plus some official letters to the Admiralty. The introduction is unsympathetic to Hood.

Hood, Dorothy. *The Admirals Hood*. London, 1942. This work contains the only reasonably full biography of Hood. Although it provides much information on the man and is a good guide to the important sources, it is not well organized.

James, William M. *The British Navy in Adversity*. London, 1926. A reliable account of the naval operations of the Revolutionary War.

Laughton, Sir John K., ed. *Letters and Papers of Charles, Lord Barham, . . . 1758–1813*. 3 vols., Navy Records Society Publications, XXXII, XXXVIII, XXXIX (London, 1907–11). The first volume contains Hood's letters to Sir Charles Middleton. It supplements the collection edited by Hannay and is, on the whole, more valuable.

Mackesy, Piers. *The War for America, 1775–1783*. Cambridge, Mass., 1964. A first-rate study of the war; strong where James is weakest— on strategic and logistical problems.

Mahan, Alfred T. *The Influence of Sea Power upon History*. New York, 1957 edn. *The Major Operations of the Navies in the War of American Independence*. Boston, 1913. Mahan's insights into strategy and tactics are still valuable. Hood's style and conduct obviously gained Mahan's admiration.

Wyndham, Maud. *Chronicles of the Eighteenth Century, Founded on the Correspondence of Sir Thomas Lyttelton and his Family.* 2 vols. London, 1924. The best printed source for Hood's early career.

A note on manuscripts.

Except for the Bridport Papers in the Additional Manuscripts of the British Museum, there do not seem to be any important unpublished collections of Hood's letters dealing with the American Revolutionary War. His letters to the Admiralty (in the Public Record Office) are, for this period, virtually all printed, though with minor variations, in the volumes mentioned above.

Sir George Rodney:

LUCKY ADMIRAL

CHRISTOPHER LLOYD

Royal Naval College, Greenwich, England

ADMIRAL GEORGE RODNEY was not a popular figure among his fellow officers. During the Revolutionary War many of his subordinates disliked the attempts he made to impose a stricter discipline upon them. Others pointed to his rapacity for prize money, which was dictated by the circumstances of his private life and at times robbed his victories of their full military impact. Some colleagues ascribed his successes to luck rather than ability, and many of his social inferiors rather resented his aristocratic airs. But during the last years of the war the British public accorded Rodney a welcome which was unrivaled until the days of Nelson, when, after a long sequence of defeats and mishaps, he twice returned victorious from the West Indies. He was certainly no ordinary naval officer. Many of his faults were common to others at this time, but the paradoxes of his public career can only be explained in the perspective of his private life and by a consideration of his personal problems. We shall find much to excuse in the man, but also much to admire.

The Royal Navy of his day attracted many officers of high birth, but none who embodied greater pride of ancestry than George Brydges Rodney. His arrogance might repel, but his conduct was sanctioned by custom and justified by his lineage. A Rodney had served as a crusader under Richard I. The Shropshire estates of Stoke Rodney had belonged to his family for six centuries before passing to Sir Thomas Brydges, who married one of the female line. From him they were inherited by James Brydges, Duke of Chandos, one of the wealthiest magnates in eighteenth-century England. It was not until a barony was conferred upon the admiral toward the end of his life, as a reward for his services during the Revolutionary War, that the estates were restored to the Rodney family.

Born on February 19, 1718, Rodney clearly owed much of his early advancement in the navy to family influence and interest. He inherited his first name from the king, who was his godfather, and his second from the Duke of Chandos. At the age of twelve he was sent to sea as a king's letter boy, a mode of entry instituted by Samuel Pepys by which boys entered under royal patronage which assured them a rapid rise in their profession. It is worth noting that Rodney was the last to enter the navy by this means. In later life he took a somewhat regal view of patronage when he made his son a captain at the age of sixteen and created a totally new post for his personal physician by appointing him physician of the fleet.

Rodney himself became a captain at the age of twenty-four and distinguished himself in the War of the Austrian Succession under Hawke and Anson. His part in the victory off Cape Finisterre was so important that Lord Anson, when he presented him at Court, remarked that "Young Rodney has been six years a captain in your Majesty's navy and I most heartily wish your Majesty had one hundred such captains, to the terror of your Majesty's enemies." [1]

At the end of the war, he was a successful and wealthy man and married Jane Compton, niece of the Earl of Northampton. Moreover, he was in high favor with the government of the day, particularly with Lord Sandwich, whose long connection with the Admiralty began at this time, and who thirty years later found in Rodney the man who might have retrieved the fortunes of an administration staggering under the weight of the reverses of the Revolutionary War. A political career was inevitable for a man of Rodney's standing in society. As he once wrote, "A man in our country is nothing without being in Parliament." [2] But that is not to say that he ever evinced any political views beyond a strong sense of loyalty to the king. Like so many placemen (for he always regarded the navy as his chosen profession), he attached himself to whatever patron he felt might further his interests. To such a man, a seat in Parliament was something to be bought or conferred for public services, as indeed a grateful government realized when they had him elected free of charge for the city of Westminster in 1780.

He entered the House of Commons in 1751 as the Admiralty nominee for the borough of Saltash. When he was dropped from the list at the next election, he transferred himself to the Duke of Newcastle, who got him in at Okehampton on the assurance that "a steady aherence to your Grace's commands shall distinguish me while I have a seat in the House." [3] In the end, however, Rodney ruined himself financially by contesting one of the most expensive elections on record. This was at Northampton in 1768. Total expenses are said to have amounted to £160,000, of which Rodney paid £30,000 and his principal supporters had to flee the country to escape their creditors.

Such folly had important consequences on his naval career. His debts, whether due to his political career or to his passion for gambling in the clubs of St. James', became so considerable that he was forced to put financial considerations first in almost everything that he did. On the other hand, he was not swayed by party prejudices which compelled men like Howe and Keppel to resign from the service and which went far to ruin the navy during the Revolutionary War. As he said in 1780, "There were officers of high rank and unquestionable courage who nevertheless bore so inveterate an animosity to the administration then existing, particularly to the First Lord of the Admiralty, the Earl of Sandwich, as almost to wish for defeat if it would produce the dismission of ministers." [4] Rodney was never a man of that stamp and any assessment of his career must take into consideration the violence of party politics, even in the fleet, during his day.

Rodney the naval officer was a very different person from Rodney the political placeman or the man about town. The Seven Years' War gave him the opportunity to rise to the top of his profession. In 1759 he was promoted rear admiral and put in charge of the bombardment of Le Havre. Two years later he was given the command of the Leeward Islands station, the most sought-after of all appointments on account of the opportunities for winning prize money in the West Indies.

His first experience on that station was a happy one because Britain's maritime strategy was to blockade the French and Spanish fleets in their European ports to prevent them from sending reinforcements to their valuable Sugar Islands. Guadeloupe had fallen to British arms by the time Rodney arrived in 1761, so he turned his attention to the conquest of Martinique in an admirably executed amphibious operation. With the subsequent conquests of St. Lucia and Grenada, he swept the board. Unfortunately, all save Grenada were restored to France by the peace treaty. During the Revolutionary War, Rodney found that all these islands had to be retaken, but under much more adverse circumstances. The same was true of the biggest amphibious operation of the war—the capture of Havana by Sir George Pocock—a campaign in which Rodney could not take part because of an attack of malaria, a disease from which he suffered at intervals for the rest of his life.

During the period between the highly successful Seven Years' War and the disasters of the Revolutionary War, Rodney reverted to his old life of man about town. The result was that his debts assumed staggering proportions. His friend, Sir Nathaniel Wraxall, has left a candid picture of him at this time—

> His person was more elegant than seemed to become his rough profession. There was even something that approached to delicacy and effeminacy in his figure: but no man manifested a more temperate and steady courage in action. I had the honour to live in great personal intimacy with him, and have often heard him declare

that superiority to fear was not in him a physical effect of constitution; on the contrary, no man was more sensible by nature to that passion than himself; but that he surmounted it from the considerations of honour and public duty. Like the famous Marshal Villars, he justly incurred the reputation of being *glorieux et bavard;* making himself frequently the theme of his own discourse. He talked much and freely upon every subject; concealed nothing in the course of conversation, regardless of who was present; and dealt his censures, as well as his praises, with imprudent liberality; qualities which necessarily procured him many enemies, particularly in his own profession. Throughout his whole life, two passions, both highly injurious to his repose, women and play, carried him into many excesses.[5]

Little is known about his love affairs, though we do know that both his marriages, first to the niece of Lord Northampton and on her death to Henrietta Clies, the daughter of a rich Lisbon merchant, were entirely happy. The frank and charming letters which he wrote in his sprawling hand to his "dear Henny" prove the depth of his family affections, and are in sharp contrast to the arrogance of the figure he played in public. Unfortunately a collation between the holographs of these letters and the printed version in the family biography shows that many endearing familiarities have been omitted, together with many parts dealing with financial matters.[6]

Rodney had been well rewarded for his services during the Seven Years' War. He had the honor of being appointed governor of Greenwich Hospital, where he took a more serious interest in the welfare of the pensioners than had his predecessors. Another distinction was the command of the Jamaica station when it looked as if war might again break out with Spain. He also held the ceremonial post of rear admiral of England, but because he ran up some debts with the Navy Board was never paid the salary.

The cost of his political career, his passion for gambling, and the dissolution of Parliament which put an end to immunity from his creditors, finally forced him to flee the country.[7] Paris was the asylum for absconding debtors and he was compelled to live there under straitened circumstances. When the American rebellion was under way, it became obvious to him that France would intervene, not so much out of sympathy with the colonists as for the chance of revenge against England. His conclusions on this score were set forth in a letter, *Observations by an Officer on the Armament making at Brest,* written toward the end of 1776, which he sent to Lord Shelburne.[8] From his own experience at Le Havre during the preceding war, he warned of the dangers of a surprise landing at Plymouth, an operation which was actually intended by the French eighteen months later. The Channel fleet was seriously under strength because of the ships deployed to American waters, and he pointed out how easily the British defense force might find itself windbound in an emergency. In his view, the danger was acute because France was already shipping arms to America.

He was anxious, of course, to be employed once more, but he dared not set foot in England. His wife and son were sent over to raise funds and to persuade the government to help him. Among the unpublished Sandwich papers there is a petition from Lady Rodney "humbly to represent to his Lordship the distressful situation of Sir George, herself and four children, who must be in danger of literally starving if his Lordship is not induced to restore him that countenance and friendship with which he has formerly been honoured." Sandwich replied in October, 1776: "If Sir George will consider things impartially, he will see that, though his merit as an officer is undeniable, there are reasons which make it impossible for me to prevail on his Majesty to appoint him to the command of a foreign station. . . . [By his debts] your husband had deprived me of the power of being useful to him." [9] Rodney continued to bombard Sandwich with letters, both on his own account and on behalf of other "hard cases," until in December, 1777, he extracted a vague promise of money; but nothing came of it.

The military situation meanwhile was steadily deteriorating. Rodney heard of American privateers being fitted out at Nantes. He knew also that the French were receiving Franklin as an unofficial ambassador and was among the first to get wind of the secret treaty of alliance between France and America. Help came with his own problem finally from an unexpected and embarrassing quarter. The Marshal de Biron, one of the grand old men of France, told Lady Rodney that his purse was at her disposal. Rodney twice declined the kind offer. But nothing was forthcoming from England, and France was on the verge of declaring war; so Rodney changed his mind in May, 1778. The children were sent home by way of Calais, but he himself chose a more obscure route to avoid any annoyance on the part of his creditors. It is satisfying to learn that he later repaid his debt and to read Biron's acknowledgment: "I was really delighted to have the opportunity to oblige so distinguished a gentleman as you, whose reputation is known throughout Europe." [10] When the storms of revolution broke over France to ruin the Biron family, Parliament recollected its indebtedness and voted an annuity to the marshal's daughter which continued to be paid until her death nearly a hundred years later.

Since all the senior naval commands had been filled on the outbreak of war—many of them with opponents of the North-Sandwich administration in order to satisfy the disaffected—there was no vacancy for Rodney at the time. He was, however, promoted admiral of the white, the highest rank on the active list, and was invited by Sandwich to advise on problems of strategy. As junior admirals continued to make mistakes, Rodney remained waiting in the wings until, by the fall of 1779, his recall became imperative. The accumulation of failures such as the battle of Ushant, d'Orvilliers' appearance in the Channel, as well as the increasing acerbity of the political faction which resulted in the refusal of many naval leaders to serve under the government of the day, compelled Sandwich to recall a man who was now sixty-one years old, in indifferent health and financially embarrassed. It is possible that Germain, a firm admirer of the admiral, may have had a hand in the matter. [11]

In October, 1779, Rodney was appointed once more to command of the Leeward Islands station—now a key position because the French had decided to make the Caribbean the center of their naval operations. The Franco-Spanish grand strategy for the following year was to include the siege of Gibraltar, the maintenance of a token force in America and in the Indian Ocean, and an offensive by the Brest fleet against British possessions in the Caribbean.[12]

The appointment was a gamble for Lord Sandwich, in part because the decision was made in the face of opposition by the West Indian merchants. Rodney encountered considerable slackness in Plymouth; fitting out his ships and the continuance of contrary winds prevented him from sailing until December 29, in spite of Sandwich's urgent demand that he go to sea immediately. He did so as soon as circumstances permitted and one of his last letters forecast his future line of conduct:

> It is astonishing—the neglect and slowness of the officers, both civil and military. The whole town of Plymouth . . . declare that more work has been done here since my arrival than had been for two months before. Such is the effect of fear. They knew there was no trifling with me and my eyes, though myself confined by the gout, were always upon them.[13]

His first duty was to escort the West Indies convoy until it was clear of the danger area, and then to take a number of supply ships to relieve the siege of Gibraltar. Luck was with him. He ran into an enemy convoy on its way to Cadiz and then followed up a report of the presence of the Spanish fleet off Cape St. Vincent. On the evening of January 16, 1780, he surprised Don Juan de Langara, whose fleet was supposed to be guarding the Straits. The ensuing clash, called the "Moonlight Battle," was the only night engagement in the war, and the conditions under which it was fought were such that only a gambler would have taken the risk: a high sea running, the darkness of a winter's night, a lee shore and an admiral who himself was confined to bed by gout.

Despite what Rodney's detractors said later, it was his decision to engage and order a general chase which made the victory possible. Tactics in warfare under sail by this date had become so stereotyped that the leading theoretician, Bigot de Morogues, was of the opinion that decisive sea actions were no longer probable. Rodney, as Hawke had done before him at Quiberon Bay, proved de Morogues wrong. De Langara's lack of reconnaissance resulted in his being overpowered by a superior force under a resolute commander. Five of eleven Spanish ships (including the flagship) surrendered during the course of the night, another blew up, and a seventh was driven ashore. The prizes were incorporated into Rodney's fleet—"as fine ships as ever swam, now completely refitted, manned and put in the line of battle," he reported. Sandwich gleefully reminded him that he had taken more ships than had been captured in any one battle during the Seven Years' War.[14] As if this were not enough, on its way home the squadron under Vice Admiral Digby, which had formed part of the fleet, overtook an outward bound convoy from French ports and took 36 merchantmen.

In his dispatch Rodney paid the conventional tribute to his officers, notably to his flag captain, Walter Young, whom he called "an excellent brave, good officer, enbued with every quality necessary to assist a commander-in chief." [15] He did not know that Young was writing to Sir Charles Middleton (later Lord Barham, but then comptroller of the navy) to claim the credit of the victory, because he urged "the ailing and irresolute admiral to make the signal." [16] That Rodney was aware that all was not well among his subordinates is shown by the covering letter, in which he wrote: "It is with concern that I must tell your Lordship that my brother officers still continue their absurd and illiberal custom of arraigning each other's conduct. My ears have been tempted to listen to their scandal; I have treated it with the contempt it deserved. In my opinion, every officer did his duty to his king and country. I have reported it so." Nevertheless, he continued, "the unhappy difference between Mr. Keppel and Sir Hugh Palliser has almost ruined the navy." [17] This sentiment was repeated in a letter to his wife in which he went even further: "Without a thorough change in naval affairs, the discipline of our marine will be lost. I could say much, but will not. You will hear of it from themselves. I have done them all like honour, but it was because I would not have the world believe that there were officers slack in their duty. Keep this to yourself." [18]

As Rodney continued across the Atlantic with the ships he was taking out to reinforce the fleet in the West Indies, he must have wondered about the state of morale he was to encounter on the other side. He could, however, take comfort that he now enjoyed the confidence of the government, since Sandwich told him, "The worst of my enemies now allow that I have pitched upon a man who knows his duty, and is a brave, honest and able officer." [19]

His arrival at Barbados on March 17 could not have been more opportune. His predecessor, Hyde Parker, who according to Rodney was a dangerous man because of his political bias and professional incompetence, had failed to inform him that the French Admiral de Guichen was daily expected from Brest with 23 sail of the line. Fortunately Rodney had, contrary to orders, retained one of Digby's ships, in addition to his own four prizes, so that the British fleet amounted to 21 of the line. His force, however, was too late to intercept the French, who arrived at St. Lucia on March 20; Rodney reached the same island a week later. The French then took refuge in their base at Port Royal, Martinique, and two of the most able tacticians of the age now faced each other across 45 miles of water.

De Guichen had a slight superiority in numbers and a much greater advantage in the highly trained corps of officers under his command. But he had a number of factors working against him. For one thing, his orders were ambiguous: "to keep the sea as much as the English forces maintained in the Windward Islands might allow him, without too much compromising his own forces." [20] For another, French tactical training encouraged skillful maneuvers aiming at immobilizing rather than destroying the enemy in action; French officers were taught to fire on the up roll in order to damage sails and rigging, and then to

bear away before the wind, in contrast to the British tradition
of close in-fighting. Rodney, on his part, realized that a knock-
out blow could only be delivered when he had maneuvered his
fleet into an advantageous position to windward, from which he
could concentrate a superior force against part of the enemy's
line. Such a maneuver required an efficient signal system and a
well-trained body of officers who knew what he intended to do.
Neither of these prerequisites was available when he challenged
de Guichen off Martinique on April 17, 1780. The result was
a classic example of the consequences of bad communications
and lack of a common doctrine.

The day before the battle, while both fleets were maneuvering
for position, Rodney gave notice that he intended to concentrate
all his ships against the enemy's center and rear. When the signal
was acknowledged by every captain, Rodney assumed they had
understood his instructions. But on the morning of the battle,
every captain interpreted the signal "for every ship to bear down
and steer for her opposite in the enemy's line, agreeable to the
21st article of the Additional Fighting Instructions" in his own
way. Some thought the word "opposite" signified (as Rodney
intended) those ships actually opposite them. Others, confused
by the ambiguity of the wording of the article, particularly the
phrase "the ship which it must be their lot to engage" thought
it meant the ship which would be opposite them if the two lines
of ships were coterminous. Rodney's own comment, in a note
scribbled in the margin of a treatise on naval tactics many years
later, was that he had created "an opportunity of bringing the
whole British fleet against part of the enemy and had his orders
been obeyed, the whole of the enemy's centre and rear divisions
had been disabled before their van could have made a motion
to assist them. But his rear tacked without his orders and his van
disobeyed and stood to windward of the enemy's van at a distance and scarce within random shot." [21]

While the admiral slowly turned his flagship towards the enemy, he saw Captain Carkett in the leading ship racing ahead to
place himself opposite the French leader; Captain Bateman was

doing nothing at all; and only three ships of Hyde Parker's squadron in the van were carrying out his plan. "Courage, mon général!" shouted someone on de Guichen's quarterdeck. "The English desert their commander!" Fortunately Rodney's defensive-minded opponent preferred to break off the action by bearing before the wind.

Rodney's fury at missing such a fine opportunity was expressed in such violent language that the Admiralty suppressed his most outspoken comments: "It is with concern inexpressible, mixed with indignation, that the duty I owe to my sovereign and my country obliges me to acquaint your Lordships that during the action the British flag was not properly supported." He wanted Bateman court-martialed and Hyde Parker recalled. On his own account he wrote blistering letters to Admiral Rowley and Captain Carkett, informing them that all he required was obedience to his orders: "the painful task of thinking belongs to me." [22]

During the next few weeks, he did his best to discipline his officers. "My eye on them," Rodney told his wife, "had more dread than the enemy's fire and they knew it would be fatal; no regard was paid to rank; admirals as well as captains, if out of their station, were instantly reprimanded by signals or messages sent by frigate—in spite of themselves I learnt them to be what they had never been before, *officers*." [23] By keeping his force constantly at sea, he drilled his men until the advent of the hurricane season made it advisable for both fleets to vacate the Caribbean. De Guichen returned to Europe instead of moving up to the American coast, as Washington had hoped. In case he had gone there, Rodney decided to sail to New York to deal with him and, if he was not there, to suppress the "piratical rebels" as he called the privateers who endangered communications along the Atlantic seaboard.

Rodney's fleet left the West Indies in a comparatively satisfactory state of health, which in those days was nothing short of a miracle. The station had an evil reputation in that era. If ships were kept at sea for any length of time, scurvy developed; if they stayed in port there was the ever-present danger of yellow fever. During his stay there was fortunately no yellow-fever epidemic as had decimated so many fleets there in the past. But the chief reason for the improved standard of health was the energy of Rodney's personal physician, Gilbert Blane, whom he had appointed to a new post of physician of the fleet without warrant from the Navy Board. This typical example of favoritism had beneficial consequences. Upon his arrival Blane discovered that the annual death rate was 1 in 7, not from combat injuries but from avoidable causes—lack of hospital accommodations, shortage of medical supplies, poor ventilation in ships and too easy an access to fiery Jamaican rum; drunken sailors lay about the streets being bitten by mosquitoes. Of course it was not yet known that these insects were the carriers of the disease, but Blane's insistence, with Rodney's support, on better hygiene saved many lives.

Blane began printing medical instructions for the use of officers, based upon the writings of Dr. James Lind, father of nautical medicine, and the more recent experiences of Captain James Cook.[24] These he distributed, with Rodney's approval, through out the fleet. Blane pointed out that "though the most laudable pains" were taken to husband and preserve from decay all manner of stores, such as ropes, blocks, spars, gunpowder and arms, little effort had been made to preserve the most valuable commodity of all—the health of the seamen. As a result of such measures, the mortality rate was reduced during the two years of Rodney's command from 1 in 7 to 1 in 29, and when the supreme test of his fleet came on April 12, 1782, "there was less sickness in this month than any of the former 23 months in which I kept a record." [25]

It was normal practice for the big British fleets to clear the Caribbean waters during the hurricane season. Rodney took his fleet to Sandy Hook, where he was welcomed by Sir Henry Clinton, the commander-in-chief of the army. Rodney always got on well with soldiers and had considerable experience in collaborating with them in amphibious operations. Such was not the case with Vice Admiral Arbuthnot, the naval commander in the area, who was junior in rank to Rodney. Arbuthnot and Clinton were on bad terms and the former resented Rodney's incursion into what he regarded as his preserve. In particular he distrusted Rodney's threat to potential prize money. Whether it was Arbuthnot's avarice, as the king thought, or Rodney's, one cannot say; but in the course of a bitter exchange of letters Arbuthnot told his senior in rank that "your partial interference in the conduct of the American war is certainly incompatible with principle of reason and precedents of service." [26]

Rodney's reply was astonishingly moderate in tone. He pointed out that he was the senior officer present and that Arbuthnot's own sphere of operations around Rhode Island remained untouched; but that since no attempt had been made to suppress the privateers to the southward, he would employ all available frigates to clear the seas between New York and the Chesapeake. "I came, indeed, so far to intervene in the American war as to command by sea in it and to do my best endeavours to put an end thereto." [27] In his view, the seas were one and the war must be viewed as a whole, now that France and Spain were engaged. He was bound to come north at this time of year, though he had no specific orders to do so, and he had expected to find de Guichen in the area. In those days commanders-in-chief on foreign stations were given far more independence of action than they are today, and their responsibility was therefore greater. Sandwich agreed with Rodney: "Unless our commanders-in-chief take the great line as you do, and consider the king's whole dominion as under their care, our enemies must find us unprepared somewhere and carry their point against us." [28]

Rodney proceeded to clear the lines of communication southward, so that Clinton was able to send General Leslie's small expedition to Virginia.[29] It is conceivable that the larger plans discussed between the two men might have changed the course of the war. Had a man of Rodney's caliber and grasp of strategic essentials remained on the coast for a longer period, the use of sea power in providing mobility for a striking force might have been more apparent. But such plans never achieved definite shape and Rodney returned south with a warning to Sandwich of the inertia which characterized the war on the American mainland:

> I must freely confess that there appears to me a slackness inconceivable in every branch of it, and that briskness and activity which is so necessary, and ought to animate the whole, to bring it to a speedy conclusion, has entirely forsaken it. It is now turned to a war of posts; and unhappily for England, when they have taken posts of infinite advantage and which, if maintained, would have brought the rebels to reason, they have unaccountably evacuated them; the evacuating Rhode Island was the most fatal measure that could possibly be adopted.[30]

The absence of the bigger ships from the Caribbean between August and December was justified, if for no other reason than the fact that they escaped the worst hurricane of the century. Rodney found the bases at Barbados and St. Lucia devastated and most of the ships which he had left behind him so crippled as to be unseaworthy. His impressive fleet of 23 ships had been thereby reduced to 9, and they were without stores. Everything depended on the arrival of a new second-in-command with a convoy from home before the French fleet made its annual appearance in those seas.

Sandwich found some difficulty in replacing "Vinegar" Parker because, as he complained, so many senior officers were "unfit by their factious connections, others from inferiority or insufficiency." [31] After juggling with the list of sea officers, he chose Sir Samuel Hood, whom Rodney welcomed as an old friend and about whom he invariably spoke in terms of the highest personal and professional approval. But Hood did not return the compliment. As soon as he arrived with the much desired convoy in January, 1781, Hood wrote private letters highly critical of his chief to his superiors in England. It is not easy to explain why Hood took up this attitude so soon after his arrival. Perhaps Rodney's run of luck had gone to his head and his aristocratic arrogance was affecting the morale of his subordinates and the fleet. At any rate, Hood and Young complained of Rodney's irresolution and frequent changes of plan. In a situation where plans had to be altered with each rumor of an invasion, however, this might equally have been called flexibility. However, there seems no doubt that his ill-health made his manner more abrupt than before, even if there is a distinct flavor of jealousy in the letters of his critics.

The turning point in Rodney's career came with the capture of the Dutch island of St. Eustatius. Although the island was supposedly neutral, it had for long been the entrepôt through which essential supplies had passed to the enemy. The Americans used it as a privateering base and obtained most of their gunpowder there in the early years of the war. The French and Spanish fleets had been supplied from it. Holland had given Britain every reason to attack the island and when the government decided to declare war Rodney and General Vaughan moved swiftly. Orders to capture St. Eustatius were dated December 20 and by February 3, 1781, the island was in British hands.[32]

Rodney was astonished at the immense amount of booty. The waterfront was lined with warehouses and the beach littered with hogsheads of sugar and tobacco. In the harbor were 130 merchant vessels, some 50 of them American, five of which were privateers. A convoy of 30 merchantmen which had just sailed for Europe with a Dutch warship as escort was overtaken and the Dutch admiral killed. There were even twelve British vessels which had come out under Hood's protection. It was these traitors who aroused Rodney's anger most: "I have seized all their effects, most of which are calculated to enable the public enemy to continue the ruinous war."[33] A hitherto unpublished letter expresses both his anger and pleasure with the prizes taken which he estimated at £3,000,000:[34]

> What terms did perjury, treason, rebels and traitors deserve? None, and none they had. France as well as America feels the blow

through their vitals. . . . Since we took the island, it has proved a trap for the Americans; no less than fifty have been taken with tobacco, and every night, though the island has been in our possession two months, they still arrive. We have taken at least £200,000 sterling from them; and I will tell you a secret: they shall cross the Atlantic for Europe. Remember their breach of the Treaty of Saratoga.

Rodney's actions were highly imprudent and on dubious legal grounds in some cases. It was pointed out to him that crews of unarmed vessels ought to be released and that an act of Parliament had legalized trade with the Dutch. For years to come, British West Indian merchants, who had opposed him from the start, plagued him with insurance claims and expensive lawsuits. He and Vaughan had seized everything in the king's name, though they were well aware that a princely share would be handed back to them in the form of prize money. As he wrote his wife, in a sentence typically deleted from the family biography, "If the capture is given to the Army and Navy, every man will make his fortune." [35]

Hood's absence from the scene prevented him from sharing in the plunder and his howl of protest was among the first of many: "They will find it very difficult to convince the world that they have not proved themselves wickedly rapacious." [36] The tale was naturally taken up by the Opposition at home. Nearly a year later, when Rodney was home on sick leave, Edmund Burke moved to appoint a committee to inquire into the affair. Burke was an interested party because of his connection with West Indian property, but to do him justice, Burke declared after the battle of the Saints, that if Rodney had a bald patch on his head he would willingly crown it with laurel. [37] When he moved his motion on December 4, 1781, he had strong political support. His charges are so similar to those advanced in Hood's letters that it may be suggested that Sir Charles Middleton, comptroller of the Navy Board, furnished Burke with some of the material. Rodney defended himself from his seat in the Commons and published the official correspondence to clear his name and Burke's motion was lost. But the irony of the whole story is that Rodney never benefited from this grand opportunity to retrieve his fortunes: most of the ships carrying the loot back to England were captured by the enemy on the high seas.[38]

The public attack on Rodney's professional reputation depended on three complaints originally made by Hood. First, that he was so busy plundering St. Eustatius that Hood's expedition to Curaçao was canceled. Rodney's reply to this charge was that rumors of de Grasse's impending arrival compelled him to keep his ships together. Second, that Tobago was lost because Rodney failed to defend it. The admiral's answer was that he was engaged in protecting a much more important base at Barbados and that he had given the inhabitants of Tobago ample means of defending themselves. The same story was to be repeated when the French recaptured St. Eustatius and it probably would have occurred at Jamaica, had that island been attacked. The inhabitants neglected to take proper measures for their defense and Rodney complained that the planters did not seem to realize there was a war on.

The third complaint by Hood was that he was given an insufficient force and the wrong orders to intercept de Grasse's arrival at Martinique in the spring of 1781. In Rodney's view, the 18 ships of the line which he had allocated for the task were sufficient, as long as Port Royal was closely blockaded, as he insisted more than once. Rodney never blamed Hood for finding himself too far to leeward when the French arrived with 20 ships and compelled him to withdraw to St. Lucia. Whether Hood could have persisted in a close blockade is doubtful. Hood may well have been right in saying that he should have been ordered to cruise to windward of the island, not to leeward. All that is clear was that the first opportunity to defeat the French was lost.

Rodney hastened to join forces as soon as he heard that De Grasse had arrived, but neither admiral was anxious to join battle. At one point the enemy were caught on a lee shore, but Rodney refrained from attacking because of navigational hazards. As the months passed, it became clear that de Grasse intended to move north. Rodney decided to take advantage of the sick leave promised him earlier in the year to return home. Blane had assured him that neither his gout nor the painful stricture from which he was suffering could be cured at sea. Leaving his fleet in Hood's hands, Rodney sailed for home in August with these words: "I am so tired that I have desired leave to go home with the convoy." [39]

Before he departed, Rodney disposed of his forces in such a way as he thought would counter any moves on the part of the enemy. His orders to Hood of July 25 indicate his grasp of the situation. Hood was to take 14 of the line and 7 frigates north to counteract an anticipated junction between the French, now off Haiti, with those at Rhode Island. He also sent two warnings to Graves (neither of which reached that admiral in time) that de Grasse might be coming north and that Rodney himself or his deputy "would endeavour to make the capes of the Chesapeake, then those of Delaware, and so to Sandy Hook." Thus, he assured Germain, the combined British forces "will be superior on the coast and prevent the enemy's designs, provided the officers who command will do their duty." [40]

Rodney's assumption in making these arrangements was that de Grasse would leave part of his fleet behind him in the Caribbean. He assumed also that Sir Peter Parker would send four ships from the Jamaican station, as he had been asked to do. Events proved him wrong. But the fleet of 19 ships of the line which encountered de Grasse's 24 should have proved a match for the enemy when they met in the Chesapeake had they been properly fought. Even if Rodney had sent two of the three ships of the line which he took home with him on escort duty, it is doubtful that their presence would have made any difference to the tactical handling of the battle.

On his way north, Hood missed de Grasse off the Chesapeake by the narrow margin of five days. Having joined Graves, their combined fleets sailed south again for the disastrous battle of the Virginia Capes. Even Hood declared that Rodney would have done better than Graves on that fateful day which sealed the doom of Cornwallis' army at Yorktown.

News of the disaster reached Rodney at Bath, where he was recuperating from an operation for bladder trouble. Once more Sandwich turned to him as his only hope: "The fate of this empire is in your hands." The old and ailing admiral responded to an appeal to go to sea again directly, though his gout was so bad that he could not write a letter and, according to his doctor, "debility and unequal spirits rendered him less equal to the fatiguing and anxious duties inseparable from such high responsibility." [41] Just as he sailed he was heartened by the news of Kempenfelt's success off Brest in destroying de Grasse's reinforcements on their way west, which enabled him to take a strong force of 15 ships across the Atlantic. [42]

By the time Rodney rejoined Hood at Antigua in February, 1782, the situation had deteriorated to a point where it looked as if the West Indies would go the same way as the American colonies. In his absence St. Kitts, Nevis, Montserrat, Demerara, and St. Eustatius had been taken by the French. Jamaica was being threatened by the Spanish from the north. Only a decisive fleet action could save the island and restore Britain's bargaining position in the peace negotiations about to begin in Paris. Fortunately Rodney was in a position to strike such a blow: he had a slight superiority in numbers, many copper-bottomed ships straight out from England, and healthy crews and better gunnery, thanks to the efforts of Sir Charles Douglas, the captain of the fleet.

The two fleets which confronted each other in the Caribbean were the largest ever seen in those waters. Rodney had 36 of the line, de Grasse 33, the French having recently been reinforced by a convoy as a result of a faulty disposition of his forces by Rodney. "Nothing short of a miracle can now retrieve the king's affairs in this country," wrote Hood. [43] That miracle was to occur at the battle of the Saints on April 12, 1782.

De Grasse sailed from Martinique on April 9 with a large convoy of transports and troops to join the Spanish fleet off Cuba for the conquest of Jamaica. Encumbered by his convoy, the French admiral failed to attack when he had an opportunity to cut off Hood in the van. Though some of his ships were disabled de Grasse succeeded in detaching his convoy in safety. Then, on April 11, the accidental collision of two French ships gave Rodney his chance. De Grasse made the mistake of altering course to save the damaged *Zélé* from falling into enemy hands. "I give you joy, Sir George," said Douglas as the morning of April 12th dawned. "Providence has given you your enemy broad on the lee bow." The French could be seen in disorder south of the island of Dominica and east of a group of rocks called Les Saintes.[44]

Two tactical points about the action which followed aroused controversy for years to come. The first was the extent to which Rodney was personally responsible for the innovation of breaking the enemy line—a maneuver which by Nelson's time became the formula for victory. If Rodney's reactions were slower on that day than those of his fleet captain Douglas, it should be kept in mind that he was a sick man who had not slept for four nights while chasing the French fleet. What happened was that the French line was so close-hauled that the third and fourth ships astern of the flagship *Ville de Paris*, which had been badly damaged at the first encounter with the British fleet, were taken aback when the wind veered four points to the south. A fatal gap appeared in the French line. Douglas was the first to notice it as he peered through the smoke. He sent to fetch the admiral, whom he congratulated upon a victory. "The day is not half won yet," replied Rodney. "Break the line, Sir George, the day is your own and I will insure you victory!" "No," said the admiral, "I will not break my line." Or did he say "any line"? As the argument developed, Rodney seems to have realized what Douglas meant. "Well, well—do as you like," he told Douglas. Similar permission was granted to Commodore Affleck aboard the *Bedford* to pass through a second gap which had appeared in the enemy's line.[45]

The second controversial point arose from Hood's charge that Rodney failed to follow up his victory immediately and lost a golden opportunity to deliver an even greater blow against the enemy. Hood, whose squadron in the rear had not been badly damaged, was eager to go after the greater part of the French fleet which had escaped. Rodney refused to order pursuit and made the signal to lie to during the night. Hood claimed that, had he been in command, twenty of the enemy's ships would have been taken, not just five. This comment was from the man to whom Rodney wrote on the evening of the battle: "Many thanks, my dear friend, for your kind congratulations; 'tis with sincerest truth that I must with great justice acknowledge that I am indebted to your very gallant behaviour that we have been so successful." [46]

Next morning, when Hood came aboard the flagship, he vehemently demanded that the chase be continued; but it was not until four days later that Rodney gave him permission. Hood then succeeded in capturing three more French ships, but the main body had passed through Mona Passage to safety twenty-four hours earlier. Rodney later made some notes to justify himself on this score.[47] He claimed that he did not pursue immediately because having himself experienced a night action he realized the danger of friendly ships firing into one another by mistake in the dark. Moreover, some 26 enemy vessels had escaped and he was anxious to keep his damaged fleet together to counter any possible French threat. As he noted in his first dispatch "both fleets have greatly suffered." In a later dispatch, he added that his fleet was becalmed for three days after the action, but the moment a breeze sprang up Hood's division was sent away.[48] If we accept his statement, and not Hood's, he seems to have had substantial reasons for delay.

"You may now despise all your enemies," he wrote to Sandwich. "The French have been given such a blow as they will not recover." [49] Certainly Jamaica was saved and the enemy never again attempted to dispute British superiority at sea in the war. But victory came too late to save either Sandwich or Rodney, or, of course, the situation in America. North's government fell on March 20, 1782. One of the first actions of the new administration was to dismiss Rodney. When the news of victory arrived in May, Keppel, first lord of the Admiralty, sent a messenger down to Plymouth to try to stop Admiral Sir Hugh Pigot from sailing to replace Rodney, but the message arrived too late. The first Rodney knew of these events was when he received orders on July 10 to strike his flag and return home.[50]

There, to the embarrassment of the Ministry, he received a hero's welcome. "Only the enthusiasm roused by Nelson at the Nile exceeded it," says Wraxall, who witnessed both celebrations. Rodney's victory "constituted a sort of compensation to Great Britain for so many years of disgrace, for so great an expenditure of blood and treasure and even for the loss of America itself. The country, exhausted and humiliated, seemed to revive in its own estimation, and to resume once more its dignity among nations."[51] The victorious admiral was given the barony of Stoke Rodney, the property of his ancestors, and a pension of £2000 a year. Only the West Indian merchants continued to plague him with their claims until the day of his death on May 23, 1792.

Rodney's victory in the battle of the Saints had a profound impact on the outcome of the peace negotiations of the Revolutionary War. Shelburne had already begun talks with the French two days after the battle was fought. When the news of victory arrived on May 18, Oswald, the British representative in Paris, was able to persuade Franklin to negotiate separate terms for the United States. Having failed to capture Gibraltar, Spain was equally anxious for peace. Vergennes, with the defeat of the main French fleet, and with bankruptcy staring the nation in the face, was forced to reconsider the Carthaginian terms which he had intended to force Britain to accept in Canada, India, and the West Indies. Besides Rodney's victory, Shelburne was able also to point to Howe's relief of Gibraltar and Hughes' stubborn resistance to Suffren in the Bay of Bengal. He could safely strike the attitude which he expressed: "It is enough to lose one world; it is not necessary to lose a second."[52] On the firm position guaranteed him by his admirals, Shelburne was able to conclude a satisfactory draft of the Treaty of Paris in January, 1783.

"Sea officers in general are apt to be censorious," Rodney told the head of the Admiralty in his old age. "It is their misfortune to know little of the world, and to be bred in seaport towns, where they keep company with few but themselves. This makes them so violent in party, so partial to those who have sailed with them, and so grossly unjust to others. Do them justice, and make them do their duty." [53] The tone of his remark is typically detached. It was this aristocratic hauteur which made him unpopular with so many of his colleagues. His philosophy of command expressed in the last sentence caused the inefficient to fear and dislike him. Whatever his defects of character—and there admittedly were many—Rodney became an outstanding commander-in-chief. He saw the war as a whole, imposed order on his fleet, and proved to be a fine tactician. He was not blinded by party passion. He won the admiration of his countrymen by his victories. He may have been a lucky admiral, but he earned much of the good fortune which attended him at the end of his long career at sea.

FOOTNOTES

1. Donald Macintyre, *Admiral Rodney* (New York, 1962), p. 29.
2. Godfrey B. Mundy, *Life and Correspondence of Lord Rodney* (2 vols. London, 1830), I, p. 298.
3. Lewis B. Namier, *Structure of Politics at the Accession of George III* (New York, 1957), pp. 307, 314, 339.
4. Nathaniel W. Wraxall, *Historical Memoirs of My Own Time* (London, 1904), p. 464.
5. *Ibid.*, p. 190.
6. A comparison between holographs of the letters and the printed version in the family biography shows that many of the endearing familiarities were omitted. For example, Mundy, who prints most of the letters now in the British Museum (Add. Mss. 39, 779), omits this sentence written after the victory in February, 1780: "If, my dear, they think me worthy of reward, I hope it will not

be the empty one of honours, but the more substantial provision for myself and family."

7. Piers Mackesy, *The War for America, 1775–1783* (Cambridge, Mass., 1964), p. 319.

8. William B. Willcox, "Admiral Rodney Warns of Invasion, 1776–1777," *American Neptune*, IV, p. 194.

9. G. R. Barnes and J. H. Owen, eds., *The Private Papers of John, Earl of Sandwich, First Lord of the Admiralty* (4 vols., [London] 1932–38; Navy Records Society Publications, LXIX, LXXI, LXXV, LXXVIII), III, p. 155; and unpublished transcripts in National Maritime Museum, Greenwich, England.

10. Rodney Papers, G.D. 30/20/6, Public Record Office.

11. Mackesy, *op. cit.*, p. 320.

12. William L. Clowes, ed., *The Royal Navy: A History from the Earliest Times to the Present* (7 vols., London, 1897–1903), III, pp. 447–48.

13. Mundy, *op. cit.*, I, p. 215.

14. Barnes and Owen, *op. cit.*, III, p. 199.

15. *Ibid.*, p. 195.

16. John K. Laughton, ed., *Letters and Papers of Charles, Lord Barham* (3 vols., [London] 1904–11; Navy Records Society Publications XXXIII, XXXVIII, XXIX), I, p. 65.

17. Barnes and Owen, *op. cit.*, III, p. 201.

18. Mundy, *op. cit.*, I, p. 229.

19. Barnes and Owen, *op. cit.*, III, p. 206.

20. Edouard Chevalier, *Histoire de la Marine Française pendant la guerre de l'independence Américaine* (Paris, 1877), p. 185.

21. Note to John Clerk's "Essay on Naval Tactics," in appendix to Howard Douglas *Naval Evolutions* (London, 1832).

22. Barnes and Owen, *op. cit.*, III, pp. 217, 233.

23. Rodney Mss., Add. Mss., 39, 779, British Museum.

24. Gilbert Blane, *A Short Account of the Most Effectual Means of Preserving the Health of Seamen, particularly in the Royal Navy* (London? 1781?). This pamphlet was expanded with a medical history of Rodney's fleet in Blane's *Observations on the Diseases Incident to Seamen* (London, 1785).

25. Gilbert Blane, *Observations on the Diseases Incident to Seamen* (London, 1785), p. 88.

26. Barnes and Owen, *op. cit.*, III, pp. 259 and 264; Laughton, *op. cit.*, I, p. 80.

27. Dorothy C. Barck, ed., *Letter-Books and Order-Book of Admiral*

Lord Rodney 1780–1782, New York Historical Society, *Collections,* (1932), pp. 43 and 59; Mundy, *op. cit.,* I, p. 392.

28. Mundy, *op. cit.,* I, p. 402; Barnes and Owen, *op. cit.,* III, p. 231; Mackesy, *op. cit.,* p. 352 criticizes Rodney as having "no good reason for staying" in the north and merely plundering Arbuthnot's supplies.

29. William B. Willcox, "Rhode Island in British Strategy, 1780–1781," *Journal of Modern History,* XVII (December, 1945) describes the discussions with Clinton. See also Barck, *op. cit.,* p. 25.

30. Barnes and Owen, *op. cit.,* III, p. 262.

31. *Ibid.,* p. 232.

32. *Ibid.,* IV, p. 128.

33. Quoted in Macintyre, *op. cit.,* p. 163.

34. From the Clinton Papers, in the Clements Library, Ann Arbor, Michigan.

35. Rodney Mss., Add. Mss. 39, 779, British Museum.

36. David Hannay, ed., *Letters Written by Sir Samuel Hood* ([London, 1895], Naval Records Society Publications) III, p. 18.

37. Philip M. Magnus, *Edmund Burke: A Life* (London, 1939), p. 113.

38. *The Parliamentary Register* (London, 1782), V, p. 92; Barnes and Owen, *op. cit.,* IV, p. 158.

39. Macintyre, *op. cit.,* p. 171.

40. Mackesy, *op. cit.,* p. 420; Mundy, *op. cit.,* II, p. 148. For a criticism of Rodney's dispositions, see William B. Willcox, "The British Road to Yorktown: A Study of Divided Command," *American Historical Review,* LII, (October, 1946), p. 22.

41. Blane quoted in Douglas, *op. cit.,* appendix XIV.

42. For Rodney's fleet, see Mackesy, *op. cit.,* pp. 453, 457.

43. Hannay, *op. cit.,* p. 98.

44. The earliest English plans call them The Saints, but the French spelling persists in the naming of British warships. Rodney called the battle that of April 12th, while the French refer to it as the battle of Dominique.

45. Narrative of Sir Charles Dashwood, Rodney's aide-de-camp. This narrative was printed by Howard Douglas in his *Naval Evolutions,* which also prints the evidence of Sir Gilbert Blane, who first published an account of what passed at breakfast that morning in his *Select Dissertations on Several Subjects of Medical Science* (London, 1822). In the 1804, or third edition, of his *Essay on Naval Tactics* (Edinburgh, 1804), John Clerk of Eldin claimed to have inspired Rodney's tactics, since he suggested the maneuver of breaking the line in the first edition of his book which was privately

printed in 1782. There is no evidence that Rodney ever saw this edition, but he owned and annotated the second edition of 1790; however, it is only in the third edition of 1804 that Clerk claims credit for the battle of the Saints. Douglas was at pains to rebut this claim. See also Wraxall, *op. cit.*, p. 466.

46. Laughton, *op. cit.*, I, pp. 159, 163, 179; Barnes and Owen, *op. cit.*, IV, p. 261; Hannay, *op. cit.*, pp. 104, 112; and Douglas, *op. cit.*, p. 95.

47. Mundy, *op. cit.*, II, p. 248.

48. Barck, *op. cit.*, pp. 358, 366.

49. Barnes and Owen, *op. cit.*, IV, p. 257.

50. Barck, *op. cit.*, p. 488.

51. Wraxall, *op. cit.*, pp. 462, 470.

52. Vincent T. Harlow, *The Founding of the Second British Empire, 1763–1793* (London, 1952), pp. 256, 281, 312.

53. Mundy, *op. cit.*, II, p. 358.

BIBLIOGRAPHY

Barck, Dorothy C., ed. *Letter-Books and Order-Book of Admiral Lord Rodney, 1780–1782.* New York Historical Society, *Collections,* LXV and LXVI. 2 vols. New York, 1932–33. Contains a wealth of information.

Hannay, David. *Rodney.* London and New York, 1891. A very brief biography.

Macintyre, Donald. *Admiral Rodney.* London, 1962. The most recent Rodney biography, but undistinguished.

Mackesy, Piers. *The War for America, 1775–1783.* Cambridge, Mass., 1964. Quite critical of Rodney and considers his victory at the Saints in 1782 more a matter of luck than skill. To Mackesy Rodney was a competent but standard eighteenth-century admiral.

Mundy, Godfrey B. *The Life and Correspondence of the Late Admiral Lord Rodney.* 2 vols. London, 1830. This typical nineteenth-century biography of Rodney by his son-in-law is both uncritical and incomplete.

[Rodney, George Brydges]. London, 1789. *Letters from Sir George Brydges Now Lord Rodney to His Majesty's Ministers . . . Together with a Continuation of His Lordship's Correspondence with the Governors and Admirals in the West Indies and America, during the Year 1781, until the Time of His Leaving the Command and Sailing for England.* A valuable collection of letters whose major purpose was to vindicate Rodney and to defend him against the charges of British merchants whose goods had been confiscated at St. Eustatius.

White, Thomas. *Naval Researches; or a Candid Inquiry into the Conduct of Admirals Byron, Graves, Hood and Rodney in the Actions off Grenada, Chesapeake, St. Christopher's, and of the Ninth and Twelfth of April, 1782.* London, 1830. Still a very useful account.

Willcox, William B. "The British Road to Yorktown: A Study of Divided Command," *American Historical Review,* LII (October, 1946), pp. 1–35. Is critical of Rodney's disposition of British naval forces in the West Indies and North American waters prior to Yorktown.

INDEXES
for VOLUMES 1 & 2

INDEX

A Note About the Author

George Athan Billias was born in Lynn, Massachusetts in 1919. After attending Bates College, he received his M.A. and Ph.D. from Columbia University. He has been the recipient of numerous fellowships and grants, including a Guggenheim Fellowship, American Philosophical Society Grant, National Endowment for the Humanities Grant, and Exxon Foundation Grant. He is Jacob and Frances Hiatt Professor Emeritus at Clark University. The author and editor of over ten books, Dr. Billias lives in Worcestor, Massachusetts, where he is at work on a book about the influence of American constitutionalism abroad, 1776-1900.

Other DA CAPO titles of interest